ARTISTS AND ILLUSTRATORS
OF THE ANGLO-BOER WAR
BY RYNO GREENWALL

ARTISTS AND ILLUSTRATORS
OF THE ANGLO-BOER WAR
BY RYNO GREENWALL

Above: W. Schulz's *Farewell to his sweetheart*. Opposite: A lithographic music cover.

RYNO GREENWALL

ARTISTS & ILLUSTRATORS

OF THE ANGLO-BOER WAR

INTRODUCTION BY JANE CARRUTHERS

FERNWOOD
PRESS

FERNWOOD PRESS (PTY) LTD   FIRST PUBLISHED 1992

P.O. BOX 15344

8018 VLAEBERG

REG. NO. 90/04463/07

COPYRIGHT

© (TEXT) R. GREENWALL,

J. CARRUTHERS

© (PICTURES) R. GREENWALL

UNLESS OTHERWISE STATED

EDITED BY ALLISON MURPHY
AND BEVERLEY BERNSTONE
DESIGNED BY WILLEM JORDAAN
PRODUCTION CONTROL BY BUNNY GALLIE
TYPESETTING BY DIATYPE SETTING c.c., CAPE TOWN
REPRODUCTION BY UNIFOTO (PTY) LTD., CAPE TOWN
PRINTED AND BOUND BY TIEN WAH PRESS, (PTE) LTD.,
SINGAPORE

ISBN 0-9583154-6-9 (Collectors' edition)

ISBN 0-9583154-2-6 (Standard edition)

This Book is dedicated to
my wife Evon and children,
Linda, Gillian, Mark, Peter
and Nicola.

THE SPONSOR

The publishers wish to acknowledge,
with thanks, the generous contribution made
by First National Bank towards defraying the
costs of this publication.

CONTENTS

4 THE SPONSOR

6 ACKNOWLEDGEMENTS

7 AUTHOR'S NOTE

7 THE WAR OF MANY NAMES – NOTE ON THE NAMES BY WHICH THE WAR IS KNOWN

8 IMPORTANT DATES OF THE WAR

9 LIST OF ABBREVIATIONS USED IN THIS BOOK

11 INTRODUCTION BY JANE CARRUTHERS

17 **PART ONE: ARTISTS AT THE FRONT**

18 CHAPTER 1   THE 'SPECIAL' ARTISTS

27 CHAPTER 2   THE ARTIST-CORRESPONDENTS

33 CHAPTER 3   THE SOLDIER-ARTISTS

38 CHAPTER 4   WORKS OF THE SIEGES, BRITISH P.O.W.S AND ARMY JOURNALS

44 CHAPTER 5   THE PRO-BOER ARTISTS

49 **PART TWO: NEWSPAPERS AND PERIODICALS**

50 CHAPTER 6   BRITISH HOME-BASED ARTISTS

61 CHAPTER 7   SPECIAL BRITISH BOER WAR PERIODICALS

64 CHAPTER 8   THE ILLUSTRATED PERIODICALS OF EUROPE AND THE UNITED STATES

69 CHAPTER 9   CHARITY AND SOUVENIR PUBLICATIONS

73 **PART THREE: THE SATIRISTS**

74 CHAPTER 10 CARTOONISTS AND CARICATURISTS: BRITAIN AND EMPIRE

81 CHAPTER 11 CARTOONISTS AND CARICATURISTS: EUROPE AND THE UNITED STATES

89 **PART FOUR: PICTURE POSTCARDS AND ILLUSTRATED NOVELS**

90 CHAPTER 12 THE PICTURE POSTCARDS OF THE WAR

97 CHAPTER 13 THE ILLUSTRATED NOVELS OF THE PERIOD

100 THE INFLUENCE OF THE ANGLO-BOER WAR ON EUROPEAN ARTISTS

102 **PART FIVE: THE BIOGRAPHIES**

238 ADDENDUM: MEDALLISTS

239 APPENDIX 1: ARTISTS' INITIALS

240 APPENDIX 2: BRITISH EXHIBITIONS

242 APPENDIX 3: POSTCARD ARTISTS

246 APPENDIX 4: ANGLO-BOER WAR COVERS IN MAJOR FRENCH ILLUSTRATED NEWSPAPERS

249 BIBLIOGRAPHY

255 INDEX

262 LIST OF SUBSCRIBERS

ACKNOWLEDGEMENTS

I would not have been able to write this book without the help of a considerable number of people, both in South Africa and abroad. Museums, art galleries, Regimental headquarters, archives, institutions, libraries and individuals have all readily responded to my enquiries.

Even when the required information has not been available the respondents have been most helpful in pointing me in a new direction.

I am extremely grateful to the following individuals and institutions for their assistance:

Miss J. Addleson, Curator, Durban Art Gallery, Durban
Miss P. Ainslie, Art Dept., Glenbow Museum, Calgary, Canada
Lt. Col. K. G. Allen (Ret.), Regimental Headquarters Worcestershire & Sherwood Foresters, Worcester, England
Mr Martyn Anglessa, Dept. of Art, Ulster Museum, Belfast, Northern Ireland
Mr Archie Atkinson (South African Postcard Research Group) Castletown, Isle of Man
Miss C. Jane Baker, Curator of Fine Art, Royal Albert Memorial Museum, Exeter, England
Col. J. R. Baker (Ret.), Curator, Regimental Headquarters, Royal Greenjackets, Winchester, England
Ms Mary Bennet, Keeper of British Art, Walker Art Gallery, Liverpool, England
Mr L. W. Bolze, Books of Zimbabwe, Bulawayo, Zimbabwe
Lt. Col. D. J. Bottomley, The Green Howards Museum, Richmond, Yorkshire, England
Mrs P. J. Broome, Administrator, National Trust for Places of Historical Interest, Chartwell, England
Mrs Helen Burgess, Editor *The Beaver*, Winnipeg, Canada
Dr M. H. Buys, Archivist, De Beers Consolidated Mines, Kimberley
Mr F. Casassa, Fine Arts Society London
Col. J. S. Cowley, Light Infantry Office (Yorkshire), Pontefract, Yorkshire
Brigadier J. M. Cubiss (Ret.), Regimental Secretary, Regimental Headquarters, Prince of Wales's Own Regiment of Yorkshire, York, England
The Curator, Dalemain (Historic house and gardens), Penrith, England
Mr Andrew J. L. Davies, Military Museum assistant, Museums & Art Gallery, Derby, England
Mrs R. Dillenbeck, Director, Remington Art Museum, Ogdensburg, New York, U.S.A.
Mrs Nancy E. Dillow, Director, Norman Mackenzie Art Gallery, Regina, Canada
Maj. G. E. Dodd, Curator, Museum of the Worcestershire and Sherwood Foresters Regiment, Lenton, Nottingham, England
Professor D. E. Duffey, Department of Art History, University of Pretoria
Mr C. F. Duggan, Killie Campbell Africana Library, University of Natal
Mrs H. F. du Toit, Curator, Potchefstroom Museum, Potchefstroom
Mrs Joan Evans, (daughter of Algernon Essex Capell), Zimbabwe
Lt. Col. A. A. Fairrie (Ret.), Regimental Headquarters, Queen's Own Highlanders (Seaforth & Camerons), Cameron Barracks, Inverness, Scotland
Capt. D. J. H. Farquharson, Home Headquarters, 16th/5th Queen's Royal Lancers, Stafford, England
Mr G. M. Farrar, County Archivist, County of Cambridgeshire, Cambridge, England
Col. A. V. Fennuci (Ret.), Curator and secretary R.A.M.C. Historical Museum, Aldershot, England
Prof. O. Ferreira, Dept. of History and Cultural History, University of Pretoria
Mr T. Flower, Senior assistant, Dept. of printed books, Royal Air Force Museum, Hendon, England
Mrs Moira Gibb, (daughter of Stratford St Leger), Milnerton, Cape Town
Mr R. Gillespie, Assistant Director, City of Glasgow District Council Libraries Dept., Glasgow, Scotland
The Bishop of Grahamstown, Grahamstown
Lt. Col. H. R. Gulliver, Regimental Headquarters and Museum, Gloucestershire Regiment, Gloucester, England
Maj. J. McQ. Hallam (Ret.), Lancashire Headquarters, Royal Regiment of Fusiliers, Wellington Barracks, Bury, Lancashire
Mr. P. H. Halton, Deputy Keeper, British Museum, London
Mr N. Hanson, Carlisle Museum and Art Gallery, Carlisle, England
Maj. A. G. Harfield, Deputy Director, Royal Signals Museum, Blandford Camp, Dorset, England
Capt. C. Harrison (Ret.), Regimental Headquarters, Gordon Highlanders, Aberdeen, Scotland
Mr Frank Haskett, Borough of Luton Recreation Services Dept., Luton, England
G. W. Haysom, Ministry of Defence, Eastern Ave., Gloucester, England
Dr T. A. Heathcote, Curatorial Officer, R.M.A. Collection, Sandhurst, Camberley, England
Mr George Hodgson, Secretary, Old Diocesan's College Union, Cape Town
Mrs P. Hodgson, Richmond, England
Miss Judith Holden, A. & C. Black Publishers, London
Dr Chris Hummel, Dept. of History, Rhodes University, Grahamstown
Mr John Hutchinson, Cataloguer, National Gallery of Ireland, Dublin, Eire
Maj. F. P. Kelly, Gibraltar Barracks, Northampton, England
Miss L. Kennedy, City Librarian, Johannesburg Public Library
Mr J. Killen, Deputy Librarian, Linen Hall Library, Belfast, Northern Ireland
Mr Robert Langham Carter, Kenilworth, Cape Town
Brigadier R. G. Lewendon (Ret.), Historical Secretary Royal Artillery Institution, Woolwich, England
Mr Lewis, Borough of Blackburn, Blackburn, England
Ms. Moira Long, Art Librarian, Alexander Turnbull Library, Wellington, New Zealand
T. G. Manby, Museums and Arts Service, the Museum and Art Gallery, Doncaster, England
Mrs Karen Meyer, Professional Assistant, Melrose House, Pretoria
Sir Oliver Miller, Surveyor of the Queen's Paintings, St James' Palace, London
Mr J. H. Minnie, retired chief, State Archives, Pretoria
T. J. Monby, Curator, Doncaster Metropolitan Borough Museums and Arts Service, Doncaster, England
Mr M. D. Mutsanwira, Director, National Archives, Harare, Zimbabwe
Mrs Blanche Nagelgast, Director, Africana Museum, Johannesburg
Mr Tom Oerder, Pretoria
Maj. N. J. Perkins (Ret.), Regimental Association, the Loyal Regiment (North Lancashire), Fulwood Barracks, Preston, England
Mr Gordon Phillips, Archivist, Fences Newspaper Ltd., London
Mr C. J. Pickford, Assistant Archivist, Bedfordshire County Hall, Bedford, England
M. Potgieter, Chief, Archives depot, Cape Town
L. Powell, Archival Consultant, Museum of Army Transport, Beverley, Humberside, England
Archdeacon of Queenstown, Queenstown, S.A.
Mr C. A. Rankin, Randburg, Johannesburg
Lt. Col. J. S. Reilly, Regimental Office, Royal Irish Rangers, Enniskillen, Northern Ireland
Mrs A. Renew, Curatrix, Mafeking museum, Mafikeng, Bophuthatswana
The Hon. Mrs Jane Roberts, Curator of the Print Room, Royal Library, Windsor Castle, England
The Curator, Royal Corps of Transport Collection of Army, Road, Rail Sea and Air Transport, Beverley, Humberside, England
Mr R. Schwegman, Town Clerk, Colenso
Mr William R. Sergeant, County Archivist, Suffolk County Council, Bury St Edmonds, England

Lady Elizabeth Shakespeare (daughter of Robert Hare), Chislehurst, Kent
Mrs Eve Sheldon-Williams (daughter of Inglis Sheldon-Williams), London
Maj. Smith, the Royal Regiment of Wales (24th/41st Foot), Brecon, Wales
M. Spence, Curator, Scottish National Gallery of Modern Art, Edinburgh
Miss Jenny Spencer-Smith, National Army Museum, London
Mr Hugh T. Stevenson, Assistant Keeper, Department of Fine Art, Glasgow Museums and Art Galleries, Glasgow, Scotland
Miss Marion M. Stewart, Archivist, Churchill College, Cambridge, England
Lt. Col. D. M. Stone, Curator, Devonshire Regimental Museum, Exeter, England
Mr W. Stroberg, Director, S.A. National Museum of Military History, Johannesburg
Maj. N. D. Taylor (Ret.), Secretary, the Prince of Wales's Own (West & East Yorkshire) Regimental Association, Beverley, Humberside, England
Mr Godfrey Thompson, City Librarian and Director of Art Gallery, Guildhall Library, London
Mr W. A. Thorburn, Keeper, Scottish United Services Museum, Edinburgh, Scotland
Miss Margaret Timmers, Research Assistant, Dept. of Prints & Drawings and Photographs, Victoria and Albert Museums, London
Maj. Tipping, Regimental Museum Queen's Lancashire Regiment, Preston, England
Maj. R. F. Tomlinson (Ret.), Regimental Secretary, Prince of Wales's Own Regiment of Yorkshire, England
The Curator, Towneley Hall Art Gallery & Museums, Burnley, Lancashire, England
Lt. Col. P. K. Upton, Regimental Secretary, Home Headquarters the Royal Hussars, Winchester, England
Mr Ian Uys, Rensburg, Transvaal
Mrs J. A. Verbeek, Dept. of Library Science, University of Natal, Pietermaritzburg
Ms Anna Waldmann, Curatorial assistant, Art Gallery of New South Wales, Sydney, Australia
Mr Ward, Regimental Headquarters, King's Own Scottish Borderers, Berwick upon Tweed
Miss P. Wessels, Senior professional officer, War Museum of the Boer Republics, Bloemfontein
Mr. John Westmancoat, Information officer, the British Library newspaper library, London
Mr R. Wilkinson-Latham, Hampshire, England
J. G. Woodroff, Curator, Queen's Royal Surrey Regiment Museum, Guildford, Surrey, England
Maj. J. H. Wyllie (Ret.), Curator, the Dorset Military Museum, Dorchester, England

Special thanks go to the following:
Fiona Barbour, for sharing her wonderful knowledge of the Anglo-Boer War, particularly the events that occurred in and around Kimberley.
Paul Bower, for acting as my scouting agent in England.
Frank Bradlow, for his help and encouragement.
Henrietta Dax, Paul Mills and the late Anthony Clarke of Clarke's Bookshop, Cape Town, who were always able to find the elusive books I needed.
Henrietta Jooste, Librarian and Custodian of the Mendelssohn Collection in the Library of Parliament, Cape Town.
Dr Ronald Joseph (French translation)
Mrs Peta Levin (German translation)
Julian Rollnick
Sonya Rollnick (Russian translation)
Mr Piet Westra, Director, and the Staff of the South African Library, Cape Town.

Ryno Greenwall April 1992

AUTHOR'S NOTE

In Part Five, the biographies or dictionary of Anglo-Boer War artists, starting on p. 102, references have been given below each entry to assist those who would like to do further research. A short title system has been used for each book referred to, and both the short title and the full title of the works are given in the Bibliography (p. 249).

The number next to an artist's name indicates the number of illustrations by that artist that appear in the book.

Unless otherwise stated, all illustrations that appear in this book are from the author's collection. The picture of Emily Hobhouse on the inside back cover flap is from the War Museum of the Boer Republics, Bloemfontein, and that of Pablo Picasso on the back cover is from the René Jacques Collection/Snark International, Paris.

THE WAR OF MANY NAMES

This book uses the terms 'Anglo-Boer War' and 'Boer War' throughout. The conflict has been given many labels over the years, however. The one that is considered to be most appropriate – particularly in academic circles – is 'the South African War'. The title is fitting in that it conveys the fact that all inhabitants of South Africa, including the Black population, were involved in and affected by the War. The publisher and authors accept that this term is gaining currency and that in years to come it will probably be more widely used. The older terms have been used, however, because they are more familiar to the public and their use reduces the possibility of misunderstanding or ambiguity. Some of the other names that have been used for the War are:

The Transvaal War
The War in South Africa
The 6th South African War*
The Transvaal War of Independence
The War of Independence
The Second South African War
The Great Boer War
The English-Transvaal War
The Second Anglo-Boer War
Die Tweede Vryheidsoorlog
Die Boere-oorlog
Der Boerenkrieg
Der Burenkrieg
De Zuid-Afrikaanische Oorlog
De Transvaalsche Krijg
De Transvaalsche Oorlog
Krieg in Südafrika
De oorlog in Zuid-Afrika
De Boerenoorlog
Der Südafrikanische Krieg
La Guerre des Boers
La Guerre au Transvaal
La Guerre Anglo-Boer
La Guerre Sud-Africaine
La Guerre du Transvaal
Burskaiya Voina
Anglo-burskaiya Voina
voina Burov za nezavisimost (The Boer war for independence)

*This term is used in Major N.C. Lekeman's 1935 publication *Regimental History*. Wars no. 1-3 are Frontier wars, while 4 is the Zulu War and 5 is the Transvaal War, sometimes also known as the first Anglo-Boer War.

IMPORTANT DATES OF THE ANGLO-BOER WAR, AND EVENTS LEADING TO IT

1895 DECEMBER 29 ⎤
1896 JANUARY 2 ⎦ Jameson Raid

1899 MAY 31 ⎤
JUNE 5 ⎦ Abortive peace conference, Bloemfontein

OCTOBER
7 Gen. White arrives in Natal aboard the *Tantallon Castle*
9 Kruger sends ultimatum to the British demanding withdrawal of troops from Transvaal border
11 Kruger's ultimatum rejected
14 Mafeking besieged
16 Kimberley besieged
19 Armoured train captured by Boers at Elandslaagte
20 Battle of Dundee (Talana Hill)
21 Battle of Elandslaagte
23 Death of Gen. Penn Symons at Dundee
24 Battle of Rietfontein
30 Battle of Ladysmith (Farquhar's farm or Lombard's Kop) Disaster at Nicholson's Nek
31 Buller arrives in Cape Town
Boer attack on Mafeking repulsed

NOVEMBER
1 Boers invade Cape Colony via Norval's Pont bridge
2 Siege of Ladysmith starts
10 Skirmish at Belmont. Lord Methuen takes command of troops on Orange River line
15 Winston Churchill captured at Chieveley after armoured train carrying him is ambushed by Boers
23 Battles of Belmont and Willow Grange
25 Battle of Graspan (Enslin)
26 Col. Holdsworth attacks Boers near Linchwe's territory
28 Battle of Modder River
29 First Canadian contingent arrives in Cape Town

DECEMBER
10 Battle of Stormberg
11 Battle of Magersfontein
13 Sir Charles Warren and 5th Division arrives in Cape Town
15 Battle of Colenso

During Black Week (10-15 December), Gen. Wauchope killed at Magersfontein, and Frederick Roberts at Colenso

18 Lord Roberts succeeds Buller as commander in chief with Lord Kitchener as chief of staff
19 Yeomanry battalions raised in Britain
21 Churchill reaches Lourenço Marques after his escape from Pretoria
23 Lord Roberts and Gen. Kitchener leave England for South Africa
29 German mail ship *Bundesrath* seized by Royal Navy in Mozambique Channel on suspicion of carrying contraband for Boers

1900 JANUARY
6 Battle of Caesar's Camp (Wagon Hill) in Ladysmith
Suffolk Regiment suffers reverse at Colesberg
10 Lord Roberts and Kitchener arrive in South Africa
13 City Imperial Volunteers leave England for South Africa
18 Battle of Acton Homes
23 ⎤
24 ⎥
25 ⎦ Battle of Spioenkop (Spion Kop)

FEBRUARY
5 ⎤
6 ⎥
7 ⎦ Battle of Vaal Kranz
11 French leaves Ramdam in his advance on Kimberley
15 Kimberley relieved
17 ⎤
27 ⎦ Battle of Paardeberg

24 Capt. R. de Montmorency of Montmorency's Scouts killed near Stormberg
27 Surrender of Gen. Cronje (avenging of Battle of Majuba 19 years before)
28 Ladysmith relieved

MARCH
1 Roberts arrives in Kimberley
7 Battle of Poplar Grove
Gatacre reoccupies Burgersdorp
10 Battle of Abraham's Kraal (Driefontein)
13 Bloemfontein occupied by Lord Roberts's forces
14 Gen. Pretyman appointed Military Governor of Bloemfontein
17 Boer council of war at Kroonstad
27 Gen. Piet Joubert dies. Succeeded by Gen. Louis Botha
28 White leaves Cape Town for England
30 ⎤
31 ⎦ Battle of Sanna's Post (Koornspruit)

APRIL
5 Col. Georges de Villebois Mareuil killed at Boshof
9 ⎤
25 ⎦ Wepener besieged by Boers
11 SS *Milwaukee* arrives off St Helena with 517 Boer P.O.W.s
25 Bloemfontein waterworks recaptured by British troops

MAY
3 Roberts begins his march from Bloemfontein to Pretoria
5 Battle of Vet River: Brandfort occupied
10 Zand River crossed
12 Kroonstad occupied
16 ⎤
17 ⎦ Mafeking relieved
24 Vaal River crossed by Roberts
Rundle occupies Wepener
Orange Free State annexed as Orange River Colony
28 Battle of Biddulphsberg
29 Battle of Doornkop
30 Kruger leaves Pretoria for Machadodorp
31 Johannesburg occupied

JUNE
1 Linley reoccupied by Lord Methuen
5 British flag raised at Pretoria
7 Transvaal Government announces transfer of the capital to Machadodorp
12 Battle of Diamond Hill near Pretoria
Battle of Roodewal

JULY
16 Steyn and De Wet escape from the Brandwater Basin
26 Battle of Dalmanutha
30 Capture of Gen. Prinsloo at Brandwater Basin

JULY ⎤
AUGUST ⎦ First De Wet 'hunt'

AUGUST
25 Hans Cordua executed for plotting attempted assassination of Lord Roberts
27 Battle of Bergendal
30 Release of 2 000 British prisoners at Nooitgedacht

SEPTEMBER
1 Formal annexation of Transvaal
5 Death of Gideon Theron at Gatsrand
11 Kruger leaves the Transvaal and goes into exile
13 French occupies Barberton
24 Pole-Carew reaches Komatipoort

OCTOBER
8 Sir Alfred Milner appointed administrator of the new colonies
19 Kruger leaves Lourenço Marques for Europe via the Suez Canal aboard the *Gelderland*
24 Buller leaves Cape Town for England
20 ⎤
25 ⎦ Battle of Frederikstad

OCTOBER	27	Return of the City Imperial Volunteers to England
NOVEMBER	22	Kruger reaches Marseilles
	29	Roberts hands over command to Kitchener
DECEMBER	11	Lord Roberts leaves Cape Town for England
	13	Battle of Nooitgedacht
	20	Martial law proclaimed in Cape Colony

NOVEMBER⎫
DECEMBER⎬ Second De Wet 'hunt'

1901 JANUARY	10	Death of Morgendaal, the Boer peace emissary, after his flogging by Froneman
	22	Death of Queen Victoria
	31	Smuts captures Modderfontein post
FEBRUARY	27	Middleburg peace conference ends in stalemate
APRIL	6	Scheepers captures detachment of 75 British troops at Zeekoegat near Cradock
JUNE	2	Kritzinger captures Jamestown
JULY	20	Death of Pres. Kruger's wife Gezina
SEPTEMBER	3	Smuts invades Cape Colony
	5	Commandant Lotter captured by Scobell near Cradock
	17	Smuts surprises 17th Lancers at Modderfontein near Cradock
	26	Louis Botha attacks Fort Itala and Prospect in Natal
OCTOBER	11	Lotter executed
		Scheepers captured
	29	Maritz captures a convoy between Lamberts Bay and Clanwilliam
DECEMBER	7	National Scouts inaugurated
	16	Kritzinger captured near Hanover Road
	25	Boers attack British at Tweefontein
	29	Bruce Hamilton captures Gen. Erasmus near Ermelo

1902 JANUARY⎫
FEBRUARY⎬ Last De Wet 'hunt'
JANUARY⎭

	17	Gideon Scheepers executed by the British at Graaff-Reinet
	25	Ben Viljoen captured near Lydenburg
	29	Refusal by British Government of Dutch offer of mediation
MARCH	7	Methuen captured by De la Rey at Tweebosch
	19	Sir J. Maxwell relinquishes military governorship of Pretoria
	23	Start of peace negotiations
	26	Death of Cecil Rhodes in Muizenberg
APRIL	1	Springbok (Cape) captured by Maritz
	4	O'Okiep besieged by Gen. Smuts
MAY	3	O'Okiep relieved by British forces under Col. Cooper
	15	Opening of Vereeniging Conference
	20	Gen. Lyttelton takes over command from Lord Kitchener
	31	Peace of Vereeniging
JULY	30	Generals De Wet, Botha, and De la Rey leave for Europe and England to raise funds to rebuild the country
AUGUST	16	Boer generals arrive in Europe
NOVEMBER	1	De Wet returns to South Africa
DECEMBER	13	De la Rey and Louis Botha return to South Africa

NOVEMBER⎫
1903 FEBRUARY⎬ Chamberlain visits South Africa to decide on reparations to the war-torn country

1904 JULY	14	Ex-President Kruger dies in Clarens, Switzerland
DECEMBER	16	Kruger's funeral in Pretoria

LIST OF ABBREVIATIONS USED IN THIS BOOK

A.I.F.	Australian Imperial Forces
A.R.A.	Associate of the Royal Academy
A.R.E.	Associate of the Royal Society of Painter-Etchers and Engravers
A.R.W.S.	Associate of the Royal Society of Painters in Watercolours
B.E.F.	British Expeditionary Forces
C.B.	Companion of the Order of the Bath
C.B.E.	Commander, Order of the British Empire
C.I.V.	City Imperial Volunteers
C.M.G.	Companion of the Order of St Michael and St George
C.M.O.	Chief Medical Officer
C.V.O.	Commander of the Royal Victorian Order
D.A.A.G.	Deputy Assistant Adjutant-General
D.C.M.	Distinguished Conduct Medal
D.L.I.	Durham Light Infantry
D.S.M.	Distinguished Service Medal
D.S.O.	Distinguished Service Order
ed./eds.	edition(s)
fl.	floruit (flourished) Used for artists whose birth and death dates are not known. Shows that artist was known to be living between these dates.
F.R.S.	Fellow of the Royal Society
F.S.A.	Fellow of the Society of Antiquaries
G.C.M.G.	Knight Grand Cross of the Order of St Michael and St George
G.C.V.O.	Knight Grand Cross of the Royal Victorian Order
G.S.M.	General Service Medal
H.A.C.	Honourable Artillery Company
I.S.	International Society of Sculptors, Painters and Gravers
I.Y.	Imperial Yeomanry
K.B.E.	Knight Commander, Order of the British Empire
K.C.B.	Knight Commander of the Order of the Bath
K.C.M.G.	Knight Commander of the Order of St Michael and St George
K.C.V.O.	Knight Commander of the Royal Victorian Order
K.G.	Knight of the Order of the Garter
K.S.A.M.	King's South Africa medal
L.F.	Lancashire Fusiliers

M.B.E.	Member, Order of the British Empire
M.C.	Military Corps
M.M.	Military Medal
M.S.M.	Meritorious Service Medal
M.V.O.	Member of the Royal Victorian Order
N.E.A.C.	New English Art Club
N.P.S.	National Portrait Society
O.B.E.	Officer, Order of the British Empire
O.C.	Officer Commanding
O.R.C.	Orange River Colony
P.M.O.	Principal Medical Officer
P.O.W.	Prisoner of War
Q.M.	Quartermaster
Q.S.A.M.	Queen's South Africa medal
R.A.	Royal Academy
R.A.	Royal Regiment of Artillery
R.A.M.C.	Royal Army Medical Corps
R.A.P.C.	Royal Army Pay Corps
R.A.S.C.	Royal Army Service Corps
R.B.A.	Royal Society of British Artists
R.B.S.	Royal Society of British Sculptors
R.C.A.	Royal College of Art
R.Cam.A.	Royal Cambrian Academy of Art
R.E.	Royal Engineers
R.E.	Royal Society of Painter-Etchers and Engravers
Ret.	Retired
R.F.A.	Royal Field Artillery
R.H.A.	Royal Hibernian Academy
R.H.G.	Royal Horse Guards
R.I.	Royal Institute of Painters in Watercolours
R.M.A.	Royal Military Academy
R.M.S.	Royal Society of Miniature Painters, Sculptors and Gravers
R.N.A.S.	Royal Navy Air Services
R.N.V.R.	Royal Navy Volunteer Reserve
R.O.I.	Royal Institute of Oil Painters
R.P.	Royal Society of Portrait Painters
R.S.A.	Royal Scottish Academy
R.S.W.	Royal Scottish Society of Painters in Watercolours
R.W.A.	Royal West of England Academy
R.W.S.	Royal Society of Painters in Watercolours
S.A.C.	South African Constabulary
S.R.O.	Supplementary Reserve of Officers
V.C.	Victoria Cross
W.O.	Warrant Officer
Z.A.R.	Zuid-Afrikaansche Republiek (Transvaal Republic)

P. H. Ripp's highly inaccurate illustration of a heroic Boer defender. (Note upside down vierkleur [flag], a common error among European artists.)

INTRODUCTION

Waging war is one of the most ancient and common of human activities. It is also one of the most dramatic in that it dislocates society, destroys life and property and is the harbinger of upheavals in the social and political order. For these reasons, while long periods of relative peace have been punctuated by far shorter bouts of military conflict, it is by the latter traumas that the march of history has generally been measured.

WESTERN WAR ART BEFORE THE ANGLO-BOER WAR

In the modern western tradition, military art first became important in France where it was an overt instrument of state policy. Such artwork was formal in character, generally large in size and usually commissioned by a royal or aristocratic patron to commemorate important victories. In the eighteenth century, an apogee was reached when heroism was combined with landscape to 'provide a didactic lesson in good conduct through the choice of an appropriate subject ennobled by a grand design . . . of a moralizing tenor that would encourage viewers to apprehend and emulate the virtuous actions of the depicted heroes.'[1] In England, the first significant commissions of this sort glorified the role of the Duke of Marlborough in the War of the Spanish Succession in the early eighteenth century: French-trained artists were employed to decorate Blenheim Palace with suitable murals and tapestries.[2] Artworks depicting the Duke of Wellington's victory over Napoleon at Waterloo in 1815 provided another occasion for affirming values such as righteousness, religion, monarchical legitimacy and patriotism.[3] These examples of history painting were celebratory and idealized aristocratic leaders and victors, often after the classical manner: the primary purpose of the paintings was not to convey details of war to the general public, but to supply states, in the name of kings and generals, with pictorial and public justification for military action. Although it is not abundant, the legacy of this form of war art can be seen in many products of the Anglo-Boer War.

With the Crimean War of 1854 a different style emerged and this tradition was to predominate in the work of the Anglo-Boer War. Two conditions came into alliance at the time of the Crimean War, factors which altered the course of western war art significantly. The first was the growth of the economic and political power of the middle class and the accompanying decline of the aristocracy; the second was the flowering of the mass illustrated press.

As far as the growth of the middle class was concerned, it was occasioned by the industrial revolution which wrought changes in the social order of Europe and of Britain in particular. Commerce and money replaced land as the principal source of wealth and a rich bourgeoisie class came to prominence – people who were not only wealthy but enfranchised and educated. In the field of war art, this rise of the bourgeoisie was instrumental in changing the structure of patronage. The prerogative of the upper classes as arbiters of taste waned and the middle class began to take an interest in art, seeking to own or appreciate small-scale and pleasing examples.

A new direction in artistic taste can be discerned, particularly in the desire to see depictions of the everyday, domestic and humdrum of life's events rather than only the extraordinary and glorious. War art became democratized as depictions of the ordinary Crimean soldier found favour over pictures of officers leading armies of anonymous men into battle. Because the middle class related well to this new style of subject matter, artists learnt that the death of Tommy Atkins made an equally heroic artistic subject as that of a titled officer – and, indeed, was more popular. Part of the trend towards depicting the exploits of the ordinary soldier was connected with the declining prestige of the officer class and the realization that it often lacked military expertise, as for example in the Charge of the Light Brigade. It was not so much the fact that great men could in this way be denigrated but rather the realization that noble birth was not a necessary condition of greatness.

Another indication of the growing attraction of mundane subjects involved depictions of events unrelated to historic battles, day-to-day events that showed soldiers leaving families bereft at their departure, conditions in hospitals, wounded men, and returning soldiers. It has been alleged that pandering to middle-class taste led to a diminution of subtlety and intellectual content in war art and an increase in sentimentality.[4] Even if this was so, however, abandoning traditional battle art did bring to many the benefit of depictions that were 'more realistic in terms of graphic truth to nature and more Realist in terms of the subjects chosen and the manner in which they were treated'.[5] In this way the public consciousness of warfare was altered as an anti-heroic vision of conflict entered the artistic repertoire; by the time of the Anglo-Boer War this perception was well entrenched. This less glorious view of war was effected by a new profession that came into existence at the time of the Crimean War: that of war artist and correspondent. For the first time an eyewitness version of hostilities was deemed to be vital for a realistic account, and war artists were employed to attend the theatre of war in this capacity. The price paid for this new professional approach to war was that contrived iconographic and formal devices diminished. The popular press removed war art from the category of fine art and freed it from the constraints previously imposed by academic theory.[6] A new perspective on war was given by Crimean War artists and it was one which was later to be extremely influential in depictions of the Anglo-Boer War.

The second component, the illustrated press, revitalized war illustration by bringing it into the public arena, indeed, onto every street and into almost every home. The rise of the illustrated press can be located in the social and technological conditions of the time. A desire for education and literacy became almost universal and there was a concomitant need to be kept informed of political and other matters. Developments in papermaking techniques meant that paper could be manufactured in a continuous web, and not only as individual sheets. Refinements in the production of iron allowed for improved machinery which in turn led to longer print runs of increased variety. The skill of engraving and block-making was streamlined and accelerated. Because rapid and wide distribution was possible, the illustrated press was instrumental in changing the primary function of war art from commemoration to pertinent contemporary news, allowing for a wider variety of opinions to be expressed. For the first time it was possible to give a meaningful platform to opinions opposed to the War.

WAR ART IN SOUTH AFRICA BEFORE 1899

Although products of the Anglo-Boer War dominate war art on the subcontinent, depictions of armed engagements have an age-old history. Of significance are rock paintings which portray fighting between San hunter-gatherer groups and others. In terms of chronology these were followed by pictures of conflict between early Portuguese seafarers and Khokhoi pastoralists, painted in Europe long after the event had taken place. Visits to the Cape by Portuguese and other European navigators were preludes to the establishment of a permanent post there in 1652 by the VOC or Dutch East India Company. The inexorable process of white territorial expansionism which followed brought resistance from indigenous communities which were dispossessed of their land. There was formal confrontation between Dutch and Khoikhoi in 1659 and 1673, but more usually conflict was sporadic and conducted by small groups from both sides employing guerrilla tactics. Lacking the grandeur of battle scenes and thus not conforming to the conventions of war art at the time, these clashes appear to have been considered unworthy of visual record. By contrast, however, the first serious resorts to arms between whites – the Battle of Muizenberg in 1795 and the Battle of Blaauwberg in 1806 – were rewarded with illustrations on a grand scale and in the eighteenth-century heroic style.

Military conflict was frequent between agro-pastoralists and other pre-colonial groups, particularly in the early nineteenth century. Because these scenes were not generally witnessed by western artists – or perhaps were considered by them to be unimportant – they were not recorded visually,

1 A San rock painting near Harrismith records a battle between two groups of archers.
2 A woodcut by Pieter (or Pierre) van der Aa showing conflict between the Khoikhoi and Portuguese in c.1510. Cape Archives.
3 A coloured engraving of the Battle of Blaauwberg (1806) by William Craig, an illustration on the grand scale and in the 18th-century heroic style. Reproduced courtesy of the Africana Museum.
4 'Kaffirs fighting with Kirries', a rare glimpse of a duel between two Xhosa men by Willem Paravicini de Capelli, aide-de-camp to Governor Janssens, who he accompanied on a journey to the Eastern Cape. South African Library.

oral tradition being the method employed by the societies involved. A rare glimpse of an early nineteenth-century duel between two Xhosa men, entitled *Kaffirs fighting with Kirries* was left by Willem Paravicini de Capelli. Further in the interior other communities were encountered by whites and in the mid 1830s Charles Bell, a versatile artist described at the time as a 'draughtsman fit for anything',[7] accompanied Andrew Smith on an expedition to the Transvaal. Although there is no record of his witnessing fighting, Bell's works, which are carefully constructed depictions, comprise an important source of knowledge concerning African military dress and conventions, for he painted scenes of Tswana, Sotho and Ndebele warriors in battle dress, war dances and medicine men preparing soldiers for war.[8]

The succession of wars between the white settlers and Xhosa on the eastern Cape frontier in the mid-nineteenth century gave an impetus to South African war art. There are, however, isolated examples of other work extant from this period which include the Battle of Bloukrans fought between Zulu and Voortrekkers in February 1838, painted Romantically and dramatically some years later by Thomas Baines. Another is Thomas Bowler's rendering of the Battle of Boomplaats between the forces of Sir Harry Smith and Andries Pretorius in August 1848. It was, however, the existence of an interested population and the regularity – even predictability – of frontier wars in the eastern Cape that created a market for pictures of the conflict, both in Europe and in the Cape Colony, and made them an attractive subject for artists and illustrators. Standards varied, but of all these artists, Thomas Baines is pre-eminent in the field.[9] In general, most frontier war artwork fits into the commemorative mould mentioned above, although Baines's emotional imagery demonstrates a strong Romantic streak, especially in the depiction of scenery. Frontier war art records one side of a struggle for land and landscape, and it is to be regretted that pictorial renderings from the African point of view do not exist.

Two campaigns at the end of the 1870s, the Anglo-Zulu War of 1879 and the Transvaal War from 1880 to 1881, were depicted both in individual paintings and also in the British illustrated press. While having affinities with the output of the Anglo-Boer War, the artwork of these conflicts is small by comparison.

THE ANGLO-BOER WAR

The significance of the Anglo-Boer War, which dominated popular consciousness and the popular press in many parts of the world for its duration, lies in its being a key ingredient in the shaping of the modern history of the country and in its being the root of a great deal of historical mythology. Although most commonly called the 'Anglo-Boer' or 'Boer' War, the title 'South African War' is now preferred because it refers to a neutral geographical location and does not isolate antagonists and prioritize the 'Anglo' component over the 'Boer'. It is also a more useful term for analysis of the War's pictorial material, for it indicates that, like the War itself, it was immensely complex and cannot be reduced entirely to a juxtaposition of two opposing armies (see p. 7).

Arraigned on one side there were vast numbers of British soldiers, but there were also substantial colonial detachments, and these forces were enlarged by many former Afrikaner Republican enemies who had changed sides – the so-called 'National Scouts', 'hensoppers' and 'joiners'. The men of the South African Republic (the Transvaal) and the Orange Free State were augmented by dissenters from within Natal and the Cape Colony and also by many foreigners – French, Scandinavian, Dutch, German, Swiss, Italian, Russian or Irish. World governments became involved in the conflict, expressing strong views in favour of it or against it, many lending support materially – such as horses and fodder from the United States – or morally as was the case with Holland and Germany. Furthermore, the pristine clarity of a struggle solely between British and Boer is seen to be even more inappropriate when the War is interpreted as a civil war and war of independence. Nor was it even a 'white man's war', an interpretation which has recently been re-evaluated with the elucidation of the many roles that Africans played – as servants and labourers, armed

1 *Medicine men administering the charm to Rolong warriors when going into battle.* This scene showing preparations for war was painted by Charles Bell. Reproduced courtesy of the Africana Museum.
2 Thomas Baines's depiction of the British attack on Maqoma in the Eighth Frontier war. Reproduced courtesy of the William Fehr Collection.

soldiers, informers, spies, messengers, casualties and concentration camp inmates.

The War was one of the first of the modern western world's 'total wars', involving the civilian population to an extreme degree and not merely soldiers. The War tore Republican civilian life asunder as farms were systematically destroyed and women and children were relocated in concentration camps, and male prisoners were dispatched to prisoner-of-war camps in, for example India, Bermuda, Ceylon and St Helena. British society was not, of course, affected to the same degree, but divisions in that society became increasingly apparent and many people did not give their full support to the War. In Europe civilians entered the fray as commentators as well as combatants. The conflict can be appreciated also at the level of a 'people's war', in which the Transvaal and Orange Free State mobilized not only their fighting men but all their physical and material resources. The widespread and passionate responses evoked by the War have been compared with the more recent public reactions towards the Spanish Civil War and the Vietnam War from people in countries not directly engaged.[10]

Another aspect of the War was its imperialistic and capitalist dimensions. These affected not only its outbreak and course but also the art which emanated from it: the Anglo-Boer War as a conflict of opposing ideologies is particularly evident in much of its illustrative record. At the time, the Transvaal and Orange Free State were reluctant to abandon their agricultural economies based on patronage and unfree labour, when the capitalist world was forging links around the globe and the 'scramble for Africa' had almost reached a point of saturation. Control of the gold mines of the Transvaal was a major ingredient in imperial rivalry, which then degenerated into an arms race and the intensification of complicated, fragile alliances which eventually led to the First World War. Late Victorian England was caught in the grip of a philosophy which, once vibrant, had become corrupted into moribund principles of enforcing British values upon others and glorifying power for its own sake. Those opposed to Brit-

ish imperialism demonstrated this by showing sympathy for Republican values, sympathy that was often aired publicly in the form of pictorial illustration. Thus the mosaic of complex ideologies relating to the causes of the War, the medley of combatants and civilians and the reactions of the international community underpin the richness and variety of South African war art.

The course of the War was also complicated and varied and had a significant effect on the artistic material which was produced. The conflict itself can be divided into two distinct phases: from the outbreak of war in October 1899 to the fall of Pretoria in June 1900 and then the guerrilla warfare phase from July 1900 to May 1902. The former was conducted in the traditional manner of battles and sieges, of clear victories and defeats. During this initial stage events moved quickly and artists kept pace, producing the greatest quantity of artwork concerning the War. Republican forces besieged Ladysmith, Mafeking and Kimberley and inflicted severe defeats on British forces at Stormberg, Magersfontein and Colenso in December 1899. Early in 1900, under Lord Roberts, the tide began to turn. The sieges were lifted and a major British victory occurred at Paardeberg on 27 February 1900. Roberts's enormous army forced its way up the centre of the subcontinent, ousting the enemy before it. Bloemfontein, the capital of the Orange Free State, fell in March 1900, and the Transvaal capital, Pretoria, capitulated on 5 June 1900. Many people considered the War to be over at this point and many war artists and correspondents left South Africa, presuming that their task was complete. But, far from being ended, the strategy of war merely changed and the long guerrilla war – the second phase – began. The informal military initiatives of the Republican commandos were countered by the scorched-earth policy of Lord Kitchener and a war of pacification developed which left South Africa in ruins. As can be seen from the art of this later phase of the conflict, the perception of war as inglorious and brutal, for civilian and soldier alike, became ever clearer.

WAR ART AND THE ANGLO-BOER WAR

Many general principles covering all war art can be applied fruitfully to an understanding of the artistic output of the Anglo-Boer War of 1899 to 1902. There appears to be a fundamental human impulse to record for posterity crucial times of crisis, and this may be attributed in large measure to the desire to justify action. Oral tradition is probably the oldest method of recording events of the past, but it is the least enduring. The written or printed word has enormous power, longevity and ubiquity, but requires literacy on the part of the recipient. Visual depictions – paintings, illustrations and sculptures – can be understood even without interpretive skills and have as long a pedigree as the spoken word. Three-dimensional images are extremely powerful, for they have a strength and immediacy which words often lack – as the cliché has it, 'a single picture is worth a thousand words'. In recording conflict this statement is especially apt because war art, by the very nature of its subject, is generally descriptive. Illustrations of war depict hostilities, describe background landscapes, delineate victors and vanquished, praise individuals displaying leadership or courage, and emphasize the high stakes of defeat and death. While it might be thought that these depictions present reality, this is not the case. Descriptive art depends on detail to simulate the appearances of the world, and in doing so, it lulls the viewer into believing that because the image looks real, it equates with reality. But no act of recording is ever neutral, for choice in the selection and prioritization of data for aesthetic or conceptual reasons operates at many levels.

While the rich oral and written record of the Anglo-Boer War has received considerable scholarly attention, far less prominence has been given to the formal and iconographic evaluation of pictorial material. And yet, owing to its subject matter, the social and propagandist function of war art is clear, for it deliberately serves contemporary society or segments of that society. It sets out to arouse strong passions, feelings and opinions and it is impossible to be noncommittal about it. No illustrations of the

1

2

War are utterly neutral because bellicose conditions always condense and intensify moral issues, simplify or amplify concerns of right and wrong and expose heroes and villains. The purpose of military art is to reflect these attitudes to war but it also serves to crystallize them, to mould opinion, to create awareness and to influence the ways in which people think about one another. The nexus between art and society fluctuates, however, and modern viewers will therefore not have the same reaction to the art of the Anglo-Boer War as did contemporary spectators. All art is functional in the sense that it is created in order to effect a reaction, but perhaps more importantly, war art overtly proclaims this role.

It is to be expected that there is a wide diversity in the pictorial approaches to war as a result of the variety of artistic media, talent, technique, points of view and public taste. But despite this great variation, war art is held together as a genre by its common theme, and by its aim of generating an emotional response. No matter what the artistic standard, or when or where it was produced, war art informs an audience about combative situations. Some examples of war art have a larger creative, imaginative, interpretative and symbolic component than others and can thus be considered 'fine art'.

It could be argued that the role of war art has changed in the past few decades because the task of realistic visualization has been usurped by photography and cinematography. Today's artists may now have more scope to express and to interpret their emotions – even to deliberately exaggerate or distort them – being freed from the responsibility of rendering an accurate (albeit subjective) record of events. At the time of the Anglo-Boer War cumbersome equipment made action photography difficult: the many hundreds of photographs of the War are extremely informative but are most often confined to pauses in hostilities, such as scenes of carnage after battle, soldiers at rest or recreation, siege conditions, field routines, concentration and prisoner of war camps.

The appeal of war to artists lies in its importance as an agent of swift change, but also in the highly attractive or exciting aspects of human experience which can be portrayed. These include the horror and brutality of violent death, adventure, courage, sacrifice, romantic landscapes, the action of men and horses and the poignancy of surrender or defeat, all of which are represented in illustrations of the Anglo-Boer War. Most war art is realistic because of its descriptive predisposition, but armed conflict can often be treated by artists somewhat romantically and dramatically, because it provides the individual with those 'perfect conditions of extremity and terror'[11] in which to act commendably and to earn some kind of immortality.

Although the late nineteenth century public generally preferred its art to be realistic rather than Romantic, many Romantic representations of individual heroism can be found in the South African material. Recognition of the element of realism inherent in war art does not exclude its symbolic role, for this exists in abundance, particularly in shaping the conceptual framework which makes an appeal to arms possible. In using symbols and emblems – such as flags, badges, or monuments – art provides the visual means of expressing those abstract ideas which bind an individual and his society.[12] And there is another form of symbolism to be found in profusion in Anglo-Boer War art – in cartoons and caricatures, which exaggerate (frequently in an amusing or satirical manner) the metaphors of war.

War art gives a partisan view and has a tendency towards propaganda because it ties comment to documentation. Consequently it is a highly public genre, for a wide audience is needed in order for propaganda to be effective. The responsibility of depicting war has therefore not been left to chance. War artists have played an official role for centuries and have been integrated into the mechanisms of power by serving the dominant ideology. Even within the simplest of records elements of propaganda can be detected; at the time of the Anglo-Boer War much of it was produced by artists in some paid capacity, for example as employees of newspapers or periodicals which prescribed the artist's point of view. War art can thus be interpreted as a means of social control and a device for conditioning behaviour. There seems little doubt that the social role of Anglo-Boer War art is as worthy of study as the artistic merit it might contain.

The discipline of art history has frequently placed a premium on formalist analysis and concentrated on originality and style rather than according primacy to content. Recent philosophical trends such as revisionism and post-modernism have, however, provided a broader sociopolitical base and yielded new interest in imagery which may be possessed of little formal and aesthetic merit. Because the distinction between 'fine art' and 'illustration' is becoming blurred, interest in the art of the War is increasing and the artistic production of the Victorian period – some of it having been categorized as 'kitsch' – is being reconsidered.[13] In order to illuminate culture, the relationship between the individual and society is being studied through more popular art forms. These tools of art historical analysis will refresh the study of war illustration which has until recently generally been relegated to the category of historical sources.

THE ART AND ILLUSTRATIONS OF THE ANGLO-BOER WAR
The many thousands of illustrations relating to the Anglo-Boer War pro-

3   4   5

vide a slice of life during three extremely complex and momentous years, and thus a study of them immeasurably enriches our understanding of the society which produced them. These artworks are not merely decorative or peripheral adjuncts to the printed word, but quite the contrary: they form an inextricable part of the social, military and political fabric of the time and are integral to any evaluation of it. In scanning the massive artistic output, it is sobering to remember that a process of selection has been at work. One of the most significant gaps in the artistic record is the quantitative paucity of the Republican record relative to that of the British. It was rare for commando members to illustrate their experiences or even to have access to paints and paper. By the same token, though more substantial than the Boer contribution, relatively little was produced by the ordinary soldier, the civilian record was thin, and there is meagre material from women or Africans. A second, more random, process has determined what has survived. Over the years a great deal of material has been lost, specifically intimate artistic expressions which might have taken the form of naive carvings, drawings or paintings. Many people produced one or two works and only very few – generally professional illustrators – left any great quantity. The value of intimate work is not always appreciated, particularly if no great skill is evident in it, and it is therefore likely that a substantial amount was destroyed and much has disappeared through ignorance of its significance.

By far the bulk of the surviving illustrative material relating to the War was executed in order to convey news of the hostilities to the public at large. Some extremely competent and well-trained draughtsmen – such as Melton Prior – were employed in the joint roles of special artist and correspondent, and many of them were sent to South Africa under commission in order to follow the War at close quarters. Under what were sometimes difficult and dangerous conditions, their work was dispatched with speed to Europe where the sometimes sketchy drawings were edited and completed, engravings and blocks made, and the finished product published. Some of these artist-correspondents were friendly with the military hierarchy and thus in close touch with events. Through these contacts they were often eyewitnesses to military action or favourably placed to interview participants: in this way their perceptions were sometimes extremely well informed. News illustrations provided the general public throughout the world with visual material of the War, and the prodigious output constitutes a massive resource for chronicling victories and defeats, major battles and minor skirmishes, sieges or route marches.

Although, if questioned, they would probably have considered themselves to be accurate and objective reporters, these artists all displayed a

strong point of view which cannot always be termed propaganda. They had a dual responsibility both to reflect and to influence public opinion, and because Britain was well nurtured in values of militarism, imperialism and cultural chauvinism, these standards had to be met. In addition, the Anglo-Boer War provided a source of adventure and heroism set in an exotic and alien environment which appealed to readers.[14] Press illustrators in Britain would have been rejected by their employers and readers had they concentrated on scenes of British cowardice, looting, drunkenness, violence between British soldiers or men finding solace in the arms of prostitutes – even though these events regularly found their way into official reports. Nor, for example, would French or Russian readers have welcomed the depiction of a constant anti-Republican point of view. Whatever their own views on the War, those who created drawings for the press were required to oblige the public's preference for the dramatic rather than the banal. Events were sensationalized and accordingly an unrealistic and idealized perspective of the War emerged.

Blatant propaganda is inherent in war art and can be found in abundance in the Anglo-Boer War material. It may well be that the complex ideologies underlying the War lent themselves to easy distortion, but whatever the cause, the symbolism contained in propaganda rewards detailed study. It exhibits a wealth of innuendo and exaggeration which tells later generations much about the mechanisms of contemporary propaganda and what appealed to segments of late nineteenth century

1 *The Charge of the Devons at Waggon Hill*, a stirring scene of the siege of Ladysmith by besieged correspondent William Maud.
2 The Battle of Nicholson's Nek, where the British mules stampeded causing the soldiers to think they were being ambushed. This postcard deriding the English was by Arthur Thiele.
3 *A midday rest: orderly and ponies*, by Stratford St Leger, showed a moment of rest for animals and man in the harsh South African veld.
4 Mortimer Menpes's *Dutch village near Edenburg* records the tranquillity of a rural scene in the Orange Free State.
5 A Boer soldier saying farewell to his family before leaving for the front. This German postcard illustration was one of many in this sentimental vein.

society. There is little that is subtle and much that is arrogant: favoured devices are contrasts of large against small, of civilization against backwardness, of power or greed against justice, of naked might against meekness. Religious symbolism features prominently, particularly in propaganda favouring the Republican cause. Examples of this include a depiction by Franco De Amicis showing Paul Kruger receiving the blessing of Jesus Christ and a work by Francisque Poulbot showing Kruger being crucified by John Bull. While much propaganda was outlandish, satirical and vicious, many cartoons were created as public artworks which gently lampooned the characteristics of individuals or groups. In *Vanity Fair*, features by Leslie Ward, or 'Spy' or 'Drawl', were popular with the British public, for example, while Emmanuel Poire ('Caran d'Ache') and T. T. Heine were among the many who catered for anti-British sentiments.

While a study of artwork done for a wide and immediate public audience is vital to understanding the Anglo-Boer war, very much more illustrative material was produced with personal aims in mind. The variety in this category is immense and particularly valuable because it contains insights, nuances and evaluations which would not have found favour with the general public. Some of this intimate work was done at leisure, such as that by the British officer Stratford St Leger, or the landscapes by the Australian journalist Mortimer Menpes: their watercolours have little to do with the news industry but are valuable sources of mood and atmosphere. Some men made sketches for their families at home in case they did not survive the War. A galaxy of other artists recorded their personal responses, one of whom was Erich Mayer who depicted scenes in P.O.W. camps.

The wide variety of artistic output relating to the Anglo-Boer War defies easy or simple classification because it can be viewed and appreciated in so many ways. But whether the original intended audience be private or public, all illustrative material is a rich source of contemporary details of life. For example, specific aspects of costume at the time can be clarified; the formal uniform of the regular British army can be contrasted with the everyday clothes of the Republican forces, although quite a few gave a fanciful notion of the dress worn by both sides. Civilian fashion – of Africans, women and children – is also depicted. There are renderings of the natural environment, geography, weather conditions and changing seasons. South African architectural design can be studied, and there are drawings of many small towns in Natal, the Transvaal and Orange Free State. Specific items of military and equestrian equipment are portrayed, as in military technology like armaments, transports, heliographs and observation balloons. Methods of fighting receive attention, ranging from set battle scenes to guerrilla methods of camouflage or the use of trenches.

It is also rewarding to examine the artists' lives, for they represent a cross section of late nineteenth century society. Well-known South African artists feature prominently – men such as Sydney Carter, Gwelo Goodman, Frans Oerder and Hugo Naude. Of others, we know only their initials or that they were humble people – like Mary Butler. Yet others, notably Winston Churchill, have blazed trails across world history. There are authors, such as Rudyard Kipling, and top-class graphic illustrators, such as John Tenniel or Hilda Cowham.

Examining the art and illustrations of the Anglo-Boer War provides an avenue through which late nineteenth century culture can be accessed. Evidence of the all-too-frequently undocumented positions of women and Africans are to be found, and other rifts in society are also exposed, such as a patronizing attitude of many artists towards the working class soldier. More significant are the divisions in British society, shown in anti-war illustrations, a point of view which became more strident as the War progressed. These pictures served also to bare the nature of imperialism – perhaps even contributed to its success[15] – and of opposition to it. Scenes of social disorder are frequent, and relate particularly to the second part of the War when the thrill of conflict had passed and the harsh realities of farm burning, concentration camps, blockhouses and barbed wire were impossible to ignore. In lighter vein, a Victorian love of narrative is given

vent both in subject matter and picture titling – some titles being long enough almost to qualify as short stories. Sentimentality and poignancy abound in depictions of wounded soldiers or of women peering at casualty lists: poignant scenes of soldiers saying farewell to their families were also popular.

Victorians shared the enduring fascination for individual heroes and found them in people ranging from young bugler Dunne at Colenso, to recipients of the Victoria Cross and portraits of generals and commanders. The more ephemeral aspects of late nineteenth century society, including war games, advertisements, educational material, music covers, fundraising techniques, and a contemporary taste for postcards, souvenirs and mementos are also shown.

An evaluation of the art of the Anglo-Boer War from a modern perspective and distance in time records a society at a point of transition. The War came at a time when a greater schism than war itself was taking place – that between the self-confident and rigid values of the nineteenth century and the growing doubts and uncertainties of the twentieth. And consequently, much that was held dear to those alive at the time of the Anglo-Boer War disappeared or was discredited in the wake of the new culture which emerged. Events of the twentieth century have demonstrated repeatedly that war impoverishes society. This knowledge enhances the value of art, for it is one of the few creative and positive results of war.

JANE CARRUTHERS
JOHANNESBURG, APRIL 1992

REFERENCES
1 Matthew P. Lalumia, *Realism and Politics in Victorian Art of the Crimean War* (Ann Arbor, Mich., 1984), p. 18.
2 *Ibid.*, p. 6.
3 *Ibid.*, p. 27.
4 William Fleming, *Art and Ideas*, 6th edn. (New York, 1980), p. 373.
5 Lalumia, *Realism and Politics*, p. xxi.
6 *Ibid.*, p. 57.
7 A. Gordon-Brown, *Pictorial Africana*, (Cape Town, 1975), p. 122.
8 William F. Lye, (ed.), *Andrew Smith's journal of his expedition into the Interior of South Africa* (Cape Town, 1975), *passim*.
9 Jane Carruthers, *Thomas Baines: Eastern Cape Sketches, 1848 to 1852* (Johannesburg, 1990).
10 M. van Wyk Smith, *Drummer Hodge: The Poetry of the Anglo-Boer War, (1899-1902)*. (Oxford, 1978), p. 250.
11 Ken Baynes, *War*, (London, 1970), p. 34.
12 *Ibid.*, p. 57.
13 K. Bendiner, *An Introduction to Victorian Art* (New Haven, 1985), pp. 4-5.
14 J. M. McKenzie, *Imperialism and Popular Culture* (Manchester, 1986), p. 49.
15 *Ibid.*, p. 49.

PART ONE

ARTISTS AT THE FRONT

CHAPTER ONE

The 'Special' Artists

Previous page: *The Scout*, a watercolour by *The Sphere* correspondent W. B. Wollen. He used the same title on a different illustration, from which a photogravure was made.
Right: Black scouts on the side of the British depicted by Mortimer Menpes in his book *War Impressions*.

For thousands of years artists have been representing war, in works ranging from the monumental friezes of the Assyrians through to the heroic canvases depicting the victories of Napoleon and Nelson. Yet most of these pictorial records were painted not by eyewitnesses but by artists working much later and at a great distance from the scene. The Crimean War (1854-6) was the first notable struggle to be covered by an artist specifically commissioned for this purpose – a so-called 'special' artist. (This term is distinct from the 'artist-correspondent', who was usually the local representative of a newspaper.) The first 'special' artist was William Simpson, who earned the nickname of 'Crimean Simpson' for his accurate representations of that war. The lithographs he produced were published in 1856 in *The Seat of War in the East*. He went on to report for *The Illustrated London News* in 1866.

Thereafter, virtually every colonial war, skirmish or rebellion in the far-flung British Empire was covered by a faithful band of 'specials', all competing for the momentous scoop that would boost their newspaper's circulation and reputation. However, travel was not so easy then and few of the 'special' artists were able to get to the battle scene in time to make live-action sketches. They were frequently reduced to using reconstructions based on the evidence of other eyewitnesses, but at least the 'specials' had the advantage of seeing for themselves the details of terrain and clothing which made their drawings more realistic and reliable than interpre-

tations done from afar. In South Africa, Thomas Baines depicted the seventh and eighth Frontier Wars against the Xhosa, although he was an eyewitness only during the eighth. John North Crealock produced striking watercolours of the Zulu War, including scenes of Isandhlwana, Rorke's Drift and the death of the Prince Imperial. The First Boer War (1880-1) was covered by Charles Fripp and Melton Prior, who had also been in South Africa during the Zulu War, but unfortunately neither artist witnessed any of the major battles. Towards the end of the nineteenth century, Melton Prior captured the dramatic failure of the Jameson Raid, the abortive attempt by Rhodes's protégé, Dr Leander Starr Jameson, to invade the Transvaal and lead the Uitlanders in revolt against Kruger.

When the Boer War broke out in 1899 most British newspapers were well prepared for the event. Though few of their correspondents were actually present when the first shots were fired, there were enough of them in the field to supply Britain with reasonably accurate portraits of the War from the beginning. The home-based artists, employed at the newspaper offices, redrew the hasty sketches sent from the front by the 'special'.

Thanks to the pioneering work of Roger Fenton, photography had been used in warfare as early as the Crimean War. The American Civil War (1861-5) was covered in great detail by Matthew Brady, who when asked why he photographed so many dead men, replied: 'Dead men don't move'. This was of course a reference to the long exposures required to produce acceptable photographs.

Although photography and even cinematography were used to excellent advantage during the War, the difficulty of processing film meant that photographers such as H. C. Shelley, W. Dickson, René Bull and David Barnett found it virtually impossible to take live action shots. It was left to the artist to depict live action. Any examination of the art of the Boer War must begin with a close look at the illustrated newspapers that employed these artists, for it was the existence of these newspapers – and their readers' voracious appetite for sensational news and dramatic images – that unleashed the flood of illustrations that characterized this war.

The Illustrated Newspapers

Attempts to launch regular illustrated periodicals on a large scale began in Europe and the United States in the early part of the nineteenth century. But the time was not then ripe for an enterprise that demanded vast financial resources, a large literate readership prepared to buy the papers, and an efficient system for distributing the news before it became stale. The situation changed dramatically in Britain with the advent of the Industrial Revolution which not only spawned a network of railways but also bred a large, educated middle class who were eager for information about the world around them and, more importantly, had enough money and time to enjoy periodicals.

Charles Knight (1791-1873), founder of the Society for the Diffusion of Useful Knowledge, exploited this demand as early as 1828, producing large quantities of cheap recreational literature, both fiction and non-fiction, in his *The New Penny Magazine* and *The Penny Cyclopaedia*. But it was not until 1841 that *The Illustrated London News*, the first of the illustrated weeklies, was launched by Herbert Ingram, a successful Nottingham newsagent who had previously made a fortune out of the manufacture of patent medicines. Ingram originally intended to produce a weekly crime sheet of a lurid and sensational nature but Henry Vizetelly, the man he hired as his art adviser, engraver, special artist and printer, convinced him of the difficulty of providing a good murder to order every Saturday.

Instead, Vizetelly proposed a more factual newspaper, which would not only report news events but also illustrate them – and would employ the finest artists and engravers available to do so. After some persuasion, Vizetelly's concept won the day. The first issue of *The Illustrated London News* appeared on 14 May 1842, with E.W.N. 'Omnibus' Bailey as editor, a Mr Monaghan as his sub-editor and John Gilbert as chief artist. By the time it reached its seventh issue, the circulation of *The Illustrated London News* was 20 000. By the end of 1842 it was 66 000, and by the end of the decade it passed the 100 000 mark. Significantly, and in direct contrast to the more ephemeral dailies, the weekly *The Illustrated London News* encouraged subscribers to save back issues, providing binders and indexes every six months.

On the Continent and in the United States illustrated newspapers followed closely on the heels of *The Illustrated London News*. *L'Illustration* was launched in Paris in 1843, the same year that the Leipzig-based *Leipziger Illustrierte Zeitung* appeared. *La Illustración* made its debut in Madrid in 1849. Across the Atlantic in New York, *Frank Leslie's Illustrated Newspaper* and *Harper's Weekly* were first published in 1855 and 1857 respectively. Also in 1857, *Le Monde Illustré* was published in Paris, while the first Russian illustrated news weekly, *Vsemirnaya Illyustratsiya*, based in St Petersburg, appeared in 1867.

In 1869, after a virtual monopoly of 27 years, *The Illustrated London News* received its first serious challenge on home ground when William Thomas launched *The Graphic*. Thomas was a well-known engraver and illustrator who had been elected a member of the Royal Institute of Painters. The success of *The Graphic* inspired him to embark on an even more ambitious project, a daily illustrated paper, and the first issue of *The Daily Graphic* appeared on 4 January 1890. The logistics of such a venture were considerable, but new, improved methods of reproduction enabled the paper to succeed despite the many initial doubts and reservations. Another major illustrated news weekly which was to have a strong influence in Britain, *Black & White*, first appeared on 6 February 1891. A budget edition known as *Black & White Budget*, costing twopence, was published at the start of the Boer War.

The Sphere made a late entry onto the scene in January 1900, the last of the 'Big Four' British illustrated periodicals that were to depict the War in all its detail. By the last quarter of 1899 the editors of the 'Big Four' were predicting that the 'Transvaal Crisis' would not be resolved peacefully and were busily engaging and despatching 'special' artists to South Africa. The illustrated newspapers which were not represented in South Africa borrowed extensively from the 'Big Four' – sometimes with, but more often without, any acknowledgement of the original source. The 'special' artists, although few in number, comprised by far the most important group of artists depicting the War. Not more than 20 artists fall into this category and only a handful were in South Africa at the start of the War.

Several established artists were already working in England, most of whom had experience of foreign wars. They were not always loyal to their employers and some of them sold their services to the highest bidder. The top 'specials' were given a free rein as far as equipment, transport and expenses were concerned and some were rumoured to earn as much as £1 000 a year in peacetime, rising to £2 000 in wartime. The American Frederic Remington was one of the highest paid artists, demanding up to $100 per illustration and the right to keep and sell the original, which he invariably succeeded in doing. Freelancers were paid £100 a month and/or a set fee per column inch for all sketches and drawings accepted.

'SPECIALS' FOR THE ILLUSTRATED LONDON NEWS
MELTON PRIOR

In September 1899 *The Illustrated London News* recalled its top artist Melton Prior from France, where he had been covering the Dreyfus retrial in Rennes, and ordered him to South Africa. An experienced and highly paid 'special' artist, Prior paused only to assemble his equipment, which included liberal supplies of champagne, Scotch whisky and tinned delicacies. When he boarded the SS *Norman* in Southampton at the end of September, it was to be his fifth trip out to South Africa. He had covered the last of the Frontier Wars in the Eastern Cape in 1878, the Zulu War in 1879, the First

'The making of *The Illustrated London News*: How the paper is produced each week'. This full-page illustration by Samuel Begg appeared in the newspaper on 2 September 1911. It depicts many of the home-based artists who drew Anglo-Boer War scenes. At the table on the left are, from left to right, S. Begg, M. Cowper, C. de Lacy, and on the right-hand side of the table are, from fromt to back: A. Forestier, F. de Haenen and H. Koekkoek. Caton Woodville is in front of the easel in the background, Cyrus Cuneo at the easel in the front, and behind him is Norman Wilkinson.

Boer War in 1881 and the Jameson Raid in 1895-6. On the last occasion Prior had been tipped off by his editor that trouble was likely and he had arrived in time to scoop the capture of Jameson and his men. Prior also interviewed and sketched them during their captivity and throughout the trial that followed.

Now in September 1899 Prior was fortunate enough to be sailing to South Africa on the same ship as Maj. Gen. John French and his staff. On his arrival in Table Bay, Prior found Cape Town agog with the news that war was imminent. It was even rumoured that the Boers had already invaded Natal.

Prior went to Durban, where he teamed up with Ernest Smith of *The Morning Leader*; the pair bought horses and set off by train for Ladysmith. There, by lucky chance, they were able to join a troop train going to the front, so that their first taste of the War was the Battle of Elandslaagte.

After Elandslaagte, Prior joined Gen. Sir George White and his forces in their withdrawal to Ladysmith and their subsequent incarceration there. At first Prior and the other correspondents in Ladysmith were confident that help would arrive within a week or two. A large press corps had gathered, including Henry Pearse (*The Daily News*), George W. Steevens (*The Daily Mail*), Henry Wood Nevison (*The Daily Chronicle*), Ernest W. Smith (*The Morning Leader*), William Maud (*The Graphic*), Joseph Smith Dunn (Central News Agency), George Lynch, Earl Robert, Harry McCormick, Bennet Burleigh and Lionel James. When they realized that imminent relief was unlikely they began to send out smuggled messages and drawings using black runners, a method that was not only expensive but also extremely dangerous for the runners. In due course the military authorities and the press censor organized a weekly postal service at the much lower cost of £15 per letter.

When the relief column reached Ladysmith, Prior was loaned a pony by Maj. Gen. Sir Archibald Hunter and so was able to ride out and sketch the historic meeting of Lt. Gen. Sir George White and Gen. Sir Redvers Buller. Two days later, on 2 March 1900, Prior left Ladysmith, travelling by wagon to Colenso and Durban, by steamer to Cape Town and by train to Bloemfontein. There he joined Field Marshal Lord Roberts's 'Grand Army' and collaborated with Julian Ralph, Rudyard Kipling and others in producing *The Friend*, the newspaper started at the suggestion of Roberts. Mindful of the number of famous journalists in the city, Roberts considered that a newspaper written specially for the soldiers who would have to remain in Bloemfontein ought to be a resounding success.

Though Prior claimed that the rest of his stay in South Africa provided no further 'exciting incidents', he followed Roberts through the Free State to Johannesburg, where he depicted the *Unfurling of the British Flag in the Gold Reef City* and he was with Roberts when he entered Pretoria. Soon after this, believing like most of the other war artists that the War was over, Prior returned to England. His next foreign assignments were the Delhi Durbar in December 1902 and the Somali Campaign in 1903. But he worked in the offices of *The Illustrated London News* before going out to India and Somalia, often drawing 'fillers' of a general nature based on his experiences in South Africa. He also portrayed the rousing welcome given to the City Imperial Volunteers at Paddington Station when they returned to Lon-

don in late October 1900. Still later, Prior collaborated with Spenser Wilkinson to produce the souvenir publication *The Transvaal War*, and was one of the signatories to the special limited edition.

FREDERIC VILLIERS

Frederic Villiers, another special artist for *The Illustrated London News*, was on a lecture tour in Melbourne, Australia, when he ran into a fortune-teller whom he had met on the voyage out from England. She predicted that war would break out in South Africa and that Villiers would travel to the battlefields via Port Elizabeth; he would carry an important despatch and, despite being involved in a British disaster and possibly falling ill, would survive the war – provided he carried the lucky token which she was about to give him. Villiers and his wife heard the news of the outbreak of war on 12 October 1899. They left Sydney on a troopship bound for Cape Town, but on their arrival in Algoa Bay learned that Lt. Gen. Sir William Gatacre was about to advance on Stormberg, and disembarked at once in Port Elizabeth. Villiers, counting Gatacre as a personal acquaintance, was all set to join him until he learned that Lt. Gen. Lord Methuen was about to relieve Kimberley. Instead he opted for what he considered would be the greater scoop: to be present at the relief of Kimberley, with the possibility of being the first reporter to interview Rhodes.

Travelling with Frederick Wilkinson of *The Sydney Daily Telegraph*, Villiers left his wife behind in Port Elizabeth and took the train for De Aar junction. The commandant of the area arranged a pass for the two men to the Orange River, but there Villiers was told that Methuen was so 'fed up' with war correspondents that he was no longer prepared to allow any of them to join his forces. However, Villiers had been with Methuen in Egypt in 1882 and he felt he might dare to impose on this friendship. He therefore sent a personal telegram to Methuen. Back came the reply: 'Glad to see you, come at once'. This time lack of transport threatened to thwart Villiers. When at last he was able to catch a train, to his surprise another of the fortune-teller's predictions came true: an official asked him to carry a despatch to Methuen personally, in the absence of a suitable officer for the task. Villiers reached Methuen's headquarters just as battle with the Boers commenced. He joined Col. Thomas Pilcher's command in its advance towards Belmont until, hearing that there was to be a fight at Coleskop, he hastily hired a Cape cart and was soon on his way to Noupoort. Along the way he was stopped and searched by a party of Suffolks, then released only to be fired at by another party of British troops who mistook him for a Boer. Afterwards the troops claimed that Villiers had not answered their call when challenged.

Still Villiers was not landing the scoops he had dreamed of. In his frustration he thought he would be better off linking his fortunes with Buller, who, he now heard, was about to make his third attempt to relieve Ladysmith. Villiers went back to Port Elizabeth by goods train, and sailed with his wife on the B.I.S. *Lindula* to Durban. Villiers was dismayed when he arrived in Durban to be met with the news of Buller's defeat at Spioenkop and subsequent withdrawal to safer regions on the far side of the Tugela River. Incredibly, Villiers went back to Port Elizabeth again, making yet another attempt (as if echoing Buller's ill-fated Ladysmith advance) to reach Kimberley.

1 Melton Prior, 'special' artist for *The Illustrated London News* and one of the most prominent correspondents of the War.
2 *With the Flag to Pretoria* published this photograph of some of the war correspondents on their return to England after the fall of Pretoria.
3 Samuel Begg painted this scene of Melton Prior sketching the Battle of Nicholson's Nek on 30 October. It was published in the *Illustrated London News* on 16 December 1899.
4 Melton Prior wrote this letter explaining the problems of sending his sketches home to his head office in London. *The Illustrated London News* published it in facsimile.

At Modder River, Villiers joined the *Black & White* artist Mortimer Menpes, who was sharing his cart with photographer Edward Daniel Scott of *The Manchester Courier* (who later died in the War). Twelve miles from Kimberley their exhausted horses refused to move. Villiers left his companions, later claiming that they had preferred to remain behind, and cadged a ride from an old friend, a local farmer by the name of Bisset.

In his book *War Impressions*, Menpes tells a different story. Without mentioning Villiers's name, Menpes refers to him sarcastically as 'the Veteran' and implies that he was sneaky and underhand. According to Menpes, Villiers had promised to send help the moment he reached Kimberley, but in fact hoped to steal a march on his *Black & White* rival in scooping early sketches of Roberts and Rhodes in Kimberley. (In the event, Roberts was not there.) Menpes took his revenge later, when he described Villiers's dishonourable act to Rhodes while they were all lunching together, causing Villiers great embarrassment.

When the untiring Villiers finally reached Kimberley, he made at once for Rhodes's hotel. The great man was in the bath, but he sent assurance that Villiers was welcome to interview him – after his ablutions. At last Villiers was in luck, not least when Rhodes insisted that his secretary share his breakfast steak with the hungry newcomer.

Unlike many other correspondents, Villiers did not stay on in South Africa until Pretoria was occupied, but left for England soon after the relief of Kimberley. His two-volume memoir *Villiers: His Five Decades of Adventure* (1921), outlines his long and illustrious career.

FRANK STEWART

Frank Stewart was a young artist of 22 when he joined the staff of *The Illustrated Sporting & Dramatic News*, whose proprietors were also the publishers of *The Illustrated London News*. Naturally, Stewart's work appeared in both papers. The precise date of Stewart's arrival in South Africa is unknown, but his first illustration (in facsimile, dated 1899) appeared in *The Illustrated London News* on 20 January 1900. It featured the Battle of Colenso, which had been fought on 15 December 1899. It is possible that Stewart, who was later to become famous for his equestrian paintings, had been sent out as a replacement for Melton Prior, who was besieged at Ladysmith. Stewart remained with Buller's Natal field force throughout the campaign; his last illustration appeared on 20 October 1900. Most of his 34 illustrations appeared in facsimile, often accompanied by extracts from his letters. Like many of his colleagues Stewart was invalided home, probably suffering from typhoid. The date of his departure is not known, but none of his illustrations was published during June and July 1900. This was probably because of his convalescence and subsequent return to Britain. His later illustrations were done in the offices of his employers. Many of Stewart's sketches were used again in John Black Atkins's book *The Relief of Ladysmith*, and several also in *The Sketch* and *The Illustrated Sporting & Dramatic News*.

HENRY CHARLES SEPPINGS WRIGHT

As another experienced and well-known artist for *The Illustrated London News* and *The Illustrated Sporting & Dramatic News*, Henry Charles Seppings Wright set out for South Africa with Buller on the *Dunottar Castle* in October 1899, but in Madeira for some unexplained reason he was ordered to get off the ship and return to England. In his report, published in *The Illustrated London News* on 11 November 1899, Wright expresses regret at being forced to leave the ship. However, he did feel that his 'mission' was already complete. He had visited the South African diamond fields in the 1870s, and had represented *The Illustrated London News* in Ashanti and Dongola in the 1890s, in the Spanish-American War of 1898, and the Russo-Japanese War of 1904-5. Most of

F. A. Stewart

R. C. Woodville

Samuel Begg

Spenser Wilkinson

Frederic Villiers

1   2

Wright's Boer War illustrations were done in the offices of the newspaper. Since he possessed considerable naval experience, the bulk of these illustrations, not surprisingly, had a maritime theme.

'SPECIALS' FOR THE GRAPHIC AND THE DAILY GRAPHIC

The Graphic and *The Daily Graphic* shared a team of highly experienced artists, including William Theobald Maud and Charles Fripp.

WILLIAM MAUD

Prior to the Boer War Maud had seen service in Armenia, Crete, Egypt, India and Sudan. In September 1899 he boarded the *Tintagel Castle* bound for South Africa (René Bull of *Black & White* was a fellow passenger) and received the famous signal 'War last Wednesday' from the outward bound *Dunvegan Castle*. Maud's impression of the incident was redrawn by H.M. Paget and published in *The Graphic*.

Maud rushed off to Natal but was trapped in Ladysmith. Writing in *The Graphic*'s special double number, published on 2 April 1900, Maud gives a very lucid account of the Battle of Lombard's Kop on 29 October 1899 which resulted in the British forces under White being besieged in Ladysmith. The sketches that reached home were few and far between and had to be smuggled out by black runners, many of whom never made it to the British lines. Maud's depiction of life in Ladysmith, in a letter he wrote home, was grim.

> We have had a horrible time of it, one I shall never forget as long as I live. The number of fine men that have gone under since the siege is simply appalling to think of. What with the deaths from shot, shell, starvation and disease we have but a shattered remnant of the fine force that came here last October. Now I write to ask for your approval of a step which I took here on February 1. It is one that is probably without precedent. The attack on January 6 left the garrison terribly weak, especially in officers. In fact our position, as you know, became critical. I then volunteered my services, which were readily accept-

ed by Sir George White and General Ian Hamilton appointed me as his A.D.C. in place of Lord Ava, who was killed.

G.W. Steevens, *The Daily Mail* correspondent, was a close friend of Maud's and shared the same house before he took ill and eventually died in Maud's arms. After the relief Maud resigned his commission but was so affected by typhoid that he had to recuperate in Durban for a while before being allowed to return home. He continued to work as a home-based artist for *The Graphic* and *The Daily Graphic* on his return to England.

CHARLES FRIPP

Fripp was another experienced war artist employed by *The Graphic* and *The Daily Graphic*. His artistic ability was regarded very highly and two of his military paintings, one titled *The last stand at Isandhula* (sic), were exhibited at the Royal Academy. As a young man of 23 he had covered the last Frontier War and a year later the Zulu War. Like Prior he was back in South Africa for the First Boer War, and for the Matabele Rebellion in 1896. Fripp was in the Philippines covering the revolution when he was recalled to South Africa and, judging by the dates of his illustrations (mostly in facsimile), he seems to have arrived later than the other 'special' artists. He may have accompanied a contingent of City Imperial Volunteers and, as one of his illustrations depicts members of the C.I.V. returning to England on the *Aurania*, which docked on 28 October 1900, he may well have returned with them. One of his best-known sketches depicts Roberts riding into Pretoria on 5 June 1900. Fripp was small but quick-tempered. Both Melton Prior in *Campaigns of a War Correspondent* and A.S. Hartrick in *A Painter's Pilgrimage* describe an incident during the Zulu War when Fripp was ordered to return to the safety of the British camp while he was busily sketching on the far bank of the Umfolozi River and, in the opinion of the commanding officer, too close to the Zulus for comfort. Fripp obeyed the order but demanded to know from Buller why he had been given such a severe dressing down. Lord William Beresford, twice Fripp's size, intervened and threatened to horsewhip him if he did not show more respect to an officer. Fripp literally flew at him and it took the combined strength of Archibald Forbes and Melton Prior to separate the two and to drag off the still-furious artist.

OTHERS

Major Godfrey Douglas Giles, another Royal Academy exhibitor of military paintings, represented *The Graphic* and was attached to French's column. In his chapter 'With French to Kimberley and Roberts to Bloemfontein' in *The Graphic History of the South African War*, Giles recalls how he, along with other correspondents, was forbidden to move forward from Modder River until Roberts had done so. Representations to the censor reversed this decision subject to certain conditions. Later, Giles was able to portray and describe in detail the surrender of Cronje at Paardeberg, the relief of Kimberley and the raising of the British flag in Bloemfontein.

The fourth member of *The Graphic* special artist team was Harry McCormick, a South African-born artist and illustrator who reputedly accompanied the relieving forces into Ladysmith. *The Graphic* special double number for 2 April 1900 reproduced several illustrations by McCormick, one of which shows *The correspondents Maud, Lynch and Steevens watching the Big Gun duel at Ladysmith*. The subject matter of this illustration and the two others seems to indicate that McCormick was indeed in Ladysmith during the siege. A more positive proof is Lionel James's comment that 'McCormick the war artist' was present at G.W. Steevens's funeral on 13 January 1900.

'SPECIALS' FOR BLACK & WHITE AND BLACK & WHITE BUDGET

Black & White, whose editor was not known for his modesty, claimed to have an unprecedented 15 'reliable correspondents', although only four were artists. *Black & White Budget* announced on 13 January 1900 and again in greater detail on 3 February that 'The chief of our correspondents . . . is Mr René Bull a talented Franco-Hibernian who has done work for us since 1896'. Bull and Bennet Burleigh of *The Daily Telegraph* managed to take the last train out of Ladysmith after the Battle of Lombard's Kop. *Black & White* boasted that 'Mr Bull had been sagacious enough to keep to the open country hopping about at his own sweet will'. This of course was meant as a dig at Lionel James, W.T. Maud and Melton Prior who were unable to make their escape. For some inexplicable reason Bull has the comment next to his name in Capt. F.B. Maurice's register: 'licence revoked'. (Maurice, the son of J.F. Maurice, the author of the eight-volume *History of the War in South Africa 1899-1902*, was a press censor. His register contained a list of all accredited correspondents.)

Continuing its announcement *Black & White Budget* reports:

Accompanying Lord Roberts to chronicle what we all hope will be a triumphant progress over the South African Karoo, over the Inter-State boundaries and on to Pretoria is Mr S.M. Laurence a young American artist who has already had experience of warfare during the great Spanish-American War. He is a seascapist of great power, and his pictures of men fighting are full of life, as our readers will find when the first work comes to hand.

With Lord Methuen's force is Mr Lester Ralph, also an American, the son of the well-known journalist Mr Julian Ralph, who is now sending home to *The Daily Mail* such admirable word pictures of camp life and fighting on the Modder River. Mr Ralph is already known to the readers of *Black & White* by his fine impressionist work and to readers of the *Budget* he is known by the living sketches he has sent home of the fighting at Belmont, Graspan, the Modder River and Magersfontein.

Accompanying the City of London Imperial Volunteers to the front is an artist whose name is known the whole world over, because he is first of all an artist, and secondly a reporter of events. This is Mr. Mortimer Menpes, who is entitled to tag after his name a list of honours and titles of which few artists can boast. Mr. Menpes is the inventor of a process of colour etching, in which, to the sharpness and definition attained by the tools of the etcher, he has added the softness and brilliance of all the rich colours that may be laid on the painter's palette. Mr Menpes will be able to send us from the front portraits of all the principal Generals and notabilities of the war and when his work appears in our pages we know that there will be but one verdict on it; what that verdict will be modesty forbids us to say.

In addition to these gentlemen we have a number of military correspondents whose names the unwritten laws of military etiquette forbid us to record. They are sending us pictures which appear in our pages from time to time. With such a staff of able assistants we contend that *Black & White* and *Black & White Budget* provide the *only complete and absolutely faithful pictorial* record of the war.

To this little bit of self-advertising was added the name of David Barnett, the photographer whom *Black & White Budget* refers to as a 'true Uitlander and brother of the photographer who acted for us during the troublous times of the Jameson raid'. His brother Joseph died in 1897.

Laurence arrived in South Africa aboard the RMS *Moor* and Bull left for South Africa aboard the *Tintagel Castle* on 29 September 1899, hearing the news of the outbreak of war from a signal from the *Dunvegan Castle* 600 miles north of Cape Town. Lester Ralph eventually reached Bloemfontein but, like many others, he became severely ill with typhoid and he returned home. He later illustrated his father's account of *The Friend* newspaper, *War's Brighter Side*. It was therefore left mainly to Mortimer Menpes to represent *Black & White Budget* in the field.

MORTIMER MENPES

Australian-born Mortimer Menpes, unlike the other artists, had not covered a war before the Anglo-Boer struggle and he was somewhat apprehensive about accepting *Black & White*'s offer to send him to South Africa. He sailed from Southampton on 14 January 1900 on the SS *Briton*, which was also carrying Gen. Archibald Wavell, who was later to embarrass the rather prudish Menpes with his colourful language, well loaded with four-letter words. Also aboard were Col. Hugh Cholmondeley and his mounted City Imperial Volunteers, the Yeomanry regiment raised by the City of London, and many 'correspondents of fortune' – freelance journalists dreaming of scoops and personal fortunes.

1 Drawings of the contributors to *The Illustrated London News*'s Record of the Transvaal War, featured in the special numbered edition. They are, from top to bottom, A. Stewart, Richard Caton Woodville, Samuel Begg, Spenser Wilkinson (the author), and Frederic Villiers.
2 C.E. Fripp's wash drawing *Bargaining for Geese*. Reproduced courtesy of the National Army Museum, London.
3 This pen-and-ink sketch by Frank A. Stewart was reproduced in *The Illustrated London News* on 24 March 1900. It depicts the taking of Monte Cristo a month before.

2

1

In Cape Town Menpes spent some time finding out how best to reach the front and with what provisions. One of his purchases was a white helmet which he stained khaki and wore until he realized that every soldier and officer was saluting him: unwittingly he had adopted the headgear of a field marshal. In his ignorance he also spent £12 on a ticket to Modder River, only to learn that all accredited correspondents were granted free rail passes. Finally, at the end of the arduous five-day journey to the Orange River, a young staff officer told him that his pass was not in order and ordered Menpes to return to Cape Town on the next train. Dejected, Menpes returned to Cape Town, prepared to resign his appointment and sail for home on the next ship. Then, as in the case of so many of the 'special' artists, a friend with influence materialized. Admiral Frederick Maxse introduced Menpes to Maj. Walter Bagot, the military censor based in Cape Town, and Bagot fired off a telegram to Lord Stanley, the censor at the front, insisting on 'Menpes's importance as chief representative of *Black & White*'. Back came the reply: 'Menpes can go anywhere he likes'.

Despite his frustration at kicking his heels in Cape Town, Menpes did not waste his time but produced many sketches of local tourist sights, some of which are reproduced in his book *War Impressions*. But at last he returned to the Orange River, from where he proceeded to Kimberley. In his version of the famous brush with Frederic Villiers, 'special' artist for *The Illustrated London News*, Menpes adds a touch of extra colour, describing his arrest by soldiers he believed to be Boers, and claiming to have been relieved when his 'captors' turned out to be merely members of the Kimberley town guard, delighted to escort Menpes and Scott into Kimberley. Rhodes granted Menpes an interview and gave him many opportunities to sketch him in the two weeks he spent in Kimberley.

A stay at Maj. Gen. Pole-Carew's camp at Klip Drift

was enlivened by the arrival, under City Imperial Volunteers escort, of Gen. Piet Cronje and the 4 000 Boer prisoners taken at Paardeberg. Menpes was able to capture the impressive sight of this weary column of prisoners in his sketchbook and describes how moved he was by the spontaneous singing of a psalm by the prisoners. Psalm-singing by prisoners and women refugees had a profound effect on British onlookers unused to such religious fervour.

An eventful trip in a damaged cart took Menpes on into Bloemfontein with Roberts's forces. Here he was able to secure an interview with Roberts, again through the good offices of Admiral Maxse. He was given considerable help by Col. Neville Francis Chamberlain, Roberts's military secretary, who was himself an artist and an admirer of Menpes's work. And though Menpes confessed shyness in Roberts's presence, the august commander-in-chief soon put him at his ease, saying 'Ah Mr Menpes, don't talk of presumption. It is a great privilege to sit to you, and I am delighted that we have you with us to secure a record of what will be a historic event'.

During his stay in Bloemfontein, Menpes met and sketched several leading generals and personalities on the British side.

When Menpes returned to Cape Town he interviewed and sketched Milner in Government House on many different occasions, and renewed his acquaintance with Rhodes. A visit to Rhodes's fruit farms may have inspired the Menpes Fruit Farms, established in 1907 at Pangbourne in England. (See also pp. 172-173.)

'SPECIALS' FOR THE SPHERE

The Sphere was a latecomer to the illustrated weekly newspaper scene, with the first issue appearing on 27 January 1900. The editor, Clement Shorter, had placed advertisements in its main rivals *The Graphic* and *The Illustrated London News*. Besides promising that it

3

1 *The Sphere* featured pictures of several artists and correspondents on 4 August 1900. Among them were (from top to bottom) Prater, Paxton, Schönberg and Lynch.
2 *Boer prisoners led into Klip Drift by C.I.V.*, a watercolour by Mortimer Menpes. Menpes commented that this was one of the most impressive sights that he ever saw in South Africa.
3 *Saving the guns at Colenso*, a watercolour by Sidney Paget. It was in this battle that Lord Roberts lost his only son Freddie. Lieutenant Roberts had volunteered to save the guns. He was mortally wounded in the attempt and was awarded a posthumous Victoria Cross. A similar watercolour by Paget was reproduced in the first issue of *The Sphere* on 27 January 1900.
4 As part of the entertainment for British troops held up in Bloemfontein during the typhoid epidemic, some of the illustrators produced lightning sketches of war personalities. Here Robert Paxton illustrated William Wollen sketching Lord Roberts.

would 'take its place in the front rank of illustrated newspapers' and that 'it would not be overcrowded with advertisements', he emphasized that the paper would provide 'the most interesting pictures of the war in South Africa, from sketches and photographs by our six "special" war artists'. These 'special' artists were Gilbert James, William Wollen, Ernest Prater and Johann Schönberg, with the Earl of Rosslyn of the Imperial Yeomanry and Col. F.H. Hoskier of the 3rd Middlesex Volunteers listed as photographers. *The Sphere* goes on to say that 'Hoskier has had very considerable experience as an artillery draughtsman and may supplement his photographs by sketches'. Hoskier had gone out to South Africa as a volunteer without a commission but obtained this when he joined Maj. Gen. Brabant under Gatacre. Later, while doing service with Montmorency's Scouts, he and his leader were killed in a skirmish near Stormberg. None of Hoskier's sketches, if any were done, has been traced, though *The Sphere* gave generous credit to his photographs.

WOLLEN, PRATER AND PAXTON

William Wollen was an artist and illustrator of considerable experience and ability. He had exhibited regularly at the Royal Academy from 1879, and on his return from South Africa in 1900 he drew on his experiences as inspiration for works that were exhibited at the R.A. in 1901, 1902 and 1903. While most of his paintings were of a sporting or military nature, the Boer War was the only conflict of which he had personal experience. Both Wollen and Prater had been sent out aboard the *Dunottar Castle* before the first issue of *The Sphere* appeared. Virtually from the first page the paper carried illustrations from Wollen (with Methuen) at Modder River and Prater (with Buller) at Colenso. Both these artists continued to send sketches home regularly, and many of them were reproduced in facsimile.

Wollen was present at Magersfontein and the relief of

Kimberley and travelled with Roberts through Bloemfontein and Kroonstad to Pretoria. While in Bloemfontein he, like Menpes, Prior and others, contributed articles and letters to *The Friend*. On one occasion in the letters column he defended the position of the war artist vis-à-vis the war photographer, whose superiority was claimed by H. Owen Scott and later by H. Shelley of *The King*. (See also pp. 233-234.)

Prater remained with Buller's forces in their advance to the relief of Ladysmith, but he too fell victim to typhoid and was hospitalized for a month before returning home. (See also pp. 187-188.)

Robert Paxton was also a member of the team aboard the *Dunottar Castle*. *The Sphere* reported on 7 April 1900 that Paxton had been sent 'to Lord Roberts whose forces may have to be divided for strategic reasons' and later announced his 'safe arrival in Bloemfontein'. Paxton sent back several illustrations of the campaign in the western Transvaal, including a self-portrait. (See pp. 182-183.)

The Sphere remarked on 4 August 1900: 'Most of the war artists and correspondents have now returned from the front bringing with them a great many sketches which will bear fruit as thrilling pictures in oils at the Galleries in the Autumn.' On their return many of the artists, including Wollen, Prater and Paxton, returned to the more mundane positions of home-based artists and continued to publish illustrations based on their own sketches and memories or the works of soldier-artists who had remained at the front. Others, such as George Lynch and Johann Schönberg, both of whom changed allegiance to other newspapers, were sent off to China to cover the Boxer Rebellion. The story of Johann Schönberg is probably one of the most bizarre of the War.

JOHANN SCHÖNBERG

In November 1899 the management of the yet unborn *The Sphere* decided that they could score an exceptional scoop by having an artist right in the heart of enemy

4

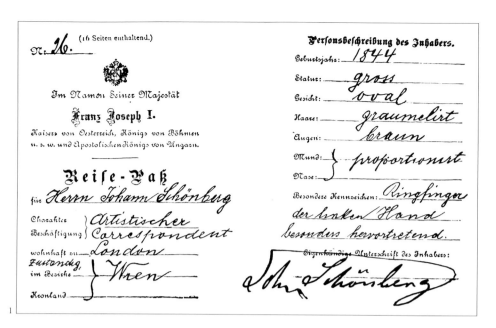

1 Johann Schönberg's Austrian passport.
Note that despite instructions from *The Sphere*
to disclose nothing of his British associations,
he gives his home address as London and
signs his name as John, the English version
of Johann.
2 Austrian Johann Schönberg, sent by *The
Sphere* to report from behind the Boer lines.

territory in Pretoria. The problem was, of course, that no Englishman would ever be allowed to fulfil such a role. Clement Shorter had heard about the talents of the Austrian illustrator Johann Schönberg, who had worked for English and European illustrated journals since the Austro-Prussian War of 1866. Schönberg, who had lived in England since 1879, agreed to accept the commission and was told that he was to revert to his original name (he was known as John in England), renew his Austrian passport and speak only German. He was instructed to obtain a temporary appointment from a German newspaper and to maintain the utmost secrecy.

Schönberg sailed for Cape Town in November 1899 aboard the *Guelph* with a commission from the German illustrated weekly *Gartenlaube*. His secret was not well kept, however, as it appears that the nurses and other correspondents aboard were aware of his true role. He travelled on to Durban but when trying to obtain a passage to Lourenço Marques he ran into considerable difficulties. Despite the fact that the true story was explained in confidence to Capt. Percy Scott of the H.M.S. *Terrible*, who was in charge of passenger regulations to Lourenço Marques, Schönberg was accused of being a German officer who was going to 'teach the Boers how to make bombs' and he was given 24 hours to leave. Undaunted, he changed his name to Jean Beaumont (the French version of his name) and boarded the French steamer *Catalan*, bound for Beira. Despite his problems with the authorities he succeeded in sending back sketches of life aboard the *Guelph* which were redrawn in *The Sphere* offices.

On the eve of his departure for Mozambique on 1 January 1900 his vessel came alongside the German freighter *Bundesrath*, which had been seized by British frigates in the Mozambique Channel on suspicion of carrying contraband for the Boers. This incident, which angered Germany especially as no contraband was found, was reported by Schönberg in *The Sphere* after he returned to England in June 1900. The journey from Lourenço Marques to Pretoria presented no problems at all but he was thwarted because the Boers did not seem to understand what a special war artist was supposed to do, and he was not permitted to continue to work for his 'German newspaper'.

However he was introduced to Transvaal state secretary Grobler, who referred him to F.W. Reitz, who in turn sent him along to Louis de Souza, Gen. Joubert's secretary. Finally he was granted a permit for 'sketching and drawing'.

Schönberg was granted an interview with Joubert himself and sketched him at his headquarters at Modderspruit. He was impressed by Joubert and says that he was the model of courtesy, offering to place his carriage at Schönberg's disposal. Their conversation was, however, rather limited as Joubert knew no German and had to rely on De Souza's translation. One complaint expressed by Joubert was that the British press, probably to excuse the British defeats during Black Week, had exaggerated the strength of the Boers considerably. After accompanying the Boer forces for a few days Schönberg returned to Pretoria and sketched various scenes and incidents in the city, including the British prisoners and the State Model School from where Winston Churchill had escaped. Then for some inexplicable reason Schönberg received a telegram from Germany saying 'London requests you to remain'. Naturally the Boers smelt a rat and Schönberg made a hasty but safe exit from the Transvaal through Lourenço Marques and back to England.

All the while the paper had published Schönberg's drawings, many in facsimile, with his signature carefully erased. On 16 June 1900, however, when Schönberg was safely back in London, they published his story under the headline: 'The return of our special artist from Pretoria – some account of the adventures of Johann Schönberg'. From then on his illustrations carried his full signature and Schönberg was given credit for them. *The Sphere* also published a facsimile of Schönberg's Austrian passport. It is interesting to note that while his name is entered in his passport as 'Johann', he must have forgotten his instructions from head office and signed his name 'John' while in South Africa. This, together with the fact that he gives his permanent home address as London, makes one wonder why the Boers did not smell the rat sooner. (See pp. 200-202.)

CHAPTER TWO

The Artist-Correspondents

Working alongside the 'specials' was another group of correspondents who, though not specifically artists, possessed enough artistic ability to augment their stories with helpful sketches and photographs.

GEORGE LYNCH

George Lynch held commissions from the *Morning Herald, Echo* and *The Illustrated London News* when he arrived in South Africa. After the Battle of Elandslaagte Lynch joined the ranks of the besieged in Ladysmith. The effects of the siege weighed heavily on his mind and early in December he asked Gen. White for permission to go to the Boer lines to distribute copies of *The Ladysmith Lyre.* (Early on in the siege, army headquarters suggested that the newspaper correspondents produce a newspaper. George W. Steevens, W. T. Maud, William Maxwell and Lionel James formed themselves into a committee and produced the 'sheet' known as *The Ladysmith Lyre.*)

White must have thought Lynch had taken leave of his senses and refused permission. Undaunted he bought a white umbrella, painted his grey horse khaki on one side, and left Ladysmith carrying 50 copies of the newspaper and a bottle of whisky. He rode off in the direction of Pepworth Hill and proceeded for a mile or two without being apprehended. It occurred to him that he might yet be the first white man to bring news of Ladysmith to the outside world.

His freedom was short-lived, however, as he was arrested and, after some lively discussion on the pros and cons of the War with his captors (whom he found courteous and surprisingly fluent in English), he was sent by rail to Pretoria. Lynch's capture caused a flurry of telegrams from both sides, as revealed in Louis de Souza's book *No Charge for Delivery.* Lynch claimed in his own book *The Impressions of a War Correspondent* that he had decided to leave Ladysmith because he was 'short of copy as well as food and wished to exchange *The Ladysmith Lyre* for the *Digger's News'.* His status as a noncombatant was finally confirmed and he was released and returned to England. He then went on to China to report for *The Sphere.* Much later, Lynch gained recognition as the inventor of special gloves for handling barbed wire.

Many of Lynch's photographs and sketches were used by *The Illustrated London News,* which had them redrawn by its home-based artists. The illustrations included scenes of his capture and pictures of his train journey to Pretoria where he is depicted playing cards with his guards. He later used this material to illustrate *The Impressions of a War Correspondent. The Illustrated London News* reported on 10 February 1900 that Lynch was forced to destroy many of his sketches in Pretoria 'lest they should give information to the enemy' and so they reproduced one 'non-controversial' sketch of Boer prisoners in Ladysmith Jail. (See p. 164.)

LIONEL JAMES

Lionel James joined Reuter's news agency in the 1890s. He had previously reported on military actions in India, where he had been actively involved in the fighting, and in 1898 he was with Kitchener in the Sudan. In 1899 Charles Moberly Bell of *The Times* asked him to represent the newspaper in South Africa, where it was obvious that trouble was brewing. Accordingly James left Southampton aboard the *Tantallon Castle* in mid-September with Lt. Gen. Sir George White and his staff. On his arrival in Cape Town, friends arranged an interview with Milner who informed him of the pending trouble in Natal and of the fact that departure of the *Scot* had been delayed in Cape Town to facilitate White's urgent passage to the front.

Teaming up with William Maxwell of *The Standard,* he took the overloaded train to East London to catch up with the *Scot.* Luck was on their side – they made the connection and in Durban took the first available train to Pietermaritzburg. James was annoyed to discover that he was not the only representative of *The Times.* He discovered from Moneypenny, the local *The Times* correspondent, that Moberly Bell had permitted anyone who was prepared to go to South Africa at his own expense to represent his newspaper. This, of course, caused numerous problems for the accredited representatives. Nevertheless in Pietermaritzburg Maxwell and James met up with Adin Coats, a young English refugee from the Transvaal, who offered to act as their guide, servant and interpreter. The three travelled on to Ladysmith, which they thought would be the ideal headquarters from which to report the impending conflict. Being an

A caricature of Winston Churchill in his army uniform by Stanley Cock (see page 119). The drawing appeared in *The Sketch* on 10 October 1900.

1 *Fix Bayonets Jack!*, a watercolour and wash drawing by the American artist Frederick J. Waugh. The painting was reproduced in *After Pretoria: the Guerilla War.*

2 The signatures of correspondents and artists who intended to hold a dinner at the Transvaal Hotel in Pretoria on Monday 11 June 1900, a few days after the city was occupied by the British. Among the artists planning to be present were Lionel James, Melton Prior, Winston Churchill, A. B. Paterson and W. B. Wollen. At this time almost all the British newspaper editors believed the War would soon be over and they recalled their special correspondents or sent them to China to cover the Boxer Rebellion.

3 Major F. D. Baillie provided the material for William Small's famous illustration *The Relief of Mafeking: The march past of the Relieving forces before Lieut.-Gen. Baden-Powell.* It was published in *The Graphic* on 30 June 1900.

experienced judge of military situations James was not impressed with the strength of the Natal Field Force and felt that he would need at least three months' supply of food and forage as the supply lines were very precarious. Having procured this vast quantity of stores, he buried them in the grounds of a boarding house where he had obtained lodgings. He also had the foresight to order a basket of carrier pigeons from Durban. Unfortunately for James the birds were despatched too late and were captured by the Boers.

James employed the standard method of sending his despatches off in triplicate to Pietermaritzburg by means of black runners and claimed that, unlike his colleagues, he never lost a message in transit. Leo Amery, who was later to edit *The Times History of the War in South Africa* (James also collaborated on this publication), received these messages for distribution back home. Every reporter was waiting for the first troops to ride into town but James's interpretation of the event was at odds with the popular theory at the time. It was generally thought that Winston Churchill and Lord Dundonald were at the head of the relieving force but James insisted that this distinction fell to Maj. Gough of the 16th Lancers and Maj. Duncan McKenzie of the Natal Carbineers.

James now found himself in a race against his colleagues to the nearest telegraph station with the news scoop of the year. To his surprise he came across Buller's headquarters at Pieter's Hill, a mile outside Ladysmith. Buller would not agree that the siege was over until his scouts had signalled that Bulwana Mountain was free of Boers. James offered to act as guide if Buller would arrange for his and Maxwell's telegrams to be despatched. Buller kept his word and *The Times* and *The Standard* carried the first news of the relief on the Saturday morning even though Churchill tried hard to usurp James's right of priority.

On his way to Pietermaritzburg James received a congratulatory wire from *The Times* ordering him to join Roberts as the paper's chief correspondent as soon as possible. He returned to Ladysmith to wind up his affairs and his partnership with Maxwell and then set off for Cape Town via Durban. He reached Cape Town on 16 March 1900 and after a brief stay at the Mount Nelson Hotel, he travelled to Bloemfontein via Bethulie, where the bridge had been destroyed. There, James renewed his childhood acquaintance with Roberts.

Like most of the other correspondents James remained in Bloemfontein for two months and contributed to the 'bringing of *The Friend* into its daily being'. He was also one of two correspondents who witnessed the British defeat at the Battle of Sanna's Post; the other was Howell Arthur Gwynne of Reuter's.

The march to Johannesburg and Pretoria with Roberts was 'journalistically uninteresting' according to James, who now believed that the War was over. He then received an order to travel to China to cover the Boxer Rebellion. On his arrival in Cape Town the order was rescinded and with heavy heart he returned to England. There, Leo Amery asked him to collaborate on *The Times History of the War in South Africa* and James soon set about 'laying the keel' of the second volume. Realizing that the War was not over and needing information for the book, James returned to South Africa in January 1901 where he joined Lt. Col. Bethune's Mounted Infantry as an intelligence officer. He spent 10 weeks with the unit and his experiences formed the basis of the book he wrote (under the pseudonym The Intelligence Officer) entitled *On the Heels of De Wet.* The unit's operations were not successful and in one incident James almost lost his life in an ambush. When it was discovered in August 1901 that he was doubling as a correspondent for *The Times* he was dismissed and ordered home.

James later represented *The Times* in Bulgaria, Greece and Japan. In 1903 he went to the United States to study American army methods of training. Here he learned the De Forest system of wireless telegraphy,

3

which he used to good effect when he chartered the Japanese ship *Haimun* for transmitting his copy during the Russo-Japanese War. During World War I James commanded King Edward's Horse. He was mentioned in despatches twice and was awarded the D.S.O. and the Crown of Italy. He also collaborated with *The Graphic* and *The Daily Graphic* for many years and at least 27 of his sketches formed the basis for illustrations in those newspapers during the Boer War.

James says in his book, *High Pressure*, that 'nature had equipped me with a useful pencil and apart from my newspaper connections, a steady stream of cheques came fluttering in from *The Graphic*'. Many of James's sketches were also reproduced in *After Pretoria: the Guerilla War* and other Boer War publications but unfortunately none of his original drawings has been traced. (See p. 152.)

WINSTON CHURCHILL

After an undistinguished school career at Harrow, Winston Churchill entered Sandhurst in 1893, passing out eighth in a class of 150. By December 1894 he was fully qualified to receive the Queen's Commission and in March 1895 he was gazetted to the 4th Hussars. In November 1895, using his father's influence with Sir Henry Wolk who was the British ambassador in Madrid, he obtained permission from the Spanish military authorities to act as an observer in the Spanish-Cuban War. He was also a correspondent for *The Daily Graphic*. Churchill and a fellow lieutenant, Reginald Barnes, sailed for New York in November 1895 before going on to Havana. Churchill later travelled to India and the Sudan, where he was witness to the cavalry charge at Omdurman, and he later published two books based on these experiences entitled *The Story of the Malakand Field Force* and *The River War*.

In 1899 he was appointed correspondent for *The Morning Post* and sailed for South Africa with Buller on the *Dunottar Castle*. On their arrival in Cape Town on

31 October they learnt of the British reverses in Natal, Ladysmith and Kimberley.

Churchill decided, together with John Black Atkins of *The Manchester Guardian*, to try to reach the Natal front as soon as possible. They managed to catch the last train to Stormberg station and finally reached East London where they caught a steamer to Durban. After landing at Durban they travelled overnight by train to Pietermaritzburg. Churchill had hoped to get into Ladysmith but by the time he reached Estcourt the Boers had already occupied Colenso station and had closed the railway line to the north.

As part of the reconnaissance to the north Gen. Hildyard would send out a cavalry patrol every morning to obtain information on the position of the Boers. He also despatched an armoured train along the 16 miles of intact railway line beyond Colenso to find out more about what was happening. On the fateful morning of 15 November 1899 he decided to put a company of the Dublin Fusiliers and a company of the Durban Light Infantry into the armoured train of six trucks, together with a small six-pound naval gun manned by four sailors landed from H.M.S. *Terrible*. Captain Aylmer Haldane, an old friend of Churchill, was the officer in charge and invited Churchill to accompany him. Churchill accepted readily. The armoured train proceeded 14 miles along the track and reached Chieveley without any sign of the enemy. Stopping to use the telegraph to report to headquarters, they saw a party of Boers about 600 yards behind them. A hail of rifle and gunfire followed and an explosion derailed the train.

Churchill devised a plan which he believed would free the trapped engine and tender. He told Haldane that by ramming and pushing the derailed trucks out of the way they may be able to escape. Before Churchill was able to put this plan into operation, however, he was apprehended by a Boer soldier on horseback. Churchill, who had been armed when he boarded the train, had lost his pistol when he attempted to move the derailed

trucks, which was fortunate. As a civilian war correspondent he could have been executed for carrying arms. However, he still had two clips of Mauser ammunition on him and, realizing that this could be dangerous if discovered, he got rid of the incriminating evidence. Three years later Churchill claimed that when he was introduced to General Botha, Botha remembered having been his captor, although subsequent evidence shows that Botha was nowhere near the scene of the attack. Churchill described how it took three days on foot and by train to reach Pretoria from the front in his books *London to Ladysmith via Pretoria* and *My Early Life*. Accompanying Churchill and Haldane was a young lieutenant, T. H. C. Frankland, who became an illustrator while he was in the P.O.W. camp. The prisoners reached Pretoria on 18 November 1899 and their arrival is depicted in several publications and on a postcard published by Ed Nels of Brussels.

In Pretoria, the captured troops were taken to the 'bird' cage which had been established on the racecourse, while the officers were confined to the State Model School. A fellow prisoner, Sergeant Major A. Brockie, was in fact a South African colonist who had used his knowledge of Dutch to pass himself off as a lieutenant and so be imprisoned in the State Model School. From the start Churchill and his fellows made plans to escape and three of the four managed eventually to do so. One of their more outrageous ideas was to attack the guards and release the 2 000 prisoners held at the Pretoria racecourse and thus outnumber the able-bodied Boer troops in Pretoria. Believing this garrison to be only about 500 strong, they planned to capture Pretoria itself from within. Needless to say this plan was never put into operation.

During the first few weeks of his captivity Churchill argued with the Boer authorities that they should release him as he was a press correspondent. He contended that he had not fired a shot and had been taken unarmed. Strictly speaking this was true but the Natal papers captured by the Boers contained glowing accounts of Churchill's activities and attributed the escape of the injured and wounded at Chieveley entirely to him. Gen. Joubert explained that although he had not fired a shot, he had prejudiced the Boer operations by freeing the engine and for this reason he was to be treated as a prisoner of war.

Together with Haldane and Brockie, Churchill made an attempt to escape on 11 December 1899 by crossing the quadrangle and hiding in the toilet. It was easy enough to get into the circular toilet but trying to climb out of it and over the wall proved too hazardous and the plan was aborted. The following evening Churchill tried again although, unknown to him, his two friends had decided that the time was not right. This time, despite the fact that his waistcoat got entangled in the ornamental work on top of the railings, he was able to lift himself over the fence and into the adjoining garden. Assuming that his friends would not make it he decided to take his chances on his own. Putting his hat on, he strolled into the garden and walked brazenly past the guards' windows. He proceeded through the gate and turned left into Pretoria.

With £75 in his pocket, four slabs of chocolate, a compass and a map, Churchill set out to find the Delagoa Bay railway and proceed along it until he reached Lourenço Marques. He found the railway line without difficulty and walked along it until he came to a station. He then hid inside a goods train. Unfortunately the train was only returning empty coal sacks to a colliery so he concluded that he would have to leave his hiding place before daylight. He decided to walk along the railway line again, and he soon discovered that all the bridges and culverts were guarded by armed men. When he eventually approached a station he realized that the trucks were not travelling at night. Believing his situation was hopeless he decided to give himself up. He eventually reached the coal mine but to his surprise the manager turned out to be an Englishman who offered him shelter for the night. Mr John Howard, the manager of the Transvaal Collieries, had become a Transvaal burgher (citizen) before the War and was the only Englishman for miles around. Howard told Churchill that the

whole area was alive with Boers looking for him and that, being British, he himself was regarded with suspicion. However, Howard allowed Churchill to hide in the disused mine for a few days to allow the hue and cry to die down. Another plan was devised and Churchill was once more hidden aboard a goods train. In the meantime the papers were full of rumours that Churchill had been caught either in Komatipoort or at Waterval Boven and at this point the Boers offered a £25 reward for him, dead or alive.

Churchill finally crossed the border into Mozambique and made his way to the British consulate, where he was told by the secretary that the consul could not see him. The news of his arrival spread like wildfire through the town, however, and he was fêted as a hero. He was concerned because there were many Boers and Boer sympathizers in Lourenço Marques, and feared that there might be an attempt to recapture him. He resolved to leave as soon as possible, and a week after his arrival in Lourenço Marques he boarded the steamship *Induna*, bound for Durban. Here he was welcomed as a national hero. The reports of his triumphant return in the press helped considerably to lift the gloom of Black Week among British readers. Not everyone regarded him as a hero, though. The tale of his escape and his part in the rescue of the train at Chieveley had been greatly exaggerated by the press. *The Phoenix*, *The Daily Nation* and *Westminster Gazette* all spoke in very disparaging terms of Churchill and suggested that because he was armed while he claimed to be a noncombatant the Boers should have shot him. Churchill fuelled the controversy by sending a telegram back to his newspaper from Durban in which he praised the Boers. His criticism of the army caused *The Morning Leader* to comment sarcastically that pending the arrival of Lord Roberts, Lord Lansdowne should appoint Winston Churchill to command the troops in South Africa, with Gen. Redvers Buller as his Chief of Staff.

Despite all this unfavourable comment Churchill sought an appointment from Buller with the Natal Field Force. Since he was still under contract to *The Morning* *Post* as a correspondent Buller was very reluctant to give him a commission – the War Office had decided that 'a correspondent could not be a soldier and no soldier could be a correspondent'. Buller, however, offered him a job with Lt. Col. Julian Byng, a captain of the 10th Hussars, as adjutant at no pay. The South African Light Horse, to which Churchill was appointed, formed part of Lord Dundonald's Cavalry Brigade. Churchill saw action at Spioenkop, where he was again critical of the British officers. He eventually reached Ladysmith with the relieving column under Lord Dundonald but his claim that he was the first into the town has been refuted. After Ladysmith, Churchill was keen to see the action in Bloemfontein and to accompany Roberts on his march to Pretoria. He left by train for Durban, where he took a ship to Port Elizabeth, and went on by train to Cape Town. His continual messages to his newspaper recommending clemency for the defeated Boers were not well received by either the British public or the British Government.

He joined Lord Roberts's column at the beginning of May 1900 for the final onslaught on Johannesburg and Pretoria, attaching himself to Ian Hamilton's force of mounted infantry. The experience resulted in his book *Ian Hamilton's March*. Churchill entered Pretoria with Lord Roberts's column and headed for the State Model School where he was instrumental in releasing some of his former comrades who were still being held prisoner. His return to the Cape from Pretoria was also touched with adventure as the train to Cape Town was ambushed outside Kopje station. However his party commandeered horses, rode south to pick up the train and again headed for Cape Town. In *My Early Life* Churchill discusses his experiences with Angus McNeill, leader of Montmorency's Scouts. On Churchill's return to England he took part in the Khaki Election of 1900. His 'heroic' exploits helped him win the Oldham seat for the Conservatives.

Churchill's escapades had been widely reported in the press and *The Graphic* used three of his sketches depicting his escape from Pretoria. (See also p. 118.)

1 Rudyard Kipling's cartoon showing an allegorical view of the De Wet 'Hunt' was published in *The Illustrated London News* on 16 March 1901.
2 Helen Wallace, a little-known South African artist, sold this oil painting of the Green Point military camp to a Sea Point resident, Mrs Spilhaus, for three guineas in 1902.

FREDERICK DAVID BAILLIE

Frederick David Baillie had formerly been a major in the 4th (Queen's Own) Hussars. At the outbreak of the War he was in Mafeking representing *The Morning Post*. While besieged in Mafeking he kept a diary which 'with the permission of the proprietor of *The Morning Post*' he republished as *Mafeking: A Diary of a Siege*. In his prefatory note Baillie also gives credit to the 'proprietors of *The Daily Graphic*' for allowing him to use his sketches to supplement his diary. Baillie left Mafeking on 20 May 1900, after the siege was lifted, and returned to England on the *Norman*, which docked in Southampton on 15 June. The majority of his sketches were used by *The Daily Graphic* while its sister paper *The Graphic* gave him credit for four. The well-known painting by William Small entitled *The relief of Mafeking: The march past of the relieving forces before Lieutenant General Baden-Powell* was inspired by Baillie. The credit is given as 'from material supplied by Major F. D. Baillie'. Even after his return to England Baillie continued to supply *The Graphic* with 'material'. He contributed a chapter on the Siege of Mafeking to Wentworth Huyse's *The Graphic History of the South African War*. Illustrations inspired by him and redrawn by the home-based artists were used to illustrate the chapter, but he is not given any credit for them. (See also p. 105.)

THE CIVILIAN ARTIST-CORRESPONDENTS

Yet another group of eyewitness artist-correspondents existed – the civilian artists living in the bigger South African towns. This group included artists such as Constance Penstone, Heinrich Egersdörfer and George Crosland Robinson in Cape Town; D. Dyer-Davies and Jeffrey Hill in Johannesburg and Henry Lea, Miss C. Tatham and Mrs Blanche Searelle in Natal. Henry Lea, who farmed in northern Natal, later claimed to have been paid almost £100 for his contributions. These artists reported on the passage of troops, dignitaries, civilians and P.O.W.s through their towns. The most famous of these civilian artist-correspondents was Rudyard Kipling. More famous as an author and poet, Kipling was a regular visitor to South Africa and during the War Roberts allowed him his first view of a battle near Bloemfontein. Kipling's only Boer War illustration appeared in *The Illustrated London News* on 16 March 1901 and was entitled *The novelist's allegorical view of the chase of de Wet*. It shows an armed steam traction engine preceded by a soldier holding a flag.

In Australia, New Zealand, Canada and even Ceylon and Bermuda, pictures of departing troops or arriving prisoners were sent to the illustrated press by civilian, amateur and professional artists. Fred Leist and Percy Spence, both well-known Australian artists, were often responsible for local scenes and both later worked in London where their work was used when illustrations of their native land were required. John Elder Moultray, who represented the New Zealand press, was the only colonial artist-correspondent. Although he was born in Scotland, his sketches and reports were widely published in the illustrated papers in his adopted country.

SOUTH AFRICAN CIVILIAN ARTISTS

Though not a correspondent, Gwelo Goodman, the famous South African painter, produced many works relating to the War. He returned to South Africa early in 1900 after studying at the Académie Julian in Paris and working in London as a painter. It seems unlikely that he enlisted but nevertheless he was granted special permission by Lord Roberts to sketch Boer War battlefields. He was allowed to go anywhere and had a few hair-raising experiences with both sides. On one occasion he was fired on by Boer snipers while sketching near Majuba Hill but was fortunately not hit. On another occasion he was shot at by a British detachment who arrested him on a charge of spying. At the end of the year he returned to Cape Town with a very large assortment of boards and canvases, all executed on his trip. An exhibition of these war sketches was held in the Technical Institute in Queen Victoria Street, Cape Town in 1901. The exhibition, which attracted nearly 1 700 people in just three days, was opened by Sir Alfred Milner.

Goodman returned to England to exhibit his Boer War paintings in the Grafton Galleries in 1901. There were 130 exhibits which filled two rooms. Colonel Heyworth-Savage and Maj. Edward Stanton, both of the Royal Welch Fusiliers who had been in South Africa, bought pictures which they presented to their regiment.

Among the paintings at the Grafton Galleries were *Colenso, Mbulwana, Mafeking* (two works with this title), *Talana Hill, Kimberley, Road into Pretoria, Spion Kop, Lombard's Kop, Ladysmith* (several views), *Majuba Hill, Matjesfontein, Colenso Bridge Rd* and *Empty convoy Impati near Dundee*. When the exhibition closed in London the Corporation of Oldham asked Goodman to exhibit the paintings in their town and Winston Churchill, the newly elected Member of Parliament for Oldham, opened the show. (See p. 138.)

Hugo Naudé was born in the town of Worcester in the Cape Colony. This was one of several towns used as a staging camps for troops proceeding north from Cape Town. He painted two watercolours showing the Duke of Wellington's West Riding Regiment marching in convoy through the town. (See p. 177.)

Helen Wallace, a little-known English-born South African artist, taught at a girl's school in East London. One of her oil paintings of Cape Town dated 1900 showed the military camp at Green Point. The painting was sold to a Mrs Spilhaus for two guineas. (See p. 227.)

Another artist of the South African school was Sydney Carter, whose Royal Academy exhibit *The list of casualties* appeared in 1902. Sydney Taylor and Edward Roworth were also to become prominent on the South African art scene, but cannot be classified as civilian artists as they served with the British forces. Taylor's painting *At dawn* is in the War Museum of the Boer Republics, Bloemfontein. Roworth arrived in South Africa with his regiment in 1902. He stayed on after the War and painted portraits of Botha, Rhodes, Hertzog and De la Rey. His most important commission was in 1909 when he was asked to paint the delegates attending the National Convention. Roworth eventually became Michaelis Professor of Fine Art at the University of Cape Town and trustee of the South African National Gallery. Roworth came under increasing criticism for his conservatism but nonetheless he had a strong influence on the South African art world.

CHAPTER THREE

The Soldier-Artists

Stiggins (mounted on Toastrack.) I prefer trekking.

1

1 A naive oil painting by an unknown soldier depicts the privations of Tommy Atkins in South Africa.
2 *Colonial Scout*, a watercolour by Trooper W. Skeoch Cumming of the Scottish Yeomanry.

A s one might expect, many of the 200 000 British troops in the field possessed some degree of artistic talent. Military education at the time included lessons in topographical sketching, given with the express purpose of training an observant eye. Lecturers at Sandhurst in the nineteenth century included Paul Sandby, George Bryant Campion and Aaron Penley, who were highly regarded in British art circles. While many of the soldiers arriving in South Africa brought with them their five-shilling Brownie in order to take 'instantaneous' photographs, the sketchbook and pencil and even occasionally the watercolour box and palette were common enough items in the trooper's knapsack.

It was not the policy of the British Government to appoint official soldier-artists in the Boer War, although the policy was to change for World War I and World War II. During the Boer War artists accompanying the troops were frowned upon and actively discouraged in their activities. The firm ruling was that a correspondent could not be a soldier and a soldier could not be a correspondent. The difference is seen quite clearly in the works of art held by the National Army Museum and the Imperial War Museum. The National Army Museum, which concentrates on army history up to the Boer War, holds mainly paintings and watercolours done purely for illustration whereas the Imperial War Museum, which starts with World War I, has several large commissioned canvases. After 1916 painters like Muirhead Bone, Eric Kensington, Paul Nash, John Sargeant, Chris-topher Nevinson and others were especially commissioned by the British Government and the military authorities to cover the conflict in Europe. By 1918 over 90 official artists had contributed, though their work was severely censored. One complained: 'I am not allowed to put dead men in my pictures because apparently they don't exist.' World War I has a far more complete pictorial record than the Boer War.

Volunteers

During the Boer War some of the volunteers, particularly those who joined the Imperial Yeomanry, had been professional artists before answering the call of duty. Others were art teachers or worked in related fields.

WILLIAM SKEOCH CUMMING

William Skeoch Cumming of the 19th Company Imperial Yeomanry had exhibited regularly at the Royal Scottish Academy from 1885 and was a scene-painter at the Theatre Royal in civilian life. He exhibited two paintings based on his South African experiences at the Royal Academy, in 1903 and 1904, and a further eight at the Royal Scottish Academy from 1903 to 1906. (See p. 122.)

INGLIS SHELDON-WILLIAMS

Inglis Sheldon-Williams was a highly competent illustrator and artist who also exhibited at the Royal Academy, although the paintings selected were based on his ex-

2

1 *The Road out of a Drift*, a watercolour by Captain Stratford St Leger. He comments: 'Great difficulty was frequently experienced in getting the heavily laden transport waggons up the rough roads leading from a drift, and at times the help of drag ropes had to be resorted to'. The painting was reproduced in his book *War Sketches in Colour*.
2 This pen-and-ink sketch from Herbert Louis Pinnock's sketchbook shows a Boer woman and her children salvaging what they can from their farmhouse, which has been set on fire by the British.
3 Sheldon-Williams's wash drawing entitled *Third Man, an Uncoveted Distinction*.

periences with the Canadian forces in World War I. During the Boer War, he resigned his post as lecturer at Frank Calderon's School of Animal Painting to join Compton's Horse Volunteers after the disasters of Black Week. He described the experiences of the 'special' artists in an article entitled 'The war correspondent then and now. Some personal reminiscences by Inglis Sheldon-Williams. One time *Sphere* Artist and a Veteran of Many campaigns' that appeared in *The Sphere* on 20 November 1937. He discusses in some detail the rise and fall of the special artist: 'what with military censorship, the advancing power of the camera, the *coup de grâce* to this breed of correspondent was finally administered'. He describes the heyday of the war correspondent's adventurous life that closed with the Boer War:

> We know that Kitchener first sounded the warning in the Sudan, and with polite ruthlessness the Japanese rang down the curtain in 1904. But in South Africa all that was required of the duly accredited war correspondent was the submitting of his copy to the censor, who entered into the sport of the thing and played the game . . .

My Boer War drawings were, on occasion, the slightest of sketches, but conveying the essentials to the artist at home. The drawings were always in outline, sketched sometimes from the top of my horse while the sergeant wasn't looking; the result could be slipped into an envelope and catch the first mail home to the office, where, if considered advisable, it could be turned into a complete double page drawing in twenty-four hours by Wal Paget. That is to say if he sat up all night. If he didn't like to do that, he would have called up another artist with a more or less similar technique and have got him to sit up only half the night doing one half of the picture while he did the other half. Then, a little before the milk delivery, they would meet at the studio and join the two halves together, each working a bit on the other man's half to get the right unity of effect, and the one who wasn't too sleepy would take it to the office and go back to bed. They would have at their fingers' ends all the equipment and so forth necessary to carry out the drawing, which would be described as 'from sketches by our special artist so-and-so'. That is how things were done at rush times before the camera came, when there was plenty of work for good professional artist's models . . . Probably the best pair of artists for this kind of team work were Gülich and Hatherell.

John Gülich, however, did not collaborate on any of Sheldon-Williams's Boer War works as he died of typhoid in 1899.

On his return home Sheldon-Williams exhibited at the Society of Fine Arts Gallery, and he said the paintings 'were sold out in a minimum of time'. He planned to write his memoirs which he had provisionally titled 'The Track of a Rolling Stone', but only the notes of his autobiography still exist. In them he reveals that on one occasion his preoccupation with sketching saved his life. He describes how when on patrol he noticed a girl talking to someone hidden in a patch of cover but did not report it to his sergeant. Two days later when it was his turn to ride again the sergeant noticed that he was working on a drawing and said he could carry on and go on patrol the following day. According to Sheldon-Williams:

> That day at the spot I have described – and where I should have been – devoid of any vestige of cover, chatting together, as likely as not joking amicably with those woman patriots, our patrol was ambushed. Two men were shot, one killed instantly, the sergeant stuck by the other until he too was dead, and escaped miraculously with the other three.

JAMES HANNAN WATSON

James Hannan Watson, of the 18th Company (Glasgow) Imperial Yeomanry, was not considered as artistically talented as some of his comrades. However, he illustrated both his own reminiscences, *The Trooper's Sketch Book of the Boer War* and A. S. Orr's *Scottish Yeomanry in South Africa*. He later exhibited some of his Boer War works in various Glasgow art galleries.

Watson's regiment left from the Clyde aboard the *Carthaginian* on 23 February 1900. They arrived in Cape Town on 19 March and, as was the custom with the Yeomanry, they encamped at Maitland soon after disembarkation. His company of Scottish Yeomanry saw action with Lt. Col. P. W. J. Le Galais through the Orange Free State and eventually took part unsuccessfully in the 'De Wet Hunt'.

In the introduction to his book Watson says:

> It was my good fortune to spend 16 weary months on the veldt as a trooper of the first lot of the Imperial Yeomanry. During that time when opportunity presented itself, I was making notes and sketches of the incidents happening round me. In doing so, I had often to contend with difficulties which would be trivial enough at home, for sometimes I was with-

out paper, sometimes there was not a pencil to be had, and sometimes when I thought myself happy in the possession of both I would find that I had no knife with which to sharpen the pencil. Then a sketch book was stolen from my saddle wallet. After this experience I sent my sketches home for safekeeping, and on my return I found a heap of dirty scraps of paper awaiting me. For my sketches I used old envelopes, anything that came my way, but such as they are they bring before me vividly the scenes they are intended to represent. Some of the more respectable sketches are on paper given me by a kindly friend in one of the hospital corps who, alas, will never again return to his native country; others are in an exercise book given me by a stationer at Kroonstadt. I had asked him to give me a pencil and a few sheets of notepaper in return for twopence. In South Africa threepence is the minimum price for a pencil or any small article, copper coins are scarcely in use, but twopence, two copper coins, represented my all – no pay had been given us for months. He kindly gave the pencils and paper and declined the twopence.

Many of those to whom I have shown my sketches have expressed the opinion that they would be of interest to the public. Then, a number which I had worked up into paintings were recently on exhibition in Glasgow and attracted a great deal of attention. So many of our countrymen have been at the Front, so many have had friends there – this is the apology for my book. The sketches are as true to life as I an eye-witness can make them, and must in this respect differ from the usual thing one sees in the illustrated papers, pictures knocked up in a London Studio. I desire also in my book to express my great admiration for the common soldier; whatever have been the mistakes in the war, the faults in his training, he is in no way to blame; he is grand, a hero, the son of heroes.

This book represents the impressions of a trooper, and should give some idea of incidents typical of life on the veldt, but it is not a history. The reader must look elsewhere for dates; I do not know them. We seldom knew whether it was Saturday or Sunday; the only difference was that on Sunday we usually expected a fight or a forced march. I have endeavoured to give some of the more amusing incidents, because in war there is a strange mixture of humour and sadness, of excitement and monotony.

But there is one feature of the country which I can scarcely convey to anyone who has not seen it, the immensity which made the largest army appear as nothing on the earth's surface. This immensity of country has undoubtedly been one of the chief causes in protracting the guerilla warfare. However badly we have managed the South African War, and our chief faults have been due to over-generosity to our enemy, no other nation would have done better, and South Africa will yet become a great country; it is well worth fighting for.

PERCY T. ROSS

Corporal Percy T. Ross joined the 69th Sussex Company of the Imperial Yeomanry soon after the outbreak of the War. In March 1900 he left the Albert Docks, London, aboard the S.S. *Delphic* with Paget's Horse.

Ross was an enthusiastic sketcher and letter writer and after his return to England on the *Aurania* in April 1901 he wrote *A Yeoman's Letters*, based on his letters and illustrated with 24 of his sketches. While the men were waiting at the Maitland camp for orders to return home a camp magazine, 'Latest Developments Gazette incorporating The Cookhouse News', was published, and Ross was responsible for the cartoons.

THE BARAGWANATH BROTHERS

Fred and Tom Baragwanath, both members of the City Imperial Volunteers, were noted Boer War artists. They were both draughtsmen in civilian life and contributed pencil sketches to *The Sphere* and *The Graphic*, which reproduced their work in facsimile. Harmsworth also published some of their sketches in *After Pretoria: the Guerilla War.* Their work was also included in the souvenir booklets of the City Imperial Volunteers published by City Press. (See pp. 105-106.)

Another well-known artist who took part in the conflict was Edward Roworth, who arrived in South Africa with his regiment in 1902 and stayed on after the War (*see* South African civilian artists, p. 32).

Professional Soldiers

Many of the professional soldiers also had considerable artistic talent. Some soldiers had already used their expertise in previous campaigns to earn a few extra pounds. Their work was used extensively by the art editors of the illustrated press, especially when their own 'special' artists had not yet been despatched to the con-

1 An original watercolour collage by Lieutenant George Mclean, who recorded scenes from the War in his diary. Among his duties was the burning of farmhouses and the rounding up of Boer women and children to be sent to the concentration camps. The first collage depicts Mclean hiding behind a rock as he feared he was about to be attacked. His 'assailant' turned out to be a tree trunk.
2 Harold Collison-Morley's watercolour *Souvenir of the Christmas cake you made me. Boxing day 1900. The feast in camp at Waterval North.* Collison-Morley acted as artist-correspondent for *The Graphic* while on active service in South Africa during the War.
3 Thomas Baragwanath's pencil sketch *Incident in the South African War 1900*, first published in *The Sphere*, is now in the Africana Museum, Johannesburg, by whose courtesy this picture is reproduced.

flict. After the fall of Pretoria most of the editors believed the War was over and recalled their 'specials' for duty elsewhere. Coincidentally the Boxer Rebellion broke out and many were sent to the East. When it became apparent that the War was not over and was indeed going to last at least another two years the work of the soldier-artists was relied upon to a much greater extent.

ANGUS JOHN McNEILL

Angus John McNeill, who was later to become a brigadier general and to be awarded the D.S.O., had already gained experience in the field before the Boer War. His pencil sketches had appeared in facsimile in both *The Illustrated London News* and *The Graphic* during the Sudan Campaign. During the Boer War his experiences with Montmorency's Scouts (he succeeded Captain Raymond de Montmorency as leader) were used both in facsimile and as preliminary sketches for the home-based artists.

JOHN FARQUHARSON

John Farquharson of the Seaforth Highlanders was another soldier whose sketches had been used by the illustrated press in previous campaigns. He was demoted from sergeant to private for neglect following an incident in the Sudan Campaign. Nevertheless, he provided a steady stream of pencil drawings and watercolours to the offices of *The Illustrated London News*. Farquharson accompanied Roberts into Bloemfontein and he submitted pencil drawings of this experience which were published in facsimile in *The Illustrated London News*.

STRATFORD EDWARD ST LEGER

One of the best-known and most competent of the professional soldier-artists was Stratford Edward St Leger. He was the son of Frederick York St Leger, who was founder and editor of *The Cape Times*, and was born in South Africa when his father was Bishop of Queenstown. He was educated at the Diocesan College (Bishop's) in Rondebosch, Cape Town and began his military training in 1890 when he joined the 18th Foot of the Royal Irish Regiment.

When the War broke out St Leger was appointed to the command of the Cork Company of the 1st Mounted Infantry Regiment. They were aboard the *Gascon* which reached Table Bay on 11 November 1899. From Cape Town they went on to De Aar, Philipstown, Prieska and the Orange River. The unit saw action for the first time on 12 February at Waterval Drift before arriving with French at the relief of Kimberley a few days later. St Leger was dismayed to discover on returning to camp one day that his saddlebag containing his sketchbook had been stolen. This sketchbook had contained all the sketches done during his stay in Prieska.

From Kimberley his company set out for Bloemfontein, which they reached on 13 March. Two days later three companies of the Irish regiment were sent off to guard the waterworks on the Modder River at Sanna's Post about 22 miles east of Bloemfontein. The Royal Irish section of the Cork Company served in the rearguard covering the retreat of the broken force at the Battle of Sanna's Post on 31 March. St Leger does not mention his own heroic act during the battle in his book *War Sketches in Colour* (1903), but an account of his brave rescue of Corporal Parker of the 1st Life Guard is given in *The Campaigns and History of the Royal Irish*

Regiment written by Lt. Col. G. Le M. Gretton in 1911.

St Leger describes in *War Sketches in Colour* the regiment's northward advance to the Vaal after an irritating week's delay in Kroonstad which they left on 20 May. They crossed the Vaal at Viljoensdrif and the Rietspruit on 26 May but encountered fierce opposition at Klipriviersberg Ridge and were forced to bivouac at Doornkop where Jameson had surrendered four and a half years previously. St Leger says that he was carried into Pretoria by his colleagues and taken to hospital, probably suffering from typhoid. He was later transferred to Wynberg military hospital in Cape Town before being invalided back to Britain. He relates how he spent most of his leisure time sketching and drawing while the rest of his colleagues were relaxing. In the preface to his book he gives credit to *Black & White* for allowing him to use the sketches which had originally appeared in that periodical. Occasionally his facsimile illustrations appeared in *The Sphere* as well. (See pp. 214-216.)

Other soldier-artists

Of all the illustrated weeklies *The Graphic* and *The Illustrated London News* seem to have accepted (and given credit to) the greatest number of sketches provided by the greatest variety of soldier-artists. Most of these soldiers provided only one or two drawings, which in turn were converted into illustrations by the home-based artists.

Captain Philip Urban Walter Vigors of the 2nd Devonshire Regiment had a namesake in Capt. Percy Urban Walter Vigors of the Royal Irish Regiment, who was mentioned for bravery in the *History of the Royal Irish Regiment*. However it was the Devonshire Vigors who was responsible for photographs used by *The Graphic* and a topographical drawing of the Battle of Monte Cristo (19 February 1900) which appeared in *The Illustrated London News* on 31 March 1900.

Lieutenant Talbot Neville Fawcett Davenport was a member of the Royal Irish Rifles whose sketches were published in *The Illustrated London News*. Davenport arrived in South Africa with his regiment aboard H.M.S. *Britannic* on 13 November 1899. He commanded the company that drove off a strong attack by commandants Philip Botha and Sarel Haasbroek at Zand River.

Harold Duke Collison-Morley was one of *The Graphic* contributors. He was only 23 when he arrived in South Africa from Australia in June 1900. He acted as a scout in the Transvaal. *The Regiment* and *Pick-Me-Up* also used Collison-Morley's work, reproducing his drawings in facsimile. In 1915 *The Graphic* published some illustrations by Collison-Morley which had been sketched only a few days before he was killed in action in France on 25 September that year.

Among other *The Graphic* and *The Daily Graphic* contributors were Capt. R.C. Gibb of the King's Own Scottish Borderers, Lt. Colin Campbell of the Cape Garrison Artillery, Lt. W.M. Griffith of the 3rd Volunteer Battalion of the South Wales Borderers, Maj. B.R. Dietz of the 7th (Princess Royal's) Dragoon Guards, Lt. Chandos Leigh of the King's Own Scottish Dragoons, Capt. E.S. Jackson of the 6th Inniskilling Borderers, Lt. W.G. Stoner, Lt. H. Percy Emmerson of the Royal Dublin Fusiliers, Capt. Ward Sausmarez Careye of the Prince of Wales' Own West Yorkshire Regiment, Capt. Marcus Beresford of the 7th Hussars, Capt. Arthur Festing and

A Transvaal Burgher. From the up-country districts, a watercolour by Captain Stratford St Leger. It was used in his book *War Sketches in Colour*.

'Trooper George' and Trooper Hugh Cleaver (whose work was often redrawn by his namesakes Ralph and Reginald Cleaver, indicating a possible relationship).

Besides those already mentioned, *The Illustrated London News* also accepted contributions from Quartermaster Sergeant W. Morris who arrived in Cape Town on the *Arundel Castle* on 16 September 1899, Private P. Kennedy of the King's Own Scottish Borderers and Lt. Richard Hennessey of the 2nd Gordon Highlanders. Hennessey sent a series of eight pencil sketches to *The Sketch* which were done in Ladysmith in 1899, indicating that he was probably in the town during the siege. Captain Louis Bols of the Devon Regiment and Maj. Gen. John Talbot Coke, who commanded the 10th Brigade, also contributed sketches and drawings. Coke provided sketches of Natal battlefields which were published on 7 July and 18 August 1900. He is the highest-ranking soldier-artist noted (Baden-Powell was only a colonel at Mafeking). There were also the soldiers like Trooper Charles Gurnell Jennis who was on board the SS *Canada* with Roberts on his return to England in January 1901. Jennis, who eventually worked for *Pick-Me-Up* and *Punch*, had a field day reporting on everything Roberts did aboard. He was also granted an exclusive sitting by the commander-in-chief. *The Illustrated London News* snapped up all Jennis had to offer and featured many of his pencil sketches in the issues of 5 and 12 January 1901.

The Royal Army Medical Corps had at least three artistically inclined members. Ernest Blake Knox had just qualified as a doctor when he came out to South Africa aboard the *Dilwara* in December 1899. He accompanied the officers and men of the Royal Lancaster Regiment. Eventually he became an authority on typhoid and spent much of his time on the passage to South Africa inoculating troops against the scourge. Knox's artistic talent was reflected in the several illustrations that he submitted to *The Graphic*. These illustrations later accompanied the text of his book *Buller's Campaign with the Natal Field Force 1900*, which was published in 1902.

Another member of the Royal Army Medical Corps who contributed to *The Illustrated London News* was Maj. Harold George Hathaway of the 10th Cavalry Division. He was severely wounded at Colesberg and one of his sketches done on top of Coleskop was published in *The Illustrated London News* on 17 February 1900. Colonel James Francis Supple, who was principal medical officer at Cape Town, submitted a sketch of Isambulwana Hill and Lombard's Kop near Ladysmith which was drawn just before the start of the siege. This sketch appeared in *The Illustrated London News* on 13 March 1900. Watercolour scenes of Cape Town painted by Supple during his stay are still in existence. Hazel Supple, who sent pictures of war graves in Wynberg to *The Graphic* in early 1900, was possibly a relative.

Captain J.L.C. Booth of the Prince of Wales' Own Yorkshire 1st Volunteer Regiment was present at Spioenkop and acted as artist-correspondent for the short-lived weekly periodical *War Pictures*. Despite the editor's claim that '*War Pictures* had a staff of 50 artists and photographers now in South Africa', only Booth seems to have been in their employ even though references are made in the magazine to 'our "special" artists Frederic Villiers, Frank Stewart, Melton Prior and George Lynch'. Booth, Grant of *Leslie's Weekly* and Lester Ralph of *Black & White* had facsimile sketches published in *War Pictures* and Booth contributed a two-page story on Spioenkop on 5 May 1900.

Even then *War Pictures'* claim of exclusivity to Booth is challenged by the fact that his work also appeared in the American news magazine *Harper's Weekly*. However home-based artist Lawson Wood was responsible for most of the cover illustrations, which do appear to be original. His namesake Stanley Wood, another home-based artist, contributed one on 19 May 1900 but this illustration had first appeared in *Black & White*.

Apart from the published and exhibited work of the soldier-artists, countless examples of sketches and drawings and even oil paintings done by the rank and file to while away the long hours are still to be found today. Many examples are found in military museums, private collections or still in the possession of descendants of the artists. Letters and diaries depicting scenes, events, and personalities drawn with varying degrees of skill are also still in existence. Some of the artists had been, or were later to become, professional illustrators or cartoonists.

Herbert Louis Pinnock kept a sketchbook which contained over 70 sketches of his experiences in the War as a member of the South African Light Horse. The sketches are full of humour and pathos. Some were used as illustrations in Cedryl Greenland's book *A Century in Shreds*. After the War Pinnock joined the police force and eventually became the cartoonist for the police magazine *Nonquai*.

George McLean was a young lieutenant of 20 when he arrived in South Africa with the Royal Inniskilling Fusiliers. He wrote a series of letters to his parents which he later used to augment his diary. The diary, which was richly illustrated with photographs and watercolour drawings, covers his service in the Boer War through to his active service in Mesopotamia in World War I. One of his regiment's duties in South Africa was to enforce Kitchener's scorched earth policies and he described and illustrated the destruction of farmhouses and the arrest and detention of Boer women and children.

The Africana Museum, Johannesburg, has examples of works by many soldier-artists. Captain Meredith Bleach, a pupil of John Amshewitz, became an official Union war artist during World War II. Other soldiers represented in their collection include Lance Corporal Harold Harvey of the 30th Company Imperial Yeomanry and Maj. Hugh Rose. Others in the collection are either unidentified or identified by initials only, such as 'I.R.F.' Among the National Army Museum's collection of watercolours and drawings by amateur soldier-artists are those by Maj. L.C. Ross.

As far as can be ascertained most of the soldier-artists survived the War. Some were wounded and others were laid low with dysentery or enteric fever. Lieutenant Thomas Nesham of the Royal Field Artillery, who contributed at least one sketch to *The Sphere*, was one exception. He was killed in a gallant action near Tweebosch on 7 March 1902. Others, including T.H. Frankland, Cecil Morgan, Clive Dixon, Harry McCormick and Harold Collison-Morley, survived the Boer War but died in action during World War I.

■

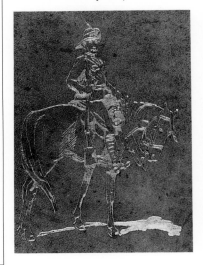

Trooper James Hannan Watson illustrated fellow trooper A. S. Orr's *Scottish Yeomanry in South Africa*. The gold embossed pictorial leather cover of the book was probably his work.

CHAPTER FOUR

Sieges, British P.O.W.s and army journals

1

1 *The Leaguer of Ladysmith* by Captain Clive Dixon of the 16th Lancers. The aide-de-camp to Sir George White, Dixon was besieged in Ladysmith. A competent artist, he produced several watercolours during his enforced stay there. Some of these were used to illustrate his book, which was published by Eyre & Spottiswoode a few months after the relief of the town.
2 and 3 Christmas and New Year greeting cards published in Ladysmith during the Siege. The artist was Earl Robert, the editor of *The Ladysmith Bombshell*.

2

The sieges of Ladysmith, Mafeking and Kimberley and the enforced idleness and boredom of the besieged acted as a stimulus to many of the inhabitants to write long letters, keep detailed diaries, make sketches and cartoons and even to publish newspapers to while away the time. Likewise the British soldiers in P.O.W. camps at Nooitgedacht and the State Model School in Pretoria provided a few extremely interesting items of pictorial Africana.

Ladysmith

Of all the siege towns Ladysmith, with its 21 000 military and civilian inhabitants, provided the richest source of material.

Several artist-correspondents had chosen or been forced to remain within its perimeters and they took every opportunity to send their sketches, drawings and reports out by hiring black runners to slip through the Boer lines.

THE LADYSMITH LYRE

To break the monotony of the siege Lionel James and fellow correspondents William Maxwell and W. T. Maud produced *The Ladysmith Lyre*, with George Steevens as editor. Steevens provided much of the humour, with Maud acting as cartoonist. The first issue appeared on 27 November 1899 and altogether four issues were produced at an issue price of sixpence. James later noted

sombrely in his book *High Pressure* that the fourth and last issue of this 'cultural' journal appeared after Steevens's death. In the third issue a paragraph appeared entitled 'Where to spend a happy day' giving details of a proposed excursion:

> To the ladies of Pretoria Messrs Kook and Son beg to announce a personally conducted tour, Saturday to Monday, to witness the siege of Ladysmith. Full view of the enemy guaranteed. Tea and shrimps (direct from Durban) on the train. Four-in-hand ox waggon direct from Modder River to Bulwan. Fare 15s return. One guinea if Long Tom is in action.

Maud produced an accompanying cartoon which showed the women and children of Pretoria pouring out of a train while Joubert invited them to try three shots at the Ladysmith Town Hall from Long Tom for a penny. The advertisement caused quite a stir. *The Defence of Ladysmith and Mafeking* quotes the journal of Capt. William Thwaites referring to the passage. McCormick sent a second sketch with a report to *The Graphic*, which was redrawn by Robert Macbeth and published in *The Graphic* Special Double Number on 2 April 1900. A facsimile edition of *The Ladysmith Lyre* was published by *The Daily Graphic* in 1900.

THE LADYSMITH BOMBSHELL

Another publication was the cyclostyled *The Ladysmith Bombshell*, which first appeared on 18 November 1899. The subsequent seven issues appeared on 26 November, 2 December, 9 December, 16 December, 23 December, 1 January 1900 and 8 January. George Walter Lines was the publisher and the news sheet was distributed free. Earl Robert produced a fine series of cartoons, which appeared on the front cover, and his work also featured inside in some of the later issues. In 1900 Robert published a facsimile version which varied slightly from the original. Lines, too, reproduced *The Ladysmith Bombshell* in a different format in his book *The Ladysmith Siege*, which also appeared in 1900.

EARL ROBERT

Earl Robert is an enigma. He arrived in South Africa in 1892 and worked for the *Cape Times* and *The Illustrated London News*. He also provided the illustrations for the book *A Souvenir of the Record Reign: Illustrations of the Jubilee Festivities*, which was published in Johannesburg in 1897. Why or how he went to Ladysmith is not known, but besides his contributions to *The Ladysmith Bombshell* he was almost certainly the artist responsible for the cartoons on the famous Ladysmith Siege postcards, which exist in various forms and were probably produced to celebrate the victory of the Devonshires at Wagon Hill on 6 January 1900. Robert's work is also found on the Christmas and New Year cards which were published in Ladysmith towards the end of 1899 and the Valentine's card published prior to 14 February 1900. (See pp. 196-197.) On 31 March 1900, soon after the siege was lifted, *The Illustrated London News* published two illustrations by 'our correspondent E. Robert' in facsimile. The illustrations depicted damage done to a shop and house during the Boer bombardment.

CLIVE MACDONNELL DIXON

Clive MacDonnell Dixon was commissioned in 1890, at the age of 20, as a second lieutenant in the 16th Lancers. He was the son of wealthy shipbuilder Sir Raylton Dixon, who had quite a reputation as an amateur artist. Clive Dixon, who had been made a captain a few months earlier, was appointed aide-de-camp to Sir George White almost immediately after the 16th Lancers arrived in Ladysmith and only three days before the outbreak of hostilities.

Dixon was the author and illustrator of *The Leaguer of Ladysmith*, published by Eyre & Spottiswoode in 1900. Writing in his foreword, dated 3 March 1900, Dixon says: 'in publishing the following sketches done in idle hours during the siege, I beg to tender my sincerest apologies to all those who appear in them, and as a souvenir of a somewhat trying four months spent together in a beleaguered town borne cheerfully by soldiers and civilians alike for the sake of the Empire'. Dixon, who must have inherited some of his father's artistic and caricaturist talent, produced 17 humorous coloured sketches, each with a letterpress description of the depicted incident. *The Sphere*, reviewing the publication on 8 September 1900, was very enthusiastic:

> When the hastily-published lucubrations of many of the war correspondents have gone the way of all waxwork, as Mr Swinburne would say, *The Leaguer of Ladysmith* by Captain Clive M. Dixon (which Messrs Eyre & Spottiswoode have issued) will remain, for it is highly humorous and shows a touch of real comic sketching genius. Beautifully reproduced in colours [the sketches] must have made the days less dreary for his comrades in distress. They illustrate humorously real incident . . . *The Leaguer of Ladysmith* is a cheap three-and-sixpence worth.

Lieutenant Colonel Henry Rawlinson was another soldier whose Ladysmith sketches survive. His panoramas drawn while aloft in a captive balloon were reproduced in the book *Anti-Commando* in 1931.

Besides the illustrators whose work was published, many of the inhabitants kept diaries. Others illustrated their letters or envelopes with cartoons and drawings which they later smuggled out. Many of these fascinating items are found in private collections all over the world. One such envelope, done by Lt. Reginald Gwynn of the 5th Royal Irish Lancers, is still in existence. The letter, posted four days before the siege was lifted, shows a soldier weeping over his horse which is being boiled to make 'Chevril' – the equestrian version of its better known cousin Bovril.

Mafeking

The artistic contribution from the Siege of Mafeking was made almost exclusively by the commander of the beleaguered town, Col. Robert Stephenson Smyth Baden-Powell. (See also pp. 104-105.)

ROBERT BADEN-POWELL

Robert Baden-Powell was encouraged from an early age by his widowed mother to pursue his artistic leanings. After leaving Charterhouse, where he had been since 1870, he had planned to go to Oxford but circumstances (probably a failed entrance exam) led him to embark on a military career. This provided many avenues for his artistic talent and throughout his life he illustrated his letters and diaries with sketches.

In September 1876 he joined the 13th Hussars as a sub-lieutenant and sailed with them for India. In 1883 he was promoted to captain. En route to England in 1884 he disembarked at Natal because trouble was brewing in Bechuanaland. When the crisis was over he spent six months hunting in East Africa before returning to England.

In 1888 he returned to the Cape as aide-de-camp to his uncle Lt. H. A. Smyth, taking part in the Zulu Campaign against Dinizulu. Towards the end of 1889, having been promoted to brevet major, he acted as secretary to the mixed British and Transvaal Commission in Swaziland and sent sketches of the negotiations to *The Illustrated London News*.

In 1895 he was ordered to organize a native levy for the Ashanti Expedition. Soon after this very successful campaign he was promoted again, this time to brevet lieutenant colonel and was gazetted for special duties in Matabeleland when the rebellion broke out in 1896.

In June 1899 he was once again sent to South Africa, to raise two regiments for the defence of Bechuanaland and Matabeleland. When war broke out on 11 October 1899, one regiment was despatched to protect the Rhodesian border while the other remained with him in Mafeking. The town was almost immediately surrounded by General Cronje and an army, at Baden-Powell's estimate, of 9 000 men.

During the Siege of Mafeking Baden-Powell found time to illustrate many of the incidents and his Boer War sketches were reproduced in *The Daily Graphic*, *The Sphere*, *The Illustrated London News*, *After Pretoria: the Guerilla War*, *With the Flag to Pretoria*, *Black & White*

The Siege Valentine

A card issued in besieged Ladysmith to celebrate Valentine's Day 1900, only two weeks before the relief of the town. The artist was Earl Robert. Note the reference to 'Chevril' — a meat extract made from horse meat by the hungry inhabitants.

and many other illustrated newspapers. For security reasons the sketches were not signed but merely bore the inscription 'from a sketch by a British officer brought by runner to Bulawayo'. Whether in fact Baden-Powell was ever paid for these contributions is not known and regrettably none of the original sketches has been traced.

Some of his work was considered to be of outstanding quality and in 1900 *The Sphere* remarked that 'A glance through these notebooks gives rise to a vision of a Baden-Powell turned R.A. with pictures on the line in the present academy exhibition. While his work would do no discredit to one or two of the artists who might be named'. In fact in 1907 a sculpture by him was accepted by the Royal Academy. One of the remarkable things about Baden-Powell was that he was adept at drawing with his left (his writing hand) as he was with his right hand. To quote from *The Illustrated London News* of 2 June 1900:

> It is even said that he can work on a picture with both hands at the same time, drawing the outline with one hand and doing the shading with the other. When he first showed signs of this remarkable capacity in his boyhood, his mother was rather anxious, thinking that he might harm himself in some way or other by the double application of both hand and brain. She consulted Mr Ruskin, then at the height of his fame as an art critic, then and always a great friend of the Baden-Powell family. He reassured her telling her it would do the boy no harm whatever to follow his bent!

His artistic ability was so well recognized that, although not a professional artist, he became a member of the London Sketch Club. In an article in *The Studio* by Walter Churcher, written in 1915, this exception was 'amply justified by such admirable sketches as his many engagements admit of his executing, and his keen interest in the club's aim'. During the siege arts and crafts exhibitions were organized and prizes were donated by various prominent citizens including Baden-Powell. In the *Mafeking Mail Special Siege Slip*, no. 103 which appeared on 29 March 1900 (168th day of the siege) it was reported that in 'Class 10, prize of £5 presented by Mr Whiteley for the best painting was taken by Colonel

Baden-Powell, the humour of whose sketches *Find the policemen, Making disparaging remarks etc., The market square when the bell rings, Siege fed* etc. was very much appreciated by the visitors'. The judges were Mrs Nicholas, Miss Friend and Captain Goodyear. Albert Carter, writing in *The Work of War Artists in South Africa*, says:

> It can be stated without contradiction that to General Baden-Powell was left the discovery of the cheery side of war, and this came as no surprise to those who had known him either as schoolfellow or comrade in arms. For a long time these had felt that in the soldier had been lost both a capable artist and a clever actor. Happily for England the opportunity came to vindicate the soldier's choice in spite of other inducements. The *vis comica*, which he possesses to such a high degree, stood him in good stead throughout the hardy defence of Mafeking. It helped him to make light of hardships and to inspire his forces with breezy confidence and determination.

Every communication that came through was alive with this hearty humour and the British public prayed and waited for the happy ending. Just a month before the relief came he wrote the following characteristic note: 'All blooming and booming here. We shan't know what to do with ourselves if we get relieved, we're so accustomed to our imprisonment now. Perhaps they'll forget about us and leave us to our little fun with the Boers, who, by the way, seem far more tired of the game than we are. I hope in a few days to make them still more tired of it. Hoping this may get through to you (our last two runners came back with bullet holes in them)'. Accompanying this was a funny sketch of *The washerwoman's son* depicting the trials of a Mafeking baby whose mother, infected by the general indifference to danger, insisted on prosecuting her calling, notwithstanding the nearness of bursting shells . . .

Another clever sketch was that devoted to Lord Edward Cecil's bright 'Cadet Corps', which rendered such useful service as boy messengers and powder monkeys during the siege. It requires little examination to show that General Baden-Powell is no tyro in art and that it is long ago since he passed the stage of the amateur. As the author of one of the best works of military observation, 'Scouting', it was only natural that he should be quick to perceive how to turn all his resources to the best account.

The sketch 'Siege games in Mafeking', with his own notes, illustrates this. He explains how, by watching the native children's precision in throwing lumps of clay with whipping sticks, he adopted the effective method of throwing dynamite bombs from the end of a long bamboo into the enemy's trenches. Another sketch shows the use of a home-made megaphone.

In January 1900, probably as the result of hoarding, currency became scarce and Baden-Powell ordered the issue of special currency which would be redeemable when the siege was lifted. On 25 January 1900 *The Mafeking Mail* announced the issue of new small denomination notes (three shilling, two shilling, one shilling, ninepence, sixpence and threepence). Soon it became apparent that new ten shilling and one pound notes would also be required. Baden-Powell designed and made a copperplate for the one pound note showing a man with a field gun and another with a Maxim gun. When it came to printing, however, there was insufficient pressure to give a clear reproduction even though a mangle was used. The local watchmaker, Mr C. Riesle, was then asked to engrave a wood block based on Baden-Powell's design. He used a croquet mallet cut in half as the wood block but this too proved ineffectual. Eventually after certain technical modifications the ten shilling note was issued in March. Riesle's initials appear on the note.

Baden-Powell then designed a different one pound note showing the Union Jack flying above the defenders, the Wolf (the locally made gun) with shells and a woman holding a baby. This drawing and the printed text were photographed, a glass negative was obtained and the image was printed onto ordinary notepaper by Edward Ross. This method was similar to that used to produce the Mafeking stamps which were issued in April and May. Today these notes are eagerly sought after by collectors, particularly the ten shilling note where the 'd' is missing from 'commanding'. Baden-Powell was probably the only besieged commander to come out of the War with any credit but it is said that he annoyed Queen Victoria by using his own likeness and not hers on the siege stamps.

Many of Baden-Powell's Mafeking sketches and drawings were later used to illustrate his book *Sketches in Mafeking and East Africa* which was published in 1907. He also included works used by *The Graphic* which had been redrawn by home-based artists.

The only other work of art that seems to have been produced during the Mafeking siege was the carefully executed oil painting by Mrs Gemmell entitled *John Bull on the 100th day of the Siege*, which was shown at the exhibition where Baden-Powell scored his triumph. It is likely that Mrs Gemmell was the wife of Lt. H.B. Gemmell of the Bechuanaland Rifles.

Kimberley

From an artistic point of view, Kimberley was the most disappointing of the siege towns. Despite the fact that nearly 45 000 people were trapped there, very few, if any, made sketches or drawings that have survived. Only one or two private unpublished diaries have been found with the occasional drawing within their pages.

The Diamond Fields Advertiser featured a page of cartoons drawn by an unidentified cartoonist 'L.C.' or 'C.L.'. These ten cartoons, which showed the humorous side of the siege, were reproduced on page 66 of the post-siege publication *The Siege of Kimberley*.

Prisoner-of-war camps

The British P.O.W. camps also yielded their fair share of illustrated news sheets and occasional sketches.

NOOITGEDACHT

Algernon Essex Capell joined the Cape Mounted Rifles in 1889 and became a member of Bethune's Mounted Rifles in 1899. Capell, who had submitted sketches to *The Graphic* prior to his capture, was taken prisoner at Scheeper's Nek on 20 May 1900. During the action he tried to rescue a wounded trooper by placing him on his own horse but the Boers surrounded him and he was taken off to Nooitgedacht where he joined another 900

British prisoners, consisting mainly of Gloucesters and Irish Fusiliers who had been captured at Nicholson's Nek and Modderspruit. *The Graphic* depicted a redrawn version of one of Capell's drawings which later appeared in *The Graphic History of the South African War*. In a note with the sketch Capell said that the prisoners were having rather a rough time of it and he added: 'Mr Graham, correspondent of the Central News is here and about to be released and by his kind favour I hope you will receive this sketch.'

On 25 August 1900 *The Sphere* depicted British prisoners at Nooitgedacht. The sketches, which were redrawn by Alfred Pearse, carried the following description of the P.O.W. camp:

Nooitgedacht is the next station below Waterval-boven on the Delagoa Bay Railway. The prisoners are kept a few hundred yards from the line in an enclosure about an acre in extent, surrounded by a barbed wire fence about 7 feet high. Among them are the Irish Fusiliers, Gloucesters, and Suffolks taken at Nicholson's Nek ten months ago. One officer, (Lieut. Essex Capell) and ten men of Bethune's Mounted Infantry; one officer (Lieut. Bertram) of the E.P.H. (Eastern Province Horse); forty men of Brabant's and Border Horse; and eleven men of the Imperial Yeomanry. The Boers keep strict watch day and night, lighting lamps or torches every 30 yards after dark. The prisoners make a sort of tent out of blankets, as none are provided, and many sleep in the open. The food is very indifferent, and usually scarce. The hospital train holds many cases of enteric fever and dysentery. The place is a hot bed of fever in summer, and is quite bad enough in winter. Several prisoners have escaped.

After the Boer defeats at Bergendal and Dalmanutha some prisoners were released. Capell, however, was taken on to Barberton before he too was finally sent back to his unit.

PRETORIA

By far the greatest number of British P.O.W.s were housed in Pretoria: the officers at the State Model School and Waterval and the N.C.O.s and privates at the racecourse. The Earl of Rosslyn, (James Francis Harry St

1 *Flooded Out*, one of Captain Clive Dixon's cartoons reproduced in his book *The Leaguer of Ladysmith*, shows the artist Melton Prior being forced out of his secure shell-proof hideout by the rising waters of the Klip River.

2 Robert Baden-Powell, commander of Mafeking during the siege of that town, produced several sketches of people and events in this period. This sketch was reproduced in his book *Sketches in Mafeking and East Africa*, published in 1907.

1 *Field Cornet Potgieter, OFS 1900*, by John Beer. Reproduced by courtesy of the Africana Museum, Johannesburg.

2 Trooper Owen Harris produced the front cover of The *Mexican Mercury*, a shipboard 'magazine' brought out to entertain the troops of Loch's Horse and others travelling to South Africa on the *Mercury* in March 1900.

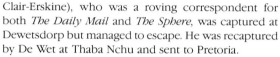

Clair-Erskine), who was a roving correspondent for both *The Daily Mail* and *The Sphere*, was captured at Dewetsdorp but managed to escape. He was recaptured by De Wet at Thaba Nchu and sent to Pretoria.

His book *Twice Captured* was the object of some controversy when Rosslyn and the publishers Wm Blackwood and Sons were threatened with legal action by Churchill over disparaging remarks made about his escape from the State Model School. In the book, published soon after his release in 1900, Rosslyn describes how the prisoners decided to put together a magazine to overcome the boredom of captivity. Major W. E. Sturges of the 5th Fusiliers suggested the title *The Gram* which was accepted unanimously. *The Gram* was decided upon because all the items of news they received from outside were from tradesmen, so they dubbed them 'Kaffirgram' (sic), 'Bakergram', 'Butchergram' and so on.

On 12 May the first issue appeared. Using a hectograph (a primitive copying machine) 62 copies of the first issue were produced. On 24 May 70 copies of the second issue were published. The third issue was prepared by Rosslyn at the end of May but was edited by Maj. Sturges because Rosslyn was released from the camp before its publication in June.

Captain Geoffrey H.A. White ('G.H.A.W.') of the Royal Horse Artillery, who was captured at Sanna's Post on 31 March, did all the covers as well as other illustrations. Lieutenant Thomas Hugh Colville Frankland ('T.H.C.F.') of the 2nd Royal Dublin Fusiliers, who Rosslyn describes as 'only twenty and really very clever', contributed illustrations depicting the escape of Brockie, Haldane and Le Mesurier among others from the State Model School on 16 March 1900. Frankland had been captured with Churchill at Chieveley (*The Gram*'s 'Roll of Officers and civilians' refers to the place as Blaukrantz). Churchill used extracts from Frankland's diary (with acknowledgement) for chapter 16, 'Held by the enemy', in his book *Ian Hamilton's March*. Besides his illustrations in *The Gram* Frankland provided an illustration, *Portrait*

of the author in prison, for the Revd. Adrian Hofmeyr's book: *The Story of My Captivity During the Transvaal War 1899-1900*. Hofmeyr, who was born in the Cape, had been arrested by the Boers at Lobatse on 15 October 1899 on suspicion of being a traitor. He was a fellow prisoner in Pretoria and he too collaborated on *The Gram*. Frankland also contributed *Prisoners at Pretoria* to *The Illustrated London News* (16 June 1900) and *Disaster of armoured train near Estcourt* to *The Graphic* (13 January 1900). Frankland, who eventually reached the rank of colonel, was killed at Gallipoli in 1915.

Second Lieutenant G.R. Wake ('G.R.W.') of the 5th Northumberland Fusiliers was captured at Stormberg on 10 December 1899. He contributed five illustrations. A biographical sketch is given in the first issue of *The Gram*. Lieutenant Alfred Haserick of the Rhodesian Regiment was captured at Rhodes Drift on 2 November 1899 and a biographical sketch of him is given in the second issue of *The Gram*. Among his illustrations was one on the inside back cover of the second issue where he depicts a true incident when he attached a Union Jack, made out of a tie, to the neck of a young hawk and released the bird over Pretoria to celebrate the Queen's birthday. Haserick, who had an M.A. degree from Oxford, also wrote poetry for the magazine. Lieutenant Colonel Charles James Blomfield ('C.J.B.') of the Lancashire Fusiliers did the back cover of the second issue. He was wounded and captured at Spioenkop on 25 January 1900. Captain Charles M. Grenfell came to Pretoria from Colenso on 24 December 1899. He did the cartoon for the page devoted to the chess tournament in the second issue.

In a footnote on page 351 of *Twice Captured* Rosslyn states that 'a limited facsimile edition of *The Gram* is in production at a price of one guinea'. In a letter from Stafford House, London, dated 10 August 1900, Rosslyn appealed for subscribers 'to this ingenious memento of the Boer Campaign', adding that 'there will certainly not be more than 500 printed'. He says in his introduction to

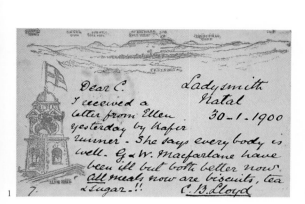

the facsimile edition that 'he fears that the ink of the original may fade' and explains that he has had the original work reproduced by lithography. He also pays tribute to those who helped with the production and mentions the illustrators and artists by their full names instead of just using initials.

The Waterfall Wag was a P.O.W. paper published by the prisoners at Waterval between 8 May and 2 June. A facsimile edition was published by Clement's Publishing Works in London in 1900. *The Times*, reviewing the facsimile edition, says that the 'illustrations are almost all admirable . . . a decorative border of thumbnail or rather little fingernail sketches of various military types – British, Colonial, and Boer shows in high degree the gift of seizing a man's character and portraying it with a few scratches of the pen'.

LOCAL ARMY JOURNALS

The Cossack Post was not a P.O.W. journal but a news sheet brought out by B Squadron of Paget's Horse who were stationed on De la Rey's farm in Lichtenburg. Paget's Horse had originally come out to South Africa aboard the SS *Tagus*, arriving on 21 March 1900. Eleven issues, originally written in a ledger, appeared between February and May 1901. The editor says that the journal was published in order to compensate for a 'lack of general literature on the Veldt'. The journal also carried illustrations. A facsimile edition was published by the Junior Army and Navy Stores Ltd in 1901. Regrettably the illustrators and cartoonists are not identified in either journal.

St George's Gazette was the regimental journal of the Northumberland Fusiliers. First published in Ireland in 1884, it had become quite popular by the time of the War as shown by the editor's apology for certain issues going out of print. The paper used cartoons and illustrations by Matthew Hewerdine, Roy Sumner and 'H.T.C.'. The identity of H.T.C. is still a mystery but evidence seems to indicate that he was Capt. H.T. Crispin. As well

as cartoons and illustrations the editor often published pictures of illustrated postal covers from the front which readers had sent in.

Another interesting cyclostyled magazine running to 32 pages, including the covers, was *The Mexican Mercury*. This one-off publication, illustrated with caricatures, was produced aboard the Union SS *Mexican* under Capt. B. Copp while en route to South Africa: 'Edited and published on the High Seas crossing the line March 10 1900.' Aboard were the number two contingent of Loch's Horse (five officers and 98 men), 2nd Volunteer Battalion of Seaforth Highlanders (three officers and 113 men), drafts from the 3rd, 5th and 6th Battalion of the Gordon Highlanders (three officers and 112 men) and 1st and 2nd Battalions of the Royal North Lancashire Regiment (five officers and 113 men). The ship's complement was made up of a crew of 141. The editors were Gordon Daniell and troopers 'Dicky' Church, E. E. Brandon and Owen Harris. Church and Harris also provided the cartoons and caricatures, signing 'R.C.' and 'O.H.' respectively, and Harris did the front cover, signing his name in full.

Although this 'Kharki Edition' was titled 'No. 1 vol. 1' it appears from the text that it was the only issue planned. The *Mexican* arrived in Cape Town on 14 March 1900. Ironically after the editor's generous praise of Captain Copp for never having been involved in any disaster at sea in his 28 years as a sailor, the *Mexican* collided with the SS *Wingfield* and sank on 5 April 1900 80 miles north of Cape Town while on her return journey to Southampton. This was to have been Copp's last voyage. The incident was illustrated and described in *The Graphic* on 12 May 1900 by Maj. George Hale who was en route to Cape Town aboard the *Wingfield* when the incident occurred.

Other illustrated news sheets were undoubtedly published by the troops in various locations. Because of their ephemeral nature, however, most have not survived. ∎

1 One of the several varieties of Ladysmith Siege cards by Earl Robert. While most were used after the siege, this one has a postmark of 30 January 1900.
2 Capt. Geoffrey White did the front cover illustration of *The Gram*, a P.O.W. magazine produced in Pretoria during the War.

CHAPTER FIVE

The Pro-Boer Artists

Anton van Wouw, the well-known sculptor, did a series of charcoal drawings of leading members of the postwar Boer delegation to Europe, namely generals De la Rey, Botha and De Wet. This postcard shows General 'Jac De la Rey'.

Paintings done from the Boer point of view during the War are much rarer than those from the side of the British. There are many reasons for this, not least the almost total absence of Boer artist-correspondents in the field and the smaller numbers involved on the Boer side – and perhaps the fact that art had a low priority in the list of needs among the Boer families at home.

A Mr S. Lapedus of Dublin was obviously worried by the one-sidedness of the illustrations appearing in the pages of *Black & White Budget* and wrote to them accordingly. On 4 August 1900 in the correspondence column of the newspaper came the editor's reply: 'The Boer proper does not draw. He knows a lot about farming and shooting.' Though this is rather a categorical statement it is interesting to note that the great majority of art works from the Boer side were done by foreign-born burghers.

FRANS OERDER

Frans Oerder, who was born in Rotterdam in 1867, is considered to be the first and possibly the only official artist of the Zuid-Afrikaansche Republiek (South African Republic). Despite opposition from his father, Oerder pursued his art education in Rotterdam and later in Brussels. He came to South Africa in 1890 and was employed by the decorating firm of De Wijn and Engelenburg. He spent some time painting telegraph poles on the newly commissioned railway between Komatipoort and Krokodilpoort. He became a Zuid-Afrikaansche Republiek burgher in 1896 and in 1899 was appointed by Kruger to act as official war artist with the Boer forces. Whether this appointment came about at Oerder's instigation or Kruger's is unclear.

Judging from the titles of Oerder's Boer War drawings in the Africana Museum and the War Museum of the Boer Republics, he must have been present at Ladysmith and Magersfontein. It is not known when Oerder left the Boer commandos but he was in Pretoria in 1900 and 1901, when he produced at least three oil paintings showing British mounted infantry. His interest in the British troops was obviously not considered a danger to their security as he was allowed to complete these paintings without any restrictions. It is claimed, however, that he had been under house arrest for part of 1901 and after the War he returned to Holland for a short period. Unfortunately not all of Oerder's Boer War work survived. His son Tom took an album of his father's Boer War sketches to school to show his teacher and fellow pupils and during the night the school was gutted by fire, which destroyed the album. (See also p. 179.)

JOHANNES POTT

Johannes Pott was an official in the office of the Staats-secretaris of the Zuid-Afrikaansche Republiek. He served with the Boer forces during the War but was wounded at Ladysmith. He accompanied Kruger to Europe, remaining with him until his death in July 1904.

The Africana Museum has a bound volume of Pott's cartoon sketches with the title page inscribed: 'Die Groot Sukses van Tommy Atkins in Zuid-Afrika. Twaalf platen geteekend door Een Transvaler'. (See also p. 187.)

OTHERS

Anton van Wouw, the Dutch-born sculptor who became renowned for his bronzes and the statue of Paul Kruger that is now in Church Square, Pretoria, produced some fine charcoal drawings of De Wet, De la Rey and Botha in 1901. These drawings were reproduced on postcards published to mark the arrival of the postwar Boer delegation to Europe. (See also p. 223.)

Fritz Wichgraf had also arrived in the Transvaal Republic before the War. His painting *De Deputatie* was commissioned by the Z.A.R. Government and intended for the Paris Exhibition in 1900 but for various reasons it was not exhibited. Prints were later made of this painting, which included portraits of Kruger, Cronje, Burger and Reitz. (See also p. 231.)

Boer prisoner-of-war camps

Virtually all the existing paintings, sketches and drawings produced by the Boers were done in the P.O.W. camps in Ceylon (now Sri Lanka), Bermuda, India, St Helena and Portugal that housed the 27 000 prisoners. Some were done in the transit camps in South Africa – at Green Point, Port Alfred and Bellevue in Simon's Town – where the prisoners stayed before being shipped out.

NEWSPAPERS

Roneoed camp newspapers were published in Ceylon and St Helena. *De Strever*, the organ of the Christian Endeavour Society, first appeared in Ceylon on Saturday 19 December 1901 and ran until Saturday 26 July 1902. *De Krijgsgevangene* (Diyatalawa) was produced from 1901-2. *De Prikkeldraad*, *Diyatalawa Dum Dum* and *Diyatalawa Camp Lyre* were also published in Ceylon while *Kampkruimels* and *De Krijgsgevangene* came out in St Helena. As far as is known only *De Krijgsgevangene* (Diyatalawa) was illustrated but the identity of the artist is unknown. Deel 1 No. VI dated '9th Januari 1902' has the name of J.G. Walton, Hut 59A, under the usual publisher's imprint which appears adjacent to the illustrated heading 'Dit Blad verschyn eenmaal per week subscriptie 25 cent per maand'. Walton was probably the editor but he may also have been the illustrator. One issue of *De Krijgsgevangene* carried the advertisement: 'J.G. Bantjies the "painter of the Battle of Sanna's Post" invites orders for pictures in oil or watercolours. His studio is Grass House residence hut 43.' Bantjies was captured at Paardeberg and left Ceylon on 28 August 1902. Regrettably none of his works has been traced.

CURIOS

The main activity of the Boer P.O.W.s, besides trying to

F. D. Oerder is regarded as the Transvaal Republic's only war artist, having supposedly been appointed by Paul Kruger himself. After the occupation of Pretoria, when he was presumably no longer employed in this capacity, he did at least three oil paintings of British Mounted Infantry.

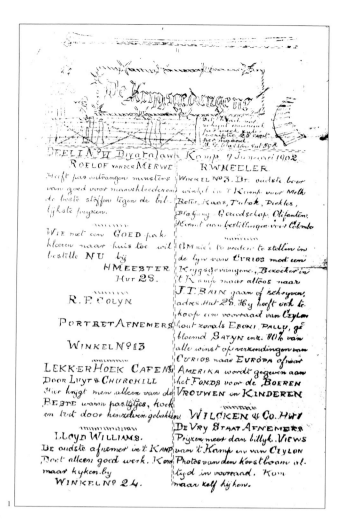

1

1 *De Krijgsgevangene*, a bilingual weekly newspaper produced by Boer P.O.W.s at Diyatalawa Camp, Ceylon. The editor, J. G. Walton, may have been responsible for the illustrations.
2 A facsimile of a drawing and P.O.W. signatures by Jan G. Reijenga (Rewenga). This card expresses thanks to the firm of Weinthal & Co., the Rotterdam cigarette manufacturers who apparently provided comforts for the prisoners at Deadwood Camp on St Helena.
3 A handpainted card by Ernest Douwes Dekker, a P.O.W. at Diyatalawa, Ceylon.
4 Maurice Le Gall, a French P.O.W., drew this caricature of an unidentified individual on a St Helena postal stationery card while he was imprisoned on the island.

escape, was the production of curios. Many examples of these fine pieces of handiwork still exist, including chairs, walking sticks, serviette holders, pipes, paper knives, pen holders, bookends, toys and even a barrel organ. Ingeniously constructed lathes and carving tools were devised, but by far the most common tool used was the penknife. The prisoners were actively encouraged to produce these items. In an article in *The Illustrated London News* of 23 November 1901 Frank Vizetelly says that the 'men set to work at camp fatigues, cleaning tents, airing bedding, washing tent flooring (this is done twice weekly) or at other work which the Industrial Association maintained in each camp has assigned them. This work consists of making all sorts of souvenirs that are sold for their benefit at the Boer Toy agency in the city of Hamilton.'

The Bermuda curio shops were on the tourist circuit and near to the United States and so were able to dispose of these items quite easily, enabling the Boer manufacturers to purchase a few luxuries with the proceeds. Prisoners at the other camps on islands – which had no curio shops or were not regularly visited by tourists – were not so fortunate, but attempts were made to develop a market for the curios in England. Emily Hobhouse, whose watercolours done after the War are housed in the War Museum of the Boer Republics, Bloemfontein, suggested that depots be opened 'in London and other towns where curios made by the prisoners of war could perhaps be sold'.

The work usually began soon after the prisoners were captured and postcards exist showing examples of the curios made by the prisoners at the Bellevue camp in Simon's Town. An advertisement in the *Cape Times*

of 15 February 1901 stated that a bazaar was to be held where Boer curios would be offered for sale in aid of Dutch Reformed Church funds. *The Sphere* on 6 April 1901 carried an illustration by Ernest Prater showing prisoners aboard the *Kildonan Castle* 'spending their time by making toys'.

Among the most interesting items of artistic merit made on St Helena were the three, or possibly four, chessboards made and illustrated by Johannes Marte Mante. Mante, who was born in Amsterdam, was captured at Elandslaagte on 21 October 1899 and sent to St Helena. He was a building contractor in civilian life. The cedarwood chessboards have alternate light-coloured blocks, each depicting a watercolour view of St Helena. Mante gave one of the boards, beautifully framed, inscribed and glazed, to the famous Dutch philanthropist Mr K. Zwaardemaker as a token of appreciation for his work in helping the Boers. The other two boards created solely by Mante are in the Totius Museum, Potchefstroom, and the Africana Museum, Johannesburg. The fourth board is in private hands but although the board itself is thought to be by Mante the watercolours were painted by D. Jansen (see p. 152).

ARTISTS

A limited number of very fine pieces were produced by the Boer prisoners in the camps. Many of the artists were born overseas, coming to South Africa and joining the Boer forces for varying reasons.

Ernst Karl Erich Mayer was born in Karlsruhe, Germany, in 1876. He originally intended to be an architect and only later studied art. He came to South Africa for health reasons and worked as a land surveyor but in De-

cember 1899 he joined the Boer forces. In May 1900 he was captured during an assault on Mafeking and sent to St Helena where he was imprisoned for two and a half years. During this time he produced a large number of paintings, drawings and sketches, all with a Boer War theme. His first attempt at painting with oils was a portrait of Kruger copied from a photograph and executed using home-made paints. This portrait now hangs in the War Museum of the Boer Republics in Bloemfontein. When the other prisoners were paroled and repatriated to South Africa, Mayer was deported to Germany in December 1902. He eventually returned to South Africa in 1911. (See also pp. 168-169.)

Ernst Evert Lindberg was a Finnish-born decorator who emigrated to the United States in 1892, establishing himself in New York. He came to South Africa to work in the mines. At the outbreak of the War he joined the Scandinavian Corps as a member of the ambulance unit. He was at the Siege of Mafeking and fought at Magersfontein but was wounded and captured at Paardeberg and sent off to Deadwood camp on St Helena. After his release in 1902 he returned briefly to Finland and wrote a book based on his experiences there. He returned to South Africa with his family in 1902. Two of his oil paintings done on St Helena are still in existence. One, in the possession of the McGregor Museum, Kimberley, is a portrait of Cronje taken from a photograph and the other shows the Deadwood camp at night. This painting was sold by Sotheby's, Johannesburg, on 24 May 1983 and is now in the Africana Museum.

A rather curious memoir of St Helena is held by the Mendelssohn Collection in the Library of Parliament,

Cape Town. This is a sketchbook depicting scenes of the island done by G. den Hertog whose name has not been found in the list of prisoners.

Painting was obviously a popular pastime on St Helena and at the Industrial Exhibition held in 1900 a photograph of the 'Section contributed by Boer Prisoners of War' shows at least 38 paintings displayed on the wall of the exhibition room. This photograph appears in T. Jackson's publications *Pictorial views of St Helena* and *Picturesque and Descriptive Souvenir of St Helena*.

The only identifiable artist imprisoned on Bermuda, besides Percy Mather of Darrell's Island (who did a pen-and-ink sketch of fellow prisoner Jan van Tonder receiving his mail), was François van der Merwe, otherwise known as 'Rooi Faan' because of his flame-red hair. Van der Merwe was born on a farm in the Fauresmith district in 1877. He was captured at Jagersfontein on 16 October 1900 and for unspecified reasons was sentenced to death by a military court under Maj. Kinghall, who was commander of the local garrison. He was released after the Boers had retaken the town but was once again recaptured by the British and, as was the custom with prisoners whose death sentences were commuted, sent to Bermuda. These prisoners were distinguished from their fellows by being made to wear 'marksmen's hearts' on their tunics. This rather macabre practice probably served as a reminder to them to behave themselves. Van der Merwe spent much of his spare time doing artistic woodcarvings. He also worked in copper, iron and leather but he is best known for the beautiful sandstone monument which he carved in the memory of the 35 prisoners who died in Bermuda during their captivity.

The War Museum of the Boer Republics, Bloemfon-

1 A hand-drawn postcard of St Helena by
French P.O.W. Captain Victor du Framont.
Du Framont produced several other similar
cards which he seems to have given or
sold to other Boer prisoners.
2 Boer P.O.W. Ernest Douwes Dekker painted
this watercolour of the P.O.W. staging camp
at Green Point after he was sent off to Ceylon.
He also painted several illustrations and
cartoons on postcards, which he disposed of
to fellow prisoners. The Africana Museum
has several other postcards illustrated by him.

tein, has a large pencil drawing of a British soldier done
by A. C. Brandsma who is reputed to have been a Boer
P.O.W., but again his name has not been traced in the roll
of prisoners.

Besides the work of known artists there are many
other sketches and paintings done by unidentified prisoners. Examples are found on postcards, letters, scraps
of paper and envelopes, some still bearing the censor's
markings. Some are by identified artists, including J. G.
Engela on Diyatalawa and J. Reijenga (or Rewenga) on St
Helena who illustrated postcards advertising the firm of
Weinthal and Co. of Rotterdam, a cigarette manufacturing firm. (See p. 193.)

Captain Victor du Framont, a French P.O.W., produced a series of hand-drawn cyclostyled postcards,
some of which were signed in full while others were
only initialled. All were dated 1902 and some were inscribed 'Souvenir des prisonniers de Guerre Français'. A
fellow prisoner, Maurice Le Gall, drew several caricatures which are housed in the Mendelssohn Collection
in the Library of Parliament, Cape Town. Louis François
was another Frenchman whose works are still in existence, including an album of watercolours of birds and
flowers, painted in Diyatalawa, which is in the Africana
Museum, Johannesburg.

Ernest Dekker produced a series of postcards showing various scenes and events at Ragama and at the
camp in Green Point. These hand-drawn watercolours
were probably done for sale to his fellow prisoners and
were numbered and initialled D.D. Many of these cards
are in the Africana Museum together with a suite of
hand-illustrated playing cards bearing the same initials.

J. H. Venter, who was captured at Paardeberg on
27 February 1900, is responsible for at least two naive
paintings, one showing a stylistic impression of the
Green Point camp and another giving an interesting impression of the Battle of Modder River. Venter appears
to have remained in Green Point, unlike most of his fellow prisoners who were sent out of South Africa.

An illustrated diary kept by E. van Korsinsky in
Diyatalawa has recently come to light. Van Korsinsky,
who hailed from Bethlehem in the Orange Free State,
dated the title page of his diary April 1901 and dedicated
it to 'His honour President Steyn as a token of admiration'. The diary which continues to 1902 has numerous
cartoons, sketches and watercolours with comments in
English. It hardly touches on his time in captivity and
mainly attacks British and Cape colonial politicians and
their policies.

The National Army Museum possesses a naive watercolour entitled *Naby Ladysmith in Januarie 1900*, bearing the inscription 'Van Moerkerken from the original
drawing by W. du Toit' but there is no information available on these two men.

While the contribution of South African artists who
were either born in the country or fought on the side of
the Boers or who later worked in South Africa was relatively small, it nevertheless forms an important part of
the artistic story of the Boer War. Most of the work was
done by amateurs, who because of natural reticence or
other reasons, did not sign their pictures. The result is
that many of these works remain unidentified.

PART TWO

NEWSPAPERS AND PERIODICALS

CHAPTER SIX

British Home-based Artists

Previous page: *The Queen listening to a despatch from the front*, a photogravure by Samuel Begg that was published by *The Illustrated London News*. The original painting was given to the National Bazaar for War Funds for its auction in May 1900. A limited edition of 1 000 copies was offered for sale, at a price of half a guinea per print.
1 Richard Caton Woodville's 1904 illustration of a trooper, Cape Mounted Police, done for the Imperial Army series of postcards.
2 and 3: Editors sometimes used seemingly straightforward pictures for propaganda purposes. An example was the drawing by F. Patterson (2) reproduced in the *Illustrated London News* of 9 December 1899. Entitled *Firing on the Ambulance: a scene during the Battle of Lombard's Kop*, the drawing was a section of the double-page panorama of the Battle of Lombard's Kop by Melton Prior (3) that the newspaper had featured in its 2 December 1899 issue that Prior had marked with a cross, showing a shell bursting near an ambulance cart.

F oreign wars had always been the lifeblood of the British illustrated press but when the Boer War started the papers became noticeably thicker and supplements and special issues were published frequently. Consequently many more illustrators were employed and better working conditions and more attractive salaries were offered. The home-based illustrators in general were a fickle lot. They changed allegiances frequently, although most stayed with the same company at least for the duration of the War. Besides having to draw well they were also expected to work quickly, to be available at all hours, to have intimate knowledge of military uniforms and accoutrements and, in particular, to be able to draw horses in every conceivable pose. Sometimes two or even more artists would sit up all night working on the same illustration to meet a deadline. Often two such illustrators would establish a good working relationship, for example Stephen Dadd and Frank Dadd of *The Graphic*.

By far the greatest contribution to the art of the War came from these home-based artists, although the art editors often resorted to blatant propaganda, and so-called Boer atrocities were played up as much as possible. Many of the scenes and events featured in the illustrations were highly exaggerated. Working from photographs, drawings and sketches from 'special' artists, or even their own fertile imaginations, the home-based artists often produced illustrations which depicted what the public wanted or needed to see. One well-known

panoramic facsimile illustration of the Battle of Lombard's Kop by Melton Prior appeared in *The Illustrated London News* in December 1899. As was his custom, Prior drew attention to certain incidents by making crosses which referred to annotations in the margin. One such incident showed the upsetting of an ambulance cart. A week later F. Patterson redrew this tiny portion of Prior's illustration much enlarged and captioned it: 'Firing on the Ambulance: A scene during the Battle of Lombard's Kop at Ladysmith 30 October' (see pp. 188-191).

Another artist whose work fell into this category and was regarded as controversial was Richard Caton Woodville, who worked for *The Illustrated London News*. His technical knowledge was admired by many, including Queen Victoria, but some of the titles he used, such as *All that was left of them* and *Conquered but not subdued* were unashamedly jingoistic. Roy Compton, writing in *The Idler* in 1896, said 'There is scarcely a soldier to say nothing of civilians whose pulse does not beat higher as he looks on the realistic production of Mr Caton Woodville's wonderful brush'. Not so complimentary was the unnamed correspondent who remarked in the 1880s that 'Caton Woodville's illustrations were an artist's victory over many a British defeat'. Another artist working in similar vein was Archibald Hartrick who worked for *The Sphere*.

H. C. Shelley, the photographer for *The King* (whose editor Walter Smith had promised no *imaginary* draw-

2

3

ings, only realistic photographs) joined the controversy raging in the correspondence columns of *The Friend* about whether using photographs was better than using the illustrations by the war artists. He ridiculed some of Caton Woodville's and Archibald Hartrick's work although he does not mention them by name:

I saw the other day a picture in one of the leading papers by one of the best illustrators. It showed the British storming a Boer position. In the middle ground was a Boer battery and the only gunner left alive was standing up with a bandage round his head, while smoke and flame and flying fragments of shells filled the air in his vicinity. In the rush of the instant he must have been bandaged by the same shot that struck him, and as for smoke and debris in the air there were more of this in a corner of that picture than I have seen in all the four battles we have fought . . .

There is a picture of two gunners standing to attention. The man nearest the gun is looking straight in front of him, with a bandage round his head, a bullet-wound in his face (close to the left ear), two in the right side of his chest and one in his right leg, some distance above the knee. Within a yard of him is a bursting shell. But that man ignores such trivial things. Still he stands. I suppose the weight of so much lead in him keeps him up. One wonders whether he is hollow inside so that the bullets drop down into his feet.

The second description refers to the illustration by Archibald Hartrick which appeared in *The Sphere* on 10 February 1900 entitled *The lost Guns at Colenso: The last two Gunners* (see p. 52).

Caton Woodville's heroic illustrations were often used by the Continental press with completely different captions, giving the opposite meaning to the one he intended. In an illustration appearing in *The Illustrated London News* on 2 December 1899 titled *Incident at Elandslaagte* he shows 'a British veterinary corporal spearing two Boers with one thrust'. The same illustration is reproduced in *Oorlog in Zuid Afrika* with a Dutch caption that can be translated as follows: 'Battlefield hyenas: The Lancers murdering unarmed Boers who have surrendered, thereby disregarding their international rights as combatants'.

The soldier in the field who looked forward to receiving his copy of *The Illustrated London News*, albeit a good few weeks after publication, was often also critical of the bias of some of the illustrations. But not all comment was critical. In an interview given to Marie Belloc of *The Strand Magazine* in 1900, Eduard Detaille, the well-known French military painter, admitted that he admired the 'really splendid black and white work which is being done by those who so modestly style themselves as war specials and war sketchers'. He also expressed great admiration for Richard Caton Woodville but felt that in general he lacked real experience of war. It was the job of the illustrated newspapers to bring

1 *The Battle of Elandslaagte* by Richard Caton Woodville was published in *The Illustrated London News* with the caption: 'An incident at Elandslaagte: A veterinary corporal of the 5th Lancers spearing two Boers with one thrust'. It appeared in *De Oorlog in Suid-Afrika* with the caption (roughly translated): 'Battlefield hyenas – the Lancers murdering unarmed Boers who have surrendered, thereby violating international law'. It is a good example of how one's interpretation of a picture depending on one's point of view.
2 The French 'special' artist Paul Frenzeny produced this illustration entitled *Inspection of Commando of Boers* for *The Illustrated London News* and it was later used on a postcard in the Picture Postcard Co. series 2d.
3 *The Lost Guns at Colenso: The Last Two Gunners* by Archibald Hartrick, published in *The Sphere* on 10 February 1900 from a description by Bennet Burleigh, correspondent of *The Daily Telegraph*. Hartrick's Boer War illustrations were criticized by some for being overly heroic, not to mention inaccurate.

this experience of war to their readers and, though they aroused controversy at times, they employed a wide range of talents to do just this.

The Illustrated London News

Once again this newspaper led the field and some of the illustrations were so popular that they were reproduced in special editions.

RICHARD CATON WOODVILLE

American-born Richard Caton Woodville was the most prolific of *The Illustrated London News* home-based artists. He had seen action for *The Illustrated London News* in Turkey in 1876 and in the Egyptian campaign of 1882 but thereafter all his work was done in the offices of the newspaper. *The Illustrated London News* often reproduced his illustrations as photogravures which also appeared in the sister publication *The Sketch* and in 'Holly Leaves', the special Christmas number of *The Illustrated Sporting & Dramatic News*. Among these photogravures was the extremely patriotic *All that was left of them*, a title that was in fact given to two separate prints. One referred to the Highland Brigade at Magersfontein and the second to an incident at Modderfontein on 17 September 1901 when C Squadron of the Lancers was surprised and surrounded by Boers.

In 1900 *The Illustrated London News* published Spenser Wilkinson's *The Transvaal War*, which was advertised as the 'Complete account of the whole campaign' and included eight photogravures of Caton Woodville's paintings. A deluxe numbered edition was published in January 1901 signed by Woodville, Melton Prior and Samuel Begg and advertised in *The Illustrated London News* on 5 January 1901. This issue also announced the forthcoming publication of *Generals of the New Century* at a selling price of five shillings. These colour prints 'on Rembrandt Art Board with gold mounts' featured Roberts, Kitchener, Buller, Baden-Powell, Hector McDonald, French, Rundle and Ian Hamilton. Also offered was *Bobs as schoolmaster* – a 'high-class' reproduction in colour from the 'clever' drawing by Cecil Aldin, at a selling price of two shillings

and sixpence. Inspired by Roberts's recent return from South Africa, the advertisement included *Lord Roberts at the front* by Caton Woodville – 200 artist's proofs at three guineas each. The list went on to include *The Queen's Garden Party*, *The Surrender of Cronje to Lord Roberts* and *The Queen Listening to a Despatch* – all at a price of half a guinea (artist's proofs at one guinea) and *Sons of the Blood* at five shillings (artist's proofs at half a guinea). (See pp. 235-236.)

SAMUEL BEGG

According to James Thorpe, the author of *English Illustration: The Nineties*, Samuel Begg's transcriptions of photographs were so close to that medium as to be almost unnecessary. Nevertheless Begg was a very important illustrator for *The Illustrated London News* although very little is known about him after he left the paper. Born in London in 1854, he emigrated with his parents to New Zealand. In 1877 he was in Australia working for the *Sydney Bulletin* and *Illustrated Australia*. By 1895 he was employed by *Black & White* in London, but a year later he joined *The Illustrated London News*, where he stayed for at least 17 years. Begg does not seem to have had any military experience and his Boer War work, while being very prolific, seems to have been concerned mainly with local English scenes and particularly matters to do with the Royal Family. In fact the illustration *The Queen listening to a despatch from the front* was donated to the National Bazaar for War Funds. The painting itself was on offer and a limited edition of 1 000 photogravures was produced and offered for sale at half a guinea while a few artist's proofs were available at one guinea. Another photogravure by Begg entitled *Sons of the Blood* (also featured in Spenser Wilkinson's book *The Transvaal War*), exceeded even Caton Woodville's efforts at patriotism.

OTHERS

The Illustrated London News, like its rivals, also employed foreign-born illustrators. Conditions of employment must have been better in England than on the Continent as many of them left their positions with the European illustrated weeklies to contribute to the Brit-

ish ones. Georges Montbard and Amedée Forestier were both French-born illustrators who supplied many illustrations to *The Illustrated London News*. Both often used monograms, so credit is not always given to their work. Gennaro Amato, also known as D'Amato, was born in Naples and, besides contributing to *L'Illustration*, provided Italian scenes as well as the occasional Boer War illustration. Paul Frenzeny, the well-known Western artist, worked for *The Illustrated London News* and contributed occasionally to *The Sphere*.

Charles de Lacy, the marine artist who exhibited Boer War seascapes at the Royal Academy, and Henry Charles Seppings Wright, who had visited South Africa in the 1870s, were called upon by *The Illustrated London News* whenever shipping scenes were required. Seppings Wright's work was used extensively for other Boer War situations as well.

The services of William Robinson, F. Patterson, George Rowlandson, Godfrey Merry, Ernest Shérie, Louis Edwards and Gunning King were used to a lesser extent. Holland Tringham, who had been a Royal Academy exhibitor in 1894 and 1895, was employed as a photo retoucher as well as an illustrator. The retouching of photographs was a vital though menial task in the newspaper art department. On 18 November 1899 an attempt was made to erase Tringham's signature from an illustration entitled *Gordon Highlanders on their way to Elandslaagte*. Instead the credit states that the illustration was a 'photograph (enlarged) taken by our special correspondent Mr G. Lynch'. Despite this ignominy Tringham contributed many illustrations, mostly of rural scenes in South Africa. As he often signed only his initials H.T. he is not always given credit for his work.

The 'younger' brother of *The Illustrated London News* was *The Sketch*, founded on 15 February 1863. At the time of the War most of its visual material was photographic although a few artist-drawn illustrations were reproduced, usually supplied by T.W. Holmes, Alexander Finberg, H.M. Wilson and Lance Thackeray. Some cartoons were also used, mainly from the pens of Hilda Cowham, Hutton Mitchell, Tom Browne, Charles Potts, Charles Pears and Dudley Hardy. A cartoon by Hutton Mitchell published on 14 February 1900 demonstrates

their policy quite clearly. It depicts an artist asking if he can show the editor some war drawings, to which the office boy replies: 'Actuality first . . . we go in for war photos.'

Many contemporary illustrated books and other publications such as *Cassell's History of the Boer War*, Louis Creswicke's *South Africa and the Transvaal War* and Harold Brown's *War with the Boers*, not to mention the many Continental and American publications which published illustrations, all lifted directly from the pages of *The Illustrated London News*. In most cases no acknowledgment whatsoever was given to the copyright holder. In many cases not only are the captions altered but the illustrators' signatures are cropped so as to make them almost unidentifiable.

The Picture Postcard Company was another publisher that borrowed freely from *The Illustrated London News*. At the end of November 1899, soon after the outbreak of war, a series of 30 postcards was issued in five sets. The morale-sapping British defeats at Stormberg, Magersfontein and Colenso, known collectively as Black Week (10-15 December 1899), had not yet taken place. Propaganda was therefore considered unnecessary and the cards themselves were objective, giving almost equal prominence to Boer and British forces.

Altogether 12 of the 30 illustrations came directly from *The Illustrated London News*, although half of these were originally published before the War. Sometimes only part of the illustration was used and in a few cases the signature or monogram had been cropped. Besides Caton Woodville's eight illustrations, one each by Amedée Forestier, Paul Frenzeny, Georges Montbard and Louis Edwards was used. (Louis Edwards worked occasionally for *The Illustrated London News* and was responsible for the illustrations in Lt. Col. Nathaniel Newnham-Davies's *The Transvaal under the Queen*.) One further unsigned illustration was that of General Buller, which has been traced to Charles Mills Sheldon. Credit is, however, given on the card to *Black & White*, who employed Sheldon at that time.

Other *Illustrated London News* illustrations were used without credit on at least two different sets of lantern slides by unidentified publishers. The sets are

1 Hutton Mitchell depicts the problems experienced by the freelance artist trying to sell his 'war drawings' to publications in this *The Sketch* cartoon. The artist asks the office boy if he can show the editor some war drawings, and the haughty boy replies that *The Sketch* uses only war photos.
2 A view of Colonel Baden-Powell and his troops reconnoitering outside Mafeking by Oliver Paque (pseudonym of William Pike), home-based artist for *The Graphic* and *The Daily Graphic*.

Wash drawing by Henry Paget entitled
Lord Roberts inspecting rescued prisoners at Pretoria. It appeared in *The Graphic, The Graphic History of the South African War* and *Cassell's Illustrated History of the Boer War*.

titled respectively *Boer War of 1900 Series* and *Juvenile Lantern Series*.

Lantern slides were very popular at the time and *Black & White Budget* frequently advertised various sets for hire from their 'slide department' at a charge of 35 shillings for the first night and 20 shillings for every subsequent night. Included in the price was a 'type written Lecture illustrative of the most recent events of the war accompanying 60 slides full explanatory thereof'. Without the lecture the slides were for hire at five shillings per dozen. A later advertisement on 5 May 1900 even offered to supply a lecturer if required: 'The complete exhibition, 100 slides, Lantern, oxy hydrogen gas, screen, operator and all accessories' could be had for two pounds, seven shillings and sixpence. Their list of 128 slides was also available 'for sale at one shilling each (post and packing extra)' while coloured slides were offered at two shillings and sixpence. The advertisement adds that the slides were taken from original sketches, drawings and photographs supplied by *Black & White* special correspondents. A further set of at least 200 slides covering the period up to the Boer surrender at Paardeberg was published by W. D. Hughes early in the War. All the illustrations used were artist-drawn and credit was given to *The Graphic* for the majority while a few were taken from *The Sphere*, again with acknowledgement.

The Graphic and The Daily Graphic

The Graphic and *The Daily Graphic* employed a greater number of illustrators than *The Illustrated London News* as in most cases the artists for the two sister papers were employed separately. One reason for using two sets of artists was that the techniques and methods of reproduction were completely different. *The Graphic* used mainly wash drawings whereas *The Daily Graphic* favoured pen-and-ink drawings, which were quick and easy to reproduce using the technique of line engraving. *The Daily Graphic* occasionally used halftone screen blocks when reproducing photographs but more often employed a process known as the 'American' method. This process involved drawing over the highlights on the photographic plate with Indian ink. The plate was then put into a bath of bichloride of mercury, which dissolved all traces of the photograph leaving only the Indian ink remaining. An 'English' method was also available and this was superior to the 'American' method in that the Indian ink was applied on tracing paper placed over the photograph, with the result that the photograph was not destroyed and could be used again.

When William Thomas first started *The Daily Graphic* he advertised for black and white artists, stating that there was 'a good opening for young men to make an income of from £400 to £2 000 per annum this way'. Archibald Hartrick joined *The Daily Graphic* soon after it was founded, but during the War he sought the greener pastures of *The Sphere*. Writing in his book *A Painter's Pilgrimage*, which was published in 1939, he describes how on arrival at *The Daily Graphic* offices the applicants were interviewed by Thomas himself and then placed under the supervision of the 'elderly Frenchman Godefroi du Rand' who acted as instructor and adviser. George Kingston Jones, Hartrick adds, was already established as a 'toucher-up of photographs or utility man'. Of the original staff who saw the start of the paper on 1 January 1890, only Herbert Johnson, Reginald Cleaver, Alexander Stuart Boyd, William Ralston, Jones and 'Mars' (Maurice Bonvoisin) were still employed at the time of the War. Hartrick (*The Sphere*) and Leonard Raven-Hill (*Punch*) had changed employers. 'Mars', a Frenchman, reported on the arrival of Kruger in Marseilles in November 1900 and his subsequent stay in Paris, and his illustrations were used by both *The Graphic* and *The Daily Graphic*.

By 1900, Douglas McPherson, Stephen Dadd, T.C.C. Crowther, Arthur Kemp Tebby, F. Young, J. Duncan, Sidney Higham, 'Oliver Paque', Miss S.A.H. Robinson and Jan van Papendrecht Hoynck, the Dutch artist, were contributing regularly to *The Daily Graphic* with

an occasional illustration from *The Graphic* team as well. Oliver Paque was the pseudonym of the Devonshire watercolourist William Pike. Pike was a prominent member of the Savage Club, as were many of the other illustrators, and was a frequent designer and illustrator of their house menus, including the one for the dinner held to welcome home the war correspondents from South Africa on Saturday 13 July 1901. Of *The Daily Graphic* staff Crowther and Higham were frequently used as outside illustrators and were spared the monotony of indoor work by attending various functions and processions in and around London, where they made their preliminary sketches.

The Graphic had the largest team of illustrators on its staff. Unlike the artists on *The Illustrated London News*, not many had covered previous foreign wars for the illustrated press. Sidney Prior Hall visited South Africa with the Duke and Duchess of Cornwall and York's world tour on *The Ophir* in 1901. Hall, who was made a member of the Royal Victorian Order, was *The Graphic*'s 'special' artist in France during the Franco-Prussian War in 1870. One of his specialities was Royal tours, and he accompanied at least three foreign tours, including one to Canada in 1881.

Henry Marriot Paget was the eldest of three artistic brothers, the others being Walter and Sidney. Henry Paget had travelled widely in Italy and the Middle East and later in Canada, and he had been a member of the 20th Middlesex (Artists') Corps from 1875 to 1884. Despite his age he volunteered in World War I and was promoted to captain in the British Expeditionary Force and mentioned in despatches in 1916. He also acted as 'special' artist for *The Sphere* in the Balkan War of 1912-13. During the Boer War *The Graphic* published many of his illustrations, which are identified only by the initials H.M.P. His two younger brothers Sidney and Walter (Wal) are probably better known. Sidney was the original illustrator of Conan Doyle's *Sherlock Homes* and he is reputed to have used Walter as his model for the hero. Both Sidney and Wal worked for *The Sphere* during the

War but two of Wal's illustrations were used in *The Graphic* in 1899. (See pp. 180-181.)

French-born Frederic de Haenen was a regular contributor to *The Graphic* during the Boer War. Very little is known about him except that he came to London in 1899 at the start of the War and left *The Graphic* to join *The Illustrated London News* in 1909. Besides his contributions to *The Graphic* many of De Haenen's illustrations appear in *L'Illustration*. His work is highly distinctive and recognizable even when his signature has been cropped or erased. (See p. 125.)

Frank Dadd was undoubtedly the most prolific of *The Graphic*'s Boer War artists as over 100 illustrations are credited to him. Dadd was a cousin of Kate Greenaway and a nephew of the well-known artist Richard Dadd, who did most of his work in an institution for the criminally insane. Richard had been committed to the asylum after murdering his father, Frank's grandfather. Most of Frank Dadd's work was signed F.D. and occasionally he did double-page spreads in conjunction with Stephen Dadd, who was probably a relative. Dadd started his career with *The Illustrated London News* in 1878 and Zulu and Basuto War illustrations appeared with his signature in the paper until he joined *The Graphic* in 1884. (See p. 123.)

John Charlton was a brilliant equestrian illustrator who exhibited over 30 paintings at the Royal Academy, including two of South African military interest. Charlton contributed nearly 50 Boer War illustrations to *The Graphic*, often signing with his initials only. Most of these, as could be expected, showed stirring equestrian scenes. Frank Craig was another well-known Royal Academy exhibitor who was kept busy by *The Graphic*. His 40 illustrations were praised by Albert Carter in his book *The Work of War Artists in South Africa*. Gordon Frederick Browne ('G.B.') was the son of Hablôt Knight Browne ('Phiz'), who was Dickens's original illustrator. Gordon Browne worked for both *The Graphic* and Harmsworth's *With the Flag to Pretoria*. Joseph Nash ('J.N.') jnr. was another less well-known son of a more

Gallant defence of derailed train near Alkmaar, a wash drawing by Frank Dadd, shows an incident on 20 May 1901 in which Lt. Duncan Lorn Campbell and four men of the First Royal Welsh Regiment held out against Boer commandant Hindon and 50 Boers. Campbell received the D.S.O. for his gallantry.

1

2

1 Joseph Nash jnr. was one of the many artists who depicted Winston Churchill's dramatic escape from captivity and his arrival in Durban. In this sketch he is depicted climbing over the fence of the Model School, Pretoria.
2 This picture by Joseph Nash jnr. shows Churchill climbing onto the goods train to make good his escape. Churchill did the preliminary sketches for both of these pictures.

famous father. Nash Junior had been working for *The Graphic* as early as 1874 but had a habit of not signing his work so he probably produced many more illustrations than he is given credit for.

George Soper worked principally for *The Golden Penny*, 'The illustrated weekly family Journal' which was also published by *The Graphic*. Among his other paintings Soper contributed an illustration each week to the series 'Heroes of the war'.

When maritime scenes were required *The Graphic* called on the services of William Lionel Wyllie and more especially Charles Dixon. Another illustrator who was later to become a famous marine artist was the American Frederick Judd Waugh, who had come to Britain in 1894. After spending a while on the island of Sark, financial pressures forced him to move to London in 1899. Despite the acceptance of his paintings by the Royal Academy he needed an extra income and accepted contracts both from Harmsworth and the proprietors of *The Graphic*. His biographer George Havens, in *Fredrick Judd Waugh: American Marine Painter*, gives a vivid description of his work with *The Graphic*: 'Despatches and sketches came to him by courier from the front every Friday, and he worked under great pressure each weekend so that the finished pictures would reach the office of *The Graphic* at 190 The Strand by Monday morning. The rest of the week was his own to paint as he wished, or to freelance.' Havens adds that Waugh was paid 'one guinea an inch'. It is unclear, however, whether this measurement was linear or square or whether the size referred to the original or the smaller printed reproduction.

Other well-known artists whose Boer War illustrations were featured occasionally in *The Graphic* included Balliol Salmon, Robert Macbeth, William Hatherell, George Percy Jacomb-Hood, William Small and John Hassall, the comic artist who later became so well known for his World War I posters and postcards. Scottish-born William Ralston contributed sketches showing the lighter side of the War. Fortunino Matania, the Italian illustrator, was only 21 when he made his debut for *The Graphic* with an illustration of President Steyn in August 1902.

Not to be outdone by *The Illustrated London News*, *The Graphic* also published a history of the War in 1900, giving it the title *The Graphic History of the South African War* 'a complete narrative of the campaign containing about 300 illustrations'. There were many illustrations but more emphasis was placed on the text than in the *Illustrated London News*'s *The Transvaal War*. The artists are not generally identified by name and in some instances existing signatures and monograms have been cropped. All the illustrations used in this publication originally appeared in *The Graphic* and many were taken from the special double issue that appeared out of sequence on 2 April 1900. This special issue, which covered the sieges of Mafeking and Ladysmith, is often absent from the bound volume of *The Graphic* January to June 1900 (Volume 41).

Several of the Boer War illustrations in *The Graphic* were reissued as 'supplementary prints' – unbound prints with no text on the reverse. Occasionally these prints were coloured. The original drawings that had been used for reproduction in the early years were usually destroyed during the transfer to wood blocks by the engraver. With the advent of the photoengraving process in the late 1880s and early 1890s all this changed and the original drawings were preserved, though they were sometimes defaced by instructions from the art editor to the printer. The question soon arose what was to be done with the vast quantity of illustrated 'Bristol board' that was rapidly accumulating in the offices of the magazines and newspapers. Soon the art departments were building galleries to house, exhibit and hopefully to sell them. *The Graphic* often used its pages to advertise the sale of these works. The 8 March 1902 issue carried the following notice:

To Artists, Collectors, officers and others. Now on view, a splendid collection of Black and White original Drawings executed for and published in *The Graphic* and of Pen and Ink sketches reproduced in *The Daily Graphic*. On sale at moderate prices. The Graphic Gallery 195 Strand London W.C. Admission Free. Hours 10 to 5p.m. Saturday 10 to 1 p.m.'

Important visitors to the newspaper offices were often presented with a gift of a painting to commemorate

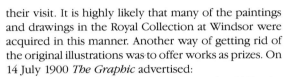

1

2

their visit. It is highly likely that many of the paintings and drawings in the Royal Collection at Windsor were acquired in this manner. Another way of getting rid of the original illustrations was to offer works as prizes. On 14 July 1900 *The Graphic* advertised:

> Valuable 'Graphic' original drawings, value £112 to be given away. These signed original drawings, by such famous artists as J. Charlton, F. Craig, A. S. Boyd and others form the prizes in *The Golden Penny* plebiscite in which the readers are voting for the six men deserving most Honour and Reward for their services in South Africa. Add your vote. You may possibly win one of these fine drawings (all of which are framed). They are all of war subjects and there is not one that would not be a possession to be proud of.

Despite all the efforts made to get rid of them, the stock of paintings held by *The Graphic* continued to increase and in 1904 it was decided to put them up for auction and the firm of Puttick and Simpson (later part of Phillips Neale and Son) was commissioned.

The sale was held on Thursday 9 and Friday 10 June 1904. The catalogue described the works as 'a valuable collection of original oil paintings, watercolours and Black and White Drawings formerly published in *The Graphic* and *The Daily Graphic*'. The artists were listed as follows:

C. Burton Barber A.R.A.	Wm Hatherell R.I.
Tom Browne R.I.	Seymour Lucas R.A.
Frank Brangwyn A.R.A.	R. W. Macbeth R.A.
Lance Calkin	Percy Macquoid R.I.
Reginald Cleaver	W. H. Margetson
John Charlton	J. Nash R.I.
M. Cot	P. Renouard
Frank Dadd R.I.	C. T. Staniland R.I.
Arthur Hacker A.R.A.	J. R. Weguelin R.W.S.
Arthur Hopkins R.W.S.	C. W. Wyllie
St George Hare R.I.	Balliol Salmon
Gordon Browne R.W.S.	Wm Small
Frank Craig	W. T. Maud (the late)
Chas Dixon R.I.	A. S. Boyd
and others.	

On the first day of the sale 181 lots were offered, of which at least 70 were of Boer War interest. Several lots included two or more items and the prices realized for the Boer War pictures were generally lower than those for the others. Some of the non-Boer War watercolours reached the fantastic sum of one pound and eighteen shillings, but the highest price raised for a Boer War painting was one pound and two shillings – for Frank Craig's *Search for wounded after a Battle, Natal*. Charles Fripp's *Compton's Horse bivouacking* which was 'an original war sketch' realized only three shillings, with Fred Whiting's *A Sortie by the Natal Volunteers* going for only two shillings. The grand total received on the first day for the 181 lots was 88 pounds and fifteen shillings with the Boer War paintings averaging out at about six shillings each. Heinrich Egersdörfer's *Boer Commando near Johannesburg* was one of the three items in lot 181, which fetched ten shillings. Three individuals identified only as Curtis, Levine and Gunn snapped up most of the bargains on offer, but it is not known whether they were collectors or dealers. Some of the paintings sold at the auction can still be traced. Joseph Nash's *Cronje's Laager at Paardeberg*, which is in the National Army Museum, fetched twelve shillings. The Africana Museum's *News from the outer World* by William Small was lumped with his *Entry of troops into Mafeking* and both were snapped up by a Mr Bright for ten shillings.

On the Friday even bigger bargains were to be found but because of the exceptionally large number of items the titles of individual paintings were not given. Altogether another 192 lots were on offer, mainly in folios in groups of up to 100. Identification was merely 'by Frank Dadd, H.M. Paget, John Charlton etc.' or 'drawings from *The Daily Graphic*' and sometimes just plain 'various'. Prices of six or eight shillings per lot were not unusual. A record price of nine pounds and five shillings was paid for *His First Voyage*, a watercolour by Frank Brangwyn, but this was not connected with the Boer War. It is interesting to note that listed among the buyers was a Mr Charlton who was particularly active when John Charlton's work was on offer, and he may well have been the artist himself repurchasing the fruits of his hard labours – and at those prices who could blame him? At the end of the second day £463.13s.6d. was

1 To get rid of some of the many original drawings that were accumulating in the archives of *The Graphic* and *The Daily Graphic*, an auction was held on 9 June 1904. This advertisement for the sale appeared on 4 June.
2 John Charlton's oil on canvas entitled *Routed! Boers retreating* was exhibited at the Royal Academy in 1900.

BOVRIL WAR PICTURE

"THE RELIEF OF LADYSMITH." BY JOHN H. BACON.

A Magnificent Historic War Gravure, 28 in. by 18½ in., printed on fine plate paper 40 in. by 30 in., free from advertising matter.

FREE TO PURCHASERS
OF BOVRIL IN BOTTLES

BOVRIL Limited, having secured the finest Oil Painting yet executed in connection with the South African War, entitled "THE RELIEF OF LADYSMITH," painted by John H. Bacon, and representing SIR GEORGE WHITE in the act of shaking hands with LORD DUNDONALD, have made arrangements to present a handsome and finely executed Gravure of the same to all purchasers of Bovril in accordance with the following plan:—

From the 1st February until the 31st May, 1901, every bottle of Bovril (from 6½d. to 5s.) sold to the public will bear a coupon, and this coupon will vary in value in proportion to the size of the bottle.

The 1oz. Bottle will bear a Coupon for 6½d.		The 4oz. Bottle will bear a Coupon for 1 9
" 2oz. " " 1 -		" 8oz. " " 3 1
	The 16oz. Bottle will bear a Coupon for 5/-.	

Every person sending in to Bovril Ltd., 152, Old Street, E.C., before the 31st of May next, Coupons to the aggregate face value of not less than 21s. will become entitled to one of these Bovril War Pictures.

The advertisement of the Bovril offer of Bacon's *Relief of Ladysmith*.

taken and added to the receipts of the first day, and the proprietors of *The Graphic* were richer by £852.6s.6d., less auctioneer's commission.

Black & White and Black & White Budget

Black & White and the twopenny *Black & White Budget* ('worth sixpence', crowed the advertisement) did not employ as many home-based illustrators as their rivals. Although expense was probably the main reason for this, it was also partly because they produced the work of their frontline 'specials' in facsimile and relied more on photographs. René Bull was as adept with his camera as he was with his pencil and David Barnett and Angus Hamilton (in Mafeking) had been appointed as special photographers.

Some of the early illustrations in *Black & White Budget* have no signature and are poorly reproduced, which may indicate some form of plagiarism. Nevertheless the work of a few well-known artists was used from time to time, including that of John Henry Bacon. Bacon was a respected exhibitor at the Royal Academy and four of his paintings were directly inspired by the Boer War. In 1901 the manufacturers of Bovril advertised in *The Illustrated London News* that the photogravure of Bacon's painting *The Relief of Ladysmith* would be offered in exchange for 21 shillings worth of coupons, which were supplied with each bottle of Bovril. The advertisement assured the readers 'that the photogravure would be printed on fine paper and would be free of advertising matter'.

Stanley L. Wood, another exhibitor of military paintings at the Royal Academy, was a prolific illustrator of adventure stories. Many of his illustrations in *Black & White* depict equestrian scenes. Christopher Clark, who exhibited two Boer War paintings at Burlington House, was used by both *Black & White* and *Black & White Budget*. Clark saw military service in the Royal Navy Volunteer Reserve during World War I. Shipping scenes were provided by Norman Wilkinson and Thirkell Pearce, Arthur Garratt, Charles Taffs, Hal Hurst, Arthur Nevison, Enoch Ward, Albert Wilkinson. Léon Daviel, C. Dudley Tennant, G. Davis, Joseph Barnard Davis and G. Grenville Manton provided the rest of the home-based illustrations. Adrian Jones, the veterinary surgeon who was in South Africa during the First Boer War and who later became a famous, if controversial, sculptor, provided one illustration.

Cartoons from S. Howard, Harry Parkes, Charles Pott, Henry Mayer, the German-born American cartoonist, and Archibald Forrest, who illustrated *Ten Little Boer Boys*, also appeared very occasionally. These cartoons were probably borrowed from publications such as *Pick-Me-Up* and *Moonshine*.

The Sphere

The Sphere, the latecomer to the illustrated weekly scene, must have had to spend considerable sums to entice illustrators to join its ranks. Poaching was mainly from *The Graphic* and Archibald Hartrick, Paul Renouard, Balliol Salmon and Ralph Cleaver worked at *The Sphere* at various times. The principal illustrators from the outset were Stanley Berkeley, Sidney Paget, Joseph Finnemore, Bernard Partridge, Alfred Pearse, James Greig, William Douglas Almond and the noted postcard artist Lance Thackeray. Many of these illustrators worked for Harmsworth's Amalgamated Press's periodical *With the Flag to Pretoria* at the same time. It is likely that their contracts permitted a certain amount of freelance work, which enabled them to boost their incomes. Others who contributed the occasional Boer War drawing were:

Fred Pegram, Paul Thiriat, Cecil Aldin, F. H. Townsend,

Charles Simpson, Thomas Walter Wilson, John Sanderson Wells, Lionel Sabattier, Paul Frenzeny, and T. Newton Shepard. Georges Bertin Scott, the *L'Illustration* artist, also had his work published in *The Sphere* as did Ernest-Auguste Bouard of *Le Monde Illustré*.

A reproduction of Thérèse Schwartze's painting of General Joubert appeared in the new weekly, but it is unlikely that she was employed by *The Sphere*. Charles Wyllie provided maritime scenes when required and Walter Paget joined the staff in May 1900. Inglis Sheldon-Williams was reputed to have been artist-correspondent for *The Sphere* during his tour of duty in South Africa but none of his works has been noted in the paper during the Boer War. His postwar views of the Delhi Durbar and the Russo-Japanese War dominated the reporting of these events in *The Sphere*.

A series of numbered lantern slides based on some of the early illustrations from *The Sphere* was also available. Postcards bearing different numbers but identical illustrations were also produced at about the same time by an unknown publisher.

Other Illustrated Periodicals

While almost completely dominating the illustrated news scene, the 'Big Four' were not the only British illustrated weeklies in existence at the time. Among the lesser-known weeklies was *The Illustrated Mail*, published by Harmsworth. It was first issued, on very cheap paper, in June 1899 at a cost of one penny (Vol. 1 No.31 was dated 13 January 1900). Ernest Smythe, who also supplied illustrations to *Under The Union Jack*, was one of the principal illustrators with Edward Lintott ('E.L.'), who had previously spent some time working in New York, and H. Arthur Hogg ('H.A.H.') making up the team. Copies of centrefolds and front pages were also available. According to the paper:

We are receiving countless applications for copies of the picture forming our front page from week to week. We have now made arrangements to meet these wishes. Below will be found a front page coupon. Cut three of these out of *Any one week's issue* of the papers and enclose together with a half-penny stamp and your name and address to the Art Editor, *The Illustrated Mail* Room 41 Harmsworth Building Carmelite Street, E.C. and we will forward you a superb copy of the drawing on art paper suitable for framing. The pictures are in every respect equal to the original drawing and framed or bound in an album will form a unique black and white art gallery.

If the reader wanted the centrefold, continued the advert, a penny stamp was required. Another special offer was a 'magnificent map of South Africa', together with a 'set of model soldiers, Boers, natives, flags, guns, encampments and men of war'. It was suggested that by moving the models on the map, which was printed on art paper, a 'complete panoramic view of the whole country and disposition of troops may be obtained'.

Another one-penny paper was *Shurey's Illustrated*, which, although cheap, was printed on art paper. The editor, Charles Shurey, boasted to his readers in the first issue on Saturday 14 October 1899 that they 'will acknowledge that I have brought out a first class illustrated paper for one Penny'. He comments also on the absence of advertisements, assuring his public that he could have let half the space for a considerable sum but declined the many tempting offers so as to 'give away every line to the British Public'.

He mentions too that he has been overwhelmed with illustrations and material from his war correspondents. However he did not name them and it is doubtful if he ever had any, but original illustrations were provided each week by a number of home-based artists.

Copies of *The Relief of Ladysmith* by John Henry Frederick Bacon were offered free to consumers of Bovril in exchange for coupons provided with the bottles.

Ernest Shérie, who eventually became art editor of *The Strand Magazine*, often provided the cover illustrations. J.H. Thornely and Arthur J. Gough, both of whom worked for Harmsworth as well, and Frank Feller ('F.F.') provided centrefolds. Edgar Holloway, who later became well known as a postcard artist, and Malcolm Patterson produced other drawings. By the 55th issue on 27 October 1900 Shurey proudly proclaimed an audited annual circulation of 9 920 500.

Shurey, who started *Sketchy Bits* with his brother in 1895, also published *Shurey's Pictorial Budget*. The first issue was on Monday 19 February 1900 and cost one and a half pence. Several illustrators were employed on the paper, which had no text besides the captions to the photographs and artist-drawn illustrations. Among the illustrators not previously mentioned were Frank Hardy (Dudley's brother), Frank M. Barton and Savile Lumley ('S.L.').

The Weekly Telegraph was yet another penny paper, but printed on inferior newsprint. Illustrations were mainly anonymous but Edward Wigfull's signature or initials W.E.W. appeared on some and 'S.M.T.G.' put his initials on photographs that had been retouched and converted to line engravings.

Lesser known still was *The Penny Illustrated Paper*, which first appeared in 1861. It was published by *The Illustrated London News* and *The Sketch* and at the time of the War John Lately jnr. was editor. Many full-page wash drawings were done by the regular artists from *The Illustrated London News*, including Richard Caton Woodville, Melton Prior and Samuel Begg. Original contributions, however, came from T.W. Holmes ('T.W.H.') and Ernest Ibbetson, who later illustrated many of the Gale & Polden 'History and Military Tradition' postcards in 1909. Other artists working for *The Penny Illustrated Paper* included Alexander Finberg, Thirkell Pearce, John Proctor, Dudley Hardy and Sidney Higham. Finberg was unusual because although he contributed to *The Illustrated London News* and *The Graphic*, illustration was very much a secondary career for him. He was best known as an author of books on art history and as an art critic for several newspapers. He was also an official valuator of art for the British tax authorities.

A coloured publication entitled *Illustrated War Special* was printed by *The Penny Illustrated Paper* and Volume 1, No. 17 appeared on 14 March 1900. The illustrations in this issue were mainly by artists employed by *The Penny Illustrated Paper* and *The Illustrated London News* but contributions from Edward Wigfull, Earl Robert and cartoonist 'Popini' were also included.

Lloyd's Weekly News was another penny paper, first published in 1842 and featuring illustrations and cartoons by Tom Merry, Sayers, Edward Lintott and 'E/c'.

As the War drew to a close the illustrated newspapers became considerably smaller. Many illustrators found themselves without employment and sought careers elsewhere. Some were lucky, such as Fred Waugh, who returned to his first love, fine art, and became America's best-known marine painter.

■

CHAPTER SEVEN

Special British Boer War Periodicals

Because of the intense public interest in the War many publishers issued magazines devoted exclusively to the subject. Naturally as interest in the War waned so the number and frequency of these publications diminished.

Cassell's Illustrated History of the Boer War

Cassell's Illustrated History of the Boer War was first published on 21 March 1900 and the first issue was given away free with No. 73 of *The New Penny Magazine*. The second issue, costing one penny, followed on 28 March. Thereafter the magazine was published weekly until No. 44 (25 January 1901). From then on, 'In order to present our readers with a record of the later phases of the war in South Africa in its correct proportion' it appeared monthly until the concluding issue (No. 49) appeared on 26 June 1901. This last issue announced that cloth covers were available for binding the work into one volume, at a cost of one shilling and sixpence. Individual issues were useless on their own as the text often stopped in mid-sentence and was continued in the following number. Cassell republished the complete set, revised and updated, in 1902-3 with Richard Danes as editor. With the exception of the illustration by Paul Hardy (P.H.) that was repeated on all the front covers, it seems that illustrations were liberally borrowed without acknowledgement.

War Pictures

War Pictures, C. Arthur Pearson's publication, was launched on 10 February 1900. It was priced at twopence and appeared weekly on Wednesdays until its abrupt demise with No. 16 on 26 May 1900. Despite the editor's claim to have a 'staff of 50 photographers and artists in South Africa' most of the illustrations were borrowed, without acknowledgement, from its rivals. However it did publish facsimile drawings by Gordon Grant and J. C. L. Booth. Nevertheless it seems as if Fred Howard, Clement Flower and Lawson Wood were the only original home-based contributors. The later issues carried a claim by a newsagent, Mr G. Vicary, that of all the Boer War periodicals displayed in his shop the Princess of Wales preferred *War Pictures*, remarking that 'it was very good indeed'. C. Arthur Pearson also published *Pearson's Weekly* and the English editions of three of Julian Ralph's books on the War: *Towards Pretoria*, *At Pretoria* and *War's Brighter Side*.

Under the Union Jack

On 11 November 1899 George Newnes's *Under the Union Jack* appeared. Besides the newspaper *The King*, Newnes produced many other publications with a Boer War theme (some issued in parts) such as *With Roberts to the Transvaal*; *Navy & Army Illustrated*; *The Transvaal War Album*; *Celebrities of the Army* and *A Pictorial*

Disaster at Nooitgedacht: the End of a Brave signaller, a wash drawing by Frederick Waugh depicting this stirring battle in the Magaliesberg mountains in December 1900. The painting was reproduced in *After Pretoria: the Guerilla War* and in several other books on the War.

History of the Transvaal. But *Under the Union Jack* was the only one with original artist-drawn illustrations (together with numerous photographs). Original wash drawings came from Ernest Smythe, John Jellicoe (J.J.) R. Savage, Frank Brindley and John Hassall. Towards the end of the run of *Under the Union Jack* (which ceased publication on 14 July 1900) original drawings were in short supply and previously published pictures by T.S. Crowther and Frank Stewart were used. These works, which first appeared in *The Graphic* and *The Illustrated London News*, were not acknowledged. Many contemporary cartoons were also published and given full acknowledgement. *Khaki in South Africa*, also published by Newnes, was originally scheduled to appear in 12 weekly parts but only six were in fact published. The first issue was published on 9 June 1900 and promised 'an album of pictures and photographs illustrating the chief events of the war under Lord Roberts'. Each issue cost sixpence. Only the covers designed by Alan Wright were original; the other illustrations were borrowed from various British sources.

With the Flag to Pretoria

'On Tuesday March 6', read the advertisement in *The Illustrated Mail* of 24 February 1900, 'There will be published by the Messrs. Harmsworth the first part of their latest publication – a really sumptuous production entitled *With the Flag to Pretoria*. This work will be issued fortnightly in sixpenny parts and those who desire to possess a permanent record of the progress and romance of the Transvaal War will order a copy of the publication at once from their newsagents.' The advertisement continues with a report on the editor Herbert Wrigley Wilson: 'Mr H.W. Wilson is the author of *Ironclads in Action* and joint author of *Nelson & His Times*.' It goes on to say that 'Accompanying the story, reliable yet romantic and realistic – of the war are numerous photographs and sketches of actual scenes and events on the battlefields which have been supplied by Messrs. Harmsworth's correspondents all over South Africa. The pictures have been well selected, they are beautifully printed on the finest art paper . . .'

By 1900 Alfred Harmsworth, later Lord Northcliffe, had worked himself up to a position of importance in the publishing world. He had already acquired *The Evening News* in 1894 and founded *The Daily Express* in 1896. It was an obvious move for his publishing company, Amalgamated Press (founded in 1887), to join its rivals in exploiting the public interest generated by the War, and so *With the Flag to Pretoria* was born on 6 March 1900. In all, four volumes were issued, in 72 separate parts: Volumes 1 and 2 consisted of 15 issues each, Volume 3 consisted of 22 issues and Volume 4 of 20. The second part, published on 21 March 1900, advertised a magnificent binding case at a price of two shillings and sixpence which could be ordered from any bookseller or agent.

The cover illustration for Part 1 was *Sounding the Charge* by Richard Caton Woodville and on 17 April 1900 Part 4 had on its cover a facsimile of a painting by Joseph Finnemore entitled *The March on Bloemfontein March 12 1900*. The delay between the actual event and publication of the illustration was a mere five weeks (although it must be said that this illustration could just as well have been of the march on Khartoum as there was

nothing in it to show that the Highlanders were marching on Bloemfontein). Part 12 (7 June) carried the announcement that 'In order that the publication of this work may be completed with as little delay as possible, the remaining parts will be issued at intervals of ten days instead of a fortnight'. It also urged the reader to 'Insist on having Harmsworth's copyright design as along with it will be presented the title page and contents to the Volume'. A promise to complete the history of the War in two volumes was given. Part 14 announced that a choice of binder colours could be had: 'the design is in gold and black and can be had in either a pretty pale grey green cloth or bright red silk grained cloth'. The preface and contents table of Volume 1 were available free with the copyright cases, read an announcement in Part 15, or if purchased separately they would cost eightpence.

Part 20 was issued on 30 October 1900 and dealt with 'the thrilling story of the relief of Ladysmith'. The delay between event and publication was now eight months and this issue carried no announcement of when the next part would be ready. Instead readers were promised that an excellent map of the Orange River and Transvaal colonies would be given with Part 30. Part 27 directed subscribers to the back cover where there was an announcement of the forthcoming publication of *After Pretoria: the Guerilla War*. 'It was hoped,' continued the advertisement, 'that this volume, which was to be issued fortnightly at 6d per part, would be a small one.' This hope was in vain, however. Part 30 (the last of the originally advertised parts) announced that 1 March 1902 would be the publication date of Part 31 (and the start of *After Pretoria: the Guerilla War*).

The 42 parts of the next two volumes continued as promised and sold at the same price of sixpence; even the binders which were to be uniform with Volumes 1 and 2 were still at the old price of two shillings and sixpence. It is impossible to be sure when the final part actually came out. It is assumed that it appeared 84 weeks after 1 March 1902, about 10 October 1903. Further information is unavailable as the records of Amalgamated Press for this period, along with those of *The Illustrated London News*, *The Graphic* and *The Sphere*, were destroyed in 1941 during the Blitz.

From Part 65 onwards the editors were apparently short of photographs and an appeal was made to 'Subscribers and others having photographs relating to events in South Africa since December 1901' to send them *immediately* (their italics) to the editor at Carmelite House E.C., adding that 'All photographs accepted are liberally paid for'. Whereas most of the covers in the first two volumes featured portraits of generals from both sides, the later illustrations depicted facsimiles of stirring scenes, mostly British victories or pseudovictories. For these covers the works of Inglis Sheldon-Williams and Fred Waugh were used frequently, together with those of Richard Caton Woodville, Hermanus Willem Koekkoek and J.H. Thornely.

The reproduction of the facsimiles was by a photomechanical or photoelectric process and the firm employed was acknowledged by means of an imprint on the actual facsimile (for example, Wm Ward & Co., Half Tone Co.). It is interesting to note that different printing firms were used for the different parts. H. Virtue & Co. must have started off with the original contract, but by Part 3 Eyre & Spottiswoode had taken over and by

1 The pictorial cover of Cassell's *Illustrated History of the Boer War* by Paul Hardy.
2 The front cover of part 2 of C. Arthur Pearson's *War Pictures* was illustrated by Clarence Lawson Wood. Most of the covers used works by Wood.
3 Frederick Waugh's painting entitled *Gen. Beyers attacks the 'faithful picket' at Zuurfontein near Pretoria on 11 January 1901*. The painting was reproduced in *After Pretoria: the Guerilla War*.
4 The advertising poster for *With the Flag to Pretoria* (part 6, 12 June 1900) showed this stirring illustration by Caton Woodville entitled *First on the top*, which no doubt encouraged readers to rush out and buy their copies.

3

Part 15 six different firms had been used and re-used.

Harmsworth's first two volumes are among the commonest illustrated books to be found on the War, although the second two are not quite as common. The individual parts of all volumes are very much rarer, however, and like *Cassell's Illustrated History of the Boer War* the individual parts often finished in the middle of a sentence, making it very difficult for the reader to follow the story if he had missed a part. Nevertheless they were popular and judging from the large number of bound volumes in existence today, particularly of *With the Flag to Pretoria*, literally thousands must have been printed. Among other interesting bits of Boer War ephemera are the posters advertising the various parts of *With the Flag to Pretoria* and *After Pretoria: the Guerilla War*. These posters reproduced the front covers of the individual parts but because of their large size (75 x 50 cm) and poor quality paper very few have survived.

Only a few artists worked exclusively on the project as there were many others who, although working for other publications, were willing to contribute original illustrations for Harmsworth. These included Richard Caton Woodville, Frederick Waugh, F.W. Burton, W. Dewar, John Bacon, Charles Sheldon, James Greig, Joseph Finnemore, Charles Taffs, John Sanderson Wells, George Soper, J.H. Thornely, Arthur Gough and Lance Thackeray.

Many of the artists involved also worked for the sister monthly *Harmsworth Magazine*, including Edward Read, who became an official war artist in World War I, and Steven Spurrier and Alec Ball, who went on to work for *The Graphic*. Another was Albert Morrow, one of the three highly respected Irish-born artist brothers, who had already built a reputation as a poster artist. The illustrator of numerous novels, American-born Simon Harmon Vedder, was among the original contributors together with Lancelot Speed, who also illustrated William Johnston's *The Kopje Farm*. John Cameron and Inglis Sheldon-Williams also worked for Harmsworth but only on *After Pretoria: the Guerilla War*. Others about whom very little is known included E.M. Rigg, T. Ivester Lloyd and Harry Dixon.

Even with this wealth of talent, Wilson still needed to borrow work from other sources, especially when frontline work was required. Sometimes acknowledgement was given to the artists but more often than not the caption was altered from the original and no credit was given to the original source at all.

As public interest in the War waned so did the circulation of the 'special publication'. Some ceased to appear while the War was still in progress while others lingered on for a few months after the end. A brief revival in the fortunes of the 'special publication' occurred at the start of the Russo-Japanese War in 1904 but it did not make a major comeback until World War I. Unfortunately by this time the camera was tending to oust the work of the home-based and frontline artists. ■

WITH THE FLAG TO PRETORIA

Part 8.

Price 6^d

SOLD HERE.

4

CHAPTER EIGHT

The Illustrated Periodicals of Europe
and the United States

Above: *Le Petit Journal* for 20 January 1901 published this illustration of Boer women and children in one of the concentration camps. The illustration is unsigned.

There were also many European illustrated news magazines, although they did not give as much coverage to events in far-off South Africa as the British ones did. Being generally more sympathetic to the Boer cause, they gave a great deal of prominence in the early part of the War to the Boer victories and capture of prisoners. The British counterattacks and the relief of Kimberley, Ladysmith and Mafeking were not given much coverage but Kruger's arrival in Marseilles in November 1900 and his subsequent tour of Europe and ultimate exile were reported extensively. The postwar visit of the 'Boer heroes' De la Rey, De Wet and Botha was also featured very prominently.

France

LE PETIT JOURNAL

In France *Le Petit Journal* featured a weekly coloured supplement which depicted a Boer War scene on its front or back cover almost every week. These covers were sometimes removed and later mounted and framed. The magazine, which was first published in 1889, used a variety of artists on these supplements. Engravers were also still used, and often the name of the engraver was featured alongside that of the artist. The Jameson Raid had been featured in the 19 January 1896 issue with an illustration by H. Meyer showing Jameson's capture (the engraver was P. Michel).

The issue published on 8 October 1899, three days before the ultimatum expired, contained an illustration by Uruguayan-born Eugène Damblans depicting a meeting in London in favour of peace. Damblans also worked for *Le Journal Illustré*, which was advertised in *Le Petit Journal*. It is likely that both were owned by the same proprietor. Another artist who shared his services was Henri Rudaux, who also worked for *Armée et Marine*. His work appeared regularly on the front cover of *Le Petit Journal* at the start of the War. For the first two months of the Boer War a relevant illustration appeared almost every week. On 19 November 1899 an unsigned cartoon (which was unusual for *Le Petit Journal*), appeared showing the victory of the Boer bull (Kruger) over the British lion. Another cartoon by Damblans, again featuring Kruger and a British soldier, appeared on 24 December 1899. Before the year was out Italian-born Oswaldo Tofani and Frenchman José Belon had also contributed illustrations to the coloured supplements.

Throughout 1900, 1901 and 1902 *Le Petit Journal* continued to exercise its pro-Boer stance. Among the incidents depicted were the death of Joubert, the Battle of Spioenkop, the surrender of Cronje, and the arrival of Kruger in Marseilles. In 1901 the plight of the concentration camp victims was featured on more than one occasion, as well as the isolated Boer victories. In 1902 Methuen's surrender at Tweebosch and De Wet's exploits were depicted, as well as the execution of Scheepers by a British firing squad (9 February 1902). The

1 2 3

4 5 6

peace proclamation and the visit to Europe by De Wet, De la Rey and Botha were also featured prominently. At this stage the work of an obscure illustrator, Domani, was used.

LE PETIT PARISIEN

Le Petit Parisien was similar to *Le Petit Journal* and had, in fact, appeared a year earlier in 1888. At first no colour was used and again the engraver's signature appeared alongside that of the artist. In many cases the illustrator was Fortuné-Louis Méaulle, although some earlier illustrations had come from Bertrand Dete ('B.D.'), including his portrayal of Jameson's capture in 1896. The coloured supplements from January 1900 onwards were mainly the work of Adolphe-Louis-Charles Crespin, Méaulle and P. Carrey. Towards the end of the War Alfred-Louis Andrieux joined the paper and his work appeared on a few covers. Besides using the work of the artists already mentioned, *Le Petit Parisien* also published contributions from Maurice Mahut and Paul Thiriat, who also worked for *The Sphere*.

L'ILLUSTRATION

L'Illustration was a much more expensive periodical than either *Le Petit Journal* or *Le Petit Parisien*. It was priced at 75 centimes compared to its contemporaries' price of 5 centimes. *L'Illustration* was into its 57th year at the start of the War with Lucien Marc as editor (although he died in 1903). Equal numbers of photographs

and artist-drawn illustrations were use and the skills of the engravers were utilized to a high degree. Many European artists who were contributing to the British illustrated weeklies were employed, including Gennaro Amato, Lionel Sabattier ('L.S.'), Georges Bertin Scott ('G.B.S.'), Frederic de Haenen and François Kupka. Amato was an eyewitness to Kruger's arrival in Marseilles in November 1900 and sent in 'live' illustrations to the home office. Works by H.M. Brock and Douglas Macpherson also appeared, which may indicate that *The Graphic*, *The Daily Graphic* and *L'Illustration* had some sort of working arrangement. However, an illustration showing the celebrations of the relief of Ladysmith, by *The Illustrated London News* artist Samuel Begg, has also been noted.

It is interesting to note that several of the illustrations, both photographic and artist-drawn, which appear in *L'Illustration*, also appeared on contemporary postcards and in many cases no acknowledgement was made either in the periodical or on the card to the artist, engraver or photographer. However, a series of cards published by Adolphe Weick of St Die in northern France entitled 'La Guerre Transvaal' gave credit to 'Gravures du Journal *L'Illustration*'. The exact number of cards in the series is not known but number 1671 has been noted (*Général de Wet*) with the lowest number recorded 738 (*Transport du long Tom*). Most of the illustrations are photographic in origin but the work of Scott, Sabattier, De Haenen, Kupka and Amato has been

1 H. Meyer's illustration on the front cover of *Le Petit Journal* for 10 January 1896 shows the capture of Leander Starr Jameson by the Boers, an incident that brought the Transvaal closer to war.
2 The Uruguayan cartoonist Eugène Damblans had this cartoon *Heads or Tails* published on the front cover of *Le Petit Journal* on 24 December 1899. Cartoons were not normally used on the front covers of this magazine.
3 Oswaldo Tofani's front cover of *Le Petit Journal* for 14 January 1900. Most of the front page illustrations of this French weekly were devoted to the War, especially in the early stages. This cover shows Gen. Joubert.
4 G. Lion produced this representation of Kruger and Chamberlain for *La Caricature*.
5 P.H. Ripp produced this cover showing the Battle of Spioenkop for *L'Impartial D'este's* 18 February 1900 issue.
6 P.H. Ripp's illustration for *La Semaine Illustré's* 1 April edition was entitled *La Liberté au Mort*. It was a common, and erroneous, belief among the European illustrators that the Boer women actively fought alongside their menfolk.

THE DREIBUND AT WORK.

1 François Kupka's depiction of the meeting between Paul Kruger and the young Queen Wilhelmina appeared on a postcard and on the cover of *L'Illustration* of 15 December 1900.
2 Colonel de Villebois-Mareuil's dying moments were depicted in this back page illustration by P.H. Ripp for *La Semaine Illustrée's* 15 April 1900 edition.
3 The cover for *L'Illustre National* on 29 July 1900 by René Le Bègue showing Queen Victoria and Chamberlain painting the map of Africa red with the blood of the Boers.
4 William Allen Rogers doubled both as cartoonist and illustrator for *Harper's Weekly*. This cartoon of a laughing Kruger was featured on the cover on 20 January 1900.
5 Kruger featured on the front cover of *Jugend* magazine on 19 February 1902. The picture was based on a painting by Thérèse Schwartze.

noted even though in many cases their signatures have been cropped on the postcard illustrations. On number 1670 (*Comment on Abreuve les Chevaux*) the unsigned work of Henry Seppings Wright appeared. The same illustration originally appeared with Wright's signature in *The Illustrated London News* on 14 October 1899.

Cartoons were not often featured in *L'Illustration* but a full-page cartoon appeared on 6 January 1900 by Louis Malteste entitled *Opinion de quelques célébrités compétentes sur la Guerre du Transvaal*. Caran d'Ache and Jean Veber were also occasional contributors but very few Boer War cartoons have been noted.

LE MONDE ILLUSTRÉ

Le Monde Illustré, founded in 1857, had both photographic and artist-drawn illustrations. The inside back often featured a series of cartoons entitled 'La Revue Comique' which was drawn by Albert Guillaume and Jehan Testevuide, the pseudonym of Jean Saurel.

On 17 November 1900 the editor, Édouard Desfosses, brought out a special number, 'Hommage au President Kruger'. Several leading artists, writers and composers were invited to contribute and among the illustrators were Étienne Berne-Bellecour, 'Job', Paul E. Mesplès, Jean Béraud, A. Rohida, Théophile Poilpot jnr., Luc-Olivier Merson, Leon Couturier, Oswaldo Tofani, L. Vallet, Jean Paul Louis Tinayre and A.O. Tubrac. Although not all the illustrations had a Boer War theme, most carried a note in the artist's hand expressing sympathy with and support for Kruger and his country's

cause. Among the more famous contributions is the message and signature of composer Camille Saint-Saëns: 'To President Kruger: right, respect and sympathy of the entire world'.

Other illustrators who contributed regularly to *Le Monde Illustré* included A. Dressel, Auguste Gérardin, Ernest-Auguste Bouard, Rud Kauffmann and A. Brun, who acted as 'special' correspondent when Kruger arrived in Marseilles.

ARMÉE ET MARINE

Armée et Marine, founded in 1888, was a weekly publication similar to George Newnes's *Navy & Army Illustrated*. Although mainly illustrated with photographs, cartoons were occasionally taken from contemporary periodicals and fully acknowledged. Illustrations from Henri Rudaux and Georges Pierre Dutriac also featured, together with work from Frank Stewart, Allan Stewart, Georges Montbard, Will Robinson and George Rowlandson from *The Illustrated London News*.

It is interesting to note that many photographers are given full credit in *Armée and Marine*, whereas the same material found in other publications appears anonymously. The magazine is therefore a valuable reference tool for researchers of Boer War photographs.

OTHERS

Au Transvaal, published by Fayard Frères at a price of 30 centimes, was specially devoted to the War and used contemporary British drawings from a broad spectrum for its illustrations. An earlier periodical *La Vie Illustrée*, founded in 1897, was published in Paris by F. Juven and, though mainly photographic, it provided some fine Boer War illustrations and cartoons by Léandre and Steinlen among others. Charles Léandre's cover illustration of Kruger appeared on 16 November 1900 in an issue devoted to Kruger's arrival in Europe. The centre page cartoon was by Théophile Steinlen and depicted Kruger surveying the golden calf. Other illustrators included Georges Redon, who acted as the magazine's 'special' artist when Kruger landed in Marseilles, and Georges Meunier, who provided the coloured front cover for the Christmas 1900 issue.

L'Illustré Soleil du Dimanche, founded and published by Baron v.d. Noirfontaine in 1887, featured the occasional illustration, often by Stanley Wood and borrowed from British sources, and a series of cartoons by Jehan Testevuide which appeared on the back page.

Another little-known series of Sunday newspapers was published by M. Vermont. The papers were identical in content but had different mastheads: *La Semaine Illustrée*, published in Paris, *L'Impartial de L'Est*, and *Le Petit Méridional* published in Montpellier. All had coloured covers and featured the work of P.H. Ripp, Paul Thiriat and M. Denis. Louis Bombled and Alfred Pronier contributed the front and back illustrations while Henri Henriot produced the cartoon series 'La Semaine Amusante' which covered the week's events.

Other French illustrated news periodicals included *L'Illustré Nationale* which featured the work of 'O'Galop', the pseudonym of Marius Rossillon; *Le Petit Brayon Illustré* which used illustrations by Hermann Paul, René Le Bègue and Henri Gerbault; and *Journal des Voyages* which employed the talents of Leclerc (Le Clerc), whose work was later published as a series of postcards.

Germany

LEIPZIGER ILLUSTRIERTE ZEITUNG

The German illustrated news periodical scene was dominated by *Leipziger Illustrierte Zeitung*, founded in 1843. Advertisements for the newspaper had promised at least 32 pages of illustrations per issue with over 1 500 per year at a price of seven marks and 50 pfennig per issue. Richard Knötel ('R.K.') and Otto Gerlach ('O.G.') were the principal illustrators and both were particularly well known in Germany for their portrayal of military subjects, although their work as it appeared in *Leipziger Illustrierte Zeitung* had been through the hands of the engraver.

JUGEND

Jugend, published in Munich from 1896, was primarily a satirical, literary and arts magazine, but portraits of Boer leaders were occasionally featured. Richard Schaupp's painting of De Wet appeared on the front cover on 29 May 1901 and copies in a portfolio were offered for 95 pfennig (see p. 200). Kruger's portrait by Thérèse Schwartze appeared on the cover on 19 February 1902, and specially printed reproductions of this painting were priced at two marks (see p. 238). Ludwig von Zumbusch's portrait of De la Rey was published on 18 March 1902 and again reproductions of the painting were available at a price of one mark. The illustration *Die Schwestern* by Alfred Zimmerman, depicting nurses

UNE PROMENADE.

Grand'maman va-t-en guerre.

as 'Sisters of Mercy' attending to wounded Boers, was published as a double-page spread on 19 June 1901 and copies subsequently went on sale for one mark and 65 pfennig.

It was stated by the publishers in an advertisement on 12 February 1902 that the popularity of the reproductions of Kruger and De Wet was evidence of the widespread sympathy of the German people for the heroic freedom struggle of the Boer people. Original paintings from *Jugend* were always on sale at the editorial offices, and in 1902 a travelling exhibition and sale of these originals was announced. The exhibition and sale started on 30 April 1902 at the galleries of Saxe and Heinzelman in Hanover. In May 1902 it moved to the Salon Neue Kunst in Konigsberg, then to Frankfurt-am-Main in June and finally to Berlin where the publisher Dr Georg Hirth hoped to sell off any remaining stocks. It is not known if any Boer War cartoons or illustrations were among the works on offer. Hirth was one of at least seven German newspaper publishers that offered their papers' offices as receiving depots for the sympathy cards sent to Kruger after his arrival in Europe in November 1900.

Holland

The Dutch illustrated news periodicals were dominated by the satirical journals *De Amsterdammer: weekblad voor Nederland*, *Die Tijd* and *Geillustreerd Polietienieuws*. However publishers Nijgh and Van Ditmar of

1 Several varieties of this card exist, addressed to President Kruger care of various newspaper editors in Germany. This one, addressed to George Hirth, the editor of *Jugend*, is by an unknown illustrator.
2 *Une Promenade: Grand-Maman va-t-en guerre* (A stroll: Grandma goes to war), was one of a series of postcards in Dutch, German and French by the Belgian artist G. Julio. This cartoon originally appeared in *La Reforme*, the Brussels weekly, on 15 October 1899.

Rotterdam produced two publications that featured the War quite prominently, including the weekly *Wêreld-kroniek*, which was first published in 1893. The illustrations were mainly photographic but an occasional artist-drawn work appeared, usually taken from *The Illustrated London News*, *The Daily Graphic* and other European publications. Special 'Extra Transvaal Nummers' were issued, as well as two 'oorlogs-nummers', both entitled 'De Vrijheids-oorlog van die Boeren in Zuid Afrika'. Another publication from Nijgh and Van Ditmar appeared in 1900 to mark Kruger's 75th birthday.

N.J. Boon, the publisher of *Boon's Geïllustreerd Magazijn*, produced nine serially issued publications. The first, which probably appeared just at the start of the War, was entitled *Transvaal Album* and was edited by H.J. Kolstee. This was followed in December 1899 by the first of six issues of *De Oorlog in Zuid Afrika*, edited by G.H. Priem. Finally came *Guerilla Oorlog in Zuid Afrika* and the editor for the two issues was Mrs J. Clant van der Mijll-Piepers who used the pseudonym 'Holda'.

While the subtitle of the publications stated 'geïllustreerd naar fotos', the cover illustrations were engravings taken from the work of unidentified artists and many of these illustrations were later reproduced on postcards. For example, the illustration on the cover of issue number 8 was by Franz Kupka and depicted Kruger being received by the young Queen Wilhelmina. This engraving originally appeared on 15 December 1900 in *L'Illustration* and also appears on a postcard published by Adolphe Weick.

OTHER EUROPEAN PERIODICALS
Other European periodicals featured occasional material on the War, including *Nuevo Mondo* (Spain); *O Seculo* (Portugal); *St Petersburg Gazette* (Russia); *La Illustra-tion* (Italy) and three in Belgium: *Nieuwe Belgische Illustratie*, *Le Illustré National* and *La Reforme*. *Het Huisgezin* borrowed the work of Ernest Bouard, Harold Collison-Morley and Herbert Johnson. *L'Illustratie Européene* depicted contemporary cartoons from other sources in its feature 'La Guerre en Caricature' appearing on the back page.

United States

In the United States illustrated papers were thriving and most prominent were the two New York papers *Harper's Weekly*, founded in 1850, and *Leslie's Weekly*, founded in 1857.

HARPER'S WEEKLY
William Allen Rogers ('W.A.R.') was both illustrator and cartoonist for *Harper's Weekly* and he recounts his experiences in his autobiography *A World Worth While* (1921). A regular contributor to the journal was Edwin Willard Deming, whose work included several Boer War illustrations signed with his elaborate monogram which resembled an electric light bulb.

Other well-known illustrators working for *Harper's Weekly* included Thure de Thulstrup and Max Klepper, both of whom contributed to Capt. Alfred Thayer Mahan's *The South African War*, which was published in 1901. G.W. Peters and R. Martine Reay also provided illustrations while frontline works by Gordon Grant and Lester Ralph were reproduced in facsimile.

A colour illustration by Frederic Remington also appears in Mahan's book. Remington worked for *Harper's Weekly* at the time of the War and some of his illustrations appear on the front covers. He makes the British soldiers look rather like American cowboys and Rough-riders. Remington's Africana work also appears in Poultney Bigelow's prewar publication *White Man's Africa*.

LESLIE'S WEEKLY
Although Gordon Grant's work appeared in several papers on both sides of the Atlantic he was principally employed by *Leslie's Weekly*. At the start of the War the paper carried illustrations by its home-based artists G.W. Peters, E.N. Blue and Edward J. Austen, but from 20 January 1900 wash and pen-and-ink sketches by Grant started to appear from Cape Town. The editor of *Leslie's Weekly* announced that their correspondent Eugene E. Easton and their 'special' artist Gordon H. Grant had arrived in South Africa:

> At last advice Mr Grant was making his way from Cape Town up to Mafeking where he hoped to arrive in good season to witness the great battle certain to take place when an attempt is made to raise the siege on that town. Mr E.E. Easton has arrived in South Africa as special correspondent to *The New York Journal*. He is a personal friend of Presidents Kruger and Steyn and may be depended upon to give the Boer side of the struggle a fair and just representation.

Leslie's Weekly also referred to a previous report it had carried about an interview Easton had had with Milner.

Grant sketched Roberts's arrival in Cape Town and followed his army through De Aar, Modder River, Magersfontein and Paardeberg. In September, however, he was back in New York redrawing sketches from China and the Philippines sent by *Leslie's Weekly*'s artist-correspondent in 'the orient', Sydney Adamson.

A serial publication *Glimpses of South Africa in Peace and War* was published by the Dominion Company in Chicago. It ran to at least nine issues (undated) and used illustrations from both *The Illustrated London News* and *The Graphic*.

In general the illustrated press of Europe and the United States depicted scenes of the Boer War that bore no resemblance to reality. Few of the papers had artist-correspondents in South Africa and their illustrations were mostly the product of fertile imaginations. Nevertheless these colourful portrayals had an important socio-historical function as they helped to gain the reader's sympathy for the Boer cause.

CHAPTER NINE

Charity and Souvenir Publications

For the duration of the War and even after it, several European organizations set about raising funds for the destitute women and children in South Africa or the dependants of the British troops fighting in the War. With regard to the Boer aid, the roving ambassador Dr W.J. Leyds was very active in encouraging the activities of the pro-Boer committees who felt that a picture was worth a thousand words. Several special editions of booklets, pamphlets and postcards were issued both to raise funds for the cause and to draw attention to the suffering of the Boer women and children. Several well-known pro-Boer writers and poets contributed to these publications.

France

Paris-Pretoria appeared in December 1901 and was intended for sale in 'all newsagents and main book shops in France and abroad'. The proceeds of the sale were to be given to the 'wounded Boers in the Transvaal war'. No price appears on the cover but it is stated that 100 046 copies were printed: '100 000 on de luxe paper, 5 on Japan paper, 10 on Whatman, 25 on China and 6 on Dutch paper'. The French committee responsible for the publication was chaired by Maxime Ridouard, a member of the French Chamber of Deputies. A. Girard acted as editor-in-chief and public relations executive and Eduard Saudry as secretary. Facsimiles of letters to Kruger and a reply from him are included among the messages of support from the 148 members of the French Chamber of Deputies. Music, poems and prose essays make up the text. The publication was illustrated by prominent artists, but few of the pictures were titled and only a handful, although obviously inspired by the War, showed scenes or events relative to it. The 21 artists who contributed were: Louise Abbéma (*Pour les Boers*), Léon Bellemont, Bernard Borione, Pierre Brouillet, Jean Brunet, (*Tu vivras*), H. de Capol, Mario Carl-Rosa (*Vue de Domrémy*), Alfred Charron, Clementél, Albert Cresswell, Louise Desbordes, Henriette Desauty, Paul de Frick (*Fructus belli*), Alexandre Guignard, Iantitzmahias (*Dans les Camps de reconcentration*), Charles Jouas (*Les Anglais Ont Brûlé les Fermes*), Désiré-Alfred Magne (*Pour vivre il Leur Faut L'Indépendance*), Henri Tattegrain, Daniel Vierge, Marie Zwiller and Maxime Ridouard.

Germany

Der Burenkrieg, which appeared in 1900, was the work of Albert Langen, the publisher of *Simplicissimus* and was dedicated to Dr W.J. Leyds. Ludwig Thoma was the editor and he received considerable support from the many writers and artists who are acknowledged in the foreword. One of the artists who collaborated was Bruno Paul, who did the coloured cover illustration. Paul also drew other cartoons showing the departure of Boer soldiers to the front, the return of the City Imperial

Frank Dadd's illustration, subtitled: 'He's an absent minded beggar but he heard his country call', from the Royal Edition of Rudyard Kipling's famous Boer War poem 'The Absent Minded Beggar'.

1

2

3

1 Jean Brunet's illustration *Tu Vivras* appeared on the cover of *Paris-Pretoria* for December 1901.
2 Theodore Heine's work *Hero Worship* featured in *Der Burenkrieg*. It shows 'English princesses decorating the youngest soldier in the British Army for having already, at the age of thirteen years, raped eight Boer women'. Queen Victoria and the Prince of Wales look on approvingly.
3 A Belgian pro-Boer postcard produced by the Algemeen Nederlandsche Verbond.

Volunteers and one entitled *Buller's triumph*. Other artists included Eduard Thöny, Wilhelm Leibl, Ludwig Steub, Wilhelm Schulz, Rudolf Wilke, Franz von Defregger, Max Liebermann, Hermann Schlittgen, Max Slevogt and F.F. Reznicek. Thomas Theodor Heine produced a coloured comic strip in four frames showing a 'trial of strength' with Queen Victoria being flattened by Oom Paul and Chamberlain looking on. Heine was also responsible for the controversial cartoon *Heldenverehrung*.

Sidney Mendelssohn's anglophile views were most offended by some of the cartoons in the publication. He commented in *Mendelssohn's South African Bibliography* (Volume 2:49):

> The most abominable caricature in this publication is one on page 24 by Th. Heine entitled *Helden-verehrung* (Hero-worship). It depicts English princesses decorating the youngest soldier in the British Army with the Victoria Cross for having already, at the age of thirteen years, violated eight Boer women. Queen Victoria and the Prince of Wales (Edward VII) stand approving in the background. Another cartoon represents the Prince of Wales in a state of intoxication whilst receiving Joseph Chamberlain, who reports the news of Cronje's surrender. This work, which has every appearance of having been issued by responsible publishers, is characteristic of a class of literature and art which was evidently popular in Germany during the South African War.

Der Burenfreund was not exactly a souvenir publication. It was published in 12 unnumbered parts during 1901 by the 'Burenhilfs' (Boer Assistance) committee and a monthly statement of funds raised was published. Most of the illustrations were photographs showing Boer leaders, families and prisoners of war, but occasional illustrations by Johann Schönberg and Heinrich

Egersdörfer also appeared. A portrait of Kruger by Johan Braakensiek is also featured, and there are cartoons by T.S. Baynes, Constance Penstone and Carruthers Gould. The well-known postcard by Franz von Defregger is advertised on page 229. It depicts Boer women and children being expelled from their burning homes by British soldiers while a black man is driving them away with a sjambok. The postcard was issued by the 'German central committee for ending the Boer War' and the card was available from the editors of *Der Burenfreund* at a price of 10 pfennig.

The publication of many souvenir publications by pro-Boer committees went hand-in-hand with the issuing of postcards. The 'sympathy to Kruger' cards are discussed in Chapter 12. It is not known if these were simply propaganda cards or whether they also had a fundraising function. They carried no imprint indicating this, whereas many others did.

Holland and Belgium

Nederland-Transvaal: Gedenkboek Opgedragen aan het volk van Transvaal en Oranje Vrijstaat was published by F.B. van Ditmar of Rotterdam and the foreword is dated December 1899. The publication was dedicated to the Transvaal and Free State people as a token of 'sympathy and admiration'. Several writers, composers, illustrators and soldiers from Holland, Germany and Belgium collaborated on the text, which is in script facsimile and contains numerous sketches. No artist is given credit, although the cover illustration showing a nurse attending to a wounded Boer is signed 'Fritz W.S.'

Between March and April of 1902 the Netherlands Boekhandel of Antwerp published the book *Antwerpen-Transvaal Gedenknummer*, which was published to

1

2

3

coincide with an exhibition of pictorial art held in the city. The artists who illustrated the book probably also exhibited at the art exhibition and included Karel Boom, J. Devriendt, Joseph Dierckx, Edgard Farasyn, Frans Hens, Joseph Janssens, Romain Looymans, J. Mees, Charles Mertens, R. Sleppe, Leo van Aken, Pierre van der Ouderaa, Frans van Kuyck, Frans van Leemputten, Alfred van Neste and Piet Verhaert. Jan Frans Deckers the sculptor and Jules Baetes the engraver completed the team. The proceeds of the sale of the publication were to 'alleviate the suffering of the unfortunate victims of the war and to help to make the lives of the thousands of women and children in the concentration camps more bearable'.

The book has the usual blend of poetic, literary, musical and artistic contributions, all of which are acknowledged and facsimile letters from Kruger, Leyds and Fischer are included. Only two cartoons – both anti-Chamberlain – by Piet van der Ouderaa have a direct Boer War theme.

Russia

In 1900 *St Petersburg-Transvaal* was published in Russian by the 'Dutch Committee to render assistance to the wounded Boers'. The appeal was organized by the Revd. Hendrik Gillot who was also editor.

Over 40 sketches and illustrations appear in the book, and photographs of the Russian-Dutch Ambulance and members of the Dutch assistance committee for the wounded Boers are also included. Of the illustrations only four may be described as having been directly inspired by the War, *Dawn of Peace* by S.V. Zivotoyskaye, *David and Goliath* by Illia E. Repina and two cartoons by Paul Robert. These cartoons have Eng-

lish captions, so Robert's work may well have appeared elsewhere first. A signed photograph of Robert also appears.

In his foreword, dated 18 November 1899, Gillot pays tribute to the donors of the 70 000 roubles already collected and singles out the newspapers *Novom Vremeni, St Petersburg Zeitung, Duna Zeitung* (in Riga), *St Petersburg Herald, Moskovskix Vedomstja* and *Southern Krae* for special mention. He goes on to say that with the proceeds of these funds a Russian-Dutch field hospital with 40 beds, six or eight doctors, and ten nurses was to be set up and if funds permitted, hospital assistants, pharmacists and servants would be employed. He reminded readers to send their donations to him at 20 Nevsky Prospect, St Petersburg. When the escaped Boer P.O.W.s Willie Steyn, George and Louw Steytler, Piet Botha and George Hausner were brought to Russia on the troopship *Cherson* after their escape from Ceylon, they were each presented with a copy of the book at a dinner in their honour in St Petersburg.

Britain

At various times during the War illustrated brochures and booklets were produced to raise money for dependants of the British troops who had been killed or wounded.

One of the earliest of these publications was the souvenir programme of the 'Grand Military and Patriotic Concert' produced by the Dangerfield Publishing Co. The concert, which took place on 5 December 1899, was organized by Ellaline Terriss and Charles Peter Little 'In Aid of the sick and wounded, the Widows and Orphans and the Families of our Troops now serving in South Africa'. The illustrations were mainly photo-

1 *Antwerpen-Transvaal Gedenknummer* number was published to coincide with an exhibition of pictorial art in Amsterdam in March and April 1902. The proceeds of the sale of the book were donated to relieving the suffering of concentration camp victims. Alfred van Neste did the cover illustration.
2 Franz von Defregger produced this anti-British postcard which was sold in aid of the Boer women and children. It was also published in the German publication *Der Burenfreund*.
3 *St Petersburg-Transvaal* was published by the 'Dutch Committee to render assistance to the wounded Boers' in 1900. The appeal was organized and the editorials written by the Revd. Hendrik Gillot, who was the pastor to the Dutch community in Russia.

The programme for the 'National Bazaar in aid of the Sufferers by the War in South Africa', which took place on 24 to 26 May 1900. The cover is by John Hassall.

graphic but some sketches were provided, including Louis Edward's *The Queen! God Bless her!!*, John Charlton's *A friend in need is a friend indeed* and an untitled pencil drawing of a drummer on horseback by Henry Harris Browne.

The Dangerfield Co. also produced the souvenir booklet for the 'Royal Naval and Military Bazaar' which was again organized by Charles Peter Little in 'aid of H.R.H. Princess Christian's homes for disabled soldiers and sailors' and held on 19, 20 and 21 June 1900. The booklet contained literary contributions from Harold Begbie, Walter Besart, Guy Boothby, Sir Francis Cowley Burnand and John Strange Winter and the 32 illustrations were provided by John Charlton. The majority of the illustrations are dated 1900 but a few, depicting Indian troops, were done at the time of Queen Victoria's Jubilee in 1897.

On 24, 25 and 26 May 1900 the 'National Bazaar in Aid of the Sufferers by the War' was held under royal patronage. The souvenir programme, published by Gale & Polden and Messrs. Langfier, ran to 158 pages and sold for two shillings and sixpence. A limited number of Morocco-bound copies were available. The designers and compilers were Louis Langfier, E. Russel Polden and Arthur J. Coke and illustrations were provided by Cecil Aldin, Max Cowper, A.J. Gough, Walter Crane and Louis Langfier, with John Hassall's work appearing on the front cover. The booklet fulsomely acknowledges the 'Ladies and Gentlemen who have kindly given pictures to be sold for the good of the fund'. Among the artists listed are A.S. Boyd, Walter Crane, C. Davidson, Louis Davis, P. Dixon, Emile Fuchs, Archibald Hartrick, Gilbert Walen, E.R. Hughes, Harrington Mann, Bernard Partridge, Laurence Phillips and Wilfred Probyn. It is interesting to note that the proprietors of *The Strand Magazine* and *The Graphic, The Illustrated London News, The Sketch* and *The King* also donated paintings. Unfortunately it is not known how many of the paintings donated had a Boer War theme.

Early in 1900 *Lest We Forget Them* was published by the Fine Art Society and Simpkin, Marshall, Hamilton, Kent and Company, and the profits from the sale were to 'be devoted to the Fund for the Relief of Widows and Orphans of our Sailors and Soldiers'. Lady Glover compiled the work, Leighton Waud did the design, and Matthew Hewerdine supplied most of the illustrations with Nora Davidson providing the illustrations of ships. Lady Glover, in her preface, gives credit to the editor of *The Sphere* for providing the blocks for the 20 portraits of 'distinguished soldiers and one sailor'. The foreword took the form of an encouraging letter to Lady Glover, dated 17 March 1900, from Lady White, the wife of Sir George White, the commander of Ladysmith during the siege.

Besides the income from the various souvenir booklets, the greatest source of revenue came from *The Daily Mail*'s fund for the benefit of wives and children of the reservists fighting in South Africa. Rudyard Kipling's poem 'The Absent Minded Beggar', and/or *A Gentleman in Kharki*, Richard Caton Woodville's painting based on the poem, appeared as a motif on all souvenir items sold in aid of the fund and performers such as Lillie Langtry, a former mistress of King Edward VII, paid the fund £100 for the privilege of reciting the poem to an audience. It is estimated that over £350 000 was raised from the copyright of *A Gentleman in Kharki*.

In 1899 the Printing Arts Co. Ltd of London produced a 'Royal Edition' booklet of 'The Absent Minded Beggar', illustrated by Gordon Browne, William Hatherell, Frank Dadd, Stanley Wood and Frank Craig. All these artists donated their services to the charity. A percentage of the proceeds of the sale of the booklet went to the *Daily Mail* fund. Reproductions of either the poem or the painting were found on all sorts of collectable items, including statuettes in silver, bronze and pewter, handkerchiefs, brass and copper plaques, porcelain plates, mugs, letter openers, tape measures, matchboxes and cardholders as well as postcards and sheet music.

Money was also raised by the rather novel method of using artists as music hall acts. George Rossi Ashton (see p. 103) packed the audiences in with his rapid sketches done in time to music. Attired in British tropical uniform, he had the crowds alternately cheering (when he drew Roberts, Buller or the Revenge of Majuba), or jeering when he depicted the 'villain' Kruger.

The European pro-Boer fundraising efforts were not so successful and even though several ambulances were financed by various committees in different countries most of these ambulance units were disbanded and sent home after the fall of Pretoria on 5 June 1900. Even after the War, when De Wet, De la Rey and Louis Botha visited Europe to raise money for the rehabilitation of the ravaged country, the results were disappointing.

On both sides, though, artists were very generous in donating their services to what they felt were worthy causes.

PART THREE

THE SATIRISTS

CHAPTER TEN

Cartoonists and Caricaturists: Britain and Empire

Previous page: Chamberlain pictured as a hung game bird by Guillaume Laplagne in one of his *Monuments Anthumes* series. This gruesome cartoon appeared in *Le Rire* on 14 May 1902. It was later reproduced on a postcard.
Above: *Chamberlain and Kruger's Ultimatum*, an original watercolour by an unknown artist, was probably based on the 'Monkey Brand' soap advertisement which was titled 'Need a little polish, Sir'.

The cartoonist played a very important role in the social life of the nineteenth century and comic and satirical art was well developed in both Europe and the United States. At the time of the Boer War virtually every British illustrated paper had a resident cartoonist and South Africa, Australia, New Zealand, Canada and India also had their share of satirical papers and 'knights of the pencil'.

The satirical papers in general flourished and far more of them existed than are published today. The British and Empire publications, while often attacking the establishment, were careful not to show any pro-Boer feelings. The Continental satirical papers, however, were very outspoken; their pro-Boer or anti-British feelings were greatly in evidence and very little attention was paid to any possible libel action by the victims of the cartoonist's pen. The United States, mindful of its own conflict with Spain in Cuba and the Philippines, and its close ties with Britain, tended to adopt a far more neutral position in its publications.

Many illustrated publications which were not devoted exclusively to satire still published cartoons taken from publications from around the world. *The King* (which also had its own cartoonist, Harry Furniss,) *Under The Union Jack* and *Review of Reviews* were among the British publications to do this regularly.

Britain

PUNCH

Most prominent of the British satirical weeklies was *Punch*, which first appeared on 17 July 1841. The first circulation figure was given as 6 000 and the price was threepence per issue, remaining so until 1917. The founding editor Mark Lemon is reputed to have coined the name when he suggested that the new paper should be a good mixture but 'like punch, it would be nothing without Lemon'.

One of the original principles of the paper was that it should exhibit religious and political tolerance. A weekly meeting of senior staff was held at a dinner where after fierce argument the cartoon or cartoons for the ensuing week were decided. It was *Punch* in 1843 that first used the word cartoon in its present meaning and its main cartoon was referred to as 'The Big Cut'. Originally calling these humorous drawings 'pencillings', *Punch* lampooned a competition for the decoration of the new Houses of Parliament and called the drawings 'cartoons', which was the technical name for mural designs. The name stuck and has been used ever since to describe any pictorial humour or satire on political subjects.

At the start of the Boer War John Tenniel was still the principal cartoonist for *Punch*. He had joined the staff in

1851 on the resignation of Richard Doyle. In 1864 he was promoted to the position he was to hold for the next 36 years and during this time he produced over 2 000 cartoons. Tenniel, who illustrated the first edition of Lewis Carroll's *Alice in Wonderland*, used a distinctive monogram, although at least six different variations are recorded. On his retirement at the beginning of 1901 at the age of 80, he was succeeded by Linley Sambourne who had been a member of the *Punch* team since 1867, providing the second weekly political cartoon. The main cartoon was always a full-page drawing, usually engraved by Swain, with no text on the reverse. Other cartoons and caricatures appeared both as full-page spreads (large engraving) or in the text (small engraving). Many regular features used the Boer War as a theme including: 'Prehistoric Peeps' by Edward Tennyson Reed ('E.T.R.'); 'Punch Museum' by George Halkett ('G.R.H.') and 'The Seats of the Mighty'.

Phil May, George Armour ('G.D.A.'), Leonard Raven-Hill ('L.R.H.'), A. Wallis Mills, Bernard Partridge ('B.P.') and A. C. Corbould were regular contributors, but only in a few instances was their work related to the Boer War. Armour was the *Punch* equestrian specialist and almost all his cartoons featured horses or sporting scenes in one form or another. Partridge became the second-string cartoonist on Tenniel's retirement but occasionally provided the main cartoon. Despite the fact that their work for *Punch* was prolific, the following well-known cartoonists did not feature the Boer War at all in their cartoons: Lewis Baumer, C. Harrison, J. H. Jalland, Tom Wilkinson, Sydney Harvey, Arthur Hopkins (Everard's brother), A. Hodgson, Gordon Browne, Starr Wood, Alexander Stuart Boyd, Charles Pott, Dudley Hardy, Charles Pears, Ralph Cleaver, Tom Browne and George Loraine Stampa. However Boer War cartoons by most of them are noted in other publications. David Wilson made his debut for *Punch* with a Boer War cartoon on 6 June 1900.

Unlike the other major publishers *Punch* did not have regular sales of original drawings, but the magazine did help its artists to sell their works when necessary.

Many *Punch* cartoonists were regarded as celebrities in their day and *The Strand Magazine*, among others, published features on them and their Continental and Australian counterparts. One article in *The Strand Magazine* in January 1902 by Frederick Dolman was entitled 'Our Graphic Humorists: Their funniest pictures as chosen by themselves'. In the article Dolman interviewed some of the best-known cartoonists and most of them worked for *Punch*: Sir John Tenniel, A. S. Boyd, Harry Furniss, Edward Reed, Bernard Partridge, Linley Sambourne, Dudley Hardy, Tom Browne, J. A. Sheppard, Phil May, J. T. Sullivan and Leonard Raven-Hill. Francis Carruthers Gould, the well-known cartoonist and editor of *The Westminster Gazette*, was also interviewed for the article.

THE WESTMINSTER GAZETTE

Francis Carruthers Gould ('F.C.G.') was actually a member of the London Stock Exchange, yet, from 1879 when his first cartoon appeared in *Truth*, he supplied cartoons to many publications. He is best known, however, for his work in *The Westminster Gazette*, the penny London evening newspaper which was first published on 31 January 1893 and claimed to have a reputation for 'fairness and impartiality'. The paper also had the exclu-

sive right to the publication of Gould's cartoons, which were sometimes more than a little controversial as he was one of the few British cartoonists to exhibit some anti-War feelings. While not exactly pro-Boer, his cartoons certainly attacked the establishment and Chamberlain in particular. Some of these anti-War cartoons were used in the pamphlets issued by the 'Stop the War Committee' under the chairmanship of William Thomas Stead. In 1895 the first volume of *Westminster Cartoons* appeared and five further volumes appeared over the next few years. Limited, signed editions of individual volumes were also available. Cartoons of Kruger and 'The Transvaal Crisis' appeared in most of the early volumes but Volume IV was devoted to 'A pictorial history of the political events connected with South Africa 1899-1900'. The preface to the volume states that the cartoons 'have been selected from *The Westminster Gazette*, *The Westminster Budget* and *Picture Politics* and they deal with the different events of the day bearing upon the difficulty between this country and the South African Republics'. Volume V, also published in 1900, is devoted to the 'Khaki Campaign' general election, which was directly influenced by the War.

Gould's other publications which had some relevance to the War included *Peeps at Parliament* by H. W. Lucy, based on the regular feature in *The Strand Magazine*. *Froissart's Modern Chronicles*, both written and illustrated by Gould, was published in 1903 and lampooned both the British and Boer leaders.

A postwar series of at least 18 political postcards entitled 'Westminster Cartoon Series' was issued in 1903. The cards which were priced at 'sixpence a packet of six, or sevenpence post free' continued the attack on Chamberlain's South African policies. (See also pp. 138-139.)

JUDY

While *Punch* was undoubtedly the most influential of the British satirical papers it was by no means the only one of its kind. *Judy*, subtitled 'The London Serio-comic Journal', had been established in 1867 and was at one time owned by the Dalziel brothers. It fell into decline after they sold it, however. At the time of the Boer War Harry Parkes was the principal cartoonist, later sharing the role with C. R. Fleming Williams, who incorporated a symbol of a palette into his elaborate signature. Contributors of cartoons with Boer War themes were Thorpe Dickson, Armand Biquard, H. L. Shindler, F. Lynch, Thomas Downey ('Thomas D.'), George James, George Whitelaw, Starr Wood, Frank Styche and H. Innes ('H.I.'), T. E. Donnison ('T.E.D.'), Popini, A. Wallis Mills, Reuben Cohen, Percy Fearon ('Poy'), Hugh Grant and John Riley Wilmer.

MOONSHINE

Moonshine, founded in 1879, had Alfred Bryan ('A.B.') as its principal cartoonist, and although he died in May 1899 some of his later cartoons depicted the 'Transvaal Crisis'. John Proctor, whose work was often unsigned, succeeded him and contributed many full-page Boer War cartoons up to 30 March 1901 when Sydney Harvey took over. Other contributors were Mosnar Yendis (the backwards pseudonym of Sidney Ransom) who also produced regular coloured lithographic caricatures of politicians, and Horace Morehen ('H.M.') who both contributed regularly with John Hassall, Archibald Forrest, John Browne and A.K. McDonald appearing less often.

1

3

In the early part of 1902 *Moonshine* ran a series of caricatures of their cartoonists and those working for other papers, including John Hassall, Edward Reed, Dudley Hardy, Phil May and Linley Sambourne.

PICK-ME-UP

Pick-Me-Up was another lighthearted weekly which first appeared on 6 October 1888, describing itself as 'A Literary and artistic force for the mind'. Leonard Raven-Hill was both a regular contributor and art editor and, according to James Thorpe in *English Illustration: The Nineties*, it was Hill who was responsible for 'carrying the paper to success'. Regular advertisements offered reproductions of its artists' work on plate paper at sixpence and Oscar Wilson, Sydney Sime and Montague Barstow are mentioned by name. Besides these prints, original drawings 'by *Pick-Me-Up*'s best artists' were also on sale: 'a splendid opportunity for collectors of black and white work'. In addition *Pick-Me-Up* ran a regular competition for aspiring young black and white artists.

The artistic team included Leslie Willson, who did the banner on the front page, Montague Barstow, Popini, Henry (Hy) Mayer, Bernard Partridge, Charles Pears, Hilda Cowham, Phil May and J. Bois. Some illustrators also produced cartoons for *Pick-Me-Up* including Malcolm Patterson, Ivester Lloyd, Ernest Shérie, Harold Collison-Morley and Oscar Eckhardt. Sydney Hebblethwaite had a regular feature 'Scenes in Mars' and F. Lynch produced a weekly caricature entitled 'Prominent Persons', featuring Kruger, Steyn and Chamberlain among others. Continental cartoonists such as Schlittgen, Caran d'Ache, Gerbault, Guillaume, Steinlen, Willette and Fernand Fau were also regular contributors but no Boer War work by these cartoonists seems to have appeared in *Pick-Me-Up*.

ALLY SLOPER'S HALF HOLIDAY

The Dalziel brothers founded another magazine in 1884 to which they gave the unlikely name of *Ally Sloper's Half Holiday*. The publication survived until 1923. The

editor once claimed that theirs had the largest circulation of any penny comic paper. The hero, Ally Sloper, was invented by the *Judy* writer Charles H. Ross and in the true tradition of the comic-strip character Sloper had a pot belly, an enormous round nose, very thin legs and large feet. Various members of his family and entourage were depicted. William F. Thomas was drawing Ally at the time of the War, having taken over from Giles Baxter as the magazine's chief cartoonist in 1890. The main cartoon, which often related to the War, appeared on the front page. Other cartoonists who contributed unsigned works to the paper were Maurice Greiffenhagen and T.R.J. Brown.

Readers were asked to write in requesting the original cartoons and the first entry opened on the following Wednesday morning (*Ally Sloper* appeared on Saturday) was declared the winner and received the cartoon of his choice. By 18 November 1899, 64 of these original drawings had been given away.

VANITY FAIR

No mention of the British cartoons and caricatures of the War can possibly be complete without reference to *Vanity Fair*, which in its day reflected the spirit of the era more accurately than any other publication. Thomas Gibson Bowles was the founder and first editor of *Vanity Fair*. Roy Matthews and Peter Mellini in their book *In Vanity Fair*, say that the magazine was: 'for those "in the know" . . . For them, *Vanity Fair* summarized each week the important events of their world. It reviewed the newest opening in the West End and the latest novel in the club's library; it aroused their curiosity and envy; it angered and amused them.' The first issue appeared on 1 January 1869 at a price of sixpence and featured a caricature of Disraeli. The chromolithographic caricatures have long remained *Vanity Fair*'s chief legacy but in its heyday the magazine was highly regarded for its features, prose, advertising and format. Many of the victims objected to being caricatured by *Vanity Fair* but Anthony Trollope is reputed to have said that 'to have

MORE MUNIFICENCE.

NEW YEAR'S DAY WITH THE BOERS.

1 Eminent punch cartoonist Sir John Tenniel drew this pencil cartoon of Paul Kruger 'shifting his capital' (a play on words). The theme was used by many cartoonists. This was one of the last cartoons that Tenniel produced for *Punch* before his retirement in 1900.
2 Francis Carruthers Gould's disturbing cartoon entitled *The Scout on the Veldt* first appeared in *Westminster Gazette* on 4 October 1899. It was later used on W. T. Stead's 'Stop the War' committee's pamphlet no. 43.
3 Mosnar Yendis (nom de plume of Sidney Ransom) produced a weekly lithograph for *Moonshine*. This one of Joseph Chamberlain was published on 7 December 1901.
4 and 5 *Ally Sloper's Half Holiday*, the humorous comic, used the Boer War as its theme in the issue for 16 December 1899. William Thomas drew Ally Sloper as a chef (4), while on 30 December he masqueraded as Paul Kruger (5).
6 This cartoon by 'Spy', the famous *Vanity Fair* cartoonist, featured Field Marshal Roberts and was published on 21 June 1900. Note the carving of Kruger in the rock in the background.

one's caricature in *Vanity Fair* was a public honour no eminent man could well refuse'. Bowles drew a sharp distinction between caricature (from the Italian *cari-cari*, meaning 'to exaggerate') and cartoon: 'Caricature was not to invent something new but to exaggerate what was already in existence.' Bowles sold the paper in 1889 to Arthur Evans for £20 000 and though the new owners tried at first to continue Bowles's independent biting satire they eventually became conformist and less anti-establishment.

Several artists contributed to *Vanity Fair* and some, such as Carlo Pellegrini ('Ape'), who died in 1889, and Leslie Ward ('Spy' and 'Drawl'), were prolific. It is said that Ward used the pseudonym 'Drawl' when he had not met the sitter. Arthur George Witherby, who was the editor at the time of the War, was also an artist and used the pseudonym 'W.A.G.'. Other caricaturists were obscure individuals and exhaustive research by Matthews and Mellini has failed to reveal the identity of many of them.

The Boer War provided plenty of new material for the caricaturists and the Boer generals and leaders were well represented. (The titles of drawings are given in brackets.) Kruger (*Oom Paul*) appeared on 8 March 1900 done by 'Drawl'. Steyn (*Ex-President Steyn*) was featured on 9 August 1900 ('W.A.G.') and De Wet (*De Wet*) on 31 July 1902 (Eardley Norton 'E.B.N.'). It is interesting that Louis Botha did not appear until 1907. The British and Colonial generals and politicians were obviously in much greater evidence and many had already appeared prior to the War. The military leaders featured during the War included Lord Strathcona (*Canada in London*) 19 April 1900 'Spy'; Sir George White (*Lady-smith*) 14 June 1900 'Spy'; Field Marshall Lord Roberts (*Bobs*) 21 June 1900 'Spy'; Captain the Honourable Hed-worth Lambton RN (*H.M.S. Powerful*) 28 June 1900 'Spy'; Gen. Robert Stephenson Smyth Baden-Powell (*Mafeking*) 5 July 1900 'Drawl'; Gen. John Denton Pink-stone French (*The Cavalry division*) 12 July 1900 by Godfrey Douglas Giles.

A double-page spread entitled *A General Group* by 'Spy' appeared on 29 November 1900 featuring Hunter, Plumer, McDonald, Buller, Baden-Powell, Roberts, Dundonald, Kitchener, Pole-Carew, Carrington, French and White. Another double page of Africana interest appeared on 25 November 1897 entitled *Of Empire Makers and Breakers* and featured Rhodes and Chamberlain, among others. The caricatures were done by 'Stuff', believed to be the pseudonym of Henry Seppings Wright.

Other military leaders drawn by 'Spy' were Gen. William Henry MacKinnon (*C.I.V.*) on 7 February 1901; Gen. Kelly-Kenny C.B. (*6th Division*) on 29 August 1901; General the Hon. Gerald Neville Lyttelton (*4th division*) on 5 September 1901; Gen. Smith-Dorrien D.S.O. (*Doreen*) on 5 December 1901; Maj. Gen. Sir Henry Trotter K.C.V.O. (*Home District*) on 9 January 1902; Gen. Plumer (*Self-reliant*) on 13 November 1902 and Gen. Forestier-Walker (*Shookey*) on 25 December 1902. Kitchener, Rhodes and Jameson had also been featured, but prior to the War. British politicians drawn by 'Spy' included Lord Salisbury on 20 December 1900; Joseph Chamberlain on 7 March 1901; Lord Rosebery 14 March 1901 and the Secretary of State for War on 18 July 1901.

Vanity Fair prints were originally issued weekly and reprints were often required. Proofs of the caricatures are still in existence but unfortunately have no captions or dates. Originally they were bound in elaborate numbered albums in green leather with gilt tooling and offered for sale or given away as prizes in the magazine's many competitions. Annual albums were compiled and sold, together with sets of caricatures such as 'Officers who had served in the Boer War'.

Original watercolours and preliminary sketches are also in existence but are rare. In 1912 many were sold at auction by Christie's and Sotheby's and still more by Puttick and Simpson in 1916. The National Portrait Gallery in London has over 300 in its collection, including originals of Gen. Kenny-Kelly and Lord Roberts. Postcard publishers often featured *Vanity Fair* caricatures

and George Stewart published 48 different cards featuring Buller, White, Chesham, French, Baden-Powell, Kitchener, Jameson, Kruger, Roberts and Chamberlain.

THE IDLER

The Idler was founded as a literary magazine in 1892 by two well-known novelists Jerome K. Jerome and Robert Burn and the list of contributors is virtually a catalogue of all the illustrators and cartoonists who were considered important at the time. The only Boer War illustrations traced, however, are four caricatures by Max Beerbohm, three featuring Kitchener and one of Kruger, which appeared in *The Idler* in January 1900. A second drawing of Kruger by Beerbohm appeared in the Christmas issue of *The Idler* in 1900.

Beerbohm was better represented in other publications, and contemporary Boer War caricatures included those of Broderick, Secretary of State for War, which appeared in *Pall Mall Magazine* in February 1902, several cartoons of Chamberlain and one of Winston Churchill reproduced in *The World* Christmas issue in 1900, which showed Churchill blowing a trumpet, entitled *My Own*. Lord Rosslyn was another who was caricatured rather contemptuously by Beerbohm, whose publication *The Second Childhood of John Bull* (1901) also featured three Boer War cartoons.

TRUTH

The liberal London weekly *Truth*, founded in 1877, tended to be anti-war in its stance. Priced at sixpence, it featured regular cartoons drawn by Rowland Hill ('Rip') and F.C. Gould, although sometimes the works were unsigned. The Christmas issues were famed for their double-page coloured cartoons and one of the best-known was published in the Christmas 1900 issue and showed Boer War notables of both sides including Kipling, Roberts, Kruger, Steyn and Baden-Powell.

THE WESTERN MAIL

Of the provincial papers *The Western Mail* (Cardiff) was the most prominent. Founded in 1869 this penny newspaper was the oldest in Wales and the principal car-

toonist was Joseph Morewood Staniforth. In 1900 the owners published a book of Staniforth's cartoons entitled *Cartoons of the Boer War*, which was priced at sixpence a copy and ran to at least three editions. The early prewar cartoons (from August 1899) reflect caution and show various fictitious individuals like John Bull and Prudence urging restraint on the British Government but thereafter, once the War had started, they were decidedly jingoistic. (See p. 211.)

South Africa

It is strange that the South African cartoonists who were working during the War should be more obscure than their overseas counterparts. One of the few exceptions was Daniel Cornelius Boonzaier ('D.C.B.'), who was very prolific and involved with virtually all the satirical publications from the 1880s onwards. Strongly influenced by Howard Schröder, Phil May and George du Maurier, he contributed to *The Owl*, *The Telephone* and *The Cape Register*. Despite his strong Afrikaner upbringing and later political connections his cartoons were surprisingly pro-British. A collection of his work entitled *Owlographs* was published by the *Cape Times* in 1901 and featured Rhodes, Brabant, Steyn, Kruger, De Wet, Botha, Milner, Schreiner and Reitz among other local politicians.

Another prolific cartoonist was Heinrich Egersdörfer, who was the local artist-correspondent for many overseas illustrated papers. Several of his drawings of local scenes were redrawn in *The Graphic* and other European weeklies. His Boer War work is found in *The Owl*, *The South African Review* and the weekly *Cape Argus*.

THE OWL

The Owl was founded in 1895 by Charles and Constance Penstone and originally published in Johannesburg. The magazine was soon transferred to Cape Town, however, because the Penstones feared that Kruger would not maintain press freedom after the Jameson Raid. The first Cape Town issue appeared on 6 June 1896 renamed *The Owl: Penstone's Weekly*. Both Penstones were cartoonists on the magazine and both

1 *A General Group* by cartoonist 'Spy' was published in *Vanity Fair* on 29 November 1900. This group of 12 caricatures portrays British Boer War generals. Group caricatures did not appear often in *Vanity Fair*.
2 *Oom Paul*, a *Vanity Fair* cartoon by 'Drawl' (Leslie Ward). It was published on 8 March 1900.
3 This cartoon by D. C. Boonzaier, entitled *Peace and Goodwill*, was published in the Christmas 1900 issue of *The Veldt*.
4 Joseph Staniforth, cartoonist for *The Western Mail* in Cardiff, gives an impression of W.T. Stead, the editor of *Review of Reviews*, who was a well-known pacifist.
5 *Lord Kitchener*, a 'Spy' caricature which appeared in *Vanity Fair* on 23 February 1899. Kitchener was represented again with a different caricature in the *General Group* on 29 November 1900.

used the initials 'C.P.', so it is not always possible to distinguish between them. Charles died in 1896 but Constance continued to manage the weekly herself, even though the ownership and editorship changed frequently. At the time of the War the publication had been taken over by Frederick York St Leger (father of Stratford St Leger) who was at that time also editor of the *Cape Times*. Constance used her own name, initials, and the pseudonym 'Scalpel' on her cartoons, which she contributed both to *The Owl* and *Cape Times*. *The Owl*, which ceased publication in 1908, employed a large number of cartoonists during the War, including regulars Constance Penstone, Boonzaier, Egersdörfer and Captain Mordaunt Cyril Richards ('M.C.R.'), who produced the series 'Army Types'. Other occasional contributors were W. Dowling, B. S. Johnson ('B.S.J.'), Walter Moorcroft Conolly ('Walrus'), M. A. Rowan, Tarquand, Binns, F. B. Ross, R. R. Musgrave and McGregor Menzies ('M.M.').

Just prior to the War *The Owl* published a bogus ultimatum from Chamberlain to Kruger. The language used was so skilfully worded that it was taken as genuine and it reputedly caused a minor stock-exchange panic in Johannesburg. Milner, who was then High Commissioner, wrote a strongly worded letter to the editor 'conveying a sharp rebuke for such untimely folly'. During the War the military authorities blacked out one of Egersdörfer's cartoons which depicted alleged American atrocities in Cuba, fearing that the Americans might be offended by it.

THE SOUTH AFRICAN REVIEW

In 1900 *The South African Review Book of 50 Famous Cartoons: A Unique Souvenir of the Anglo-Boer War 1899-1900* was published. *The South African Review* itself, edited by Alfred Palmer and priced at twopence, claimed to be the oldest weekly journal in South Africa. The cartoons were all by Heinrich Egersdörfer but towards the end of the War the work of the little-known Cape Town cartoonist Islay also appeared. Palmer stated quite categorically and unashamedly that *The South African Review* advocated Imperial principles, and the

50 cartoons by Egersdörfer in the book, dated from 29 July 1897 to 29 July 1900, are naturally anti-Boer.

OTHERS

The Telephone only ran from September 1899 to March 1900 but some leading names were employed, including Boonzaier, Roderick Heron ('R.H.'), J.B. Hess and F.B. Ross ('F.B.R.'). Ross, who often signed his work with a heart-shaped monogram, also contributed to *The South African Review* and *The Owl* and his postwar work appeared in *The Cape*. Unfortunately the magazine never really took off as J.H. Blenkin ('Johannes') described in his weekly feature 'Weekly Papers of the Past' in *The Cape* on 10 June 1910: 'Because of political differences between the interested parties after six months, *The Telephone* rung off.'

The Cape Register was founded in 1890 by Henry Dennis Edwards who was not only the proprietor but also the chief cartoonist, using the pseudonym 'Grip'. Again the paper was short-lived and lasted until 1904. Edwards had originally been sent out to South Africa by *The Graphic* as war correspondent during the Zulu War. He stayed on and besides being a respected artist he became well known as a publisher, particularly of trade and commercial directories. He also published *The Anglo Boer War 1899-1900: An Album of Upwards of Three Hundred Photographic Engravings*. This souvenir book, which did not contain any artist-drawn illustrations, cost one guinea and was available in time for Christmas 1901. An advertisement directed at 'the fighting men' in the Christmas issue of *The Cape Register* claimed it was 'The best Christmas present you can send home to the old country'. As an additional inducement to acquire a copy Edwards quotes Lord Roberts's opinion of it: 'I think the publication [is] a very instructive and interesting one and that it represents very graphically the different features of the South African campaign.'

Another Cape Town publication, this time a monthly, was *The Veldt*. It lasted from June 1900 to 1904 and had occasional cartoons by Boonzaaier, Dowling, F. B. Ross and some unknown artists. The magazine, which

THE DRAGON AND THE DESTROYER!

The cartoon *The Dragon and the Destroyer!* by Heinrich Egersdörfer depicted Great Britain, as the champion of Liberty, taking up the sword of Justice against the rebel Boer republics.

billed itself 'the best illustrated journal in all the Empire', changed its name to *The Veld* in 1902.

In Johannesburg *Mosquito* used the work of the unknown W. Gould. It is not to be confused with the late nineteenth century weekly with the same name published in Durban. *The Weekly Star* was another Johannesburg paper featuring occasional Boer War cartoons done by H. Law ('H.L.'). D. Dyer-Davies, who acted as cartoonist for *The Rand Daily Mail* from its inception in September 1902, provided *The Sphere* with an illustration of De Wet addressing burghers near Johannesburg in 1900.

A lesser known satirical paper which had offices both in Durban and Pietermaritzburg was *The Natal Caricature*: 'a Natal comic paper published on the 1st and 15th of the month'. It started its existence on 1 February 1901 with Earl Robert as owner, publisher and cartoonist. Robert even did the advertising illustrations. In his editorial Robert says '*The Natal Caricature* is a paper to please, not to offend and in no way approaches vulgarity. It is not a newspaper and therefore stands alone without a rival. Being the first comic illustrated paper in Natal (we might say South Africa) it claims the support of all and becomes a first class medium for advertising . . .'

Australia

Considering the country's relatively small population, the Australian satirical press had a long history and was well developed at the start of the War. Several English and South African cartoonists had worked in Australia, including Heinrich Egersdörfer, George Rossi Ashton, Phil May, Samuel Begg, B.E. Minns and Charles Penstone.

As far back as 1879 the *Sydney Bulletin* had come into existence. Samuel Begg was initially employed as a cartoonist but later Livingstone Hopkins ('Hop') arrived from the United States to take over as chief cartoonist, a position he held for over 20 years which included the Boer War period. Hopkins and Phil May had been good friends when they worked together for the paper during the 1880s. Melton Prior too had been in Australia at the time representing *The Illustrated London News* in Melbourne. Other cartoonists who worked for the *Sydney Bulletin* at the time of the War were Fred Leist, A. Henry Fullwood, B.E. Minns, Frank Mahoney and Will Dyson who, although only 19 at the time, contributed some Boer War drawings.

The Melbourne Punch was another humorous paper dating from 1855 and at the time of the war Alek Sass and G.H. Dancey were the regular cartoonists, with Dancey supplying full-page cartoons. It is not known if any had a Boer War theme, however.

C.E. Taylor, who later became well known as a postcard artist, worked for *The Arrow* and *The Australian Sunday Times* and on one occasion his work was reproduced in *Black & White Budget*. *The Melbourne Outpost* and *The South Australian Critic* also carried cartoons but the artists were not identified. ■

CHAPTER ELEVEN

Cartoonists and Caricaturists: Europe and the United States

Albert René's depiction of Kruger appeared on the cover of *Le Charivari*, 6 August 1899.

Europe

The reasons for the consistently anti-British stance of the Continental cartoonists and the papers they worked for were many and varied. The European governments adopted a neutral position and although Kruger was warmly welcomed by the populace when he arrived in Europe in November 1900, official welcomes were cool or non-existent. Naturally there was a certain amount of jealousy towards the Imperial British power and the underdog was warmly supported, especially when he inflicted the humiliating defeats at Stormberg, Magersfontein and Colenso. But some countries had their own particular reasons for adopting a pro-Boer stance in their popular press.

France was in the throes of an anti-military, pacifist phase with the resurrection of the Dreyfus affair. In addition she had suffered a humiliating setback at Fashoda when she had attempted to exert an influence on the countries bordering the upper Nile at the time of the Sudan Campaign in 1898. The exploits of Georges de Villebois Mareuil, who had made his own way to South Africa to fight for the Boer cause, and his heroic death at the hands of the British at Boshof in April 1900, captured the imagination of the French public.

Russia, too, was having internal problems and any setback for Britain would have enabled her both to meddle in Indian and Persian affairs in the East and to divert attention from more pressing matters at home.

Germany was still smarting over Queen Victoria's re-buke to her grandson, the Kaiser, after he had sent a congratulatory telegram to Kruger at the time of the Jameson Raid. Germany also had designs on Africa but her navy was not powerful enough to challenge British supremacy in foreign waters. The *Bundesrath* incident on New Year's Day in 1900 caused great concern in Europe. Two British warships, *Hermes* and *Terrible*, had intercepted three German ships, *Bundesrath*, *Generaal* and *Herzog* in international waters in the Mozambique Channel, suspecting them of carrying contraband to the Boers. The German vessels were escorted to Durban but after protests from Von Bulow, the German foreign minister, and on finding no weapons, the British authorities released the ships.

The Dutch of course had strong family and other ethnic and cultural ties with the Boers. The newly crowned Queen Wilhelmina had even placed the Dutch warship *De Gelderland* at Kruger's disposal to transport him to Europe after he left the Transvaal. The Swiss were neutral, but they did allow Kruger to remain in exile in Clarens. The reasons for the Belgian and Austro-Hungarian anti-British feeling were unclear but Belgium had possessions in Central Africa which bordered on British colonies and areas of influence.

Lastly, the activities of the pro-Boer committees had a very profound effect on public opinion. Added to this were the efforts of Leyds, the roving South Africa ambassador, and his deputies who had persuaded many leading personalities, including newspaper editors and

N° 276. 6ᵉ année. 17 Février 1900. — transwaal — 15 centimes.

Le Rire

JOURNAL HUMORISTIQUE PARAISSANT LE SAMEDI

Un an : Paris, 8 fr.
Départements, 9 fr. Etranger, 11 fr.
Six mois : France, 5 fr. Etranger, 6 fr.

M. Félix JUVEN, Directeur. — Partie artistique : M. Arsène ALEXANDRE

La reproduction des dessins du RIRE est absolument interdite aux publications, françaises ou étrangères, sans autorisation

10, rue Saint-Joseph, 10
PARIS

Les manuscrits et dessins non insérés ne sont pas rendus.

LE GOTHA DU RIRE. — N° XXVIII

Monsieur CÉCIL RHODES

Le complice de Chamberlain aura fait verser plus de sang en Afrique que de champagne à Kimberley.
Dessin de Ch. LÉANDRE.

1 French artist Henri Henriot's illustration *Flegme Britannique* (British unconcern) appeared in *Le Charivari*.
2 A grim depiction by Charles Léandre of Rhodes, walled up in Kimberley during the siege, from *Le Rire* of 17 February 1900. Kimberley had in fact been relieved a few days before.

postcard publishers, to support the Boer cause. In addition Austria, Russia, Holland, Belgium and Germany had voluntary ambulances helping the Boers, and nationals from these countries, together with others from Scandinavia and Ireland, fought in the international brigades alongside the Boers.

At the time of the War, European satirical publications greatly outnumbered those produced in either Britain or the United States. The fact that the libel laws in Europe were not strictly enforced may have been a reason for this. This could explain why such vicious cartoons attacking Britain, her queen, politicians and soldiers were published in Europe, particularly on postcards.

FRANCE

France already had a long history of satirical publications. *Punch*, which had the subtitle 'London Charivari', was based on the French *Le Charivari*, founded in 1831 and published daily at the price of 25 centimes. It consisted of only eight pages an issue but regularly featured the Boer War on its front cover, which was occasionally coloured. The artist Henri Henriot, who often provided the main cartoon, was also the editor. He contributed several cartoons to *Le Charivari*'s 20-page publication *Boers et Anglais*, which appeared in 1900 at a price of 30 centimes. The pro-Boer caricatures in this publication featured Georges de Villebois Mareuil on the cover by Albert René. Henriot, Jean d' Aurian, Jules Draner,

Tezier and Nicolson also contributed. Henriot also contributed a regular weekly cartoon to *L'Illustration*. This cartoon was placed on the inside cover, so it is not always present in the bound volumes of this magazine.

The weekly *Le Rire* was first published in November 1894 by Felix Juven in Paris. Priced at 15 centimes, it featured coloured cartoons on the front and back covers and black and white ones on the inside pages. The first Boer War cover cartoon appeared on 7 October 1899, depicting an overweight Queen Victoria holding a sewing needle and sitting on Kruger's head. Thereafter regular cartoons came from the brush and pens of Georges Tiret-Bognet, Henry Somm, ('Echos du Rire') Hermann Paul, Maurice Radiguet, Fernand Fau, Fertom, Pierre Jeanniot, Georges Delaw, Lucien Métivet, Henri Gerbault, Jules-Abel Faivre, François Lempereur, Adolphe Willette, Théophile Steinlen, Léonce Burret, August Roubille, George Bigot, André Rouveyre and Charles Carlegle. Added to this impressive list was their most famous cartoonist, 'Caran d'Ache'. Russian-born Emmanuel Poire adopted this pseudonym, which is a transliteration of the Russian words for 'lead pencil'. He had a long and distinguished career with *Le Rire* as well as working for many other contemporary publications, particularly *Le Figaro*. The entire issue of *Le Rire* for 17 November 1900 entitled 'Kruger le Grand et John Bull Le Petit' was devoted to his work. Charles Léandre, who was responsible for the famous cartoon of Queen Victoria and Kruger that appeared on the cover on 7 Octo-

1   2

ber 1899, was another famous French cartoonist of the period. He was honoured at a special dinner given by the proprietors of *Le Rire* in February 1900. In the foreword to their publication the editors of *Neue Burenstreiche*, the collection of anti-British cartoons, praised him for his 'ingenuity'.

Besides its own cartoons *Le Rire* ran a regular feature reproducing selected examples from its contemporaries worldwide. Most often these cartoons came from the American magazines *Life*, *Puck* and *Judge*, or from various other European sources (always with acknowledgment).

One of the best-known French satirical weeklies was *L'Assiette au Beurre*, which first appeared on 4 April 1901 and continued until 1912. More expensive than its rivals at 60 centimes, it was published by Samuel Schwarz, Paris. Schwarz, whose real name was Sigismond, was a Polish immigrant. He was a controversial character who was often in trouble with the censors, particularly with his erotic magazines *Frou Frou* and *Le Pompon*. He went bankrupt in 1902 and control of *L'Assiette au Beurre* was taken over by André de Joncires. Schwarz also published, among others, the weekly series *La Guerre au Transvaal: Anglais et Boers*, which was produced in 100 parts. Many of the *Le Rire* artists also had work reproduced in *L'Assiette au Beurre*, along with cartoonists from other French magazines. The names of Frans Kupka, Hermann Paul, Théophile Steinlen, Adolphe Willette, Léonce Burret, Georges

Jeanniot, Leal de Camara, Henri Gerbault, Hermann Vogel, Fernand Fau, Charles Leandré, Lucien Métivet, Jean-Louis Forain, August Roubille, Jules-Abel Faivre, Caran d'Ache and Noël Dorville were among those who contributed regularly. Kees van Dongen's work is also represented but no Boer War related illustrations by him have been noted.

The best-known Boer War issue was Number 26 published on 28 September 1901 entitled 'Les Camps de Reconcentration au Transvaal', which was exclusively the work of Jean Veber. At least 12 editions of this issue were published with a reputed circulation of 250 000 – ten times the average weekly run. The cartoon on the back cover entitled *L'Impudique Albion*, which depicted King Edward's face superimposed on Albion's buttocks, was eventually suppressed by the Paris police, but not before most editions were circulated. In those that were censored the cartoon was either absent altogether or a blue polka dot petticoat was printed over the offending anatomy. A German version of this publication was produced by Dr Eysler & Co. in 1901 and titled *Das Blutbuch von Transvaal*. Even though the offending King Edward cartoon did not appear, Mendelssohn in his *South African Bibliography* refers to the publication as 'one of the most atrocious collections of coloured and plain caricatures on the South African War issued in Germany'. A Dutch version published in Amsterdam by S.L. van Looy in 1901 was entitled 'De Boeren Kampen' and it, too, omitted *L'Impudique Albion*.

1 and 2 The celebrated back cover by Jean Veber of *L'Assiette au Beurre* for 28 September 1901. This issue ran to at least 11 issues and the authorities demanded that the offending portrait of King Edward be covered over with a blue polka dot petticoat. This of course rendered the cartoon meaningless. Depicted here are copies of the third and the censored tenth editions.

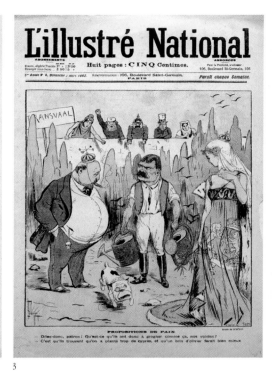

1

2

3

4

A re-issue, again without *L'Impudique Albion*, was published in Brussels in 1915 by the Germans – ostensibly to remind the French what they had thought of the English 14 years before. The re-issue carried a note on the back page to the effect that this edition was an exact copy of the original except that for 'reasons of decency' the obscene reference to King Edward VII had been omitted. *L'Assiette au Beurre* reissued some of these more controversial cartoons in a special number (Number 129) subtitled 'Vive L'Angleterre'. A series of postcards by the Paris publisher J. Picot depicting most of the cartoons (excluding the 'offensive' one) was issued at various times during the War. *L'Impudique Albion* did however make its appearance on several hand-drawn postcards. As late as 1941 German propaganda cigarette cards were still featuring examples of these cartoons showing 'British atrocities'. At least four other issues of *L'Assiette au Beurre*: Number 19, 8 August 1901; Number 41, 11 January 1902; Number 65, 28 June 1902, subtitled 'Britannique' and Number 109, 2 May 1903 subtitled 'Vive L'Angleterre', attacked King Edward and the British politicians for their conduct during the War. All these numbers except 41, which had cartoons by François Kupka, featured the work of the Portuguese cartoonist Leal de Camara exclusively. In Number 65, 'Britannique', several caricatures of Boer generals also appeared and some of these drawings were reproduced on postcards by unidentified publishers. Other artists such as A. Michäel, Fernand-Louis Gottlob, Louis Malteste, Paul Jouve and Eugène Cadel also contributed Boer War cartoons to other issues.

Le Bon Vivant commenced publication late in 1899 and used the work of R. Ener, Maurice Radiguet, S. Frick, G. Ri, Fertom, C. da Amaral and Victor Mignot. *La*

Caricature, founded in 1879, also featured Victor Mignot, some of whose coloured cover illustrations later appeared on a series of six black and white postcards published in mid-1900 entitled 'Boers et Anglais'. Both weeklies were published by the same firm, Fayard Frères.

Cartoonists working for *La Caricature* were particularly anti-British and included Georges Tiret-Bognet, Spada, Georges Grellet, Jean-Louis Plumet, G. Lion, Jean Jamet, Gann Keronec'h, Jean d'Aurian, Robert Lewis (the postcard artist), P.H. Lobel (whose virulent and bloody cartoons became a feature of his series of postcards) and, of course, C. da Amaral, whose well-known cover illustration of 'English Correction' showed Queen Victoria being spanked on her bare bottom ('Dum Dum') by Kruger, appeared on 25 November 1899. This particular issue resulted in a diplomatic protest and copies of this issue were seized by the censors. In an issue two weeks later the indignant editor P. Landragin protested that Emile François Loubet (the French President) had failed to realize that the attack on Queen Victoria was not aimed at her as a woman but as head of the British Government.

On 16 June 1902 *Le Gavroche* published a special commemorative issue in honour of the peace. The British, however, came in for much criticism and the issue was subtitled 'La Paix à la mode John Bull'. The coloured cover illustration by Francisque Poulbot showed John Bull crucifying India, Ireland and Paul Kruger. Others to contribute cartoons in similar vein were Ali Donah, Sancha, Oswald Heidbrinck, G. Monnier, La Garriage, Léon Georges, Aristide Delannoy, Moriss, Ricardo Flores, Jean Plumet, G. Ménard, Lucien Weil ('Weiluc') and Le Bocain.

One of the most famous of the French periodicals

5

6

was *Le Canard Sauvage*. Although it was first published only in 1903, it featured several cartoons relating to the Boer War. The issue for 2-8 May 1903 (Number 7) entitled 'La Promenade Anglais' featured cartoons by François Kupka, Roubille, Théophile Steinlen, Paul and the famous Swiss etcher and engraver Félix Vallotton ('F.V.'). All of these cartoons had a Boer War theme, showing De Wet and Kruger among others. Another well-known magazine was *Le Courrier Français*, founded in 1883 by Jules Roques of Paris. This journal was rather more upmarket, selling at 50 centimes and often using work by Toulouse-Lautrec. During the Boer War illustrations by Adolphe Willette often appeared on the front cover.

Over 140 different weekly and monthly satirical papers were produced in France between 1870 and 1900, while a further 94 were launched between 1900 and 1914. Some of these magazines with their principal cartoonists were *Le Sourire* (Auguste Roubille); *Le Journal Amusant* and *Lyon* (Rene Le Bègue); *Cri de Paris* and *Chronique Amusante* (Georges Tiret-Bognet 'G.T.B.'); *La Vie Pour Rire* and *Echo des Marches* (René Le Bègue, A. Sorel and Alphonse Lalauze); *Le Franc Normand Illustré* (René Le Bègue, Marius Rossillon using the pseudonym 'O'Galop', Alphonse LaLauze and the rather unlikely G. Og); *La Silhouette* (Alphonse Hector Colomb using the pseudonyms 'Bobb' and 'Moloch'); *Polichinelle* (Fertom and Jan Duch); *Le Petit Brayon Illustré* (Hermann Paul, René Le Bègue and Henri Gerbault); *Le Grelot* (Alfred Le Petit); *La République Illustrée* (Albert René, Oswald Heidbrinck, Nicolson and Jules Draner); *L'Indiscret* (Georges Tiret-Bognet, Maurice Radiguet, Leal de Camara and G. Monnier); *L'Illustré Nationale* (Hermann Paul, René Le Bègue and H. Gog);

La Vie Pour Rire (Lucien Weil, H. Gog, Jan Duch, Radiguet, Georges Tiret-Bognet, Francisque Poulbot, Lempereur and Noël Dorville); *Le Dépêche* (O'Galop, Emil Cohl, René Le Bègue and Georges Tiret-Bognet); *La Revue Mâme* ('Luc') and *La Vie en Rose* (Adolphe Willette).

As can be seen from this list, many cartoonists were not exclusively employed by one publisher but contributed to many publications at the same time. Despite this, all the works published were original and not duplicated in other magazines. Many of these periodicals, although printed on inferior paper, had coloured covers. The method of reproduction was zincography, a photomechanical process invented by Charles Gillot in 1872.

HOLLAND

The best-known Dutch Boer War cartoonist was undoubtedly Johan Braakensiek. Braakensiek, who was born in 1858, worked for many years on *De Amsterdammer: weekblad voor Nederland* and virtually every week he produced a full-page lithographed cartoon on a topical subject. It is claimed that he contributed more than 4 000 illustrations to the paper. Between 1896, the year of the Jameson Raid, and 1902, over 80 Boer War and Africana cartoons appeared. At the height of the War these cartoons appeared weekly to the exclusion of all other subjects. Needless to say the subjects chosen were always pro-Boer. In 1900 the firm of Van Holkema and Warendorf published *John Bull in Zuid-Afrika: Platen van Johan Braakensiek en andere ontleend aan De Amsterdammer: weekblad voor Nederland*. Besides those of Braakensiek, it included cartoons by Caran d'Ache, Arpad Schmidhammer, M. Feldbauer and John

1 *Das Blutbuch von Transvaal*, a German version of the *L'Assiette au Beurre* 'concentration camps' issue published by Dr Eysler & Co., omitted both the back page and another cartoon which showed Edward VII dressed in a wine barrel wetting himself. All the atrocity cartoons were retained however.
2 C. da Amaral's famous illustration *English Correction*. This front cover cartoon appeared in *La Caricature* on 25 November 1899. It was later used on Dutch postcards to celebrate one of the first British defeats, at Modder River on 28 November 1899. This battle actually took place after the cartoon was first published.
3 Réne Le Bègue riducules Edward VII's controversial love for cards in this illustration, produced for *L'Illustré National*.
4 *Le Gavroche*, the sister paper to *L'Assiette au Beurre*, published a special number on 16 June 1902 to celebrate the end of the War. The bitterness had not ended with the declaration of peace, however, and this cover by Francisque Poulbot shows Kruger as Jesus Christ being crucified by John Bull.
5 C. da Amaral produced *La Dame de Chez Maxim* for *La Caricature* of 30 December 1899.
6 Victor Mignot's series of cartoons *Nos amis Les Anglais* was featured on the front covers of *Le Caricature* between January and March 1900. These cartoons were also featured on a series of six 'Le Bon Vivant' postcards.

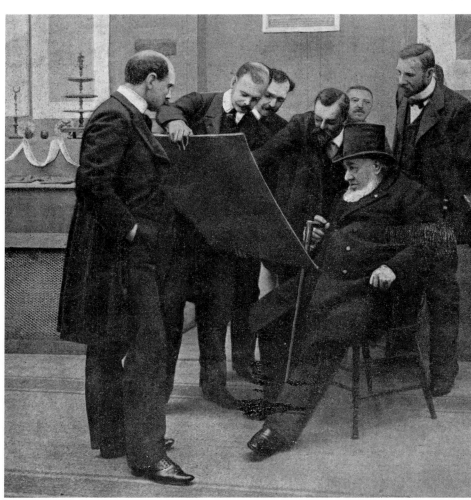

Tenniel. Postcards by Joh G. Steinlen, Jos Nuss and other Dutch publishers featured reproductions of some of the Braakensiek cartoons. Other Dutch satirical and humorous weeklies included *Humoristisch Album* founded around 1852, *Uilenspiegel* founded in 1867 in Rotterdam, and *Der Wahre Jacob*, published by the Nederlandsche Kiosken Maatschappij and edited by E. Gans, and still fairly new at the time of the War. Jan Linse was the principal cartoonist for *Humoristische Album*. Patriq Kroon, who is better known by his pseudonym 'Orion', contributed regularly to *Uilenspiegel* having started his career there in 1894. Even though he contributed to other publications his three drawings a week for *Uilenspiegel* must have kept him very busy. Boer War cartoons by 'Soranus' were also prominent in *Uilenspiegel*. *Der Wahre Jacob* employed the services of the Amsterdam journalist and cartoonist Johannes Feith. Feith, who was born in Austria in 1874, used the *nom de crayon* 'Chris Kras Kzn'. Besides his regular features he published several books of cartoons on the South African War, according to an article entitled 'Dutch Humorous Artists' by Arthur Lord which appeared in Volume 24 of *The Strand Magazine* for July-December 1902. However the only two books by 'Chris Kras Kzn' which can be traced are *Kronings-Idylle* with verses by Kees van Ponten (published by Cohen Zonen in 1902) and a similar volume entitled *Pillen Voor Joe* (published by Cohen Zonen in 1900) which credits Feith under his own name.

Another *Der Wahre Jacob* artist Jakobus Hendrikus Speenhoff, who spent his spare time writing plays, also contributed to *Woord en Beeld*, Rotterdam *Dagblad* and Rotterdam *Weekblad*. He claims to have based his cartoons on the style of Caran d'Ache and Degas, but was particularly influenced by Edward Tennyson Reed, the *Punch* cartoonist. A young artist whose work was also found in *Der Wahre Jacob* was Pieter Das. Occasionally Kees van Dongen contributed a cartoon to this weekly but as with his work in *L'Assiette au Beurre* no Boer War cartoons have been noted.

Vooruitgang, founded in The Hague around 1890, used the services of G.J. Sitjthoff and Cornelis Koppenol in their lithographic cartoon supplements. *Die Nederlandsche Spectator*, published by Martinus Nyhoff in The Hague, also featured a regular lithographic cartoon supplement, which often featured the cartoons of 'Henricus', and some of these cartoons were later reproduced on postcards. The *Amsterdamsche Courant*, *Delftsche Courant* and *De Tijd* all employed the cartoonist Petrus van Geldorp. In a similar style to Johan Braakensiek he produced a regular weekly lithographic cartoon in *Amsterdamsche Courant*. The lithographic cartoon supplements of these newspapers often took the form of loose inserts and were keenly collected. Many survive today, mounted and framed.

GERMANY
The German satirical press was in a highly advanced

5

6

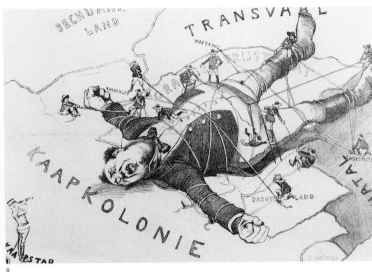

7   8

state when the War started. *Lustige Blätter*, founded in 1885, was published in Berlin by Dr Eysler & Co. with Leopold Wulf as editor-in-chief. The cartoons generally were very anti-British. *Neue Burenstreiche* featured a cartoon dated 2 January 1900, based on a news item claiming that four British soldiers had attacked a bookseller in Cape Town for stocking copies of *Lustige Blätter*. The cartoons were principally the work of Franz Jüttner ('F.A.J.'), M. Janzelow ('M.J.'), Julius Klinger, Feodor Czabran, W.A. Wellner ('W.A.W.'), Lyonel Feininger, George Tippel, F. Griebner and E. Bahr. Besides the magnificent 'Gruss vom Kriegsschauplatz' series of coloured postcards, most of which were based on cartoons from *Lustige Blätter*, Dr Eysler & Co. also published *Burenstreiche*, *Neue Burenstreiche* and *Pfui Chamberlain*, which were collections of cartoons. *Burenstreiche* featured 101 Boer War cartoons taken from the contemporary press, including works that had appeared in *Lustige Blätter*. Its successor *Neue Burenstreiche*, also published in 1900, was an enlarged edition with 175 cartoons. *Pfui Chamberlain*, published in 1902, was devoted entirely to attacking Joseph Chamberlain and his policies. The illustrations were again taken from the contemporary press and included 130 cartoons by Franz Jüttner, Jean Veber, Lyonel Feininger, Arpad Schmidhammer, W.A. Wellner, Ludwig Stutz and others.

Jugend, which was discussed in Chapter 8, was probably better known for its cartoons and caricatures. The editor Georg Hirth was considered a controversial figure in art circles, as indicated by his choice of cartoons and illustrations. Others who contributed occasional Boer War cartoons to *Jugend* were Angelo Jank, Julius Diez, Ludwig von Zumbusch, Adolf Münzer, Fritz Scholl ('F.S.') Max Hagen ('M.H.') and Max Feldbauer. Very prominent in *Jugend* during the Boer War was the work of Arpad Schmidhammer, who also worked for *Münchener Odinskarte* and *Der Scherer*. Schmidhammer used a variety of strange monograms: one appears to represent a frog, another might be a cork or a mushroom and occasionally he used his initials, 'A.S.', intertwined. The reasons for these variations are unclear, especially as several cartoons or caricatures by him often appeared on the same page with different monograms.

Ulk was founded in 1871 and used Paul Halke ('P.H.') as one of its principal cartoonists. Some of the *Ulk* cartoons annoyed Mendelssohn, and in his *Mendelssohn's South African Bibliography* (Volume 2, pages 402-403) he draws attention to one showing Kitchener and Chamberlain as two demons. Kitchener collects the starving children and deposits them in the cauldron stirred by Chamberlain. The children emerge as angels. The cartoon is entitled *Wie die Teufel für den Himmel Sorgen! Zwölftausend Burenkinder*!! Mendelssohn sarcastically refers to the cartoon as 'a work of art'. Another, which appeared on 12 July 1901, is referred to as a 'choice specimen'. This cartoon is entitled *Englische Helden* and shows British soldiers clubbing a Boer woman and her children. Having murdered them, the soldiers set fire to

1 Georges Tiret-Bognet drew this cartoon for *Chronique Amusante* on 13 February 1902. The caption reads: '*Correspondent to the Great Drunken Magazine*: Why General I don't call that an execution, but a murder! *The Glorious Sirdar*: I can't help it, dear Sir, these are my only means to get them out of my sight'. Note Kitchener's horse's 'weekly bulletins'.
2 *The Battle of Spion Kop*, a highly fanciful print by an unknown artist and publisher. Note the uniforms and gold-highlighted insignia, bandoliers and shrapnel burst. Even though the title is in English, it is probably a Continental production.
3 This photograph by W. Wolf shows Kruger viewing a series of caricatures by American cartoonists at the pro-Boer art exhibition held at The Hague in August 1902.
4 Maurice Radiguet's *Le Courageux Baiser* (The Courageous Kiss) appeared in the French publication *La Vie Pour Rire* for 22 March 1902.
5 The front cover of the Dutch anti-British publication *Pillen voor Joe* by Johannes Feith.
6 The German publisher Dr Eysler & Co. published a series of anti-British cartoons. Shown here are *Burenstreiche* with the cover depicting Kruger by Lyonel Feininger and *Neue Burenstreiche*, with an illustration of a Highlander as a mule, by M. Janzelow. Cartoonists often used mules to symbolize British troops after the Battle of Nicholson's Nek, when British pack mules stampeded during the night and the troops, fearing a Boer attack, fired on them.
7 Johan Braakensiek's *De terugtocht over de Toegela* was one of many of his lithographs printed by the Dutch publication *De Amsterdammer: weekblad voor Nederland*. Showing Joubert sending Buller back over the Tugela, it was published on 4 February 1900.
8 Petrus van Geldorp produced a series of lithographic supplements for *Amsterdamsche Courant*. This one appeared on 17 November 1899.

the house. In the sketch they are seen sneaking off, scared by a little Boer boy shouting 'Vater Kommt'.

Other German comic weeklies with their cartoonists were *Der Floh* (Arpad Schmidhammer); *Das Goldene Buchlein* (Franz Jüttner); *Simplicissimus* (Theodor Heine 'T.T.H.', Bruno Paul 'B.P.' and Eduard Thony 'E. Th.'); *Kladderadatsch* (L. Stutz and G. Brandt 'G.B.'); and *Fliegende Blätter* (Fritz Steub).

AUSTRIA

Austria was much larger at the time of the Boer War than it is today, as the Austro-Hungarian Empire took in Hungary, Czechoslovakia and other smaller countries. Austrian publications, with their cartoonists, included *Wiener Humoristische Blätter* (F. Grätz 'F.Gr.'); *Neue Glulichler* (F. Graetz); *Der Scherer* (Arpad Schmidhammer); *Figaro* of Vienna (Ernst Juch); *Humoristike Listy* (K. Krejcik); *Kiekeriki* and *Sipy*. The Hungarian publications included *Bolond Yostok*, *Borszem-Janko*, *Kakas Merton* and *Ustokos*, all produced in Budapest.

OTHERS

In Switzerland *Nebelspalter*, the only Swiss satirical magazine identified to date, used cartoons by F. Buscovitz ('F.B.') and W. Lehmann-Schram ('W.L-S.'). Belgian publications included *La Réforme* (which featured cartoons by 'G. Julio'), *L'Illustré National* (Hermann Paul), *Le Rire Belge* and *Belgische Karikatur*.

In 1900 John Grand-Carteret assembled his *John Bull Sur La Sellette* or 'One Hundred Years of Anti-British Cartoons' which was published by Libraire Strauss. As the name implies, the book consisted of anti-British cartoons from France, Poland, Germany, Austria, Russia, Italy, Belgium, Portugal, Spain, Britain, Ireland and the United States. Nearly half the cartoons had Boer War themes. Many of the English prewar cartoons urged caution, including those by Francis Carruthers Gould in *The Westminster Gazette* and one by an unidentified cartoonist in *The Morning Leader*. Others were downright unsupportive of Britain's war effort, including Phil Blake's cartoons in *Freeman's Journal*. The work of the Continental cartoonists was naturally even more scathing.

Six years later Grand-Carteret produced a similar book entitled *L'Oncle de l'Europe*, which contained cartoons and postcards featuring King Edward VII. Despite the fact that virtually all the cartoons lampooned the king, his secretary Lord Francis Knollys wrote to the author accepting a copy of the book on the king's behalf. The letter was reproduced in facsimile as a frontispiece.

United States

Most of the American papers carried cartoons portraying national and international events as a regular feature but the three main satirical papers were *Puck*, *Life* and *Judge*. *Puck* was founded in 1876 by German immigrant Joseph Keppler, who was both owner and principal cartoonist. When he died in 1894 his son Joseph jnr. succeeded him and produced several cartoons with a Boer War theme. Eugene Zimmerman ('Zim'), who had been with *Puck* at its inception, later moved to *Judge* and contributed several Boer War cartoons. Edward Kemble was one of the most prolific cartoonists at that time, working for several papers as well as both *Puck* and *Life*.

Another cartoonist working for *Life* signed himself 'Culver' and many of his cartoons appeared on postcards at a later date.

Henry (Hy) Mayer was a German-born cartoonist who came to the United States in 1886. He was truly cosmopolitan and his work appeared in virtually all the American humorous magazines as well as leading British and European publications including *Pick-Me-Up*, *Black & White*, *Pall Mall Magazine*, *Punch*, *Le Rire* and *Fliegende Blätter*. He went on to become editor-in-chief of *Puck* in 1914. (See also p. 169.)

Other American newspapers that featured Boer War cartoons included *The Des Moines Leader*, *The Chicago Chronicle*, *St Paul Pioneer Press*, *The St Louis Republican*, *Grand Rapids Morning Post*, *Detroit Free Press*, *The Philadelphia Record*, *The New York Evening World*, *The Pittsburgh Despatch*, *Chicago News*, *St Paul Weekly Gazette*, *Minneapolis Sunday Times*, *Denver Evening Post*, *Chicago Record*, *Brooklyn Eagle* and *The New York Journal*.

Other noted cartoonists were C. L. Bush (*The New York World*); W.L. Bowman (*The Minneapolis Tribune*); F. Bowers (*The Indianapolis News*) and Vic Lambdin (*The Minneapolis Journal*). The illustrated journals *Harper's Weekly* and *Leslie's Weekly* also carried cartoons, often on their front pages and occasionally with a Boer War theme. W. A. Rogers was one cartoonist whose work appeared on the front pages of *Harper's Weekly*. *Thrilling Experiences in the War in South Africa*, published in 1900 by the Educational Company in Chicago, featured contemporary cartoons from some of these newspapers, especially *St Paul Pioneer Press*, *The Denver Times* and *The Indianapolis News*.

PART FOUR

PICTURE POSTCARDS AND ILLUSTRATED NOVELS

CHAPTER TWELVE

The Picture Postcards of the War

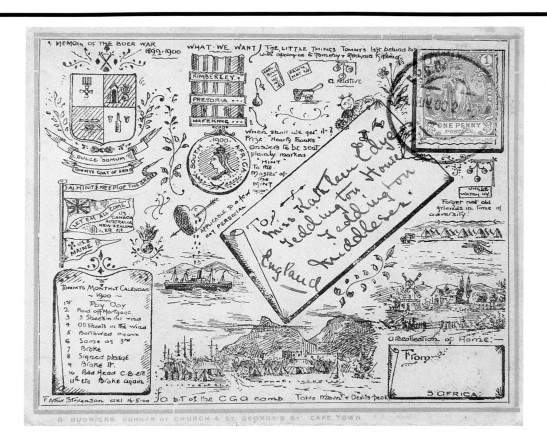

Previous page: Raphael Tuck's 'Empire Series' postcard no. 1288. The illustration, *Graced with Victory*, was copied from the original painting by B. Faustin.
Above: The large number of British troops arriving in the Mother City encouraged the Cape Town postcard publisher George Budricks & Co. to produce a pictorial souvenir envelope in May 1900. Sergeant F. A. Stevenson of the Cape Garrison Artillery was the designer, and several editions of the envelope were produced.

The postcard is reputed to have been the brain-child of Heinrich von Stephan, who first submitted the idea to the German postal authorities in 1865. However this suggestion, repeated at a postal congress in Karlsruhe in 1867, was rejected. But in 1869 the Austrian postal authorities, apparently acting on an independent suggestion by Dr Emmanuel Herrmann in a Vienna newspaper, instituted the world's first 'postal card'.

The first British postcard followed a year later and at the Berne Postal Congress in 1874 it was agreed that postcards would be allowed to travel from one country to another at a uniform rate. Up to then all legal postcards had been officially produced and pre-stamped at half the standard letter rate but in 1894 the use of privately produced cards was permitted. These new cards (sized 122 x 75 mm in Britain) could be used with an adhesive stamp purchased from the post office. Picture cards had, of course, been sent through the mail before but they had to be enclosed in an envelope and sent at the normal postal rate. In November 1899 the firm of Raphael Tuck & Sons claimed that, because of its representations, the British postal authorities would now permit the use of the larger European card (140 x 89 mm). This became the standard size for postcards.

The collecting of postcards became popular in the early 1890s and the magazine *The Post Card* appeared in the United States in 1889. The life of this magazine was regrettably short, but by the early part of the twentieth century there were at least six others to take its place, including *The Picture Postcard*. One of the earliest advertisements was placed by a collector who requested 'Foreign war cards – caricatures preferred – no English, Dutch or Common Cards'.

At the turn of the century the telephone was a luxury and the commonest and most convenient form of long distance communication was by means of the picture postcard. Inland rates for cards remained at a halfpenny for 20 years. Earlier figures are not available but it is estimated that in 1903 over 600 million cards were produced in England alone. In 1900, when the firm of Raphael Tuck & Sons offered a prize of £1 000 for the collector who assembled the largest number of their cards, they were inundated with entries and the winner was reputed to have collected over 20 000 cards.

The first South African picture postcards were produced before the turn of the century. The first locally produced cards may have been the 'Transvaal Crisis' cards which featured the Jameson Raid and its aftermath, for which a postmark of 6 February 1896 has been found. As they were produced just over a month after the event by a halftone screen-block process they could not have been manufactured abroad. Mozes Zadok Booleman, who was also South Africa's first philatelic dealer, and Sallo Epstein are credited as being the first postcard publishers in South Africa. Joseph Barnett in Johannesburg and J. C. Hubrich and W. J. Smuts in Cape Town followed soon after. Local scenes by over-

Above: Boer generals and their aides at the pro-Boer art exhibition held in The Hague during August 1902. The same illustration was widely used on several post cards published by, among others, M. M. Couveé of The Hague. The artists H. W. Mesdag and Josef Israels are standing directly behind generals De la Rey, De Wet and Botha, who are seated.

seas publishers were also produced. Early picture post-cards were published in many small country towns, in-cluding Beaufort West, De Aar, Harrismith and Klerks-dorp, to name just a few.

One of the richest sources of Boer War illustration is found on the several thousand cards depicting the War, although sadly the vast majority of these cards never ap-peared in South Africa. They originated mainly in Eu-rope and, of course, England. Advertisements in con-temporary postcard journals and messages on the cards themselves reveal that Boer War cards were actively col-lected during and after the War by schoolchildren and adults alike. In October 1900 an article appeared in the *Royal Magazine* entitled 'The War on Pictorial Post-cards' in which the author, Clive Holland, discusses sev-eral contemporary European anti-British cards. He tries to refute the messages conveyed in the cartoons and ends his article with the following remarks:

Scores of other cards have of course been published, which have been eagerly snapped up by collectors, destined ultimately to form an amusing if inaccurate and not a little scandalous pictorial record of the South African campaign. Many of these such as the horrible *Dream of the Queen of England*; *The Queen of England at the carnival*; *The Brave English* and a score or more of others are too indecorous for repro-duction – That there must be a market for such things is proved by their production, but their issue and their purchase do not indicate a national opin-

ion. That should be remembered. The coarseness of Gillray – who caricatured the English Royal Family of his time – did not represent the bulk of intelli-gent opinion. In like manner should be regarded the more scurrilous attacks which have been made on things English by the illustrated papers of the Conti-nent. A great writer has said 'the strong are ever hat-ed, the weak ignored!' This maxim may well bring some meed of comfort to John Bull in difficulties.

The proprietor and editor of *The Picture Postcard*, E.W. Richardson, was equally scathing in his attack on the publishers of anti-British postcards. In the Novem-ber 1901 issue he complains about the French postcards issued to coincide with the visit of Tsar Nicholas II to Paris:

These bitter and sarcastic cartoons are not pleasant cards and we should have preferred to ignore them but unfortunately advantage was taken of the Tsar's presence in France to bombard him with these and similar appeals to interfere with England's prosecu-tion of the war against the remnants of the Boer Army in her South African possessions. The chief card with appeals to interfere in favour of the late South African Republics was sent to the Emperor in such quantities that it was stated that trunks of these pro-Boer missives were carried to Russia with the Royal Baggage.

Even after the War had ended Richardson was still com-plaining and in November 1902, in an article entitled

1

2

3

4

'The press and picture postcards', he drew attention with some pleasure to the fact that the Dutch police were seizing postcards caricaturing Queen Victoria. Despite this threat of censorship many of these cards survive today.

The editor of *Navy and Army Illustrated* also took exception to at least one of the propaganda cards issued to welcome Kruger to Europe. In the 8 December 1900 issue of the magazine (p. 282), one of the German cards by C. Lehr was reproduced, and in the caption below he commented: 'the above is one of the postcards which were sent in shoals from various parts of Europe to meet Kruger on his arrival in Paris. On the other side they are addressed in Dutch to "His High Excellency the State President of the S.A.R." The vierkleur is for the name and address of the sender. Considering the part sea power has played in Kruger's downfall the anchor seems rather an unfortunate symbol to have selected, in spite of its being the Emblem of Hope.'

The Southern Africa Postcard Research Group has to date recorded over 100 publishers of Boer War cards alone, and this does not include the majority of cards where unfortunately no publisher is given. Many publishers, both European and British, were content merely to issue neutral and non-political cards bearing photographic reproductions of generals and other leaders of both sides as well as pictures of troops and the aftermath of various battles. Some unidentified publishers issued 'real photographic' cards but in some cases these were photographs of magazine illustrations. George Budricks produced a *Souvenir of the Anglo-Boer War* – a booklet containing 24 tipped-in photographs. Many of these photographs also appeared on postcards, so it is possible that he published the postcards as well.

Among the most interesting and sought-after cards are those which were artist-drawn or designed. While the work of such well-known illustrators and cartoonists as Harry Payne, Georges Scott, Richard Caton Woodville, Jean Veber, Adolphe Willette, Julius Arthur Thiele, Henry Seppings Wright, Georges Montbard, Paul Frenzeny, C. da Amaral, Charles Sheldon and Amedée Forestier appeared on these cards, the vast majority of the illustrations are by unidentified artists. Often the original illustrations with the artists' signatures or monograms were cropped when printing the cards with the result that the work in many cases appears anonymously. By tracing the original illustration one can often identify the artist, however. One must also draw a distinction between the cards which were specifically commissioned and those which are taken from other sources (see Appendix 3).

The British cards are of course patriotic and jingoistic while those of the European publishers are almost unanimously anti-British or pro-Boer or both.

Great Britain

One of the first British publishers of Boer War cards was the Picture Postcard Co. Ltd., which issued a series of 30 cards in five sets early in the War. At the time these cards were published (probably before Black Week of 10-15 December 1899) a swift and victorious end to the War was expected and so there was no obvious need for propaganda cards. Consequently the cards are objective in tone and content, using illustrations taken from *The Illustrated London News* (without acknowledgement) and *Black & White*. Raphael Tuck & Sons, the most prolific of the Boer War publishers, entered the field in November 1899 and soon realized that the British public needed to be persuaded that the cause was right. They launched what was known as the 'Empire Series', which consisted of over 100 cards with variants. Fortunately Tuck had a numbering system (not always consistent, however) so it is relatively easy to follow his sequence.

Among Tuck's most popular cards were those illustrated by Harry Payne commemorating the heroic feats of the defence of Mafeking, the relief of Ladysmith and the Boer defeat at Paardeberg (which was also celebrated as the avenging of Majuba). He became so well known in this field that he was described as 'the Michelangelo of military artists'. The exploits of the City Imperial Volunteers (C.I.V.) were chronicled both by Tuck and the City Press. Tuck, being a good marketing man, saw his opportunity when the C.I.V. returned from South Africa and presented Colonel Boxall of the C.I.V. depot with a 'further' packet of 160 cards for distribution among the invalided troops who were about to parade at the Guildhall. (The members of the C.I.V. who had returned before this had evidently been presented with their cards aboard their train.) Lance Thackeray, the British illustrator who worked for Tuck, conceived the idea of the 'write away' series and among the hundreds of cards produced were nine with Boer War themes. Each illustration was accompanied by a sentence which the sender then completed with his own message.

Other publishers soon followed Raphael Tuck & Sons Ltd. including C.W. Faulkner & Co. ('Patriotic Series'), George Stewart & Co., W. & A.K. Johnston Ltd., Blum & Degen Ltd. and Gale & Polden Ltd. All featured cards showing flags, heroic British generals, quotations from Shakespeare and other poets, as well as the words and music of contemporary patriotic songs.

In order to counteract the propaganda effect of the European publishers, British cards were published in European languages as well as in English. Advertisements using the Boer War as a theme were common in the illustrated press and products as diverse as Hovis bread, Dunville's Irish Whiskey and Eucaryl soap (among others) were featured on postcards. These cards were offered free to consumers who collected a specified number of wrappers or labels. The Coventry firms of W.H. Grant & Co. and Thomas Stevens produced woven silk cards and included Boer War generals in their range. However the artists responsible for these cards remain largely unidentified.

Europe

The European publishers in the main had no love for Britain and her Empire and, as their cards appeared earlier than their British counterparts, distinct phases are apparent. Only a few of the cartoons were original, most being borrowed from the contemporary press, and there was certainly no shortage of material. Their unconcealed delight at the early British defeats featured prominently in the cartoons published, for example, by the firms of Brüno Burger and Ottille (Leipzig) Ernst Rennert (Aussig), Dr Eysler (Berlin), Regel & Krug (Zurich), Cartes Postales Artistiques par Julio (Belgium), N.J. Boon, W.J. Luii, Ludwig and J.G. Vlieger (Amsterdam). Chamberlain, Queen Victoria, Edward VII, Kitch-

5

Buren im Feuer.

6

7

1 One of a series of postcards published by the firm of W. & A.K. Johnson Ltd. of Edinburgh. The cards were titled *Peace with Honour* and *Peace, Lasting Peace*, and the artist is unknown.

2 Royal Engineers building a bridge under heavy Boer fire. Neither the artist nor the publisher of this postcard has been identified. A similar image appears on a lantern slide.

3 F. O'Beirne's Imperial Yeomanry postcard no. 1668. The earlier cards in the Blum & Degen military series were produced prior to the start of the War.

4 This postcard, illustrated by Lance Thackeray and published by S. Hildesheimer & Co., shows 'pushful' Joe Chamberlain, the British Colonial Secretary, painting the Transvaal and Free State red – the British Empire colour.

5 The Patriotic Postcard Company of London produced several cards in this series, based on the words and music of popular jingoistic songs of the time. The artist is unknown.

6 *Boers firing*, a colourful depiction of Boer uniforms. The artist and publisher of this set of postcards are unknown. The same illustration appeared on a similar series of trade cards for Palais des Broderies and Chicorée de la Meuse.

7 A solidarity postcard by 'P.L.' and published by H. Däumler, Germany. It was addressed to President Kruger while he was in Brussels.

EDOUARD VII ET LE TRANSVAAL. 7 mars 1902.

Et ce n'est pas fini!

1

2

3

TRANSVAAL

OVERWINNEN OF STERVEN

4

1 *La guerre du Transvaal* series of postcards was mostly drawn by the artist 'Victa'. This one, however, is by 'Darsane'. It is entitled *Eduard VII et Le Transvaal 7 Mars 1902: Ce n'est pas fini*. It refers to one of the Boers' last victories – at Tweebosch on 7 March 1902 when Methuen was captured by De la Rey. This series of eight cards was produced in three states: a limited numbered edition, a hand-coloured and an uncoloured set.
2, 3 and 4 A series of Belgian Pro-Boer postcards, published by the Algemeen Nederlandsche Verbond (Antwerp branch). The artists of these cards were E. M. van Averbeke, K. Collens and E. van Mieghem.

ener and Lord Roberts particularly were lampooned and ridiculed. The popularity of these cards spread and soon different language versions, including Russian, appeared. In January 1901 a Boer P.O.W., Willie Steyn, and four of his comrades jumped off the *Catalonia* in Colombo Harbour and were picked up by the Russian troopship *Cherson* and brought as heroes to the Russian capital St Petersburg. This incident, together with other Russian involvement in the War, inspired the production of a rare series of at least ten cards in two editions by the Moscow firm of Scherer Nabholz & Co. in 1902 and 1903.

As the tide turned against the Boers and Kruger was forced to leave the Transvaal new sets of cards appeared, depicting firstly his arrival in Europe and then the 'solidarity' cards expressing sympathy with the 'brave Boer leaders and people' with an appeal to European leaders (including the Tsar and Queen Wilhelmina) to intercede on their behalf. The public were urged to send these cards, which had pre-printed addresses to Kruger, either at the hotels where he stayed during his European tour or to the offices of five newspapers whose editors acted as collecting agents. The pro-Boer committees were extremely active in the production of fundraising cards. One of the best-known was Franz von Defregger's card showing British troops allowing blacks to flog Boer women and children. This card was advertised in *Der Burenfreund*. The Algemeen Nederlandsche Verbond (Antwerp Branch) issued several of these cards using illustrations by identifiable artists. Edmond van Offel drew Kruger and Joubert enclosed in laurel leaves, and when Joubert died on 27 March 1900 the portrait vignette had a mourning border.

Van Offel also drew an illustration of an armed Boer soldier with a child at his feet looking at a woman in black, who may symbolize death. E. M. van Averbeke contributed an illustration of the English 'spider' trapping the Transvaal 'fly' entitled *Engeland-Transvaal*. (The same illustration was used on the back covers of Louis van Neck's *Een Noodlottige Oorlog*, and on the cover of the French version.) Jules Baetes illustrated *Zuid Afrika Nederduitsch*. K. Collens, who was both an illustrator and silhouettist, contributed three illustrations. It is possible that E. van Mieghem was the artist of three other cards signed 'E.V.M.'. It is interesting to note that variations in typography, colour and publisher's imprint occur on all these cards.

A large series of postcards was published by the 'Haagsche Pro-Boer Vereniging' (The Hague) in aid of the 'imprisoned women and children in South Africa'. Each had a photographic illustration with an elaborate border inscribed 'Amajuba Bloemen'. Others were double cards with artist-drawn illustrations and verses occupying two-thirds of the card. Unfortunately the artists are not identified. Another single card inscribed *Beinertrag zu gunsten verwundeter Buren* was published by J. A. Jetzelsberger of Salzburg and signed by M. Ruppe. Another card entitled *Zurtapferkeit der Boeren* was published by W. Havlicek of Prague and again there is no discernible artist's signature. An unsigned card entitled *Sphinx Albion* issued in 'protestation of the English war against Transvaal' was published by A. Hembo in Nice and also included German and French inscriptions. A. Beinert was the illustrator of the *Minerva* card issued in 'recognition of the freedom struggle of the Boers 1899-1900' printed by Schneider & Lux in Vienna. A series of at least 14 photographically illustrated cards was published by 'Ertrag Zum besten Nothleidender Burenfrauen'. A chromolithographic card by an unknown publisher and artist was issued for the widows and orphans of fallen Boers. The artist-drawn illustration showed Buller being branded by a Boer.

Early in the War a photolithographic card was published by Paul Bergmann in Munich with the stamp of the Orange Free State embassy in Bavaria and stated that 'five groschen was to be donated to the next of kin of fallen Boers if the official consulate stamp was present'.

When De Wet's exploits brought renewed hope and admiration in Europe the cards reflected the glory, but towards the end of the War the plight of the concentration camp victims became the rallying point of the pro-Boer committees in Europe, and cards were sold to raise funds for the relief of the women and children. Finally after the War, when the Boer delegates toured Europe in August, September and October 1902 to seek financial aid for the reconstruction of the ravaged country, appropriate cards again appeared, including cards showing portraits done by Anton van Wouw and Denizard Orens. Several artist-drawn cards, including mourning cards (1904), depicted Kruger in many heroic poses.

South Africa

The most famous of the South African cards were those depicting the Ladysmith siege. These were undoubtedly the work of Earl Robert of *The Ladysmith Bombshell* fame, and six different versions have been identified by the Anglo-Boer War Philatelic Soceity. The cards were produced in Ladysmith on or around 6 January 1900 and those with postmarks dated earlier than 28 February 1900 are the most sought after.

Herbert Guest, the Klerksdorp publisher, also produced a series of postcards issued at various times throughout the War; some were used as Christmas cards. In June 1900 a 'write away' type of card was issued by an unknown South African publisher to commemorate the occupation of Bloemfontein and Pretoria.

A rare postwar set of cards was the 'South African Souvenir' series based on *The Owl* cartoonist M.C. Richards's feature 'The Army Types', which appeared in *The Owl* for 26 consecutive weeks from March to September 1902. The cards could have been published by *The Owl* in Cape Town but it is known that the firm of E. Wrench Ltd. in England published a later series by Richards.

After the War the South African firms of Sallo Epstein, Hallis & Co., R.O. Füsslein and others issued series of cards showing battlefields, monuments and camp sites. These are mostly divided-back cards, photographic in origin and fairly common. The divided-back card was introduced around August 1902 by the British firm of F. Hartmann. It allowed the address and message to be written on the same side. Previously one side was reserved for the address only, with the result that the picture side had to be defaced in order to send the message. It is safe to say, however, that all contemporary Boer War cards were of the undivided back variety.

Empire

Cards of a patriotic nature featuring their leaders and troops and pledging loyalty to Queen and Empire were published in New Zealand, Canada and Australia. Naturally, because of their smaller print runs, they are much

1 *British troops arresting Boer women and Children.* This highly imaginative postcard illustration was drawn by an unknown artist. The publisher is also unidentified. Several other chromolithographic cards were published in this series.
2 'Homage to Kruger' cards sent to mark his arrival in Europe appeared in several languages, including Russian, Croatian, Dutch, English, Spanish, French and German. They were addressed to him care of his consulate in Paris. This particular card is in Italian and published by Kunzli Frères of Zurich. The illustration was by Arthur Thiele. Note the Vierkleur is the wrong way up, a common error by European illustrators.

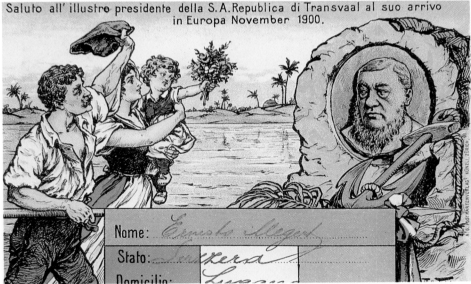

Saluto all' illustre presidente della S.A.Republica di Transvaal al suo arrivo in Europa November 1900.

Nome:
Stato:
Domicilio:

rarer than those of their British or European counterparts and many of these too were the work of unidentified artists. Other cards were produced by publishers in Bermuda, St Helena, Ceylon and India, where the Boer P.O.W. camps were based. These cards featured mainly photographic scenes depicting the prisoners and the 'tourist' attractions of the area. One rare artist-drawn issue of at least three different cards was published by P.O.W.s at Umballa in India using a cyclostyle machine for reproduction. The cards written by P.O.W.s themselves with the various censor markings are particularly sought after. Some of the prisoners painted watercolours and drew scenes of camp life on cards which they then sold to fellow prisoners.

Early in the War the firm of Ed Nels of Brussels featured a series of photographic illustrated cards. Some in

Uitgegeven door de Haagsche Pro-Boervereeniging te 's Gravenhage, Molenstraat 4, ten bate van de gevangen Boerenvrouwen en -kinderen in Z.A.

DIE MIELIEPIT.

Die mieliepiant is door Gods hand
    Aan ons Transvaal gegeven,
Dat mensch en dier nog altijd hier,
    Kan eten en kan leven.

Ons arme land is zwart gebrand
    Door d' Engelsche gebroedsel.
Maar die mieliekop raak nog nie op,
    Hij schenk ons drank en voedsel.

God zij gedaak, nie die soort drank,
    Wat door ou Marks 1) gestook wordt.
Maar mielienat die drink ons, wat
    In die koffiepot gekook wordt.

Vrijstaat het 2) brood. Ons bondgenoot
    Wensch ons geluk daarmede.
Maar voor ons deel — met mieliemeel
    Is ons al hoog tevrede.

In vredestijd — dan zonder strijd —
    Het 2) korenmeel meer waarde,
Maar met oorlog is mielies tog
    Die beste kos op aarde.

Maak kooigoed 3) van zijn blare dan,
    Zijn stronk kan vuur en pijp maak,
Zelfs met zijn as kan jij kleere wasch.
    As jij hom eerst tot zeep maak.

Of wil die Boer ook groene voer
    Aan perd of schaap of os gé' —
Dan weet hij goed wat hij doen moet,
    Wil hij hem lekker kos gé'. —

Maar die mieliepit, ja hij is dit
    Waarvoor ons God het meest moet loven.
Met hom en vlijs 4) zal ons Khaki wijs,
    Ons volk die blijf nog boven.

Op hoeveel wijs tot lekker spijs,
    Jij mielies klaar kan krijge,
Is bo' mijn gal en daarom zal
    Ik dit nu maar verzwijge.

Maar geef mij 'n hap van mieliepap,
    Dan zal ik niks meer zoeke,
Want glo 5) mij vrij, dit smaak voor mij,
    Nog lekkerder dan koeke.

Transvaal bezit die mieliepit;
    Laat Khaki ruk en plukke.
Zijn twak is nat 6); ons land te vat
    Zal hem zoo nooit gelukke.

Waarom is daar een adelaar
    Op ons Transvaalsche wapen?
Zet eers daarop een miliekop
    En laat die roofvo'el schrape.

F. W. REITZ.

1) Samuel Marks : Whisky v Hatherly distillery. 2) Heeft. 3) Matrasvulsel. 4) Vleesch. 5) Geloof. 6) ,,Zijn tabak is nat'' hetgeen beteekent ,,zijn kracht is gedaan''

1

1 *Die Mieliepit*, a Hague pro-Boer society double postcard. The illustrator is unknown.
2 *Mr Atkins*, one of a series of postwar postcard caricatures in the South African Souvenir Series by Captain Mordaunt Richards.

the third series show British prisoners arriving under escort in Pretoria and on the card Winston Churchill is clearly identified.

Besides postcards a number of illustrated Boer War postal covers are also in existence. Some of these, like those produced privately by H. Clark, were hand-painted and designed to brighten up letters sent home. Clark who signed 'H.C.' sent over 20 cartoon covers back to his family. Others were commercially produced, including seven cartoons drawn by Alfred Lyons and produced in Johannesburg to coincide with Christmas and New Year 1901; they were entitled *The Absent Minded Burgher, Xmas on the Veld: Bringing in the Boer's head* and *De Wet's Xmas pudding*.

George Budricks & Co. of Cape Town produced another popular souvenir envelope which was drawn by Sergeant F. Arthur Stevenson on 16 May 1900 and available in at least five different versions. Another possible Budricks production were the 'T.P.' covers which came in at least nine different varieties. Each one differed in some respect from the others with the same title and they were probably mass produced using a hectograph and stencil. A series of cards by Budricks based on these envelopes was issued later in the War. It is believed that these cards were the work of Corporal T. Payne.

The postcards of the War varied enormously in style and quality. Some were of an extremely high standard, especially in their colour reproduction, while others were quite crudely reproduced. The number of artists involved is extensive and a list is provided in Appendix 3.

■

2

CHAPTER THIRTEEN

The Illustrated Novels of the Period

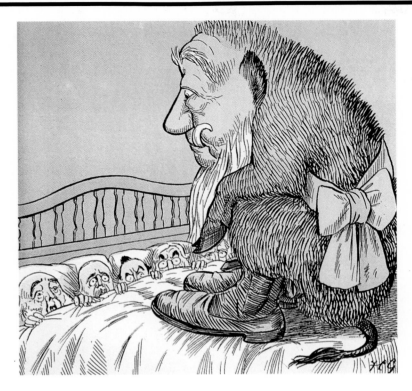

The late Victorian novelists, unlike those of to-day, relied heavily on the assistance of their illustrators to create the image of the characters or events they were trying to portray. One only has to think of Sidney Paget's drawings of his brother Wal as Sherlock Holmes in Arthur Conan Doyle's detective stories to realize that the likeness of Sherlock Holmes can never be anything else to anyone who has read those early novels. Novels, particularly adventure stories for boys and girls, were very popular and had a wide sale. It is estimated that, including modern works, over 250 novels about both Boer wars have been written.

Many of the illustrators discussed in the other chapters were employed by the publishers of these novels. George Henty, himself a cartoonist, illustrator and war correspondent of an earlier era was a prince among his contemporaries and during his working life he wrote over 70 books for boys. He died in 1902, so only a very few of his later works had the war theme. Henty's *With Buller in Natal or A Born Leader* (1901) and *With Roberts to Pretoria: A Tale of the South African War* (1902) were both published by Blackie & Son and illustrated by H. William Rainey. Rainey also did the eight illustrations for *Grit & Go* (1902), which was a collection of short stories by Guy Boothby, George Henty, D. Christie Murray, H. A. Bryden, D. L. Johnstone, Harold Bindlow, Francis O'Neill and S. Annesley. Three of the stories had Africana or Boer War relevance: Boothby's *Steven Whilledge's Revenge*; H. Bryden's *Hendrik Swanepoel's Promised Land* and O'Neill's *De Wet's First and Worst Repulse*.

William Andrew Johnston, a popular author of adventure stories for boys, wrote at least five books on

South African wars but only *The Kopje Farm* (*c.*1900) had a Boer War theme. The 'coloured' illustrations were by Lancelot Speed, although in some editions the illustrations were in black and white only.

Captain Frederick S. Brereton of the Royal Army Medical Corps wrote three adventure stories set in South Africa which were all the more authentic because he saw service there with his unit between 1899 and 1901. Stanley Wood illustrated his earlier work *With Shield and Assegaai: A Tale of the Zulu War* and also one of his Boer War stories *One of the Fighting Scouts* (1902). His other Boer War tale *With Rifle and Bayonet* had eight illustrations by Wal Paget. Bessie Marchant wrote two adventure stories about South Africa. One, a Boer War story, was titled *Tommy's Trek: A Transvaal Story* (1901) and had illustrations by Henry Brock and John Walker. Fred Whishaw also wrote two stories about South Africa, including *The Three Scouts: A Story of the Boer War* (1900), which used George Soper's illustrations. Ernest Glanville was the author of at least 20 novels on South Africa and his *Max Thornton* (1901) had eight illustrations by James Shaw Crompton.

Bertram Mitford was one of the most prolific authors of the period who used South Africa as his inspiration for his adventure stories, and over 50 had Africana relevance. However, only two were about the Boer War: *Aletta: A Tale of Boer Invasion* (1900), which had a frontispiece by A. Wallis Mills, and *A Veldt Vendetta* (1903), which used Gordon Browne's illustrations. The first novel is set in the period before and just after the start of the War.

George Manville Fenn wrote *The Dash from Diamond City* in 1901. It was published simultaneously in

Francis Carruthers Gould's illustration for Harold Begbie's book *The Struwwelpeter Alphabet* (1900). Here the letter 'O', representing the 'Ogre' Kruger is seen frightening members of Lord Salisbury's cabinet.

1

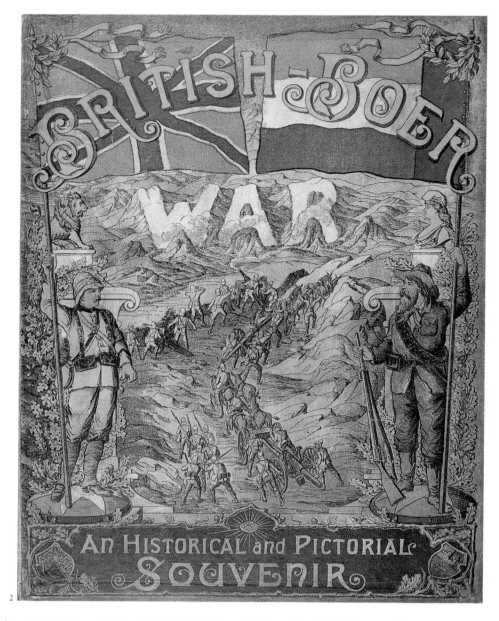

2

London by Ernest Misler and in New York by F.P. Dalton & Co. and illustrated by Frank Stewart.

The Kopje Garrison: A Tale of the Boer War (1901) had eight illustrations by William Boucher and *Charge!: A Story of Briton and Boer* (1900) used William Groome's illustrations. N. Tèstelin was the illustrator for E. Harcourt Burrage's *Carbineer and Scout*, published by Blackie & Son Ltd. in 1901 and 1902.

Joseph Finnemore did the illustrations for William Gordon Stable's *On Special Service: A tale of life at sea* (1901). Harold Piffard provided eight illustrations, including a coloured frontispiece for Tom Bevan's *Dick Dale, The Colonial Scout: A Tale of the Transvaal War 1899-1900*. Clarence Lawson Wood, one of Pearson's illustrators, provided the frontispiece for Harold Blore's 1900 novel *An Imperial Light Horseman*.

In the United States *With Lawton and Roberts: A Boy's Adventure in the Philippines and Transvaal* (1900) by Elbridge Brooks has illustrations by Emerson C. Chase. Another book published in 1900 was Edward Stratemeyer's *Between Boer and Briton* which had eight illustrations by A.B. Shute. F.A. Carter illustrated the English translation of August Niemann's *The*

Boer Boy of the Transvaal (1900).

In Holland the Dutch novelist Louwrens Penning, whose family was in South Africa during the War, wrote *De Leeuw van Modderspruit* and the 1903 edition had three illustrations by Willem Steelink. The book was dedicated to 'General Louis Botha the hero of Colenso and Spion Kop'. *De overwinnaar van Nooitgedacht* had four illustrations by Johan Isings jnr.

De Verdedigers en Verdrukkers der Afrikaansche Vrijheid, also by Penning and published in 1902, featured pen drawings by Hendrik Jan Linse, C. Koppenol and Jan Hoynck van Papendrecht.

All the editions of his *Die verkenner van Christiaan de Wet* used C. Koppenol's illustrations.

Harm Oost's three stories in *De Nieuwe Bibliotheek voor de jeugd* series were all illustrated by W.K. de Bruin.

In Germany Frederich Meister's *Burenblut. Bilder aus dem letzen Transvaalkriege* (1900) was published in Leipzig and illustrated by C. Klingebeil. The novel *Bur und Lord* (1900), based on the diary of an English officer whose author remains anonymous, had a cover illustration by Robert Haug.

4

3

5

1 Many British authors wrote schoolboy adventure novels with a Boer War theme. Their pictorial cloth covers make these books very collectable. Depicted here are F. S. Brereton's *One of the Fighting Scouts*; George Henty's *With Buller in Natal*; Brereton's *With Rifle and Bayonet*; George Hayen's *Scouting for Buller*; William Johnson's *Kopje Farm* and George Henty's *With Roberts to Pretoria*. The *Kopje Farm* illustrator Lancelot Speed has shown a moose swimming in a river — it seems that he confused the fauna of North America with that of Africa.
2 *British-Boer War* by Israel Smith Clare was published by the Souvenir Publishing Co. in 1900. The illustrator of this elaborate pictorial cloth cover is unknown.
3 *Les Jumeaux du Transvaal*, an adventure story about the War by Paul Roland, had this interesting pictorial cover, done by J. Fay, from the illustration on the title page by Paul Giffey.
4 *Kronings-Idylle* was published at the time of Edward VII's coronation by Cohen Zonen of Amsterdam. The text was by Kees van Ponten while 'Chris Kras Kzn' (Johannes Feith) was the illustrator.
5 C. da Amaral's *Le force et le droit* appeared in *La Caricature* on 21 April 1900. At the time a Boer delegation was in America attempting to win support for their cause. While they received a reasonably sympathetic hearing, it was an election year and the United States was not keen to antagonize Britain, particularly as she herself was involved in a colonial war with Spain in both Cuba and the Philippines.

In France Paul Roland wrote *Les Jumeaux du Transvaal* (1906) with illustrations by P. Giffey. Alfred Paris did the illustrations which were engraved by Deloche for *Les Libres Burghers* by G. St Ives. A children's story, *Aventures de Deux Petits Boers Contées par L'Oncle Paul aux Petits Français*, used 13 coloured illustrations by S. Pestillac and another story in a similar vein, *Les Petit Boers* by Marie Lera, had illustrations by Valerie Rottembourg ('V.R.'). *Un Hero de Treize Ans* (1902) by Leo Dex (a pseudonym of Edouard Deburaux) had 17 original illustrations by Hermann Vogel, the *L'Assiette au Beurre* artist, who used a distinctive monogram on these particular drawings. Pierre Guedy, who used the pseudonym Pierre Burel, wrote *Aventures d'un Enfant de Paris au Transvaal*. This book also appeared in weekly episodes. The illustrator was identified as 'Kees'.

Some children's poetry books of the period included: *Clara in Blunderland* (1902), *The Coronation Nonsense Book* (1902) and *Lost in Blunderland: The Further Adventures of Clara* which were written by Caroline Lewis (pseudonym) and illustrated in colour by Stafford Ransome ('S.R.'); *Ten Little Boer Boys* written by 'Norman' and illustrated by Archibald Forrest; *Pictures for Little Englanders* again illustrated by Forrest; *ABC for Baby Patriots* with verses by Ernest Ames and illustrations by his wife Mary Frances; *The Struwwelpeter Alphabet* and its companion volume *The Political Struwwelpeter* written by Harold Begbie with coloured illustrations by Francis Carruthers Gould; and one of the most sought-after children's books from this era John Hassall's *An Active Army Alphabet* (1899).

Colonel W.W. Knolly's *The Story of Earl Roberts V.C.K.G.*, a little booklet published by Raphael Tuck & Sons, has several illustrations both in black and white and colour, but the artist, who was obviously influenced by Richard Caton Woodville, remains anonymous.

A renewed interest in children's books — particularly those with coloured, albeit highly imaginary, illustrations — have made many of these books, which were plentiful in their day, much scarcer.

The Influence of the Anglo-Boer War on European Artists

Recent discoveries of art with a Boer War theme in Europe indicate to some extent the effect the War had on certain European artists. Besides the paintings done for charity productions discussed in Chapter 9, other paintings have come to light from time to time. Most of these are portraits. Kruger, of course, was a favourite subject, but despite the contention that many of these portraits were done from life it is highly unlikely; Kruger disliked having his portrait painted as this conflicted with his ultra-orthodox religious views. The portraits by Léandre and Thérèse Schwartze were discussed in Chapter 8 and recently a portrait by René Gilbert has come to light. This portrait was purchased by the South African Government. Schwartze's portraits of De la Rey and De Wet are in the War Museum of the Boer Republics, Bloemfontein, and her well-known portrait of Piet Joubert, which appeared in *The Sphere*, is also reproduced on a postcard. The Bloemfontein war museum has acquired most of Antoon van Welie's portraits that were exhibited in 1909. Among other subjects exhibited were De la Rey, Joubert, De Wet, Kritzinger, General Ferreira and his wife and Louis Botha and his wife.

In 1902 an interesting art exhibition of over 3 000 works took place in The Hague in Holland to coincide with the visit to the city by De la Rey, De Wet and Botha although the paintings do not seem to have had a Boer War theme. It is not clear if the artworks were sold in aid of the Pro-Boer Committee's funds or whether only the entrance fees were donated. An art lottery was held at the same time and tickets were sold in aid of the Boer cause. Presumably a work or works had been designated as prizes but it is unclear who the lucky winners were or what they won.

Despite the fact that the Art Nouveau movement was well established at the time and Post-Impressionists and other modern art schools and groups were functioning, not much of their influence is noted in Boer War art. There were of course notable exceptions. Pablo Picasso as an 18-year-old was obviously affected by what he had read or heard about the Boers, Chamberlain and the Highland Brigade, because he produced a series of doodles showing his impressions (see p. 185). They are highly fanciful and show pipe-smoking Boers armed with swords and bayonets, Highlanders in kilts labelled 'Ingles' and a monocled individual who is almost certainly meant to represent Chamberlain. These three sheets of doodles are housed in the Picasso Museum in Barcelona.

Paul Berthon, the Art Nouveau artist and lithographer, produced a lithograph of Kruger (not a very good likeness) with destroyed farmhouses burning in the background.

In keeping with the fashion of the times poster art was quite popular and Jules Grün's work *La Boite à Fursy* (see p. 140) stands out as one of the best examples. Among the several heads of state shown on the poster, a smiling Kruger is featured seated next to a monocled Chamberlain. Another fine example is P. Chapellier's large poster *Le Transvaal et L'Afrique Sauvage* depicting a view of Pretoria and the Long Tom cannon used at Ladysmith. Several postcard artists also produced posters including Denizard Orens whose portraits of De la Rey, Georges de Villebois-Mareuil, Louis Botha and De Wet are better known on postcards. The lesser-known lithographer Eugene Ogé was responsible for a large poster which showed a cartoon of Kruger and Queen Victoria.

Perhaps the most important recent finds are the

works of Cornelis De Bruin and Sylvester Reisacher, which have now been acquired by the South African Government.

DE BRUIN'S TABLEAU

European artists were occasionally commissioned by their patrons to produce paintings related to the War. One of the most remarkable stories is that of Cornelis de Bruin. Utrecht-born De Bruin was trained as a painter but eventually worked for De Distel and the well-known tile manufacturer Dordtsche Kunstpotterij. In 1900 a café was built in Rotterdam by a Mr C.N.A. Loots. In keeping with the pro-Boer fervour Mr Loots named his business the 'Café Transvalia'. De Bruin was commissioned to decorate the walls of the café with appropriate tiles.

De Bruin set about his task with great enthusiasm, copying whatever illustrations he could find in the contemporary press, especially C.H. Priem's *De Oorlog in Zuid-Afrika*. It is often said that he was a follower of Richard Caton Woodville but his portrayals, with the exception of *The Battle of Colenso*, which is a direct copy, do not show the British in the usual Caton Woodville-like heroic poses, so this seems unlikely. De Bruin's tableau was constructed of hand-painted tiles 15 cm square, formed into panels with an overall size of 2,3 x 1,5 m, and each scene and portrait had a Jugenstil (Art Nouveau) border. The scenes depicted were *Ladysmith, Modder River, Stormberg, Magersfontein, Colenso, Spioen Kop, Paardeberg* and *Reddersburg*. The portraits were of Louis Botha, Dr H. Coster, Col. de Villebois-Mareuil and Gen. J. H. M. Kock.

In 1969 Dr Willem Punt, the then director of the Simon van der Stel Foundation, was informed by the Nederlands-Zuidafrikaanse Vereniging that the building

Tiles by Cornelis de Bruin depicting (from left to right)
the battles of Colenso, Ladysmith, Stormberg, Magersfontein,
Spioenkop and Paardeberg. Reproduced by kind permission of
the War Museum of the Boer Republics, Bloemfontein.

containing the tiles (the café had been converted
to a theatre and then a cinema) was about to be
demolished. The tiles had in fact been hidden under
wallpaper for over 30 years. Punt went over to
Holland where he concluded a deal, ahead of
bidding from England and the United States, which
ensured that the tiles would be sent to South Africa.
He also managed to trace one of the employees at the
De Distel tile factory, 88-year old Willem van Norden,
who remembered the manufacture and installation of
the tiles, and was able to name the artist responsible
for the work. He also recalled that other generals had
been portrayed, a fact which was confirmed by
contemporary press reports. The missing panels,
which had been destroyed when the café was altered
in 1907, were of Cronje, De Wet, De la Rey, Joubert
and Penn Symons. Only Cronje's caption existed.
Eventually with the help of an expert tile restorer,
J. Curvers, who took six months to complete his task,
the 2 500 tiles were removed, packed and sent off to
South Africa. On 24 November 1970 the then
Minister of Defence, P.W. Botha, opened the
exhibition of the tiles at the new Transvaal Provincial
Administration building in Pretoria. In 1980 the
collection was installed in the Bloemfontein war
museum. The story of the rediscovery of the tiles and
their subsequent transportation piece by piece to
South Africa is told in *Historic Tableaux on Tiles*
published by the Publicity and Travel Department,
South African Railways and Airways in 1970.

THE SYLVESTER REISACHER OIL PANELS
Another remarkable story was that of the five large
Sylvester Reisacher oil panels which were also
rediscovered in Europe. These enormous panels,
which depict *The Siege of Ladysmith, The Battle of*
Colenso, The Battle of Spion Kop, The Battle and
Siege of Paardeberg and *Breakthrough of General de*
Wet through British lines were found rolled up in a
trunk in Germany by Dr C.L. de Bruyn of Pretoria.
A Mr B. Heimann of Cape Town had recalled that a
friend of his father's had commissioned the paintings
to hang in the foyer of his clothing factory. The artist
Reisacher, an inveterate traveller, was born in
Germany in 1862. he had had military art training
and because of the wealth of detail in his paintings it
was thought that he may have been an eyewitness to
the events he portrayed. However despite extensive
research no evidence has come to light that he ever
travelled to South Africa. In April 1972 the paintings
were bought for the National Cultural History
Museum in Pretoria. Tom Hennings of the National
Cultural History Museum described their discovery in
his book *Vyf Skilderye oor die Tweede*
Vryheidsoorlog which was published to coincide
with an exhibition of the paintings opened by Dr Piet
Koornhof, the then minister of Education, on
2 September 1976.

A perusal of European auctioneers' and dealers'
catalogues indicates that much Boer War
iconographic material, including pottery, books,
souvenirs, newspapers, postcards and artwork, is still
obtainable on the Continent. It is surely only a matter
of time before other exciting finds of major artworks
come to light.

PART FIVE

THE BIOGRAPHIES

·Pour les Boers·
Louise Abbéma

ABBÉMA, Louise 1858-1927 1
Painter, etcher, sculptor and Art Nouveau postcard artist. Abbéma was born at Etampes, France, on 30 October 1858. A pupil of Chaplin, Henner and Carolus-Duran, she exhibited at the Salon des Artistes Français and is best known for her portrait of Sarah Bernhardt. Her engraving entitled *Pour les Boers* appears in *Paris-Pretoria*. She died in Paris in 1927.
> *Bénézit, Dictionnaire antique, vol. 1, p. 6*
> *Holt, Tonie and Valmai, Stanley Gibbons Postcard Catalogue, (1985), p. 37*
> *Paris-Pretoria, p. 13*

ADAMS, Douglas 1853-1920
A landscape painter, mainly of Scottish subjects. Adams exhibited at the Royal Academy from 1880. In 1900 his painting entitled *Straight for the Guns*, presumably of Boer War interest, was exhibited.
> *Graves, Royal Academy, vol. 1, p. 6*

A.E.C.
This illustrator, who is credited with contributions to *The Graphic*, is probably Algernon Essex Capell. Another individual signing himself 'A.E.C.', also possibly Capell, submitted a poem entitled 'Silent Army' to *The Friend*. Julian Ralph reproduced this poem in his book *War's Brighter Side*.
> *Hofmeyr, Matton and Roets, Graphic Picture Index*
> *Ralph, War's Brighter Side, pp. 277-278*

A.F.
Postcard artist responsible for some of the Bruno Burger *Der Boerenkrieg* series. Cards 6069, 6070, 6151 and 6152 are signed 'A.F.'. No. 6153 is unsigned but similar in style. (See Kleinhempel, G.)

ALDIN, Cecil Charles Windsor 1870-1935
Sporting artist and humorous illustrator. Born in Slough on 28 April 1870, he was educated at Solihull Grammar School and Eastbourne College. He studied anatomy at the South Kensington School of Art and animal painting under Frank Calderon. His first drawing for *The Graphic* was published in 1891, forming what was to be a long association with the magazine.

He illustrated Kipling's *Jungle Stories* for *Pall Mall Budget* (1894-5) and contributed a series of sporting colour prints. Other illustrations appeared in *Pickwick Papers* (1910), *Handley Cross* (1912), and *12 Hunting Countries* (1912-13).

Aldin exhibited at the Royal Academy in 1904, and in 1918 two of his pictures, *A Land Girl Ploughing* and *Women Employed at the Remount Depot*, were purchased by the Imperial War Museum.

He published many books including *Ratcatcher to Scarlet* in 1926; *Dogs of Character* (1927); *The Romance of the Road* (1928); *An Artist's Models* (1930); *Scarlet to MFH* and – with J.B. Morton – *Who's Who at the Zoo* (1933). He published his autobiography, *Time I was Dead*, in 1934. He died on 6 January 1935.

Aldin did not do many Boer War illustrations. One photogravure in colour entitled *Bobs as Schoolmaster* was advertised in *The Illustrated London News* on 29 December 1900. It was offered for sale at 2/6d. *Bobs as Schoolmaster* was the title of quite a few illustrations by other artists including Arthur Drummond, F.J. Waugh, Lester Ralph and the unknown illustrator of Col. W.W. Knollys' *The Story of Earl Roberts V.C. K.G.*, but Aldin's was possibly the original.

Another illustration by Aldin that is of South African interest (but not to do with the Boer War) appeared in *The Illustrated London News* on 18 December 1897. It featured the giraffe presented to Queen Victoria by King Khama. Aldin's work, which is very sought after today, was used extensively on advertising posters and postcards, particularly by the firm of Valentine and Sons Ltd. Aldin was also a contributor to the souvenir programme of the 'National Bazaar in Aid of the Sufferers by the War'. One illustration depicting a wounded bulldog was entitled *Things like this, you know, must be after a famous victory.*
> *Cuppleditch, London Sketch Club, p. 42*
> *Graves, Royal Academy, vol. 1, p. 18*
> *Heron, Cecil Aldin*
> *Who was Who, vol. 3, p. 14*

ALEC, B.
Le Rire caricaturist whose portraits of Kruger and Chamberlain appeared in the publication on 10 May 1902.

ALLOM, W.J.
Australian artist who painted *SS Warrigal leaving Sydney Harbour. A Battery off to war per Warrigal 1899* (oil on canvas). This painting was offered for sale by Sotheby's, London, on 28 May 1981.

ALMOND, William Douglas 1866-1916
Illustrator. Almond was born in London on 28 April 1866 and educated at the King's College School and the Langham Life Class. He worked for *English Illustrated Magazine* and *The Illustrated London News*, where he was designated special artist of 'character subjects'. He exhibited at the Royal Academy from 1893 to 1904. Among his favourite subjects were the Cavaliers and Roundheads, featured in *In Council* (1899). He was a member of the R.B.A., Savage Club and Langham Sketching Club, acting as curator at the last-mentioned for many years. Almond exhibited at the R.O.I., R.S.A., R.B.A., Fine Art Gallery in London, Glasgow Institute of the Fine Arts, Walker Gallery in Liverpool and Manchester Art Gallery. His Boer War work appeared in *The Graphic*, *The Illustrated London News* and *With the Flag to Pretoria*. He died on 12 March 1916.
> *Graves, Royal Academy, vol. 1, p. 29*
> The Studio, 'The Langham Sketching Club', vol. 32, p. 279-298
> *Who was Who, vol. 2, p. 19*

AMARAL, C. DA (TARSILA) 4
Probably the Brazilian-born artist who was a pupil of Pedro Alexandrino and M.E. Renard and who exhibited a portrait at the Salon des Artistes Français in 1922. He worked as cartoonist and caricaturist for both *Le Bon Vivant* and *La Caricature* from 1899 to 1900. Several of his coloured anti-British cartoons appeared on the front cover of *La Caricature*, including *English correction par Amaral* 1039 (25 November 1899); *Épilogue de la Guerre du Transvaal* 1042 (16 December 1899); *Le 'Christmas' de la Reine* 1043 (23 December 1899); *La Dame de Chez Maxim* 1044 (30 December 1899); *Le Spectre de Banquo* 1047 (20 January 1900); *Le Cavalerie de Saint George* 1053 (3 March 1900); *Étrange victoire* 1058 (7 April 1900); *Avant Sainte Hélène* 1059 (14 April 1900); *La Force et le droit* 1060 (21 April 1900), and *Nouveau jeu de Football* 1063 (12 May 1900). His black and white inside full-page cartoons were: *Le Fils a Mammon* 1045 (3 January 1900); *Gâte-sauce* 1052 (24 February 1900) and *Bien Rugi, Lions* 1054 (10 March 1900). His controversial cartoon of Kruger beating Queen Victoria's bare buttocks, taken from the cover of *La Caricature* (25 November 1899), was reproduced on several postcards with the title *Die slag op Modder River*.
> *Bénézit, Dictionnaire antique, vol. 1, p. 137*

AMATO, Gennaro 1857-1949
Italian illustrator, also known as D'Amato. He was born in Naples in 1857. He worked for both *The Illustrated London News* and *L'Illustration* and exhibited at the Royal Academy in 1899. Amato illustrated scenes of Rhodes's funeral and the arrival of President Kruger at Marseilles for *The Illustrated London News*, and his illustration *La défense d'un Train Blindé* from *L'Illustration* (16 December 1899) appears as No. 1669 in the *La Guerre au Transvaal* series of postcards.
> *Osterwalder, Dictionnaire des Illustrateurs, Hubschmid and Bouret (eds.), p. 47*
> *SAPRG Newsletter, No. 13, p. 2 (August 1984)*

AMES, Mary Frances 2
Illustrator. Ames collaborated with her husband, Ernest, on two children's books: *An ABC for Baby Patriots* and *The Tremendous Twins or How the Boers were Beaten* (Grant Richards, London, 1900). She signed these illustrations 'M.A.'.
> *SABIB, vol. 1, p. 60*

ANDRÉ
The identity of this cartoonist is unknown, but examples of his Boer War work appear in *Der Floh*.

ANDRÉ, Richard fl. 1880-1907 1
Golfing and children's book illustrator. His watercolour *Kruger's Golf* was used for a poster which advertised the annual dinner of the West Hertfordshire Golf Club on 4 November 1896 held at the Café Monico in London. He was the author of *Colonel Bogey's Sketchbook Comprising an Eccentric Collection of Scribbles and Scratches Found in Disused*

Lockers and Swept Up in the Pavilion Together with Sunday After Dinner Sayings of the Colonel (Longman Green, London, 1897) and *Golf Plays and Recitations* (R. A. Everett, London, 1903).

Houfe, British Illustrators and Caricaturists, *p. 219*

ANDRIEUX, Alfred-Louis ?-1945
French painter and engraver. He collaborated with F. Méaulle, C. Crespin and P. Carrey on the coloured cover illustrations for *Le Petit Parisien* during the latter part of the Boer War.
Bénézit, Dictionnaire antique, *vol. 1, p. 173*

A.R.
A Dutch postcard illustrator whose series of eight cards published in 1900 included two with Boer War themes: *Na den oorlog afrekenen* and *John Bull as Cyrano de Bergerac*.

ARDAGH, John Charles (1840-1907)
Major General of the Claims Commission in South Africa in 1901. The painter of *Landscape surrounding Spion Kop* (watercolour), he is known to have done other South African scenes.
Verbeek, Early Natal Art
Who Was Who, *vol. 1, p. 22*

ARMOUR, George Denholm 1864-1949
Black and white artist and illustrator. Armour was born in Lanarkshire, Scotland, on 30 June 1864. He saw action in World War I, reaching the rank of lieutenant colonel. Often signed 'G.D.A.', his illustrations depicting sporting and eques-

trian scenes appeared in the magazine *Punch*, as did his Boer War work. Armour's autobiography *Bridle and Brush* was published in 1937. He died on 17 February 1949.
Armour, Bridle and Brush
Houfe, British Illustrators and Caricaturists, *p. 222*

ARONSON, Nachum
Russian-born sculptor who exhibited in Paris, Berlin and Bonn. During the Boer War he sculpted a bust of De Wet from photographs. His other works include a bust of Lenin, which was completed in 1937.
Bénézit, Dictionnaire antique, *vol. 1, p. 251*
Rosenthal, General de Wet, *p. 212*

A.S.
The cartoonist using these initials worked for the Dutch periodical *Kloods Hans*.

ASHTON, George Rossi fl. 1874-1902   1
Artist and illustrator. Ashton started his career as an artist working for *The Graphic*. In 1877 he was sent out to South Africa to represent *The Illustrated London News*. He joined the Cape Mounted Police and fought in the last Frontier War in 1878 and in the Zulu War under Gen. Buller in 1879. Three of his identified illustrations in *The Illustrated London News* are credited to J.R. Ashton. He later worked in Australia as an artist-correspondent for the English newspapers and for the *Sydney Bulletin*, where he worked with Phil May (see page 168).
    Ashton returned to England in 1894 and worked for *The*

Daily Graphic, Lika Joko, Pearson's Magazine, St James Budget, Fun, Illustrated Bits, Pall Mall Magazine and *The Sketch*. At the outbreak of the Boer War he obtained employment at the Alhambra Theatre doing a most unusual music-hall act. In time to music provided by the orchestra and attired in full tropical kit he would create a large sketch using subjects related to the War. He would finish the sketch in exactly 60 seconds while the audience cheered him on. Presumably the sketch was sold or auctioned later. Among the subjects chosen were portraits of Roberts, Buller and Kruger, but the most popular was *One for Majuba* which showed a Highlander bayoneting a Boer. A report in Arthur Pearson's *Royal Magazine* (Vol. 3, November 1899 – April 1900) stated that this picture 'is always completed amid howls of enthusiasm while that of Kruger is a favourite for derision'.
Houfe, British Illustrators and Caricaturists, *p. 223*
De Wet, Illustrated London News Index
Royal Magazine, *vol. 3, p. 401*
The Strand Magazine, *vol. 23, pp. 659 ff.*

---

1 *Pour les Boers*, the engraving by Louise Abbéma that appeared in the publication *Paris-Pretoria*.
2 *The Tremendous Twins or How the Boers were Beaten*, a children's storybook, was illustrated by Mary Ames, wife of the author Ernest Ames.
3 One of the pictures from Mary Ames's *The Tremendous Twins* shows a defeated Kruger leaving the Transvaal with his 'millions'.
4 *Kruger's Golf*, a watercolour poster by Richard André advertising a performance at the West Herts Golf Club annual dinner, 1896.
5 George Rossi Ashton is shown here producing his rapid sketches of Boer War personalities in his music-hall act.

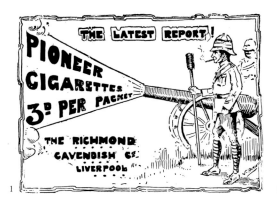

ASHWITH, William 1

Illustrator of the Pioneer cigarette advertisement: 'De Wet and Pioneer Cigarettes. Both are much sought after' appeared in *The Illustrated London News* (16 March 1901) and *The Sphere* (11 May 1901).

AULENT, A.

Sculptor of a 36-cm-high bronze statue depicting a Boer horseman holding a rifle on his thigh, inscribed 'Copie van den Boereruiter te Bratina voor Generaal Cronje en zyn Boeren'. It was presented to President Paul Kruger in 1900 by Tsar Nicholas II and is currently housed in the Kruger House Museum in Pretoria.

AUSTEN, Edward G.

Leslie's Weekly artist who provided occasional Boer War illustrations.

BACON, John Henry Frederick 1865-1914 2

Illustrator and watercolourist. Bacon was born in London in 1865, the second son of John Cardanell Bacon, a lithographer. He attended the R.A. schools, where his talent won him many distinctions. His first picture, *Dead*, was completed at the age of 23. This was followed by *The Announcement*, which was exhibited at the Royal Academy in 1889 and later shown under the new title *Young Widow*. The French Government wanted to buy this work, but the copyright had already been acquired by a firm of art publishers. Another of Bacon's pictures, *Forgiven*, was exhibited at the Royal Academy in 1891 and lent thereafter to the postwar exhibition in aid of the Guildhall fund for the widows and orphans of those who had died in the Boer War.

One of Bacon's best-known pictures is *Vive L'Empereur!*, which depicts the return of the City Imperial Volunteers from South Africa in 1900. Exhibited at the Royal Academy in 1902, this painting, which is now in the Guildhall in London, earned him A.R.A. during that year. His Boer War work was often reproduced as photogravures. *The Relief of Ladysmith* was offered in an advertisement in *The Illustrated London News* in 1901 by the manufacturers of Bovril in exchange for 21 shillings worth of coupons. Bacon also contributed many illustrations to *With the Flag to Pretoria* and *After Pretoria: the Guerilla War*, *Black & White* and *Black & White Budget*. He illustrated *The King's Empire* (Cassell & Co., 1906) and *Celtic Myth and Legend* by C. Squire (1912). *For King and Fatherland* was purchased in 1901 by the Durban art gallery. Three other paintings which were accepted by the Royal Academy were inspired by the Boer War: *Ordered South*

(1900), *The Return* (1901) and *Your Sovereign, etc.* (1902). Photogravures after these pictures were published by C. W. Faulkner and Co. Extant Boer War works by Bacon include a wash drawing entitled *Boers firing on stretcher bearers*.

Bacon's later work took the form mainly of portraiture including the memorial picture of Sir Henry Campbell-Bannerman for the Reform Club. He painted the coronation of King George V in 1911. He was awarded the M.V.O. in 1913 and died on 24 January the following year. Examples of his work are to be found in the British Museum.

Bénézit, Dictionnaire antique, *vol. 1, p. 331*
The Graphic *(1 January 1903)*
Graves, Royal Academy, *vol. 1, p. 89*
The Illustrated London News *(31 January 1903)*
The Times *(26 January 1914)*
Who was Who, *vol. 1, p. 31*

BADEN-POWELL, Frank Smyth 1850-1933

Painter and sculptor. Frank Baden-Powell was born in Oxford in 1850, the elder brother of Robert Baden-Powell (see below). He studied art in Paris under Duran and Rodin, and exhibited at the Royal Academy from 1880. A picture completed in 1888 featured his more famous brother and was entitled *Lieutenant Baden-Powell and the Camel Corps*. Another picture, with a similar subject, was exhibited at the Royal Academy and entitled *Colonel Baden-Powell at Mafeking*. (This painting is not listed in Graves.) He travelled around the world in 1902 and, according to R. F. Kennedy in *Catalogue of Pictures in the Africana Museum*, visited Johannesburg. The watercolour, *General Baden-Powell's house in Johannesburg* (1902), is presumably postwar. Baden-Powell died in London on 25 December 1933.

Graves, Royal Academy, *vol. 1, p. 90*
Kennedy, Pictures in the Africana Museum, *vol. 4, p. 96*
Who was Who, *vol. 3, p. 49*

BADEN-POWELL, Robert Stephenson Smyth 1857-1941 2

Illustrator and sculptor. Brother of Frank (see above), Robert was born in London on 22 February 1857, the sixth son of the Revd. Baden-Powell, Professor of Geometry at Oxford, and his third wife, Henrietta Grace Smyth, a niece of Lord Nelson. He was educated at Charterhouse, but failed to gain admission to Oxford. In September 1876 Baden-Powell joined the 13th Hussars as a sublieutenant and sailed to India. He was promoted to captain in 1883.

En route to England in 1884, Baden-Powell disembarked at Natal, because of trouble over Bechuanaland. Disguised as a reporter, he surveyed the lesser-known Drakensberg passes,

mapping an area previously regarded as unexplored. He then spent six months hunting in East Africa before returning to England. In 1888 he returned to the Cape as aide-de-camp to his uncle, Lt. Gen. H.A. Smyth, taking part in the Zulu Campaign against Dinizulu. In late 1889 he was promoted to brevet major, acting as secretary to the mixed British and Transvaal Commission in Swaziland. He took this opportunity to send sketches of the negotiations to *The Illustrated London News*.

Baden-Powell then spent three years in Malta as assistant military secretary, followed by two years in Ireland. In 1895 he was ordered to organize a native levy for the Ashanti Expedition. After a successful campaign he was promoted again, this time to brevet lieutenant colonel. He had been gazetted for special duties in Matabeleland when the rebellion broke out there in 1896. As chief staff officer he was stationed at Bulawayo and it was because of his skilful night-scouting that the positions of the native impis in the Matopos were discovered. These activities, described in *The Matabele Campaign* (1897), earned him the name 'Impeesa' (the wolf that never sleeps) and promotion to brevet colonel. He returned to India to command the 5th Dragoons and it was there that he published *Aids to Scouting* (1899).

In June 1899 Baden-Powell was sent to South Africa again, this time with orders to raise two regiments for the defence of Bechuanaland and Matabeleland. When war broke out on 11 October one regiment was despatched to protect the Rhodesian border, while the other remained with him in Mafeking. The Siege of Mafeking is well documented, and many books and articles are devoted to Baden-Powell's role in the siege. He is probably the only commander of the besieged towns who came out of the War with any credit, although he is reputed to have annoyed Queen Victoria by issuing postage stamps bearing his own likeness. During the siege he used his talents as an artist (the famous £1 note was produced from his design) and actor to keep the beleaguered garrison entertained. After the siege he was promoted to major general and greeted as a hero in Britain. On his return to South Africa, Baden-Powell led the forces that took part in the first 'De Wet Hunt' in the north-western Transvaal. In August 1900 he was recalled by Milner to raise and train the South African Constabulary (to serve in the areas cleared of Boer commandos) and within a year he had a force of 9 000 men ready for service.

In 1903 Baden-Powell returned to Britain as inspector-general of Cavalry, establishing the Cavalry School at Netheravon and founding the *Cavalry Journal*. In 1906 he accompanied the Duke of Connaught to South Africa, returning via

East Africa. His *Sketches in Mafeking and East Africa* (1907) commemorate this tour. In 1908 he was promoted to lieutenant general and he assumed command of the Northumbrian division of the Territorials. In the same year his book *Scouting for Boys* appeared.

Baden-Powell resigned from the army in May 1910, thereafter devoting himself to the Boy Scout movement which he had founded. He visited South Africa as Chief Scout in 1925 and 1936. In 1938 he returned to Kenya where he remained until his death in 1941. His honorary awards include the K.C.B. (1909); a baronetcy (1921); the G.C.V.O. (1923), and the G.C.M.G. (1927).

Baden-Powell is the best-known soldier-artist of the War. He is the author of 35 books (most of which he illustrated himself), including *Reconnoissance and Scouting* (1884), *Cavalry Instruction* (1885) and *Pigsticking or Hoghunting* (1889).

Throughout his life he illustrated his letters and diaries with sketches of his experiences. During the Siege of Mafeking he contributed to The Graphic, *The Illustrated London News* and *The Sphere*. His work was also reproduced in *After Pretoria: the Guerilla War*, *With the Flag to Pretoria* and *Black & White*, among others. He was a member of the London Sketch Club, and his sketches can be found in the South African Library and the Zimbabwean (formerly Rhodesian) National Archives. The Royal Collection at Windsor has two of Baden-Powell's Boer War works: *Men of the Protectorate Regiment and the Rhodesian Regiment* and *South African Constabulary*.

> *Carter,* War Artists in S.A., p. 16
> The Graphic, *26 May 1900, p. 762*
> *Grinnell-Milne,* Baden-Powell at Mafeking
> The Illustrated London News, *2 June 1900*
> Mafeking Siege Slips, *p. 103*
> The Sketch, *28 March 1900, p. 420*
> The Sphere, *Supp. 26 May 1900*

BAER, Gil
French cartoonist for *Le Supplement* and *Le Rire*.

BAETES, Jules 1861-?
Belgian artist and engraver. Baetes was born in Antwerp on 1 October 1861. His work appeared in *Antwerpen-Transvaal Gedenknummer* (March-April 1902) and on a postcard entitled *Zuid-Afrika Nederduitsch!*, which was issued by the Antwerp branch of the Algemeen Nederlandsche verbond. The postcard showed the Vierkleur and Transvaal coat of arms being threatened by a lion and an eagle. A German version was published by Hilfs-Ausschuss: 'Für Transvaal und Oranje-Freistaat zu Antwerpen'.

> *Bénézit,* Dictionnaire antique, *vol. 1, p. 338*

BAGGIE, Paul
Oil painter. His painting depicting a Boer consoling his wife can be found in the Potchefstroom Museum. It was probably copied from the Dutch postcard, *Naar Harde Strÿd* (B. Brugsma AZ, Utrecht), reputedly illustrated originally by the German artist Marie Pischon. The postcard illustration shows greater detail than Baggie's painting and was reproduced on posters in the Netherlands after the War.

> Bloemfontein War Museum Catalogue
> *Kriel and De Villiers (ed.),* Rondom die Anglo-Boereoorlog, *p. 152*

BAHR, E.
Cartoonist for *Lustige Blätter* who used the monogram 'E.B.'.

BAILEY, G. C.
Illustrator. His Boer War sketch, which appeared in *The Graphic* (4 November 1899), was redrawn by F.C. Dickinson and entitled *Churchyard at Dundee where Sir W.P. Symons was buried.*

> *Hofmeyr, Matton and Roets,* Graphic Picture Index

BAILLIE, Frederick David 1862-1924 1
Illustrator. Baillie was born in 1862, the son of Col. James William Murray Baillie. He was educated at Eton. He was a major in the 4th Queen's Own Hussars and later saw action in World War I. As the correspondent for *The Morning Post* during the Siege of Mafeking, he produced at that time *Mafeking: A Diary of a Siege* (Archibald Constable and Co. Ltd, Westminster, 1900), which includes his sketches from *The Daily Graphic*. Copies of the book usually have a facsimile siege slip bound in at the end.

He left Mafeking on 20 May 1900 after the relief and returned to London aboard the *Norman*. He continued to contribute to *The Graphic*, including the well-known work *Last attack on Mafeking* (7 July 1900). His sketches of Mafeking appeared (redrawn by home-based artists) in *The Daily Graphic*, *The Graphic* and Creswicke's *South Africa and the Transvaal War*. In Wentworth Huyse's *The Graphic History of the South African War* Baillie gives a full account of the Siege of Mafeking. His article is illustrated with sketches again redrawn by home-based artists, without giving him credit. He was responsible for the well-known illustration entitled *The Relief of Mafeking: The march past of the relieving forces before Lieutenant General Baden-Powell*, which appeared, redrawn by W. Small, in *The Graphic* (30 June 1900). Baillie received the Queen's South Africa medal on 16 February 1903.

> The Graphic *(21 October 1899)*
> *Hofmeyr, Matton and Roets,* Graphic Picture Index
> The Orders and Medals Research Society, *Summer 1986,* 'War Correspondents: South Africa 1899-1902', *by Patrick Street*

BALL, Alec C. fl.1900-1910 1
Illustrator for *Harmsworth Magazine* and *The Graphic* between 1905 and 1910. He exhibited two paintings at the Royal Academy and his Boer War illustrations appeared in *With the Flag To Pretoria* and *After Pretoria: the Guerilla War*. The author has a watercolour *Escape of one of Plumers Scouts on 13 Feb 1901*, which appeared in Vol. 1 of *After Pretoria: the Guerilla War*.

> *Houfe,* British Illustrators and Caricaturists, *p. 225*
> *Johnson and* Greutzner, British Artists, *p. 38*

BANKS, H. G.
Illustrator. Three of his lithographs appear on music covers to be found in the National Army Museum: *Songs for Soldiers, Humorous, Pathetic and Descriptive with tonic Sol-Fa setting* (Reeder and Walsh) with an illustration of a cavalry trumpeter in khaki drill uniform; *Bravo! Dublin Fusiliers! or Ireland's Reply* (Francis Day and Hunter) with a vignette showing the Dublin Fusiliers in hand-to-hand action with the Boers, and *Some Mothers Will Lose a Son* (Francis Day and Hunter) commemorating the charge of the Royal Irish Fusiliers at Colenso in 1899.

BANNERMAN, Alexander Islay
Edinburgh artist who worked for the postcard publishers George Stewart & Co. Ltd. He was probably responsible for the design of at least six of their Boer War postcards: *Relief of Ladysmith, Cape to Cairo Route, Soldiers of the Empire, Col. Baden-Powell, Siege of Mafeking* and *Kruger Staggering Humanity.*

> *Byatt,* Picture Postcards, *p. 274*

BANTJIES, Jan Gerrit 1864-?
Soldier-artist. No. 2622 of the Van Aswegen Field Cornetcy, he was recruited from Ventersdorp in the Potchefstroom district. He was captured at Paardeberg on 27 February 1900 and sent to Diyatalawa in Ceylon as a P.O.W. He advertised his services in *De Krijgsgevangene*, a weekly journal published by the Boer P.O.W.s, as follows: 'J.G. Bantjies "Painter of the Battle of Sanna's Post" invites orders for pictures in oil or water colours. Studio at the grass house residence hut 43.' He was discharged and returned to South Africa on 28

4

August 1902. None of his works appears to have survived.

> *Mendelssohn,* Mendelssohn's S.A. Biography, *vol. 2, p. 378*
> *Personal communication with M. Minnie, Director, State Archives, Pretoria*

BARAGWANATH, Fred 1875-?
Soldier-artist. Baragwanath was a draughtsman who enrolled in the C.I.V. on 8 July 1891 as a lance corporal with the First London Royal Engineers. His work is similar to that of Tom Baragwanath (see below), who is assumed to have been his brother. Both Baragwanaths were members of the first volunteer contingent that left London on 20 December 1899. The facsimile sketch showing the C.I.V. camp at Britstown and entitled *It was in the neighbourhood of Britstown that a sharp fight occurred on 6 March, in which eight of the C.I.V. were wounded and six reported missing* appeared in the C.I.V. *City Press Souvenir* No. 4. His illustration, redrawn by Frederic de Haenen and entitled *The City Imperial Volunteers in action: A reconnaissance in force near Britstown*, appeared in *The Graphic* on 21 April 1900.

> *C.I.V.* City Press Souvenir, *nos. 2 and 4*
> *Guildhall Library: Personal communication with Godfrey Thompson, City Librarian and Director*
> *Hofmeyr, Matton and Roets,* Graphic Picture Index

BARAGWANATH, Thomas P. 1871-? 1
Soldier-artist. Like his brother Fred (see above), Thomas Baragwanath was a draughtsman who enrolled with the First London Royal Engineers of the C.I.V., but in Thomas's case eight years later in 1899. The brothers were among the earliest members of the C.I.V. to arrive in South Africa. Thomas saw action at Bloemfontein, Lindley, Bethlehem, Bultfontein, Slabbertsnek, Fouriesberg and finally Pretoria. He was a member of the C.I.V. contingent which left Cape Town aboard the *Aurania* on 7 October 1900, arriving in London on Saturday 27 October 1900. His sketches were reproduced (some-

---

1 William Ashwith's Pioneer Cigarette advertisement.
2 *The Return*, an oil on canvas by John Henry Frederick Bacon, was exhibited at the Royal Academy in 1901.
3 Robert Baden-Powell's pen-and-ink and colour sketch entitled *Men of the Protectorate Regiment and the Rhodesian Regiment* is in the Royal Collection, Windsor. Reproduced by gracious permission of Her Majesty, Queen Elizabeth II.
4 *Escape of one of Plumer's Scouts* by Alec. C. Ball depicted an incident in which Plumer's Scouts attacked De Wet's farm and slowly pushed the Boers back, but two scouts on patrol were taken by surprise by four Boers at a deserted farmhouse. One scout surrendered, while the other escaped under a shower of bullets. The illustration was reproduced in *After Pretoria: the Guerilla War.*

times in facsimile) in *The Sphere* and *With the Flag to Pretoria*. *The Sphere* records that he saw action on 27 February 1900 while the majority of the C.I.V. was still aboard the *Montfort*. An original letter and accompanying pencil sketch signed 'Tom Baragwanath, 22 July 1900' can be found in the Africana Museum. The sketch is entitled *Incident in the South African War 1900*.

> *Childers,* The C.I.V.
> *C.I.V.* City Press Souvenir, *nos. 2 and 4*
> *Kennedy,* Pictures in the Africana Museum, *vol. 6, p. 5*
> *Records of the C.I.V. Guildhall Library: Personal communication with Godfrey Thompson, City Librarian and Director*
> The Sphere *(4 August 1900)*

BARNARD, J. Langton 1853-?
Genre painter. Barnard was born in London in 1853 and exhibited at principal galleries there, including the Royal Academy, from 1876 to 1902. His wife, formerly Emily Cummins, was a landscape painter. Barnard's Boer War illustrations appeared in *After Pretoria: the Guerilla War*.

> *Johnson and Greutzner,* British Artists, *p. 42*
> *Waters,* British Artists, *vol. 1, p. 21*
> *Wood,* Victorian Painters, *p. 36*

BARNES, W.
Possibly William Rodway Barnes who worked between 1885 and 1918. He provided two illustrations in *The Graphic* (25 November 1899), taken from sketches by F. W. Dimock Brown and entitled *Views of Estcourt in Natal beleaguered by the Boers*.

> *Hofmeyr, Matton and Roets,* Graphic Picture Index

BARRAUD, Allan F. fl. 1873-1908
Landscape painter, etcher and postcard artist. Barraud exhibited at the Royal Academy from 1873 to 1900, as well as at the R.B.A. and R.O.I. His Boer War work consists of two illustrations from photographs of Worcester and Burgersdorp in *After Pretoria: the Guerilla War*.

> *Johnson and Greutzner,* British Artists, *p. 43*
> *Mallalieu,* British Watercolour Artists, *p. 25*
> *Mead, Venman and Whitney,* Picton's Priced Catalogue
> *Wood,* Victorian Painters, *p. 37*

BARSTOW, Henry George Montague McLean ?-1943

British cartoonist for *Ludgate Monthly, Windsor Magazine, Royal Magazine* and *Pick-Me-Up*. According to Thorpe, his work was of a 'photographic nature'. The publishers of *Pick-Me-Up* offered 'copies of pictures for mounting and framing by Montague Barstow on plate paper at sixpence each post free'. *Burenstreiche* has a reproduction of one of his *Pick-Me-Up* cartoons. He married Baroness Emma Orczy, an artist who was best known as the author of *The Scarlet Pimpernel*. Barstow died in 1943.

> *Dictionary of National Biography, p. 2820*
> *Pound,* The Strand Magazine 1891-1950
> *Thorpe,* English Illustration

BART
Cartoonist for the *Minneapolis Journal*. Several of his Boer War cartoons were reproduced in the contemporary American publication *Thrilling Experiences in the War in South Africa* (1900).

BARTON, Frank M.
Illustrator for *Shurey's Pictorial Budget*.

BASEILHAC, Jacques 1874-1903 1
Painter and illustrator. Baseilhac was born in Trebours, France, in 1874. He illustrated *La Chanson Des Gueux* (1901). One of his Boer War cartoons, *Un episode Au Transvaal*, was a parody of the well-known Michelin tyre advertisement. It appeared in the special edition of *Le Rire* for 17 November 1900, *Kruger le grand et John Bull le petit*. He occasionally signed his cartoons 'Jacques'. He died in October 1903.

> *Bénézit,* Dictionnaire antique, *vol. 1, p. 445*

BASTIN, A. D. fl. 1883-1907
Figure painter. One of his works, *From the Front*, was exhibited at the Royal Academy in 1900.

> *Graves,* Royal Academy, *vol. 1, p. 139*
> *Johnson and Greutzner,* British Artists, *p. 45*

BATES, Harry 1851-1899
Sculptor. Bates studied at the Lambeth School of Art and the Royal Academy schools. He won a gold medal travelling scholarship to study under Rodin in Paris. He was originally apprenticed as a carver to Messrs Bridley and Farmer from 1869 to 1879. Bates became an A.R.A. in 1892. His bronze statue of Lord Roberts was unveiled by Lady Roberts at Crystal Palace in May 1901, two years after Bates's death on 30 January 1899.

> The Graphic, *1 June 1901, p. 747*
> *Johnson and Greutzner,* British Artists, *p. 46*
> Who was Who, *vol. 1, p. 46*

BAUNIER
French cartoonist responsible for occasional Boer War cartoons in *L'Indiscret*.

B.C.R.
Cartoonist for *The Minneapolis Tribune*.

BEACH, E. S.
Soldier-artist who accompanied Lord Methuen's forces. One of his illustrations, redrawn by W. Ralston, was entitled *How we nearly lost our Christmas dinner on the Modder River* and appeared in *The Graphic* on 3 February 1900.

> *Hofmeyr, Matton and Roets,* Graphic Picture Index

BEADLE, James Prinsep Barnes 1863-1947 1
Historical, portrait and landscape painter. Beadle was born in Calcutta on 22 September 1863, the son of Maj. Gen. James Pattle Beadle. He studied at the Slade School under Legros, at the École des Beaux-Arts in Paris under Cabanel, and in London under G. F. Watts. He won a bronze medal at the Paris Universal Exhibition in 1889. Beadle exhibited at the Paris Salon and is represented in several public collections, as well as the Royal Collection. He exhibited his work at the Royal Academy from 1884, including *The last Lap* which shows 'the 62nd Battery of the Royal Field Artillery coming up to the Modder River battle after a forced march' (1900). It was illustrated in *Royal Academy Pictures* (1900) and is identical to his watercolour, *The victors of Paardeberg*, which can be found in the National Army Museum. Beadle's painting, *The empty saddle, South Africa 1900*, appeared in *The Graphic* on 3 June 1911. *The Sphere* (2 June 1900) states that he was a painter who 'illustrated Tommy Atkins with particular fidelity'. He died in Kensington on 13 August 1947.

> *Dawnay and Miller,* Military Drawings and Paintings, *vol. 1, p. 234*
> *Graves,* Royal Academy, *vol. 1, p. 151*
> *Johnson and Greutzner,* British Artists, *p. 48*
> Royal Academy Pictures *(1900)*
> *Waters,* British Artists, *vol. 1, p. 26*

2   3

BEER
Cartoonist for *Borszem-Janko*.
> *Burenstreiche, p. 21*

BEER, John-Axel-Richard 1853-1906   2
Equestrian artist. Beer was born in Stockholm on 18 January 1853. In 1869 he went to America where he lived for five years. A shorter trip to Russia was followed by visit to London where he established himself as an illustrator. He worked for several British publications including *Black & White*, *The Illustrated Sporting & Dramatic News* and *The Illustrated London News*. He also worked for the German weekly *Leipziger Illustrierte Zeitung*. Beer contributed illustrations to the Earl of Rosslyn's *Twice Captured* (Wm Blackwood and Sons, 1900). Four of the original drawings from this book are in the Africana Museum: *Boers driving off with prisoners 1900*, *Field-Cornet Potgieter, OFS 1900*, *General de Wet addressing a commando after Reddersburg 1900*, *Table Mountain 1900*. It is unlikely that he was in South Africa during the War as some illustrations carry the comment 'drawn from eyewitness description'.
> *Bénézit, Dictionnaire antique, vol. 1, p. 512*
> *Kennedy, Pictures in the Africana Museum, vol. 1, pp. 128-129*

BEERBOHM, Sir Henry Maximilian (Max) 1872-1956
Caricaturist. Beerbohm was born in London on 24 August 1872, the youngest son of Julius Beerbohm and the younger brother of Sir Herbert Beerbohm Tree. He was educated at Charterhouse and Merton College, Oxford. Known primarily as a novelist and broadcaster, he was an admirer of the *Vanity Fair* caricaturist 'Ape' (Carlo Pellegrini). He wrote to his future wife Florence: 'I can draw caricatures at any moment and how I rejoice in them. They are what I was put into the world to do'. Beerbohm contributed extensively to *Pick-Me-Up*, *Vanity Fair*, *The Sketch*, *The Strand Magazine*, *Pall Mall Magazine* and *John Bull*. *The Idler* and *World* published his Boer War caricatures featuring Kruger, Kitchener, Chamberlain, Lord Rosslyn, John Broderick and a rather uncomplimentary one of Winston Churchill produced in 1901. He was the author of *The Second Childhood of John Bull* (1901) which features *Lest we forget ourselves* (showing Kimberley, Ladysmith and Mafeking), *Colenso*, *Magersfontein*, *Spion Kop* and a third drawing referring to the Kaiser's *Kroojer Telegram*.

Dictionary of National Biography, p. 2505
Hart-Davis, Caricatures of Max Beerbohm

BEGG, Samuel 1854-?   2
Illustrator and sculptor. Begg was born in London in 1854 and at the age of six he emigrated with his parents to New Zealand. In 1877 he joined the staff of Gibbs Shellard and Co. in Sydney and worked on *The Town and Country Journal* from 1878 to 1880. He then worked for the *Sydney Bulletin* and *Illustrated Australia*. Begg returned to London to join *The Illustrated London News* where he remained for at least 17 years. (He is recorded as also having worked for *Black & White* during 1895/6.)

Begg's South African illustrations appeared in *The Illustrated London News* from 1896 until 1913, and this publication described him as 'an illustrator of public functions and public events'. His Boer War work consisted mainly of illustrations of the Royal Family either visiting troops in hospital or receiving news from the front. During the War, his work was often reproduced and sold as photogravures. On 19 May 1900 a black and white painting entitled *The Queen listening to a despatch from the front* was donated to the National Bazaar for War Funds. The original illustration had appeared in *The Illustrated London News* on 17 March. This publication announced that it was producing a select edition of 1 000 photogravures 'beautifully reproduced, signed by the artist and stamped, measuring, with the mount, 37 x 27 inches'. One of Begg's wash drawings, *Gordon Highlanders embarking for South Africa*, is housed in the Victoria and Albert Museum, and of his watercolours in the Royal Collection at Windsor only one is of Boer War interest. The author has a wash drawing entitled *With Capt. Le Mesurier on the way to Pretoria: the prisoners' first halt*, which was originally published in *The Illustrated London News* (5 June 1900). His group portrait of '*The Illustrated London News* artists in the studio', which included a self-portrait, appeared on the front cover on 15 February 1911. The limited edition of Spenser Wilkinson's *The Transvaal War* is signed by Begg and features his portrait. Houfe describes Begg as 'representing the worst of the late nineteenth-century illustrators'.

Dawnay and Miller, Military Drawings and Paintings, vol. 2, p. 234
Houfe, British Illustrators and Caricaturists, p. 231
De Wet, Illustrated London News Index
Moore, The Story of Australian Art

BELLEMONT, Léon 1868-?
Born in Langres, France, on 20 August 1868. Bellemont was a pupil of Bonnat, and two of his Boer War works appeared in *Paris-Pretoria*.
> *Bénézit, Dictionnaire antique, vol. 1, p. 533*

BELO (or BELLO), Avelino Soares 1872-1927   1
Pro-Boer Portuguese ceramic artist. Belo produced tribute medals and ceramic figures in honour of the Boers. Born on 19 January 1872 in the village of Murtosa in the Aveiro district of Portugal, Belo was the son of a fisherman. At the age of 13 he was apprenticed to the famous playwright and ceramic

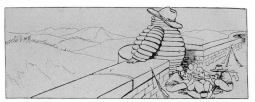

1 James P. Beadle's *To the Sound of the Guns*, of the 62 Battery R.F.A. arriving at Modder River, is now in the National Army Museum, London. Reproduced by courtesy of the Director.
2 John Beer's drawing entitled *General de Wet addressing a Commando after Reddersburg 1900* was reproduced in the Earl of Rosslyn's book *Twice Captured*. Reproduced by courtesy of the Africana Museum, Johannesburg.
3 Samuel Begg's watercolour, *With Capt. Le Mesurier on the way to Pretoria: the prisoners' first halt*, was reproduced in *The Illustrated London News*.
4 A cartoon by Jacques Baseilhac featuring the Michelin Man.

artist Rafael Bordalo Pinheiro, who had a factory in Caldas da Rainha. Belo eventually opened his own workshop, and at this time he came into contact with Boer P.O.W.s at a nearby camp. (These Boers had crossed into Mozambique in 1900 and were interned by the Portuguese in accordance with international law. Because of a lack of facilities in Lourenço Marques, they were transferred to Portugal.)

His friendship with the Boers inspired Belo to design and produce terracotta medals and an exceptional commemorative jug in their honour. Known as the 'Bilha Boer', it is 45 cm high and 17 cm wide with a cylindrical base supporting a tubular neck parallel to the handle. An outstretched eagle rises from the handle and below is a panel with the words 'Leve Kruger en Steyn, Mogen de Zuid-Afrikaansche strÿd-magten overwinnen'. The spout is formed by two panels with the coats of arms of the Transvaal and Orange Free State in bas relief. Standing on one side of the cylindrical base is a victorious Boer holding his flag. On the other side is a lion supporting a shield with two clasped hands symbolizing union between the two Boer republics and the words 'Eeuwige Broederband'. Above the lion, as if hanging from the neck of the jug, is a medallion with a bust of Kruger, bearing Belo's full signature. The work was exhibited in Oporto.

Belo produced two terracotta medals: one has a profile bust of Kruger framed in an octagonal base formed by two superimposed squares, with the coats of arms of the Free State, Transvaal, Portugal and Caldas da Rainha. On the other side is an inscription in Portuguese that translates as follows: 'To the committee which raised funds for Boer refugees', and a list of the names of some local women who served on the committee. The other medal, intended for sale to raise money for the Boers, also has Kruger on one side, but on the reverse are two clasped hands illuminated by a star. The word 'Transvaal' appears on the left, 'Orange' on the right and 'Amazade Eterna' ('eternal friendship') at the bottom.

The author has a ceramic medallion 6 cm in diameter and 5 mm thick by Belo. On one side is a relief of Kruger and bears Belo's signature. The reverse is blank.

Belo died on 24 May 1927.

Gedenkpennings ter ere van President P. Kruger, *National Cultural History and Open-Air Museum, Pretoria*
Personal communication with A. Malan, Curator Kruger House Museum, Pretoria, and Professor O. Ferreira, Department of History and Cultural History, University of Pretoria

BELON, José ?-1927

Cartoonist and poster artist. Belon was born in Alés, France. His Boer War work appeared on the covers of *Le Petit Journal*, *Le Journal Illustré*, *Le Charivari* and in the *Le Charivari Album: Boers et Anglais*.
Bénézit, Dictionnaire antique, vol. 1, p. 542

3

BENDLE, W.

Possible illustrator of a postal cover, addressed to Sgt. Bendle of the 7th Dragoon Guards, which appeared in *Black & White Budget* (5 May 1900). Reproductions of other covers that Sergeant Bendle received in Cape Town appeared in *Black & White Budget* (30 June 1900).

BENNETT, William B. fl. 1900-1913

Landscape and figure painter. Bennett exhibited at the Royal Academy from 1900. His work includes *A soldier's daughter* (1900).
Graves, Royal Academy, vol. 1, p. 181

BENYON, J. A.

Soldier-artist. His illustration, *Bivouac of the 3rd Royal Rifles on 16 January during the crossing of the Tugela*, apppeared in *War Pictures* (5 May 1901).

B., E.O. *see* E.O.B.

BÉRAUD, Jean 1849-1936   1

Painter and illustrator. Béraud was born in St Petersburg, Russia, of French parents in 1849. He studied under Bonnat. He contributed an illustration to the special issue of *Le Monde Illustré* (17 November 1900) which was dedicated to President Kruger.
Bénézit, Dictionnaire antique, vol. 1, p. 567

BERESFORD, Marcus de la Poer 1848-1922

Soldier-artist. Beresford was born on 25 December 1848. He was educated at Harrow and later joined the 7th Hussars, serving as aide-de-camp to the Lord Lieutenant of Ireland from 1874 to 1876. Beresford was made K.C.V.O. in 1918 and later appointed as extra equerry and manager of King George V's thoroughbred stables. One of his sketches, entitled *Polo in sight of a battle: an incident at Klerksdorp*, was redrawn by Percy F.S. Spence and reproduced in *The Graphic* on 13 July 1901. A book entitled *A Sporting Alphabet of African Animals* (1924) was written by a Marcus Beresford and although it was published two years after his death, the two Beresfords may well be one and the same.
Hofmeyr, Matton and Roets, Graphic Picture Index
SABIB, vol. 1, p. 75
Who was Who, vol. 2, p. 84

BERGEN, Fritz 1857-?

Illustrator and portrait painter. Bergen was born in Dessau, Germany, on 5 November 1857. He studied at the Academy of

1

2

Leipzig and worked in Munich. He illustrated *My Reminiscences of the Anglo-Boer War* (1902) by Gen. Ben Viljoen, as well as the German edition, *Die Transvaaler im Krieg mit England – Kriegserinnerungen von Generaal Ben Viljoen* (1902), with Anton Hoffman, and *Mit den Burenkommandos* (1902) by John Daniel Kestell.
Bénézit, Dictionnaire antique, vol. 1, p. 577
SABIB, vol. 1, p. 176

BERKELEY, Stanley 1855-1909   1

Painter and etcher of military subjects. Berkeley originally studied law but gave it up in 1875 to become an artist. He illustrated several books and worked for *The Sphere*, *The Illustrated London News*, *The Graphic*, *After Pretoria: the Guerilla War* and *Shurey's Pictorial Budget*. Berkeley exhibited at the Royal Academy (as did his wife, Edith, a landscape painter) from 1881 and was elected R.E. in 1884. In *The Work of War Artists in South Africa*, A.C.R. Carter praises his drawing *Saving the guns at Colenso*. Two of his works can be found in the Africana Museum: *The Death of Captain De Montmorency, V.C. 1900* and *Captain Towse at Mount Thaba 1900*, with the pencil inscriptions 'Capt. Towse V.C. at Mount Thaba (where his eyes were shattered)' and 'Captain E.B. Towse, Gordon Highlanders, winning the Victoria Cross on Mount Thaba 30th April 1900' respectively. Other works by Berkeley depicting the Boer War are housed in the National Army Museum. He was a contributor to Raphael Tuck & Sons' Empire Series of Postcards including No. 823 *C.I.V in action embarked January 1900 – returned October 1900*. He was responsible for several prewar military prints published by S. Hildesheimer and Co. Ltd. and Henry Graves. One of these prints published as a supplement to *Chums* (23 October 1901) showed Sgt. A.H.L. Richardson winning his V.C. The author has an untitled and undated wash drawing showing a party of National Scouts (who were Afrikaners fighting for the British) ambushing a group of Boers.

Berkeley is often described as a Western artist because some of his sketches in *The Illustrated London News* had Western themes. He lived in Esher and Surbiton Hill in Surrey, where he died on 24 April 1909.
British Military Costume Prints
Carter, War Artists in S.A., pp. 10 and 18
Illustrated London News (14 March, 1892)
Windsor Magazine, vol. 11, July 1899

BERNE-BELLECOUR, Etienne-Prosper 1838-1910

Military artist. Berne-Bellecour was born in Boulogne-sur-Mer, France, on 29 July 1838. He studied under Picot and

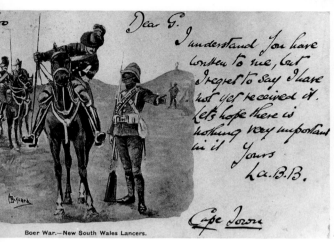

Boer War.—New South Wales Lancers.

Barrias at the École des Beaux-Arts. One of his illustrations appeared in the special issue of the periodical *Le Monde Illustré* on 17 November 1900 that was dedicated to President Kruger.

Bénézit, Dictionnaire antique, *vol. 1, p. 597*

BERNHARD, F.

Postcard illustrator for Carl Otto Hayd, Munich. One of his postcards, *Mit Gott Für Unser Gutes Recht*, shows Kruger, Steyn, Cronje and Joubert.

BERTHON, Paul Emile 1872-1909 2

Art Nouveau painter, postcard artist and lithographer. Berthon was born in Villefranche, France, on 14 March 1872. He was strongly influenced by Eugene Grasset and Luc-Olivier Merson.

In 1895 Berthon exhibited at the Salon des Artistes Français and in 1898 he worked as an illustrator for *L'Ermitage*. Berthon's only known Boer War work is a tinted lithograph of Paul Kruger, one of a series of contemporary world leaders including King Edward VII, Emperor William II, Emperor Franz Joseph and Queen Wilhelmina (three versions, 1901) done in 1902.

Barnicoat, History of Posters
Osterwalder, and Hubschmid and Bouret (eds.),
Dictionnaire des Illustrateurs, *p. 129*
The Poster, *May 1899*

BIENERT, A.

The illustrator of a postcard issued 'In commemoration of the freedom struggle of the Boers 1899/1900'. The publisher of the card was Kunsanstalt Minerva and the printer Schneider & Lux of Vienna. The card was titled *Dem Heldenvolk und seinen Führern*.

BIGOT, George

Cartoonist for *Le Rire*. Bigot's work also featured on Dutch and French postcards published by 'P.J.' or 'J.P.'. A George Bigot was *The Graphic*'s representative on the Japanese side during the Sino-Japanese War of 1894-5. Coloured reproductions of his work appeared in *The Graphic* in 1895. It is not known if the two Bigots are one and the same.

Hodgson, War Illustrators, *p. 146*
Stead (ed.), Review of Reviews, *vol. 21, Jan.-June 1900*

BINDLEY, Frank fl. 1880-1900

Born in Galway, Ireland. Bindley exhibited at the Royal Academy and R.B.A. His Boer War illustration, *Playing the*

Boer game: British scout decoying the Boers into an ambush, appeared in *Under The Union Jack*, vol. 2.
Johnson and Greutzner, British Artists, *p. 58*

BINNS

Cartoonist for *The Owl*.

BIQUARD, Armand fl. 1899-1909 4

French-born painter who exhibited at the R.A. in 1904. Biquard worked for *Pick-Me-Up* and *Judy*. He did two postcards, *Commandant Cronje and an officer on horseback* and *New South Wales Lancers*, in the Picture Postcard Co. series.

Bénézit, Dictionnaire antique, *vol. 1, p. 670*
Byatt, Picture Postcards, *p. 207*

B.J.M.

An artist with these initials illustrated Capt. J.E. Symons's article 'With the telegraph squad in besieged Kimberley' which appeared in *St Martins — Le Grand* (April 1900), the internal publication of the British postal service. This article was reproduced in *The Post Office Militant 1899-1902: The Anglo-Boer War* (A.G.M. Batten, Woking, 1981).

BLAKE, Phil

Cartoonist for the Irish periodical *Freeman's Journal*.
Stead (ed.), Review of Reviews, *vol. 21, Jan.-June 1900*
Grand-Carteret, John Bull, *p. 46*

BLEACH, C. Meredith 5

Soldier-artist who was a pupil of J.H. Amshewitz. Bleach served in the Boer War and World War I. He was appointed Union war artist in December 1940. The Africana Museum has 17 of his sketches, but only one deals with the Boer War. The caption reads: 'One of our Boer prisoners October 10/01 sketched in the blockhouse, Brussels Bechuanaland.' It is a pencil sketch, signed C. M. Bleach.

Berman, Art and Artists, *p. 484*
Kennedy, Pictures in the Africana Museum, *vol. 1,*
pp. 188-191

BLOMFIELD, Charles James 1855-1928

Soldier-artist. Blomfield was born in Bow, Devon, on 25 May 1855. He was educated at Haileybury and Sandhurst. He was promoted to captain in the Lancashire Fusiliers in 1881, to major in 1890, lieutenant colonel in 1896, colonel in 1900, and major general in 1907. He was awarded the D.S.O. in 1898 and the C.B. in 1904. He was wounded and taken prisoner at Spioenkop on 25 January 1900. During his incarceration in

Pretoria he helped to illustrate *The Gram*, the P.O.W. publication that was edited by the Earl of Rosslyn, author of *Twice Captured*. A facsimile of this 'magazine' was published by Eyre & Spottiswoode in 1900. Blomfield was responsible for the cartoon that appeared on the back cover of the second issue (24 May 1900), signed C.J.B. After the War he commanded the Harrismith and Natal subdistrict from 1902 to 1907. He delivered a lecture entitled 'Individual intelligence in modern warfare' in Pietermaritzburg, where it was published by Monro Bros. *c*.1905.

The Gram
SABIB, *vol. 1, p. 220*
Who was Who, *vol. 2, p. 100*

BLUE, E. N.

Artist for *Leslie's Weekly*. Blue contributed occasional Boer War drawings from May 1900.

BLUMELL, C.

Blumell's undated oil on canvas showing mounted infantry is a reproduction of Lucy Kemp-Welch's painting of the C.I.V. entitled *Sons of the City*, which was exhibited at the Royal Academy in 1903.

BLUNDELL, W.

A sketch by Blundell, redrawn by an unidentified home-based artist, appeared in *The Illustrated London News* on 15 September 1900. A reproduction of the same illustration appeared in *After Pretoria: the Guerilla War*, entitled *Retief's Nek and the adjacent passes, from Bethlehem*.

De Wet, Illustrated London News Index

'BOBB'

This is the pseudonym of a cartoonist who worked for *La Silhouette*. He illustrated the French postcard, *England is the most civilized nation in the world*, depicting the destruction of Boer houses and the murder of women and children.

BOGNET, Georges Tiret *see* TIRET-BOGNET, Georges

BOLS, Louis-Jean 1867-1930

Soldier-artist. Bols was born on 23 November 1867. He entered the Devon Regiment in 1887 and was promoted to captain in 1897, adjutant in 1899, and lieutenant colonel in the Dorset Regiment in 1914. He was awarded the D.S.O. in 1900, the C.B. in 1915, and the K.C.B. and K.C.M.G. in 1919. Bols was later appointed governor and commander in chief in Bermuda. He served in Burma and in South Africa from 1899 to 1902. He was mentioned in despatches three times and won the Queen's medal with five clasps and King's medal with two clasps. He fought in World War I and was mentioned in despatches 12 times. Bols was responsible for the sketch, later redrawn by H. Seppings Wright, entitled *Operations in Natal: The action of 10 April at Sunday's River*. It appeared in *The Illustrated London News* on 19 May 1900. He died on 13 September 1930.

Creagh and Humphris, The D.S.O., *p. 197*
De Wet, Illustrated London News Index
Who was Who, *vol. 3, p. 131*

---

1 Stanley Berkeley.

2 Paul Berthon, the well-known Art Nouveau artist, produced this lithograph of Paul Kruger with his devastated country in the background.

3 The illustration contributed by Jean Béraud to the special edition of *Le Monde Illustré* on 17 November.

4 The Picture Postcard Co. Boer War series included this painting by Armand Biquard, entitled *New South Wales Lancers*.

5 Soldier-artist C. Meredith Bleach produced this pencil sketch of a Boer prisoner in Bechuanaland in 1901. Reproduced by courtesy of the Africana Museum, Johannesburg.

1

2

LA SEMAINE ILLUSTRÉE

LECTURES POUR LE DIMANCHE
VERMOT, Éditeur

Bataille de Glencoe
Le général Symons mortellement blessé

3

4

5

I think I am like this, but I am told that this is nearer the truth. ISB

6

BOMBLED, Louis-Charles 1862-1927 1
Military artist. Bombled was born of Dutch parents in Chantilly, France, on 6 July 1862. His father, Karel, was also a well-known artist. Bombled exhibited at the Salon des Artistes Français, where he obtained an honourable mention in 1885. He worked for *La Caricature, Petit Journal pour Rire, Chat Noir, The Regiment, La Semaine Illustrée* and *Le Monde Illustré.* The serial publication, *Les Boers,* also featured Bombled's work in colour on its front covers.

His main Boer War work, 19 silhouettes, appeared in *La Moderne Épopée Les Boers,* (Ombres et Scénario de L. Bombled, Poème de G. Montoya, Musique de Jules Mulder), published by L. Geisler, Vosges and Flammarion, Paris. On the dedication page there appears, in facsimile, a letter from Jonkheer C. G. S. Sandberg, military secretary and aide-de-camp to Gen. Louis Botha, dated 28 January 1902 and addressed to Bombled, thanking him for his 'magnificent idea' and adding that 'his work for the Boer people and their children will ensure that right and justice will triumph'. An illustration, entitled *Kruger and his bodyguard visiting a Boer camp,* appeared in James H. Starke's *British and Boers in South Africa.* The author has one of the original black ink and wash paintings done for *La Moderne Épopée Les Boers.* Some of Bombled's other illustrations are housed in the Leicester City Museum. He died at Pierrefonds, Oise, on 9 October 1927.
Bénézit, Dictionnaire antique, *vol. 1, p. 752*
Osterwalder, and Hubschmid and Bouret (eds.),
Dictionnaire des Illustrateurs, *p. 149*

BONVOISIN, Maurice ('Mars') 1849-1912
This Belgian artist was born in Verviers in 1849. Using the pseudonym 'Mars', he worked for *The Graphic, The Illustrated London News, The Daily Graphic, The Sketch, Illustrated Bits, Le Charivari, L'Illustration, Le Journal Amusant, Revue Illustré, Vie Elegante, Le Monde Illustré* and *Petit Journal pour Rire.* During the War he provided illustrations of Kruger in Paris for *The Graphic.*
Osterwalder, and Hubschmid and Bouret (eds.),
Dictionnaire des Illustrateurs, *p. 149*
Hofmeyr, Matton and Roets, Graphic Picture Index

BOOM, Karel 1858-?
Historical painter and engraver. Boom was born in Hoogstraten, Belgium, and lived in Antwerp where he was later a professor at the Antwerp Academy. He was a member of the committee which illustrated and published the *Antwerpen-Transvaal Gedenknummer* (March/ April 1902). He signed his work 'Ch Boom'.
Bénézit, Dictionnaire antique, *vol. 2, p. 11*

BOONZAAIER, Daniel Cornelis 1865-1950 2
Cartoonist and caricaturist. Boonzaaier was born on the farm Patatsrivier, in the Carnarvon district, on 11 November 1865, the son of W.D. Boonzaaier. He began his career in the civil service as an authority on handwriting. As a cartoonist he was self taught, but he was influenced by the British artist Phil May and W.H. Schröder, who worked for the Cape Town periodical *The Knobkerrie.* Boonzaaier first contributed to *The Knobkerrie* in 1884. When it ceased publication, he contributed to *The Veldt, The Telephone, The Owl,* in which Boer War cartoons appeared, and *Cape Punch.* In 1901 he published *Owlographs: A selection of Cape Celebrities in Caricature,* which included political and military personalities of the War.

Boonzaaier took a pro-Afrikaner stance as a political cartoonist for *South African News* from 1903 to 1907, after which he joined *The Cape.* He later worked for *Observer, The Cape Argus, Sunday Post* and *De Burger.* His publications also included *South African News Cartoons* (1904), *My Caricatures* (1912), *Rand Faces* (1915), *Politieke Prente uit De Burger* (1916), and *Die Springbokke in Nu-Seeland* (1921). His diary, kept by Boonzaaier from 1904 until his death in Cape Town on 20 March 1950, is preserved in the South

African Library. His son, Gregoire, is a well-known artist.
De Kock, (ed.), DSAB, *vol. 1, pp. 93-96*

BOOTH, J. L. C.
'Special' artist. Booth was a captain in the Prince of Wales Own Yorkshire 1st Volunteer Regiment. Representing *War Pictures,* he accompanied General Buller's forces. He also contributed numerous sketches, some of which were reproduced in original form, to *Harper's Weekly.* After the War Booth contributed occasionally to *The Graphic.* His photograph appeared in *After Pretoria: the Guerilla War.*
Houfe, British Illustrators and Caricaturists, *p. 238*

BORGLUM, John Gutzon De la Mothe 1867-1941
American sculptor. Borglum was born in Bear Lake, Idaho, of Danish parents. He trained at the San Francisco Art Academy and in Paris with Rodin. Borglum worked in London from 1895 to 1901, when he became an R.B.A. He returned to New York in 1902 and became well known as a Western artist, as well as a successful sculptor. He is best known for the giant figures of Washington, Jefferson, Lincoln and Roosevelt on Mount Rushmore in Dakota. During the War Borglum contributed illustrations occasionally to *Black & White.* He died in Chicago in 1941.
Johnson and Greutzner, British Artists, *p. 66*
Samuels, Artists of the American West, *pp. 57-58*

BORIONE, Bernard Louis
French-born painter who exhibited at the Salon des Artistes Francais from 1911 to 1920. He contributed to *Paris-Pretoria.*

BOSCOVITS, Friedrich 1845-?
Painter, illustrator and postcard artist. Boscovits was born in Budapest on 6 January 1845. He studied in Vienna and worked with Alex Wagner before settling in Zurich in 1900. His Boer War cartoons, often signed 'F.B.', appeared in the Swiss publication *Der Nebelspalter.* His son, Fritz, was also an artist.
Bénézit, Dictionnaire antique, *vol. 2, p. 31*

BOUARD, Ernest-Auguste ?-1938 2
Parisian artist. Bouard was a pupil of Boulanger, Bonnat and Lefebvre and exhibited regularly at the Salon des Artistes Français, receiving an honourable mention in 1914. He contributed illustrations to *The Sphere, Le Monde Illustré* and *Het Huisgezin.* One of his illustrations in *The Sphere* (23 June 1900) had the inscription: 'The Boer armies vanish in the night but at what cost of physical strength may be judged from the accompanying picture which French artist, Monsieur Bouard, has made of the way in which they have to pull up their guns'. The author has three of Bouard's black and white wash drawings that were originally published in *Le Monde Illustré.*
Bénézit, Dictionnaire antique, *vol. 2, p. 43*

BOUCHER, William Henry ?-1906
Illustrator and cartoonist for *Judy* from 1868 to 1887. An A.R.W.S., Boucher exhibited at the Royal Academy from 1888 to 1891. He collaborated with George Fenn on *Diamond Dyke or the Lone Farm of the Veldt: A Story of South African Adventure* (W. & R. Chambers, London and Edinburgh, 1894). He contributed eight illustrations to Fenn's *The Kopje Garrison: A Tale of the Boer War* (W. & R. Chambers, London and Edinburgh, 1901).
Houfe, British Illustrators and Caricaturists, *p. 238*
Johnson and Greutzner, British Artists, *p. 67*

BOUFFIER, Marguerite
French-born illustrator. Bouffier was responsible for at least three German postcards, *Das letzte aufgebot Englands* (after a painting by Defregger), *Für die Buren,* published by Rud Bechtold and Co., Wiesbaden, and another card showing a British soldier spilling his hot chocolate when attacked by the

Boers. This card was published by L. Schellenberg'sche Hofbuchdrukerei, also in Wiesbaden.
Bénézit, Dictionnaire antique, *vol. 2, p. 56*

BOWERS, F.
Cartoonist for *Indianapolis News.* His Boer War cartoons were reproduced in the contemporary American publication, *Thrilling Experiences in the War in South Africa* (Educational Company of Chicago, Illinois, 1900).

BOWMAN, R. C.
American cartoonist for *The Minneapolis Tribune.*

BOWRING, Walter Armiger 1874-1931
Portrait and figure painter. Bowring was born in Auckland, New Zealand, on 11 March 1874. He studied art in New Zealand with Kenneth Watkins and L.J. Steel and later in London with John and Orpen. He worked as a cartoonist for *The New Zealand Observer* until 1895 and thereafter for *The Weekly Press.* Bowring's Boer War illustrations were done from sketches received from the front. He was elected a member of the R.O.I. in 1922. While in London, he contributed to *Punch.* Bowring settled in Sydney in 1925 where he married Violet Nelson, also an artist. He died on 3 November 1931.
*Personal communication with Moira Long, Librarian,
Alexander Turnbull Library, New Zealand*
Waters, British Artists, vol. 1, p. 40
Who was Who, vol. 3, p. 146

BOX, J.
An illustration by Box, *Lord Roberts talking to Colonel Spence,* appeared in *The Graphic* on 16 June 1900.

BOYD, Alexander Stuart 1854-1930 4
Landscape and genre painter. Boyd was born in Glasgow on 7 February 1854. He adopted the pseudonym 'Twym' for his humorous drawings in *Quiz* and *The Baillie of Glasgow.* He illustrated many books including Robert Louis Stevenson's *Lowden Sabbath Morn* and *Days of Auld Lang Syne;* McLaren's *Rabbi Saunderson;* Munro's *Gillian the Dreamer* and *Shoes of Fortune;* Bell's *Wee McGregor* and *Jess and Co.;* Burns's *The Cotter's Saturday night;* Haliburton's *Horace in Homespun;* and *Our Stolen Summer, A Versailles Christmastide* and the *Fortunate Isles* — written by his wife, Mary Stuart Boyd. *Our Stolen Summer* was a description of the couple's trip to New Zealand in 1898.

Many of Boyd's illustrations appeared in *The Sphere* and *Punch,* but his Boer War work appeared in *The Graphic* and *The Daily Graphic.* He contributed political cartoons regularly to *The Daily Graphic,* especially during the latter part of the War, including *Slow but sure* on the front cover (1 January 1902). The well-known illustration for *The Daily Graphic, Laus Deo — Peace with Honour,* celebrating the declaration of peace in June 1902, appeared as Raphael Tuck's postcard No. 662. Boyd's extant Boer War pen-and-ink sketches can be found in the Africana Museum, the National Army Museum, the Mendelssohn Collection in the Library of Parliament, Cape Town, and the author's collection. He often used the signature 'A.S.B.' and so sometimes his work was not recognized. He was a member of the Strand Club; his photograph

---

1 Louis Bombled's pen silhouette *Le Nombre,* reproduced in *La Moderne Epopée Les Boers.*
2 Louis Bombled's depiction of the Battle of Glencoe and the death of Gen. Penn Symons for *La Semaine Illustrée* on 12 November 1899.
3 This wash and Chinese white drawing by Ernest-Auguste Bouard shows clearly the terrible toll that the War was taking on the Boers.
4 Cartoons of De Wet and Reitz appeared in D. C. Boonzaaier's 1901 publication *Owlographs.*
5 Ernest-Auguste Bouard's drawing of Boers damaging the railway was reproduced in *Le Monde Illustré* on 28 July 1900.
6 A.S. Boyd drew himself as he would like to be (left), but added a more realistic sketch as well.

1 2 3

and an article appeared in volume 23 of *The Strand Magazine* in 1902, and a self-portrait appeared in volume 32 during 1906. He died at Takapuna, New Zealand, on 21 August 1930.

New Zealand Obituaries, *vol. 15, p. 566*
Potts, *New Zealand Artists, pp. 55-56*
The Sphere, *vol. 1, p. 604*
The Strand Magazine, *vol. 2, p. 78 and vol. 3, p. 557*
Who was Who, *vol. 3, p. 147*

BOYINGTON, F. W.

Illustrator for boys' weekly comic *Robin Hood*. During the War Boyington produced illustrations for *Black & White* and *Black & White Budget*. He often signed his work 'F.W.B.'.

BRAAKENSIEK, Johan 1858-1940 2

Painter and cartoonist. Braakensiek was born in Amsterdam on 24 August 1858. He studied at the Amsterdam Academy and worked for many years on the cartoon supplement for *De Amsterdammer: weekblad voor Nederland*, also known as 'De Groene' because of its green cover. According to *The Strand*, 'Braakensiek was something more than a cartoonist. He was an exceptionally clever and humorous book illustrator and is without question the foremost draughtsman in Holland.' He contributed to *John Bull in Zuid-Afrika* (Van Holkema and Warendorf, 1900) and illustrated other books on South Africa, including Frederick Marryat's *Het Spookschip de Vliegende Hollander* (1889) and *Onder de Hottentotten* (1890). He was possibly also the lithographer ('Gebr. Braakensiek') of the illustration for the game 'Boer-en-Rooinek-Speel'.

Braakensiek's Boer War lithographic cartoons in the *De Amsterdammer* supplements were: *Oom Paul en die uitlanders* (5 January 1896); *Na den Slag bij Krugersdorp* (12 January 1896); *De Mogendheden en de (voor't oogenblik vergeten) Armenische quaestie* (26 January 1896); *President Kruger's reis naar Engeland* (16 February 1896); *De receptie van Dr Leyds te Amsterdam* (23 February 1896); *Dr Jameson's ontvangst in Engeland* (1 March 1896); *De decoratie van de Transvalers door de Fransche Republiek* (2 August 1896); *Jameson Gestraft* (9 August 1896); *Het voorstel tot viering van Koningin Victoria's Jubileum in de Transvaal* (9 May 1897); *De herkiezing van President Kruger* (27 February 1898); *De hulde van de Transvaal aan den Grand Old Man* (29 May 1898); *Geldleeningen voor Transvaal en Egypte in Europa* (31 July 1898); *Een bod op de Delagoabaai* (18 September 1898); *Geen uitnoodiging van Oranje-Vrystaat en Z-Afr Republiek ter Vredes conferentie* (16 April 1899); *Engeland en de Transvaal* (7 May 1899); *John Bull en de hoogverraders* (28 May 1899); *Een politiek van dreigementen* (18 June 1899); *De brave John Bull!* (23 July 1899); *De Transvaalsche Kwestie* (30 July 1899); *Het adres van het Nederlandsche Volk aan het Engelsche Volk* (13 August

1899); *Engeland en Transvaal* (16 September 1899); *Holland 1569-1899 Transvaal* (8 October 1899); *Twee fantasiën over den afloop van den oorlog* (15 October 1899); *De uitwerking van den oorlogsbril* (22 October 1899); *De Eerste Oorlogsoogst* (29 October 1899); *Na den slag bij Ladysmith* (5 November 1899); *De Engelsch-Transvaalsche Oorlog* (12 November 1899); *De hypnose bedreigd* (19 November 1899); *Engelsche taktiek in Zuid-Afrika* (3 December 1899); *Na den slag aan de Modderrivier* (10 December 1899); *John Bull in Zuid-Afrika* (17 December 1899); *Kerstnacht in Zuid-Afrika* (24 December 1899); *De Prins van Wales als chef der Yeomanry* (7 January 1900); *Engeland en de Delagoa-baai* (14 January 1900); *Hulp voor Transvaal en Vrystaat en werkloosheid in Nederland* (21 January 1900); *De omtrekkende bewegingen der Engelschen* (28 January 1900); *De terugtocht over de Toegela* (4 February 1900), *Engelands pogingen om den Vrystaat ende Transvaal te scheiden* (11 February 1900); *Chamberlain en de Oorlog in Zuid-Afrika* (18 February 1900); *John Bull Trumphator* (25 February 1900); *Cronje's overgave* (4 March 1900); *Chamberlain ontvangt den gelukwensch van den Sultan* (11 March 1900); *Rhodes aan't woord* (18 March 1900); *Het verzoek op interventie aan de Mogendheden* (25 March 1900); *De toestand in Zuid-Afrika* (1 April 1900); *De annexatie van der Oranje-Vrystaat* (8 April 1900); *John Bull's triomphtocht naar Pretoria* (22 April 1900); *De Boeren-deputatie in Amerika* (13 May 1900); *Nog geen Vrede* (27 May 1900); *John Bull as heerscher in Azië en Afrika* (15 July 1900);*Engelsche overwinningen* (19 August 1900); *De Engelsche wreedheden in Zuid-Afrika* (2 September 1900); *Chamberlain na den Moord* (23 September 1900); *De Feestelijke ontvangst van Generaal Roberts* (28 October 1900); *President Kruger's aankomst in Europa* (4 November 1900); *Kruger in Europa* (25 November 1900); *De beteekenis van het telegram der Koningin aan Kruger* (2 December 1900); *Duitschland en Kruger* (9 December 1900); *Kersttijd 1900* signed Jan Linse; *De Groote industriëel* (23 December 1900); *Het onsterfelijk ideaal* (23 December 1900); *Oudejaarsavond 1900* (30 December 1900); *Roberts de feesten afzeggend* (20 January 1901); *Keizer Wilhelm's dankbaarheid aan Frederik Hendrik en bewondering voor de Ruyter* (27 January 1901); *De Boeren bij het hoeren van Edwards troonrede* (24 February 1901); *Chamberlain's kritiek op Kitchener* (7 April 1901); *Oorlogslasten in Engeland* (28 April 1901); *Uitvoerrecht of steenkolen tot dekking van Oorlogskosten* (12 May 1901); *Engelsche officieële waarheidsliefde* (19 May 1901); *De Nieuwe bondgenooten in Zuid-Afrika* (9 June 1901); *In de Keuken des Vredes* (16 June 1901); *Amerika en Engeland als leveranciers* (30 June 1901); *Tante Sannet* (28 July 1901); *Sympathie(?)* (4 August 1901); *Engeland in Zuid-Afrika* (11 August 1901); *Kitchener's proclamatie* (18 August 1901); *Engeland en het bezoek van den Czar*

aan Frankrijk (1 September 1901); *Het in werking treden der Engelsche proclamatie op 15 September* (15 September 1901); *Kitchener's dreigen met naar Engeland terug te keeren* (6 October 1901); *De oorlogspartij in Engeland en de oppositie* (13 October 1901); *Chamberlain en Kitchener in het Zuid-Afrikaansche Abbatoir* (20 October 1901); *Napoleon's denkbeeld veredeld* (27 October 1901); *Een Bondgenoot van John Bull* (3 November 1901); *Kitchener's Overwinningen* (10 November 1901); *Chamberlain's redevoering over de Duitschers in den oorlog van 1870-1871* (1 December 1901); *Duitschland, Rusland en Engeland* (8 December 1901); *John Bull's Kerstboom* (5 January 1902); *Koning Eduard leest zijn Troonrede voor* (26 January 1902); *De Oorlogslasten in Engeland* (16 February 1902); *Tusschen de Blokhuizen* (2 March 1902); *De Wet en Zijn buit* (9 March 1902); *De Nederlaag van Lord Methuen* (16 March 1902); *Vrede in Zuid-Afrika* (8 June 1902); *President Steijn in Nederland* (10 August 1902); *De drie Boeren-Generaals in Nederland* (24 August 1902); *De Boeren-Generaals te Berlijn* (19 October 1902); *Kruger's afsterven* (31 July 1904); *De oude geschiedenis van den splinter en de bulk* (14 August 1904); *Het geschenk der Transvaal voor Koning Edward* (25 August 1907).

A series of postcards issued during the War by an unidentified publisher included some of Braakensiek's cartoons taken from the *De Amsterdammer* supplements: Series 1 No. 2 *Turkije en Frankrijk China en Duitschland*; No. 3 *Het in werking treden der Engelsche proclamatie op 15 September*; No. 5 *De Fransche wapenschouwung en de Engelsche Soldatennood*; No. 6 *Kitchener's Dreigen met naar Engeland terug te keeren*; No. 7 *De Oorlogspartij in Engeland en de oppositie*; No. 8 *Chamberlain en Kitchener in het Zuid-Afrikaansche Abbatoir*; No. 9 *Napoleon's Denkbeeld veredeld*; No. 10 *Een Bondgenoot van John Bull*; No. 11 *Kitchener's overwinnigen*; No. 12 *De Franco-Turksche Kwestie en 't hof van Arbitrage*; No. 13. *Het Britsche Volk en Chamberlain*; No. 14 *Chamberlain's redevoering over de Duitscher in den Oorlog 1870-1871*; No. 15 *Duitschland, Rusland en Engeland*.

Other cards taken from his work included *John Bull: Laat mij toch los, jelui rekels wat moeten die menschen daar wel denken...!*; *In den handel gebracht door de 'Union d'indépendence'* (Joh G. Stemler and Co., Amsterdam) and *Paul Kruger* (Joss Nuss, Amsterdam), depicting Paul Kruger with an open bible on hearing of the death of his wife.

None of Braakensiek's original works, often signed 'Joh B.', appears to have survived.

Bénézit, Dictionnaire antique, *vol. 2, p. 93*
Quarterly Bulletin, *vol. 34, p. 3*
SABIB, *vol. 1, p. 269*
The Strand, *vol. 24, p. 91*

"Paradise Lost"

BRADSHAW
Designer of the Yorkshire Tribute Medal.
Hibbard, Boer War Medals, *p. 88*

BRANDSMA, A. C.
Soldier-artist. Apparently Brandsma was a P.O.W., although British archive records do not include his name. He was responsible for one large pencil drawing, depicting a British soldier, which was donated by his son to the War Museum of the Boer Republics, Bloemfontein.
Bloemfontein War Museum Catalogue

BRANDT, Gustav 1861-1919
Brandt was born in Hamburg on 2 June 1861. He was a pupil at the academies in Düsseldorf and Berlin. He contributed Boer War cartoons, often signed 'G.B.', to *Kladderadatsch*.
Osterwalder, and Hubschmid and Bouret (eds.), Dictionnaire des Illustrateurs, *p. 172*

BRANGWYN, Frank William 1867-1956
Artist, illustrator and etcher. Brangwyn was born on 13 May 1867, the son of a Welsh architect. He visited South Africa in 1891 and is reputed to have spent four or five months in the Cape executing a commission for a Mr Larkin. Fifty-one South African items were exhibited in Larkin's Japanese Galleries in March 1892. Three of Brangwyn's watercolours, *Wine pressing at Stellenbosch* (1891), *Adderley Street, Cape Town* (1891) and *Cape Town Docks* (1891), are in the Africana Museum. His only Boer War work, *Good luck to you Tommy; bluejackets at Suez cheering a Cape transport*, appeared in *The Graphic* on 31 March 1900, after a photo by E.T. Meagher. He often signed his work 'F.B.'. He died on 11 June 1956.
Houfe, British Illustrators and Caricaturists, *p. 242*
Kennedy, Pictures in the Africana Museum, *vol. 1, p. 229 and vol. 6., p. 40*

BRENNAN, G. H.
Brennan painted *The Grenadier Guards in South Africa 1899-1902*, which is housed in the Africana Museum. He always signed his work 'G.H.B.'.
Kennedy, Pictures in the Africana Museum, *vol. 6, p. 40*

BRIDGMAN, George 1
Bridgman illustrated the print *Paradise lost* (Messrs Fores, London, 1900), depicting 'Mr and Mrs Kruger' driven from Paradise by Lord Roberts.
Wood, Victorian Painters, *p. 63*

BROCK, Charles Edmund 1870-1938
Book illustrator and genre painter. The elder brother of Henry Brock (see below), Charles Brock was born in Cambridge in February 1870. He studied at the Cambridge School of Art and under sculptor Henry Wiles. He illustrated novels by Jane Austen, Charles Lamb, Oliver Goldsmith and Daniel Defoe, and also worked for *Punch*, *The Graphic*, *The Illustrated London News* and *Fun*. His Boer War work appeared in *With the Flag to Pretoria*. The two brothers often collaborated on their illustrations. He died on 28 February 1938.
Bradshaw, C. E. Brock and his Work
Hammerton, Humorists of the Pencil, *p. 74*
Houfe, British Illustrators and Caricaturists, *pp. 244-245*
Who was Who, *vol. 3, p. 164*

BROCK, Henry Matthew 1875-1960
Book illustrator and landscape painter. Henry Brock was born in Cambridge on 11 July 1875, the younger brother of Charles Brock (see above). He was educated at the Higher Grade School and the Cambridge School of Art. He exhibited at the Royal Academy and the R.I. in 1901 and was elected a member of the latter in 1906. He illustrated the reprints of old books, including works by Thackeray, Whyte-Melville and Oliver Wendell Holmes. Brock was the co-illustrator (with John Walker) of Bessie Marchant's *Tommy's Trek: A Transvaal Story*. A list of books illustrated by Brock appears in the *Bibliography of British Book Illustrators*. He also worked for *Punch* and *The Graphic*, and his Boer War illustrations appeared in *With the Flag to Pretoria*. His obituary in *The Times* described him as a 'pleasant and highly successful draughtsman and illustrator somewhat in the Hugh Thompson tradition of lightly humorous, skilfully controlled and clear-cut pen drawing'. Brock married Doris Pegram, the sister of the artist Fred Pegram. He died on 21 July 1960.
Houfe, British Illustrators and Caricaturists, *p. 245*
Wood, Victorian Painters, *p. 64*

BROUILLET, Pierre-André 1857-1920
Painter. Brouillet was born in Charroux, near Vienna, on 1 September 1857. He studied at Poitiers and the École des Beaux-Arts in 1879, before becoming a pupil of Gérôme and J. P. Laurens. His Boer War work appeared in *Paris-Pretoria*.
Bénézit, Dictionnaire antique, *vol. 2, p. 155*

BROWELL, Langton
Soldier-artist. A sketch by a Lt. Langton Browell, entitled *'Good Luck!' Homeward and outward bound at St Vincent*, appeared in *The Graphic* on 27 January 1900. It had been redrawn by J. Nash.
Hofmeyr, Matton and Roets, Graphic Picture Index

BROWN, Cecil fl. 1888-1925
Sculptor. Brown exhibited at the Royal Academy from 1893. His group sculpture, *Red Badge of Courage*, was exhibited in 1900 and is presumably of Boer War interest.
Graves, Royal Academy, *vol. 1, p. 306*
Houfe, British Illustrators and Caricaturists, *p. 246*

BROWN, Dimmock F. N. or Dimock F. W.
Soldier-artist. Brown probably served with Buller's Natal Field Force. His illustrations appeared in *The Graphic* (November 1899) and *The Illustrated London News* (January 1900).
De Wet, Illustrated London News Index
Hofmeyr, Matton and Roets, Graphic Picture Index, *p. 19*

BROWN, John Dimock
Soldier-artist. John Brown was probably with Buller's Natal Field Force, and two of his illustrations appeared in *The Illustrated London News* in December 1899.
De Wet, Illustrated London News Index

BROWNE, Gordon Frederick 1858-1932 1
Landscape painter and illustrator. Browne was born on 15 April 1858 in Banstead, Surrey, the youngest son of Dickens's illustrator, Hablôt Knight Browne ('Phiz'). He studied at Heatherley School, London, and exhibited at London galleries from 1886, including the Royal Academy, the R.I. and Suffolk Street. He became a member of the R.I. in 1896. Browne illustrated Rider Haggard's *Benita, an African Romance* (1906) and Bertram Mitford's *A Veldt Vendetta* (1903), as well as works by Shakespeare, Scott, Defoe, Swift, Bunyan, Stevenson and others. Three of his watercolour sketches, which

---

1 Alexander Stuart Boyd's famous illustration *Laus Deo* was issued as a postcard by Raphael Tuck very soon after peace was declared.
2 This pen-and-ink drawing by Alexander Stuart Boyd appeared on the front page of *The Daily Graphic* on 1 January 1902. It was captioned: 'Slow but sure: John Bull: That peace plant takes a long time to come up — seeds all right I suppose? Gardener Salisbury: The Seed's all right and should by rights have been up in 1901. It's a bit slow to sprout and takes a heap of nursing, but it'll be a fine healthy plant when it do come.'
3 This pen-and-ink drawing by Alexander Stuart Boyd entitled *Occupation of Bloemfontein* was probably reproduced in *The Daily Graphic* soon after the event, which took place on 13 March 1900. Reproduced by courtesy of the National Army Museum, London.
4 The cover of the book *John Bull in Zuid-Afrika: Teekeningen van Johan Braakensiek en Anderen.*
5 Messrs Fores of London published this chromolithograph after a work by George Bridgman in June 1900. The date coincides with the fall of Johannesburg, and the picture depicts Lord Roberts banishing Kruger and 'Eve', probably representing his wife Gezina, from Paradise. When Kruger left Pretoria a few days later he did not in fact take his ailing wife into exile with him.

were originally reproduced in *With the Flag to Pretoria* and the special double number of *The Graphic* (2 April 1900), can be found in the National Army Museum, including *The Boer attack on Caesar's camp: A hot corner with the Border Mounted Rifles*, after a sketch by H. McCormick. Fifteen other illustrations by Browne appeared in *The Graphic*. His Boer War work was reproduced in *The King, With the Flag to Pretoria* and *After Pretoria: the Guerilla War*. Some of his works were only initialled, but are identifiable by the tag placed on the 'G' which underlines the 'B'. Browne lived in Richmond, Surrey, where he died on 27 May 1932. See p. 168.

Bénézit, Dictionnaire antique, *vol. 2, p. 163*
Graves, Royal Academy, *vol. 1, p. 316*
Johnson and Greutzner, British Artists, *p. 81*
SABIB, *vol. 1, p. 309*
The Strand Magazine, *vol. 10, p. 790*
The Times, *30 May 1932*
Who was Who, *vol. 3, p. 175*

BROWN(E), Henry Harris 1864-1948

Brown(e) contributed a sketch to the souvenir programme of the 'Grand Military and Patriotic Concert' at the Royal Albert Hall on 5 December 1899. The proceeds were in aid of 'our sick and wounded soldiers, for our women and children, for the families of the Reserve'. Waters and Johnson and Greutzner record a Henry Harris Brown who was born in Northamptonshire on 29 December 1864, studied in Paris under Bouguereau and Tony Fleury, and exhibited at the Paris Salon and the Royal Academy from 1888.

Johnson and Greutzner, British Artists, *p. 80*
Waters, British Artists, *vol. 1, pp. 47-48*

BROWNE, Thomas Arthur (Tom) 1870-1910   3

Painter, illustrator and postcard artist. Browne was born in Nottingham in 1870. In about 1884 he was apprenticed to a firm of lithographers where he remained for several years. He later founded his own printing firm in Nottingham. Browne went to London in 1895, and he exhibited at the Royal Academy from 1897. He was elected a member of the R.B.A. in 1898 and the R.I. in 1901. Browne published his own paper called *Tom Browne's Comic Annual*; his other publications include *Tom Browne's Cycle Book* and *Khaki Alphabet*. He worked for *Punch*, but the only work by Browne influenced by the Boer War and published by this magazine was a cartoon entitled *Time revenges*, which appeared on 12 March 1902. Some of his Boer War work that was published by *The Sketch* included an illustration, on 10 October 1900, lampooning

ACTIVE SERVI

Kruger's 75th birthday. Browne was also a prolific postcard artist from 1900, the year in which he produced advertising cards for Peak Frean and Eucaryl soap, including *A Transvaal Bath* and one depicting a British soldier in Boer War uniform. His travels through Europe, the United States and the Far East inspired many postcards. Browne signed his work in full, or used 'T.B.', or, more often, 'Tom B.'.

Hammerton, Humorists of the Pencil, *p. 80*
Johnson, Tom Browne
Lawson and Warr, Postcards of Tom Browne
Who was Who, *vol. 1, pp. 94-95*

BRUCE-JOY, Albert 1842-1924

Sculptor. Albert Bruce-Joy was born in Dublin in 1842, the elder brother of George William Joy (see page 155). He studied at the Royal Academy schools and in Paris and Rome. He exhibited work at the Royal Academy from 1888, including a bronze bust of 'Field Marshal Lord Roberts of Kandahar VC' in 1900. Bruce-Joy died on 22 July 1924.

Graves, Royal Academy, *vol. 4, p. 291*
Johnson and Greutzner, British Artists, *p. 82*
Waters, British Artists, *vol. 1, p. 49*

BRUESTLE, George M. 1872-?

Bruestle was born in New York in 1872. *Harper's Weekly* featured his landscape of Majuba Hill (21 October 1899) and a portrait of General Penn-Symons (11 November 1899).

Fielding, American Painters, etc., *p. 46*

BRUN, A.

'Special' artist for *Le Monde Illustré*. Brun's illustration of Kruger arriving in Marseilles appeared on the front cover of *Le Monde Illustré* on 24 November 1900. An Alexander Brun, born in Marseilles, exhibited at the Royal Academy in 1881 and 1882 and may be the same person.

Bénézit, Dictionnaire antique, *vol. 2, p. 176*

BRUNET, Jean   1

French painter born in Mézières-en-Brenne. His Boer War work appeared in *Paris-Pretoria*.

Bénézit, Dictionnaire antique, *vol. 2, p. 180*

BRYAN, Alfred 1852-1899

Caricaturist and illustrator. Bryan's cartoons featuring the 'Transvaal Crisis' were published in *Moonshine* and *Judy*. He also worked for *The Illustrated Sporting & Dramatic News*. He used the initials 'A.B.' to sign his work. *Cartoons by A.B. 1897-1898* is a collection of Bryan's caricatures which originally appeared in *Entr'acte*, including one of Marie Lloyd and President Kruger (13 March 1897).

SABIB, *vol. 1, p. 316*
Thorpe, English Illustration, *p. 66*

BUCHANAN, Fred

Cartoonist for *Fun, The Graphic* and *The Strand Magazine*. Buchanan was responsible for the postwar postcard *Well over South Africa*.

KRUGER.

« Pour l'Indépendance du Transvaal »

6

7

Houfe, British Illustrators and Caricaturists, p. 250
Mead, Venman and Whitney, Picton's Priced Catalogue 1983

BUCKLAND, William Harold 1870-1941

Soldier-artist. Buckland was a corporal in the New Zealand 4th Contingent in South Africa. His Boer War diary, including sketches of scenery and military life, can be found in the Alexander Turnbull Library, Wellington, New Zealand.
Personal communication with Moira Long, Librarian, Alexander Turnbull Library, Wellington, New Zealand

BUCKNALL, Ernest Pile 1861-?

Landscape painter. Bucknall was born in Liverpool on 2 April 1861. He studied at the Lambeth and South Kensington schools of art. Bucknall exhibited at the Royal Academy, the R.B.A. and the R.I., and his Boer War work appeared in *With the Flag to Pretoria*.
Waters, British Artists, vol. 1, p. 51

BUELINKX, Henry 1

Belgian sculptor whose work is featured on the postcard *Pour l'Independence du Transvaal.*

BULL, René 1870-1942 1

Artist-correspondent for *Black & White*. Bull was born of French parents in Dublin on 11 December 1870. He studied engineering in Paris (where he met the cartoonist Caran d'Ache), but gave it up to become an artist in 1892. His assignments as a war artist included the campaign in Armenia, the Turko-Greek War, the Indian Frontier and Tirah campaigns, and the Atbara and Omdurman wars in the Sudan. He set a record by enduring three campaigns on three different continents in 10 months. Bull received medals for both the Sudan and Boer wars, including the Queen's South Africa medal on 23 February 1903.

Bull was sent to South Africa aboard the *Tintagel Castle*, and his illustration that was published in *Black & White Budget* on 19 November 1899 depicts the first news of the War signalled from the *Dunvegan Castle*, about 600 miles north of Cape Town. Bull spent the early days of the War with Melton Prior, but when Ladysmith was surrounded he escaped with Bennet Burleigh on one of the special medical trains. He joined the Ladysmith relief column which set out under General Buller from the advance base on 14 December 1899, but was invalided back home some time during 1900. He collaborated with H.S. Boorman on improvements to the Maxim gun, which he patented in 1901.

In March 1916 Bull joined the R.N.V.R. as a lieutenant attached to the R.N.A.S. He was drafted to France in July 1916 and promoted to lieutenant commander of the R.N.V.R. in June 1917. He was transferred to the R.A.F. in April 1918, and was later promoted to major, having been mentioned in des-

patches. In 1940 he entered the Air Ministry.

Bull's Boer War sketches and photographs were sent back to England for publication in *Black & White* and *Black & White Budget*, many being reproduced in facsimile. He also worked for *Lika Joko, Pick-Me-Up, The Sketch* and *Pall Mall Magazine*. The author has the original painting *The Battle of Farquhar's Farm – returning into the town October 30 1899*, which was completed just prior to the Siege of Ladysmith and was reproduced in *Black & White Budget* (9 December 1899).

Bull later became well known as a comic and sporting postcard artist. He died in March 1942.
Black & White Budget, 3 Feb. 1900, p. 6
Personal communication with G.W. Haysom, Ministry of Defence, Eastern Avenue, Gloucester
The Orders and Medals Research Society, Summer 1986, 'War Correspondents: South Africa 1899-1902', by Patrick Street
Who was Who, vol. 4, pp. 158-159

BURN, Gerald Maurice 1862-1945

Marine painter. Burn was born in London on 1 April 1862. He studied in London, Cologne, Düsseldorf, Antwerp and Paris. He exhibited in London galleries from 1881, and four of his paintings were shown at the Royal Academy. Burn's works include *Field Marshal the Earl Roberts proceeding ashore at Cowes from H.M. Troopship Canada upon his return from the Cape with H.M.S. Australia firing a salute.*
Graves, Royal Academy, vol. 1, p. 351
Parker Gallery Catalogue, 1984, no. 14
Waters, British Artists, vol. 1, p. 53
Wood, Victorian Painters, pp. 73-74

BURRET, Jean-Leonce 1866-1915

French cartoonist, illustrator and lithographer. Burret was born in Bordeaux on 20 April 1866. He worked for several French periodicals including *Le Sourire, Chat Gris, Fantasio, La Vie Parisienne* and *L'Assiette au Beurre*. His Boer War work appeared in *Le Rire*. Burret died in Paris in 1915.
Fanelli and Godoli, Art Nouveau Postcards
Osterwalder, and Hubschmid and Bouret (eds.), Dictionnaire des Illustrateurs, p. 202

BURTON, F. W. 1

Illustrator who contributed to *The Sphere, The Illustrated London News* and *With the Flag to Pretoria*. Burton also produced one of the well-known Bovril advertisements using the Boer War as a theme. The illustrator could have been Sir Frederick William Burton, but this is unlikely as the latter died in 1900 at the age of 84.

BUSH, C.L.

Cartoonist for *The New York World*.

BUTLER, Elizabeth Southerden 1846-1933

Military painter. Elizabeth Butler (née Thompson) was born in Lausanne, Switzerland, in 1846. She married Lt. Gen. Sir William Francis Butler in 1877 just before his first tour in South Africa. In 1898 she returned to South Africa with Butler, who was acting as High Commissioner while Milner was home on leave. This period was marked by controversy, as Sir William was blamed for not informing the British Government of the Boers' military strength. He was also accused of pro-Boer sentiments. Both accusations were disproved at an official enquiry. Sir William returned once again to South Africa in 1906. Her equestrian portrait of her husband with a backdrop of Table Mountain, done in June 1899, was engraved for the frontispiece of Sir William's atuobiography, published posthumously in 1911.

Some of Lady Butler's paintings were exhibited at the Royal Academy. They included: *The defence of Rorke's Drift* (1881), *Floreat Etona!* (1882), from which prints and lithographs were made, and *Within sound of the guns* (1903). Two preliminary sketches, *Running the gauntlet, Boer War* and *The relief*, under the general title *A despatch bearer, Boer War and the Horse Gunners*, can be found in her book *An Autobiography* (1923). *Yeomanry Scouts on the Veldt*, an oil on canvas, is owned by the Downside Abbey. *Within sound of the guns*, also an oil on canvas, is in the Army Staff College. A watercolour version of this painting was done in 1929. All these paintings were exhibited, together with several others,

1 Gordon Browne's illustration *He is out on active Service wiping something off a slate and he's left a lot of little things behind him*, which he donated to the Royal Edition of Rudyard Kipling's poem 'The Absent Minded Beggar'.
2 Tom Browne drew the illustration for this postwar 'On Active Service' postcard, published by Davidson Bros. Pictorial Postcards.
3 Paul Kruger's 75th birthday was marked by the publication of this satirical cartoon by Tom Browne in *The Sketch* on 10 October 1900.
4 The versatile Tom Browne produced this sketch of himself.
5 Pro-Boer card showing a frieze by Henry Buelinkx entitled *Pour l'Independence du Transvaal.*
6 René Bull's pen-and-wash drawing *The Battle of Farquhar's Farm* was reproduced in *Black & White Budget* on 9 December 1899. Bull was present at this battle, which preceded the Siege of Ladysmith, but got away before the siege began.
7 The famous Bovril advertisement drawn by F. W. Burton.

at a retrospective exhibition of her work at the National Army Museum in 1987.

Lady Butler died in Ireland on 2 October 1933.
Art and Antiques, *1979, no. 5, p. 83*
Butler, An Autobiography
From Sketch-Book and Diary
Usherwood and Spencer-Smith, Lady Butler: Battle Artist 1846-1933
Waters, British Artists, *vol. 1, p. 55*
Who was Who, *vol. 3, p. 201*

BUTLER, Mary Emily
Described by Verbeek as 'an impoverished gentlewoman who taught art in Pietermaritzburg in the last two decades of the nineteenth century'. Butler sent three sketches from Natal to *The Graphic: A Colonial welcome to British troops: A scene at Zwartkop station* (3 February 1900), redrawn by Arthur Garratt; *Enlisting stretcher-bearers for the front at Pietermaritzburg* (17 February 1900), redrawn by Percy F. S. Spence, and *Nearing Ladysmith: view from Longwood farm* (4 March 1900), redrawn by Frank Dadd.
Hofmeyr, Matton and Roets, Graphic Picture Index
Verbeek, Early Natal Art

BUVAL, E.
Responsible for the lithographic cover of *Les Boers à la Reine,* a pro-Boer French song.
Africana Notes and News, *June 1981, p. 211*

CADEL, Eugène
French painter. Cadel studied at the École des Beaux-Arts and exhibited widely throughout Europe. He was a member of the French Society of Humorists. He worked for *L'Assiette au Beurre,* and one of his cartoons, which was entitled *Les 'Morts aux gosses'* and compared Kitchener to a milk adulterator, appeared in the special issue 'Les Empoisonneurs Patentes'.
Bénézit, Dictionnaire antique, *vol. 2, p. 224*

CALKIN, Lance 1859-1936
Portrait painter. Calkin was born in London on 27 June 1859, the son of George Calkin, a musician and composer. He studied at the South Kensington, Slade and Royal Academy schools. A member of the R.O.I., he exhibited at the Royal Academy, and his portraits include King Edward VII, King George V, Sir Joseph Chamberlain, Marquis Camden, Sir John Tenniel and Captain Scott. Calkin's Boer War work includes a portrait of General De Wet in *With the Flag to Pretoria,* contributions to *War Pictures,* and three illustrations in *The*

Graphic (January – June 1900). He died on 10 October 1936.
Graves, Royal Academy, *vol. 1, p. 378*
Hofmeyr, Matton and Roets, Graphic Picture Index
Who was Who, *vol. 3, p. 209*

CAMARA, Tomás Júlio Leal de 1877-1948 1
Painter, sketcher and cartoonist. Camara was born in New Goa, India, on 30 November 1877. His Boer War work appeared in *L'Assiette au Beurre* and *Le Rire*; in fact two issues of the former – 'Britannique' (28 June 1902) and 'Vive L'Angleterre' (2 May 1903) – were taken up entirely by his anti-British contributions. Several of Camara's postcards showing Kruger and King Edward VII were produced by an unidentified publisher during the War and included some of his unsigned illustrations taken from *L'Assiette au Beurre.* Some of his Boer War work also appeared in the Spanish periodical *Nuevo Mundo.* Camara's Art Nouveau postcards are much sought after, especially those depicting bicycles. He died in Lisbon on 21 July 1948.
Bénézit, Dictionnaire antique, *vol. 2, p. 272*
Fanelli and Godoli, Art Nouveau Postcards
Holt, Tonie and Valmai, Stanley Gibbons Postcard Catalogue 1983
Weill, Art Nouveau Postcards

CAMERON, J. G.
His cartoon lampooning British patriotism appeared in *Le Rire* on 2 December 1899.

CAMERON, John J.
Cameron's illustrations appeared in *The Graphic* and his Boer War work in *After Pretoria: the Guerilla War.*

CAMPBELL, Colin
Soldier-artist. Campbell was probably a member of the Cape Garrison Artillery. Three of his illustrations appeared in *The Graphic* (May 1900 – April 1901), as did a portrait of a Lt. Campbell on 5 May 1900. His work also appeared in *After Pretoria: the Guerilla War.*
Hofmeyr, Matton and Roets, Graphic Picture Index

CAMPBELL, John F. 1
Postcard illustrator. Campbell's work appeared in the V.C. series (W. and A.K. Johnston Ltd, Edinburgh and Glasgow, 1906), including *How General Buller won his Victoria Cross in the Zulu War March 1879* and *How Lt J. Norwood 2nd D.G. won his Victoria Cross, Boer War October 1899.*
Byatt, Picture Postcards, *p. 144*

CAPELL, Algernon Essex 1869-1952
Soldier-artist. Capell was born in Tettenhall, near Wolverhampton, on 1 November 1869 and educated at Felsted School. In 1889 he joined the Cape Mounted Rifles as a trooper and remained in the corps until 1899 when he joined Bethune's Mounted Rifles as lieutenant, having served in Pondoland during the annexation. Capell also served in the Boer War and was promoted to captain in 1900 for 'gallantry in the field' at Scheeper's Nek. He joined the South African Constabulary (S.A.C) during that year, was created D.S.O., and was promoted to major in 1902. He was mentioned in despatches, twice by Gen. Buller and once each by Lord Roberts and Lord Kitchener. Capell was 'ejected' from the S.A.C by the Boer government in 1908 and was appointed Assistant District Commissioner in British East Africa. From 1910 to 1912 he served as Chief of Police in Grenada, where he was awarded the King's Police Medal, and in 1913 as Assistant Commissioner of the British South African Police in Southern Rhodesia. Capell also served in World War I during which he commanded a column in German South-West Africa. He was captured at Schuckmannsburg, the capital of the Caprivi. In 1914 he was given command of the 2nd Rhodesian Regiment with the rank of lieutenant colonel. He was mentioned in despatches by Gen. Smuts and received the Croix de Guerre. His daughter,

Joan Evans, is a well-known Zimbabwean artist.
Capell was taken prisoner at Scheeper's Nek on 20 May 1900 and sent to Nooitgedacht from where he submitted sketches to *The Sphere* and *The Graphic.* One illustration appeared in *The Graphic History of the South African War.* On 25 August 1900 *The Sphere* depicted British prisoners at Nooitgedacht using Capell's sketches which had been redrawn by Alfred Pearse. Following the defeat of the Boers at Bergendal and Dalmanutha many prisoners were released, but some, including Capell, were sent to Barberton. His family still possesses some of his watercolours, oils and sketches, including one of a bunker completed after his release from Nooitgedacht. Some of Capell's papers can be found in the Zimbabwean Archives.
A Capt. Essex Capell who wrote *Rhodesian Regiment in East Africa* (1923) and the illustrator A.E.C. (see p. 102), who worked for *The Graphic* are possibly Algernon Capell.
Debrett's Illustrated Peerage, p. 433
Hofmeyr, Matton and Roets, Graphic Picture Index
Personal communication with Joan Evans

CARAMBA
Cartoonist for the Turin publication *Il Fischetto.*
Grand-Carteret, *John Bull, p. 38*

CARAN D'Ache 1858-1909 1
Pseudonym of French cartoonist Emmanuel Poiré. Caran d'Ache was born in Moscow of French parents. In 1875 he went to Paris and studied under Eduard Detaille, the military painter. He enlisted in the French army and adopted the pseudonym 'Caran d'Ache', which is the phonetic translation of the Russian for 'lead pencil'. He admired the work of Phil May, Linley Sambourne, Dudley Hardy and John Tenniel. His work for the production of *L'Épopée* at the 'Chat Noir' was extremely well received: he produced hundreds of shadow silhouettes depicting, in 30 tableaux, the leading people in the Napoleonic drama. Copies were sent to the Tsar of Russia, one of his most avid fans. Caran d'Ache was described by Marie Belloc as 'the greatest caricaturist of France, if not of the whole world' in *The Strand Magazine* (January 1898). The cartoonist said in an interview that 'I am a great believer in telling stories silently and by means of pen or pencil alone'. This is borne out by the fact that most of his cartoons have no caption. Caran d'Ache's work appeared in *Le Journal du Lundi, Chronique Parisienne, L'Assiette au Beurre, La Vie Parisienne, Le Rire, Le Figaro, La Caricature* and *Chat Noir,* among others. During the Dreyfus affair he was associated with the journal *Ps'itt.*

3

According to John Raphael in *London Magazine* (1902), 'during the Boer War [Caran d'Ache] devoted himself largely to portraying British imperfection, which he did with a bitterness that must have satisfied Oom Paul himself'. His Boer War work appeared in *Punch, Le Figaro, Journal d' Illustration, The King* and *Pick-Me-Up*. The special edition of *Le Rire* (17 November 1900), entitled 'Kruger le Grand et John Bull le Petit', was devoted almost entirely to his cartoons. Most of his work was reproduced by *Le Figaro*, including a cartoon (which also appeared in *Lustige Blätter*), depicting a maid bringing a parcel of anti-British postcards to a frustrated John Bull, who attacks the parcel with his whip and dog. The maid remarks: 'Poor man, he becomes a raving lunatic when the post arrives from Germany.' (This cartoon is captioned 'John Bull and the *Lustige Blätter* postcards'.)

Although Caran d'Ache often signed his work 'C d'A', most of his postcard cartoons relating to the Boer War were unsigned. The author has a signed, untitled brush and pencil cartoon depicting a group of British soldiers holding aloft the sign 'Victory', while a Boer boy sits nonchalantly behind his rifle (see above).

Bateman, Caran d'Ache the Supreme
Bénézit, Dictionnaire antique, *vol. 2, p. 306*
The King, *15 Sept. 1900, p. 658*
London Magazine, *vol. 9, p. 150*
Le Rire, *9 June 1900 (cover)*
SABIB, *vol. 3, p. 697*
The Strand, *vol. 15, p. 158 and vol. 22, p. 678*
Weill, Art Nouveau Postcards, *p. 10*
Who was Who, *vol. 1, p. 178*

CAREY, John
Carey's Boer War illustration in *The Graphic* (23 June 1900) depicted a banquet for Sir George White in Belfast.
Hofmeyr, Matton and Roets, Graphic Picture Index

CAREYE, Ward Sausmarez 1867-1940
Soldier-artist. Ward Sausmarez Careye (the *Army List* and *The Graphic* always omitted the final 'e' from his name) was commissioned into the Prince of Wales' Own West Yorkshire Regiment from the militia on 14 November 1888. He was promoted as follows: lieutenant 24 September 1890, captain 20 March 1895, brevet major 29 November 1900, and major 14 November 1908. He was transferred to the army pay department on 1 July 1901 and served with the army accounts department as second class assistant accountant from 1 May 1905 until 31 December 1919. He retired from the army on 2 March 1920.

Careye served with the 2nd Battalion of the Regiment throughout the Boer War. He was present at the relief of Ladysmith and the Battle of Colenso. He was active in Natal from 17 to 24 January 1900, where he took part in the Battle of Spioenkop, and from 1 to 7 February 1900 at Vaal Kranz. Careye was involved in the operations at Tugela Heights between 6 and 9 June 1900 and on active service in the Transvaal from July 1900 until 31 May 1902. He was mentioned in despatches and received the Queen's medal with five clasps and the King's medal with two clasps. Two of Careye's sketches were reproduced in *The Graphic: Panoramic view of the battle of Colenso: the fight against a hidden enemy* (27 January 1900), redrawn by C. E. Fripp and F. C. Dickinson, and *The taking of Ladysmith Hill by Kitchener's Brigade and the West Yorkshire Regiment* (7 April 1900), redrawn by George Soper. Careye died in Oxford on 18 February 1940.
Hofmeyr, Matton and Roets, Graphic Picture Index
Personal communication with Maj. R. F. Tomlinson (Ret.), Regimental Secretary, Prince of Wales' Own Regiment of Yorkshire

CARLEGLE, Charles-Emile 1877-1940
Cartoonist and illustrator. Carlegle was born in Switzerland on 30 May 1877. He was a member of the French Society of Humorists. He worked for *L'Assiette au Beurre, Les Humoristes, La Vie Parisienne, L'Illustration, Le Sourire* and *Le Rire*. Carlegle's Boer War work appeared in *Le Rire*.
Osterwalder, and Hubschmid and Bouret (eds.), Dictionnaire des Illustrateurs, *p. 218*

CARLETON, Clifford 1867-?
Illustrator. Carleton was born in Brooklyn, New York, in 1867. He studied under Mowbray at the Art Students' League of New York and became a member of the Society of Illustrators in 1901. He illustrated Julian Ralph's *Pembroke* and Howell's *Wedding Journey*. Carleton's Boer War work appeared in *Harper's Weekly*, including a cover illustration of General De Wet taken from a well-known photograph (26 January 1901).
Fielding, American Painters, etc., *p. 56*

CARL-ROSA, Mario Cornelleaiu Raoul 1855-1913
Landscape artist. Carl-Rosa was born in Loudun, Vienna, in 1855. His Boer War work appeared in *Paris-Pretoria*.
Bénézit, Dictionnaire Antique, *vol. 2, p. 316*

CARNEGIE, Robert Francis
Soldier-artist. Carnegie was made second lieutenant in the Gordons on 28 June 1890, lieutenant on 10 October 1892, captain on 4 November 1898 and brevet major on 29 November 1900. He served in the Boer War from 1899 to 1901 in Natal, participating in the defence of Ladysmith and Laing's Nek. He was mentioned twice in despatches and was severely wounded in January 1900. In 1902 Carnegie served as regular adjutant of the Gordons 1st Volunteer Battalion, but he does not appear in the *Army List* after 1905. His Boer War illustrations appear, with acknowledgment, in Capt. Aylmer Haldane's *How we Escaped from Pretoria*.
Personal communication with W. A. Thorburn, Keeper of the Scottish United Services Museum

CARONTE
Cartoonist for the Turin publication *Il Fischetto*.

CARREY, P.
Illustrator and engraver. Carrey provided, usually in collaboration with F. Méaulle or Charles Crespin, several coloured and uncoloured cover illustrations for *Le Petit Parisien*.

CARRUTHERS GOULD, Francis see GOULD, Francis Carruthers

CARTER, F. A.
Illustrator of August Niemann's *The Boer Boy of the Transvaal* (Penn Publishing Co., Philadelphia, 1900) which was translated from the German by Kate Milner Rabb.
SABIB, *vol. 3, p. 545*

CARTER, Sydney 1874-1945
Carter was born in Enfield, Middlesex, on 2 April 1874, the son of artist Richard Carter. He studied at the Royal Academy schools and exhibited at the Paris Salon, the R.O.I., and the Royal Academy from 1894. One of his exhibited works, entitled *The list of casualties* (1902), is presumably of Boer War interest. He was employed as a postcard illustrator by Raphael Tuck & Sons and S. Hildesheimer & Co. Ltd. Carter fought in World War I, and some years later, in October 1924, he emigrated to South Africa. His work can be found in most South African galleries and his illustrations in a number of books, including one by Dorothea Fairbridge. Carter died on 21 December 1945 while on a painting trip to Lesotho.
Byatt, Picture Postcards, *p. 131*
Carter, Sydney Carter
Graves, Royal Academy, *vol. 2, p. 7*

CARTER, T. J.
Cartoonist for the *Minneapolis Sunday Times* and *The New York Journal*.

CATON WOODVILLE, Richard see WOODVILLE, Richard Caton

CAUTY, Horace Henry 1846-1909
Genre and historical painter. Cauty exhibited at the Royal Academy from 1870, including *The Advance Guard* (1901), which was probably of Boer War interest.
Graves, Royal Academy, *vol. 2, p. 16*
Waters, British Artists, *p. 62*

---

1 The controversial cartoon entitled *L'Impudique Albion* by Jean Veber was censored in September 1901, but the cartoonist Leal de Camara would not let the matter rest and produced this cartoon in *L'Assiette au Beurre* on 2 May 1903. It shows King Edward VII viewing Veber's work at an art gallery and being shown the offending cartoon.
2 John F. Campbell's *How Lt. J. Norwood 2nd D.G. won his Victoria Cross* was published by W. & A. K. Johnson Ltd. Norwood won his V.C. on 30 October 1899 when he went out from Ladysmith with a small patrol of 5th Dragoon Guards. They came under heavy fire and one of the men was hit. Norwood galloped back and brought him to safety.
3 Caran d'Ache's cartoon *Victory* was produced for publication, possibly in *Le Figaro*.

C.G.
An artist-correspondent using these initials contributed six illustrations to *The Graphic* (April – June 1900). It is possible that he was with Roberts's forces at Bloemfontein and saw action at Brandfort, Norval's Pont and Driefontein.
Hofmeyr, Matton and Roets, Graphic Picture Index

CHAMBERS, Mrs M.A.
A sketch attributed to Mrs Chambers, entitled *Off to South Africa: The 2nd Gordon Highlanders leaving Bombay*, was redrawn by Frank Dadd and appeared in *The Graphic* on 21 October 1899.
Hofmeyr, Matton and Roets, Graphic Picture Index

CHAPELLIER, P. 1
Chapellier was the designer of the poster *Le Transvaal et L'Afrique Sauvage* (Courmont Frères, Paris), depicting the 'Long Tom' with Pretoria in the background. It carried the inscription 'Rue de La Federation (Avenue de Suffren) Gare du Champ de Mars Quai D'Orsay'.

CHARBERT
The illustrator of a French card entitled *Le Lion Britannique et le coq Gallois* (fable).

CHARLTON, John 1849-1917 2
Animal and battle painter and illustrator. Charlton was born in Bamburgh, Northumberland, on 28 June 1849. He first received art lessons from his father when he was four years old, and he started work for a bookseller at the age of 12. He later studied at the Newcastle School of Art under W.B. Scott and at the South Kensington School of Art under J.D. Watson. In 1870 his first work, *Harrowing*, was accepted by the Royal Academy.

It was during the Egyptian Campaign (1882) that Charlton's interest in battle scenes developed. His earliest important military work was *British artillery entering the enemy's lines at Tel el Kebir* (1883). Between 1870 and 1904 over 36 of his paintings were exhibited at the Royal Academy, including *After the charge: 17th Lancers, Ulundi, July 4 1879* (1888) and *Routed! Boers retreating* (1900). Charlton worked for most of the illustrated weeklies during the Boer War, especially *The Graphic*, which he had joined in 1876. Some of his illustrations in *The Graphic*, including *Hot chase* and *Into the jaws of death*, were published as supplementary prints. His work also appeared in *With the Flag To Pretoria*.

The author has a Boer War wash drawing, *Keep quiet, signs of the enemy*, which was reproduced in *The Graphic* (27 January 1900) and *The Graphic History of the War* (1900).

A postcard depicting De Wet breaking through the blockhouse lines was published by the Dutch firm of C.J. Dalmeijer. Thirty-two paintings were reproduced as colour plates in the programme for the 'Royal Naval and Military Bazaar in aid of Princess Christian's Home for Disabled Soldiers and Sailors', which was held from 19 to 21 January 1900. The booklet was published by the Dangerfield Printing Company, London. Charlton contributed the illustration *A friend in need is a friend indeed* to the programme of the 'Grand Military and Patriotic Concert' held on Tuesday 5 December 1899, in aid of wounded and ill soldiers and their dependants, as well as soldiers' widows and orphans.

Queen Victoria commissioned Charlton to paint the Jubilee procession in 1897, and 10 of his watercolours are still in the Royal Collection at Windsor. Charlton's work is often unidentified, as he sometimes signed with the initials 'J.C.' only. His second wife, Edith, was a painter of miniatures and also exhibited at the Royal Academy.
Art Journal, 1982, pp. 33 ff.
British Military Costume Prints
Carter, War Artists in S.A.
Dawnay and Miller, Military Drawings and Paintings
Graves, Royal Academy, *vol. 2, pp. 46-48*
Hofmeyr, Matton and Roets, Graphic Picture Index
Who was Who, *vol. 2, p. 191*

CHARRON, Alfred-Joseph 1863-?
Sculptor. Charron was born in Vienna on 8 July 1863. He contributed a sketch of one of his sculptures to *Paris-Pretoria*.
Bénézit, Dictionnaire antique, *vol. 2, p. 453*

CHASE, Emerson C.
Illustrator of Elbridge Streeter Brooks's *With Lawton and Roberts: A Boy's Adventure in the Philippines and Transvaal* (Boston Lothrop Publishing Co., 1900).
SABIB, vol. 1, p. 300

C., H.T. *see* **H.T.C.**

CHURCH, Richard (Dicky)
Soldier-artist. Church, a trooper with Loch's Horse, was one of the editors of *The Mexican Mercury*, produced and published aboard the SS *Mexican* which sailed to South Africa in March 1900. He was responsible for some of the caricatures, which he signed 'R.C.'.

CHURCHILL, Winston Leonard Spencer 1874-1965
Winston Churchill was born at Blenheim Palace in Oxfordshire on 30 November 1874, the elder son of Lord Randolph

Churchill. His biographical details and Boer War activities are well documented in numerous publications. His Boer War sketches are limited to just three illustrations, which appeared in *The Graphic* (3 February 1900 and 24 February 1900), redrawn by home-based artists.

Churchill arrived in South Africa in October 1899 as correspondent for *The Morning Post*. While attempting to get to the besieged town of Ladysmith he was captured by the Boers and sent to the State Model School in Pretoria, which served as a P.O.W. camp. In December he managed to escape, and his three published Boer War illustrations all relate to this escape. One of them, which was redrawn by Frederic de Haenen, was titled *Mr Winston Churchill's escape from Pretoria: Waiting for the night to come.* Joseph Nash redrew *Mr Winston Churchill's escape from Pretoria: Boarding the goods train* and also *Mr Winston Churchill's escape from Pretoria: Scaling the prison wall.* These illustrations were subtitled 'from sketches by Winston Churchill', and appeared on 3 February 1900. They were later reproduced in *With the Flag to Pretoria*. Churchill eventually became well known as an artist and had works accepted by the Royal Academy. He was also a member of the British Society of Water Colourists. It is generally claimed that he only began painting seriously after 1915 and neither Churchill College, Cambridge, nor the International Trust at Chartwell, Churchill's home, can trace any of his early sketches.
Churchill, From London to Ladysmith
Ian Hamilton's March
My Early Life
Haldane, How we Escaped from Pretoria
SESA, *vol. 3, p. 220*

CINIRIN
Cartoonist for the Turin publication *Il Fischetto*.

C., J.A.H. *see* **J.A.H.C.** 1

C.L.
This cartoonist was responsible for ten cartoons entitled *Humorous Sketches of Some Incidents of the Siege* in *The Siege of Kimberley 1899-1900* published by *The Diamond Fields Advertiser*. He may also have used the monogram 'L.C.'.

CLACY, Ellen fl. 1872-1916
'Domestic' painter. Clacy exhibited 27 works at the Royal Academy, including *War news in the streets of England 1900* (1900).
Graves, Royal Academy, *vol. 2, pp. 63-64*
Johnson and Greutzner, British Artists, *p. 10*

CLARK, Christopher 1875-1942
Military and historical painter. Clark was born in London on 1 March 1875. He exhibited at the Royal Academy from 1900, including *The attempt to save the guns at Colenso* (1900) and *Ubique* (1901). He was made a member of the R.I. in 1905. Clark served in the R.N.V.R. during World War I and was noted for his drawings of the Royal Scots Greys. He worked as an illustrator for the popular, but short-lived, weekly *The Regiment*, but most of his Boer War work appeared in *Black & White* and *Black & White Budget*. The watercolour of Maj. H.S.H. Prince Francis of Teck, First Royal Dragoons (c.1902) can be found in the Royal Collection at Windsor. Clark died on 9 February 1942.
> *Dawnay and Miller*, Military Drawings and Paintings, *p. 237*
> *Graves*, Royal Academy, *vol. 2, p. 64*
> *Houfe*, British Illustrators and Caricaturists, *p. 260*
> *Waters*, British Artists, *vol. 1, p. 66*

CLARK, H.C. 1
Soldier-artist. Clark sent a series of illustrated postal covers to Mr and Mrs Clark at 25 Seaford Road, South Tottenham, London between April 1900 and November 1901. Another cover was addressed to Miss H. Clark in Brighton. All the covers are signed with the monogram 'H.C.' and include the month and the year. (Recent discoveries indicate that 'H.C.' was producing similar covers as early as 13 October 1897.) Most of these covers have watercolour drawings, some of which are copies of popular postcards, such as *Gentleman in Kharki* and *With the Flag to Pretoria*. One illustrated cover featuring the C.I.V. implies that Clark may have been a member of this corps.

CLARK, Joseph 1834-1926
Genre painter. Clark was born in Cerne Abbas, Dorset, on 4 July 1834. He was elected a member of the R.O.I. He exhibited at the R.A. from 1857, including the work *War news at St Cross* (1899), which is presumably of Boer War interest. Clark died in August 1926.
> *Graves*, Royal Academy, *vol. 2, p. 71*
> *Waters*, British Artists, *vol. 1, p. 69*

CLEAVER, Dudley
Illustrator who contributed to *The Penny Illustrated Paper* and *Illustrated War Special*. One of his illustrations depicted Churchill's escape from Pretoria.

CLEAVER, Hugh
Soldier-artist. Cleaver was responsible for illustrations entitled *In the bush veldt with the Imperial Yeomanry* which appeared in *The Graphic* on 17 November 1900. The credit reads 'from the diary of a trooper in the Montgomeryshire (49th) Company'. The sketches had been redrawn by Reginald Cleaver (see below), who may have been a relative.
> *Hofmeyr, Matton and Roets*, Graphic Picture Index

CLEAVER, Ralph fl.1893-1923
Black and white artist. Ralph Cleaver was the brother of artist Reginald Cleaver (see below). He worked for many of the illustrated papers, particularly *The Graphic*, *The Daily Graphic* and *Punch*. He served in the R.N.V.R. during World War 1. Ten Boer War illustrations by Cleaver appeared in *The Illustrated London News* from 1900 to 1903, including *Reception on the Stock Exchange of the news of Cronje's surrender* (3 March 1900). His Boer War work also appeared in *With the Flag To Pretoria* and *After Pretoria: the Guerilla War*.
> *De Wet*, Illustrated London News Index
> *Houfe*, British Illustrators and Caricaturists, *p. 262*
> *Spielmann*, History of Punch
> *Thieme and Becker*, vol. 2, p. 75
> *Thorpe*, English Illustration

CLEAVER, Reginald Thomas ?-1954
Black and white artist. Cleaver worked for *The Daily Graphic*, *The Graphic* and *Punch*. Thorpe refers to him as 'the bright star of *The Daily Graphic*. No artist has ever translated photographs into lines with more success.' Only five of Cleaver's Boer War illustrations appeared in *The Graphic* — his work was more prolific in *The Daily Graphic*. The National Army Museum has two of Cleaver's Boer War pen-and-ink drawings: *Relief at last* and *Staff officers mounted and dismounted*, which probably appeared in *The Daily Graphic*. The author has two original pen-and-ink drawings, reproduced in *The Daily Graphic*, one depicting Sir Evelyn Wood and his daughter, and the other an untitled illustration featuring Rhodes, Jameson, Capt. Tim Tyson and Lord Randolph Churchill, dated 1892, which was also reproduced in Randolph Churchill's *Men, Mines and Animals*. The Royal Collection has four of this artist's non-Boer War works. Cleaver was considered an excellent portrayer of 'women in the social scene' and highly regarded for his parliamentary drawings.
> *Hofmeyr, Matton and Roets*, Graphic Picture Index
> *Houfe*, British Illustrators and Caricaturists, *p. 262*
> *Peppin and Micklethwait*, British Book Illustrators, *p. 73*
> *Spielmann*, History of Punch
> *Thorpe*, English Illustration

CLEMENTEL
A contributor to *Paris-Pretoria*.

C.L.G.-C.
Identity unknown. The author has a montage of pen-and-ink and watercolour sketches by this artist dated 1899-1900, depicting Elandslaagte, the Tugela River, Spioenkop, Ladysmith, the Howick Falls, Willow Grange and Estcourt.

C., M.L. *see* M.L.C.

COCK, Hylton
Cartoonist and caricaturist. Cock produced a series of musical comic strips for *Black & White Budget*, including 'Merry Moments in Mafeking' (26 May – 2 June 1900) and 'Pickings from Pretoria' (30 June – 7 July 1900).

COCK, Stanley 1
Cartoonist for *The Sketch*. His caricature of Churchill in army uniform, entitled *Mr Winston Churchill, M.P. for Oldham. A baby of the House of Commons. Truly a promising child!* appeared in *The Sketch* on 10 October 1900.

COHEN, Reuben
Cartoonist who contributed Boer War cartoons to *Judy*.

COHL, Emile 1857-1938
Pseudonym of E. Courtet. Cohl was born in Paris on 4 January 1857. He worked for *La Caricature*, *Le Charivari*, *Le Courrier Français*, *L'Hydropathe* and during the War for *La Dépêche*. He was involved in the early days of cinema, working for Gaumont. Cohl died in Orly on 27 January 1938.
> *Osterwalder, and Hubschmid and Bouret (eds.)*,
> Dictionnaire des Illustrateurs, *p. 251*

---

1 This large poster (160 x 112 cm) by P. Chapellier was published by Courmont Frères in Paris in 1900. A series of postcards with this title was published by the same firm.
2 *Keep quiet, signs of the enemy*, a wash drawing by John Charlton, was first published in *The Graphic* but later reproduced in at least four other contemporary publications under various titles. Harry Payne used a mirror image of the work as his illustration in the Tuck Oilette postcard series 3163.
3 Winston Churchill in the uniform of the 4th Queen's Own Hussars.
4 *The Royal Horse Artillery*, a watercolour by the unidentified artist 'J.A.H.C.'. The Africana Museum, Johannesburg, has a similar watercolour by the same artist.
5 This illustrated postal cover, one of several sent by a soldier, H. Clark, to his family in England, was based on Rudyard Kipling's poem 'The Absent Minded Beggar'.

um, and Julius Weil, the Mafeking siege benefactor, in the Mafikeng museum. Collier also did a portrait of Rudyard Kipling, which appeared on souvenir brochures featuring Kipling's famous poem 'The Absent Minded Beggar'. He died on 11 April 1934.

> *Kennedy,* Pictures in the Africana Museum, *vol. 2, p. 158*
> Who was Who, *vol. 3, p. 273*

COLLISON-MORLEY, Harold Duke 1877-1915 2

Soldier-artist. Collison-Morley was educated at St Paul's School, London and studied art at the Slade School and the Académie Julian in Paris. Collison-Morley joined the Queensland Bushmen, after he had obtained a commission from the Lancashire Fusiliers. He arrived in South Africa from Brisbane in June 1900 and acted as scout in the Transvaal for Kitchener, Hamilton, Mahon, Pilcher, Clements and Delisle. He was awarded the Queen's medal with three clasps. He served as captain in the Buffs in 1911 and adjutant to the 7th Battalion of the Lancashire Fusiliers at the start of World War I.

Collison-Morley worked for *The Regiment, Pick-Me-Up, The Graphic* and *The Daily Graphic.* His work in *The Graphic* included illustrations from Gibraltar completed during 1903, and four coloured lithographs of Hong Kong appeared in *The South China Morning Post* in 1909. Collison-Morley's Boer War work, completed between 15 September 1900 and January 1902, appeared in *The Graphic,* including a series of three sketches from the front (8 December 1900) and illustrations of the 'Queensland Outlaws' in facsimile (26 January 1901 and 16 November 1901). His Boer War work which appeared in the Belgian weekly, *Het Huisgezin,* was probably taken from *The Daily Graphic.* The author has the watercolour *Souvenir of the Christmas cake you made me Boxing Day 1900. The feast in camp at Waterval North.*

Collison-Morley was killed in action in France on 25 September 1915. *The Graphic* published his last sketches in facsimile posthumously in October 1915.

> The Graphic, *19 January 1901, p. 90 and 9 October 1915, p. 470*
> *Hofmeyr, Matton and Roets,* Graphic Picture Index

COLOMB, Alphonse Hector 1849-1909

French cartoonist. Colomb started his career as a cartoonist during the Franco-Prussian War when he took the side of the Commune. He took a pro-Dreyfus stance in cartoons for *Le Sifflet.* During the Boer War Colomb's caricatures in *La Silhouette* appeared under the pseudonym 'B. Moloch'.

> *Feaver,* Masters of Caricature, *p. 92*

COMERFORD, E.

His illustration *Ferry over the Vaal River near Kimberley* appeared in *The Graphic* (4 November 1899), redrawn by Frederic de Haenen.

> *Hofmeyr, Matton and Roets,* Graphic Picture Index

CONOLLY, Walter Moorcroft

Cartoonist who contributed to *Cape Argus* and *The Owl* under the pseudonym 'Walrus'. Eight of his cartoons can be found in the Africana Museum, including those depicting Chamberlain returning to England after his postwar tour of South Africa, and the departure of Milner.

> *Kennedy,* Pictures in the Africana Museum, *vol. 2, p. 168*
> *Schoonraad,* Spot- en Strookprent Kunstenaars, *p. 43*

COOKE, W. H.

Soldier-artist. The following Boer War drawing was offered by the Parker Gallery in its 1980 catalogue: *The Queen's Own (Royal West Kent) Regiment Officer and Private,* with inscription 'to Q.M.S. Powell the Srgt of the 4th? Batt R N Kent .. in remembrance of the kindness received during S.A. campaign 1900 – 2 W.H. Cooke, Sergt Kitchener's Horse.'

COOPER, William Sidney fl. 1871-1908

Landscape painter. From 1871 Cooper exhibited at all the prin-

---

COKE, John Talbot 1841-1912

Soldier-artist. Coke was born on 9 August 1841. He was educated at Harrow. He entered the army in 1859, and, after serving in Canada in 1866, he took part in the Sudan Campaign and saw action in Suakin. As major, he commanded the 10th Brigade, Natal Field Force, from 1899 to 1901, excelling himself at Spioenkop – he was mentioned in despatches and was awarded the Queen's South Africa medal with six clasps. Two of Coke's illustrations appeared in *The Illustrated London News: Almon's Pass. The Boer's last stand in Natal* (18 August 1900) and *Historical battle ground Ingogo, Inkwelo, Majuba and Laing's Nek, the scene of hostilities in 1881 and again the battle ground for the Natal Field Force in May 1900.* Coke was the highest-ranking soldier-artist of the War, as he was promoted to major general on 13 November 1899. He died on 2 February 1912.

> Black & White Budget, *23 June 1900, p. 361*
> *De Wet,* Illustrated London News Index
> Who was Who, *vol. 1, p. 146*

COLE, C.W.

Humorous artist. Cole worked for *The Graphic* from 1884, collaborating with C.J. Staniland on 'Views of Japan'. Cole's Boer War drawing *His first medal: a bluejacket's return home* appeared in *The Graphic* (11 October 1902), redrawn by Sydney Hall.

> *Hofmeyr, Matton and Roets,* Graphic Picture Index
> *Houfe,* British Illustrators and Caricaturists, *p. 264*

COLE, Philip Tennyson fl. 1880-1930

Portrait and domestic painter. Cole exhibited at the Royal Academy from 1887, including *Lord Milner G.C.M.G., G.C.B., High Commissioner for South Africa* (1902).

> *Graves,* Royal Academy, *vol. 2, p. 101*

COLLENS, K. 1869-1901 1

Caricaturist and silhouettist. Collens was born in Antwerp in 1869. He was a member of the 'Skalden' Club, a group of young avant-garde artists who illustrated books and postcards. Collens's silhouettes on postcards were published by the Algemeen Nederlandsche Verbond (Antwerp Branch). Three cards were of Boer War interest, depicting: an armed Boer leaving his farm house; the British worshipping the Golden Calf (signed 'K.C.'), and mounted Boers on the attack.

> *Bénézit,* Dictionnaire antique, *vol. 2, p. 580*
> The Studio, *vol. 20, p. 60 (1900) 'Studio Talk'*

COLLIER, John 1850-1934

Figure, portrait and landscape painter. Collier was born in London on 27 January 1850, the younger son of Judge Robert Collier, later the third Lord Monkswell. He was educated at Heidelberg and studied art at the Slade School and in Paris and Munich. He was encouraged by Alma-Tadema and Millais and exhibited at the Royal Academy from 1874 to 1934. Collier was the author of *The Primer of Art* (1882), *A Manual of oil Painting* (1886) and *The Art of Portrait Painting* (1905). His portraits include Kitchener, to be found in the Africana Muse-

4

schools under E. A. Abbey. Craig exhibited at the Royal Academy from 1895. He worked for many publications including *Pall Mall Budget*, *The Graphic*, *Harper's Weekly* and *Scribner's*. Craig also illustrated poems by Rudyard Kipling, including the Royal Edition of 'The Absent Minded Beggar'. Over 40 of his Boer War illustrations appeared in *The Graphic*, and several were issued as supplementary prints. The two works *Communion on the veld* and *The battle of Colenso* appear in *The Work of War Artists in South Africa*, by A. C. R. Carter. The former picture once formed part of the Durban art gallery's collection. The watercolour *The crossing of the Riet River*, originally drawn for *The Graphic* after a sketch by G. D. Giles, can be found in the National Army Museum, and the wash drawing, *Royal Army Medical Corps in South Africa*, reproduced in *The Graphic* on 25 August 1900, can be found in the Africana Museum, Johannesburg. The *Dictionary of Military Painters* records another Boer War watercolour, entitled *R.A.M.C. watching an engagement through field glasses*. Craig died of tuberculosis on 9 July 1918 in Sintra, Portugal.

> *Bénézit*, Dictionnaire antique, *vol. 2, p. 714*
> *Carter*, War Artists in S.A.
> *Graves*, Royal Academy, *vol. 2, p. 190*
> *Hofmeyr, Matton and Roets*, Graphic Picture Index
> *Kennedy*, Pictures in the Africana Museum, *vol. 6, p. 181*
> *Thieme and Becker*, pp. 49-50
> *Verbeek*, Early Natal Art
> Who was Who, *vol. 2, p. 241*

CRAIG, Stuart E.
Possibly a relative of Frank Craig. His illustration, *Into the jaws of the enemy: a letter from the front*, appeared, redrawn by Frank Craig, in *The Graphic* on 18 August 1900.

CRANE, Walter 1845-1915
Painter, designer and book illustrator. Crane was born in Liverpool on 15 August 1845. He was largely self-taught before being apprenticed to W.J. Lynton in London in 1857. He eventually became principal of the Royal College of Art (1898-9). He was also a member of the R.W.S. and the R.I. Crane was considered a fine exponent of the Art Nouveau style in books and postcards. His Boer War work consists of a small pictorial poster, *Stop the War*, which also appeared on the cover of an unnumbered pamphlet issued by the Stop the War Committee. His illustration, *England's emblem*, depicting St George slaying the dragon, appeared in the *Souvenir and Official Programme of the National Bazaar in Aid of Sufferers by the War* (May 1900). Crane died in Kensington on 14 March 1915.

> Art Nouveau Prints, Illustrations and Posters, *pp. 86-87*
> *Fanelli and Godoli*, Art Nouveau Postcards
> Who was Who, *vol. 1, pp. 165-166*

CRESPIN, Adolphe-Louis-Charles 1859-?
Crespin was born in Brussels on 17 May 1859, where he was later honorary professor at the École des Beaux-Arts. His Boer War work, usually produced in collaboration with F. Méaulle and P. Carrey and signed 'ch Crespin', appeared in *Le Petit Parisien*.

> *Bénézit*, Dictionnaire antique, *vol. 2, p. 727*

cipal London galleries, including the Royal Academy and the R.I. His Boer War work appeared in *The Sphere*.

> *Waters*, British Artists, *vol. 1, p. 75*

COPE, Arthur Stockdale 1857-1940
Portrait and landscape painter. Cope was born on 2 November 1857, the son of Charles West Cope, R.A. He studied at Carey's and at the R.A. schools, and he exhibited at the R.A. from 1876. Cope became an associate of the R.A. in 1899 and a full member in 1910. He was knighted in 1917 and made K.C.V.O. in 1927. His portraits included King Edward VII, King George V, Lord Kitchener and World War I naval officers. Cope's painting of Lord Kitchener of Khartoum was exhibited at the Royal Academy in 1901, illustrated in *The Royal Academy Pictures* (1901), and reproduced in *The Graphic* (19 December 1908). The Autotype Company held the copyright and produced photo-engravings. Cope died on 5 July 1940.

> *Graves*, Royal Academy, *vol. 2, p. 155*
> Royal Academy Pictures, *1901*
> Who was Who, *vol. 3, p. 287*

COPNALL, Frank T. 1870- c.1948
Copnall was born in Ryde, Isle of Wight, on 27 April 1870. He exhibited at the Royal Academy, the R.S.A., the R.E., the N.P.S. and the I.S. He was a member of the Liverpool Academy of Fine Arts and the London Portrait Society, and president of the Liver Sketching Club and the Liverpool Art Club. The only Boer War work credited to Copnall is a sepia halftone print, *For the Queen and old Ireland, a wounded infantryman, Field Service Order*, which appeared in *The Spear* (1900). A copy of the print can be found in the National Army Museum.

> *Waters*, British Artists, *vol. 1, p. 76*

CORBOULD, Aster Chantrey ?-1920
Sporting artist and illustrator. Corbould was the nephew of the *Punch* illustrator Charles Keene. Although he worked regularly for *Punch* during the War, only one Boer War cartoon (13 June 1900) is recorded.

> *Houfe*, British Illustrators and Caricaturists, *p. 266*

CORE
Russian cartoonist who worked for *Novoe Vremya*. Core's work appeared in *Revue des Revues* (1 February 1900), which contained cartoons from a worldwide spectrum of newspapers.

COURTET, E. *see* **COHL, Emile**

COUTURIER, Léon-Antoine-Lucien 1842-1935
Couturier was born in Mâcon, France, on 28 December 1842.

He studied under Danguin at the École des Beaux-Arts in Lyon and later under S. Cornu and Cabanel in Paris. Couturier exhibited at the Salon des Artistes Français from 1868. His illustration, *Au Président Kruger, hommage*, appeared in the special issue of *Le Monde Illustré* on 17 November 1900 that was dedicated to Kruger.

> *Bénézit*, Dictionnaire antique, *vol. 2, p. 698*

COWHAM, Hilda 1873-1964
Author and book illustrator. Cowham was born in Westminster in 1873. She studied at the Wimbledon Art School and under Alfred Drury at the Lambeth School of Art. Her work appeared in *Pick-Me-Up* and *The Queen* while she was still at school. Described by a contemporary art critic as 'our only petticoated humorist', Cowham had work published in *Queen*, *Pick-Me-Up*, *Moonshine* and *Punch*, and particularly in *The Sketch*, which reproduced her only Boer War related cartoons in March 1900. Cowham became well known as a postcard artist specializing in children and cats. She married artist Edgar Lander.

> *Hammerton*, Humorists of the Pencil, *pp. 156-160*
> *Holt, Tonie and Valmai (compilers)*, Stanley Gibbons Postcard Catalogue
> *Houfe*, British Illustrators and Caricaturists, *p. 268*

COWPER, Max fl.1892-1911 3
Figure painter and illustrator. Cowper worked in Dundee during 1893, in Edinburgh during 1894 and in London from 1901, contributing illustrations to *Punch*, *St Paul's*, *Fun*, *Pick-Me-Up*, *Illustrated Bits* and *The Strand Magazine*. His Boer War work appeared in *With the Flag To Pretoria* and *Black & White Budget*. The illustration *Aye ready* was published in the *Souvenir and Official Programme of the National Bazaar in Aid of Sufferers by the War* (May 1900). Cowper also contributed to *The Muster Roll of Angus* and was one of the subscribers.

> *Thorpe*, English Illustration

COX, A.
Probably a home-based outside artist for *The Graphic*. Most of Cox's sketches depict troops embarking or ships leaving ports. His Africana work appeared in *The Graphic* from 1896 to 1899.

> *Hofmeyr, Matton and Roets*, Graphic Picture Index

CRAIG, Frank 1874-1918 2
Genre and historical painter and illustrator. Craig was born in Abbey Wood, Kent, on 27 February 1874. He studied at the Lambeth School of Art, Cook's Life School, and the R.A.

---

1 Frank Craig's painting *Communion on the Veld* was bought by the Durban art gallery in 1902 but is now missing.
2 Soldier-artist Harold Collison-Morley.
3 The black and white work of illustrator and figure painter Max Cowper appeared in many contemporary publications.
4 The stirring work by Frank Craig entitled *The crossing of the Riet River*. Reproduced by courtesy of the National Army Museum, London.

CRESSWELL, Albert
Parisian painter who contributed to *Paris-Pretoria*.

CROFTS, Ernest 1847-1911
Military and historical painter. Crofts was born in Yorkshire on 15 September 1847. He was educated at Rugby and in Berlin, and he studied art in London and Düsseldorf. Crofts exhibited at the Royal Academy from 1874. He became an A.R.A. in 1878 and R.A. in 1896. The subjects he adopted were usually chosen from the English Civil War, the Napoleonic Wars or the Franco-Prussian War. The Parker Gallery once offered a coloured photogravure, entitled the *Presentation of medals by H.M. Edward VII on the Horse Guards Parade after the Boer War*, 'which was published in 1902 after a painting by E. Crofts'. Crofts died on 20 March 1911.

> *Waters*, British Artists, *vol. 1, p. 80*
> Who was Who, *vol. 1, p. 170*

CROMPTON, James Shaw
Crompton was the illustrator of both editions of Ernest Glanville's Boer War novel, *Max Thornton*, (1901 and 1908).
> SABIB, *vol. 2, p. 356*

CROWTHER, T. S. C. fl. 1891-1902 2
Illustrator for *The Daily Graphic*, who also worked for other publications. *The Idler*, *Windsor Magazine* and *The Temple Magazine* made use of Crowther's illustrations. His Boer War work appeared in *Under The Union Jack* and *Navy & Army Illustrated*. Crowther's illustrations also appeared in the Jubilee publication, *60 years a Queen* (1897), and 20 of his chromolithographs depicting naval uniforms appeared in *The British Navy 1837-97* (George Berridge's and Co.). The illustration, *Off to fight the Rooineks 1899*, which can now be found in the Africana Museum, was reproduced in *The Daily Graphic* (30 October 1899) and the Dutch newspaper *Wêreldkroniek* (4 November 1899). The author has a group of four pen drawings, *Mafeking celebrations in the provinces, rejoicings at Liverpool*, which was reproduced in *The Daily Graphic* (22 May 1900). Each has a subtitle: *The Lord Mayor acknowledging the cheers of the crowd at the town hall*; *The Lord Mayor addressing the crowd in the exchange news room*; *The hero's portrait crowned with laurel*, and *Illuminated ferry boats at 'the landing stage'*. Crowther often signed his work 'T.S.C.C.'.

> British Military Costume Prints, *p. 2584*
> *Kennedy*, Pictures in the Africana Museum, *vol. 6, p. 182*
> *Thorpe*, English Illustration

CUCUEL, Edward 1875-?
Painter and illustrator. Cucuel was born in San Francisco in 1875. He studied in Paris under Constant, Laurent and Gérôme. Cucuel was a 'special' artist for *The Illustrated London News* in Berlin during the postwar visit by De la Rey, De Wet and Botha. Illustrations of their welcome at the station on 16 October 1902 and their address at the Great Philharmonic Hall

on 17 October appeared in *The Illustrated London News* (25 October 1902).

> *Bénézit*, Dictionnaire antique, *vol. 2, p. 748*
> *Fielding*, American Painters, etc., *p. 83*

CULVER
American cartoonist for *Life*. Culver's cartoon depicting Kruger on a Dutch postcard, published by Gebroeders Stein Jacob W. V., advertised 'Distileederij en Likeurstokerij de Zon'.

CUMMING, William Skeoch 1864-1929 2
Figure and military painter. Cumming was born in Edinburgh on 28 December 1864, the fourth son of John Cumming and Jane Skeoch, cousin of Horatio McCulloch. Cumming studied at the Edinburgh School of Art and the R.S.A. and later began his art career as a scene painter at the Theatre Royal. His first important painting, *The royal archers of Holyrood Palace*, depicts Queen Victoria leaving the palace to open the first Edinburgh Exhibition in 1886 and now hangs in the Royal Archer's Hall. Over 48 of Cumming's works were exhibited at R.S.A. from 1885, and his illustrations of Scottish life later appeared in *Black & White* (1896).

Cumming joined the Lothian and Berwickshire Yeomanry which became the 19th Company Imperial Yeomanry during the Boer War, commanded by Sir James Miller whose equestrian portrait Cumming painted. The 19th joined with the 17th Ayrshire and Lanarkshire Co., the 18th Glasgow (Queen's Own) and the 20th, the Fife and Forfarshire Light Horse, to form the 6th Battalion under the overall command of Lt. Col. C.R. Burn. On 23 February 1900 three of the companies boarded the *Carthaginian* on the Clyde. At Las Palmas they received news of the relief of Kimberley and the surrender of Cronje at Paardeberg. They arrived in Table Bay on Monday 19 March 1900 and were sent immediately to the Maitland camp, and then on to Stellenbosch and Worcester before proceeding to the front. Judging from the titles of his paintings, Cumming probably saw action at Diamond Hill, Wepener and Frederikstad and took part in the first De Wet 'hunt'. He contracted severe enteric fever but recovered enough to remain on the active list.

Cumming returned from South Africa and joined the Scottish Horse. Prior to the War he had met James Roddick, a drummer in the 92nd Gordon Highlanders, who became Cumming's principal model and his likeness appears in many paintings. Cumming's Boer War paintings exhibited at the R.S.A. include: *Foragers* (1903); *The gun pit – colonials working the guns – defence of Wepener* (1903); *Frederikstad – October 1900, Charge of the Scots Fusiliers* (1903); *The Black Watch on the trek* (1903); *Over the veldt – the Argyll and Sutherland Highlanders* (1904): *Defence of a kraal: 1st Life Guards at Diamond Hill 11 June 1900* (1904); *Guns moving to the front* (1906); *Heliographing Col. Thorneycroft's column* (1906); *Inspanning*; *Lost on the veldt* (1906).

Sir James Guthrie, the then president of the R.S.A., commented on Cumming's work: 'It was something new in the

way of light and shade, the strong South African sun being of course accountable for this.' Two of his watercolours, *Scout – Brabant's Horse* (1901) and *Mess time in the veldt*, can be found in the Africana Museum. Other works include *Slaapkrans 28 July 1900 Prinsloo's surrender* (1903), which can be found in the National Army Museum; *Officers of the 6th (Scottish) Battalion Imperial Yeomanry*, in the Edinburgh City Art Gallery, and watercolours and sketches held in the Scottish United Services Museum. Bénézit records two other Boer War works, *Convoy fording a river in South Africa* and *Transvaal 1901*. The author has two watercolours, *Night patrol South Africa* (1902) and *Boer soldier* (1904).

Cumming also took over 300 photographs, which are now in the Imperial War Museum, and many of his paintings were based on these photographs. Cumming was responsible for at least one postcard: *The Royal Scots Fusiliers at Frederikstad, South Africa, 1900*, published by Geo. Falkner and Sons. In 1911 he was commissioned by the Marquis of Bute to design tapestries of Scottish subjects.

Cumming married Belle Sutton, also a well-known watercolourist. He died in Edinburgh on 10 April 1929.
> Africana Notes and News, *(Sept. 1984) vol. 23, p. 3*
> *Bénézit*, Dictionnaire antique, *vol. 2, p. 193*
> British Journal of Photography Annual 1987
> *Caw*, Scottish Painting, *p. 272*
> *Graves*, Royal Academy, *vol. 2, p. 223*
> *Paton*, Memoir of W. Skeoch Cumming
> *Personal communication with W. Thorburn, Keeper Scottish United Services Museum; M. Veals, Assistant Librarian, Royal Scottish Academy, and J. Carmichael, Keeper of Photographs, Imperial War Museum*
> *Waters*, British Artists, *vol. 2, p. 16*

CUNDAL, James A.
Responsible for the lithograph 'Volunteer souvenir', which was published in the *Natal Mercury* after the War.

CUNEO, Cyrus Cincinnato 1879-1916
Genre and portrait painter. Cuneo was born of Italian parents in San Francisco in 1879. He studied in Paris under Girardo Prenet and Whistler in 1900. Cuneo financed his early art career by fighting as a professional boxer. He later settled in London (in 1902), although he had exhibited at the Royal Academy earlier in 1900. He became a member of the R.O.I. in 1908. The only recorded Boer War works by Cuneo accompanied an article by Talbot Mundy, entitled 'Three helios, a story of the Boer War', which appeared in *The Strand Magazine* (Vol. 46, July 1913). Cuneo was included in a group portrait of *The Illustrated London News* artists illustrated by Begg, published in *The Strand Magazine* on 2 September 1911 (see page 9). Cuneo's son, Terence, is better known as an artist and his work can be found in the Africana Museum. Cuneo snr. died of blood poisoning in 1916.
> *Samuels*, Artists of the American West, *p. 117*
> *Waters*, British Artists, *vol. 1, p. 82*

CUSINS, A.G.T.
Soldier-artist. A Lt. Cusins of the Royal Engineers supplied a sketch, entitled *The use of the searchlight in war: the armoured train Ubique in action at Brugspruit*, which appeared, redrawn by Charles Dixon, in *The Graphic* on 24 August 1901.

Army List *(1901)*
Hofmeyr, Matton and Roets, Graphic Picture Index

CYNICUS (Martin Anderson) 1854-1932
Political and social cartoonist and postcard designer. Cynicus was the pseudonym of Martin Anderson, who was born in Leuchar, near Dundee (Scotland), in 1854. His satirical cartoons appeared in *The Idler* and others. Cynicus is best known for his postcards, particularly those he drew and published himself between 1902 and 1916. His Boer War illustration, *Mars and Venus*, appeared in *The Muster Roll of Angus* (Brodie & Salmond, Arbroath, 1900).

Byatt, *Picture Postcards*

CZABRAN, Feodor 1867-?
Illustrator. Czabran was born in Dresden on 9 April 1867. He worked for many periodicals, but his Boer War work appears mainly in *Lustige Blätter* and on postcards for Dr Eysler's Gruss vom Kriegsschauplatz series.

DA COSTA, Joseph Mendes
Dutch sculptor. Da Costa's bust of De Wet can be found in the National Park near Arnhem in the Netherlands and a copy thereof in the Kroller-Muller Collection in The Hague.

Rosenthal, *General de Wet, p. 212*

DADD, Frank 1851-1929 4
Black and white artist. Born into a family of artists in London on 28 March 1851, Dadd was a cousin of the illustrator Kate Greenaway, and his brother married her sister. His uncle, Richard Dadd, was a well-known British painter who murdered his own father and spent the rest of his life in an asylum for the insane. Frank Dadd studied at the South Kensington and R.A. schools, and started his career illustrating boys' adventure stories. He exhibited at the Royal Academy from 1878 to 1885 and he was elected a member of the R.I. in 1884 and the R.O.I. in 1888. In 1878 Dadd joined *The Illustrated London News*, covering the Zulu War and various Basuto wars. He was employed by *The Graphic* from 1884, often using the initials 'F.D.' to sign his work.

Dadd's output of Boer War work was prolific. He produced over 100 illustrations for *The Graphic*, several of which were issued as supplementary prints, and his work was also noted in the Belgian paper *L'Illustration Européenne*. He also did work for the Royal Edition of Kipling's poem 'The Absent Minded Beggar'. Three of his illustrations can be found in the Africana Museum, but none is of the Boer War, although the originals of 10 Boer War drawings, reproduced in *The Graphic*, can be found in the Mendelssohn Collection in the Library of Parliament, Cape Town. The author has four of Dadd's Boer War works, all of which appeared in *The Graphic: Traitors: The Irish Brigade serving with the Boers*, taken from a photograph by Emile Andreoli depicting the men of the Irish-American Brigade who left Johannesburg at the outbreak of war to fight the British (18 November 1899); *An oath of vengeance at the funeral of a victim of Boer treachery* (24 November 1900); *Gallant defence of derailed train near Alkmaar* (10 August 1901), and *War preparations: Military activity at Portsmouth* (14 October 1899). Three of Dadd's prewar paintings can be found in the Royal Collection at Windsor, while others are housed in the Rand Club, Johannesburg, and the Exmouth Art Gallery. Dadd spent his later years in Devon and died in Teignmouth on 7 March 1929.

Carter, *War Artists in S.A., p. 21*
Dawnay and Miller, *Military Drawings and Paintings*
Graves, *Royal Academy, pp. 229 & 325*
Hofmeyr, Matton and Roets, Graphic Picture Index
Houfe, *British Illustrators and Caricaturists, p. 278*
Personal communication with C. Lejeune, Secretary of the Rand Club
The Times, *9 March 1929*
Who was Who, *vol. 3*

DADD, Stephen Thomas fl. 1879-1914 1
Figure painter and illustrator. A relative of Frank Dadd (see above) with whom he often collaborated, Stephen Dadd was trained in wood engraving by John Greenaway, father of the artist Kate Greenaway.

Dadd's early work consisted mainly of domestic animal subjects, but he later took up the topic of the Boer War and his work appeared in *The Graphic*, *The Daily Graphic* and *With the Flag to Pretoria*. He was also responsible for several Elliman's Embrocation advertisements in which the Boer War was occasionally used as a theme. The author has three of Dadd's pen-and-ink drawings which were published in *The Daily Graphic* on 7 October 1899. Dadd often used the initials 'S.T.D.' to sign his work.

Hofmeyr, Matton and Roets, Graphic Picture Index
Houfe, *British Illustrators and Caricaturists, p. 279*
Phillips Catalogue: English and European Drawings and Watercolours, *June 1986*

DAMBLANS, Eugène 1865-? 1
Watercolourist, illustrator and postcard artist. Damblans was born in Montevideo, Uruguay, on 14 July 1865. He was a pupil of Buland and Celez. His Boer War work could often be found on the front or back pages of the coloured supplements of *Le Petit Journal* and also in *Le Journal Illustré*.

Bénézit, *Dictionnaire antique, vol. 3, p 19*
Holt, Tonie and Valmai, *Stanley Gibbons Postcard Catalogue, p. 52*

DANIEL, Vincent
Daniel's Boer War illustrations can be found in *South Africa in Peace and War* (Miles and Miles, London).

1 This composite four-part drawing in pen and ink by T. S. C. Crowther, showing the celebrations in Liverpool after the relief of Mafeking, was published in *The Daily Graphic* only a few days after the event.
2 A pen-and-ink drawing by T. S. C. Crowther entitled *Off to fight the Rooineks 1899*. Reproduced by courtesy of the Africana Museum.
3 This watercolour by W. S. Cumming, entitled *Mess time in the veldt*, is found in the Africana Museum, Johannesburg, by whose kind permission this picture is reproduced.
4 Frank Dadd's illustration, entitled *Traitors: The Irish Brigade serving with the Boers*, was published in both *The Graphic* and *Leslie's Weekly*. There was much resentment in Britain about the participation of an Irish Brigade on the side of the Boers, and *The Graphic* commented that they were 'some of the worst sweepings of Johannesburg' and 'all loafers'.
5 *The Transvaal Crisis*, a pen-and-ink drawing by Stephen Dadd, appeared in *The Daily Graphic* on 7 October 1899. It shows the preparations of the Balloon Section of the Royal Engineers for their departure to South Africa.
6 This drawing by Frank Dadd shows soldiers cheering the bluejackets from the ships H.M.S. *Terrible* and *Powerful*, among others, who took the guns from their ships by train to Ladysmith to help in the relief of the siege.

DARSANE 1

Postcard artist. Darsane's cartoon, *Eduard VII et le Transvaal 7 Mars 1902. Et ce n'est pas fini*, appeared in the 'La Guerre du Transvaal' series of eight cards issued in a special limited numbered edition.

DAS, Pieter 1881-1937

Das was born in Koudekerk, Netherlands, on 21 April 1881. He was a cartoonist for *Der Wahre Jacob*. Das worked in The Hague, Dordrecht, Utrecht, Cologne and the United States. He died in New York in 1937.

> The Strand, *(1902) vol. 24, p. 97*
> Scheen, *Nederlandse Beeldende Kunstenaars, p. 244*

D'AURIAN, Jean-Emmanuel 2

French painter, illustrator and cartoonist. D'Aurian exhibited at the Salon des Humoristes in 1910. His Boer War work appeared in *Le Sourire*, *Le Charivari* Album: *Boers et Anglais*, *La Caricature* and *Le Bon Vivant*. Two of D'Aurian's coloured cartoons, *Un qu'elle n'aura pas* (17 November 1900) and *Le Napoleon du Cap* (12 April 1902) appeared on the cover of *La Caricature*.

> Bénézit, *Dictionnaire antique, vol. 1, p. 295*

DAVENPORT, Talbot Neville Fawcett ?-1905

Soldier-artist. Davenport was commissioned to the Royal Irish Rifles on 4 January 1899 and promoted to lieutenant on 4 March 1900. During the Boer War he served with the 2nd Royal Irish Rifles, arriving on H.M.S. *Britannic* in Cape Town on 13 November 1899. In March 1900 the company joined the Mounted Infantry Company, and Lt. Davenport served in the 2nd Company under Major Festing.

Two of his illustrations were reproduced in *The Illustrated London News* (27 January 1901), and his sketch, *Retreat from Stormberg*, appeared in *With the Flag To Pretoria*. He often signed his work with the initials 'T.N.F.D.'. Davenport died from accidental poisoning on 3 March 1905.

> Personal communication with Lt. Col. W. R. H. Charley, Regimental Headquarters, Royal Irish Rifles, Belfast.

DAVIE, K. M. 1868-

Soldier-artist; major in Gloucester Regiment. He completed Capt. W. Erskine's freehand drawings for Maj. Gen. Sir F. Maurice's *History of the War in South Africa* after Erskine was killed in 1901.

DAVIEL, Léon fl. 1893-1930

Portrait painter, wood engraver, illustrator and miniaturist. Daviel was born in Paris. A one-time pupil of Carolus-Duran, he exhibited at the Royal Academy in 1893 and at the Salon des Artistes Français in 1927. Daviel worked for several British periodicals, including *Good Words*, *Pearson's Magazine* and *The Temple Magazine*. His Boer War work appeared in *Black & White* and *Black & White Budget*. He also illustrated the Pioneer Tobacco advertisement, which featured Kruger saying 'Well I'll take your parcel as full material moral and intellectual compensation' and John Bull replying 'I'm here and civilisation is coming so you had better come to terms'. It appeared in *The Illustrated London News* on 7 July 1900.

> Bénézit, *Dictionnaire antique, vol. 3, p. 73*
> Houfe, *British Illustrators and Caricaturists*

DAVIES, D. Dyer-

Dyer-Davies was the first cartoonist for *The Rand Daily Mail*. His work appeared soon after the first issue of 29 September 1902, but he was replaced a few months later by Joseph Gould. Dyer-Davies's illustration, *De Wet addressing the Burghers on the scheme for invading the Cape Colony*, appeared in *The Sphere* with caption: 'This picture was made by Mr Dyer-Davies from a snapshot taken by a Boer prisoner illustrating the events. The artist has also in his possession a series of portraits of the officers under De Wet and from these he made life-like portraits. De Wet's portrait was finished from a photograph supplied by Mrs De Wet who lives near Johannesburg. The picture is considered so life-like that its copyright has been purchased by Mr John Fox and Mr James Bonthrone of Johannesburg. De Wet's chief of staff, his secretary and Jonas his chief scout are identified in the picture.'

> Kennedy, *Pictures in the Africana Museum, vol. 2*
> Schoonraad, *Spot- en Strookprent Kunstenaars*

DAVIS, Joseph Barnard 1861-?

Landscape painter and illustrator. Davis was born on 19 July 1861 in Bowness-on-Windermere. From 1890 he exhibited at leading London galleries, including the Royal Academy, the R.I. and the R.B.A. His Boer War illustration, *With Lord Roberts in the Free State: searching for arms and ammunition*, appeared in *The Graphic* on 19 May 1900.

> Hofmeyr, Matton and Roets, *Graphic Picture Index*
> Waters, *British Artists, vol. 1, p. 87*

DAVIS, Lucien 1860-?

Portrait and landscape painter. Lucien Davis was born in Liverpool on 7 January 1860 into a family of artists, including father William Davis and brothers W.P. and Valentine Davis. Lucien Davis was educated at St Francis Xavier College, Liverpool, and the R. A. schools. He began his career as an illustrator with Cassell's Publications in 1878, but he later worked for *The Graphic* (1880-81) and *The Illustrated London News*, which he joined in 1885, remaining there for the next 20 years and specializing in social subjects and Christmas numbers. Davis was elected a member of the R.I. in 1893. His Boer War illustration, *Invalided home, the wounded C.I.V.'s return*, appeared in *The Illustrated London News* (18 August 1900).

> Houfe, *British Illustrators and Caricaturists*

DAVISON, Nora fl. 1881-1905

Landscape and marine painter. Davison illustrated hospital ships in *Lest We Forget Them* (Fine Arts Society), which had been compiled by Lady Glover. The profits of the sale of the

publication were 'devoted to the Fund for the Relief of Widows and Orphans of our Sailors and Soldiers'.

Johnson and Greutzner, British Artists, *p. 138*
Waters, British Artists, *vol. 1, p. 87*

DE AMICIS, Franco   1

De Amicis was the illustrator of a postcard depicting a seated Kruger being blessed by Jesus Christ, inscribed 'your cause is just, universal sympathy from all over the world. Prayers for triumph of right raised to the sky. God is with us and will not abandon us.' It was issued in 1901 by an unidentified publisher, and French and Dutch versions also exist.

DE BEAUVAIS, Lubin

French children's book illustrator. De Beauvais exhibited works at the Exposition des Humoristes in Copenhagen in 1909 and at the Salon des Humoristes in Paris in 1910. He was the illustrator of the cover for the 100-part series *La Guerre au Transvaal: Anglais et Boers* (published by S. Schwarz, Paris).

Bénézit, Dictionnaire antique, *vol. 1, p. 497*

DE BRUIN, Cornelis 1870-1940   1

Tile painter. De Bruin was born in Utrecht on 7 April 1870. He trained under Professor Augustus Allebe, director of the Amsterdamse Rijks-Academie van Beeldende Kunsten, and was later employed as a tile painter by De Distel and the Dordtsche Kunstpotterij. His Boer War contribution was a magnificent set of tiles, depicting, in eight tableaux, battles of the Boer War: Spioenkop, Colenso, Ladysmith, Stormberg, Reddersburg, Magersfontein, Modder River and Paardeberg. He also did portraits, which still exist, of Louis Botha, Kock, Coster and De Villebois-Mareuil, as well as Cronje, De Wet, De la Rey, Joubert and Penn-Symons, which are lost. The story of the rediscovery of the tiles after they had been forgotten for decades and their purchase by the South African Government is told in *Historic Tableaux on Tiles* (Publicity and Travel Dept, South African Airways, 1970). The collection has been kept in the War Museum of the Boer Republics, Bloemfontein, since 1980. De Bruin died in Amsterdam on 27 August 1940. (See also pp. 100-101.)

Historic Tableaux on Tiles *(SAA, 1970)*
Antiek, *7 February 1987: Cornelis de Bruin*

DE BRUIN, W. K.

De Bruin illustrated three stories by Harm Oost in the *Die Nieuwe Bibliotheek voor de jeugd* series: *Gevonden. Een verhaal uit den Zuid-Afrikaanschen Vrijheidsoorlog, Geroepen. Een verhaal uit den Zuid-Afrikaanschen Vrijheidsoorlog* and *Gestreden. Een verhaal uit den Zuid-Afrikaanschen Vrijheidsoorlog.* (Oost fought with the Boers during the War, was captured and sent to St Helena. Later he returned and became a well-known politician and journalist.)

SABIB, *vol. 3, p. 588*
De Kock (ed.), DSAB, *vol. 4, p. 1426*

DE CAPOL, H.

Contributor to *Paris-Pretoria.*

DECKERS, Jan Frans 1835-?

Sculptor. Deckers was born in Antwerp on 20 March 1835. He was a professor at the Antwerp Academy and he contributed to *Antwerpen-Transvaal Gedenknummer.*

Bénézit, Dictionnaire antique, *vol. 3, p. 99*

DEFREGGER, Franz Von 1835-1921

Genre and portrait painter. Defregger was born in Stronach, Bavaria, on 30 April 1835. His Boer War work appeared in *Der Burenfreund.* Active in the pro-Boer movement in Germany, Defregger also produced a postcard depicting Boer women and children being driven from their homes by whip-wielding blacks and British soldiers, which was sold by the Deutsche Centrale f. Bestrebung z. Beendigung d. Burenkrieges. His correspondence with W.J. Leyds can be found in Leyds's *Correspondentie.*

Bénézit, Dictionnaire antique, *vol. 3, p. 109*
Leyds, Correspondentie

DE FRICK, Paul 1864-?

Painter. Born in Paris in 1864, De Frick was a contributor to *Paris-Pretoria.*

DE HAENEN, Frederic fl.1896-1920   3

French-born illustrator and postcard artist. De Haenen worked mainly for *L'Illustration* and *The Illustrated London News,* which he joined in 1910. During the Boer War he worked for *The Graphic,* contributing over 60 illustrations, several of which were issued as supplementary prints. The Africana Museum has six of De Haenen's wash drawings which were reproduced in *The Graphic: A Sortie from Mafeking 1899* (13 January 1900); *Boer Ambulance train 1900* (20 January 1900) subtitled *A Sad Home-coming: Arrival of the Boer Red Cross Train with wounded at Pretoria; Boer War 1900 night attack on a kopje* (24 March 1900); *Lady Sarah Wilson at Mafeking 1900* (16 June 1900); *Any washing today? Dutch laundresses visiting English troops in the Transvaal* (2 November 1901) with the caption 'Any washing Today? Little laundresses in Transvaal', from a sketch by Capt. Ronald C. Gibb, and *Funeral of Cecil Rhodes — Coffin entering cathedral Cape Town 1902* (3 May 1902). One of his Boer War drawings can be found in the Mendelssohn Collection, and there are four works in the Royal Collection at Windsor, including *The coronation of King Edward VII: a review by the Prince of Wales of the Indian Cavalry contingent: Horse Guards Parade on 2 July 1902.* The author has the De Haenen wash drawing *How Bethune's Mounted Infantry crossed the Tugela: in midstream on a kaffir boat,* which appeared in *The Graphic* (30 June 1900). De Haenen's portrait appeared, with other *Illustrated London News* artists, in *The Illustrated London News* of 2 September 1911, drawn by Samuel Begg (see page 107).

Bénézit, Dictionnaire antique, *vol. 4, p. 545*
Collecting Postcards in Colour
Dawnay and Miller, Military Drawings and Paintings
De Wet, Illustrated London News Index
Hofmeyr, Matton and Roets, Graphic Picture Index
Kennedy, Pictures in the Africana Museum, *vol. 2, p. 200*
Thorpe, English Illustration

DE JOLAR, Marie

De Jolar was the artist responsible for the undated, hand-coloured lithograph *Groupe de Boers.* The style of dress depicted in the lithograph is earlier than that of the Boer War and this work could be early or mid-19th century.

DEKKER, Ernest François Eugène (also known as Douwes Dekker) 1879-1950   2

Soldier-artist. Dekker was a Boer prisoner of war housed at the Ragama Camp, Ceylon. The Africana Museum has a complete suit of spades from a pack of playing cards drawn by Dekker. On the face of each card are the number of spades and a watercolour and pen-and-ink vignette depicting: 2: a Boer shooting from behind a rock; 3: a British soldier staggering after being shot; 4: an armed Boer on horseback; 5: a kilted British soldier running; 6: an armed Boer kneeling; 7: a British soldier taking aim; 8: a dead British soldier lying on ground; 9: an armed Boer facing forward; 10: back view of Boer firing; Jack (marked B for Boer): a bust of Lord Roberts; Queen (marked D for dame): a Red Cross nurse marked 'Liefdezuster'; King (marked K for koning): a portrait of Louis Botha, and Ace: the Battle of Modderspruit 30 November 1899. Hidden away in most of the pictures is the artist's monogram. The design on the back consists of the four colours of the Vierkleur in diagonal lines with two interlaced capital Ds in the centre. In the top left corner is the legend 'Fijnste Ragama' and at the foot on the right 'Speel-kaarten'.

A series of hand-drawn numbered postcards signed 'D.D.' can be found in the Africana Museum and in the author's collection. It is possible that these postcards were sold to fellow prisoners by the artist.

Africana Notes and News, *vol. 25, no. 5, March 1983, p. 182*

---

1 Frederic de Haenen's wash drawing *Boer Ambulance train 1900* was reproduced in *The Graphic* on 20 January 1900. Louis van Neck of the Belgian ambulance team took the photograph on which the drawing is based. The original photograph was published in Van Neck's book *Een Noodlottige Oorlog in het Boerenland.* Reproduced by courtesy of the Africana Museum.
2 Frederic de Haenen's wash drawing showing how Bethune's Mounted Infantry crossed the Tugela River was published in *The Graphic* in June 1900.
3 *La Caricature* 17 November 1900 by Jean D'Aurian shows Kruger being protected from Queen Victoria by Queen Wilhelmina of the Netherlands. Kruger reached Europe aboard the *Gelderland* a few days later.
4 Jean D'Aurian's portrayal of Cecil Rhodes as *Le Napoleon du Cap* on the front page of *La Caricature* on 12 April 1902. Rhodes had died in Cape Town only a few days before.
5 Franco de Amicis did the illustration for this 1901 pro-Boer postcard of Kruger being blessed.
6 This drawing by Frederick de Haenen shows a vulture watching Winston Churchill while he hides out waiting for night to come. The incident took place after Churchill's escape from Boer captivity.
7 A handpainted card by Ernest Dekker, a P.O.W. at Diyatalawa, Ceylon. He produced several similar cards which he either sold or distributed to other prisoners.

DE LACY, Charles John fl. 1885-1930
Landscape, marine and portrait painter who was born in Sunderland. Trained as an engineer before joining the army and navy, De Lacy also studied art at the Lambeth and South Kensington schools. He exhibited at the R.B.A. and Royal Academy from 1889, and his R.A. exhibits included *With the troops for Table Bay: Transport leaving Royal Albert Docks* (1900). De Lacy was a special artist for the Russian fleet in 1897 and later worked for *The Graphic*, acting as a special artist for the Admiralty and Port of London Authority. He also worked for *The Illustrated London News* and *Pall Mall Magazine*. His Boer War seascape *The outbreak of the war: Transport leaving England for the Cape*, which appeared in *The Illustrated London News* on 16 February 1900, was reproduced in Louis Creswicke's *South Africa and The Transvaal War*. De Lacy also produced the oil painting *Waiwera leaving New Zealand for South Africa 1899* (the *Waiwera* was a New Zealand troopship). He also illustrated *A Book about Ships* (1914) and J. S. Margerison's *Our Wonderful Navy* (1919).
De Wet, Illustrated London News Index
Graves, Royal Academy, *vol. 2, p. 295*
Houfe, British Illustrators and Caricaturists, *p. 282*
Thorpe, English Illustration
Waters, British Artists, *vol. 1, p. 89*

DE LAMARRE, A. F.
French cartoonist who illustrated a series of limited edition satirical French and British postcards dated 1903.

DELANNOY, Aristide 1874-1911
Delannoy was born in Béthune, France, in 1874. He contributed to several periodicals: his cartoon, *Ouf*, depicting a drunk Edward VII, appeared in the special number of *Le Gavroche* (16 June 1902), subtitled 'La Paix à la mode John Bull'. Delannoy died in Paris in 1911.
Bénézit, Dictionnaire antique, *vol. 3, p. 140*

DELAW, Georges 1874-1929
Cartoonist, illustrator and artist. Delaw was born in Sedan, France, in 1874. He contributed to *Le Rire* during the Boer War.
Bénézit, Dictionnaire antique, *vol. 3, p. 149*
Fanelli and Godoli, Art Nouveau Postcards

DEMING, Edwin Willard 1860-1942
Western artist, sculptor and animal painter. Deming was born in Ohio in 1860. He studied in the United States before going to Paris for a year to work with Boulanger and Lefebvre. His first painting trip to the West was in 1887 and this was followed by a second trip in 1893 with fellow Western artist De-Cost Smith, resulting in the articles 'Sketching among the Sioux' and 'Sketching among the Crow Indians' in *Outing*. Deming also collaborated with Frederic Remington. His Boer War illustrations appeared in *Harper's Weekly*, and his work can be found in many art galleries and museums in the United States. Deming's monogram resembles an electric light bulb. He died in New York in 1942.
Samuels, Artists of the American West, *p. 136*

DEN HERTOG, G.
Soldier-artist. His sketchbook depicting scenes from a Boer P.O.W. camp on St Helena can be found in the Mendelssohn Collection, Library of Parliament, Cape Town.

DENIS, Maurice 1870-1945
Painter, draughtsman and writer. Denis was born in Granville, France, in 1870. He travelled widely in Europe and was highly regarded in Art Nouveau circles. A cartoon of Kruger signed 'Dennis', but possibly by this artist, appeared in *Black & White Budget* on 12 May 1900. Denis died in Paris in 1945.
Hofstätter, Art Nouveau Prints, etc., *p. 22*

DENIZARD, Charles O. *see* ORENS

DE OSARADA, A.
Nothing is known about this artist except that he worked for *The Sphere* during the Boer War. Two of his illustrations, under the title *Back from the war: a wounded officer on his way home*, appeared on 17 November 1900. One illustration featured a wounded soldier on board ship holding a letter, presumably from his family, and later with his family on a train.

DE SAULLES, George William 1862-1903 2
Sculptor and medal designer who exhibited at the Royal Academy between 1897 and 1903.
De Saulles was born in Birmingham in 1862 and died in London on 21 July 1903. He designed the Kings's and Queen's South Africa medals. The Queen's medal was first presented in early 1901, reputedly to Lord Roberts on behalf of his son Freddie, who had been killed at Colenso while attempting to save the British guns on 15 December 1899.
Bénézit, Dictionnaire antique, *vol. 7, p. 534*
Graves, Royal Academy
Personal communication with M. G. Hibbard

DESAUTY, Henriette
Paris-born genre painter who contributed to *Paris-Pretoria*.
Bénézit, Dictionnaire antique, *vol. 3, p. 197*

DESBORDES-JONAS, Louise-Alexandra
French artist who studied with Alfred Stevens. Desbordes-Jonas exhibited at the Salon des Artistes Français in 1876. During the Boer War she contributed to *Paris-Pretoria*.
Bénézit, Dictionnaire antique, *vol. 3, p. 198*

DE STA, Henri 1
French cartoonist and caricaturist who worked for *Chronique Amusante*. Most of De Sta's Boer War work was done as a series of full-page comic strips. The author has one such strip — probably done for reproduction in *Chronique Amusante* — which consists of nine separate black and ink and blue crayon panels. Each cartoon is captioned and the main title is *Chacun Mon Tour*.
Osterwalder, and Hubschmid and Bouret (eds.),
Dictionnaire des Illustrateurs, *p. 1003*

DETE, Bertrand
French illustrator who worked for *Le Petit Parisien*. Dete's work is found almost exclusively on the uncoloured pre-1900 supplements of this journal. Occasionally he signed just with his initials ('B.D.').

DE THULSTRUP, Thure (Bror Thure) 1848-1930
The son of the Swedish secretary for naval defence, De Thulstrup was born in Stockholm, where he was later trained as a soldier. In 1871 he became a captain in the French Foreign Legion serving in Algeria and also took part in the Franco-Prussian War. After studying art in Paris, De Thulstrup emigrated to Canada where he worked as a topographical engraver. He later moved to Boston and then New York where he attended the Art Students' League. At that stage he changed his name from Thulstrup to De Thulstrup. He is rated as a Western artist, even though he probably never visited the American West.

Initially De Thulstrup worked as an illustrator for *The New York Graphic*, but later also contributed to *The Graphic*, *Leslie's Weekly* and *Harper's Weekly*, with which he had a 20-year association, covering the inauguration of four presidents. In 1888 he visited Russia and reported on the Kaiser's visit to that country. He became a member of the Society of Illustrators and of the American Water Colour Society. His Boer War illustrations are represented in A.T. Mahan's *War in South Africa*. De Thulstrup died in New York on 9 June 1930.
Bénézit, Dictionnaire antique, *vol. 8, p. 300*
Fielding, American Painters, etc., *p. 367*
Samuels, Artists of the American West, *p. 137*

DE V, E.
Possibly Eduard de Vries. Four cartoons signed 'EdeV' were featured on postcards published by J. C. auf der Heide, S.H.D. Amsterdam. They were: 1. *'Chamberlain and Rhodes' bericht brengende van Ladysmith*; 2. *John Bull in een Holl Café*; 3. *Slapeloze Nachten de nederlaag van Generaal Buller*; and 4. *Slag bij de Modderrivier*.

DE VERNON, Frederick Charles Victor *see* **VERNON, Frederick Charles Victor de**

DEVRIENDT, Julien 1842-?
Belgian-born genre painter who contributed to *Antwerpen-Transvaal Gedenknummer*, which was published in aid of Boer concentration camp victims.
Bénézit, Dictionnaire antique, *vol. 3, p. 240*

DEWAR, W.
Nothing is known about this artist, but he could be William Germond Dewar. His Boer War work appeared in *Black & White* and *With the Flag to Pretoria*. Verbeek lists a watercolour done by Dewar, entitled *Queen's own Cameron Highlanders (79th Foot) Foreign Service 1901*. This painting was offered for sale by the Parker Gallery in 1972. Thorpe mentions that W. Dewar also worked for *Pick-Me-Up* and *Illustrated Bits*.
Thorpe, English Illustration
Verbeek, Early Natal Art

DICKINSON, F. C. fl. 1898-1906 1
Dickinson worked extensively for *The Graphic* and *The Daily Graphic*, and his illustrations are also found in *With the Flag to Pretoria*, *Follow the Flag in South Africa* and Creswicke's *South Africa and the Transvaal War*. Thorpe records that he also worked for *Quarto*. Over 53 of Dickinson's works relating to the Boer War are recorded in the *Index to Pictures of South African Interest in The Graphic*.

The Victoria and Albert Museum has one work by Dickinson, entitled *Scene outside the Mansion House, London 1st March 1900, The Announcement of the Relief of Ladysmith*. This was reproduced in *The Graphic* on 10 March 1900. On 30 January 1981 Sotheby's, London, offered two works by

Dickinson, entitled *The View of crowds at Mansion House celebrating the Relief of Mafeking* and *The War Balloon used in Ladysmith during the siege on exhibition at the Crystal Palace*. The latter was signed with initials and both were reproduced in *The Graphic*. The National Army Museum has a sketch by Dickinson of Lord Roberts. The Mendelssohn Collection in the Library of Parliament, Cape Town, has two paintings by F. C. Dickinson, one of which appeared in *The Graphic* on 6 November 1901, entitled *Result of the Boer raiding in Natal* and done after a sketch by Henry Lea. The other, which appeared on 5 May 1900, is entitled *Commandeered: bringing in supplies for Lord Roberts's force* and was done from a photograph by Reinhold Thiele. The author has one work by Dickinson, entitled *The Dying Embers of the War: the final stage of the fight that led to the capture of Barberton*. This illustration appeared in *The Graphic* on 24 November 1900, in *After Pretoria: the Guerilla War* and in Cassell's *History of the Boer War*. The National Army Museum has two photogravures which were published by Dickinson and Foster. The first one bears the title *The relievers of Ladysmith Natal Field Force. Portraits of officers taking part in the Campaign* and the other *Officers of the Highland Brigade 1900*. The caption reads 'photogravure from a painting by Dickinson published by Messrs Dickinson April 9 1906'. It has, however, not been confirmed that the painter is in fact F. C. Dickinson.
Thorpe, English Illustration
Hofmeyr, Matton and Roets, Graphic Picture Index

DICKSEE, Herbert Thomas 1862-1942
Painter, etcher and mezzotinter. Born on 14 June 1862, he was the son of artist Thomas Francis Dicksee and brother of the artist Frank Bernard Dicksee. He studied at the Slade School of Art and exhibited at the R.A. from 1885 onwards. He was elected R.E. in 1865. His etching exhibited in 1901 at the Royal Academy, entitled *In the enemy's country*, is presumably of Boer War interest. Dicksee died in London on 20 February 1942.
Graves, Royal Academy, *vol. 2, p. 325*
Waters, British Artists, *vol. 1, p. 92*

DICKSON, Thorpe
Cartoonist for *Judy*.

DICKSON, William Kennedy Laurie 1861-1932
The author of *The Biograph in Battle* (T. Fisher Unwin, 1901). Dickson illustrated his book (which describes the use of the biograph [movie camera]) with photographs and a few sketches.

Dickson accompanied Buller when he sailed for South Africa on the *Dunnottar Castle*, which left Southampton 14 October 1899, and followed him through Natal until the relief of Ladysmith. He was also present at the occupation of Bloemfontein and Pretoria and, like many other correspondents who believed the War was over, left Cape Town for home on the *Carisbrook Castle* on 18 July 1900. During his stay in South Africa, he was the accredited representative of the Mutoscope Biograph Company.
Dickson, Biograph in Battle
Gutsche, Motion Pictures in S.A., *p. 54*
SABIB, *vol. 2, p. 73*

DIERCKX, Joseph 1865-?
Historical painter, sculptor and architect. Dierckx was born in Brussels on 4 October 1865. He was a member of the committee of the *Antwerpen-Transvaal Gedenknummer*, which was published in 1902 in aid of Boer concentration camp victims.
Bénézit, Dictionnaire antique, *vol. 3, p. 261*

DIETZ, B. R.
Soldier-artist. Maj. Dietz was a member of the 7th (Princess Royal's) Dragoon Guards. He arrived in South Africa with

the regiment aboard the SS *Armenian* on 1 March 1900.

He provided sketches (signed 'B.R.D.') of the Battle of Diamond Hill and other engagements for Charles Thompson's *Seventh (Princess Royal's) Dragoon Guards: The Story of the Regiment*. The book is also illustrated with several photographs taken by Dietz while on duty in South Africa. The regiment only returned to England in June 1902 after the signing of the Peace Treaty of Vereeniging.

One of Dietz's illustrations appeared in *The Graphic* supplement of 11 August 1900. Entitled *Driving General Botha from one of his positions near Pretoria*, this illustration, which was reproduced in facsimile, depicts the engagement in which Ian Hamilton was injured.
Hofmeyr, Matton and Roets, Graphic Picture Index
Thompson, Seventh (Princess Royal's) Dragoon Guards: The Story of the Regiment

DIEZ, Julius 1870-1957
Diez was born in Nuremberg on 8 September 1870, the nephew of the painter Wilhelm Diez. Julius Diez studied at the Munich School of Applied Art (where he was made professor in 1925) and under G.V. Hackl and R.V. Seitz at the Munich Academy. His Boer War cartoons appeared in *Jugend*, for which he had worked since 1896. Although as yet no Boer War postcards credited to Diez have been traced, he is much sought after as a postcard artist. He died in Munich on 13 March 1957.
Bénézit, Dictionnaire antique, *vol. 3, p. 268*
Fanelli and Godoli, Art Nouveau Postcards
Hofstätter, Art Nouveau Prints, etc., *p. 162*

DIXON, Charles Edward 1872-1934
Marine painter. The eldest son of Alfred Dixon, the genre and historical artist, Charles Dixon was born in Goring-on-Thames on 8 December 1872. He exhibited at the Royal Academy from the age of 16 and was later a prolific contributor to *The Graphic*, mainly of naval scenes. He was a member of the Langham Sketching Club and was elected a member of the R.I. in 1900. It is said that he was influenced by W.L. Wyllie. While Dixon was not an official war artist during World War I, several of his works are in the Imperial War Museum.

Ten Boer War related naval illustrations by Dixon appeared in *The Graphic*. One of them, *The Mariposa burning in Algoa Bay*, is used by Thorpe in his *English Illustration: The Nineties* as an example of Dixon's work. He was also responsible for the full-page coloured illustrations of naval scenes in *Britannia's Bulwarks* (George Newnes, 1901). (C.J. Staniland did the black and white illustrations.) Other Boer War related illustrations by Dixon include *The Good Hope in Table Bay* and *H.M.S. Powerful steaming up channel on her return from South Africa*. Dixon died at Itchenor on 12 September 1934.
Antique Collecting, *April 1986, p. 20*
Hofmeyr, Matton and Roets, Graphic Picture Index
Personal communication with E. Dixon (artist's granddaughter)
Thorpe, English Illustration, *p. 75*
Waters, British Artists, *vol. 1, p. 93*
Who was Who, *vol. 3, p. 369*

DIXON, Clive MacDonnell 1870-1915 3
Soldier-artist. The son of Sir Raylton Dixon (a keen amateur artist and caricaturist), Clive Dixon was born on 10 February 1870. He was appointed as a second lieutenant in the 16th

---

1 The French artist Henri De Sta produced this Boer War comic strip for *Chronique Amusante*.
2 *The Dying Embers of the War* by F. C. Dickinson appeared in several contemporary publications. The vertical lines on the picture are for the key that appeared above the picture in *After Pretoria: the Guerilla War*.
3 This watercolour by soldier-artist Clive M. Dixon entitled *Boers Ladysmith 1900* is now in the Africana Museum, by whose courtesy it is reproduced.

Lancers on 8 October 1890 and promoted to lieutenant on 27 January 1893 and captain on 28 January 1899. He was appointed aide-de-camp to Sir George White on 9 October 1899.

Dixon was the author and illustrator of *The Leaguer of Ladysmith* (Eyre & Spottiswoode, 1900), which was published 'as a souvenir of a somewhat trying 4 months spent . . . in a beleaguered town, borne cheerfully by soldiers and civilians alike for the sake of the Empire'. The book itself consisted of 18 coloured illustrations with the text printed on the opposite page. The sketches were entitled: 1. *The first shell*; 2. *The last shell*; 3. *Mr Bester's Poultry*; 4. *Boer picnic on Middle Hill disturbed by our Howitzer*; 5. *The sight of our men washing so infuriated the Boers that they immediately opened fire*; 6. *Defence Commanders proving each to his own entire satisfaction, that the two 6.3 inch howitzers are absolutely necessary in his particular section*; 7. *Troglodytic Conchologists* (this is followed by the note 'Question: What is a Troglodytic Conchologist? Answer: One who lives in a cave and sallies forth at intervals to collect shells'); 8. *The Town Guard*; 9. *The Volunteers' ponies*; 10. *A choice of Evils*; 11. *Flag of Truce after Surprise Hill*; 12. *Flooded out* (followed by the note 'Bomb Proof shelters excavated by the river banks, though secure from shell fire, were at the mercy of the Klip River when it came down in flood. A certain veteran war artist [probably Melton Prior] was evicted from his commodious dwelling by one exceptionally high flood); 13.

The Cattle Guard; 14. *The ADC and the goats*; 15. *Between the hours of 7 and 8 a.m. the Boer prisoners are expected to perform their ablution*; 16. *Jemoet die Town Hall skit*; 17. *Allemachtij*; 18. *Chevril Factory.*

Dixon's work was also used in *The Ladysmith Lyre*, which was published in Ladysmith during the siege. A facsimile version of the *Lyre* was published by *The Graphic* on 28 March 1900. Most of the illustrations were unsigned, except for one with the initials 'CMD'. *The Sphere* (8 September 1900) favourably reviewed the book, saying 'it [was] highly humorous and show[ed] a touch of real comic sketching genius'.

Verbeek notes two original Boer War works by Dixon: *Sketches in a war diary* and *Boer skirmishing party taking a break*. Several watercolours by Dixon, including some done during the War, can be found in the Africana Museum. The author has an unsigned watercolour portrait by Dixon dated 23/02/02, of Capt. (later Field Marshal) Philip Walhouse Chetwode (1869-1950) of the 19th Hussars who was with Dixon in Ladysmith.

Dixon was killed in action in Europe in February 1915, after he had attained the rank of major.

> *Personal communication with Kintracers*
> The Sphere, (8 Sept. 1900) vol. 2, p. 286 and (15 Feb. 1915) vol. 50, p. 190
> Under The Union Jack, (5 May 1900) p. 619
> Verbeek, Early Natal Art

DIXON, Harry
Illustrator whose work appeared in *With the Flag to Pretoria* and *After Pretoria: the Guerilla War*.
> *Waters*, British Artists, *vol. 1, p. 93*

DIXON, Percy 1862-1924
Landscape painter. Dixon exhibited at the Royal Academy from 1890 until 1909. He was elected a member of the R.I. in 1915. In 1900 his painting, *On the road to Ladysmith*, was exhibited at the Royal Academy. The Africana Museum has four watercolours completed by Dixon during a visit to South Africa in 1893.
> *Kennedy*, Pictures in the Africana Museum, *vol. 6, p. 195*
> *Verbeek*, Early Natal Art
> *Waters*, British Artists, *vol. 1, p. 93*

D., J.A. *see* J.A.D.

D., N. (N.D.)
Cartoonist for *Moonshine*.

DOMANI
Illustrator whose Boer War work appeared in the coloured supplement of *Le Petit Journal*.

DONAH, Ali
French cartoonist who provided the illustration *L'erbe cache et la pluie effacer* for the special number of *Le Gavroche* of 16 June 1902, entitled 'La Paix à la mode John Bull'.

DONNISON, T. E. 1
Irish-born cartoonist who signed his work 'T.E.D.'. He contributed to *Boy's Own Paper*, *Moonshine*, *Puck* and *Longbow*, and his Boer War cartoons can be found in *Judy*. Sawyers offered a cartoon of Kruger and Chamberlain signed 'T.E.D.' for sale in 1899; it was probably by Donnison. This cartoon is very similar in style to the unsigned 'Monkey Brand' advertisement − 'Need a little polish Sir' − which appeared regularly in the contemporary illustrated press.
> The Illustrated London News, *21 Oct. 1899*
> *Thorpe*, English Illustration

DORVILLE, Noël
French cartoonist whose work appeared in *Le Journal Amusant*, *L'Indiscret* and *L'Assiette au Beurre*. A postcard depicting one of his cartoons from *Le Journal Amusant* was published by an unknown Dutch publisher.

DOWLING, W.
The Owl (Cape Town) cartoonist who also provided *The Illustrated London News* with a sketch of Chamberlain speaking at a banquet at the Wanderers Hall in Johannesburg on 17 January 1903. Dowling drew attention to the centrepiece on the main table which was meant to represent a blockhouse, but the French chef had misunderstood his instructions and had modelled a Martello tower instead. The sketch was redrawn by Samuel Begg (see page 107).
> *De Wet*, Illustrated London News Index

DOWNEY, Thomas fl. 1890-1935
Cartoonist and illustrator. Downey contributed to *The Daily Graphic*, *Holly Leaves*, *The Sketch*, *Moonshine*, *The Idler*, *The Illustrated Sporting & Dramatic News* and *Boy's Own Paper*. His Boer War work appeared in *Judy*. He signed his illustrations 'Thomas D'. Downey was a pupil of Alfred Bryan and succeeded him as principal cartoonist for *Judy* on the latter's death in 1899.
> *Thorpe*, English Illustration

DOYLE-JONES F. W. ?-1938
British sculptor who exhibited at the Royal Academy. Doyle-Jones was commissioned to do five Boer War memorials: 1. *Men of Llanelly* (1905); 2. *Men of West Hartlepool* (1905); 3. *Men of Gateshead* (1905); 4. *Men of Middlesbrough* (1905); 5. *Men of Penrith* (1906).
> *Gildea*, For Remembrance
> *Waters*, British Artists, *vol. 1, p. 97*

DRANER (Jules Renard) 1833-1926
Painter and cartoonist. Draner was the pseudonym of Jules Renard, who was born in Liège on 11 November 1833. He lived and worked in Paris, contributing to many satirical periodicals including *La Caricature*, *Le Charivari*, *Le Journal Amusant*, *L'Eclipse*, *L'Illustration*, and *Le Petit Journal pour Rire*. His Boer War work appeared in the *Le Charivari* Album: *Boers et Anglais*.
> *Bénézit*, Dictionnaire antique, *vol. 3, p. 332*
> *Osterwalder, and Hubschmid and Bouret (eds.)*, Dictionnaire des Illustrateurs, *p. 324*

DRESSEL, A. 1862-?
A. Dressel (possibly August Dressel, the German-born illustrator) was responsible for an illustration in *Nieuwe Belgische Illustratie*, which depicted Boer prisoners making toys on

board ship while being transported to P.O.W. camps.
Bénézit, Dictionnaire antique, vol. 3, p. 335

DRUMMOND, Arthur 1871-1951
Genre and historical painter. The son of the marine painter John Drummond, Arthur Drummond was born in Bristol in 1871. Drummond first studied under Alma-Tadema and later under Constant and J. P. Laurens in Paris. He exhibited at the Royal Academy from 1890. In 1986 his large untitled oil showing another version of 'Lord Roberts and the Innkeeper's child' was offered for sale by the Everard Read Gallery in Johannesburg for R24 000. Drummond died in West Molesey, Surrey, on 1 January 1951.
Waters, British Artists, vol. 1, p. 98

DRUMMOND, N.
Artist who produced some of Raphael Tuck's military postcards during the Boer War.
Holt, Tonie and Valmai, Picture Postcards, p. 81

DRURY, Edward Alfred Briscoe 1856-1944
Sculptor of figure subjects, mainly in bronze and marble. Drury was born in London on 11 November 1856 and he was educated at the New College School, Oxford. He also studied art in Oxford, as well as in Paris under Dalou. Drury exhibited at the Royal Academy from 1885. He designed six Boer War memorials: 1. the monument to Maj. Gen. Sir William Penn-Symons in Saltash, Cornwall (1900); 2. New College, Oxford (opened 1903); 3. the statue in memory of Old Cliftonians, Clifton College, Bristol (1904); 4. the memorial to the South Lancashire Regiment, Queen's Gardens, Warrington (1907); 5. Harrow School chapel memorial to those soldiers who were educated at Harrow; 6. the memorial to the Gordon Highlanders, Castle Esplanade, Edinburgh. Drury died in Wimbledon on 24 December 1944.
Gildea, For Remembrance
Waters, British Artists, vol. 1, p. 98

DU BOIS
Cartoonist for *Pick-Me-Up*.

DUCH, Jan
Polichinelle cartoonist who also worked for *Le Rire, La Vie Pour Rire* and *Le Bon Vivant*.

DUDENEY, Henry Ernest 1857-1930
Dudeney who was born in Mayfield, Sussex, on 10 April 1857. Initially Dudeney worked for George Newnes's *Tit Bits*, using the pseudonym 'Sphinx' for the first time. He was later known as the 'puzzle king' of *The Strand Magazine*, where he remained on the staff for many years. He is reputed to have been the first person to have made puzzle-solving a profession. *The Strand Magazine* paid Dudeney 10 guineas a month for his efforts, which elicited correspondence from all over the world.

Dudeney's Boer War related contribution was a board game, one of a weekly series, which appeared in *The Golden Penny* on 27 January 1902. The illustration depicted an outline of the map of the Transvaal and Orange Free State showing towns occupied by British and Boers. The object was to occupy as many of the opponent's towns as possible.

Dudeney's publications included *The Canterbury Puzzles* (1907), *Amusements in Mathematics* (1917) and *Modern Puzzles* (1926). He died on 24 April 1930.
Pound, Strand Magazine 1891-1950, p. 140
Who was Who, vol. 3, pp. 387-388

DU FRAMONT, Victor Albert 1855-? [1]
Du Framont lived in Tournon, France, before coming to South Africa. A captain in the French legion fighting on the side of the Boers, he was captured and sent to St Helena where he produced a number of hand-drawn cyclostyled postcards. Some of these were marked 'Souvenir des Prisonniers de Guerre Français', while one is inscribed 'Maison de Napoleon à Longwood' and another is addressed to 'Monsieur Le Commandant Snyman, Deadwood camp'. Another depicts the Battle of Colenso. Four of the cards bear a map of the island. Some of the cards are signed in full, others are only initialled. All are dated 1902 and have either the French or English inscription 'prisonnier de Guerre' or 'prisoner of war'.
Mabbet, St Helena
Transvaal Archives, TKP 156, p. 142

DU FRESNE, Paul
Illustrator for *Le Petit Journal*. His *Arrivée des Généraux Boers à Paris* appeared on the front cover of *Le Petit Journal* (No. 623) on 26 October 1902.
Bénézit, Dictionnaire antique, vol. 3, p. 382

DUNCAN, James Allen fl. 1894-1910
Illustrator and postcard artist. Duncan was a prolific illustrator for *The Daily Graphic*, although occasionally his work also appeared in *The Graphic* and *The Evergreen*. Duncan's illustrations were also found on comic postcards, usually with a Scottish theme. He often used the pseudonym 'Hamish' or 'Hamish Duncan'.
Hofmeyr, Matton and Roets, Graphic Picture Index
Houfe, British Illustrators and Caricaturists, p. 281
The Studio, vol. 15, pp. 184-189
Thorpe, English Illustration
Holt, Tonie and Valmai, Stanley Gibbons Postcard Catalogue 1983, p. 53

DUPRAY, Henri (Henri-Louis) 1841-1909 [1]
Military painter. Dupray was born in Sedan, France, on 3 November 1841. He was a colleague of Alphonse de Neuville and Eduard Detaille. Dupray illustrated the British publication, *British Battles* (Charles Ketts and Co., 1902), written by William Maxwell. Three of Dupray's illustrations were of Boer War interest: 1. *The Battle of Colenso, 1899; who will save the guns*; 2. *Surrender at Paardeberg, 1900: Dark Cronje at Bay*; 3. *Siege of Mafeking, 1900, A memorable defence*. Dupray died in Paris in April 1909.
Bénézit, Dictionnaire antique, vol. 3, p. 421
British Military Costume Prints, p. 1084

DU RAND, Godefroy 1832-?
Illustrator. Du Rand was born of French parents in Düsseldorf in 1832. He settled in London in 1870, joining the permanent staff of *The Graphic*, after studying with Leon Cogniet. He exhibited pictures of the siege of Paris at the R.B.A. in 1873. He supplied *The Graphic* with illustrations on military and horse subjects, as well as on foreign affairs. His Boer War work appeared in *Battles of the 19th Century*.

DU TOIT, W. (Junior)
Du Toit provided the original watercolour for a sketch by Van Moerkerken entitled *Naby Ladysmith Januarie 1900*, which can be found in the National Army Museum.

DU TRIAC, Georges-Pierre
Painter and illustrator who worked for *Armée et Marine*, producing illustrations which were probably done from photographs.
Bénézit, Dictionnaire antique, vol. 3, p. 454

D., W.B. see W.B.D.

DYER-DAVIES, D. see DAVIES, D. Dyer-

DYSON, William Henry 1880-1938
Dyson was born in Ballarat, Australia, on 3 September 1880, (both *Who was Who* and Waters give the incorrect date of 1883). He was ninth of eleven children: his brother, Ted, became a writer and Ambrose, another brother, was an artist and cartoonist.

Dyson originally joined the *Sydney Bulletin* in 1899. Later, however, believing that there was little scope for his talents as an artist and cartoonist in Australia, he went to London to work for the *Daily Herald*.

Dyson was only nineteen at the start of the Boer War, but some of his caricatures for the *Sydney Bulletin* received some praise. One of these caricatures, *The Boer at Heaven's gate*, earned him three guineas. In 1913, while working for the *Daily Herald*, he produced some very anti-South African cartoons. These cartoons attacked the prime minister, Louis Botha, and his government for declaring martial law and deporting the leaders of the miners' strike. One of his cartoons urged dockers not to handle South African produce until the deportees had been allowed to return to their adopted country. He signed his work 'Will Dyson'.

During World War I Dyson volunteered his services as a war artist and, despite being wounded twice, he produced several remarkable paintings and drawings of members of the Australian contingent and their exploits. He returned to Australia in 1925 and developed his talents as an etcher.

In September 1909 he married Ruby Lindsay. The couple's daughter, Betty, also showed artistic talent. Dyson died on 21 January 1938.
McMullin, Will Dyson
Waters, British Artists, vol. 2, p. 18
Who was Who, vol. 3, p. 399

EBBUTT, Phil fl. 1886-1903
An illustrator of humorous subjects, Ebbutt began his career as a draughtsman by working for and studying with the Dalziel brothers. He later worked for *The Daily Graphic* and *The Graphic*, and also contributed to *Fun, The Quiver* and *Lady's Pictorial*. Ebbutt's limited Boer War work is found in *The Illustrated London News* (26 May 1900, supplement), and the illustration shows the 'Mafeking night' celebrations.
Houfe, British Illustrators and Caricaturists, p. 293
Thorpe, English Illustration

E.C.
An unknown artist who contributed to *Lloyd's News*. An original sketch bearing these initials, dated 12 August 1900, is in the author's collection.

ECKHARDT, Oscar 1872-1904
Oil painter and illustrator. Eckhardt was born in Sunderland in 1872. He exhibited at the R.O.I. and the R.B.A. He worked for *Black & White, St Pauls, The Daily Graphic, The Sketch, Pick-Me-Up* and *The Strand Magazine*. His Boer War work appears in *With the Flag to Pretoria* and in *Cassell's Illustrated History of the Boer War*.
Thorpe, English Illustration
Waters, British Artists, vol. 2, p. 18

EDWARDS, George Wharton
Painter and illustrator. Edwards was born in Fairhaven, Connecticut. He studied in Antwerp and Paris and lived for a while in New York. He illustrated several books and was responsible for the mural decoration at the United States Military Academy. In 1900 Edwards became the art editor for *Collier's* and persuaded his friend, Frederic Remington, to switch allegiance from *Harper's Weekly* to his paper. Edwards designed the pictorial cloth covers of A.T. Mahan's *The War in South Africa*.
Fielding, American Painters etc., p. 108
Samuels, Frederic Remington

---

1 French military painter Henri Dupray's depiction of Cronje surrendering at Paardeberg. The illustration appeared in William Maxwell's 1902 book *British Battles*.
2 The Monkey Brand soap advertisement. Several artists did reproductions of this famous cartoon, including T. E. Donnison.

EDWARDS, (Henry) Dennis 1861-1921
Cartoonist. Edwards was born in England in 1861. He was sent out to South Africa as a war correspondent for *The Graphic* in 1879 to cover the Zulu War. Edwards was later employed by the Cape of Good Hope Bank, but left their employ and started his own printing and publishing business in Cape Town. He produced several directories.

On 25 April 1890 the first issue of *The Cape Register* appeared. Initially its eight pages consisted mainly of advertisements, but Edwards later expanded the scope of the weekly by publishing his own cartoons, often under the pseudonym 'Grip', although some of his work was unsigned. Over 600 cartoons, including many attacking Rhodes, appeared during the 14-year duration of the publication. It is claimed that Edwards's paper was the first to reproduce cartoons by process block instead of the more cumbersome method of lithography.

The Africana Museum in Johannesburg has several original non-Boer War cartoons by Edwards.

The Cape, *20 May 1910*
Rosenthal, National Biography, *p. 111*
Schoonraad, Spot- en Strookprent Kunstenaars

EDWARDS, Lionel Dalhousie Robertson 1878-1966
Equestrian painter, illustrator of and writer on sporting subjects. Edwards was born in Clifton on 9 November 1878. His art education was acquired at the Frank Calderon School of Animal Painting in Kensington. Edwards worked for *The Graphic* and for *Punch*. He was elected a member of R.I. in 1927. Edwards's Boer War work can be found in *Under The Union Jack*. In 1984 the Parker Gallery offered a coloured photogravure entitled *A scene during the South African War* (c.1900), which was done after a drawing by Edwards. He died on 13 April 1966.

Waters, British Artists, *vol. 1, p. 103*

EDWARDS, Louis
British illustrator, who contributed military subjects to *The Illustrated London News*. Two of his illustrations, *Boer War: the 10th Hussars* and *1st Royal Regiment of Dragoons*, were reproduced in the Picture Postcard Co.'s series on the War. Edwards also contributed a chromolithograph cover to sheet music and provided eight chromolithographs, including the frontispiece, to *The Historical record of the Third (King's Own) Hussars* (W. P. Griffith and Sons, 1903). Edwards' illustrations are dated 1899 and 1900.

On 5 December 1899, a 'Grand Military and Patriotic Concert' was held at the Royal Albert Hall, in aid of sick and wounded soldiers and their dependants. The souvenir brochure was illustrated and one sketch, *The Queen! God Bless her!*, was by Louis Edwards.

British Military Costume Prints
SAPRG Newsletter, *no. 8*

EGERSDÖRFER, Heinrich 1853-1915 1
Illustrator and cartoonist. Egersdörfer was born in Nurem-

berg in 1853. Trained as a lithographer, he went abroad in the 1870s, taking part in the Franco-Prussian War and spending much time in England. He arrived in South Africa in 1879 and in 1884 founded *The South African Illustrated News* in Cape Town. His black and white sketches recorded a fascinating cross section of Victorian Cape Town. He was also responsible for many early South African postcards, including *In the days of the Mail Coach*. Egersdörfer went to Australia in the late 1880s, after the demise of *The South African Illustrated News*, but returned, this time to Johannesburg, in 1895.

Egersdörfer's original illustrations can be found in many South African art galleries and the Africana Museum. He often used the signature 'Heiner Egersdörfer' or just 'E.H.'. His most important work of Boer War interest was entitled *The South African Review Book of 50 famous cartoons: A unique souvenir of the Anglo-Boer War 1899-1900*. Published in 1900, it was based on the cartoons which he drew for *The South African Review*. Egersdörfer also acted as a local correspondent for *The Graphic*, and many of his illustrations appeared in this weekly between 1899 and 1901. His South African work continued to appear in *The Graphic* until 1908. *Cassell's Illustrated History of the Boer War* used his illustrations second-hand. Egersdörfer died in England in 1915.

Hofmeyr, Matton and Roets, Graphic Picture Index
Rosenthal, Heinrich Egersdörfer
Schoonraad, Spot- en Strookprent Kunstenaars

E.H.
An unidentified *Jugend* illustrator whose postcards, including one showing 'Spion's Kop', were based on illustrations taken from that paper.

EMMERSON, H. Percy
Second lieutenant Emmerson's sketch appeared in *The Graphic* on 20 September 1902, entitled *A snowstorm in the Cape Colony. A camp of the Cape Mounted Rifles on a spur of the Drakensberg* and redrawn by W.T. Maud.

Hofmeyr, Matton and Roets, Graphic Picture Index

ENER, G.
French cartoonist who contributed to *La Caricature* and *Le Bon Vivant*.

ENGELA, J. G.
Engela was a Boer prisoner at the Ragama Camp who did a watercolour portrait of a man who was probably a fellow prisoner in 1902. This is in the author's collection.

E.O.B.
Two sketches by this artist and redrawn by Frank Dadd appeared in *The Graphic* on 2 June 1900.

ERSKINE, W. C. C. ?-1901
A captain in the Field Intelligence Dept. who started the free-hand sketches for Maj. Gen. Sir F. Maurice's *History of the*

War in South Africa. He was killed in action on 7 October 1901 and the sketches were completed by Capt. K. M. Davie (see p. 124).

ESPINASSE
Cartoonist who drew a series of French postcard cartoons in 1902, attacking Edward VII. The unnumbered cards were: 1. *Le Rêve D'Edouard, Edouard César. P Krüger Vercingétorix* (signed 'Essanipse'); 2. *Couronnement d' Edouard VII 1902 Commémoratief*; 3. *Une Conquête – Le départ*; 4. *Une Conquête – Le Retoer*; 5. *Une Conquête – Le Nouveau Timbre-poste Sud-Africain*; 6. *Le Triomphe – Le Matin du 9 août 1902*; 7. *Le Triomphe – Le Soir du 9 août 1902*; 8. Untitled, but shows Edward surrounded by skulls on a shilling postage stamp. An earlier card, published in 1900, shows President Kruger and is titled *Gloria Victis*.

ETTLING, L. E.
Private Ettling was a member of the Post Office Corp in Pretoria. An illustrated postal cover depicting Kitchener and addressed to Ettling's mother appeared in Batten's *Post Office Militant*.

EVANS, A.
A sketch by him, showing the Australian Contingent departing from Melbourne, appeared in *The Sphere* 14 July 1900.

EVANS, Harry
A picture by Harry Evans, entitled *War's pathetic Side*, appeared in *War Pictures*.

FAIRHURST, Enoch 1874-1945
Miniaturist, illustrator, etcher and oil and pastel artist. Fairhurst was born in Bolton, Lancashire, on 1 May 1874. He exhibited at the Royal Academy, the R.S.A., the R.C.A. and the R.W.A. His best-known work is a large drypoint of the Halle Orchestra done in 1933. Fairhurst's Boer War contribution was the illustrations to the story, 'Brothers in Arms', by Edward Stratemeyer, which appeared in volume 2 of *Boys of Our Empire*. Fairhurst died in Bolton on 31 October 1945.

Houfe, British Illustrators and Caricaturists, *p. 295*
Waters, British Artists, *vol. 1, p. 109*

FAIVRE, Jules-Abel 1867-1945
Caricaturist and genre and portrait painter. Faivre was born in Lyon on 30 March 1867. He was a pupil of J.B. Poncet at the École des Beaux-Arts of Lyon and Benjamin Constant and Jules Lefebvre in Paris. Faivre was associated with Grün, Léandre, Steinlen and Willette of the artistic group 'Taverne de Paris'. He was renowned for his savage satire, which he used to good effect on postcards, and for his work which appeared in *L'Assiette au Beurre*, *Le Rire* and *Le Bon Vivant* and is signed 'Abel Faivre'. He died in August 1945.

Bénézit, Dictionnaire antique, *vol. 3, p. 653*
Fanelli and Godoli, Art Nouveau Postcards, *p. 336*
The Strand, *vol. 22, p. 679*

FARASYN, Edgard 1858-?
Landscape, marine and genre painter. Farasyn, also known as Edgar Farazÿn, was born in Antwerp on 14 August 1858. He was a professor at the Academy in Antwerp, a founder of the 'de Dertienen' movement, and a contributor to *Antwerpen-Transvaal Gedenknummer* (March/April 1902).

Bénézit, Dictionnaire antique, vol. 3, p. 670

FARQUHARSON, David 1838-1907
Landscape painter. Farquharson was born in Blairgowrie, Scotland, in 1838. He was mainly self-taught and exhibited at the R.S.A. from 1868. He was elected A.R.S.A. in 1882 and A.R.A. in 1905. One of Farquharson's oil paintings which was exhibited at the Royal Academy in 1900 appeared in *Royal Academy Pictures* (1900). The title of the picture (*War News*), but not its content, suggests the influence of the Boer War. Farquharson died in Bernam on 12 July 1907.

Bénézit, Dictionnaire antique, vol. 3, p. 675
Waters, British Artists, vol. 1, p. 110

FARQUHARSON, John 1866-? 1
Soldier-artist. Farquharson was born in Blairgowrie, Scotland, in May 1866. He joined the Seaforth Highlanders on 17 February 1894. He was promoted to lance corporal on 6 September of the same year, to corporal on 4 January 1897 and to lance sergeant on 8 October 1898. His military record reveals that, for reasons described only as 'neglect', he was demoted to private by the regimental court martial on 29 May 1899. Farquharson served in the occupation of Crete (1897) and the Nile Expedition (1898), and, undeterred by his demotion to private, served in the Boer War receiving the Queen's S.A. medal (1899-1902) with Paardeberg, Driefontein, Witteberg, Cape Colony and Transvaal clasps. (This medal was in addition to those he had received in Egypt in 1898.) He finally left the service on 16 February 1906, apparently without regaining his original rank.

Farquharson had been an artist before he joined the Seaforth Highlanders, although no record of any early work or exhibitions has been found. He provided facsimile sketches of the Sudan to *The Illustrated London News* in 1898. During the Boer War he also submitted sketches to *The Illustrated London News*, many of which were published in facsimile. On 13 January 1900, *The Illustrated London News* published 'a picture from the able pencil of Private Farquharson of the E Company 2nd Seaforth Highlanders – whose Sudan sketches many will remember with interest'. The report goes on to describe the heroic stand of the Northamptons at Enslin, which Farquharson depicted in his sketch. In the 12 May issue a report appeared entitled *With Roberts in the Orange Free State* and it was illustrated with three facsimile sketches 'drawn by Private Farquharson, 2nd Seaforth Highlanders'. They were: *An early morning wash in the Riet*; *A thunderstorm passing over the camp*, and *In the market square, Bloemfontein, the pipes and drums of the Black Watch*.

The Africana Museum has 24 loose sketches by Farquhar-son which originally formed part of an album. On 28 October 1981 Christie's offered three of Farquharson's Sudan Campaign watercolours. The author has one of his watercolours, entitled *A night patrol, Modder River 1899*.

Correspondence with the Africana Museum, 1 Sept 1982
De Wet, Illustrated London News Index
Personal communication with Kintracers

FAU, Fernand
Fau was a French caricaturist who worked for the English magazine *Fun* as well as for *Le Rire*, in which his Boer War contribution appeared.

Houfe, British Illustrators and Caricaturists, p. 298

FAUSTIN, Betbeder 1847-? 1
Born in France in 1847, Faustin worked in London as a painter and caricaturist. A painting by him of Lord Roberts and 'Peace' was used by Raphael Tuck on two postcards, *Veni Vidi Vici* (No. 1286) and *Graced with Victory, a hundred thousand welcomes* (No. 1288). The latter was coloured. On both cards credit is given to the 'Proprietor of *Ludgate Magazine*' who must have held the copyright. It is assumed that they issued engravings of this painting.

Bénézit, Dictionnaire antique, vol. 3, p. 683

FEARON, Percy ('Poy') 1874-1948
Fearon was born of American parents in Shanghai on 17 March 1874. He spent much time in England where he became a cartoonist for *Judy*, in which his Boer War contribution appeared. Fearon was an active member of the Savage Club, and he derived his pseudonym from the American pronunciation of Percy. Fearon died on 4 November 1948.

Norgate and Wykes, Not So Savage, p. 54
Personal communication with the Savage Club
Thorpe, English Illustration

FEININGER, Lyonel 1871-1956
Landscape and marine painter and caricaturist. Feininger was born of German parents in New York on 17 July 1871. Before devoting himself exclusively to painting and later working as an avant-garde artist with Kandinsky, Klee and Gropius, Feininger was employed as a cartoonist by French, German and American magazines. He also drew comic strips for the *Chicago Tribune* from 1906. Feininger's Boer War cartoons were published in *Lustige Blätter* and *Ulk*, and his cartoon of Kruger, dated 1899, appeared on the front cover of *Burenstreiche*. Feininger died in New York on 13 January 1956.

Bénézit, Dictionnaire antique, vol. 3, p. 700
Fanelli and Godoli, Art Nouveau Postcards
Feaver, Masters of Caricature, p. 129

FEITH, Johannes (Jan) jnr. ('Cris Kras Kzn') 1874-1944 2
Illustrator. Feith was born in Amsterdam on 12 May 1874. He was well known in the Netherlands for his illustrations in the series *De Geschiedenis van ons Vaderland*. He was also a journalist and editor-in-chief of *De Kampioen*.

His Boer War work is found in *Pillen Voor Joe* by Kees van Ponten, published by Cohen Zonen (Amsterdam 1900) and *Kronings-Idylle* with verses by Kees van Ponten. In the latter publication Feith used his pseudonym. At least one postcard, probably taken from *Der Wahre Jacob*, was published by Dr van den Ende of Rotterdam. It was entitled 'Der Wahre Jacob' 'John Bull op Majoeba, scene op die Maasbrug Rotterdam'.

Feith was a regular contributor to *Der Wahre Jacob* and, according to Arthur Lord's article, 'Dutch Humorous Artists', in *The Strand* (vol. 24, 1902), he illustrated several books on the War. Lord also mentions that, besides being a cycling champion, Feith produced several 'book covers, posters and caricatures'. He died in The Hague on 2 September 1944.

SABIB, vol. 3, p. 701
Scheen, Nederlandse Beeldende Kunstenaars, vol. 2, p. 335
The Strand, vol. 24, p. 95

FELDBAUER, Max 1869-?
Illustrator. Feldbauer was born in Neumarkt, Germany, on 14 February 1869 and he later worked in Munich for the magazine *Jeunesse*. His Boer War work appeared in *Jugend* and in the Dutch publication *John Bull in Zuid-Afrika*.

Bénézit, Dictionnaire antique, vol. 3, p. 701

FELLER, Frank 1848-1908 2
Illustrator and postcard artist. Feller was born in Bümpliz, Switzerland, on 28 October 1848 and he was educated in Geneva, Munich and Paris. He went to London in 1870 and became an illustrator of periodicals and books. He exhibited at the Royal Academy between 1883 and 1885.

Feller was one of the principal illustrators for *Shurey's Pictorial Budget* and *Shurey's Illustrated*, in which double-page features often appeared. Feller's illustrations also appeared in *The Strand Magazine*, *Boy's Own Paper*, *New Budget*, *Chums* and *Black & White*.

Four of Feller's Boer War watercolours can be found in the Africana Museum: 1. *Surrender of the Boers at Paardeberg 1900*; 2. *The Fall of Bloemfontein 1900*; 3. *The Relief of Kimberley*; 4. *British troops crossing the Zand River 1900*. The National Army Museum also has work by Feller, but not concerning the Boer War. The Parker Gallery has also offered works by Feller from time to time. One of Feller's large oils, entitled *No Surrender*, was sold by Stephan Welz and Co. in Johannesburg in April 1990. The painting depicted the Highlanders at Magersfontein.

---

1 The cartoon *Le Triomphe – Le Soir du 9 août 1902* by Espinasse was one of a series lampooning Edward VII.
2 *A night Patrol, Modder River 1899*, a watercolour by Private John Farquharson of the Seaforth Highlanders.
3 *Surrender of the Boers at Paardeberg* by Swiss illustrator Frank Feller. Reproduced by courtesy of the Africana Museum.
4 The soldiers depicted in Frank Feller's watercolour *British troops crossing the Sand River 1900* have an almost manic zeal in their eyes. Reproduced by courtesy of the Africana Museum.

Feller was well known as a postcard artist, and one of his Boer War illustrations was featured in Raphael Tuck's Empire series no. 840, entitled *Earl Roberts and Viscount Kitchener on the South African Battlefields*. Feller often signed his work with the monogram 'F.F.'. His full signature was often not very distinct and his postcard illustrations have often been described incorrectly as being by 'Teller' or 'Geller'. He died in London on 6 March 1908.

Kennedy, Pictures in the Africana Museum, *vol. 3*
Thorpe, English Illustration

FENWICK
Designer of the Ratby Tribute Medal.
Hibbard, Boer War Medals, *p. 65*

FERTOM
Cartoonist. His cartoons of Louis Botha appeared in *Polichinelle* on 6 January 1901 and his work lampooning Roberts and Kitchener on 13 January the same year. During the War he also worked for *La Caricature* and *Le Rire*, although his cartoons in the latter were not about the War.

FESTING, Arthur Hoskyns 1870-1915
Soldier-artist. Festing was born on 9 February 1870. (Creagh and Humphris in *The D.S.O.* give the date as 1869.) He was educated privately and on the Continent before going to Sandhurst. He was gazetted to the Royal Irish Rifles on 11 February 1888 and served with the regiment during the Nile Campaign in 1889, being promoted to lieutenant on 3 July of that year. He served in the Niger-Sudan Campaign (1896-7). He was awarded the brevet rank of major on his promotion to captain on 15 January 1898. He served with the combined Imperial Troops in the West African Frontier Force and with the Royal Niger Company's troops in 1898 and 1899.

Festing served in South Africa from 1899 to 1900. He commanded the 11th Mounted Infantry and was on the staff of the Rhodesian Field Force, taking part in the operations in the Orange Free State from February to May 1900; those in the Cape Colony south of the Orange River during 1900; those in Rhodesia in May 1900, and those in the Transvaal, west of Pretoria, from July to November 1900. He retired from the army in 1905 on receiving a civil appointment with the Colonial Office, but served again during World War I. He was killed in action in 1915.

Festing's Boer War work appeared in *The Graphic* on 6 June 1900, entitled *Defence of Wepener: the scene of Colonel Dalgety's successful resistance* and *The operations at Dewetsdorp: a sketch from the right of the Boer position*. Sketchmaps drawn by Festing appeared in facsimile in *The Daily Graphic* on 27 June 1900.

Creagh and Humphris, The D.S.O., *p. 92*
Hofmeyr, Matton and Roets, Graphic Picture Index
Who was Who, *vol. 1, p. 242*

F.H.Y.
Illustrator of Max Marcus of Berlin postcard no. 837, entitled
Für Nord und Süd, für Ost und West,
Wird jener Tag ein frohes Fest,
An dem – was bald geschehen sollt',
Den Chamberlain der T... b . . .!]

FICKENSCHER
Cartoonist responsible for the Boer War postcard published by L. Schlaf, Salzburg and Munich, in 1900. The card was addressed to 'Herrn Praesidenten Paul Kruger in Pretoria, Transvaal'.

FIELD, C. R. M.
Major C. R. M. Field was the author and illustrator of 'Kruger's Cruiser' ('Our great war story'), which appeared serialized in 16 parts in *The Golden Penny* from 17 February to 14 April 1900.

FIELD, D. H.
Cartoonist for *Pittsburgh Press*. Examples of his work were reproduced in *The King* during the War.

FINBERG, Alexander Joseph 1866-1939 2
Black and white artist, and art critic, advisor and writer. Finberg was born in London on 23 April 1866. He studied art at the Lambeth School of Art and in Paris, and he exhibited at the Salon des Artistes Français in Paris, and at the New English Art Club.

Finberg's black and white work appeared in *The Graphic*, *The Illustrated London News* and *The Penny Illustrated Paper*. Later he became art critic for *The Morning Leader*, *The Star*, *The Manchester Guardian* and *The Saturday Review*. In 1905 he catalogued the drawings of the Turner bequest at the National Gallery and became the recognized authority on the artist. Finberg was also lecturer on the history of painting to the Education Committee of the London

A HUNDRED THOUSAND WE

County Council and the University of London, but his main contributions to the art world at that time were his writings on the history of English art. He also had the doubtful distinction of being the art adviser to the Board of Inland Revenue in the matter of picture evaluation for tax purposes.

Finberg wrote articles for, among others, *Edinburgh Review*, *The National Review*, *Burlington Magazine*, *The Studio*, *The Art Journal* and *Les Arts*. His publications include *English Watercolour Painters* (1906); *The Drawings of David Cox*; *Ingres*; *The Watercolours of J. M. W. Turner*; *Inventory of Turner's Drawings in the National Gallery* (1909); *Turner's sketches and drawings* (1910); *The History of Turner's Liber Studiorum, with a new Catalogue Raisonné* (1924); *An abridgment of Ruskin's Modern Painters* (1927); *Introduction to Turner's Southern coast* (1929); *In Venice with Turner* (1930); and *The Life of J. M. W. Turner* (1939, published posthumously).

Some of Finberg's work can be found in the Victoria and Albert Museum. He often used the initials 'A.J.F.' to sign his illustrations. The author has two of his Boer War works, both signed and dated 1900: *The HAC (Honourable Artillery Company) Contingent of the City's Own with their Vickers Maxim quick firing field guns* and *The King of the Castle*. Both paintings were reproduced in *The Penny Illustrated Paper* and bear the *P.I.P.* stamp on the reverse. *The Sketch* also reproduced a few of Finberg's Boer War illustrations. He died on 15 March 1939.

Dictionary of National Biography, *p. 2631*
Thorpe, English Illustration
Who was Who, *vol. 3, p. 443*

FINNEMORE, Joseph 1860-1939   2

Figure painter, etcher, illustrator and postcard artist. Finnemore was born in Birmingham on 8 January 1860. He studied at the Birmingham Art School and at the Antwerp Academy under Verlat. He returned to England in 1881 and exhibited at the principal London galleries from 1885, including the Royal Academy from 1891 to 1901. He was elected a member of the R.B.A. in 1890, the R.I. in 1898, and the R.B.S.A. in 1901.

Finnemore spent 18 months travelling in Malta, Greece, Turkey and Russia, and in 1884 worked as an illustrator for *The Graphic*, *The Sphere* and *Black & White*. Finnemore's first black and white work appeared in *Boy's Own Paper* in 1885. From its inception in 1891 *The Strand Magazine* used his work regularly to illustrate short stories. An article about him, with photographs, appeared in the December 1895 edition.

Finnemore's work can be found in both the Queen's and the Duke of Windsor's collections. The Chilean Government owns one of his paintings, and another, entitled *The signing of the Treaty of Peace at Versailles*, is in Australia.

Finnemore's Boer War contribution was extensive, and his work, including *A meeting of General and Lady White*, appeared in *The Sphere*. A Boer War postcard, signed 'J.F.', as

was much of Finnemore's work, was published by Raphael Tuck (No. 838) and featured the return of Kitchener. There are two different versions of this card, which is entitled *A hundred thousand welcomes*. A painting which was listed in *R.B.A.Exhibitors* in 1902, entitled *Peace: a Boer Vrouw of North Holland*, may have been of Boer War relevance.

Finnemore was responsible for the eight illustrations in William Gordon Stables' Boer War related work, *On Special Service: A tale of life at sea* (Hodder and Stoughton, London, 1901). Finnemore's work for *With the Flag to Pretoria* and *After Pretoria: the Guerilla War* is extensive and many of his illustrations are used on the covers of the individual parts. The McGregor Museum in Kimberley possesses the watercolour, *Funeral of General Wauchope CB CMG commanding officer of the Highland Brigade killed at Magersfontein 11 December 1899*, which was reproduced in *The Sphere* on 17 February 1900.

Finnemore lived for a time in Northwood in Middlesex, where he died on 18 December 1939.

Carter, War Artists in S.A., *p. 16*
The Strand, *1895, vol. 10, p. 788*
The Times, (obituary) *22 December 1939*
Who was Who, *vol. 3, p. 447*

F., I.R. *see* I.R.F.

FLORES, Ricardo ?-1918

French artist and cartoonist who worked for *Le Rire*, *La Vie Pour Rire* and *L'Assiette au Beurre*. He provided two cartoons, *Edouard VII Victoreuse* and *Conclusion* to the special number of *Le Gavroche* of 16 June 1902, entitled 'La Paix à la mode John Bull'. Flores died in France on 20 October 1918.

Bénézit, Dictionnaire antique, *vol. 3, p. 789*

FLOWER, Clement fl. 1899-1908

Portrait and figure painter. Flower worked at Bushey, Herts, between 1899 and 1908. A painting of his, *Market day in Bavaria*, was reproduced in *Nieuwe Belgische Illustratie*, vol. 10, no. 2 (1902/1903). One Boer War illustration by Flower appeared in *The Graphic*, but his major contribution concerning the War can be found in *War Pictures*.

Houfe, British Illustrators and Caricaturists, *p. 306*

FORBES, Stanhope Alexander 1857-1947

A genre, landscape, town and figure painter. Forbes was born in Dublin on 18 November 1857. He studied art at the' Lambeth School of Art, at the Royal Academy schools (1874-8) and in Paris for two years under Bonnat. Forbes and his wife, Elizabeth Armstrong, founded the Newlyn School of Art in 1899. He became a member of the N.E.A.C. in 1886, an A.R.A. in 1892 and R.A. in 1910. His Boer War contribution consists of a painting entitled *A tale of the Veldt*. A photoengraving after this painting was offered in *The Graphic* (Christmas 1900), having been advertised in *The Golden Penny* in November 1900. Forbes died in Newlyn on 2 March 1947.

Dictionary of National Biography, *p. 2635*
The Golden Penny, *vol. 15, p. 421*
Waters, British Artists, *p. 117*

FORESTIER, Amedée 1854-1930   1

Illustrator and postcard artist. Forestier was born in Paris in 1854 and worked principally for *The Illustrated London News*. Despite his French nationality he lived mainly in London but travelled widely in Europe, Canada and North Africa. In 1896 Forestier was sent by Queen Victoria to Moscow to paint commemorative pictures of the Tsar's coronation and in 1908 he acted as special artist for the Quebec tercentenary celebrations. During World War I he did pictorial work for the French and British Red Cross and in 1920 he accompanied the French official mission to Morocco. A keen archaeologist, he was commissioned to illustrate the history of London for the London Museum and to do similar work for the Field Museum of Chicago. Among other commissions were the large

paintings of Roman Britain done for the Royal Ontario Museum of Archaeology in Toronto. The author has several of Forestier's wash drawings of Roman soldiers, done for an unidentified publication.

Among Forestier's publications are *Brabant and East Flanders*; *Liège and the Ardennes*; *Bruges and West Flanders*, and *The Roman Soldier*. He illustrated works by many well-known novelists, including Anthony Hope, Robert Hichens, Besant, 'Q' and Seton Merriman.

Forestier's work with a South African context appeared in *The Illustrated London News* from 1885 until 1929, and no less than 34 Boer War illustrations appeared at various times. In July 1986 Bonhams offered the watercolour *Celebration after the Boer War*.

Two of Forestier's works appear in the Royal Collection at Windsor, but are not to do with the Boer War. Forestier often signed his work with an elaborate monogram.

Carter, War Artists in S.A., *p. 18*
De Wet, Illustrated London News Index
Illustrated London News, *22 Nov. 1930*
Who was Who, *vol. 3, p. 463*

FORMILLI, Cesare T. G. fl.1887-1913

Italian-born decorative artist. Among his several works was *My son's regiment*, which was exhibited at the Royal Academy in 1903. The painting was reproduced in *The Illustrated London News* on 30 May 1900 (sup. VIII, vol. 122).

Graves, Royal Academy, *vol. 3, p. 140*
Johnson and Greutzner, British Artists, *p. 181*

FORREST, Archibald Stevenson 1869-1963

Landscape and figure painter and illustrator. Forrest was born in Greenwich in 1869. He studied art at the Westminster School, the City and Guilds College and the Edinburgh Art School. Besides working for *The Idler*, he illustrated several books. During the Boer War Forrest worked for *Moonshine*, but he is best known for his illustrations in *Ten Little Boer Boys* by 'Norman'.

SABIB, *vol. 2, p. 265*
Waters, British Artists, *vol. 1, p. 118*

FOSTER, Arthur J. fl. 1800-1905

Portrait and landscape painter. Foster exhibited at the principal London galleries. Of his 14 Royal Academy exhibits, his oil *Our young defenders. Children collecting for the Widows and Orphans Fund, May, 1900* (1904) was of Boer War interest.

Graves, Royal Academy, *vol. 3, p. 144*
Johnson and Greutzner, British Artists, *p. 182*

FOUCAR, George

Three works by this unknown artist were used by *The Graphic*. He was probably a trooper with Buller's Natal Field Force. On 23 June 1900 the illustration, *General Buller's advance: pursuing the fleeing Boers after the fight on Helpmekaar Heights* appeared, redrawn by J. Nash jnr. *General*

1 Frank Feller's depiction of the attack by the Royal Artillery on the Boers near the confluence of the Riet and Modder rivers on 25 November 1899. Though the illustration was entitled *The Relief of Kimberley*, the town was actually only relieved nearly three months later. Reproduced by courtesy of the Africana Museum, Johannesburg.
2 Well-known artist, critic and art writer Alexander Finberg produced this watercolour and wash work entitled *The HAC Contingent of the City's Own with their Vickers Maxim quick firing field guns*. The painting was reproduced in *The Penny Illustrated Paper*.
3 Famous postcard artist Frank Feller produced this illustration of *Earl Roberts and Viscount Kitchener on the South African Battlefields* for Raphael Tuck's Empire series.
4 Alexander Finberg's wash drawing *The King of the Castle* showed the first Briton to reach the top of Spioen Kop. It was published in *The Penny Illustrated Paper* on 10 February 1900.
5 Joseph Finnemore's painting depicting Britannia welcoming Lord Kitchener back from the War was reproduced on a Raphael Tuck Empire postcard. There is another variant of this card.
6 French illustrator Amedée Forestier had a long association with *The Illustrated London News*.

Ne pleures plus Grand-Mère tu peux compter sur moi.

Buller's advance: An unexpected treat while on the march was redrawn by G. Soper and published on the same day. *The railway accident near Vlakfontein: Boers in ambush attacking the relief train* was published on 8 December 1900, after being redrawn by Frank Dadd.

Hofmeyr, Matton and Roets, Graphic Picture Index

FRAMPTON, George James 1860-1928
British sculptor. Frampton won several prizes and medals for his work. Besides his design for the C.I.V. medal which was illustrated in both *The Studio* (1901) and *The Graphic* on (20 July 1901), he designed two Boer War memorials: the Lancashire Fusiliers, Bury, and the figure of St George above the memorial to Old Radleins, St. Peter's College, Radley, Berkshire.

Hibbard, Boer War Medals, pp. 48-49
The Sketch, vol. 32, p. 501
The Studio, vol. 21, p. 261
Who was Who, vol. 2, p. 376

FRANÇOIS   1
An artist by this name produced three very fine pencil sketches which can be found in the National Army Museum. In spite of intensive investigations it has been impossible to verify the identity of this artist. His signature is not dissimilar to that of Leo Auguste François, the South African artist who was born in Luxembourg, but no conclusive proof can be established that they are the same person.

The National Army Museum also has two unidentified works attributed to François, but which are different to his signed pencil sketches. As all these drawings show Boers in victorious situations it is possible that he was involved in the conflict on the side of the Boers.

FRANÇOIS, Louis 1872-?
François was a prisoner at the Diyatalawa Camp in Ceylon. Listed as 'number 3,238 of Johannesburg', he was a member of the French Corps. An album, produced while François was a P.O.W. and illustrated with flowers and birds, can be found in the Africana Museum. Two extant photographic postcards, depicting the camp at Diyatalawa and decorated with flowers, are signed 'L. Francois, P.O.W. Diyatalawa camp'. These postcards were either sold or given to other inmates and guards in the camp.

FREDILLO   1
French postcard artist. Fredillo was responsible for the cartoons in a series of six anti-British postcards (published before February 1900). Four of the postcards were signed 'Fredillo', the fifth 'Fredil', and the sixth 'Fredillo invent'. The unnumbered cards were entitled: 1. *Oh no moà* (sic) *pas vouloir prendre votre or de ce façon*; 2. *Les Enrolements Volontaires au Cap*; 3. *Chamberlain fuyant le remords*; 4. *David and Goliath* (Kruger and Buller); 5. *Ne pleures plus Grand-*

Mère tu peux compter sur moi; 6. *Sortie décisive du glorieux White*.

FRENZENY, Paul c.1840-1902   1
French-born 'special' artist and illustrator. Frenzeny served in the French Cavalry in Mexico in 1865. From 1869 he worked as illustrator for *Harper's Weekly*. He became a member of the Bohemian Club in San Francisco in 1874, and from 1882 to 1887 he worked for *Leslie's Weekly*. He was the illustrator of William Luscombe Searelle's *Tales of the Transvaal* (1896), and in 1889 he illustrated *Fifty years on the trail*. He exhibited at the R.I. in 1898.

During his time with *Harper's Weekly*, accompanied by Jules Tavernier, another French artist, Frenzeny made a 'long excursion on horseback to the Pacific, traversing regions where railroads have not yet penetrated'. This journey, which took place in 1873, resulted in many illustrations which were reproduced in *Harper's Weekly*. Frenzeny is highly regarded as a Western artist, and a painting entitled *Indians by a river bank* was sold by Christie's in 1981 for £12 000.

Frenzeny is listed as one of *The Illustrated London News* 'special' artists during the Spanish-American War in 1898, having worked for the paper since 1887. Much of his work for the paper also concerned the theatre. At the time of the Boer War six of his illustrations appeared in *The Illustrated London News*. *The Sphere* also reproduced a Frenzeny Boer War related illustration in January 1900. One of his pre-war illustrations from *The Illustrated London News* was used on a postcard published by Picture Postcard Co. Ltd. (No. 2d), entitled *The crisis in the Transvaal: Inspection of the assembled 'Commando' of Boers in the market place of a dorp*. In *The Story of 'South Africa' Newspaper and its founder as Told by Others*, a 'corner of a menu at a South African Dinner' is reproduced, and the cartoon featured is signed 'P. Frenzeny'. It shows an ostrich holding a copy of *South Africa* and watching a Boer and Britannia on a see-saw which is tipped in Britannia's favour.

De Wet, Illustrated London News Index
Houfe, British Illustrators and Caricaturists, p. 310
Johnson, Front Line Artists, p. 57
Samuels, Artists of the American West, p. 178
SAPRG Newsletter, 6 Nov. 1978

FRKBCH, C.J.
Artist of *Gruss aus Afrika* postcard which has a Boer War theme.

FRIPP, Charles Edwin 1854-1906   3
'Special' war artist for *The Graphic* and *The Daily Graphic*. Fripp was born on 4 September 1854, the fourth son of George Arthur Fripp, the landscape painter. Charles Fripp's art education was acquired in Nuremberg and Munich and at the R.A. schools, London, as well as in his father's studio. He

worked as war correspondent for *The Graphic* during the last Frontier War, the Zulu War and the first Boer War and during the Eastern Sudan Campaign of 1885. In addition, Fripp held a commission in the 20th Artists' M.R.V. Fripp's exhibits at the Royal Academy included the paintings *The last stand at Isandhula* (sic) *(1885)* and *The attack on General Sir John's McNeills' force near Suakim* (1886). He also exhibited at the Japanese Gallery in Bond Street in 1891.

The Graphic sent Fripp to the Far East to cover the Sino-Japanese War (1894-5), after which he returned to South Africa and was present during the Matabele Rebellion of 1896. In 1897 Fripp held a personal sketching interview with Paul Kruger. He was sent to the Klondike in Alaska in 1898 by *The Graphic* and he covered the Philippine War in 1899 before being recalled to South Africa at the start of the Boer War.

Nearly 100 of Fripp's illustrations to do with South Africa appeared in *The Graphic* and of these 70 were Boer War related. Judging from the date of Fripp's Boer War illustrations, it appears that he arrived in South Africa later than most other correspondents. He probably arrived with a contingent of City Imperial Volunteers, and as one of his illustrations depicts the Volunteers returning to England on the *Aurania*, he might have sailed aboard that vessel. In the interim he drew some excellent scenes of the C.I.V. in action near Pretoria. He also accompanied French's column on its march to the north.

Five of Fripp's Boer War originals can be found in the National Army Museum. Four of these were published in *The Graphic* and one appeared in *After Pretoria: the Guerilla War*. The author has one wash drawing by Fripp: *The relief of Vryheid: The fighting at Scheepers Nek* which was published in *The Graphic* on 9 February 1901. The drawing was done from a sketch by 'A.E.C.' (see page 102). The Africana Museum has a pencil sketch of Fripp and other artists done by an unknown artist, probably during the Zulu War. Two of his Zulu War canvases can be found in the Sydney Art Gallery: *The last stand of the 24th Foot at Isandlwana* and *On the march, Zulu War 1879* (a watercolour). Fripp was awarded the Queen's South Africa medal on 12 February 1903.

After the War he lived in Montreal where he died in 1906.

Graves, Royal Academy, vol. 3, p. 170
Hartrick, A Painter's Pilgrimage, p. 71
Hofmeyr, Matton and Roets, Graphic Picture Index
Prior, Campaigns of a War Correspondent, pp. 114-116
Samuels, Artists of the American West, p. 179
The Orders and Medals Research Society, Summer 1986, 'War Correspondents: South Africa 1899-1902', by Patrick Street
Who was Who, vol. 1, p. 261

FRITSCH, Hans 1870-?
Born in Dresden on 2 May 1870. He was a cartoonist who worked for *Lustige Blätter* during the War.

Bénézit, Dictionnaire antique, vol. 4, p. 95

FRITZ, W.S.
Illustrator responsible for the cover of *Nederland Transvaal Gedenkboek opgedragen aan het Volk van Transvaal en Oranje Vrijstaat*, (F.B. van Dittmar, Rotterdam, 1899).

FRITZCHEN
German or Austrian naive postcard cartoonist whose speciality seemed to be using wooden toylike figures to portray his caricatures. Six of his photo-lithographic cards, which formed part of his political series, had a Boer War theme, depicting, among others, Roberts and Buller. No publisher was credited on these cards, although the date, March 1902, could be seen. Both French and German inscriptions appeared on the backs of the cards, while the fronts had a facsimile of German script that was difficult for the untrained eye to read.

F.,R.M. *see* R.M.F.

FRUMENT, Dudley
Nothing is known about this artist except that illustrations by him appeared in *With the Flag to Pretoria* and *After Pretoria: the Guerilla War*.

F.S.
Münchener Odinskarte cartoonist whose work also appeared in *Lustige Blätter*. A similar monogram appeared in the Eysler postcard *Vom Spionskop*.

FUCHS, Emil 1866-1929   1
Sculptor of portraits and figure subjects; medallist. Fuchs was born on 9 February 1866 in Vienna. He studied at the Royal Academy in Berlin. He received an honourable mention in 1907. He was recorded in *The Graphic* (2 August 1902) as having designed a commemorative medal of the War. Hibbard attributes the St John's medal to him. Fuchs is also well known for his design of postage stamps during King Edward VII's reign. After the War he was commissioned to sculpt two memorials: the memorial to Prince Christian Victor, the Bray Chapel, Windsor, and the Boer War Memorial, Plymouth, which includes a frieze of the charge of the Devons at Wagon Hill. Onslow Whiting collaborated with Fuchs on this memorial and it was unveiled by Lady Elizabeth Butler (see pp. 115-116) on 8 August 1903. Fuchs died on 13 January 1929.
Gildea, For Remembrance
Hibbard, Boer War Medals, *pp. 239-240*
Waters, British Artists, *vol. 2, p. 21*

FULLER, Edmund G. fl. 1890-1930
Landscape and marine painter. Fuller exhibited at the principal London galleries. Of his 23 paintings at the Royal Academy, *Peace! be still!* (1902) was presumably of Boer War relevance.
Graves, Royal Academy, *vol. 3, p. 181*

Johnson and Greutzner, British Artists, *p. 189*
Waters, British Artists, *vol. 1, p. 122*

FULLWOOD, Albert Henry 1863-1930
Cartoonist, postcard artist, illustrator and painter and etcher of landscapes and architectural subjects. Fullwood was born in Birmingham in 1863. He studied at the Birmingham School of Art. In 1881 he went to Australia, but returned to England in 1899. He exhibited at the Salon des Artistes Français, Paris, in Australia and in the U.S.A. He also exhibited three works of South African interest at the Royal Academy: *Table Bay, South Africa, during the Boer War, 1900* (1901), *The Castle, Cape Town* (1904) and *Cape Town from the Malay quarter* (1904). Fullwood is credited with the largest block engraved for reproduction in Australia. To be found in the library of the *Sydney Morning Herald*, it is 90 x 60 cm in size and depicts a panorama of Sydney. He was also well known as a postcard artist, although he did not produce any cards of Boer War interest.
Fullwood's Boer War work for *The Graphic* consisted of four illustrations which appeared in December 1899 (and one on 10 March 1900) that depicted Australian troops leaving either Sydney or Melbourne for South Africa. The author has a painting, by Sydney Prior Hall, which bears a label on the back stating that it was presented to his 'Fellow artist Fullwood at *The Graphic* on his marriage to Miss Donaldson'. Fullwood died in New South Wales on 1 October 1930.
Graves, Royal Academy, *vol. 3, p. 181*
Hofmeyr, Matton and Roets, Graphic Picture Index
The Strand, *vol. 23*
Waters, British Artists, *vol. 2, p. 21*

FURNISS, Harry 1854-1925   1
Caricaturist, postcard artist, illustrator, writer of 'photoplays' and black and white artist. Furniss was born in Wexford, Ireland, in 1854. From a very early age he submitted work to *Zozimus*, the Irish version of *Punch*, and later came to work for *Punch* itself. (While at school he had produced a magazine called *The Schoolboy's Punch*.) At various times he contributed to *The Graphic*, *The Illustrated Sporting & Dramatic News*, *The Illustrated London News* and *The Strand Magazine*, among others.
Furniss was a humorous lecturer and toured the U.S.A., Canada and Australia, where he was in great demand. He illustrated several books, including works by Lewis Carroll. After his disagreement with *Punch* he resigned in 1894 and founded *Lika Joko* and *The New Budget*.
Among Furniss's publications were the following: *Romps*; *Flying Visits* (1887); *Royal Academy Antics, Humours of Parliament*; *P & O sketches* (1898); *America in a Hurry* (1900); *Illustrated London letter*; *Peace with Humour*; *Confessions of a Caricaturist* (1901); *Harry Furniss at Home* (1903); *Poverty Bay*, a novel (1905); *How to draw in pen and ink* (1905);

and *Friends without faces*, a book for children (1905). He illustrated *All the works of Charles Dickens* (1910); *All the works of W.M. Thackeray* (the Harry Furniss Centenary edition, 1911); *Our Lady Cinema* (1914); *More about How to Draw in Pen and Ink* (1915); *What You are Thinking About*; *The Frightfulness of Humour*; *The Blue Moon; An Intermittent Publication for Concrete Objects*; *A Crank's No. (Brewers)*; *Peace in War* (Salvation Army War work fund, 1917); *Deceit*; *A reply to Defeat*, (1917); *My Bohemian Days*; *The Byways and Queenways of Boxing* (1919); *Stiggins* (1920); *Some Victorian Women (Good, Bad and Indifferent)* (1923); and *Some Victorian Men* (1924).
Furniss wrote many 'photoplays' for the cinema. He produced and acted in these plays both in the U.S.A. and in England.

1 A pencil drawing by 'François' entitled *Boers repulsing a British Attack*. Nothing is known about this artist. Reproduced by courtesy of the National Army Museum, London.
2 Fredillo produced this series of six anti-British cards. This card, with a postmark of 7 December 1900, shows the Kaiser embracing his grandmother Queen Victoria. Note the Kaiser's telegram about sending his warships to Lourenço Marques, and the bottle of cognac around Queen Victoria's neck.
3 Charles Edwin Fripp, 'special' war artist for *The Graphic* and *The Daily Graphic*, provided numerous illustrations for the papers during the War.
4 *The Relief of Vryheid*, a wash drawing by 'special' artist C. E. Fripp from a sketch by 'A.E.C.'. Fripp did the drawing at *The Graphic*'s offices after his return from South Africa.
5 The memorials in Plymouth to Prince Christian Victor, Queen Victoria's grandson, and the members of the Devon Regiment. The memorials were designed by Emil Fuchs and Onslow Whiting respectively.
6 *The Lion Tamer* by Harry Furniss, a postwar card published by John Walker & Co.

Furniss's Boer War work appeared mainly in *The King*, which commenced publication on 6 January 1900. He contributed a weekly full-page cartoon, very often signed 'HyF'. Furniss was also responsible for a series of six postcards (John Walker and Co. Ltd, London, 1903), entitled *Harry Furniss Political postcard* 'people series'. All of the cards lampooned Chamberlain, but only cards 1, 3 and 4 had any Boer War relevance. Included in Furniss's Boer War oeuvre was his 'New Century Envelope and Card'. These envelopes and accompanying insert cards were published by John Walker & Co of London. A portfolio containing six envelopes and six cards was priced at one shilling.

Furniss died in Hastings on 14 January 1925.

> Book World, *vol. 25, p. 3 (Feb. 1984), 'An imp of a Victorian Caricaturist' by D. Cuppleditch*
> *Furniss*, Confessions of a Caricaturist *and* Harry Furniss at Home
> *Houfe*, British Illustrators and Caricaturists, p. 311
> The Strand, *vol. 23, p. 78*
> Who was Who, *vol. 2, pp. 386-387*
> *Personal communication with Ian Shapiro, Argyll Etkin Ltd., London*

F.W.

The illustrator of a peace card inscribed 'Zur Erinnerung am den Frieden in Süd Africa'. It was published by S. & G. Saulsohn of Berlin. The card is numbered '605 Dessin 1'.

GANDY, Herbert fl. 1879-1920

Landscape painter of historical and classical subjects. Gandy exhibited several works at the Royal Academy from 1879, and he designed the cover of Spenser Wilkinson's *The Transvaal War*.

> *Houfe*, British Illustrators and Caricaturists, p. 313
> *Waters*, British Artists, vol. 1, p. 124

GANN KERONEC'H *see* KERONEC'H, Gann

GARRATT, Arthur Paine 1873-?

Portrait and historical painter. Garratt was born in London on 17 July 1873. He was educated at the City of London School and is thought to have taught drawing at the Leys School in Cambridge. He spent some time in America, eventually returning to England and settling in Chelsea. During the early part of his career Garratt was a prolific illustrator and contributed extensively to *The Graphic* and *Black & White*. His work also appeared in *Punch*, *The Quiver*, *Pall Mall*, *The Sphere* and *Pearson's Magazine*. He specialized in scenes of London life. Garratt exhibited at the Royal Academy and at the Paris Salon.

His Boer War illustrations, which are few in number, appeared in *The Graphic* (only three between February and November 1900) and *Black & White*, and second-hand in *Cassell's Illustrated History of the Boer War*.

Garratt's exhibits at the Royal Academy included three oils of Boer War interest: *Wounded men at Wynberg, South Africa: A shady corner* (1900); *Veterans reading the war news in Chelsea Hospital* (1900); and *The King's Yeoman* (1901).

One of Garratt's paintings is in the Royal Collection at Windsor and is entitled *King Edward VII Robing in the House of Lords, 1902*.

> *Graves*, Royal Academy, vol. 3, p. 211
> *Thorpe*, English Illustration

GARRATT, R.?

An artist using this signature illustrated a work for *Cassell's Illustrated History of the Boer War*. It is possible that it was an illustration by A. Garratt and signed with an unclear signature.

GAUL, William Gilbert 1855-1919

Military and Western painter. Gaul was born in Jersey City, U.S.A., on 31 March 1855. He was educated at the Claverack Military Academy. He studied under J.G. Brown and L.E. Wilmarth, and became a National Academician in 1882. He obtained a commission from *Century* magazine to illustrate *Historical Battles and Leaders of the Civil War* (1887). Gaul spent much time in the West during the 1880s, on Indian reservations or at army posts, and produced several paintings depicting battles in this region. One of these, *Charging the Battery*, was awarded a medal at the Paris Exposition of 1899.

His Boer War work appeared in the American publication *The War in South Africa* by Capt. A.T. Mahan. Gaul died in New York in 1919.

> *Fielding*, American Painters, etc.
> *Samuels*, Artists of the American West, p. 184

G.B.

Initials used by G. Brandt, the *Kladderadatsch* cartoonist. *The Graphic* artist, Gordon Browne, also used these initials.

G.C *see* C.G.

GEMMEL, Mrs

Very little is known about Mrs Gemmel except that she was probably the wife of Lt. H.B. Gemmel of the Bechuanaland Rifles who was besieged in Mafeking during the War.

Verbeek lists one painting which was possibly by Gemmel, entitled *Nursing Sister 1901*. The only record of Mrs Gemmel is that on the *Mafeking Siege Slip* no. 103 she is reported to have won the prize at an exhibition sponsored by Baden-Powell on 25 March 1900, with a picture entitled *John Bull on the 100th day of the Siege*.

> *Personal communication with A. Renew, Curatrix, Mafikeng Museum*
> *Verbeek*, Early Natal Art

GEORGE

A Trooper George is listed as having contributed sketches for reproduction in *The Graphic*.

GEORGE, Edward 1866-?

French caricaturist. George was born in Sète on 21 April 1866. He occasionally used the pseudonym 'Teddy'. His work appeared infrequently in *Le Rire*. He produced a series of nine pen-and-ink and blue crayon caricatures of women in various national costumes for an unidentified publication. (This sheet, which is signed and dated 1901, is in the author's collection.) Two of the women depicted are *Jeune Boer* and *Soldat Anglais*.

> *Bénézit*, Dictionnaire antique, vol. 4, p. 209

GEORGES, Leon

French cartoonist who provided two charcoal drawings, *Le condition de la Paix* and *Un Boer exigeant*, for the *Le Gavroche* special number of 16 June 1902 that was entitled 'La Paix à la mode John Bull'.

'GEOYO'

Le Rire cartoonist whose occasional naive Boer War related cartoons were based on drawings by 'seven-year-old Berthe'.

GÉRARDIN, Auguste 1849-?

Still life, landscape and portrait painter. Gérardin was born in Mulhouse in France on 31 July 1849. His Boer War illustrations appeared in *Le Monde Illustré*.

> *Bénézit*, Dictionnaire antique, vol. 4, p. 21
> *Osterwalder, and Hubschmid and Bouret (eds.)*, Dictionnaire des Illustrateurs, p. 419

GERBAULT, Henri 1863-1930

Caricaturist, postcard artist and watercolourist. Gerbault was born in Châtenay, France, in 1863. Marie Belloc, in an article on French humorous artists in *The Strand*, placed him among the most important French caricaturists. Gerbault worked as a cartoonist for many illustrated periodicals, including *Le Rire*, *Le Bon Vivant* and *La Caricature*. He also became well known as an Art Nouveau postcard artist. His Boer War work appeared in *Le Petit Brayon Illustré*.

> *Bénézit*, Dictionnaire antique, vol. 4, p. 215
> *Fanelli and Godoli*, Art Nouveau Postcards
> *Osterwalder, and Hubschmid and Bouret (eds.)*, Dictionnaire des Illustrateurs, p. 420
> The Strand, *vol. 22, p. 676*

GERLACH, Otto 1862-1908

Painter, sketcher and illustrator. Gerlach was born in Leipzig, Germany, on 3 August 1862 and he later studied at the Academy there. Gerlach produced several illustrations for *Leipziger Illustrierte Zeitung*. Some of these were reproduced in G.L. Klepper's *De Zuid Afrikansch Oorlog*. In 1904 his work appeared in *The Illustrated London News*. In the same year he was an eyewitness in the Russo-Japanese War, contributing sketches of the war to *The Sphere*. Gerlach signed his work 'O.G.' He died in Teheran on 15 August 1908.

> *Bénézit*, Dictionnaire antique, vol. 4, p. 219

4

GIBB, Arthur

A watercolour by A. Gibb, depicting a memorial plaque in Farnham Church, can be found in the National Army Museum. An illustration by Arthur Gibb appeared in *The Sphere* on 2 June 1900, but it is not known if the illustration is by the same Gibb. Arthur Gibb also produced several pen-and-ink cartoons with a Boer War theme which appeared in the pages of *The Sketch*.

GIBB, R. C.

One sketch by this soldier appeared in *The Graphic* entitled *Garrison life in South Africa: a game of water polo in the Mooi River*. This appeared on 14 June 1902 and was redrawn by George Soper. A Capt. R. Gibb of the King's Own Scottish Borderers appeared in the *Army List* for June 1902.

> Army List, *June 1902, p. 224*
> *Hofmeyr, Matton and Roets*, Graphic Picture Index

GIBSON, Charles Dana 1867-1944   1

Illustrator and caricaturist, magazine editor. Gibson was born in Roxbury, Massachusetts, U.S.A., on 14 September 1867. He studied at Flushing High School and at the Art Students' League in New York. He later attended the Académie Julian in Paris. He is best known as a chronicler of American high society and he received acclaim on both sides of the Atlantic. He became famous for his 'Gibson Girl' who epitomized glamour at the turn of the century. His wife, Irene Langhorne, on whom he is said to have modelled the Gibson Girl, was the sister of Lady Astor. His postcards and drawings are collectors' items, particularly in the U.S.A.

Gibson worked extensively for *Life, Cosmopolitan* and *Collier's* and was friendly with Phil May and George DuMaurier. He acquired *Life* and served as its editor until 1930. He died in New York on 23 December 1944.

His only Boer War related cartoon is *Studies in expression while a hero describes the horrors of War*, which appeared on page 32 of the May 1902 issue of *Pictorial Comedy*. This magazine, which purported to show 'The humorous Phases of Life depicted by eminent artists', was published by James Henderson and Sons of Fleet Street, London.

> *Fanelli and Godoli*, Art Nouveau Postcards
> *Hammerton*, Humorists of the Pencil
> *Houfe*, British Illustrators and Caricaturists, *p. 315*
> *Pitz*, American Illustration, *p. 421*
> Who was Who, *vol. 4, p. 430*

GIFFEY, P.

Illustrator of Paul Roland's *Les Jumeaux du Transvaal* (1906). Giffey did several coloured illustrations, published by an unknown French firm in 1899, for a series of children's school books. (Not all were signed, however.) These illustrations appeared on the front cover, while a map of South Africa appeared on the back. The cover illustration titles are as follows (unnumbered): 1. *Les mules emportent l'artillerie Anglaise à Ladysmith*; 2. *Bombardement de Ladysmith*; 3. *Les Boers attaquent un train blindé envoyé par les Anglais*; 4. *Les Prisonniers Anglais à Pretoria*; 5. *Devant Ladysmith – en parlementaire*; 6. *Après la bataille de Modder-River une Eglise transformée en ambulance*; 7. *Embarquement de l'armée Anglaise*; 8. *Escaramouche entre un avant poste de Gordon's* (sic) *Highlanders et une avant-garde Boer*; 9. *Mort du Général Simons* (sic); 10. *Combat de Modder River*; 11. *Départ des Volontaires Boers*.

GILBERT, René Joseph 1858-1914

Portrait painter. Gilbert was born in Paris in 1858. He was strongly influenced by Maurice-Quentin de la Tour, and because of this influence he tended to use pastels in preference to oil for his portraits.

In January 1983 the Kunskamer in Cape Town offered a large pastel portrait of Paul Kruger by Gilbert. This portrait was reputedly done from life during Kruger's exile in the south of France. There is, however, no documentary evidence of this fact. Because of Kruger's strong religious objection to graven images, it is unlikely that he ever sat for his portrait. Even Anton van Wouw claimed that he had to work from photographs when doing his numerous sculptures, busts and portraits of the president.

Gilbert died in Paris on 24 September 1914.

> The Argus, *3 Jan. 1983*
> *Bénézit*, Dictionnaire antique, *vol. 4, p. 247*

GILES, Godfrey Douglas 1857-1941   1

'Special' war artist for *The Graphic* and *The Daily Graphic*; military and sporting artist. Giles was born at Kurrachee, India, on 9 November 1857, the son of Capt. Edward Giles who was stationed there as a naval officer. His formal art education took place in Paris under Carolus-Duran in 1885. His works were exhibited at the Royal Academy between 1884 and 1888. These paintings included battle scenes such as *The Battle of Tamai* (two paintings) and *El Teb*. Giles lived in Newmarket for many years where he painted local racing scenes. Besides his work for *The Graphic*, his illustrations appeared in *Black & White* in 1891.

In 1875 Giles went straight from Sandhurst to India on army service. He also fought in the Afghan War and commanded the Turkish cavalry at the Battle of El Teb. Later he served as a captain in the Loyal Suffolk Hussars (Imperial Yeomanry) and in the Artists' Rifle Corps.

Giles was sent out to South Africa by *The Graphic* and *The Daily Graphic* and attached himself to French's column. He was present at the capture of Cronje at Paardeberg and at the relief of Kimberley. Subsequently Giles wrote the chapter 'With French to Kimberley and Roberts to Bloemfontein' in *The Graphic History of the South African War*. He also contributed over 31 sketches which appeared in *The Graphic*, including the special double number of 2 April 1900.

Giles's existing Boer War work includes one in the Africana Museum, entitled *Under their own Flag*. It was drawn for reproduction in *The Daily Graphic* of 20 February 1900. The printed caption on the back reads: 'Under their own flag: Commandeered Scotchmen, escaped from the Boer lines, being conducted into the British Camp at Rensburg'.

The National Army Museum has four works by Giles; two pen-and-ink drawings, one entitled *With French in the Cape Colony: Scenes in the camp at Naauwpoort* and the other untitled. An oil bearing the title *Advance of the Cavalry to Kimberley* and a similar watercolour make up the collection. The home headquarters of the Loyal Hussars in Hampshire has a watercolour entitled *Patrol of the 10th Hussars, SA War.*

The De Beers company headquarters in Kimberley houses an oil painting completed by Giles in 1901 and entitled *To the relief of Kimberley. A cavalry division under General French riding to the relief of Kimberley on February the 15th 1900.* A personal communication from Dr M. Buys, the archivist at De Beers, relates how the picture was presented to Lt. Gen. French on 15 February 1903 by 30 officers who served on his staff during the War. (A list of these officers is given.)

One of Giles's works was offered for sale by Sawyer's in 1960, and Christie's sold the large oil, *The Battle of Springfontein*, on 25 May 1983. The author has an oil by Giles, dated 1905 and entitled *The 2nd Worcestershire Battalion attacking the Boers at Slingersfontein.*

Several of Giles's non-Boer War paintings were reproduced as prints, and four caricatures by him (signed 'GDG') appeared in *Vanity Fair* in 1899, 1900 and 1903. General French was one of the subjects caricatured by him in *Vanity Fair* in 1900. He was awarded the Queen's South Africa medal on 12 February 1903.

Giles died on 1 February 1941.

> *Carter*, War Artists in S.A., *p. 21*
> *Graves*, Royal Academy, *vol. 3, pp. 237-238*
> *Kennedy*, Pictures in the Africana Museum, *vol. 3, p. 86*
> The Orders and Medals Research Society, *Summer 1986*, 'War Correspondents: South Africa 1899-1902', by Patrick Street
> *Thorpe*, English Illustration
> *Waters*, British Artists, *vol. 1, p. 130*
> Who was Who, *vol. 4, p. 434*

GILL, Arthur J. P.

Cartoonist who contributed to *The Sketch, Pick-Me-Up* and *Judy*. His Boer War work appeared in the last-named magazine.

> *Houfe*, British Illustrators and Caricaturists, *p. 317*
> *Thorpe*, English Illustration

---

1 French caricaturist Edward George's cartoon series of women in national costumes included one of a 'Jeune Boer' (top left) pointing a gun at a 'Soldat Anglais' (top centre).
2 Major Godfrey Douglas Giles produced this pen-and-ink drawing entitled *Under their own Flag* for *The Daily Graphic*. Reproduced by courtesy of the Africana Museum, Johannesburg.
3 Charles Dana Gibson, the well-known American artist and illustrator, produced this cartoon, entitled *Studies in expression*, for the May 1902 edition of *Pictorial Comedy*.
4 Godfrey Giles, who was probably present at the engagement, painted this depiction of the 2nd Battalion Worcester Regiment under Major General Clements at Slingersfontein (near Colesberg) on 12 February 1900. Giles was commissioned to do this painting by the officer commanding the Worcester Regiment, Col. Hackett Pain, in 1905.

GILLAM, F. Victor

English-born cartoonist who worked for both *Harper's Weekly* and *Judge* in the U.S.A. Boer War cartoons by Gillam appeared in the latter magazine and were reproduced in *Review of Reviews* in 1901. Fielding suggests that John Tenniel influenced the work of Gillam and his more famous brother, Bernard Gillam, who died in 1896.

Fielding, American Painters, *p. 138*

GILLETT, Edward Frank 1874-1927

Sporting illustrator and cartoonist. Gillett was born in Worlingham, Suffolk, on 23 July 1874. In the mid-1890s he joined the staff of *The Graphic* and *The Daily Graphic*. Later he became known for his cricket and rugby illustrations. In 1908 he joined *Black & White* and then *The Illustrated Sporting & Dramatic News*. His work also appeared in *Fun*, *Judy* and *The Idler*.

Gillett did few Boer War works, and most of them appeared in *The Daily Graphic* and *The Golden Penny*.

Thorpe, English Illustration
Waters, British Artists, *vol. 1, p. 131*

GILSON, T. 1

Gilson is a little-known artist whose main claim to fame is as a postcard artist for J. Salmon (1922-8) and E. G. Hey and Co. Some of these cards bear the legend 'This is a genuine Gilson Post Card', indicating a unique type of illustration. He is also noted for his 'Kute Kids' comic cards produced during World War I.

In 1984 the Parker Gallery offered two watercolours by Gilson, done in about 1900: *Canadian Light Horse Mounted Trooper* and *South African Mounted Rifles, Mounted Trooper*. (The latter is in the author's collection.)

Holt, Tonie and Valmai, Stanley Gibbons Postcard Catalogue, *1985*
Parker Gallery Catalogue, *1984, nos. 441 and 445*

G., K. see K.G.

GOCY, E.

An artist of this name is referred to by Anna H. Smith in her article 'French Pro-Boer Songs' in *Africana Notes and News* (June 1981). She mentions the sheet music 'Bienvenue à Kruger', which was written by Antonin Louis. The cover has an uncoloured portrait of Kruger by Gocy, published by Edition Musicale Française.

Africana Notes and News, June 1981, p. 211

GODFIN

Cartoonist responsible for French postcard cartoon showing Kruger being strangled by a British knight in armour.

GODFREY, Herbert

A cartoon illustration, signed 'H.G.', of 'Fancy dress costumes worn by Mr Herbert Godfrey at the Roller Skating Carnival, Crystal Palace' was reproduced in *Black & White Budget* on 10 March 1900. These Boer War related cartoons make use of a play on words and attack the War Office for neglecting British soldiers.

GOG, H.

French cartoonist whose work, often in colour, appeared in *Le Franc Normand*, *La Caricature*, *Le Bon Vivant* and *L'Illustré National*.

GOODMAN, Robert Gwelo 1871-1939

Goodman was born in Taplow on the Thames on 1 July 1871. He was 15 when his family came to Cape Town, but he returned to Europe to study art and was sponsored by J.S. Morland. Early in 1900 Goodman returned to South Africa to make sketches of the Boer War battlefields. He is the subject of a book by Joyce Newton-Thompson entitled *Gwelo Goodman: South African Artist*. It is unclear whether he was actually an enlisted soldier at the time of his return to South Africa, but it appears unlikely. According to Newton-Thompson, Goodman had obtained special permission from Lord Roberts for this tour of South Africa. While he was painting at Majuba Hill he was fired at by Boer snipers who had killed two men on the same spot the previous night. He was lucky to escape unscathed. On another occasion he was fired on by the British and was surrounded by a detachment who arrested him as a spy. He also relates a story of how he had watched a British sentry on guard duty hand his rifle over to a Boer prisoner while he, the sentry, went to quench his thirst. Toward the end of the year he returned to Cape Town with a large assortment of boards and canvases covered by sketches made in various parts of South Africa.

An exhibition of Goodman's Boer War sketches was held in the Technical Institute, Queen Victoria Street, Cape Town, in 1901. This exhibition was opened by Sir Alfred Milner who was then governor of the Cape Colony. In three days nearly 2 000 people visited the gallery. It was at this time that Goodman adopted the name Gwelo after the then Rhodesian town. Henceforth he signed his work Robert Gwelo Goodman or 'R.G.G.'

When he returned to England in 1901 he showed his Boer War works in the Grafton Galleries, London, where the 130 items filled two rooms. The popular show gave the people of England a very clear idea of the conditions under which their men were fighting. Various officers who had taken part in campaigns in South Africa bought pictures and Col. Heyworth-Savage and Maj. Stanton, both of the Royal Welch Fusiliers,

bought pictures which they presented to their regiments. According to Newton-Thompson, this was the first occasion on which an exhibition consisting entirely of pictures of South Africa had ever been seen in London.

Among the paintings at the Grafton Galleries were *Colenso*, *Mbulwana*, *Mafeking* (two works with this title), *Talana Hill*, *Kimberley*, *Road into Pretoria*, *Spion Kop*, *Lombard's Kop*, *Ladysmith* (several views), *Majuba Hill*, *Matjiesfontein*, *Colenso Bridge Rd* and *Empty Convoy Impati near Dundee*. When the exhibition closed in London the Corporation of Oldham asked Goodman to exhibit the paintings in their town.

The people of Oldham had a special interest in the Boer War as their newly elected Member of Parliament, Winston Churchill, had served as a war correspondent in South Africa. When the exhibition closed in London the Corporation of Oldham invited Goodman to send his pictures to them and Churchill was asked to open the show.

Goodman went on to become a very well-known South African painter. He died in Cape Town on 11 March 1939.

Newton-Thompson, Gwelo Goodman

GOTTLOB, Fernand-Louis 1873-1935

Gottlob, who was born in Paris, exhibited at the Paris Salon from 1890. He was on the staff of *Gil Blas*, *Le Rire* and *Le Sourire*. He also worked for *L'Assiette au Beurre*, and one of his illustrations was of Boer War interest.

Osterwalder, and Hubschmid and Bouret (eds.),
Dictionnaire des Illustrateurs, *p. 441*

GOUGH, Arthur J. fl. 1897-1914

Landscape painter and illustrator. Gough exhibited several pictures at the Royal Academy, one of which, entitled *Removing the limbers of the Guns at Tafel Kop*, appeared in 1903. At various times he contributed to *Sketchy Bits*, *Pearson's Magazine*, *Royal Magazine* and *Rambler*. His numerous Boer War illustrations appeared in *Black & White*, *With the Flag to Pretoria*, *Shurey's Illustrated* and *Budget*. In May 1900 Gough provided an illustration for the official souvenir programme for 'The National Bazaar in aid of Sufferers by the War'. The full-page illustration was entitled *The spirit of war*.

Graves, Royal Academy, *vol. 3, p. 281*
Houfe, British Illustrators and Caricaturists, *p. 320*
Johnson and Greutzner, British Artists, *p. 208*
Thorpe, English Illustration

GOULD, Francis Carruthers 1844-1925 4

Gould was born in Barnstaple, North Devon, on 2 December 1844. His first cartoons appeared in 1879 when he illustrated the Christmas number of *Truth*.

During the Boer War Gould worked for the *Westminster Gazette* doing parliamentary sketches and other work. He also contributed to *The Strand Magazine*, *Vanity Fair* and *The Sketch*. He founded his own paper, *Picture Politics*, which ran from 1894 until 1914. For many years he illustrated a series by H. W. Lucy called *Behind the speaker's chair*. This appeared regularly in *The Strand Magazine*. *Peeps at Parlia-*

ment (1903) by H.W. Lucy was also illustrated by Gould. *Froissart's Modern Chronicles* (published 1903) 'was told and pictured' by Gould. This chronicled the principal political events of the years 1901 and 1902. Chapters 4 and 5 of the 1902 volume are devoted to 'The War in Africa' and 'The Ending of the War'.

For over 20 years Gould was member of the London Stock Exchange. Among his other publications were a large number of Stock Exchange sketches and caricatures for private circulation: *Who killed Cock Robin?* (1897), *Tales told in the Zoo* (1900), and six volumes of *The Westminster Cartoons*. Volume IV of this series featured 'A pictorial history of political events connected with South Africa 1899-1900', and volume V the 'Khaki Campaign' general election of 1900 and the politicians involved in the War. (*The Sphere* also carried examples of Gould's posters during the Khaki election.) The other volumes also featured some cartoons relevant to South Africa.

In a tipped-in note to volume II of *The Westminster Cartoons* readers were invited to apply to the assistant editor to purchase the original cartoon drawings. One such cartoon, *Birds of a feather*, featuring the Duke of Bedford and Paul Kruger, can be found in the Woburn Abbey Collection. Another, entitled *Too good to be true*, is in the author's collection. Gould's Boer War work also featured in the 'Westminster cartoon series' of postcards.

Other publications with a South African theme to which Gould contributed included *The Political Struwwelpeter* (1899) by Edward Harold Begbie, *The Struwwelpeter Alphabet* (1900) by the same author, and *The Westminster Alice* (1902) by Hector Munro. *Cartoons in Rhyme and Line* by Sir Wilfred Lawson was published in 1905. A pamphlet (no. 46) put out by the Stop the War Committee (4 Clock House, Arundel St, Strand, London W.C.) featured one of Gould's cartoons, *The Scout on the Veldt*.

For many years Gould was editor of *The Westminster Gazette*. He often signed his work 'FCG'. He was knighted in 1906 and died on 1 January 1925.

Houfe, British Illustrators and Caricaturists, *p. 320*
SABIB, *vol. 2, p. 377*
The Strand, *vol. 10, p. 789*
Who was Who, *vol. 2, p. 424*

GOULD, W.
A cartoonist, with the name that appears to be 'W. Gould', did cartoons for the *Weekly Star* (Johannesburg).

GOURSAT, Georges *see* SEM

GOUSSE, Henri
Le Rire cartoonist whose contribution of one Boer War related work appeared on 22 March 1902.

GRANDJOUAN, Jules-Felix 1875-1968
Cartoonist and illustrator. Grandjouan was born in Nantes, France, on 22 December 1875. He was a controversial character who was known for his pacifist views. He worked for *L'Assiette au Beurre*, *Canard Sauvage* and *Conscrit*. His Boer War work appeared in *Le Rire*. A double-page cartoon, *Au Transvaal: Happy Christmas*, appeared on 29 December 1900. Grandjouan died in Nantes on 12 November 1968.

Osterwalder, and Hubschmid and Bouret (eds.), Dictionnaire des Illustrateurs, *p. 445*

GRANT, Gordon Hope 1875-1962   1
Illustrator, watercolourist and cartoonist. 'Special' for U.S. newspapers during the Boer War. Grant was born of Scottish parents in San Francisco in 1875. He was sent to England to study art at the Heatherley and Lambeth schools. On his return to America he worked for *The San Francisco Chronicle* and *The Examiner*. Many of his watercolours, which included nautical subjects, are in the Metropolitan Museum of Art and the Library of Congress.

Grant was a frontline artist for the American press during

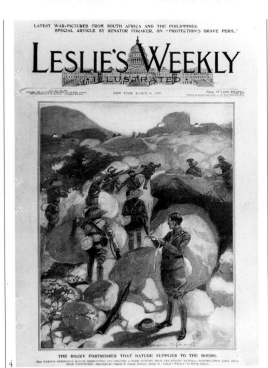

LATEST WAR-PICTURES FROM SOUTH AFRICA AND THE PHILIPPINES.
SPECIAL ARTICLE BY SENATOR FORAKER, ON "PROTECTION'S GRAVE PERIL."

Leslie's Weekly
ILLUSTRATED

NEW YORK, MARCH 31, 1900.

THE ROCKY FORTRESSES THAT NATURE SUPPLIES TO THE BOERS.

the U.S. conflicts with Pancho Villa on the Mexican border. His cartoons also appeared in the London magazine, *Pictorial Comedy*, in 1902.

During the Boer War Grant represented both *Harper's Weekly* and *Leslie's Weekly*. His first illustration appeared in 20 January 1900, showing Roberts's arrival in South Africa. Thereafter he accompanied Roberts's army to De Aar, Modder River, Magersfontein and Paardeberg. By September 1900 he was back in New York as a home-based artist for *Leslie's Weekly*, and even though the magazine became mostly photographic in character he was still contributing in 1903. During the War all his work (pen-and-ink sketches and wash drawings) appeared in facsimile.

Grant's Boer War work also appeared in Pearson's *War Pictures* and *The Golden Penny*.

Fielding, American Painters, etc., *p. 144*
Osterwalder, and Hubschmid and Bouret (eds.), Dictionnaire des Illustrateurs, *p. 449*
Pitz, American Illustration, *p. 421*

GRANT, Hugh
A cartoon by this artist appeared in *Judy* on 5 April 1899, before the outbreak of the War. It depicts Rhodes as a locomotive pushing Kruger off the Cape to Cairo railway track.

GRÄTZ, Fritz Georg Friedrich 1875-1915
Cartoonist. Grätz was born in Frankfurt-am-Main, Germany, on 5 August 1875. He studied at the Stadel Institute and the Frankfurt Academy. Grätz worked primarily for *Der Fliegende Blätter*, *Der Humoristische Blätter*, *Der Floh* and *Wiener Humoristische Blätter*. His cartoons were reproduced in *Burenstreiche* and *John Bull Sur la Sellette*. Redrawn designs based on his cartoons can be found on a series of French postcards. These cards were published in numbered sets and the pirating artist, A. Rouilly, sometimes used his initials in monogram form ('RA'), as well as signing his name in full. The series of Dutch postcards featuring cartoons from the contemporary European and American press used Grätz's *Transvaalsche Nachtmerrie* from *Wiener Humoristische Blätter*. His cartoons are often signed 'F.G.' or 'F.Gr'. Grätz died in Serbia in 1915.

Bénézit, Dictionnaire antique, *vol. 4, p. 399*
Grand-Carteret, John Bull
The Strand, *(1901) vol. 21, p. 450*

GRAY, Tristram
Evening News cartoonist.

GREENFIELD, D.G.
One of this untraced civilian medical doctor's illustrations appeared on 2 June 1900 in *The Illustrated London News*. The caption reads 'Open-air concert for patients at the Imperial Yeomanry Hospital, Deelfontein'. It was redrawn by H. C. Seppings Wright (see pp. 236-237).
De Wet, Illustrated London News Index

GREIFFENHAGEN, Maurice 1862-1931
Painter and illustrator. Born in 1862, Greiffenhagen studied at the Royal Academy schools. In 1906 he became headmaster of the Life School at the Glasgow School of Art, A.R.A. in 1916 and R.A. in 1922.

Greiffenhagen's early career was devoted almost entirely to illustration and he worked for most of the illustrated journals from 1889. He is also known for his illustrations in Sir Rider Haggard's novels. He was influenced by Phil May.

Greiffenhagen was responsible for only a few Boer War illustrations: those depicting Kitchener and his troops returning to England after the War appeared in *The Sphere*.
Houfe, British Illustrators and Caricaturists, *p. 325*

GREIG, James 1861-1941
Illustrator and watercolourist. Greig was born in Arbroath, Scotland, in 1861. After an early training in journalism on the local newspaper, Greig contributed both text and illustrations.

He went to London in 1890 where he was employed as a freelance contributor to several journals, including *Punch*. In 1895 he went to Paris to complete his artistic education and to fulfil a commission to supply a London weekly journal with illustrated articles on life in general. Greig returned to London in 1896 and after various journalistic experiences joined the staff of *The Morning Post*, later succeeding Robert Ross as art critic. During World War I he drew maps for the journal to illustrate the aspects of the different fronts.

Greig edited the manuscript of *Farrington's Diary* (the early history of the Royal Academy) and the successive volumes as they were published. The research involved made him one of the leading authorities on art in England during the late 19th and early 20th centuries.

Greig's most important publications were his *Life of Gainsborough* and the *Life of Raeburn*. Among his other contributions to the literature of art were 'The Art of Henry Woods RA' in the *Art Annual* of 1915 and (Frederic Cayley) 'Robinson' in the *Old Water Colour Society Club Annual* for 1928. In addition he published *Diaries of a Duchess* and *Drawings for Punch*.

Greig's Boer War work appeared in *Black & White*, *The Sphere* (including *Boers looting dead Britishers*) and *King*, and in Cassell second-hand.

Greig became president of the Savage Club after having been a popular member of that society for many years. He died in Brighton on 13 October 1941.

Carter, War Artists in S.A., *p. 17*
Caw, Scottish Painting
Waters, British Artists, *vol. 1, p. 141*
Watson, The Savage Club
Who was Who, *vol. 4, p. 468*

1 *South African Mounted Rifles*, a watercolour by T. E. Gilson.
2 Francis Carruthers Gould produced this pen-and-ink sketch for an unknown publication. Entitled *Too good to be true*, its subject is the Lord Chancellor, Lord Stanley Hardinge Gifford. The caption reads 'It is not true that the Lord Chancellor, fired by the example of the Duke of Norfolk, has resigned the Woolsack and gone to the front'.
3 Francis Carruthers Gould depicted himself as a bloodhound in this drawing entitled *F.C.G. on the old trail*.
4 Gordon Hope Grant, accompanying Lord Methuen's forces, represented newspapers in England and the United States. This front page illustration by Grant, entitled *The rocky fortresses that nature supplies to the Boers*, appeared in *Leslie's Weekly* on 24 March 1900.

GRELLET, Georges
La Caricature cartoonist. One of his coloured cartoon illustrations appeared on the cover of issue 1054 on 10 March 1900. Entitled *Allo Allo*, it showed a defeated Buller using the telephone with Albion looking on.

GRELLIER, Henry Harley 1879-1943
Postcard artist. Grellier was born at St Catherines, Ontario, Canada, on 14 November 1879. He immigrated with his family to South Africa, via England, in 1895. Grellier snr. was offered the parish at Pietersburg.

Grellier worked for a bank in Natal, but in 1902 he decided to study art. He left for London to attend the Slade School. He returned in 1904 after a sojourn in Italy. (The earliest postmark on a card by Grellier is May 1904.) In 1907 he joined the Natal civil service and was appointed magistrate in Zululand. He fought in World War I. He later became a magistrate in Queenstown where he married Joyce Ordbrowne, the Johannesburg artist. She exhibited a portrait of her husband in 1941.

At least 29 Sallo Epstein cards have been credited to Grellier. Some, although postwar, have Boer War relevance and one depicts a scene from the Zulu War.

Grellier died in Stellenbosch on 14 March 1943.
Kennedy, Pictures in the Africana Museum, *vol. 4, p. 44*
SAPRG Newsletter, *(Nov. 1983) no. 10, p. 9*

GRENFELL, Charles
Capt. Grenfell was a prisoner of war after his capture at Colenso on 24 December 1899. He was a member of the 2nd Buckinghamshire Yeomanry Brigade. He was given credit in the P.O.W. publication *The Gram* for illustrations which appeared on page 33 of the second number.

GRIEBNER, F.
An artist of this name had Boer War cartoons published in

Lustige Blätter. They also appeared in *Burenstreiche*.

GRIFFITH, W. M.
A Lt. Griffith was responsible for illustrations which appeared in *The Graphic* on 14 December 1901, 18 January 1902 and 24 March 1902. The illustrations were redrawn by George Soper and Frank Dadd.
Hofmeyr, Matton and Roets, Graphic Picture Index

GRISET, Ernest-Henry 1844-1907
Illustrator and comic draughtsman. Griset was born in Boulogne-Sur-Mer, France, in 1844. He studied under Louis Gallait. He went to London in the 1860s and worked for several illustrated magazines including *Fun* and *Punch*. He was also closely associated with the Dalziel brothers. Griset was responsible for two extant Boer War watercolours entitled *The last stand; Nicholson's Nek* and *The Ambuscade; Nicholson's Nek*.
Bénézit, Dictionnaire antique, *vol. 4, p. 437*
Houfe, British Illustrators and Caricaturists, *p. 326*
Osterwalder, and Hubschmid and Bouret (eds.), Dictionnaire des Illustrateurs, *p. 462*
Wood, Victorian Painters, *p. 192*

GROOME, William Henry Charles fl. 1881-1914
Landscape painter and illustrator. Groome became a member of the R.B.A. in 1901. He worked for *The Illustrated London News* from 1889 until 1892, as well as for *Chums*. He was responsible for the illustrations in George Manville Fenn's *Charge! The story of Briton and Boer* (W. & R. Chambers, London, 1900).

Houfe, British Illustrators and Caricaturists, *p. 327*
SABIB, *vol. 2, p. 235*

GROSSI, A.
Italian cartoonist who worked for the Bologna satirical publication, *Le Perroquet*.
Grand-Carteret, John Bull, *p. 39*

GRÜN, Jules-Alexandre 1868-1934
Poster, postcard and silhouette artist. Grün was born in Paris on 25 May 1868. He was greatly influenced by Felix Vallotton and he studied under Guillemet. His Art Nouveau postcards are very sought after.

Grün provided illustrations for *L'Assiette au Beurre, La Caricature, Le Courrier Français, Fin de Siècle, Le Rire* and *Le Sourire.*

His only known Boer War related work is his 1899 poster *La Boîte à Fursy: 12 Rue Victor-Massé, Ancien Hotel du Chat Noir.* It was produced in his studio (Atelier Grün) and published by Chaix, 20 Rue Bergère, Paris. The poster – which depicts several characters of the period including Tsar Nicholas, Kaiser Wilhelm, Abu Hamid of Turkey, and President Loubet of France – shows a smiling Kruger seated next to Chamberlain in the front row of a night club.

Grün died in Paris on 15 February 1934.
Barnicoat, History of Posters, *p. 150*
Bénézit, Dictionnaire antique, *vol. 4, 458*
Fanelli and Godoli, Art Nouveau Postcards
Osterwalder, and Hubschmid and Bouret (eds.), Dictionnaire des Illustrateurs, *p. 463*
Schardt, Art of the Poster

GUIGNARD, Alexandre-Gaston 1848-?
French genre artist who was responsible for a painting which was reproduced on page 25 of *Paris-Pretoria*. The illustration shows the desolation of a ruined farmhouse in the moonlight.
Bénézit, Dictionnaire antique, *vol. 4, p. 498*

GUILLAUME, Albert-André 1873-1942
Painter, cartoonist and illustrator. The son of Edmond Guillaume, professor of architecture at the École des Beaux-Arts, Guillaume was born in Paris on 14 February 1873. He studied at the Atelier Gérôme. He exhibited as a 17-year-old before becoming a soldier. While he contributed to several French illustrated and satirical periodicals and to *The Graphic*, his Boer War cartoons appeared only in *Le Monde Illustré*. These cartoons on various subjects were a regular feature (with Jehan Testevuide) on the inside back cover of the magazine.

His sister, Mrs Lami, was also a well-known cartoonist. Guillaume died in Faux in the Dordogne in 1942.
Bénézit, Dictionnaire antique, *vol. 4, p. 501*

5

6

Fanelli and Godoli, Art Nouveau Postcards
Houfe, British Illustrators and Caricaturists, *p. 327*
The Strand, *vol. 22, p. 676*

GULLY, C.

Army Service Corps major whose pictorial postal cover from Modder River to Mr C. Turvey in London was reproduced on 31 March 1900 on p. 252 of the *The Golden Penny.*

GUNN, D. D.

Gunn was a lieutenant in the King's Own Scottish Borderers. One of his sketches was reproduced in *The Graphic* on 24 February 1900 and entitled *On The Road To Kimberley: View of the Boer positions from one of our pickets.* It had been redrawn by Percy F. S. Spence.

GWYNN, Reginald P. J.   1

Gwynn was a lieutenant in the 5th Royal Irish Lancers which were besieged in Ladysmith. He had joined the Lancers on 31 May 1890 as 2nd lieutenant and was promoted to lieutenant in 1900 when he was seconded to the 7th Fusiliers. During the siege he sent a hand-illustrated envelope from Ladysmith to his father, Col. Gwynn, Chief Constable at Bath. The sketch shows a dejected Lancer mourning the fact that his horse had been converted to 'Chevril' (the equestrian version of the better-known Bovril).

Willcox, The Fifth (Royal Irish) Lancers

HAGEN, Max 1862-1914

Landscape artist and caricaturist. Hagen was born in Flensbourg, in Schleswig-Holstein, on 25 October 1862. He studied at the Munich Academy. He contributed occasional cartoons and caricatures to *Jugend,* often signing them with his initials only. He died in Schliersee in Bavaria in 1914.

Bénézit, Dictionnaire antique, *vol. 4, p. 549*

HALE, George Ernest 1861-1933

Marine painter. Hale was born in Eastbourne, England, on 13 June 1861. Educated at Cheltenham College, he qualified with his M.R.C.S. and L.R.C.P. (the latter at Edinburgh).

Hale joined the army on 31 January 1885 and served with the Sudan Frontier Force (1885-6). He was present during the action of Ginnis where he won a medal and the Khedive's Star. He saw action in Burma (1889-91), where he received a medal with two clasps, and he was mentioned in despatches for the Pounkhan Expedition in 1889. For the Tonhon Expedition he was recommended for a V.C., but received the thanks of the government instead. Hale was awarded the D.S.O. on 18 March 1892 in recognition of his services. He was promoted to sergeant major in 1897 and served in South Africa from 1900 until 1902 as officer commanding the Imperial

Yeomanry Bearer Company and senior medical officer for Gen. Mahon's column. He was mentioned in Lord Roberts's despatches. Later he became the officer commanding the 23rd Bearer Company and senior medical officer for Col. Sitwell's column. He was awarded the Queen's medal with three clasps and the King's medal with two clasps.

Hale became honorary surgeon to the Viceroy of India in 1908 and retired in 1912. He was re-employed on 7 June 1915 when he joined the British Expeditionary Field Force as the officer commanding the 45 Field Ambulances and senior medical officer for 45th Brigade 15th Scottish Division. He was present at the Battle of Loos. He won the 1915 Star, the General Service medal and the Victory medal.

Hale exhibited in London and the provinces, as well as abroad. Only one of his Boer War works is recorded. It appeared in *The Graphic* on 12 May 1900 and is entitled *The loss of the SS Mexican 80 miles from Cape Town.* It was redrawn by Charles Dixon. Hale was eyewitness to the event.

Hale died on 11 January 1933.

Creagh and Humphris, The D.S.O., *p. 45*
Drew, Officers in Medical Services, *vol. 1, p. 532*
The Graphic, *12 May 1900, p. 702*
Waters, British Artists, *vol. 1, p. 146*
Who was Who, *vol. 3, p. 376*

HALKE, Paul 1866-?

Portrait and genre painter. Halke was born in Bukowicz on 27 October 1866. He studied at the Berlin Academy. He was the principal cartoonist of *Ulk* and often used the initials 'P.H.' as his signature.

Bénézit, Dictionnaire antique, *vol. 4, p. 558*

HALKETT, George Roland 1855-1918

Cartoonist, artist and art writer. Halkett was born in Edinburgh on 11 March 1855. He was educated privately and studied art in Paris. He later became a regular contributor to art magazines. Halkett became the art critic for the *Edinburgh Evening News* in 1876 and the joint compiler and artist of the *New Gleanings from Gladstone* and *Gladstone Almanac.* In 1887 he wrote and illustrated *The Irish Green Book.* He joined the *Pall Mall Gazette* in 1892 as political cartoonist and writer on art. Halkett, who travelled widely, also contributed many drawings and caricatures to *Punch* and wrote the *Phil May Picture Book.* He became art editor of the *Pall Mall Magazine* in 1897 and general editor of the same magazine from 1900 until 1905.

Halkett often signed his work 'GRH'. Several Boer War cartoons of his were reproduced in *Punch,* where his 'The Seats of the Mighty' was a regular feature. The Africana Museum has three original pen-and-ink cartoons, signed 'G.R.H.': *Oom William – More Krugerite then Kruger* (probably pub-

lished in *Pall Mall Gazette*); *On commando! Joseph the Trekker; oh that Jesse could see me now; Joe his mark* (original in *Punch,* 11 February 1903).

Africana Notes and News, *vol. 25, p. 5 (March 1985, p. 192)*
Hammerton, Humorists of the Pencil, *p. 43*
Kennedy, Pictures in the Africana Museum, *vol. 3, p. 117*
Who was Who, *vol. 2, p. 452*

HALL, Sydney Prior 1842-1922   3

Caricaturist, Western and 'special' artist, illustrator and painter of royalty. The son of Harry Hall of Newmarket, a well-known sporting painter, Sydney Hall was educated at Merchant Taylors' School and Pembroke College, Oxford. He travelled widely for *The Graphic,* for which he had been working almost from its inception in 1869. He was a 'special' artist during the Franco-Prussian War and he travelled with Edward VII, then Prince of Wales, on his voyage to India (1875-6). Hall also accompanied the Marquess of Lorne and his wife, Princess Louise, when he was sent to Canada to become governor general in 1879. It was at this time that Hall did some of his large oils of Canadian scenes and became known as a Western artist. He also accompanied the Marquess of Lorne on his journey to the Canadian north-west frontier in 1881, and he was a member of the then Duke and Duchess of York's suite on board the H.M.S. *Ophir* in 1901 when they visited South Africa.

Hall's work was highly regarded by royalty and he accompanied the German emperor on a visit to Palestine. He painted the marriage of the Duke and Duchess of Connaught for Queen Victoria and the marriage of the Princess Royal and the Duke of Fife for King Edward, for whom he also painted the *Investiture of King Haakon of Norway with the garter.* He received the M.V.O. in 1901.

While at Oxford Hall earned a reputation as a caricaturist; several of his caricatures were later issued under the title of *Oxford Sketches* and found an appreciative public. This also led to a commission from MacMillan in 1874 to illustrate *Tom Brown's School Days.*

Hall's 13 paintings exhibited at the Royal Academy (1875-1904) were mainly to do with royalty. A sumptuous volume produced in 1877 by Sampson and Low, entitled *Prince of Wales Tour,* was illustrated by Hall with letterpress by W.H. Russell. The *Ophir* book was similarly illustrated in conjunction with Chevalier De Martino and was written by Sir D. MacKenzie Wallace of *The Times.* It was called *The Web of Empire* and was published in 1902. Hall also received fame for his sketches of the Jameson Raid Inquiry and the Parnell Commission. Six of Hall's paintings can be found in the Royal

1 *La Boîte à Fursy* was the title of this poster by Jules Grün, done in 1899. Kruger can be seen seated next to Joseph Chamberlain. President Loubet of France is directly behind Kruger. Other personalities depicted are the Kaiser and the Tsar of Russia, Nicholas II.
2 Distinguished soldier-artist Major George Hale depicted the liner *Mexican* after her collision with the transport ship *Wingfield* (or *Winkfield* in dense fog north-west of Cape Town. Hale, who was a member of the R.A.M.C., was an eyewitness to the collision. The sketch was redrawn by Charles Dixon for publication in *The Graphic.*
3 Four days before the relief of Ladysmith Lieutenant Reginald Gwynn of the 5th Royal Irish Lancers wrote to his father Colonel Gwynn in England. The sketch on the envelope depicts the fact that his horse had apparently been converted to the meat extract named 'Chevril', an equine version of the more famous 'Bovril'.
4 A portrait of Sydney Prior Hall, published in *The Graphic* on 6 December 1890.
5 Sydney Prior Hall's wash painting entitled *Transvaal Crisis* showed men flocking to a recruiting station in Cape Town. The painting was based on a sketch by Cape Town artist Heinrich Egersdörfer.
6 Sydney Prior Hall based this melodramatic rendering entitled *Only a Pawn* on a sketch by Lionel James. It appeared in *The Graphic* on 14 July 1900.

Military Collection at Windsor, but are not of Boer War relevance.

Hall was a very prolific artist for *The Graphic* and he became well known for his sketches of politicians drawn from life. *In the Houses of Parliament* appeared regularly. At least 38 Boer War drawings by Hall appeared in *The Graphic* and some of these were drawn when he was with the Duke of Cornwall and York in Pietermaritzburg in 1901. The author has one of Hall's works which was drawn from a sketch by Heinrich Egersdörfer entitled *Transvaal Crisis: besieging a recruiting station at Cape Town*. This appeared in *The Graphic* just before the start of the War, on 30 September 1899.

Art Journal, *1905, p. 277*
The Graphic, *6 Dec. 1896*
Graves, Royal Academy, *vol. 3, p. 357*
Hofmeyr, Matton and Roets, Graphic Picture Index
The Times Obituary, *16 Dec. 1922*
Who was Who, *vol. 2, p. 454*

HALSTED, A. E.

Four sketches by this unidentified artist, who was probably a soldier, appeared in *The Graphic* between 26 November 1899 and 2 June 1900.

Hofmeyr, Matton and Roets, Graphic Picture Index

HAMPE, T.

One of the illustrators of *British and Boers in South Africa* by James H. Birch jnr. (P. W. Ziegler and Co., Philadelphia and Chicago).

SABIB, *vol. 1, p. 198*

HARCOURT, George 1868-1947   1

Portrait and figure painter. Harcourt was born in Dumbartonshire on 11 October 1868. He exhibited at the principal London galleries from 1893 and also at the Paris Salon where he won a gold medal in 1923. He was elected A.R.A. in 1919 and R.A. in 1926.

Between 1893 and 1904 Harcourt exhibited 10 pictures at the Royal Academy. One of these paintings, exhibited in 1900, was entitled *Goodbye! The 3rd Battalion Grenadier Guards leaving Waterloo station, October 21 1899*. This painting was reproduced on the front cover of *Nieuwe Belgische Illustratie* (vol. 18, p. 34, 1901/1902).

Harcourt's wife, Mary Lascelles Leesmith, whom he married in 1919, was also a artist. He died on 30 September 1947 in Bushey, Hertfordshire.

Graves, Royal Academy, *vol. 3, p. 378*
Waters, British Artists, *vol. 1, pp. 149-150*

HARDY, Dudley 1867-1922   1

Genre portrait, landscape and historical painter. The elder son of the marine painter T.B. Hardy, Dudley Hardy was born in Sheffield on 15 January 1867. His art education was received initially from his father and later at the Düsseldorf Academy where he studied under Crola and Lowenstein. He worked for a time under his father, under Verlat in Antwerp, and under Collin and Rossi in Paris. Hardy was a prominent member of the London Sketch Club, eventually becoming its president. He exhibited at the Royal Academy between 1884 and 1903 and became a member of the R.I. and R.O.I. in 1897.

As an illustrator Hardy contributed to *The Illustrated London News*, *The Sketch*, *Pictorial World*, *Lady's Pictorial*, *Gentlewoman*, *Pick-Me-Up*, *Black & White* and *The Graphic*. At one time he acted as 'war correspondent' in the Sudan while living in London.

Hardy became known for his posters which include at least one with a Boer War theme: *Briton, Boer and Black* advertised a show at Olympia in 1900. His Boer War illustrations can be found in *The Sphere*, *With the Flag to Pretoria* and *The King*. One of his drawings, *Mafeking Night*, appears in A. C. R. Carter's *The Work of War Artists in South Africa*. His comic postcard illustrations are now collectors' items.

Carter, War Artists in S.A., *pp. 16-17 and 31*
Cuppleditch, London Sketch Club,
Graves, Royal Academy, *vol. 3, p. 385*
Holt, Tonie and Valmai, Stanley Gibbons Postcard Catalogue
Johnson, Dudley Hardy
The Studio, *vol. 30*
Thorpe, English Illustration
The Times (obituary), *12 Aug. 1922*
Waters, British Artists, *vol. 1, p. 150*
Who was Who, *vol. 2, p. 462*

HARDY, E. Stewart

Illustrations by this artist appeared in *Cassell's Illustrated History of the Boer War*.

HARDY, Frank C.

Brother of Dudley Hardy, Frank Hardy worked for *Longbow*. During the War he contributed to *Shurey's Pictorial Budget*.

Thorpe, English Illustration

HARDY, Norman H. fl. 1864-1914

This artist, who worked for the *Sydney Herald* in 1896, was

responsible for Boer War illustrations in *Cassell's Illustrated History of the Boer War*.

Houfe, British Illustrators and Caricaturists, *p. 333*

HARDY, Paul fl. 1886-1901

Historical painter and illustrator. Hardy was a prolific illustrator of books, but he also worked at various times for *English Illustrated Magazine, The Illustrated Sporting & Dramatic News, The Quiver, Black & White, Gentlewoman, Cassell's Family Magazine, Chums, Boy's Own Paper, St Pauls, The Rambler, St James Budget* and *The Strand*.

During the War Hardy did the illustration that was used on the pictorial covers of the 49 individual parts of *Cassell's Illustrated History of the Boer War*.

Hardy provided illustrations for Jane Spettigue's *A Trek and a Laager: A borderland story* (Blackie and Co., London, 1900). The story deals with the Frontier wars, however, and not the Boer War. *An Africander Trio: A story of adventure for Boys and Girls* (1898), by the same author, carried two of Hardy's illustrations.

Hardy worked in Bexley Heath, Kent. He often signed his work 'P.H.'. His wife, Ida Wilson Clarke, was also an artist.

Houfe, British Illustrators and Caricaturists, *p. 333*
SABIB, *vol. 4, p. 365*
Thorpe, English Illustration

HARE, Robert William 1872-1953   1

Soldier-artist. Hare was born on 14 November 1872. He was educated at Harrow and joined the Norfolk Regiment on 19 November 1892, becoming lieutenant on 7 March 1896. In 1896, he served in southern Africa with the Mounted Infantry, earning the Mashonaland medal, and was in South Africa during the Boer War. He was a special service officer (including service with the Rhodesian Regiment) from 15 July 1899 to 22 July 1900 and was present at the relief of Mafeking. Thereafter he was staff officer to a brigadier general from 3 July to 28 August 1900. He was promoted to captain on 16 February 1901. Hare was mentioned in despatches in September 1901 and on 29 July 1902. He received the Queen's medal with five clasps and the King's medal with two clasps. He was placed on the list of officers considered qualified for staff employment because of their service in the field and he was created a D.S.O. on 27 September 1901. He was aide-de-camp to the lieutenant governor of the Orange River Colony, Sir Hamilton Goold Adams, from 15 November 1902 to 22 January 1905, at a salary of £250 per year. Hare was staff captain at the headquarters of the army from 16 January 1906 to 27 September 1908 and brigade major of 17th Brigade Irish

To my friend Hartrick

Phil May
- /9-

5

Command from 28 September 1908 to 27 June 1911. He was promoted to major on 30 March 1912 and was G.S.O. at the War Office from 8 October 1913 to 4 August 1914. Hare served in World War I, and by February 1919 had reached the rank of brigadier general. He was twice mentioned in despatches and awarded the C.M.G. in 1919.

According to a eulogy which appeared in *The Times* in early January 1954 and which was written by 'G.H.S.', Hare spent his leisure time during his retirement 'sketching and painting and in expert craftsmanship in wood and metal'. It continues: 'On several occasions he exhibited at the Model Engineers Exhibition complete engines, every part of which he had fashioned himself.'

A personal communication from his son, Lt. Col. R.G.D. Hare, who lives in Norwich, mentions that his father did not have much artistic training except at Harrow. He says that he owed much to his art master and he seems to remember that Winston Churchill was also at Harrow at the same time. He mentions further that his father was too modest to exhibit even though he had been prevailed upon on many occasions to do so. Hare jnr. describes how some of his father's drawings were published in the Kipling Society Journal during the 1930s. His father had become good friends with Kipling after meeting him on a Union Castle liner returning from Cape Town in about 1904. As Sir H. Goold Adams' aide-de-camp, he had a seat at the captain's table at which Kipling was also a guest. Kipling was very interested in Hare snr.'s drawings, and a verse or two of his poem, *Ubique* (about the Royal Artillery), was inspired by Hare snr.'s drawing entitled *Guns and Dust*. This is one of the pictures that is still in Hare jnr.'s possession. In later years his mother and father stayed with Kipling in Sussex.

One of Hare's sketches sent from Rhodesia in 1896 was redrawn by A.S. Boyd in *The Graphic* in January 1897; it was entitled *Tommy Atkins in Rhodesia – leaves from an officer's sketch book*. The author has a pencil sketch drawn on blotting paper which is inscribed on the reverse: 'Drawn by one Hare of the army ADC Lieutenant to Sir Hamilton Goold Adams about the year 1902 in Lord Milner's office on a bit of blotting paper picked up and framed by 'H.A.W.'. Boer farmer on Commando exactly true to life'. The Norwich Museum has six Boer War pencil sketches by Hare.

Hare died in Norfolk on 29 December 1953.

Creagh and Humphris, The D.S.O., *p. 230*
Debrett's Illustrated Peerage, p. 727
Peerage and Baronetage, *pp. 1629-1630*
Personal communication from Lt. Col. R.G.D. Hare
Who was Who, *vol. 5, p. 484*

HARE, St George 1857-1933

Portrait, genre and nude figure painter. Hare was born in Limerick, Ireland, on 5 July 1857. He studied at the R.C.A. after moving to London in 1875. He exhibited at the Royal Academy from 1884 and was elected a member of the R.I. in 1892.

One of Hare's illustrations appeared in *The Graphic* on 10 March 1900. Entitled *The Girl he left behind him*, it shows the Ceylon contingent leaving Colombo for South Africa and is from a sketch by E. F. van Dort.

Hofmeyr, Matton and Roets, Graphic Picture Index
Waters, British Artists, *vol. 1, p. 151*

HARINGUS, Lui-Même

This is the nom de plume of a wealthy Dutch cartoonist whose work appeared in *L'Agonie d'Albion*.

HARRIS, E. S.

A Boer War watercolour by this artist is in the author's collection. In true heroic style it shows Britannia riding a chariot surrounded by soldiers representing the British Empire.

HARRIS, Owen   1

Trooper Owen Harris of Loch's Horse was one of the editors

of *The Mexican Mercury*, which was produced and published aboard the Union liner SS *Mexican* which sailed with his contingent to South Africa in March 1900. He was responsible for the front cover, as well as some of the caricatures, many of which were signed 'O.H.'.

HARTRICK, Archibald Standish 1864-1950   2

Hartrick was born in Bangalore in Madras, India, on 7 August 1864. His father, Captain William Hartrick, had been stationed there with his regiment, the 7th Royal Fusiliers. At the age of two Hartrick and his family returned to Scotland. He was educated at Fettes College where he excelled in art.

After school Hartrick attended Edinburgh University and then the Slade School, where he studied under Legros between 1884 and 1885. He moved to Paris a year later where he studied under Boulanger at the Académie Julian and under Cormon at the latter's studio.

With several friends from the Académie Julian he spent his first summer in France painting at Pont-Aven, the well-known artists' resort. It was here that he came to know Paul Gauguin and Vincent van Gogh, with whom he became quite friendly.

Hartrick returned to Scotland in 1887, but in 1889 W.L. Thomas's advertisement for artists for his newly founded *The Daily Graphic* caught his eye. The advertisement offered 'a good opening to young men to make an income of from £400 to £2 000 per annum'. He applied and was interviewed by Thomas and 'the elderly Frenchman Godefroi Durand'. He was accepted and was placed under the guidance of G. K. Jones, 'a London youth of about our own age who was already established as a toucher-up of photographs and general utility man'. E. J. Sullivan, 'a lad of just nineteen', was also on the staff.

During his sojourn with *The Daily Graphic*, Hartrick came into close contact with several other artists and correspondents, including Charles Fripp, Fred Villiers, Bennet Burleigh, Reginald Cleaver, A. S. Boyd and Herbert Johnson. The last three were 'founder' artists of *The Daily Graphic*, having been on the staff since its inception. Hartrick also became closely associated with Paul Renouard, who, although he spoke no English, acted as French artist-correspondent for *The Graphic* and *The Daily Graphic*. Phil May (see p. 168) was another of his close friends, as was Ed Sullivan.

At the start of the War Hartrick had left *The Graphic* and moved to Frenham to continue his fine art. Clement Shorter, the editor of the newly founded *The Sphere*, sent him sketches from the front to be worked up into drawings for his paper. The local postman had been wounded at Paardeberg and Hartrick used him as his model.

Besides the papers mentioned above Hartrick also worked for *Pall Mall Budget, Daily Chronicle, The Quiver, New Budget, Cassell's Family Magazine, Fun, The Strand Magazine, Ludgate Monthly, Pearson's* and *Pall Mall Magazine*. Hartrick's *Lithography as a fine art* was published in 1932, and his autobiography *A Painter's Pilgrimage through Fifty years* in 1939.

1 George Harcourt's oil painting of the 3rd Battalion Grenadier Guards leaving for South Africa was exhibited at the Royal Academy in 1900. Station 'farewells' were a popular subject for artists of the period.
2 A humorous drawing of illustrator Dudley Hardy, who is well known for his Boer war posters and contributions to several contemporary periodicals.
3 Soldier-artist Robert William Hare, who served as aide-de-camp to Sir Hamilton Goold Adams during the War.
4 A pencil sketch on blotting paper by soldier-artist Robert Hare. The back of the sketch has a note stating that he drew the sketch, of a mounted Boer, in Lord Milner's office and that it is 'exactly true to life'.
5 A sketch of A. S. Hartrick by cartoonist Phil May.

Hartrick was elected a member of the N.E.A.C. in 1893 and the I.S. in 1906. He became an A.R.W.S. in 1910 and R.W.S. in 1920. He was a founder member and vice-president of the Senefelder Club. Hartrick had works on exhibit at the Royal Academy from 1895 to 1907. During World War II he was appointed as an official war artist.

The author has a pen-and-wash drawing by Hartrick entitled *Tom Sutherland's Ghost at Port Elizabeth*. The mount of the drawing bears the inscription 'This pen-and-wash and watercolour drawing is by A. S. Hartrick and was the original for an illustration to a story about an incident in the Boer War, the appearance of Tom Sutherland's ghost at Port Elizabeth. Hartrick gave me the drawing when I visited him in 1935 but the drawing was done at the beginning of the century; [signed] Ronald Horton'. No details of this story have as yet been established, but it is possible that it appeared in *Pall Mall Magazine*.

One of Hartrick's unsigned illustrations was used as the frontispiece for Herbert Hayen's *Scouting for Buller*. This illustration is similar to one which appeared on page 85 of *The Sphere* on 10 February 1900. It is also probably the drawing referred to by Julian Ralph as quoted by H.C. Shelley, the well-known photographer, in a letter to *The Friend* in 1900.

This letter is reproduced on page 461 of Julian Ralph's *War's Brighter Side*. He criticizes the fanciful illustrations appearing in the contemporary press. Some of Hartrick's Boer War illustrations were characterized by very dramatic representation which today seems quite ludicrous.

Hartrick's association with several well-known artists and illustrators has given his work a certain quality, particularly his chalk drawing. According to his own modest assessment, however, his work 'never quite amounted to much'.

His wife, Lily Blatherwick, a relative of his stepfather, was also an artist. Hartrick died in London on 1 February 1950.

Hartrick, A Painter's Pilgrimage
Houfe, British Illustrators and Caricaturists, *p. 334*
Thorpe, English Illustration
Waters, British Artists, *vol. 1, pp. 152-153*
Who was Who, *vol. 4, pp. 509-510*

HARVEY, Harold

A lance corporal in the 30th Co. Imperial Yeomanry, 9th Battalion, Harvey is reputed to be the artist responsible for four sketches which can be found in the Africana Museum. Two are seascapes, one a landscape, and the fourth is initialled 'H.H.' and shows a mounted British infantryman. It is as-

sumed that the initials are those, not of the sitter, but of the artist, whose name, rank and company appear on the reverse of the drawing.

Kennedy, Pictures in the Africana Museum, *vol. 7, p. 3*

HARVEY, Sydney fl. 1897-1907

Moonshine cartoonist whose Boer War works appeared in that magazine from 1901. He also contributed to *Punch* between 1899 and 1902, but not on Boer War themes.

Houfe, British Illustrators and Caricaturists, *p. 334*
Thorpe, English Illustration

HASERICK, Alfred E.

Soldier-artist. Haserick was a lieutenant in the Rhodesian Regiment. He was captured at Rhodes Drift on 2 November 1899. While being held as a prisoner of war in Pretoria he collaborated with his fellow prisoners on *The Gram*, the P.O.W. magazine, providing illustrations for issue no. 2 (pages 9 and 10 and the inside back cover). The back cover illustration, according to Rosslyn, the editor, in his 'Notes for guidance in reading no. 2' in the facsimile edition, 'represents a true incident, when Lieut. Haserick, having been given a young hawk by one of our guards, attached a Union Jack (made out of his

tie) to the bird's neck, and sent it out over Pretoria on the Queen's Birthday'.

After he was released Haserick did civilian duties in the 'Native pass office' but ultimately became a member of the Pietersburg Light Horse in March 1902. He had previously been involved with the Bushveldt Carbineers and knew Capt. Hunt, whose death lead to the courts martial of Lts. Breaker Morant, P.J. Handcock and G. R. Witton.

Davey (ed.), Breaker Morant and the Bushveldt Carbineers
The Gram

HASSALL, John 1868-1948 2
Illustrator, caricaturist, and poster and postcard artist. Hassall was born in Walmer, near Dover, on 21 May 1868. He was the son of Lt. Christopher Clark Hassall, a naval officer who died when his son was eight years old. John Hassall was educated at Newton Abbot College in Devon and in Neuenheim College in Heidelberg, Germany. He spent his early adult life as a farmer in Manitoba, Canada, from where he sent a few sketches of prairie life to the infant *The Daily Graphic.* He went to Antwerp and Paris between 1891 and 1894 to study under Van Havermaet and Bouguereau respectively. Hassall was well known for his theatrical and commercial posters, particularly those done for the firm of David Allen. He later became famous for his postcard illustrations and those done for boys' books and nursery rhymes. He was a prominent member of the London Sketch Club. He was elected as a member of the R.I. and the R.M.S. in 1901.

Hassall's Boer War work is not prolific, but probably his best known is *An Active Army Alphabet* (Sands and Co., London, 1899). As its name implies, this children's book illustrates each letter of the alphabet as representing something related to the Boer War. Five of his illustrations appeared in *The Graphic* between 3 February and 22 September 1900. One of these illustrations was reproduced in *Under The Union Jack* on 2 June 1900. Hassall contributed caricatures to *The King* and on 15 December 1900 illustrated Mostyn Pigott's article on 'The meeting of the centuries' in that paper. Caricatures of Kruger and Chamberlain are represented among other personalities. Hassall also provided the cover illustration for *The Souvenir and Official Programme of the National Bazaar in aid of sufferers by the War.* One of his Boer War postcards (a write away type) has been noted. Hassall married twice, and Joan, his daughter from his second marriage, is a well-known wood engraver.

Cuppleditch, The John Hassall Lifestyle
Houfe, British Illustrators and Caricaturists, *p. 335*

ANGLIA

5

The Strand, *vol. 32, p. 87*
Waters, British Artists, *vol. 1, p. 153*
Who was Who, *vol. 4, p. 512*

HATHAWAY, Harold George 1860-1942
Soldier-artist. Hathaway was born on 13 June 1860 in Kensington. He was educated at the King's School, Rochester, and St Bartholomew's Hospital in London. He joined the army in 1885 soon after he qualified. Hathaway saw active service in Burma between 1885 and 1889. Experience with the Chitral Relief Expedition (1895) was followed by the Punjab Frontier and Tirah expeditions and eventually service in South Africa during the Boer War. Major Hathaway was appointed medical officer of the Cavalry Division staff and he took part in all the engagements with this division throughout the War. He was seriously wounded at Colesberg but was promoted for distinguished conduct in the field, receiving the Queen's medal with five clasps. Hathaway served in World War I, during which he was mentioned in despatches, awarded the C.B., and promoted to major general.

He was responsible for at least one illustration in *The Illustrated London News.* Entitled *Peep from Coles Kop,* it appeared on 17 February 1900.

De Wet, Illustrated London News Index
Drew, Officers in Medical Services, *vol. 1, p. 538*
Who was Who, *vol. 4, p. 513*

HATHERELL, William 1855-1928 2
Illustrator and painter of historical, literary and figure subjects. William Hatherell was born in Westbury-on-Trym on 18 October 1855. He was educated privately and then later at the Royal Academy schools. His work was exhibited at the Royal Academy and the R.W.S. from 1879 until 1902. His illustrative work appeared in *The Graphic, The Quiver, Black & White, English Illustrated Magazine, Pall Mall Budget, Cassell's Family Magazine, Chums, Harper's Magazine* and *Scribner's.* Hatherell was elected a member of the R.I. in 1888, the R.O.I. in 1898 and R.W.A. in 1903. He was made an honorary member of the Langham Sketching Club in 1900 and a member of the American Society of Illustrators in 1905. He often signed his work with the initials 'W.H.'. His illustrations of Shakespeare's *Romeo and Juliet* received strong praise when the play was published in 1892. He illustrated the four volumes of Cassell's *Picturesque Australia.* He often formed a 'pictorial duet', working on double-page illustrations with F. Dadd, W. Small, Frank Craig, Balliol Salmon or H. M. Paget.

Hatherell contributed at least 18 Boer War illustrations to *The Graphic.* His work also appeared second-hand in Creswicke and *Follow the Flag in South Africa.*

On 29 November 1902 *The Graphic* advertised the publication of 'Another Bovril War Picture: Owing to the great success of their celebrated war picture "The Relief of Ladysmith" Bovril Ltd. have arranged to present another splendid gravure – 'Lord Kitchener's Home-coming' reproduced from the original painting of William Hatherell, RI. The gravure will form a magnificent companion to "The Relief of Ladysmith" picture and will also be quite free from advertising matter. A coupon and leaflet with full particulars will be found wrapped with each bottle of Bovril (1 oz to 16 oz).' The advertisement also reproduced Hatherell's painting. This photogravure was produced by W. C. Faulkner and Co., London E.C. In spite of Bovril's claim of no advertising the picture had the inscription 'published by Bovril Limited' on the bottom left.

The Royal Collection at Windsor has five contemporary Hatherell pictures. The subjects are British royalty and are not connected with the Boer War as such.

Carter, War Artists in S.A., *pp. 21-22*
Hofmeyr, Matton and Roets, Graphic Picture Index
Houfe, British Illustrators and Caricaturists, *pp. 336-337*
Waters, British Artists, *vol. 1, p. 154*
Who was Who, *vol. 2, p. 475*

HATOS, Sandor 1868-1907 1
Hungarian cartoonist. None of his publications has yet been traced. The Mendelssohn Collection in the Library of Parliament, Cape Town has an original cartoon by Hatos entitled *Anglia (a cartoon of John Bull).* He died in Budapest in 1907.

Bénézit, Dictionnaire antique, *vol. 4, p. 610*

HAUG, Robert 1857-1922
Historical and genre painter. Haug was born in Stuttgart on 27 May 1857. He illustrated the pictorial cover of *Bur und Lord* (Eugen Salzer, Heilbronn, 1900), a German novel about the War based on the diary of an English officer. The author of the book remained anonymous.

Bénézit, Dictionnaire antique, *vol. 4, p. 612*
SABIB, *vol. 1, p. 331*

HAYWARD, Lucy Pearson
A work by Lucy Hayward can be found in the Exeter Museum collection. An oil on canvas entitled *Her Majesty's last recruit,* it is inscribed, signed and dated 'L.P. Hayward 1901' at the bottom right. The picture shows a man in khaki trousers, green jumper and khaki bush hat trimmed with red, white and blue ribbons sitting on a table in a room with the newspaper on the table and a recruiting picture on the wall for 'V.R. Regular Army'. A note in the museum's catalogue indicates 'that this probably refers to "just normal" army recruitment and he supposedly being the last soldier recruited before Queen Victoria's death'. The painting was presented to the museum by the artist herself.

Personal communication with the Curator, Exeter Museum

H.E.
The illustration entitled *A blow for a fallen friend: a scene at the Modder River* by an artist using these initials was redrawn by Sydney Hall and reproduced in *The Graphic* on 31 March 1900. The original artist may have been Heinrich Egersdörfer (see page 130).

Hofmeyr, Matton and Roets, Graphic Picture Index

HEDLEY, Ralph 1848-1913
Portrait, landscape and genre painter. Hedley was born in Richmond, Yorkshire, in 1848. He studied at the Newcastle Art School and exhibited at the Royal Academy from 1874. In 1900 his *The Reservist's wife* was shown at the Royal Academy.

Graves, Royal Academy, *vol. 4, p. 61*
Johnson and Greutzner, British Artists, *p. 240*
Waters, British Artists, *vol. 1, p. 157*

---

1 *Lord Kitchener's Home-coming,* a photogravure by William Hatherell, was offered free by the makers of Bovril to consumers who collected coupons provided with their product. The print was a companion to J. F. Bacon's *The Relief of Ladysmith.*
2 John Hassall.
3 John Hassall produced this rare cartoon of Kruger and his 'millions' for *The King* on 15 December 1900.
4 William Hatherell's illustration *There are girls he walked with casual,* which he donated to the Royal Edition of Rudyard Kipling's War poem 'The Absent Minded Beggar'.
5 This pen-and-ink cartoon by Hungarian Sandor Hatos shows a wounded British Lion licking his Queen's chocolate. The New Year's gift of chocolates by Queen Victoria to her troops in South Africa was a source of amusement to many European cartoonists. Reproduced courtesy the Mendelssohn Collection, Library of Parliament, Cape Town.

1

2

HEIDBRINCK, Oswald 1860-1914
Caricaturist. Heidbrinck was born in Bordeaux in 1860. He studied art under Bonat. He worked for *L'Assiette au Beurre*, *Le Courrier Français*, *Chat Noir*, *Mirliton*, *La Vie Parisienne* and *Le Charivari*. During the War his work appeared in *Le Gavroche* and *La République Illustrée*. Heidbrinck died in Paris on 5 March 1914.
Osterwalder, and Hubschmid and Bouret (eds.), Dictionnaire des Illustrateurs, p. 486

HEINE, Thomas Theodor 1867-1948 2
Graphic artist, illustrator and poster artist. Heine was born in Leipzig on 28 February 1867. He studied at the Düsseldorf Academy where he was a pupil of Jansen. His work showed a strong element of the grotesque and fantastic. Heine was a regular contributor to *Simplicissimus*, *Fliegende Blätter* and *Jugend*, and he is believed to have been one of the founders of the first-mentioned magazine.

Some of Heine's Boer War cartoons from *Simplicissimus* were reproduced in *Burenkrieg, Neue Burenkrieg* and *John Bull Sur la Sellette* and on a series of postcards. He contributed over 2 500 drawings to *Simplicissimus* and his work appeared on the front cover more than that of any other artist. Sidney Mendelssohn comments on his 'obscene and lewd' cartoons of Queen Victoria in *John Bull Sur la Sellette*, describing him as a 'notorious Anglophobe'.

Heine signed his work with a distinctive monogram. His anti-Nazi activities forced him to leave Germany in 1933 when Hitler came to power and he emigrated to Prague. He died in Stockholm in 1948 when in 1945 he had published his memoirs, *I am waiting for miracles*.
Barnicoat, Art Nouveau Posters and Prints, pp. 180-181
Bénézit, Dictionnaire antique, vol. 4, p. 640
Feaver, Masters of Caricature, p. 130
Lucie-Smith, Art of Caricature, pp. 93-94
Mendelssohn, Mendelssohn's Bibliography, vol. 1, p. 624

HELOURE RINS, P.
The illustration on a pro-Boer postcard published by A.B., Paris, entitled *La Paix en Marche*, was done by this artist.

HELYAR, C.W.H.
Helyar was a lieutenant colonel commanding a battalion of Imperial Yeomanry. Two illustrations by him appeared in *The Graphic* in May and August 1902, both showing Boer P.O.W.s. Considering the subject of the illustrations, it is possible that Helyar was stationed in Bermuda and in charge of one of the P.O.W. camps there.
Hofmeyr, Matton and Roets, Graphic Picture Index

HENCKE, A.J.
Hencke was one of the illustrators responsible for some of the illustrations in Israel Smith Clare's *British Boer War*. The author claims that 'none of these illustrations can be found in any other publication as they have been drawn by our special artists from photographs and personal descriptions of the scenes portrayed at an expense of many thousands of dollars ... the entire work is unique'. This is obviously untrue as the illustrations are almost without exception plagiarized from contemporary French, German and British newspapers.

HENNESSEY, Richard
Hennessey was a lieutenant in the 2nd Gordon Highlanders who was besieged at Ladysmith. *The Sketch* reproduced eight of Hennessey's pencil sketches, entitled *Scenes in beleaguered Ladysmith*, done in 1899. *The Sketch* remarked 'on the very morning when England heard with unbounded satisfaction of Sir George White's noble victory at Ladysmith a number of sketches of the beleaguered town itself came to hand from Lieutenant Richard Hennessey of the 2nd Gordon Highlanders (wounded at Elandslaagte) who in a letter particularly desired that *The Sketch* should reproduce them in its pages. The editor takes this opportunity of congratulating the gallant officer upon his enterprise and *The Sketch* renders on the realistic glimpses of the besieged garrison that they thus obtain'. Two of his illustrations appeared in *The Illustrated London News* on 29 September and 20 October 1900. Richard Caton Woodville and Henry Seppings Wright respectively redrew these illustrations.
De Wet, Illustrated London News Index
The Sketch, vol. 29, 17 Jan. 1900

HENRIOT, Henri Maigrot 1857-? 1
Painter and caricaturist. Henriot was born in Toulouse, France, in 1857. He worked extensively for *La République Illustrée, L'Illustration* and *Le Journal Amusant*. In 1890 he was made a director of *Le Charivari*. Henriot's Boer War work appeared mainly in *Le Charivari*, including the special edition of *Le Charivari* Album: *Boers et Anglais*. He produced a weekly comic strip in *La Semaine Illustrée*, entitled 'La Semaine Amusante'. Henriot occasionally signed his work just with the initial 'H'.
Bénézit, Dictionnaire antique, vol. 4, p. 660

HENS, Frans 1856-?
Marine painter and engraver. Hens was born in Antwerp on 1 August 1856. He was a founder of the Society of Thirteen there. His Boer War work is found in *Antwerpen-Transvaal Gedenknummer*, the Belgian publication in aid of concentration camp victims. Hens served on the committee of this publication.
Bénézit, Dictionnaire antique, vol. 4, p. 663

HERING, E.
An American illustrator who was responsible for some of the illustrations in *The South African War* by Capt. A.T. Mahan.

HERKOMER, Hubert (von) 1849-1914
Herkomer was born in Waal, Bavaria, on 26 May 1849, and he and his family emigrated to England in 1857. From 1866 he studied art at the South Kensington School. In 1883 he founded the Herkomer School of art at Bushey. Between 1885 and 1894 he was the Slade Professor of Art at Oxford.

Herkomer was a prolific illustrator and contributed to *The Illustrated London News, The Graphic, The Quiver, Good Words for the Young, The Cornhill Magazine, London Society, The Sunday Magazine, Black & White* and *Fun*. He also illustrated Hardy's *Tess of the d'Urbervilles* in 1891.

Herkomer was a very influential and sought-after painter in Victorian times: he became an A.R.A. in 1879 and an R.A. in 1907, the same year he was knighted. Kaiser Wilhelm honoured him in 1899 by allowing him to add 'von' to his name.

His *Autobiography* was published in 1890. His more than 50 Royal Academy exhibits included: *General H.R.H. The Duke of Connaught K.G.* (1900); *The Earl of Albemarle CB MVO Lieut. Colonel commanding City Imperial Volunteers, South Africa* (1902); and *Maj. General R.S.S. Baden-Powell, CB* (1903). The National Portrait Gallery has a painting of 'Kitchener of Khartoum' done in 1890. The National Army Museum has reproduced this painting on a postcard.
Graves, Royal Academy, vol. 4, p. 85
Houfe, British Illustrators and Caricaturists, p. 339
Mallalieu, British Watercolour Artists, p. 133
Who was Who, vol. 1, pp. 333-334

HERLE, D.
An artist by this name did illustrations for Cassell's Publications.

HERMANN-PAUL 1874-1940
Painter, poster artist and illustrator. Hermann-Paul was the pseudonym used by René Georges Hermann-Paul. Born in Paris in 1874, he was a follower of Paul Cézanne and a member of the Salon des Humoristes. Hermann-Paul's Boer War contributions consist of cartoons which appeared in the French publications *Le Figaro, Le Petit Brayon Illustré* and *L'Illustré National*. On 9 October 1915 *The Graphic* reviewed an exhibition of French anti-German cartoons at the Leicester Galleries in London which featured, among others, Hermann-Paul's work, often signed with a distinctive monogram or the initials 'HP'. He died in Paris in July 1940.
Bénézit, Dictionnaire antique, vol. 4, p. 672
Osterwalder, and Hubschmid and Bouret (eds.), Dictionnaire des Illustrateurs, pp. 496-497

HERON, Roderick
Cartoonist for the Cape Town-based magazine, *The Telephone*. Heron's Boer War cartoons were reproduced in *Review of Reviews* vol. 20, July–December 1899.
Schoonraad, S.A. Cartoonists, p. 161

HESS, J.B.
Hess provided a sketch for an illustration which was redrawn by D.C. Boonzaier for *The Telephone*.

HESTER, Edward Gilbert ?-1903
Engraver. Hester exhibited more than 20 items at the Royal Academy. In 1902 his *In time of War*, after a painting by G.D. Leslie, was exhibited there.
Graves, Royal Academy, vol. 4, p. 90
Johnson and Greutzner, British Artists, p. 245

HEWERDINE, Matthew Bede 1871-1909 1
Book illustrator and artist. Hewerdine was born in Hull in 1871. He later worked there and in Oxford, and at one time for *Gentlewoman*, but Thorpe says 'he could not be considered a good draughtsman'.

Hewerdine is best known for his illustrations in *Lest we Forget Them*, compiled by Lady E. Glover and published by The Fine Art Society and by Simkin, Marshal, Hamilton, Kent and Co. Ltd. in London in 1900. The profits on the sale of this

3

work were donated to the 'Fund for the Relief of the Widows and Orphans of our Sailors and Soldiers'.

Hewerdine's work also appeared in *St George's Gazette*, the regimental journal of the Northumberland Fusiliers. An editorial in *St George's Gazette* on 30 April 1902 said 'Lt. H.B. Hewerdine (sic) of the 4th Volunteer Battalion the King's Royal Rifle Corps has kindly offered his services and joined our staff. Two pictures by him appear in this number, one 'Old and Bold' will be seen illustrating Depôt Notes, (p. 64) whilst the other 'St. George's Day 1838' occupies p. 74. Both pictures as will be seen possess much artistic merit, and we take this opportunity of thanking Mr Hewerdine for his kind assistance, feeling sure that his efforts will be appreciated. We hope he has many more pictures in store for us.' In spite of the incorrect initial the signature on the illustration is the one used by M.B. Hewerdine.

He also illustrated William Stables' *On War's Red Tide: A tale of the Boer War* (James Nisbet, London, 1900) and C. Reade's *Cloister and the Hearth* in 1904. The six postcard illustrations in C.W. Faulkner & Co.'s 24 series were all done by the same hand. The two signed 'MBH' are *Scots wha hae* and *News from the front*. Hewerdine often used his initials in his drawings and it is almost certain that these illustrations were done by him. In addition Hewerdine was known to have done the 108 and 109 series (*Typical Dancers* and *New Pierrots*) by the same company.

Byatt, Picture Postcards, *p. 345*
Houfe, British Illustrators and Caricaturists, *p. 340*
Mallalieu, British Watercolour Artists, *p. 133*
SABIB, *vol. 2, p. 358* and *vol. 4, p. 373*
St George's Gazette, *30 April, 1902*
Thorpe, English Illustration, *p. 75*

HICKSON, Robert Albert 1848-1934

Soldier-artist. Hickson was born in Ballintaggart, Ireland, on 15 September 1848. He was responsible for some of the pre-Boer War sketches, done in 1876, which can be found in the Africana Museum's collection. He is reputed to have worked for *The Illustrated London News* and *The Graphic*. He was in South Africa during the Boer War, but no works of his to do with that conflict can be traced. Later in his career he became a brigadier general. Hickson commanded the Buffs and saw action at Paardeberg (in command of the 13th Brigade), at

the relief of Kimberley, and at Driefontein. For his actions in the last-mentioned engagement he received a mention in despatches and Queen's medal with four clasps. He was awarded the C.B. in 1900 and the D.S.O. in 1917.

Kennedy, Pictures in the Africana Museum
Who was Who, *vol. 3, p. 636*

HIGGINS, Herbert

A soldier by this name was responsible for four sketches which were redrawn by W.B. Robinson and appeared on 28 April 1900 in *The Illustrated London News*. These illustrations were entitled *Views from the Rhodesian armoured train (in Bechuanaland)*.

De Wet, Illustrated London News Index

HIGHAM, B.

Soldier-artist. Trooper Higham was probably a member of the Imperial Yeomanry. Two sketches by him appeared in *The Graphic*: *With the 62nd Imperial Yeomanry: their first fight, twenty miles from Kroonstad* (1 September 1900) and *The Imperial Yeomanry hospital at Deelfontein: Lunch time in the convalescent camp* (27 October 1900). It is possible that this artist was the Bernard Higham (fl. 1895-1925) who, according to Houfe, later became an illustrator and exhibitor at the Royal Academy.

Hofmeyr, Matton and Roets, Graphic Picture Index
Houfe, British Illustrators and Caricaturists, *p. 340*

HIGHAM, Sydney fl. 1890-1905

Postcard and comic artist in black and white. Higham worked for a number of magazines and contributed to *The Daily Graphic*, *The Penny Illustrated Paper* and *The Graphic*.

Just after the Jameson Raid, in February 1896, Higham was sent by *The Graphic* to Las Palmas to meet Jameson and his henchmen who were being deported to England aboard the *Harlech Castle*. His sketches done on board the vessel were published in facsimile. One of his sketches, published on 29 February 1896, was entitled *Jameson's men on their way home on board the Harlech Castle*.

Higham's Boer War work was done probably as a home-based outside artist for *The Graphic*. One illustration, which appeared on 8 December 1900 and had been redrawn by

Frederic de Haenen, was entitled *Three cheers for the Queen: the Canadian troops from South Africa at Windsor*.

Higham visited Canada in 1904 to report on immigration to that country for *The Graphic*. The articles were entitled *An artist's tour through Canada*. According to Houfe, he may have emigrated to Canada in about 1905. He is classified as a Western artist.

Hofmeyr, Matton and Roets, Graphic Picture Index
Houfe, British Illustrators and Caricaturists, *p. 340*
Samuels, Artists of the American West, *p. 224*

HILL, F. Jeffrey

Hill was probably in Johannesburg during the Boer War. He supplied nine illustrations to *The Graphic* that were redrawn by home-based artists. Two of his illustrations showed shipping scenes in Lourenço Marques, indicating that at an early stage of the War he might have been in the town.

The Africana Museum has an original pen-and-ink drawing by Hill entitled 'The fort search light Johannesburg answering the search light to the South of the town over the Race Course'. The illustration was published on 28 October 1899.

Hill's original work also appeared in *The Golden Penny* (24 February, 1900) and *The Daily Graphic*.

Hofmeyr, Matton and Roets, Graphic Picture Index
Kennedy, Pictures in the Africana Museum, *vol. 3, p. 156*

HILL, Rowland 1873-1925

British cartoonist who used the pseudonym 'RIP'. Hill was born in Halifax in 1873. He studied art at Bradford School of Art and at the Herkomer School in Bushey. Hill went to South Africa in 1910 to be a cartoonist for *The Rand Daily Mail*. He only stayed for a year.

Hill's work can be found in *Black & White*, *Truth* and *The Sketch*. In the last-mentioned magazine one cartoon has been noted: entitled *From Bobs to Kruger with best wishes for a Happy Easter*, it was published in vol. 29, p. 569 on 18 April 1900. *The Evening News* also published the occasional 'RIP' Boer War cartoon. The Africana Museum has two cartoons by 'RIP', one dated before the Boer War (1896) and the other 1910.

Houfe, British Illustrators and Caricaturists, *p. 434*
Kennedy, Pictures in the Africana Museum, *vol. 3, p. 156*

HILLINGFORD, Robert Alexander 1828-? 1

Historical painter. Hillingford was born in London in 1828. He studied art in Düsseldorf and Munich. He lived in Italy for many years and returned to London in 1864 when he exhibited at the Royal Academy for the first time. Over 18 of his paintings appeared at the Royal Academy up to 1902. His oeuvre included many battle pictures, mostly with a historical flavour.

His only Boer War work at the Royal Academy, exhibited in 1901, was entitled *South Africa 1901: The dawn of Peace*. This picture shows Lord Roberts seated on his horse in the centre surrounded by troops and nurses, with Boers in the right foreground being pursued by British soldiers. The painting was illustrated on p. 91 of *Royal Academy Pictures* (1901).

Hillingford's chromolithographic plate *Farewell*, an emotional station departure scene, was published by *Black & White*.

Graves, Royal Academy, *vol. 4, p. 105*
Royal Academy Pictures, *1901*
Waters, British Artists, *vol. 1, p. 163*

---

1 Thomas Heine's *Simplicissimus* cartoon postcard no. 27, *England's Traum in Sud Afrika*, shows Queen Victoria plucking ostriches. This particular card was addressed to President Kruger c/o Dr George Hirth, the editor of *Jugend*.
2 M.B. Hewerdine, who probably served in South Africa with the Northumberland Fusiliers, drew the illustrations for this series of postcards for C.W. Faulkner & Co.
3 Robert Hillingford's 1901 Royal Academy exhibit *South Africa 1901: The dawn of Peace*.

1

HIRST, Norman 1862-1956
Mezzotinter and engraver. Hirst was born in Liverpool in 1862. He studied with Herkomer at Bushey and eventually became an A.R.E. in 1931. Of his 44 exhibits at the Royal Academy, *The Capture* (1902), after Herbert Draper, may well be of Boer War relevance.
Graves, Royal Academy, *vol. 4, p. 111*
Johnson and Greutzner, British Artists, *p. 250*
Waters, British Artists, *vol. 1, p. 164*

HOBHOUSE, Emily 1860-1926 1
Emily Hobhouse was a well-known British humanitarian who was active both during and after the Boer War. She drew the attention of the British public to the plight of Boer prisoners and concentration camp inmates.

She was born in St Ives, Cornwall, on 4 April 1860. From 1895 until September 1896 Emily devoted herself to working among Cornish miners who had emigrated to the U.S.A. She was engaged for a short while to an American businessman, but the engagement was broken off in 1898. In that year she started working for the Women's Industrial Committee in London and studied the position of the child in English society from the beginning of the Industrial Revolution.

Emily Hobhouse became associated with the South African Conciliation Committee which attempted to reconcile the differences between the Imperialists and the Afrikaners. At the request of her uncle, Leonard H. Courtney M.P., she became secretary of the women's branch of the committee. When the implications of the British 'scorched earth' policy in the latter half of 1900 became apparent, she became determined to

Sieg!

2

Lith. K. Anst. v. Hub. Köhler, München, Buchwaren 13.

Anton HOFFMANN, München

to take steps to alleviate the distress which this policy was causing to civilians. In September 1900 she asked permission to form a non-political, non-sectarian Benevolent Fund to help Boer, British and other women in South Africa. She collected £300 in Britain and decided to visit South Africa herself.

Arriving in Cape Town on 27 December 1900, Emily Hobhouse got permission from Lord Kitchener and Sir Alfred Milner to visit the camps. She left Cape Town on 22 January 1901. She gave a great deal of encouragement to the inhabitants of the refugee camps, promising to do whatever she could to improve the conditions in which they were languishing. On 7 May 1901 she sailed from Cape Town on the same ship as Milner who was returning home on leave. Milner had promised to help her, but after receiving no assistance from him and acting on the advice of her brother and other prominent Liberals, she decided to take her case to higher authorities. She arrived in England on 24 May 1901 and ten days later had an interview with the Secretary of State for War, John Brodrick.

Emily Hobhouse also met the Liberal leader Sir Henry Campbell-Bannerman and there can be no doubt that it was her description of the conditions in South Africa which prompted him to use the phrase 'methods of barbarism' that same evening in a speech which had wide political repercussions. Following the report of the committee of the Distress Fund, the government sent a commission of women led by Millicent Fawcett to investigate conditions in the camps. Emily Hobhouse was not invited to join this committee as she was considered to be biased towards the Boers. She returned to South Africa at the beginning of October 1901, accompanied by her personal maid, Elizabeth Phillips. She was refused permission to go to the front and placed under arrest when she landed in Cape Town on 27 October, and, as she refused to re-board the ship to return to England, she was forcibly put aboard a troopship and taken to Europe. On her return she considered instituting legal action against Kitchener and the military authorities, but her counsel advised against it. She succeeded in focusing attention on the conditions in the concentration camps, and the consequent wave of indignation in Britain and other countries played an important part in forcing the authorities to make improvements.

Emily Hobhouse spent April 1902 at the French resort of Talloires where she wrote *The Brunt of the War and Where it Fell*. She returned again to South Africa after the War in May 1903 and she travelled extensively through the conquered republics, trying to draw the attention of the authorities to the tardy payment of compensation. It was at this time that she produced the watercolours of ruins of churches and farms which are now in the War Museum of the Boer Republics in Bloemfontein. She returned once again to South Africa in February 1905 and established the first spinning and weaving school, at Philippolis in the Orange River Colony. During and after World War I she was also engaged in relief work, chiefly in connection with the Save the Children Fund.

She also prepared a collection of short narratives about the War and these were published after her death as *War without Glamour* (London, 1927). The originals of some of the illustrations that she had used can be found in the War Museum of the Boer Republics, Bloemfontein.

The watercolours which Emily Hobhouse donated to the Bloemfontein war museum are as follows (each carries a comment in her handwriting on the reverse):
1. *Ruins of Dullstroom church*. Inscription: 'Ruin of Dullstroom Church in Transvaal as left by the British troops. Sketched by me in 1903 in winter time.'
2. *Ruin of the farm Enkeldoorn*. Inscription: 'Farm Enkeldoorn between Roos-Senekal and Witpoort — Transvaal where I slept in the stable not far off in the late winter of 1903. It is early *sunrise*. The house is a long way off — it is a large one — with a frontage of about 70 feet.'
3. *Ruin of the church at Lindley*. Inscription: 'Lindley church after destruction by the British Troops. It had taken £4,000.00 to build it. The whole town was destroyed — I slept there on a sheet of corrugated iron in 1903.'
4. *Ruin of General de Wet's farmhouse*. Inscription: 'The ruin of de Wet's farm as left by the British army and as sketched by me in 1903 when I stayed with him and Mrs de Wet in the bare new building they had hastily put up. The house was first burnt and then dynamited. Fruit trees all cut down in and around the garden where you see the remains of barley and mealies. His 6 cows are about 2 miles off.'
5. *Cemetery at Brandfort concentration camp*. Inscription: 'Graveyard of the concentration camp at Brandfort OFS. The ground newly turned up is red and becomes gradually yellow as it dries. Sketched by me in 1903.'
6. *A scene near Thaba'nchu OFS*. Inscription: 'Scenes in the Free State near Thaba'nchu looking towards Springkaansnek. Sketched by me in 1903.'
7. *Graveyard of Middelburg concentration camp, Transvaal*. Inscription: 'Graveyard of the Concentration Camp at Middelburg — when the sun had just set and the moon had risen. Sketched in the Transvaal winter of 1903 by me.'
8. *The ruin of the farm "Wonderhoek" Transvaal*. Inscription: 'Farm Wonderhoek — Transvaal near Witpoort. The red ruins stand in ground still blackened by the flames of the destroying army. The story of the destruction is told by Mrs v. d. Berg. Sketched by me in the *early* Transvaal spring of 1903.'
9. *Ruin of the farm Bultfontein O.F.S.* Inscription: 'Farm Bultfontein — Martiens Rheeder — on Modder River between Bloemfontein and Boshoff — as I saw it in 1903. The adjoining stable had been patched up for use — is seen on the left. I slept in a lean to at the back of the burnt house.'
10. *Ruin of a farm nearby Roos-Senekal*. Inscription: 'A farm near Roos-Senekal in Transvaal where I passed the night in 1903, as left by the British troops. Sketched by me in very early Spring.'
11. *Ruin of the farm Kruger's Drift (near Bloemfontein)*. Inscription: 'Kruger's Drift. A burnt farm on the Modder River. Sketched by me in 1903. (June).'

The illustrations used in *War without Glamour* include:
1. *Witpoort, the burnt farm of Mrs van den Berg*.
2. *A farm near Roos-Senekal*.
3. *Moonrise in the burial ground of Middelburg camp*.

Emily Hobhouse died on 8 June 1926. Her ashes were brought back to South Africa where they were buried at the foot of the Women's Monument, Bloemfontein, one of the most sacred shrines of Afrikanerdom.
Bloemfontein War Museum Catalogue
De Kock (ed.), DSAB, vol. 2, p. 306

HODGSON, Michael R.K.
Hodgson was a 2nd lieutenant in the 2nd Royal Fusiliers, City of London Regiment. His Boer War illustrations appeared in *The Graphic*, as well as *The Illustrated London News*, in which four redrawn illustrations were published between 2 June and 25 August 1900.
Army List, *Feb. 1900, p. 576*

3

De Wet, Illustrated London News Index
Hofmeyr, Matton and Roets, Graphic Picture Index

HOEK, Henri Frits Marie 1877-1901
Hoek was born in Leyden on 8 May 1877. He worked mainly in The Hague, where he contributed to *Tabaksnieuws*. He died there on 25 August 1901.
Scheen, Nederlandse Beeldende Kunstenaars, *vol. 1*

HOFFMANN, Anton 1863-? 1
Book illustrator. Hoffmann was born in Bavaria on 10 April 1863. He exhibited in Berlin in 1909 and spent a great deal of time in Munich. Hoffmann illustrated five publications related to the War:
1. *Der Burenkrieg in Bild und Wort* by Fritz Bley (1901).
2. Associated with Fritz Bergen, the German illustrated edition of General Ben Viljoen's *Die Transvaaler im Krieg mit Engeland: Kriegserinnerungen von General Ben Viljoen* (1902).
3. *Die Buren in der Kap Kolonie im Kriege Mit England* by A.G. De Wet (1902).
4. *Präsident Steijn: ein Lebensbild* by Frederick Rompel (1902).
5. *Mit den Burenkommandos im Felde* by J.D. Kestel (1902).
   Hoffmann's illustrations also appeared on at least five chromolithographical postcards published in early 1900 by Hub Köhler, 13 Bluthenstrasse, Munich: 1. *Vorwarts*; 2. *Verwundert*; 3. *Sieg*; 4. *Im Feuer*; 5. *Artillerie*.
SABIB, *vol. 2, p. 573*

HOFMEYR, Adriaan Jacobus Louw 1854-1937
Hofmeyr was a Cape-born Afrikaner clergyman who was arrested by the Boers on 11 October 1899, just after the outbreak of the War, while he was in Lobatse in Bechuanaland. He was suspected of being a traitor to the Boer cause when correspondence found on him was deemed to be pro-British and anti-Boer. He persuaded his captors that he was not a spy and avoided the threatened summary execution; nevertheless he was taken to Pretoria where he was imprisoned at the Model School with British prisoners. Hofmeyr eventually wrote *The Story of My Captivity* (Edward Arnold, London, 1900). He also made contributions to *The Gram* magazine. These contributions were literary and possibly pictorial.
   In his book Hofmeyr describes why the paper was called

The Gram. The name referred to the sources of the information they received; that from the black servants which was called 'Kaffirgrams' (sic), and there were also 'Butchergrams', 'Bakergrams', 'Hospitalgrams' etc. The production of the paper gave much work to the publisher and great excitement to the prisoners. The first number appeared on 12 May 1900 and the illustrations, Hofmeyr claimed, compared 'favourably with the cartoons and pictures of any published paper'. Two full numbers were published and the third number was well in hand when they were released from their camp. The editor, Lord Rosslyn, realizing the interest which the newspaper had generated, arranged for a facsimile of the published numbers to be re-published.
   Hofmeyr also mentions in his book that the editors persuaded the caterer to advertise and, being the only advertiser, he was given a full page for the sum of £5 sterling.
   Hofmeyr was released when the British entered Pretoria on 5 June 1900 and travelled by way of Lourenço Marques back to the Cape.
The Gram
SABIB, *vol. 2, p. 575*

HOGG, H. Arthur
Boer War illustrations by Hogg appeared in *The Illustrated Mail*. Hogg also worked for *Punch* and *Fun* up to 1907.
Houfe, British Illustrators and Caricaturists, *p. 341*

HOLDING, J. W.
This individual may have been a photographer. He is responsible for two illustrations which appeared in *The Graphic*:
1. *The British influence among the natives in South Africa: a wedding in native high life in Zululand*. It was redrawn by Frank Dadd, and appeared on 14 October 1899. 2. *Black element in Natal: collecting the hut and dog taxes*. Redrawn by Frank Dadd, 16 December 1899.
Hofmeyr, Matton and Roets, Graphic Picture Index

HOLLOWAY, Edgar A.
British illustrator of military subjects who became well known for his military postcards, especially those published by Gale & Polden. At one time he worked for *The Regiment*.
   Holloway illustrated Jesse Page's *Christians in Khaki* (Marshall Bros., 1900) and Owen Vaughn's Boer War novel

Old Fireproof: being the Chaplain's Story (by 'Owen Rhoscomyl' [pseudonym], Duckworth, 1912). Occasional illustrations by Holloway appeared in *Shurey's Illustrated* and *Shurey's Pictorial Budget*. Some of these were signed 'EAH'.
Byatt, Picture Postcards
SABIB, *vol. 4, p. 647*

HOLLOWAY, W. H. ?-1919
One illustration by this artist appeared on p. 60 of *The Graphic* special double number and is entitled *Cronje's men arriving at prison at Cape Town*. The illustration is signed with a monogram. An artist with these initials is listed in Johnson and Greutzner with the annotation that he exhibited in 1919 at the Walker Art Gallery in Liverpool. Houfe lists a Herbert Holloway as having illustrated *Fairy Tales from South Africa* (1908).
Houfe, British Illustrators and Caricaturists, *p. 342*
Johnson and Greutzner, British Artists, *p. 254*

HOLMES, T. W. 1
Illustrator for *The Penny Illustrated Paper*. The author has an illustration, signed by Holmes, entitled *At bay Spionkop: January the 24th*. This illustration must have been done for *The Penny Illustrated Paper*, as the letters 'P.I.P.' appear on the reverse. Holmes's address also appears on the back as 'Oxford Villas Shipperton on Thames', indicating that he might have been working as a freelance artist for this paper. Thorpe mentions that he also worked for *Chums*.
   Holmes did an illustration of White and Dundonald meeting in Ladysmith for *The Sketch* on 7 March 1900.
Thorpe, English Illustration

HOLYOAKE, Rowland fl. 1880-1917
British genre artist and portrait painter. Son of William Holyoake R.B.A., he exhibited over 20 paintings at the Royal Academy. Illustrations by him appeared in *The Quiver*.
   In 1984 Clarke's Bookshop (Cape Town) had a bound folio of 15 pen-and-ink drawings advertising 'Horlicks'. The drawings all had a Boer War theme. Facsimiles of these drawings have been reproduced in vol. 4 of *The British Empire*.
Bénézit, Dictionnaire antique, *vol. 4, p. 744*
Johnson and Greutzner, British Artists, *p. 256*

HOPKINS, Everard 1860-1928
Hopkins was born in Hampstead, London, in 1860 and educated at Charterhouse and the Slade School of Art. His illustrative work appeared in *The Graphic*, *The Illustrated London News*, *Black & White* and *Punch*. (His brother, Arthur, also worked for *Punch*.) It is in the last-named magazine that his very occasional Boer War cartoons appeared, including one on 6 February 1901 which featured Kitchener. According to Sidney Mendelssohn, Hopkins also provided one of his 'original' drawings for Edward Harold Begbie's *The handy man* (Lamley & Co., London, 1902). The other drawings in this six-page publication were by Richard Caton Woodville. Hopkins often used a monogram with initials 'E.H.'
Houfe, British Illustrators and Caricaturists, *p. 345*
Mendelssohn, Mendelssohn's Bibliography, *vol. 1, p. 109*
SABIB, *vol. 1, p. 161*
Who was Who, *vol. 2, p. 514*

---

1 *Ruin of the Farm Bultfontein, O.F.S*, by Emily Hobhouse. Reproduced by courtesy of the War Museum of the Boer Republics, Bloemfontein.
2 The German book illustrator Anton Hoffmann produced this stirring illustration of a mounted Boer, entitled *Sieg!* (Victory), for a postcard published by Hub Köhler of Munich.
3 A wash drawing by T. W. Holmes showing British soldiers at Spioenkop, published in *The Penny Illustrated Paper* on 3 February 1900.

HOPKINS, Livingston(e) ('Hop') 1846-1927   1

Cartoonist. Hopkins was born in Ohio, U.S.A., and served in the American Civil War. While working successfully as a cartoonist for *Wild Oats* in New York he was persuaded to join the staff of the *Sydney Bulletin*. He was appointed in 1882 on a three-year contract, but, as he liked the Australian climate, he stayed for over 20 years. He was the first staff artist to be employed by this paper. 'Hop', as he signed his cartoons, had a distinctive style and a keen perception of the comic possibilities of a political situation and did more than any other cartoonist to give the *Sydney Bulletin* its national character. He was not considered a good draughtsman but he had a high degree of humour and imagination and a well-developed sense of invention.

A cartoon taken from the *Sydney Bulletin* and entitled *An Australian View: The attempt to trap the Australian colonial troops, with land-grant bait, into permanent residence in South Africa*, was reproduced in *The King* on 27 October 1900.

Doris June Hopkins wrote a biography of her father entitled *Hop of the Bulletin* (Angus Robertson, Sydney, 1929). He died in New South Wales on 21 August 1927.

Feaver, Masters of Caricature, *p. 98*
The Strand, *vol. 23, pp. 658-659*
Who was Who, *vol. 2, 515*

HOUGHTON, J. H. fl. 1886-1900

Fun and *Judy* cartoonist. It is in the latter magazine that his Boer War cartoons and caricatures can be found. Occasionally Houghton signed with an elaborate 'JHH' monogram.

Houfe, British Illustrators and Caricaturists, *p. 346*
Judy, *29 Nov. 1899, p. 573*
Thorpe, English Illustration

HOWARD, S.

An illustrator by this name did Boer War illustrations for *Black & White Budget*.

HOYNCK VAN PAPENDRECHT, Jan 1858-1933   1

Illustrator, landscape and watercolour artist, and painter of military subjects. Hoynck was born in Amsterdam on 18 September 1858. He lived and worked in Amsterdam at first, and later in Rotterdam, Antwerp and Munich. Hoynck was responsible for *Gedenksboek Van het eeuwfeest der Rijdende Artillerie*. He was co-illustrator of L. Penning's *Die Verdedigers en Verdrukkers der Afrikaansch Vrijheid*. Several exhibitions of his work were held.

Hoynck worked for the Dutch periodical *Eigen Haard*, although during the War he was a regular contributor of pen drawings to *The Daily Graphic*. The author has the pen drawing, *Private Northumberland Fusiliers*, which was published in *The Daily Graphic* on 15 September 1899. Occasionally Hoynck's work was published in *The Graphic* which issued 10 of his illustrations as special prints from 1898 to 1903. From 1904 to 1907, however, his illustrations appeared regularly in this periodical.

Hoynck's work is found in many Dutch museums, including the Rijksmuseum. He died in The Hague on 11 December 1933.

Bénézit, Dictionnaire antique, *vol. 5, p. 7*
British Military Costume Prints, *p. 460*
Scheen, Nederlandse Beeldende Kunstenaars, *vol. 2, p. 521*

H.R.

This artist was responsible for a series of lithographed cartoons and postcards during the War. The cartoons include the following (some are hand coloured):
1. *Can I Venture (Veni vidi vici)* (not signed)
2. *Real Patriotic Randites* (signed 'HR')
3. *I Yield. Nil desperado* (not signed)
4. *Sagacity Activity Courage.* 'We'll run them in'. (not signed)
5. *I Made Railways (UNIQUE)* (not signed)

The postcard, *Our Volunteers C.I.V. Are you a boab!* (not signed), was taken from the top half of *Can I Venture*.

H.T.C.

A cartoonist using these initials drew several cartoons which appeared in *St George's Gazette*, the regimental journal of the Northumberland Fusiliers. One cartoon, which was entitled *Overheard near Thaba'N Chu during the late campaign*, shows Tommy Atkins and a Boer woman exchanging pleasantries. The original of this cartoon can be found in the National Army Museum. It appeared in vol. 20 of *St George's Gazette*, on 3 September 1982.

H.T.C. was probably Lt. H. T. Crispin of the Northumberland Fusiliers who reached that rank on 21 July 1895. He was promoted to captain on 17 February 1900. He returned to England on 21 January 1901. His return coincided with the appearance of H.T.C. cartoons and sketches, lending further credence to the identification of the artist as Crispin.

St George's Gazette, *vol. 19, p. 28 (28 Feb. 1901) and vol. 19, p. 206 (31 December, 1901)*

HURST, Henry William Lowe (Hal) 1865-1938

Portrait and genre painter and etcher. Hurst was born in London on 26 August 1865. Early in his career he went to the U.S.A., where he worked for *Philadelphia Press* and later for several New York newspapers. He returned to Europe and studied art at the Académie Julian in Paris and at the Royal Academy schools. He exhibited at the Royal Academy and was elected a member in 1898. Hurst's Boer War illustrations appeared in *Black & White Budget*. It is possible that he was the *Vanity Fair* caricaturist who used the *nom de crayon* 'How'. Hurst was well known for his comic postcards.

Matthews and Mellini, In Vanity Fair
The Sketch, *vol. 32, p. 18 (24 Oct. 1900)*
Who was Who, *vol. 3, pp. 683-684*

HUTCHISON, Robert Gemmell 1855-1936

Genre painter. Hutchison was born in Edinburgh in 1855. He studied at the Board of Manufacturers School of Art there. (He had previously studied as a seal engraver.) He exhibited at the R.S.A. from 1879 and at the Royal Academy from 1881. He was elected to the R.W.A. in 1895 and became an associate of the R.S.A. in 1901 and a full member in 1911.

Hutchinson's large oil (approximately 110 x 60 cm) depicting White and Buller meeting at the relief of Ladysmith, was offered for sale by the Everard Read Gallery in 1986. The asking price was R48 500.

Waters, British Artists, *vol. 1, p. 176*

HUTTON, R. W.

Judy cartoonist. The Africana Museum has an original pen-and-ink cartoon by Hutton featuring Joseph Chamberlain and John Bull. According to the vendor, C.J. Sawyer, the cartoon was published in *Judy* in 1902.

Kennedy, Pictures in the Africana Museum, *vol. 7, p. 24*

H.W.

Regel & Krug of Leipzig postcard illustrator. At least three cards were produced by this artist. Both Dutch and German variations have been noted. The titles are *Ohm Paul vom Burenkrieg* ('Oom Paul van den Boerenoorlog'), *Der Militärische Spaziergang der Engländer Nach Pretoria* ('De Militaire Plaiziertocht der Engelschen naar Pretoria') and *Durchgekende Maulesel: Die Ursache Der Englischen Niederlagen im Boerenkrieg* (Dutch caption, double card).

HYDE-KELLY, W.

The Royal Military Academy has two paintings by this artist:
1. A sepia wash drawing with touches of Chinese white, showing a blockhouse with horizontal loopholes and a corrugated iron pitched roof, protected by stone breastwork and a ditch, and surrounded by a double line of barbed wire. One soldier, in short sleeves with a bandolier and a sunhelmet, stands guard, while two others relax beside a camp fire with open tin cans and a boiling kettle. Six rifles are piled nearby in two sets of three. In the background another blockhouse can be seen, as well as the veld and the mountains.
2. Watercolour. Delagoa Bay, Christmas Day 1902. The painting depicts the harbour with three-masted sailing vessels, merchant steamers, and a British man-of-war with two buff funnels. Various buildings and a pier can be seen, as well as foliage and a butterfly in the foreground.

Personal communication with Dr T.A. Heathcote, Curatorial Officer, Royal Military Academy Collection, Camberley, England

IANTITZMAHIAS

An artist, probably of Greek origin, who contributed a pen-and-ink drawing to *Paris-Pretoria*. This illustration, which appeared on p. 13, was entitled *Dans les Camps de Reconcentration*.

IBBETSON, Ernest   1

Figure painter and postcard artist. Ibbetson, who lived in Yorkshire, had one painting exhibited at the Royal Academy in 1903. The Africana Museum has five pictures (numbered

3

I223 to I227) of military scenes by Ibbetson, who was commissioned by a Johannesburg collector of military prints and paintings, P. W. Cahill. Ibbetson became well known for his comic and military postcards and he collaborated with J. Mc-Neill (c.1909) in the Gale & Polden History and Tradition series of postcards. According to Byatt, Ibbetson was still producing illustrations for postcards up to the end of World War II.

The author has two Boer War wash drawings done by Ibbetson in 1900. They appeared in *The Penny Illustrated Paper* on 10 February 1900, on pages 83 and 89 respectively. The first was entitled *New South Wales Lancers caught in an ambush*. The other shows a panorama of Ladysmith with the Boer positions under attack by the relieving British forces and was done 'from a sketch by Melton Prior'.

Byatt, Picture Postcards
Johnson and Greutzner, British Artists, *p. 268*
Kennedy, Pictures in the Africana Museum, *vol. 7, p. 24*

INGRAM, Joseph Forsyth 1858-1923

The Durban museum has a series of 21 Boer War sketches done in northern Natal during the War by this Belfast-born artist. Ingram is better known, however, for the several books he wrote about Natal. He served in both the Zulu and Boer wars, in the latter as a field intelligence officer. He was appointed magistrate of Dundee (Natal) in 1903.

SABIB, *vol. 2, pp. 648-649*
Verbeek, Early Natal Art, *pp. 29-30*

INNES, H.

Judy cartoonist who signed his work with a distinctive 'IH' monogram.

I.R.F.

A watercolour (no. FI) by this unknown artist appears in the Africana Museum catalogue. The inscription on the top in pencil reads 'After Magersfontein' and it is signed 'I.R.F.'. On the back is written in ink: 'I am writing this to certify my delight in seeing it; being present when the actual copy of this was taken. I may here state that I belong to the Seaforth Highlanders and many of my intimate friends were laid in the trench (All for Queen and country) Sergeant William Mackenzie 2nd Seaforth Highlanders.'

Kennedy, Pictures in the Africana Museum, *vol. 3, p 66*

ISINGS, Johan Herman (jnr.) 1884-?

Isings was born in Amsterdam on 31 July 1884 and lived and worked in his native city. His Boer War related illustrations

appeared in Louwrens Penning's *De Overwinnaar van Nooitgedacht* (J. N. Voorhoeve, 1903). Two subsequent editions, one published as late as 1917, also used Isings's illustrations.

SABIB, *vol. 3, p. 649*
Scheen, Nederlandse Beeldende Kunstenaars, *vol. 1, p. 560*

ISLAY

Cape Town cartoonist whose work appeared in *The South African Review* towards the end of the War. Schoonraad records that Islay worked for *The Cape* in 1910.

Schoonraad, S.A. Cartoonists, *pp. 177-178*

JACARRIERE

A French artist who was responsible for the crudely drawn, coloured cover illustrations of the pro-Boer French songs *Gloire à Kruger* and *Gloire au President Kruger* (published by Leon Hayard). (The latter credits Hayard as co-artist of the picture as well as publisher.) The tune for both of the songs is given as *La Paimpolaise*. *Gloire à Kruger* shows the head of Kruger surrounded by oak and laurel leaves. The title *Gloire au President Kruger* is followed by the words 'Hommage à la reine Wilhelmine, Le Vieillard et la jeune fille, l'Union fait la force'. The illustration depicts Kruger and Queen Wilhelmina and the coat of arms of the Transvaal and Orange Free State and a head marked Gen. Cronje. Above the words 'Le Salut de la France, au Président Kruger' is the legend 'Arrivée du President Kruger en France'.

Africana Notes and News, *vol. 24, no. 6. (June 1981)*
'French Pro-Boer Songs' by Anna H. Smith

JACKSON, E.S.

Captain Jackson, possibly of the 6th Inniskilling Dragoons, was responsible for an illustration which appeared in *The Graphic* on 24 November 1900, entitled *The Dying Embers of the War: The final stage of the fight that led to the capture of Barberton*. His illustration was redrawn for publication by F. C. Dickinson. (The author has Dickinson's original drawing.) The same illustration was also reproduced in *Cassell's Illustrated History of the Boer War* and in *After Pretoria: the Guerilla War*.

Hofmeyr, Matton and Roets, Graphic Picture Index

JACKSON, F.S.

After Pretoria: the Guerilla War attributes a picture on p. 136 to F.S. Jackson. This is possibly a misprint and should be E. S. Jackson (see above).

JACKSON, Murray Cosby

A sergeant in the 7th Mounted Infantry, Murray Cosby Jackson wrote and illustrated *A Soldier's Diary, South Africa 1899-1901* (Max Goschen Ltd, 20 Great Russell St, London, W.C., 1913).

Jackson left Southampton with his colleagues aboard the P. and O. steamer, *Assaya*, some time after Christmas 1899. He was present at Jacobsal, Ramdam and Poplar Grove and entered Bloemfontein with Roberts. He also saw action at Diamond Hill and was with the occupying forces in Johannesburg and Pretoria. He later saw action with McDonald, and at Bultfontein. Jackson also took part in the operations against De Wet. Like many others he contracted typhoid but was fortunate enough to recover and to remain on the active list throughout the War. Jackson immigrated to South Africa after the War.

Jackson's book was based on manuscript notes and illustrations which he had sent back to his family in England. The publisher mentions in a preface that the author was offered a commission twice but declined. He apologizes for Jackson's expressive illustrations: 'if they should be subjected to an academic criticism which they were not expected to face, it should be mentioned that he has never had a drawing lesson in his life'.

SABIB, *vol. 2, p. 662*

JACOMB-HOOD, George Percy 1857-1929

Illustrator. Jacomb-Hood was born in Redhill, Surrey, on 6 July 1857. He was educated at Tonbridge School and the Slade School of Art, and under J. P. Laurent in Paris. He exhibited annually at the Royal Academy and at the Grosvenor Gallery from 1880 onwards. He was prolific in illustrating stories for *The Graphic* and *The Illustrated London News*. Jacomb-Hood was sent to Greece by *The Graphic* as correspondent to illustrate the first Modern Olympics in 1896, and to Delhi in 1902 for the Durbar accompanying the Prince of Wales. In 1905 and 1906 he returned to India, and went there once again in 1911 while on the staff of the King and Queen. He published *With Brush and Pencil: A Book of Reminiscences* (John Murray, 1925) and was responsible for the illustrations in several novels. He was an R.B.A., R.I., R.O.I., R.B.C., N.E.A.C. and M.V.O.

Jacomb-Hood's Boer War work appeared mainly in *The Graphic* and in *The Illustrated London News*. One of his illustrations appeared on the cover of *The Ladysmith Special Double Number* (2 April 1900). He often signed his work with a distinctive monogram. He died on 11 December 1929.

Peppin and Micklethwait, British Book Illustrators,
pp. 159-160
Who was Who, *vol. 3, p. 701*

J.A.D.

Initials of the unidentified illustrator who provided the illustration for the pictorial cloth cover of the eight volumes of Louis Creswicke's *South Africa and the Transvaal War*. The T. C. Jack of London and Edinburgh edition and the rarer Blackwood, Le Bas and Co. edition have a completely different cover illustration.

J.A.H.C.

The Africana Museum has an oil painting, *The Royal Horse Artillery in South Africa*, signed with the monogram 'J.A.H.C.'. The author has a similar untitled watercolour.

Kennedy, Pictures in the Africana Museum

---

1 'Hop' Hopkins produced this cartoon for the *Sydney Bulletin*, and it was later published in *The King* and *Harper's Weekly*. It satirizes official attempts to trap the Australian troops fighting in South Africa to become permanent residents there.
2 Jan Hoynck van Papendrecht, the Dutch artist produced this pen-and-ink sketch of a private in the Northumberland Fusiliers for *The Daily Graphic*, to which he contributed during the War.
3 Ernest Ibbetson's wash drawing *New South Wales Lancers caught in an ambush* was reproduced in *The Penny Illustrated Paper* on 10 February 1900.

JAMES, George E.
Judy cartoonist.

JAMES, Gilbert fl. 1886-1926
Illustrator. James was born in Liverpool where he later became friendly with the artist Sidney Sime. He moved to London in about 1892 and received a commission from *The Sketch*. At various times he worked for *The Butterfly, Ludgate Monthly, English Illustrated Magazine, The Idler* and *Pick-Me-Up*, as well as illustrating several books between 1900 and 1926. Thorpe praises his work as does Arthur Lawrence in an interview given in *The Idler* in 1900.

On 27 January 1900 *The Sphere* mentioned that 'Mr Gilbert James, another artist of considerable repute in a certain fantastic way, will, no doubt, give very striking illustrations of what he sees on South African battlefields, whither he has gone as a representative of the Artists' Corps in the City Imperial Volunteers'. A photograph of James appeared on the same page. On 20 October 1900 *The Sphere* published another photograph of James on p. 72 with the caption 'One of the C.I.V.'s Mr Gilbert James. Few people will recognise in his khaki uniform Mr Gilbert James, the brilliant decorative artist who has illustrated *Omar Khayyam* with such charm. Mr James, who is a member of the Artists' Corps, went out with the C.I.V.'s and was invalided home the other week from enteric fever'.

The records of the C.I.V. kept at the Guildhall Library make no mention of James's being invalided home from this disease. Their records do show a G. James, Private, aged 27, a draughtsman, enrolled on 4 February 1896. He was '4 years efficient with no knowledge of riding and he was number 323 in F. Company'.

Houfe, British Illustrators and Caricaturists, *p. 353*
Peppin and Micklethwait, British Book Illustrators, *p. 161*
The Sphere, *27 Jan. and 20 Oct. 1900*
Thorpe, English Illustration
Waters, British Artists, *vol. 2, p. 30*

JAMES, Lionel 1871-1955
Artist-correspondent; illustrator. James was the fourth son of Lt. Col. L. H. S. James, R. A. Lionel James was educated at Cranleigh and at the age of 17 went to India to become an indigo planter. He developed a gift for writing and he contributed to some of the Indian newspapers. He used the money he earned in this way for training horses and polo ponies and for racing. As the result of one particular race, however, he found himself, at the age of 24, compelled to sell his stable and look for some other means of livelihood.

James volunteered to represent Reuter's agency, *The Times of India* and *The Englishman* on the Chitral relief expeditions and was accepted. He became personally involved in the fighting at the Malakand Pass, and Reuter sent him on the Mohmund and Tirah expeditions and with Kitchener to Omdurman in 1898. He was unable to reach a permanent agreement with Reuter and was about to return to India in 1899, when he received an offer from Moberly Bell, manager of *The Times*, to become the newspaper's principal war correspondent in South Africa. Having been alerted to the fact that trouble was brewing in South Africa, James sailed on the *Tantallon Castle* from Southampton in mid-September 1899.

James arrived in Ladysmith on 6 October. He was present at the Battle of Elandslaagte and sent a very vivid account of this to *The Times* before the final retreat into Ladysmith, which cut off his communications for the duration of the siege.

In spite of this, James never lost any of his despatches, which were sent south by black runners. He did, however, issue his despatches in triplicate, sending each on a separate day. His colleague, Leo Amery, who eventually edited *The Times History of the War*, was stationed at Pietermaritzburg and he intercepted James's despatches and immediately telegraphed them to *The Times* in London.

The army headquarters in Ladysmith suggested that the newspaper correspondents should produce a newspaper and

Steevens, Maud, Maxwell and James formed themselves into a committee and produced a sheet which was known as *The Ladysmith Lyre*. Four issues of this newspaper appeared.

When Ladysmith was finally relieved, James wasted no time in riding through the Boer lines, reaching Buller's headquarters at Pieter's Hill. Buller was not sure that the siege had been lifted – his men had not yet signalled that they had occupied Bulwana Mountain – but he promised to send James's despatches as soon as he had official confirmation that the siege had ended. At this stage James had a disagreement with Winston Churchill who had believed that he was the first man out of Ladysmith and had expected that his despatches with *The Morning Post* would be given priority. Back in Pietermaritzburg James received instructions from *The Times* to join Lord Roberts as soon as possible as the newspaper's chief correspondent in the field.

In Bloemfontein James met Lord Roberts who had in fact known him previously and had the unenviable job of breaking the news of James's father's death to him. James snr. and Lord Roberts had served together in India many years before.

During their enforced two months' stay in Bloemfontein while Lord Roberts' forces were recuperating, James and a few other correspondents founded *The Friend*. He was also one of the few correspondents to be present at the Battle of Sanna's Post. From Bloemfontein he followed Roberts' Grand Army on to Johannesburg and Pretoria. As with most other correspondents, his head office believed that the War was now over and James was instructed to return home. On his arrival there he was asked to collaborate with Leo Amery in the writing of *The Times History of the War*, in particular volume 2. The continuing success of the Boer guerrillas, however, made *The Times* feel, unlike the other newspapers, that they still needed someone in South Africa and James was sent back. Early in January 1901 James returned on a Castle liner to Cape Town. Proceeding once again to De Aar, which was the scene of the operations against De Wet, he talked himself into an appointment as intelligence officer to Gen. Bethune and his mounted infantry. James spent 10 weeks with this outfit. His experiences with them formed the basis of the book which he later wrote under the pseudonym 'the Intelligence Officer', entitled *On the Heels of De Wet*. When Headquarters heard that James was doubling as a correspondent for *The Times* while acting as intelligence officer, he was dismissed. From Bloemfontein he finally went to Pretoria to cover the tentative peace negotiations then in progress. These negotiations were unsuccessful and he was finally ordered home, leaving South Africa in August 1901.

James continued to represent *The Times* for quite a few years and he was in Bulgaria and Greece for that paper before going to Japan and Manchuria to cover the Russo-Japanese War.

During World War I James was appointed in command of King Edward's Horse Regiment, which, under the name of the King's Colonials, had come into existence at the end of 1901. During the war he was mentioned in despatches twice and was awarded the D.S.O. and the Crown of Italy. James's love of horses later led to his becoming manager of a racing stable and stud farm between 1921 and 1931. Still later, in 1930, he was appointed Governor of the Imperial Service College, Windsor. He retired from public service in 1946 but made occasional broadcasts for the BBC.

Among his publications were 4 or 5 volumes of short stories; *With the Chitral Relief Force* (1895); *Indian Frontier War* (1897-8); *On the heels of De Wet* (1902); *The Boy Galloper* (1903); *The Yellow War* (1905); *A study of the Russo-Japanese War* (1906); *A subaltern of Horses* (1908); *Side Tracks and Bridle Paths* (1909); *With the conquered Turk* (1913); *The History of King Edward's Horse* (1921); *High Pressure* (1929); *Times of Stress* (1929); *Green Envelopes* (1929); as previously mentioned he collaborated on *The Times History of the War in South Africa*, volumes 2 and 3.

James's artistic contribution to the Boer War took the form of sketches which he sent from the front to *The Graphic* and *The Daily Graphic*. Many of these were used by other

papers and periodicals and appeared, redrawn by home-based artists, in *After Pretoria: the Guerilla War* as well. James mentions early in his book, *High Pressure*, that 'nature had equipped me with a useful pencil and, apart from my newspaper connection, a steady stream of handsome cheques came fluttering in from *The Graphic*.' This relationship with *The Graphic* lasted for many years. Over 27 of James's sketches were redrawn in *The Graphic* by, among others, Sydney Hall, Joseph Nash jnr., Fred Waugh, Frank Dadd, George Soper, W.T. Maud, S. A. Robinson and Fred Whiting. One of the most famous pictures by James was entitled *Only a Pawn*, which appeared, redrawn by Sydney Hall, in the *The Graphic* on 14 July 1900 (see page 141).

In spite of intensive efforts by the archivist of *The Times*, none of James's original sketches and drawings has as yet been traced. He was awarded the Queen's South Africa medal on 20 February 1903.

James died on 30 May 1955.
Creagh and Humphris, The D.S.O., *pp. 122 and 277*
Navy and Army Illustrated, *vol. 12, p. 319*
The Orders and Medals Research Society, *Summer 1986, 'War Correspondents: South Africa 1899-1902', by Patrick Street*
The Times (obituary), *1 and 3 June 1955*
Who was Who, *vol. 5, pp. 577-578*

JAMET, Jean
French cartoonist who worked for *La Caricature*. One coloured illustration by Jamet and entitled *Mieux Vaut Douceur* appeared on the cover of this magazine on 5 July 1902.

JANK, Angelo (also known as Janck) 1868-1940
Painter, postcard artist and cartoonist. Jank was born in Munich on 30 October 1868. He became a member of 'Die Scholle' group of artists in 1894. As a painter he received an honourable mention in 1900 and a medal at the Munich exhibitions in 1901 and 1905. Jank taught at the Ladies' Academy of the Munich Association of Lady Artists between 1899 and 1907. He worked as a cartoonist for *Jugend* and *Simplicissimus*. Jank was also known as an Art Nouveau postcard artist.

One cartoon of Boer War interest that is credited to Jank appeared in *Jugend* on 20 November 1901. The cartoon shows Britain being chained to South Africa while Germany, Russia, Greece and America are carving up Europe, China, Samoa, Nicaragua, Yangtse, Manchuria and parts of the Balkans.

Jank often signed his work with the initials 'A.J.'. He died in Munich on 9 October 1940.
Bénézit, Dictionnaire antique, *vol. 5, p. 119*
Fanelli and Godoli, Art Nouveau Postcards
Hofstätter, Art Nouveau Prints etc., *pp. 173-174*

JANSEN, DIRK 1
A Boer P.O.W. on St Helena, Jansen manufactured and decorated a framed chess board (39 x 39 cm) with squares 42 x 42 mm in size. Thirty-two watercolours were placed on the lighter sections of the board. It was given to Mr B.G. Verselewel de Witt Hamer, a fellow prisoner on the island. Mr de Witt Hamer had organized schools and carpentry facilities, ran the post office, organized church services and put on concerts for the prisoners. Similar boards made by Johannes Marte Mante have given rise to the speculation that Jansen may have been working under Mante's supervision. This board is in the author's collection. See pp. 165-166.
Quarterly Bulletin, *vol. 36, nos. 3 and 4 (March and June 1982), 'Some Artefacts and Curios made by Boer Prisoners of War' (Parts 1 and 2) by Frank R. Bradlow*

JANSEN, Hendricus ('Henricus') 1867-1921
Etcher, lithographer and illustrator. Jansen was born in The Hague on 2 January 1867. During the War he worked for *Die Nederlandsche Spectator*. Jansen died on 5 February 1921.
Scheen, Nederlandse Beeldende Kunstenaars, *vol. 1, p. 550*

JANSSENS, Joseph-Marie-Louis ('Joz') 1854-?
Historical and portrait painter. Janssens was born in St Nicholas, Belgium, in 1854. He was a pupil of Jean Saverts and d'Ittenbach. His Boer War contribution appeared in the *Antwerpen-Transvaal Gedenknummer*, which was published to commemorate an exhibition of paintings in Antwerp in March and April 1902. The proceeds were in aid of the 'unfortunate suffering women and children in the concentration camps in South Africa'.
  Bénézit, Dictionnaire antique, *vol. 5, p. 126*

JANZELOW, M.
Lustige Blätter cartoonist whose work was often featured on the cover of this magazine. One of Janzelow's cartoons appeared on the front cover of *Neue Burenstreiche*. He often signed his work with the initials 'M.J.'.

JAQUOT, L.
An illustration redrawn from a photograph by this artist appeared in *La Vie Illustrée*.

JAY, Harry R.
The Owl cartoonist who often signed his work with the initials 'H.R.J.'.

JEANNIOT, Pierre-Georges 1848-1934
Painter, engraver, illustrator and cartoonist. Jeanniot was born in Geneva of French parents on 2 July 1848. He was a member of the Society of French Artists. Jeanniot served in the French army from 1868 to 1881 and saw action in the Franco-Prussian War. His Boer War work, in the form of illustrations and cartoons, appeared in *Le Rire, Le Monde Illustré* and *L'Illustration*.
  Bénézit, Dictionnaire antique, *vol. 5, p. 138*
  Le Collectionneur Français, no. 201, p. 14 (May 1983)
  Who was Who, *vol. 3, p. 707*

JELLICOE, John F. fl.1865-1903
Figure painter and illustrator. Jellicoe worked for *The Illustrated London News, The Sporting and Dramatic News, Good Words, New Budget* and *Windsor Magazine*. His Boer War illustrations appeared in *Black & White, Under The Union Jack* and *The Battles of the British Empire*. Jellicoe often signed his work with the initials 'J.J.'.
  Houfe, British Illustrators and Caricaturists, *p. 354*
  Thorpe, English Illustration

JENEER, J.
Artist who drew Dutch postcards showing a statue of Kruger and Wilhelmina (Salon Blanc).

JENNIS, Charles Gurnell 1874-1943
Black and white artist, etcher and soldier-artist. Jennis was elected A.R.E. in 1914. He contributed work to *Pick-Me-Up* and *Punch* from 1913 to 1922 and to *The Graphic*.
  During the Boer War Jennis was a trooper and the desig-

nated special artist for *The Illustrated London News* on board the SS *Canada* with Lord Roberts on his return to England. His drawings of this were published in the magazine on 5 and 12 January 1901 and most of the illustrations were done in facsimile and included several pictures of Lord Roberts. *The Illustrated London News* mentioned that 'one of our portraits was obtained by the kindness of Lord Roberts who granted our artist, a trooper of the Yeomanry, a sitting. It may seem strange that Lord Roberts should have granted this favour when correspondents were excluded from the vessel, but the Field Marshal wishes it to be understood that he did so solely on the consideration that our representative was an artist not a writer'.
  Jennis must have returned to South Africa later as he contributed sketches of the colonial tour by the Duke and Duchess of Cornwall and York. Five of these illustrations appeared in *The Illustrated London News* on 21 September 1901: *A Levée in Khaki at Government House: Duke of Cornwall at Cape Town* (redrawn by R.C. Woodville) and *The Royal Colonial Tour: the Duke of Cornwall at Cape Town* (which consists of four sketches redrawn by Reginald Cleaver).
  Jennis was awarded the Queen's South Africa medal on 17 February 1903.
  De Wet, Illustrated London News Index, *p. 108*
  Houfe, British Illustrators and Caricaturists, *p. 354*
  The Orders and Medals Research Society, *Summer 1986*, 'War Correspondents: South Africa 1899-1902', by Patrick Street
  Thorpe, English Illustration

JENSEN, A.
Artist of an early German postcard (December 1899) showing Boer using a sjambok on British soldier and entitled *Heil und sieg den Boeren*.

JILENO
Gédéon (Madrid) cartoonist. His cartoon *Gulliver en de Lilliputters* was reproduced on a series of Dutch postcards featuring cartoons from the contemporary press. The cartoon originally appeared in *Gédéon* on 6 November 1899.

JOB
French caricaturist and illustrator who contributed an illustration to the special number of *Le Monde Illustré* (17 November 1900) dedicated to President Kruger.

JOHN, William Goscombe 1860-1942 2
Sculptor. John was born in Cardiff on 21 February 1860. He was educated at the Cardiff School of Art, the City and Guilds School and the Royal Academy schools. He won a gold medal and a travelling scholarship that enabled him to travel widely in Europe and the Middle East. He worked in Paris under Rodin from 1890-91 and he exhibited at the Royal Academy from 1884. He was elected A.R.A. in 1899 and R.A. in 1909. In 1901 he won a gold medal at the Paris Salon and in 1942 he was awarded the R.B.S. gold medal.

John's Boer War work in South Africa includes the memorial to Capetonians who died while fighting on the side of the British. This memorial stands opposite the Drill Hall in Darling Street, Cape Town. Another statue by John which is situated near the memorial is that of King Edward VII, on the Parade. This statue, dated 1904, was unveiled on 12 April 1905. A study for this statue was exhibited in the Royal Academy in 1904. It featured in *Royal Academy Pictures* in 1904. In the same year an eight-foot bronze statue of Prince Christian Victor, Queen Victoria's grandson who died of typhoid in South Africa, was erected at Windsor. This, too, featured in *Royal Academy Pictures*.

John's finest work, however, was probably the memorial to the officers, non-commissioned officers and men of the Coldstream Guards who died in South Africa. This memorial can be found in St Paul's Cathedral, London. A large congregation attended the unveiling which was described in *The Graphic* on 30 July 1904:

  The band of the regiment and many of its officers and rank and file gathered in the nave to witness this ceremony and to take part in the memorial service. The tablet which represents in gilt bronze two men of the Coldstream Guards, one of the 1st and the other of the 2nd Battalion, the former mortally wounded, dying in his comrade's arms. Above them, in the clouds, as in a vision, is a group of the Coldstream men of former days, looking down upon their successors with pride in their courage and devotion, and behind them, on horseback, is General Monk, the first Colonel of the Coldstream Guards.

  The landscape background shows the South African veldt, with distant kopjes behind which the sun is setting. Below the sculptured panel, upon a riband, is a Garter star, the badge of the regiment, the motto *Nulli Secundus*, and an inscription which reads as follows: "To the memory of Lieut-Colonel H. Stopford, commanding the 2nd Battalion, Major the Marquis of Winchester, Captain S. Earle, Captain T. H. E. Lloyd, Lieutenant A. C. Burton, Captain R. A. S. Benson, Lieutenant and Quartermaster W. Girling, Drill-Sergeants F. Seager, T. Evans, Colour Sergeants F. Band, R. Clifford, A. Panter, Sergeant-Instructor of Musketry, A. G. Mill and 207 non-commissioned officers and men of the Coldstream Guards, who died for the Empire in South Africa 1899-1902. Erected by their comrades".

The illustration of the unveiling by Gen. S.F. Stephenson was drawn by A. Kemp Tebby.
  Among John's other Boer War memorial works are:
1. The figures on the Royal Army Medical Corps memorial at Aldershot (unveiled by Edward VII on 24 May 1905)

1 William Goscombe John's memorial to Cape Town citizens who gave their lives during the War. The memorial, on the Parade, was unveiled by Sir Walter Hely Hutchinson on 15 March 1908.
2 The memorial in St Paul's Cathedral, London, to the special correspondents who were killed in the War. The memorial, designed by W. Goscombe John, includes the names W. T. Maud and Horace Spooner.

2. The memorial to Major the Marquis of Winchester at the Amport St Mary Parish Church
3. The King's Liverpool Regiment Memorial, Liverpool (unveiled by Sir George White on 9 September 1905)
4. The Memorial in St Paul's Cathedral to the special correspondents who died during or just after the War
5. The memorial to Dr Alfred Hughes, who died of fever during the War, Corris, Wales (unveiled on 9 September 1905)

John lived in London where he died on 15 December 1942.

Gildea, For Remembrance
SESA, *vol. 3, p. 806*
Waters, British Artists, *vol. 1, pp. 182-183*

JOHNSON, B. S.

Owl cartoonist who signed his work with the initials 'B.S.J.'.

JOHNSON, Herbert 1848-1906   3

Figure and landscape painter and illustrator. Johnson was a student at the Royal Academy where he won several prizes and a life studentship. He worked principally for *The Daily Graphic* (from its inception) and *The Graphic,* but he also contributed to *Girls' Own Paper* and *Windsor Magazine* As 'special' artist he accompanied the Prince of Wales to India in 1875 where he received the Indian medal from the prince. Johnson did several Indian paintings for the prince and his friends, and these were hung in the Royal Academy. Eleven of his paintings were exhibited there between 1868 and 1888. In 1882 he went to Egypt as one of the 'special' artists for *The Graphic* and he designed the War Correspondents' Memorial in St Paul's Cathedral. He was elected a member of the Savage Club in 1876.

During the War Johnson's work appeared almost exclusively in *The Daily Graphic.* Often, however, he either did not sign his illustrations or else used the indistinct monogram 'HJ'. Only three of his illustrations were reproduced in *The Graphic* during the War. The Royal Collection at Windsor has one picture by Johnson, showing Queen Victoria decorating two soldiers with the Victoria Cross at The Royal Victoria Hospital, Netley, on 14 May 1898. The National Army Museum has some pen-and-ink drawings which were reproduced in *The Daily Graphic,* including: *Mending the Telegraph Wires at Ladysmith; Carrying goods over the bridge at Tugela River; The 1st Grahamstown Volunteers entering Steynsburg; Free State Boers passing through Steynsburg;* and *Pouring shells for the war effort.* Another two depicting the C.I.V.s at Green Point were reproduced in the special C.I.V. number of *The Daily Graphic.*

The Africana Museum has a pen-and-ink drawing of General Botha signed 'HJ' which also appeared in *The Daily Graphic.* The author has another entitled *Bugler Dunne,* which was published in *The Daily Graphic* on 12 February 1900. It had been drawn 'from a photograph by Stephen Cribb of Southsea'.

Dawnay and Miller, Military Drawings and Paintings
Graves, Royal Academy, *vol. 4, p. 254*
Houfe, British Illustrators and Caricaturists, *p. 355*
Personal communication with the Secretary, The Savage Club
Thorpe, English Illustration
Waters, British Artists, *vol. 1, p. 183*

JOHNSTON

Pittsburgh Press cartoonist.

JOHNSTONE, Agnes M.

A Pietermaritzburg-based artist by this name was responsible for 10 sketches which were sent from South Africa and redrawn by home-based artists for *The Graphic.* The illustrations in *The Graphic* date from 28 October 1899 to September 1900. One dated 4 November 1899 was reproduced in *The Illustrated London News.*

De Wet, Illustrated London News Index
Hofmeyr, Matton and Roets, Graphic Picture Index

JONES, Adrian 1845-1938

Soldier-artist; sculptor and painter. Jones was born in Ludlow, Shropshire, on 9 February 1845. He was educated at Ludlow Grammar School. He became a veterinary surgeon and served in the army for 23 years – in the 3rd Hussars, Queen's Bays and 2nd Life Guards. In 1868 he saw active service in Abyssinia, where he received a medal, and in 1881 in the first Anglo-Boer War. Thereafter he took part in the Nile Expedition, during which he won a medal and clasp, and the Khedive's Star.

Jones came out to South Africa with the Inniskilling Dragoons aboard SS *Nemesis.* After many delays they finally reached Durban and were sent up to Pietermaritzburg and later to Newcastle where they arrived in time for the peace declaration. In Newcastle Jones made sketches from which he later painted a large picture of General Gore leading the Inniskillings over Bennet's Drift. Jones had been keen on art throughout his army career, but when he returned to England he became friendly with the sculptor, C. B. Birch, who encouraged him, especially with his vast knowledge of equine anatomy, to take up sculpture.

Jones exhibited regularly at the Royal Academy, but in 1892 he was involved in a serious incident in which he was falsely accused of exhibiting work which was not entirely his own.

Jones, who had sent an illustration to *The Graphic* of the conference between a Zulu chief and Sir Evelyn Wood in 1881, did one Second Anglo-Boer War illustration which was published in *With the Flag to Pretoria.*

He is better known for his sculpture and was commissioned to do the Royal Marines Memorial in London (unveiled on 25 June 1903), the South Australian National Memorial in Adelaide (unveiled on 6 June 1904), and The Carabineers South African War Memorial in London (unveiled 23 June 1906). Statues of Redvers Buller in Exeter and the Duke of Cambridge at Whitehall were executed by Jones. In addition large portraits of Lord Roberts, Horatio Kitchener and Gen. Smuts are in collections in England.

Jones wrote *Memoirs of a Soldier Artist* in 1933. He was an active member of the Savage Club and came in close contact with Melton Prior, John Hassall and Phil May. He died in London on 24 January 1938.

Hofmeyr, Matton and Roets, Graphic Picture Index

5   6

Jones, Memoirs of a Soldier Artist
Watson, The Savage Club
Who was Who, vol. 3, p. 723

JONES, George Kingston fl. 1890–1924   3
Painter and illustrator who worked principally for *The Daily Graphic*. He also contributed to *Windsor Magazine* between 1896 and 1899. Two of his illustrations appeared in *The Graphic* between September 1899 and June 1900. Jones exhibited at the Royal Academy.

Hartrick, in *A Painter's Pilgrimage*, mentions that when he arrived at *The Daily Graphic* 'G.K. Jones, a London youth of about our own age, who was already established as a toucher-up of photographs and general utility man, was also there to show us the ropes of the place'.

The Africana Museum has two of Jones's pen-and-ink sketches. One, entitled *Hands up for annexation*, has the inscription 'Hands up for annexation: the meeting in Green Market Square, Cape Town, in support of the Government's attitude regarding the Boer Republics (From photographs by Field and Lowe, Cape Town, delayed in the wreck of the Mexican).' The date stamp on the reverse, '1st May 1900', and the pencilled note, '3 cols immediate', indicate that it was probably used as an illustration for *The Daily Graphic* on that date. The other sketch, *On the Way to the Peace Conference 1902*, has an inscription on the newsprint pasted below the drawing: 'On the way to the Peace Conference: General Delarey and other delegates arriving at a British outpost. (From a sketch by a British Officer).' It is signed 'G.K. Jones'. 'Boer Peace delegates', '4 cols' (in blue) and a date stamp, '4th July '92', appear on the back. This obviously should have read '02' and the sketch was probably reproduced in *The Daily Graphic* on that date.

The author has one of Jones's pen-and-ink sketches, entitled *Engineers constructing a temporary bridge over the Modder River*. The reverse bears a pencil inscription, '3 cols', and a date stamp, '18th January 1900'. Once again, this is probably the date of its appearance in *The Daily Graphic*.

The Queen's Royal Surrey Regiment Museum also possesses a pen-and-ink sketch by Jones.
Hartrick, A Painter's Pilgrimage, p. 67
Hofmeyr, Matton and Roets, Graphic Picture Index
Graves, Royal Academy, vol. 4, p. 274
Kennedy, Pictures in the Africana Museum, vol. 7, pp. 32–33
Personal communication with J. G. Woodroff, Curator, the Queen's Surrey Regiment Museum, Guildford, Surrey
Thorpe, English Illustration

JOUAS, Charles 1866–1942
Painter, illustrator and etcher. Jouas was born in Paris on 5 December 1866. He illustrated several books and became president of the etching section of the Société National des Beaux-Arts. Jouas contributed an illustration to *Paris-Pretoria*, entitled *Les Anglais Ont Brulée les Fermes*.
Bénézit, Dictionnaire antique, vol. 5, p. 181

JOUVE, Paul 1880–?
Painter and lithographer. Jouve was born in Marlotte, France, on 16 March 1880. He is believed to have done the illustrations for the French edition of Kipling's *Jungle Book*. He worked for *L'Assiette Au Beurre* at the time of the War and at least two of his illustrations were Boer War related: *Le Coq — Je suis déplumé, c'est possible . . . mais tu l'es encore plus que moi* (27 June 1901,) and *Au Transvaal — le sang, c'est de l'argent* (published with issue 34, which was devoted entirely to his 'Vengeances Sociales', on 23 November 1901). Jouve often signed his work with a monogram.
Bénézit, Dictionnaire antique vol. 5, p. 186

JOY, George William 1844–1925
The brother of Albert Bruce-Joy (see p. 114), George William Joy was born in Dublin on 7 July 1844. He was educated at Harrow and studied art at the Kensington School of Art, the Royal Academy and in Paris under Charles Jalabert and Bonnat. Joy served in the Artists' Corps for 21 years, representing them at Wimbledon, Bisley etc. In 1904 he published an autobiographical sketch entitled *The Work of George W. Joy*.

One work with reference to the Boer War has been noted. Entitled *Dreams on the veld*, it was reproduced in *The Sphere* on 16 March 1901.
Waters, British Artists, vol. 1, p. 185
Who was Who, vol. 2, p. 568

J.R.W.
Caricaturist who depicted Steyn and Kruger leaving Pretoria on a donkey. A copyright print was published in 1900 by E. Cross and Co., Designer and Colour Printers, 35 Crutch Friars, London E.C. The same caricature appeared on a postcard by an unknown publisher.

JUCH, Ernst 1838–1909
Artist, sculptor and caricaturist. Juch was born in Gotha, Austria, on 25 April 1838. He worked initially for the Vienna publications *La Râpe* and *L'Air Viennois*. Later he joined *Figaro* (Vienna) and *Kikeriki*. During the War his work was featured in *Figaro*. Juch died in Vienna on 5 October 1909.
Bénézit, Dictionnaire antique, vol. 5, p. 191
Grand-Carteret, John Bull, p. 26

JULIO, G.
Belgian artist who produced a series of 12 anti-British postcards ('Cartes postales artistique par Julio'). Dutch (or Flemish), and French and a much rarer German version have been noted and it is likely that all of these cartoons were originally published in the Brussels journal *La Reforme*, from as early

as 1897. *John Bull Sur la Sellete* and *Dum-Dums der Publieke Opinie* also reproduced some of his cartoons. Grand-Carteret refers to him as the 'Belgian Caran d'Ache'.

The titles of the unnumbered cards are as follows:

Dutch version	French version
1. Een Vreeslijke Nacht	Une nuit terrible
2. Een Fiasco	Un Four
3. Echtscheiding	Divorçons
4. Verzuchting voor een Doodskop	Réflexion devant une Machoire
5. De Goede Boerin	La Bonne Fermière
6. Een Flinke Oude Heer	Un Rude Bonhomme
7. De Jager Vervolgd	Le Chasseur Chassé
8. De Toestand	La Situation
9. Een Uitstapjie	Une promenade
10. Een oude Deun	Musique Connue
11. De Vervlogen Hoop	L'Espoir Déçu
12. Dum Dum! All right!	Dum Dum! All right!

No. 4 appeared in *La Reforme* on 28 September 1899 and no. 9 on 15 October 1899 with the title 'Grand Maman va-t-en guerre'.
Grand-Carteret, John Bull, pp. 4 & 29
SAPRG Newsletter, 21 Sept. 1986, 'The cartes postales par Julio' by R. Greenwall

---

1 Herbert Johnson's two composite pen-and-ink sketches of the C.I.V. at their camp in Green Point, drawn for *The Daily Graphic*'s special C.I.V. edition on 27 October 1900. Reproduced by courtesy of the National Army Museum, London.
2 British engineers build a new bridge over the Modder River after the Boers destroyed the old bridge during the battle. A pen-and-ink sketch by George Jones, reproduced in *The Daily Graphic* on 18 January 1900.
3 A portrait of Herbert Johnson, artist for *The Daily Graphic*.
4 A pen-and-ink drawing of Louis Botha by Herbert Johnson which was drawn for *The Daily Graphic*, the publication that featured most of Johnson's Boer War work. Reproduced by courtesy of the Africana Museum, Johannesburg.
5 The Boer general De la Rey leading the delegation to a British outpost for peace talks was drawn by George Jones for reproduction in *The Daily Graphic*. Reproduced by courtesy of the Africana Museum, Johannesburg.
6 George Jones produced this pen-and-ink drawing entitled *Hands up for annexation*, showing a meeting held in Cape Town in support of the British Government's attitude towards the Boer Republics. Reproduced by courtesy of the Africana Museum, Johannesburg.

GRUSS VOM KRIEGSSCHAUPLATZ

Der englische Zinnsoldat
unter der Sonne Afrikas.
„Wenn Menschen aus-
einandergehn,
So sagen sie: Auf Wieder-
sehn!"

1

GRUSS VOM KRIEGSSCHAUPLATZ

CECIL RHODES.

2 | Dem Protz sieht man es an | Er war ein fleiss'ger Mann
Er hat viel Geld und ob! | Und ist ein fauler Kopp.

3

JÜTTNER, Franz Albert 1865-? 2

Painter, illustrator and cartoonist. Jüttner was born in Lindenstadt, Germany, on 23 April 1865. His Boer War cartoons appeared in both *Lustige Blätter* and *Das Goldene Buchlein*, his Boer War work in the latter. Several of these cartoons were reproduced in *Burenstreiche* and *Neue Burenstreiche*. *The Studio* described Jüttner as 'already well known as one of the humorists whose fun proves always victorious whether he takes up politics or social weaknesses and he commands esteem by his technical development'.

The series of *Gruss Vom Kriegsschauplatz* postcards published by Dr Eysler was based on anti-British cartoons which had appeared in *Lustige Blätter*. Many of these anti-British cards featured the work of Jüttner, either signed in full or initialled 'F.J.'. Jüttner's cards in the series were: no. 11 *Die Maulthiere* (not signed); no. 17 *Cecil Rhodes* (signed 'F.J.'); no. 18 *Chamberlain in der Falle* (signed 'F.J.') and no. 21 *Vorgefühl* (signed 'F. Jüttner Dez 1899').

J.C. Auf der Heide, the Amsterdam publisher, used a Jüttner caricature of Chamberlain, *Chamberlain en de Muilezels*, in his 'Engeland-Transvaal' series no.19. *Aujourd'hui, Hier, Après La Paix et après Ladysmith*, another card by an unknown French publisher, was unsigned but based on his *Lustige Blätter* cartoon *Moral vom englischen Geldmarkt*. The card is unsigned.

Bénézit, Dictionnaire antique, *vol. 5, p. 201*
Burenstreiche, *p. 46*
SAPRG Newsletter, *Aug. 1983 'Gruss vom Kriegsschauplatz cards' by R. Greenwall*
The Studio, *vol. 51, p. 165*

KASTER, M.

Postcard artist who made a crude copy of C. da Amaral's caricature of Paul Krüger smacking Queen Victoria's bare bottom; the card was entitled *English correction par Amaral*.

KAUFFMANN, Rud

Designer, illustrator and publisher of postcards in both German and Dutch, including those entitled *Den Trouwen vader Zijns Volks onze Hulde* and *Unser Mitgefühl dem Treuen Vater Seines Volkes*. Some of these cards were addressed to Kruger in Brussels. It is assumed that Kauffmann, whose firm was in Krefeld, Germany, was the illustrator of the cards as they are initialled 'R.K.' with the 'R' in reverse.

An R. Kauffmann, who may have been the same individual, did illustrations for *Le Monde Illustré*, one of which appeared on 27 January 1900.

KEAN, W. R.

The Cape Register cartoonist who occasionally used the initials 'W.R.K.' to sign his work. Kean's original Boer War cartoons can be found in the Mendelssohn Collection in the Library of Parliament, Cape Town.

KEES

Pseudonym of an unidentified artist who illustrated Pierre Burel's *Aventures d'un Enfant de Paris au Transvaal*. (Pierre Burel was the pseudonym of Pierre Guedy [1872-1903].) The publication, which appeared each Tuesday at a price of 10 centimes, was published at 5 Rue de Croissant, Paris. The back cover frequently had an anti-British cartoon taken from the contemporary press.

Kees van Dongen, the Dutch artist, was working in Paris at the time, but the poor quality of the illustrations and the different signatures make it unlikely that he was the artist.

SABIB, vol. 1, p. 333 and vol. 3, p. 458

KEMBLE, Edward Windsor 1861-1933 1

Kemble was born in Sacramento, U.S.A., on 18 January 1861. He had no formal art education but nevertheless became a well-known magazine illustrator and was particularly noted for his pen drawings of the deep South. His cartoons appeared mainly in the American magazines *New York Daily Graphic*, *Puck*, *Life* and *The Illustrated Graphic News*, as well as in the British publication *Moonshine*.

One of Kemble's cartoons appeared in *Under The Union Jack* on 30 June 1900. Entitled *Modern Warfare*, it bears the caption 'Commandant Hansoff: 'Now den sing Hymn Fifty-two und vhen you come to de vords "mit peace und lofe" blaze avay eferybody!'

Osterwalder, and Hubschmid and Bouret (eds.),
Dictionnaire des Illustrateurs, *p. 550*
Pitz, American Illustration

KEMP TEBBY, Arthur *see* TEBBY, Arthur Kemp

KEMP-WELCH, Lucy Elizabeth 1869-1958 2

Kemp-Welch was born in Bournemouth on 20 June 1869. She studied art at the Herkomer School in Bushey, Herts., and she later became principal of the Kemp-Welch School of Painting there. She was elected a member of the R.B.A. in 1902 and the R.I. in 1907. Kemp-Welch became president of the Society of Animal Painters in 1914 and had paintings bought by the Chantrey bequest in 1897 and 1917. She exhibited at least 14 paintings at the Royal Academy between 1895 and 1914.

In 1901 she exhibited *'In sight'; Lord Dundonald's dash on Ladysmith* at the Royal Academy. This work was painted from Lord Dundonald's personal account of the event, and the picture shows Capt. Birdwood, Winston Churchill, Lord Dundonald, Lt. Cleeves and other troopers. This oil on canvas is now in the Royal Albert Museum in Exeter. The Royal Albert Museum also has sketches and letters from the artist relating to this painting. There are also other preliminary sketches for this work in an unnamed private collection. The museum has the correspondence about the picture between Kemp-Welch, her secretary, H. Goffy, and a trustee of the museum, F.R. Rowley. On 29 January the artist replied to the museum's enquiry about which pictures were available and mentioned that *In sight*, *Ploughing on the Coast* and *The Incoming tide* were all available. By this time she had reduced her price for *In sight* to £200 (the original price at the Royal Academy was £1 000).

The National Army Museum in London has a photogravure after Kemp-Welch, which was published by the Fine Art Publishing Company, Charing Cross House, London, in 1905; it was entitled *Sons of England. The line of Imperial Yeomanry drawn up in the veld in South Africa* (c.1900). In

4 SPION KOP LAAGER

1902 *The Morning* was exhibited at the Royal Academy and *Sons of the City* during the following year. The latter was illustrated in *Royal Academy Pictures* (1903) and is probably the painting from which the National Army Museum's photogravure was made.

Kemp-Welch died in Watford on 27 November 1958.

Graves, Royal Academy, *vol. 4, p. 310*
Messum, Lucy Kemp-Welch
Personal communication with the Curator, Royal Albert Museum, Exeter
Waters, British Artists, *vol. 1, p. 188*

KENNEDY, P.

Private Kennedy of the King's Own Scottish Borderers sent a sketch with a letter to *The Illustrated London News*. The picture, which was redrawn by W.T. Smith, appeared on 3 August 1901 entitled *War in South Africa: Music in camp*. An extract of his letter was also published: 'We have just had ten families of refugee women and children brought into camp. One of them has an American organ, and I began to play "Wait till the clouds roll by"'.

De Wet, Illustrated London News Index

KEPPLER, Joseph (jnr.)

Cartoonist. Joseph Keppler snr. emigrated from Austria to the U.S.A. in 1868 and founded the well-known satirical magazine, *Puck*, in 1876. After his death in 1894, his son, Joseph jnr., took over his role as leading cartoonist. During the Boer War several cartoons appeared under his signature. One of his best-known cartoons, showing the British Lion being repulsed by Kruger in the guise of a porcupine, was reproduced in several European magazines, as well as appearing on a postcard.

Feaver, Masters of Caricature

KERONEC'H, GANN

La Caricature cartoonist whose work appeared in issue number 1094 on 15 December 1900. The cartoon was entitled *Les Étrennes de Chamberlain*.

K.G.

These were the initials of a postcard artist who provided the illustration for a German card entitled *Chamberlain as Friedensengel*, showing Chamberlain and Edward VII at the latter's coronation. The card was published by Illig & Moller, Göppingen.

KIENERK, Giorgio 1869-?

Italian painter and sculptor born in Florence on 5 May 1869. He studied under Cecioni and Signorini and was influenced by the Impressionists. Kienerk was responsible for a cartoon on an Italian postcard (E.T.P.G. Obsner, Florence) entitled *After the Victory*.

Bénézit, Dictionnaire antique, *vol. 5, p. 248*

KING, Frank C.

The Royal Collection at Windsor has two works by this artist: *Sowar, 1st (Duke of York's Own) Bengal Lancers (Skinner's Horse), 1902* ('1st Bengal Lancers' is inscribed on the painting) and *New Zealander 1902* ('a New Zealander' is inscribed in pencil on the back and in ink on the front). Both are watercolours and are signed 'Frank C. King'. The subject of the second painting wears a Boer War period Mounted Infantry dress of khaki with Stohwasser leggings and bandolier. This uniform was worn in London for the coronation of King Edward VII. Nothing is known about the artist.

Dawnay and Miller, Military Drawings and Paintings, *vol. 2, p. 243*

KING, J.

The J. King who was responsible for several Natal landscapes depicting Boer War battle sites was possibly the landscape painter John Baragwanath King (1864-1939) who was born near Penzance in Cornwall. Formerly an engineer, Baragwanath King later took up art and exhibited at the R.I., in Paris and in other galleries on the Continent. Some of his work was purchased by King Edward VII and Queen Alexandra. He published *Arthur and others in Cornwall* and other works.

Verbeek lists 21 watercolours by 'J. King':
1. *Amajuba, from Mount Prospect road, 1902*
2. *Boer gun emplacements, Gun Hill, Ladysmith, showing Nicholson's Nek*
3. *Colenso, 1902*
4. *Colenso bridge and road to Ladysmith*
5. *Colenso looking east – Lt. Robert's monument*
6. *Colenso looking west, showing Shooter's Hill and Tugela River*
7. *Fort Wylie and the Railway line*
8. *From Gun Hill, Ladysmith, showing Umbulwana and Table Hill*
9. *Grobblaars Hill, Natal, 1902*
10. *Gun emplacement, Gun Hill, showing Boer water tanks*
11. *Hart's Hill, between Ladysmith and Colenso*
12. *Ladysmith, 1902*
13. *Ladysmith, from the top of Gun Hill, 1901*
14. *Looking north from Talana Hill, 1901*
15. *Pieters Hill, looking south, 1901*
16. *Smith's farm, Talana, 1901*
17. *Spion Kop at dawn from Taba Imnyana*
18. *Table Imnyana and Spion Kop*
19. *Tugela River at Colenso*
20. *View from Green Hill – Grobbelaar's Hill 1901*
21. *View from Tugela Falls, 1901*

The Africana Museum possesses numbers 1, 3, 9, 12 and 21. In 1985 Clarke's Bookshop, Cape Town, offered two similar watercolours dated 1901 and 1902. Both showed landscapes of the countryside near Ladysmith.

The author has seven watercolours by J. King: two seascapes and five landscapes. Two of the landscapes are entitled *Spion Kop South Africa* and *Hlangwani and Monte Cristo, Colenso*; the other three are untitled but depict Natal landscapes.

Kennedy, Pictures in the Africana Museum, *vol. 3, pp. 209-210 and vol. 7, p. 2*
Verbeek, Early Natal Art
Waters, British Artists, *vol. 1, p. 190*

KING, (William) Gunning 1859-1940

Genre painter, postcard artist and illustrator. King was born in South Kensington on 2 September 1859. He studied art at the South Kensington School of Art and the Royal Academy schools, where he received a silver medal for drawing. He ex-

1 A satirical German postcard published by Dr Eysler & Co. making fun of the British 'tin soldier'. The unsigned illustration was probably by F. A. Jüttner.
2 A caricature of Cecil Rhodes reproduced on a German postcard drawn by Franz Jüttner.
3 This poignant oil on canvas by Lucy Kemp-Welch is entitled *The Morning*. It was exhibited at the Royal Academy.
4 American artist Edward Windsor Kemble drew this cartoon, showing Boers preparing for a battle, for *Harper's Weekly*. Entitled *Modern Warfare*, it was also reproduced in *Under the Union Jack*.
5 Lucy Kemp-Welch's 1901 Royal Academy exhibit *'In sight'; Lord Dundonald's dash on Ladysmith*.
6 Gann Keronech'H drew this cartoon, entitled *L'Etrennes de Chamberlain* for *La Caricature* on 15 December 1900.

hibited at the leading London galleries from 1878, at the Royal Academy, the R.P., the R.B.A. and also in the provinces. At various times King worked for *The Illustrated London News, The Graphic, Windsor Magazine, Punch, The Sketch, The Illustrated Sporting & Dramatic News, English Illustrated Magazine, Pick-Me-Up* and *The Quiver*. Both he and his brother Edward were well-known postcard artists for both Tuck (Oillettes) and Hildesheimer.

The Illustrated London News featured three of King's illustrations: of Boer War interest were *Boers entraining in Johannesburg for the Natal border* (18 November 1899) and *From the Battle field* (2 June 1900), showing the 'aristocratic' and 'working class' soldiers being welcomed home to the 'Hall' and 'cottage'.

Holt, Tonie and Valmai, Picture Postcard Artists
Houfe, British Illustrators and Caricaturists, *vol. 2, p. 360*
Waters, British Artists, *vol. 1, pp. 190-191*

KIPLING, Rudyard 1865-1936   1

Rudyard Kipling is, of course, far better known for his literary talents than his artistic ones. Nevertheless he was a competent illustrator and some of his tales, like the *Just So Stories*, he illustrated himself.

Born in Bombay in 1865, Kipling was influenced by his father, J. Lockwood Kipling, who was a student of Indian art and culture. He was educated at the United Services College, Westward Ho!, North Devon, but he spent his vacations with the family of his uncle, the artist Sir E. Burne-Jones. Another uncle, Sir Edward Poynter, director of the National Gallery, was also a famous artist.

Kipling was employed as a journalist from 1882 to 1889 and after early successes travelled to the U.S.A. Kipling's poem 'The Absent Minded Beggar' — first published in *The Daily Mail* in October 1899 — was the inspiration for Richard Caton Woodville's painting, which was reproduced in virtually every illustrated periodical of the day, as well as being issued separately as sheet music (written by Sir Arthur Sullivan), on handkerchiefs, postcards and many other types of souvenirs. The royalties raised from the proceeds of the recital of the poem were donated to the Soldiers' Widows and Orphans Fund.

Kipling spent 10 consecutive summers in South Africa (between 1898 and 1908) and was present during part of the War. Only one Boer War illustration by Kipling has been noted. This drawing, which reflects his fascination with machines, was first published in *The Illustrated London News* but was also reproduced in most of the illustrated journals. On 16 March 1901 *The Illustrated London News* featured an article entitled 'Rudyard Kipling as an artist: the novelist's allegorical view of the chase of De Wet'. The illustration shows a traction engine complete with gun and anchor preceded by a soldier with a red flag chasing De Wet. *The Illustrated London News* comments: 'The father's artistic mantle rests not ungraciously on the shoulders of the son'.

Lord Roberts, ever mindful of his image, invited selected journalists to accompany him during certain engagements. This coincided with one of Kipling's visits to South Africa and he was present at the skirmish at Karee Siding and later spent time with Roberts in Bloemfontein, where he contributed several articles to the war correspondents' newspaper *The Friend*. He wrote other very pro-British articles about the War, including 'The Sin of Witchcraft', a direct polemic against what he called 'Free State and Cape Traitors'. He also contributed 'a back handed olive branch' entitled 'Piet', which was a tribute to the defeated Afrikaner. Another poem written at this time was entitled 'The Comprehension of Private Copper'.

At one time Cecil Rhodes gave his estate, Woolsack, in Mowbray to the Kiplings on a life tenancy for their use during their stays in South Africa and it was here that Kipling wrote the first of the *Just So Stories*. The memorial to those who died in the Kimberley siege bears an inscription composed by Rudyard Kipling. The bronze tablet on the memorial to George Labram, the designer of the famous Long Cecil gun, was designed by J. Lockwood Kipling (Rudyard's father).

Kipling died in London on 18 January 1936.
Gildea, For Remembrance
Illustrated London News, *16 March 1901*
Fido, Rudyard Kipling

KIRTON, Walter

Soldier-artist. One of Kirton's illustrations appeared in *The Illustrated London News* on 24 March 1900. The sketch, redrawn by H.C. Seppings Wright, was entitled *'Klip Drift on the morning of the Relief of Kimberley: General French sweeping aside the enemy'* from a sketch made on horseback by Mr W. Kirton, of Rimington's Horse. Kirton was responsible for another Africana illustration in *The Illustrated London News*; it appeared on 15 September 1906, entitled *Back from the compound: the coolies return from S. Africa (to Hankow)*.

According to Kennedy a drawing by J.D. McPherson, which can be found in the Africana Museum collection, was done from a sketch by Kirton while in Shanghai in 1905/6. In the note Kirton relates that, in response to a question, he replied that 'the Chinese in South Africa were very happy and certainly not treated as slaves'.

De Wet, Illustrated London News Index
Kennedy, Pictures in the Africana Museum, *vol. 4, p. 8*

KLEINHEMPEL, G. 1875-?

Designer of jewellery, posters and devices for books and business cards. Gertrud Kleinhempel was born in Leipzig in 1875. Her brothers, Fritz (1860) and Frederich or Erich (1874), were artists. Kleinhempel studied at schools in Dresden and Munich. She lectured on textiles and handwork at private schools, and became a professor in 1929.

It is possible that Kleinhempel illustrated the well-known *Der Boerenkrieg* postcards published by Bruno Bürger and Ottilie of Leipzig. In many cases these cards, which were published early in November 1899, had a signature which could possibly be interpreted as 'G. Kleinhempel'. Other cards in the series are unsigned and at least four are by a different hand and signed 'A.F.'. J. Pompen Veendam published a similar series in Dutch.

The cards are as follows:
6058 *England im Wurstkessel* (not signed);
6059 *Überreichung des Bürgerbriefes* (not signed)
6060 *Ein gutes Schwein Frisst Alles* (not signed)
6061 *Komm'se rein in die gute Stube* (not signed)
6062 no title ('Dum Dum' on soldier's bandolier — not signed)
6063 *Der Erste Erfolg* (not signed)
6064 *Ja die Esel sind an allem Schuld* (signed)
6065 *Deutsche Männer, Deutsche Frauen, Helft den Englishman verhauen!* (signed)
6066 *Wie die Buren Momentaufnahmen von den in Durban ankommenden Engländern machen* (signed)

6067 *Junge, willste 'runter von dem Appelboom* (signed)
6068 *Burenwäsche* (signed)
6069 *Au weh! Das hatte ich mir anders vorgestellt* (signed 'A.F.')
6070 *Mr Chamberlain beim Empfang der Telegramme v Kriegsschauplatz* (signed 'A.F.')
6102 *Eendracht Maakt Magt* (signed)
6107 *Wie Sich Onkel Krüger von den Herren Buller, Methuen u Gatacre verabschiedet* (signed)
6108 *Extrablatt! Heimkehr der Englischen Esel* (not signed)
6138 *Paul Kruger Präsident von Transvaal aus Süd Afrika* (not signed)
6151 *O, dass sie ewig grünen bliebe Die schöne Zeit der Burenbiebe!* (signed 'A.F.')
6152 *Extrablatt! General Warren in der Tinte!* (signed 'A.F.')
6153 *Es is Erreicht Lady-Smith is gefallen* (not signed)

The next three cards are probably not part of the series but have Boer War or Africana relevance:
2156 *Die Schwiegermutter Als Lyddit-Bombe* (signed)
6305 *Die Krieg in China. Na, es wird schon luft 'John Bull in Nökten'* (In spite of the title a Boer is depicted — not signed)
7496 *Der Aufstand in Deutsch Südwestafrika* (not signed)
The Studio, *vol. 26, pp. 306-307*

KLEPPER, Max Francis 1861-1907

Illustrator. Klepper was born in Germany in 1861. He went to the United States in 1876 and settled in Toledo, Ohio. After establishing himself in New York he worked as a magazine illustrator and was noted for his animal pictures.

Klepper's Boer War work appears in Capt. A.T. Mahan's *The War in South Africa*. He also contributed illustrations to *Harper's Magazine*, one of which is entitled *Inside a Boer Laager*. One of his works, an original illustration for *Harper's Magazine* (but not relating to the War), fetched $5 000 at an auction on 28 September 1973.

Klepper died in Brooklyn, New York in 1907.
Fielding, American Painters, etc., *p. 202*

KLINGEBEIL, E.

German illustrator whose work appears in Frederich Meister's *Burenblut. Bilder aus dem letzten Transvaalkriege* (Abel & Müller, Leipzig, 1900) and Paul Groningen's *Der Heldenkampf der Buren und die Geschichte Süd-afrikas* (1902). Klingebeil contributed four coloured and 20 black and white illustrations to the former.

Klingebeil often signed his work with the initials 'E.K.'. Neudin refers to him as a postcard artist.
Neudin, L'officiel international des Cartes Postales De Collection
SABIB, *vol. 2, p. 450*

KLINGER, Julius 1876-1950

Cartoonist, Art Nouveau postcard artist, and illustrator. Klinger was born in Vienna on 22 May 1876. He contributed occasionally to *Lustige Blätter* during the War.
Bénézit, Dictionnaire antique, *vol. 5, p. 268*
Fanelli and Godoli, Art Nouveau Postcards
The Studio, *vol. 51, p. 165*

KNÖTEL, Richard 1857-1914

Historical painter, illustrator and lithographer. Knötel was born in Glogau, Prussia, on 12 January 1857. He worked for *Leipziger Illustrierte Zeitung* and other German papers, and became famous for his military prints. Many of Knötel's Boer War illustrations from these sources were reproduced in G.L. Klepper's *Zuid Afrikaansche Oorlog*, as well as many other contemporary European publications about the War.

A catalogue of over 1 000 military uniform prints by Knötel, *Uniforms Kunde*, was published by Hans Dietrich v. Diepenbroick-Grüter in 1932. Herbert Knötel (possibly a relative) was the compiler.

Knötel often signed his engravings with the initials 'R.K.'.

A postcard published by C. Auf der Heide had an illustration with these initials. The illustration had formerly appeared in *Leipziger Illustrierte Zeitung*.

Knötel died in Berlin on 27 April 1914.

Bénézit, Dictionnaire antique, *vol. 5, p. 278*

KNOX, Ernest Blake 1874-1927

Soldier-artist. Knox was born at Black Rock, Dublin, on 20 September 1874. He enlisted on 17 November 1899 in the Royal Army Medical Corps and took his passage out to South Africa in the H.M.T. *Dilwara*, accompanying officers and men of the Royal Lancaster Regiment and the 11th Brigade in conjunction with Captain Tyacke, also of the Royal Army Medical Corps. He arrived in South Africa in December 1899 and stayed until February 1901. During this time, besides sketching and writing, he did research into the effects of typhoid inoculations and wrote a treatise for *The Medical Journal* on his return to England. This was published in a more technical form in the *Medical Press and Circular* of 28 August 1901. Knox saw action at Tugela, Thaba Nyama, Spioenkop, Vaal Kranz, Colenso, Hart's Hill, Pieter's Hill, Laing's Nek and Belfast. He was invalided home in 1901. His subsequent promotions were to captain on 17 November 1902, major on 17 August 1911 and lieutenant colonel on 26 December 1917. He saw action in World War I and was mentioned in despatches.

Knox was the author of *Buller's Campaign with the Natal Field Force 1900* (R. Brimley Johnson, London, 1902). In the preface to his book he gives the reasons why a doctor should write a book on war. 'An army surgeon with a fighting unit,' he says, 'has opportunities of observation second to none should he care to use them . . .; his professional education as a doctor will have supertrained the faculty of observation — impartial observation, too . . . .'

During lulls in his professional work Knox made a point of entering all items of interest in his diary of the day; this he illustrated with sketches, battle maps and photographs, afterwards tearing out those pages and sending them home as part of his weekly letters to his parents. These different types of illustrations form the basis of the book, and many of those which he sent to *The Graphic* are re-used to enhance the book. Other illustrated papers, such as *With the Flag to Pretoria* and *The Illustrated London News*, also used his sketches and photographs.

The author has a topographical sketch of the area around Laing's Nek, reputed to be Knox's work.

Drew, Officers in Medical Services, *vol. 2, p. 13*
Hofmeyr, Matton and Roets, Graphic Picture Index
Knox, Buller's Campaign

KOCH, F.

Illustrations by this artist, showing mounted Boers, appeared in 'The Road of Honour' by E.A. Gillie, one of a series of short stories in *Valour and Victory* (John T. Shaw and Co., Paternoster Row, London [undated]). Work by the same illustrator also appeared in *Revue Mâme* for 18 February 1900.

KOEKKOEK, Hermanus Willem 1867-1929 1

Hermanus Koekkoek was a member of the well-known family of Dutch land- and seascape artists. He lived and worked in Amsterdam from 1887 to 1891 before going to London where he lived and worked for 20 years.

Koekkoek's illustrations, which were often done in the unusual medium of oil, appeared in *The Illustrated London News*, *The Sketch* and *With the Flag to Pretoria*. He also contributed to Spenser Wilkinson's *The Transvaal War*, his portrait appearing in the frontispiece of the special edition.

On 13 September 1902 *The Illustrated London News* advertised in its series of fine art plates the publication of *Lord Kitchener at the Front*. Two hundred artist's proofs were sold at two guineas, and special frames were also available at prices ranging from one to three guineas.

In 1908 Koekkoek illustrated Herbert Stang's *Barclay of the Guides* and during World War I he contributed several

illustrations to *The Illustrated London News*.

The author has nine Koekkoek watercolours featuring the Zulu War, probably done for a later, as yet unidentified, publication, possibly an adventure story.

Koekkoek died in Amsterdam on 9 September 1929.

De Wet, Illustrated London News Index
Wilkinson, Transvaal War
Scheen, Nederlandse Beeldende Kunstenaars

KÖHLER, Gustav 1859-?

Köhler was born in Dortmund, Germany, on 20 July 1859. His only known Boer War contributions were the caricatures and cartoons illustrating 'Das Lied Der Tapfern Buren'. This 'humorous' song sheet in praise of the Boers was published by C.L. Krüger in Dortmund *c.* early 1900. The lyrics were composed by Karl Prümer and the sheet sold at 25 pfennig.

Bénézit, Dictionnaire antique, *vol. 5, p. 287*

KOPPENOL, Cornelis 1865-1946

Koppenol was born in Zoetermeer, Holland, on 29 December 1865. He was well known for his portraits, etchings, lithographs and illustrations. He was a member of the 'Pulchri Studio' in The Hague.

During the War Koppenol worked as a cartoonist for *Vooruitgang*. In addition he illustrated *De verkenner van Christiaan de Wet* by Louwrens Penning and he co-operated on *Die Verdedigers en Verdrukkers der Afrikaansch Vrijheid*, also by Penning.

Scheen, Nederlandse Beeldende Kunstenaars

KOSKI

Cartoonist and postcard artist. One of his cards forms part of the French set by an unknown publisher that was also illustrated by Marnix and A. Romilly.

KREJCIK, K.

Hungarian cartoonist who contributed to the Prague periodical *Humoristike Listy*.

KROON, Patriq Heleen Joan 1867-1941

Kroon was born in Gelderland, the Netherlands, on 17 March 1862. He used the pseudonym 'Orion' for his political cartoons, as well as the names 'Wyers' and 'Joan'. He is best known as the political cartoonist for *Uilenspiegel*, in which his cartoons were signed 'Orion'. He started work for *Uilenspiegel* in 1894. At the time of the War Kroon was producing three cartoons a week. Beside his work in other periodicals he also had cartoons published in *Humoristisch Album*.

Besides drawing Kroon also taught, because, as he explained in an interview with Arthur Lord in *The Strand* magazine for July 1902, 'in Holland it is not yet possible for an artist to live entirely by his brush and pen'.

Kroon died in The Hague on 26 November 1941.
Scheen, Nederlandse Beeldende Kunstenaars
The Strand, *vol. 24, pp. 93-94*

KRÜGEN, A.

Illustrator of a postcard ('sympathiekaart') published by 'Deutschen Michel' of Leipzig. The card had a printed address to 'Präsident Paul Krüger, Pretoria, Transvaal, Süd Afrika'.

KUPKA, François (also known as Frank or Frantisek) 1871-1957 1

Art Nouveau and abstract artist. Kupka was born in Opocno, Bohemia, on 23 September 1871. He was a student at the École des Beaux-Arts in Prague and worked for a time in Scandinavia. Several illustrated magazines, such as *Frou Frou*, *Squire*, *Le Rire* and *Les Temps Nouveau*, published his illustrations, many of which were anti-war and anti-capitalist.

Kupka's Boer War cartoons and illustrations appeared in *Canard Sauvage*, *L'Illustration* and *L'Assiette au Beurre*. Issue No.41 of the last-named magazine, published on 11 January 1902 and titled *L'Argent*, was devoted entirely to Kupka's

work. Anti-British cartoons appeared on pages 646, 647, 649, 650, and 654 of this issue.

An illustration of Kruger and Queen Wilhelmina by Kupka, which appeared on the cover of *L'Illustration* on 15 December 1900, was reproduced on postcard No. 1304 of the Adolphe Weicke *L'Illustration* series of postcards. His signature is distinctive and is reproduced in Bénézit.

Kupka died in Puteaux, France, in 1957.
Bénézit, Dictionnaire antique, *vol. 5, p. 330*
Hofstätter, Art Nouveau Prints, etc.
Osterwalder, and Hubschmid and Bouret (eds.), Dictionnaire des Illustrateurs, *p. 576*
Piper, Dictionary of Painting, etc., *p. 100*
Shikes and Heller, The Art of Satire, *p. 53*

K.,V. see V.K.

'L.' 1

A monochrome series of 12 artist-drawn cards showing, among other things, concentration camp victims, Cecil Rhodes, Chamberlain, trouserless British troops and the burning of a Boer farmhouse, was produced by an unknown publisher. All the cards are signed 'L.' or Lenny.

LA GARRIAGE

French cartoonist who provided one cartoon, *L'Arbitrage*, to the *Le Gavroche* special number of 16 June 1902, entitled 'La Paix à la mode John Bull'.

LALAUZE, Alphonse 1872-?

Historical painter. Alphonse Lalauze was born in Paris on 21 June 1872. He was the son of Adolphe Lalauze (1838-1906), the better-known painter and etcher. Lalauze jnr.'s Boer War work appeared in *Soleil du Dimanche*.

Bénézit, Dictionnaire antique, *vol. 5, p. 367*

LAMBDIN, Vic

Denver Times cartoonist. Several of Lambdin's Boer War cartoons were reproduced in the American contemporary publication *Thrilling Experiences in the War in South Africa* (The Educational Company, Chicago, 1900).

LANDER, Edgar

Capt. Lander worked for *Pick-Me-Up* as a cartoonist and his Boer War related work appeared in that magazine from 16 September 1899. He later worked for *Punch* and *Windsor Magazine*.

Both Houfe and Johnson and Greutzner maintain that Lander was born in 1883. This is unlikely as his cartoons of 1899 show considerable maturity — beyond that of a 16-year-old. He is better known as the husband of the famous illustrator, Hilda Cowham (born 1873), who also contributed to *Pick-Me-Up*.

Houfe, British Illustrators and Caricaturists, *p. 364*
Johnson and Greutzner, British Artists, *p. 299*

LANGA, Rata (?)

Cartoonist who worked for *L'Asino*, the Rome satirical weekly during the War, and *Der Wahre Jacob*. Langa's work also appeared in *Burenstreiche*. His cartoon *England Transvaal*, which was published on 15 October 1899, was reproduced in a series of Dutch postcards with illustrations taken from the contemporary press. The postcard illustration was not signed.

Burenstreiche, *p. 87*
Grand-Carteret, John Bull, *p. 41*

Dutch artist Hermanus Koekkoek.

LANOS, Henri fl. 1886-1916

Genre and watercolour painter. Lanos was secretary of the Society of French Artists from 1886. He was probably also one of *The Graphic*'s French correspondents.

At least two illustrations of Kruger by Lanos were reproduced in *The Graphic*: *Waiting for Mr Kruger: A poet of the pavement at Marseilles (selling a portrait of ex-president Kruger)* (24 November 1900), and *Kruger at Marseilles* (1 December 1900).

The Royal Collection includes a pen-and-wash drawing of Queen Victoria's Diamond Jubilee (in 1897) done by Lanos.

Bénézit, Dictionnaire antique, vol. 5, p. 403
Dawnay and Miller, Military Drawings and Paintings, vol. 2, p. 243
Hofmeyr, Matton and Roets, Graphic Picture Index
Houfe, British Illustrators and Caricaturists, p. 364
Osterwalder, and Hubschmid and Bouret (eds.), Dictionnaire des Illustrateurs, p. 588

LAPLAGNE, Guillaume   2

Sculptor who was born in Ervy, France. Laplagne was a member of the Society of French Artists from 1894 and received an honourable mention in 1896.

His work appeared on at least five Boer War postcards published by A.N., Paris. They all have signed reproductions of what appear to be clay models by Laplagne:
1. *La vraie Couronne* (King Edward VII);
2. *Posture de Heros Les Anglais* (Kitchener, Chamberlain and Roberts);
3. *Posture de Heros Les Boers* (De la Rey, Botha, de Wet) ('Pour Nos Freres') (poor likeness of each);
4. *Bain de Sang* (Kitchener);
5. An untitled card with a poem, showing Chamberlain as a bird being strung up against a fence. This card gives credit to *Le Rire*. See page 73.

The illustration on card no. 1 appeared in *Le Rire* on 10 May 1902 under the title *Monuments Anthumes 11. – S.M. Edouard VII – Buste Commemoratif du Couronnement*. The illustration on card no. 5 appeared on 14 June 1902 with the title *Monuments Anthumes III. Joe Chamberlain*.

Bénézit, Dictionnaire antique, vol. 5, p. 409

LASZLO DE LAMBOS, Philip Alexius De 1869-1937

Lambos was born in Budapest on 30 April 1869. He won several medals throughout Europe for painting. He married Lucy Guinness in 1900 and became a naturalized Englishman. In spite of this he was interned between 1917 and 1918. He was commissioned by King Edward VII to do a portrait of Gen. George White. In 1930 he became president of the R.B.A. Lambos died in London on 22 November 1937.

Bénézit, Dictionnaire antique, vol. 5, p. 423
Waters, British Artists, pp. 197-198
Who was Who, vol. 3, p. 781

LAURENCE, Mervin

Unknown sculptor who modelled a bronze statuette of a British soldier in tropical (probably Boer War) kit. The bronze is signed, and dated 1903.

LAURENCE, (Lawrence or Lawarence) Sydney Mortimer 1865-1940

Western artist. Laurence — whose name was also spelt Lawrence or Lawarence — was born in Brooklyn, New York, in 1865. He received an honourable mention at the French Salon in 1894. After working in England, he was elected a member of the R.B.A. in 1895. He also spent some time in Anchorage, Alaska. One of his works is reputed to have fetched $210 000 at an auction.

On 13 January 1900 *Black & White Budget* announced in a black-bordered notice entitled 'What we are doing' that '. . . following Lord Roberts, to join him at Cape Town and accompany him on what we all hope will be a triumphal progress, is Mr S.M. Laurence, a young artist of American birth, whose brilliant work in recent war-times has been prominent in Transatlantic journals . . .'.

On 3 February 1900 a photograph of Laurence appeared in *Black & White Budget*, entitled *Mr S.M. Laurence with General Gatacre*. Laurence arrived in South Africa aboard the R.M.S. *Moor* and sent several sketches to his head office. Many were reproduced in facsimile in *Black & White* and *Black & White Budget*.

Bénézit, Dictionnaire antique, vol. 5, p. 432
Samuels, Artists of the American West

LAUTERBURG, Emil 1861-1907

Landscape and postcard artist. Lauterburg was born in Berne, Switzerland, on 25 May 1861. He studied in Munich and Vienna. Later he became well known as a postcard artist whose military and bear subjects have become much sought after.

Lauterburg published one of his postcards himself in Berne. It had a Boer War theme and was entitled *Kindlifresser – Brunnen in Prätoria*. The 'EL' monogram Lauterburg used is distinctive. He died in Berne in 1907.

Bénézit, Dictionnaire antique, vol. 5, p. 441

LAW, H.

Cartoonist whose work was published in the Johannesburg *The Weekly Star*. He often used the initials 'H.L.' to sign his work.

Schoonraad, S.A. Cartoonists

LAWRENCE, Jack

The author has three unsigned watercolours showing Boers, and, according to the vendor, Shelton and Co., they were reputedly done by an artist with this name.

LAWTON, W.C.

Sculptor who modelled signed Parian statues (about 20 cm high) for the firm of Leadbetter and Co. The subjects included: Baden-Powell (c.1903.); Lord Roberts (signed and dated Jan. 1900. 'Copyright "R.&L." (Robinson and Leadbetter)'); General White ('Copyright, Feb. 24th 1900'); General Buller ('Copyright, Oct. 30th 1899'); and Lord Kitchener.

Oosthuizen, Boer War Memorabilia
Sotheby's Catalogue, 7 Feb. 1985

L., C. *see* C.L.

LEA, Henry (Harry)

During the early 1890s Henry Lea arrived in South Africa with his twin brother, Frank, intending to work on the Transvaal goldfields. A slump at the time caused them both to look for employment in Durban. Frank found a job as 'night stationmaster', while Henry was paid six shillings a day for painting railway wagons. He later came to work as an assistant to a veterinary surgeon.

The brothers had an ambition to farm but, being short of capital, they returned to the Transvaal where they established a store in an area they called Brereton, after their ancestral home in Cheshire. Brereton was 60 miles from the Natal border and they travelled there regularly to collect goods for their store.

Henry Lea married Eve, the sister of his lifelong friend Horace Evans, in Cape Town in February 1901. (Horace had studied with him at the Manchester School of Art.) The couple did not return to Brereton until after the War but hired a farm in northern Natal, where they lived until hostilities were over. They returned to their devastated Transvaal home after the War.

Lea was made a Justice of the Peace and in 1913 returned to England with his wife and two small sons, leasing his farm and store.

LA VIE ILLUSTRÉE
et l'Univers Illustré réunis

- « L'Oncle Paul », par Ch. Léandre -

LE PRÉSIDENT KRUGER EN EUROPE

He stayed abroad until 1920. He joined the 22nd Royal Fusiliers as a private at the start of World War I and saw action at Vimy Ridge and at the Somme. In 1918 reorganization in the army had all the over-aged transferred to the 100th Field Ambulance. (Lea claimed he fell into this category.)

He was a keen and enthusiastic artist and produced a large range of oil paintings, watercolours and lithographs. During the Boer War he provided *The Illustrated London News* and *The Graphic* with several sketches done in Natal. At least 14 are credited to him in both papers between 1899 and 1906. One of these sketches was done in Ladysmith soon after the relief. Lea earned about £100 from the papers for his efforts. A picture published in *The Spear* showed a wounded man saluting the statue of the Queen in Pietermaritzburg. He sent the original to the Queen which was 'particularly graciously acknowledged'.

Lea did not volunteer for active service in the Boer War as his brother had become a Transvaal burgher (citizen) and was liable to commando service. He claimed that he did a deal with the local veld cornet in which his brother would not be called up if he didn't join the Colonial forces. This claim was treated with disdain and he was suspected of spying. Lea's book, *A Veld Farmer's Adventures*, has Boer War illustrations, including one depicting an incident during which he and his wife were robbed of their bedding and clothing by a party of Boers while staying at the local hotel towards the end of the War.

During World War I, despite official disapproval, Lea continued to sketch and some of his work was published as 'full pagers' in *The Graphic*, earning £5 per illustration. Several of his World War I illustrations are in the Imperial War Museum, London, and a lithograph of a Voortrekker force in action was presented to the Royal United Services institution by Lord Roberts in 1912.

Lea also illustrated *Otjie and Piet*, the Van Schaik publication written by C.M. Welsford in 1932. He is known to have exhibited works at the South African Academy between 1928 and 1940.

De Wet, Illustrated London News Index
Hofmeyr, Matton and Roets, Graphic Picture Index
Kennedy, Pictures in the Africana Museum, *vol. 3, p. 220*
Lea, A Veld Farmer's Adventures

LEADER, H. P.
Captain Leader was possibly a member of the 5th Dragoon Guards (Carbineers). Two of his illustrations appeared in *The Graphic*: *With General French's force: General view of the Boer position at Taaibosch laagte before our advance on Colesberg* (27 January 1900) and *The Morning tub on the veldt* (17 February 1900).

Army List
Hofmeyr, Matton and Roets, Graphic Picture Index

LÉANDRE, Charles-Lucien 1862-1930 2
Cartoonist and painter in oils and pastels. Léandre was born at Champsecret, Orne, France, on 23 July 1862. He studied art under Bin and Cabanel. He exhibited at the Salon des Artistes Français where he received an honourable mention in 1888. He worked extensively for *Le Rire*, *La Vie Illustrée*, *Chat Noir*, *Gaulois*, *Le Journal Amusant* and *L'Illustration*. During World War I, on 9 October 1915, Léandre held an exhibition of anti-German cartoons at the Leicester Galleries.

Léandre was also known for his Art Nouveau postcards. He was a member of the Society of Humorists.

Léandre's Boer War work appeared in *Le Rire* and *La Vie Illustrée*. The cover of *Le Rire*, October 1899, displayed a cartoon of a very overweight Queen Victoria sitting on a somewhat squashed Kruger. The issue of *La Vie Illustrée* of 16 November 1900 was devoted entirely to Kruger with the cover by Léandre engraved by Reymond. This illustration was also reproduced as a postcard by an unknown French publisher. The cartoon on the cover of this book is by Léandre.

An article by Madeline Murgatroyd which appeared in *The Argus* on 10 October 1981, entitled 'Who painted this portrait?', discussed the possibility that Kruger's portrait, which appeared in *La Vie Illustrée* on 16 November 1900, was drawn by Léandre from life. As Kruger only arrived in France six days later, this is unlikely. The portrait was exhibited in April 1954 at the Greenwich Galleries in Rosebank, Johannesburg, and at the Witwatersrand Agricultural Show. The description of Kruger's face which was given in *La Vie Illustrée* was based on information supplied by Jean Carrere, a French war correspondent who had worked in South Africa, but who confessed that he had never met or even seen the president.

The author has two small non-Boer War portraits by Léandre, who died in Paris in 1930.

Africana Notes and News, vol. 11, pp. 96-97
The Argus, 10 Oct. 1981
Bénézit, Dictionnaire antique, vol. 5, pp. 451-452
Fanelli and Godoli, Art Nouveau Postcards
Feaver, Masters of Caricature, pp. 118-119
Neue Burenstreiche

LE BÈGUE, René 1
French illustrator whose work appeared in *Echo des Marches*, Lyon (Republican Supplement), *Le Petit Brayon Illustré*, *L'Illustré National* (coloured front covers), *Le Franc Normand Illustré* and *L'Assiette au Beurre*.

Bénézit, Dictionnaire antique, vol. 5, p. 454

LE BOCAIN
French cartoonist who contributed to the special number of *Le Gavroche* of 16 June 1902, entitled 'La Paix à la mode John Bull'.

LECLERC (LE CLERC)
Nothing is known about this artist, who was responsible for an illustration on a French postcard entitled *Les Femmes Boers*. The illustration depicts Boer women loading rifles. The card is inscribed 'Journal des Voyages' and it is possible that Léon Le Clerc, a French artist who exhibited at the Salon des Artistes Français from 1896, worked for this publication.

Bénézit, Dictionnaire antique, vol. 5, p. 465

LE GALL, Maurice 1872-? 1
Le Gall was a Parisian who volunteered for service with the Boers during the War. He was captured at Mafeking on 12 May 1900, while serving in Captain du Framont's commando, and sent to St Helena. While in captivity he drew several cartoons and caricatures, occasionally on postcards. Some of these caricatures are in the Mendelssohn Collection in the Library of Parliament, Cape Town.

The author has in his collection postcards which were sent by Le Gall from the P.O.W. camp on St Helena to addresses in France, including one with a pen-and-ink illustration of a man in formal dress.

Transvaal Archives, TKP 156 (p. 143)

LEGAND, Jules
The Mendelssohn Collection in the Library of Parliament, Cape Town, possesses a series of watercolours by Legand. Only one, however, entitled *Night Patrol*, depicts a scene from the Boer War. This watercolour is similar to an illustration entitled *With BP in Mafeking*, which was published on page 6 of *The Daily Graphic Special Mafeking Number*. The illustration in the paper was done by Georges Scott and it is possible that Legand copied it. Nothing is known about Legand.

Verbeek, Early Natal Art

LEHMANN-SCHRAM, W.
Swiss cartoonist whose work appeared in the Zurich weekly, *Nebelspalter*. He often signed his work with the initials 'WL-S'.

LEHR, Christian Wilhelm Jacob 1856-?
Lehr was born on 25 March 1856 in Berlin. Even though he was a sculptor it is assumed that he may have been responsible for the illustrations of some of the postcards 'sent in shoals' to welcome Kruger on his arrival in Europe during November 1900. The quotation 'sent in shoals' was taken from *Navy & Army Illustrated* which featured this postcard. The article with its disparaging comments about Kruger appeared in the magazine on 8 December 1900. While several variants of this particular card exist in several languages, Lehr's signature (with a date assumed to be '2,7', [2 July]) appears on those with a dark background. French, German, Dutch, English, Croatian, Italian and Russian versions have been noted. Other cards with an almost identical illustration (light background with palm trees, however) are signed by Arthur Thiele and were published by Kunzli of Zurich.

Bénézit, Dictionnaire antique, vol. 5, p. 489
SAPRG Newsletter, no. 11, Feb. 1984

LEIBL, Wilhelm Maria Hubertus 1834-1900
Leibl was born in Cologne on 23 October 1834. His Boer War work appeared in *Der Burenkrieg*. One of his sketches was reproduced on p. 3 under a poem entitled 'Burenland' by Hermann Lingg. Leibl died in Würzburg on 4 December 1900.

Bénézit, Dictionnaire antique, vol. 5, p. 489

---

1 His Majesty King Edward VII: Commemorative bust of his coronation. An illustration of Guillaume Laplagne's plasticine sculpture appeared in *Le Rire* on 10 May 1902 as part of his '*Monuments Anthumes*' series. It shows the bitterness the French felt towards the British, although the War was over.
2 One of a series of six cards illustrated by a French cartoonist identified only as 'L' or Lenny. No publisher's imprint appears. Towards the end of the War clothing for the Boers was at a premium, and most British prisoners were debagged before being released. This illustration refers to this practice.
3 Charles Léandre's cartoon of an overweight Queen Victoria sitting atop Paul Kruger has the ironic title: *England the eternal champion of Justice, upholder of the weak*. This cartoon appeared on the front cover of *Le Rire* on 7 October 1899, just four days before war was declared.
4 Charles Léandre's celebrated portrait of Paul Kruger which appeared on the cover of the special number of *La Vie Illustrée* on 16 November 1900. It also appeared on a postcard.

LEIGH, Chandos 1873-1914

Soldier-artist. Leigh was born during August 1873. The son of Sir E. Chandos Leigh K.C., he was educated at Harrow and Cambridge. He joined the King's Own Scottish Borderers through the Warwickshire Militia on 29 May 1895, becoming lieutenant on 22 September 1897. During the Boer War he served with the Mounted Infantry and took part in the relief of Kimberley and operations in the Orange Free State. He was present at Paardeberg, Poplar Grove, Houtnek, Vet River and Zand River. He was in the Transvaal during June 1900 and saw action near Johannesburg and Diamond Hill. He was also in the Orange Free State in 1900 where he saw action at Wittebergen and Bothaville, and was in the Transvaal, Free State and Cape from 30 November 1900 to 31 May 1902.

Leigh was mentioned in despatches (*London Gazette*, 10 September 1901) and received the Queen's medal with six clasps. He was created D.S.O. on 27 September 1901 for his services in South Africa.

Leigh was promoted to captain on 1 April 1901 and spent the following 10 years in the Egyptian Army. During World War I he went to France with his regiment and was reported missing on 23 August 1914 at Mons. According to reports, even though wounded he was seen to be encouraging his men and telling them not to mind about him. Six months later returning wounded prisoners reported that he died in August 1914 of wounds received in action during this battle. He had the dubious distinction of being the first Harrovian to die in the War. His only brother, Lt. E.H. Leigh of the 2nd Battalion of the Rifle Brigade, was killed on the Aubers Ridge in May 1915 and his grief-stricken father died three days later.

A sketchbook of the Boer War done by Leigh is in the Regimental Museum of the King's Own Scottish Borderers in Berwick-on-Tweed. Leigh's only other Boer War work traced is a sketch which appeared in *The Graphic* on 16 March 1901, redrawn by Frank Dadd and entitled *In pursuit of De Wet: An engagement with the enemy's rearguard at Thabacsburg* (sic).

Creagh and Humphris, The D.S.O., *p. 233*
Hofmeyr, Matton and Roets, Graphic Picture Index
Personal communication with the Curator of the Regimental Museum, King's Own Scottish Borderers, Berwick-on-Tweed

LEIGHTON, Frederick

Designer. Leighton did several heraldic designs for the postcard firm of C.W. Faulkner and Co. The heraldic designs on the 'Patriotic Postcard' series of Boer War cards (numbers 19, 21, 22 and 23) were probably by him. All of these cards had Boer War relevance. In 1903 Leighton exhibited a design for a bookplate at the Royal Academy. It is not known if the artist Lord Frederic Leighton, who died in 1896, was a relative.

Byatt, Picture Postcards
Graves, Royal Academy, *vol. 5, p. 33*
Johnson and Greutzner, British Artists, *p. 308*

LEIST, Frederick William 1877-1945

Painter and cartoonist. Leist was born in Sydney on 21 August 1877. Educated at the Crown Street Public School he studied art under Julian Ashton. For several years he was on the staff of *Sydney Bulletin* and *The Sydney Mail*. His work for *Sydney Bulletin* was noted for 'having a strong and individual style'. Leist went to London in 1908 and was commissioned by *The Graphic* to do a series of drawings. His first success as a painter was *The Mirror*, which was hung at the Royal Academy in 1911. The following year one of Leist's paintings was accepted by the Paris Salon. While living in London Leist exhibited regularly at the Royal Academy and also at the International Exhibition in Venice. During World War I he was appointed official artist with the A.I.F. in France and later painted two large murals for the Australian Pavilion at the Wembley Exhibition.

In 1925 Leist went to America where he painted murals for the Church of St Augustine in Florida. He travelled through Texas, New Mexico and Arizona. When he returned to settle in Australia in 1926 he was appointed lecturer in painting at the East Sydney Technical College.

Leist was a member of the R.B.A. and the Royal Society of Painters in Oils in England. He was a founder member of the Royal Society of Arts in Sydney, the Australian Academy of Art, a member of the Australian Watercolour Institute and the '15 Group'.

Examples of his work are found in art galleries in Sydney, Melbourne and Bendigo, the National Australian Collection at Canberra, and the Sheffield and Bradford Galleries in England. In *Art in Australia* (March 1927), Leon Gellert wrote 'Fred Leist is one of the most resourceful artists this country has produced — illustrator, figure painter and war artist. He was the first to portray the Australian girl as a definite type.'

Leist's Boer War contribution can be found in *After Pretoria: the Guerilla War* and consists mainly of frontline work done in Australia showing troops parading in Australian cities or embarking for South Africa.

Houfe, British Illustrators and Caricaturists, *p. 370*
The Strand, *vol. 23, p. 663*

LEMPEREUR, François (?)

Lempereur's Boer War cartoons appeared in *Le Rire* and *La Caricature*. A François Lempereur is listed in Bénézit as a French-born sculptor who died in 1904. It is possible, but unlikely, that the two Lempereurs are the same artist.

Bénézit, Dictionnaire antique, *vol. 5, p. 508*

LENBACH, Frans-Seraph von 1836-1904

Portrait painter. Lenbach was born in Schrobenhausen, Germany, on 13 December 1836. He was a pupil at the Academy at Munich. His portrait of President M. T. Steyn appeared on the front cover of *Jugend* in April 1902 (issue 14). Lenbach died in Munich on 6 May 1904.

Bénézit, Dictionnaire antique, *vol. 5, p. 510*

LENNY: see 'L.'

LE PETIT, Alfred 1841-1909

Caricaturist. Le Petit studied art in Rome and Paris. In 1870 he published and contributed to *La Charge*, an anti-Empire satirical weekly. Because of its offensive nature it was banned by the authorities. At this time Le Petit often used the pseudonym 'Zut' or 'Alfred Le Grand'.

He contributed at various times to *Le Journal Amusant*, *La Fronde*, *Le Charivari*, *Sans-Coulotte* and *Le Petard*, and by the time the Boer War was in progress he was working for the Paris weekly *Le Grelot*. According to his son, Alfred Marie, he wished to devote his career to painting but complained 'I am condemned to the torture of producing caricatures forever'. Le Petit died on 15 November 1909.

Feaver, Masters of Caricature, *p. 87*
Osterwalder, and Hubschmid and Bouret (eds.),
Dictionnaire des Illustrateurs, *p. 622*

LEROY, Hippolyte 1857-?

Sculptor and medal designer born in Liège on 4 April 1857. He studied at the academy at Gand and at Falguire in Paris. He designed a medal which was struck in commemoration of the 'courageous protection given by the Queen of the Netherlands to the President of the Transvaal, his Excellency Paul Kruger'. The medal was depicted on two separate postcards produced by Albert Sugg of Gand.

Bénézit, Dictionnaire antique, *vol. 5, p. 536*

LESLIE, George Dunlop 1835-1921

Landscape and genre painter. The son of C. R. Leslie R.A., George Leslie was born in London in July 1835. He studied with his father and at the Royal Academy schools. He is listed as a Royal Academy exhibitor from 1857 and was elected A.R.A. in 1868 and R.A. in 1876. In 1900 Leslie's oil, *In time of war*, was exhibited and is presumably of Boer War interest. It shows a lady sitting in a formal garden with her head in her knees. The painting was illustrated in *Royal Academy Pictures 1900*, p. 98.

Graves, Royal Academy, *vol. 5, p. 44*
Waters, British Artists, *vol. 1, p. 203*

LEVERING, Albert

Harper's Weekly and *Life* cartoonist.

LEWIN, Frederick George fl. 1901-1930

Punch cartoonist who produced very occasional illustrations of Boer War related subjects in 1901 and 1902. He was elected a member of the R.W.A. in 1906.

Houfe, British Illustrators and Caricaturists, *p. 371*

LEWIS, Robert

La Caricature cartoonist and postcard artist. Lewis's coloured front cover illustration, *Golgotha*, showing Kruger as a crucified Jesus Christ appeared in that magazine on 8 February 1902 and his *Le Don Quichotte Sud Africain* appeared on 6 December 1902. One of his postcards was published by A.B., Paris, in both coloured and uncoloured forms. The card, which carried the title *Bruits de Paix*, lampooned Edward VII and Chamberlain.

LIEBERMANN, Max 1847-1935

Genre, landscape and portrait painter. Liebermann was born in Berlin on 20 July 1847. He became an extremely prolific and well-known artist and illustrator. One Boer War painting by Liebermann was reproduced on p. 20 of *Der Burenkrieg* and shows a Dutch farmhouse.

Bénézit, Dictionnaire antique, *vol. 5, pp. 571-572*
Osterwalder, and Hubschmid and Bouret (eds.),
Dictionnaire des Illustrateurs, *p. 632*

LINDBERG, Ernst Evert 1864-?

Lindberg was born in Helsinki, Finland, on 3 January 1864. He and his family emigrated to New York in 1892 where he obtained work as a decorator. In Finland he had been trained as a bookbinder, mechanic and decorator.

Lindberg came out to South Africa before the War and worked on the mines. At the outbreak of War he joined the Scandinavian Corps, and as a member of the ambulance unit he was involved in the conflict at Mafeking and later at Magersfontein.

Lindberg was captured at Paardeberg where he was slightly wounded and was sent to St Helena. In 1902 he was repatriated to his native land where he wrote a book about his experiences; it was entitled *Suomalaisen Seikkailuja buurisodassa ja muistoja van keudesta St. Helenan saarella*. He returned to South Africa with his family in 1903 and once again worked on the gold mines.

During his captivity on St Helena Lindberg painted at least two oils. One, of Gen. Cronje done from a photograph, is in the McGregor Museum. The other, of Deadwood Camp, was offered for sale in Cape Town by Sotheby's on 24 May 1983 and is now owned by the Africana Museum, Johannesburg.

Personal communication with Fiona Barbour,
Ethnologist, McGregor Museum, Kimberley

LINDSAY, Norman Alfred William 1879-?

Cartoonist. Lindsay was born in Creswick, Victoria, Australia on 23 February 1879. He joined the staff of the *Sydney Bulletin* in 1901 and later became the newspaper's chief cartoonist. He was considered to be Australia's finest black and white artist. His Boer War cartoons appeared in the paper towards the end of the War.

Houfe, British Illustrators and Caricaturists, *p. 372*
Review of Reviews, *vol. 23, Jan.-June 1902*

LINSE, Hendrik Jan Carel 1843-1906

Watercolourist, etcher and lithographer. Linse was born in Amsterdam on 30 April 1843. He worked in Rotterdam, The Hague and Amsterdam. He was an illustrator for *Humoristich*

1 'Royal Dragoons - S Africa

Album at the time of the War and in 1902 worked for *Nederlandsche Spectator*. He also contributed to *Der Wahre Jacob* and *Abraham Prikkie*, as well as illustrating several books including Louwrens Penning's *De Verdedigers en Verdrukkers der Afrikaansch Vrijheid*. One of his lithographs, *Kersttijd 1900: De groote industriël*, was published in the supplement to *De Amsterdammer: weekblad voor Nederland* on 23 December 1900. (This issue also carried the usual supplement by Braakensiek [see page 112].)

SABIB, *vol. 3, p. 649*
Scheen, Nederlandse Beeldende Kunstenaars, *vol. 1, p. 714*
The Strand, *vol. 24, p. 91*

LINTOTT, Edward Barnard 1875-1951
Portrait and landscape painter. Lintott was born in London on 11 December 1875. He was educated at the Académie Julian, the Sorbonne and the École des Beaux-Arts. He won the Carnegie Prize for work exhibited at the Salon des Artistes Français. During the War he worked for *Lloyd's News* and *The Illustrated Mail*. Lintot died in Chelsea in 1951.
Houfe, British Illustrators and Caricaturists, *p. 373*

LION, G. 1
Cartoonist. Lion worked for *Le Bon Vivant, La République Illustrée, L'Indiscret, Le Charivari* and *La Caricature*. One coloured cover cartoon by him appeared in *La Caricature* on 27 October 1900, entitled *à Lourenço Marques*; it showed Chamberlain attempting to shave Kruger in Lourenço Marques. Two divided-back Lion postcards with Boer War relevance have also been noted. One, published by P.L. of Paris with a signed illustration, is entitled *Edouard VII, son rêve, son cauchemar*. The other, *Jeu de Cartes des souverains*, obviously part of a set, also shows Edward VII; the publisher is unknown.

LIONEL
One of the illustrators of *La Guerre du Transvaal: Anglais et Boers*.

LLOYD, T. Ivester 1
Very little is known of this artist. One of his illustrations appeared on p. 335 of *With the Flag to Pretoria*, entitled *A race for life — Two newspaper correspondents risk their lives in attempt to escape capture*. The author has one watercolour entitled *First Royal Dragoons South Africa*. The Regimental Museum of the Gordon Highlanders in Aberdeen has six pen-and-ink drawings by Lloyd depicting the War.
Lloyd is also listed as a military and general postcard artist. He illustrated the 'Our friends and Allies' series by W.N. Sharpe Ltd., Bradford, and he signed some of these cards with the initials 'T.I.L.'. Equestrian and sporting paintings by Lloyd have been noted at English auctions.
Byatt, Picture Postcards, *p. 249*
Personal communication with Capt. C. Harrison (Ret.), Curator, Regimental Museum, Headquarters, Gordon Highlanders, Aberdeen, Scotland

LOBEL, P. H. 1
Lobel was a French cartoonist who was virulently anti-British. One of his cartoons which attacked Chamberlain, entitled *Le 'Happy New Year' de La Reine* appeared on the front cover of issue 1096 of *La Caricature*, dated 29 December 1900.
Lobel was also responsible for at least two series of chromolithographed postcards. These cartoons attacked Chamberlain and King Edward VII and portrayed the suffering of the Boers. Lobel was particularly fond of adding as much blood as possible to his coloured illustrations. One series of cards was entitled *La Paix des Lâches. Revue de fin d'année par un Lâche anonyme. 2me series* and the other *Fruits de la Conférence de la Paix Transvaal – Chine. 10 cartes postales*. The titles do not appear on the cards themselves but have been obtained from their packaging. Neudin, in identifying Lobel's signature, refers to him erroneously as 'Solal'.

LOCHARD
Illustrator of lithographed music cover *Hommage au President Kruger, Gloire au Peuple Boer*. The music was written by Victor Thieles and created by Moullett and Berard, and the songs were sung by Mesdames Dufresne, Jeanne Dubray and Cecile d'Aulnay and Messrs Gasty, Dartagnan and Flories.

LOMAX, John Arthur 1857-1923
Genre and historical painter in oil. Lomax was born in Manchester in 1857. He studied in Stuttgart and exhibited several paintings at the Royal Academy from 1880. In 1900 his painting *A Soldier ever! Assassin never!* was shown and is presumably of Boer War interest. Lomax lived in St John's Wood where he died on 13 December 1923.
Graves, Royal Academy, *vol. 5, p. 84*
Johnson and Greutzner, British Artists, *p. 317*
Waters, British Artists, *vol. 1, p. 208*

LONGSTAFF, William Francis
British artist who was responsible for the oil, *The Battle of Diamond Hill*, which hangs in the museum at the Regimental Headquarters of the Worcestershire and Sherwood Foresters Regiment in Nottingham.
Johnson and Greutzner, British Artists, *p. 318*
Personal communication with Maj. G. F. Dodd, Curator, Museum of the Worcestershire and Sherwood Foresters Regiment

LOOYMANS, Romain 1864-1914
Landscape, interiors, religious and genre painter. Looymans was born in Antwerp on 3 February 1864. He was a member of the committee that produced the *Antwerpen-Transvaal Gedenknummer* in aid of wounded Boers. Looymans died in Antwerp on 14 June 1914.
Bénézit, Dictionnaire antique, *vol. 5, p. 629*

LORAINE, Nevison Arthur fl. 1889-1903
Figure and landscape painter. Lorraine was elected to the R.B.A. in 1893. He contributed to *The Illustrated London News* in 1895. Loraine's Boer War work appeared on p. 17 of *Black & White Budget* on 24 February 1900. A double-page spread entitled *Lions of The Empire*, it shows lions representing the countries of the Empire taking part in the War.
Houfe, British Illustrators and Caricaturists, *p. 374*

LOURDEY, Maurice 1860-1934
Lourdey was the pseudonym of M. Lefèbvre-Lourdet, who was born in Paris on 8 April 1860. He exhibited at the Salon des Artistes Français from 1885 until 1892 and at the Salon des Humoristes between 1907 and 1915. Lourdey contributed at various times to *Le Courrier Français* (1888), *Le Bon Vivant*, *Gil Blas Illustré*, *Le Journal*, *Le Sourire* and *Le Rire*. His Boer War cartoons have been noted in *Le Petit Bleau*. Lourdey died in Paris in 1935.
Grand-Carteret, John Bull
Osterwalder, and Hubschmid and Bouret (eds.), Dictionnaire des Illustrateurs, *p. 642*

LOVETT, Alfred Crowdy 1862-1919
Lovett was gazetted to the Gloucester Regiment in 1883 and was promoted to captain in 1891, major in 1903, lieutenant colonel in 1911 and colonel in 1915. He was instructor at the Royal Military College from 1901 to 1906. He served in World War I and was mentioned in despatches. Lovett was awarded the C.B. in 1915 and was eventually promoted to brigadier general. He was a member of the Navy and Army Club.
Lovett was responsible for at least three watercolours of Boer War interest (c.1902). All three show soldiers in Boer War dress and can be found in the National Army Museum.
Mockler Ferryman's book, *Military Sketching and Reconnaissance*, features a topographical sketch by Lovett, dated 30 March 1903.
Lovett is best known for his military uniform prints. *Types of the British Army and Navy*, published as supple-

---

1 The little-known British artist T. Ivester Lloyd did this original watercolour of a trooper in the 1st Royal Dragoons.
2 The French cartoonist Lobel, who was known for producing very gory cartoons, was responsible for this rather mild postcard.

2

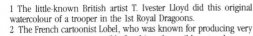
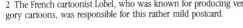

La Vieux Boer - Je ne marcherais jamais pour plus que cela !.....

ments to *The Graphic* on 29 April 1893, featured *The Madras Army and Troops* by Lovett. In 1911 *Lovett's Armies of India* was published, 73 plates of which were done by him.

British Military Costume Prints
Mockler Ferryman, Military Sketching and Reconnaissance, *p. 152*
Who was Who, *vol. 2, p. 646*

L., P. *see* P.L.

L., R. *see* R.L.

LUC
Revue Mâme cartoonist whose 'Petits échos du mois' occasionally feature the Boer War.

LUCAS, Henry Frederick Lucas ?-1943
Painter of hounds, horses and other equestrian scenes. Lucas was born in Louth in Lincolnshire. In 1878 he settled in Rugby where he had a studio. His Boer War related oil painting, *Rhodesian scout 1901*, was offered for sale at Ashbey's Galleries on 12 June 1986.

Waters, British Artists, *vol. 1, p. 210*
Who was Who, *vol. 4, pp. 703-704*

LUCAS, John Seymour 1849-1923
Historical portrait, genre and landscape painter. Lucas was born in London on 21 December 1849. (His uncle, John Lucas, was a well-known portrait painter.) He was educated at the Royal Academy schools. He was elected R.I. in 1877, A.R.A. in 1886 and R.A. in 1898. Over 180 of his works were exhibited at the Royal Academy. In 1914 Lucas was commissioned to do a fresco for the House of Commons.

In 1899 his *News from the front*, presumably of Boer War interest, was exhibited at the Royal Academy.

Graves, Royal Academy, *vol. 5, p. 104*
Johnson and Greutzner, British Artists, *p. 320*
Waters, British Artists, *vol. 1, p. 210*

LUCAS, Sydney Seymour fl. 1893-1940
Portrait painter and illustrator. Sydney Seymour Lucas was the son of John Seymour Lucas (see above) with whom he collaborated occasionally on certain illustrations. Lucas jnr. contributed, among others, numerous military sketches to *The Graphic* from 1893. He was often used as an illustrator of serialized stories in the paper, and occasionally these illustrations were in colour.

His Boer War work is restricted, however, to five illustrations: *A corps of gentlemen: Paget's Horse preparing for the front* (this consisted of four sketches which appeared on 3 March 1900) and *The living and the dead* (this was drawn from a photograph by E. Blake Knox and appeared on 2 June 1900).

Hofmeyr, Matton and Roets, Graphic Picture Index
Thorpe, English Illustration

LUI-MÊME, Haringus
Caricatures by this cartoonist appeared in *L'Agonie d'Albion*, which was written by Eugène Demolder and published by Mercure, Paris, in 1901.

SABIB, *vol. 2, p. 47*

LUKER, William (jnr.) 1867-?
Painter and illustrator of animal portraits and figures. The son of William Luker who was also a portrait, genre and animal painter, Luker jnr. was born in Kensington in 1867. He studied art at the R.C.A. schools. He exhibited at the principal London galleries from 1886 and he illustrated several books.

In 1901 one of his works, entitled *Earl Roberts arriving at Buckingham Palace*, was exhibited at the R.B.A. The painting fetched £52.10s.

Waters, British Artists, *vol. 1, p. 211*

LUMLEY, Augustus Savile fl. 1899-1950
Genre painter and illustrator who contributed Boer War illustrations to *Shurey's Pictorial Budget*. Lumley also worked for the other Shurey publication *Sketchy Bits*. He occasionally signed his work with the initials 'S.L.'.

Lumley became well known as a children's book and magazine illustrator, but his best-known work was his World War I recruitment poster *Daddy, what did YOU do in the Great War?*.

Houfe, British Illustrators and Caricaturists, *p. 376*
Johnson and Greutzner, British Artists, *p. 321*
Peppin and Micklethwait, British Book Illustrators, *pp. 187-188*
Thorpe, English Illustration, *p. 122*

LYNCH, Frank
Cartoonist and caricaturist who contributed regularly to *Fun* and *Judy*. During the War some of these cartoons were reproduced in *Burenstreiche*. His 'Prominent personages' series in *Pick-Me-Up* featured among others: No.14 Kruger (24 June 1899); No. 19 Chamberlain (29 June 1899); No. 26 Rudyard Kipling (16 September 1899). Lynch often signed his work with the initials 'F.L.'.

Houfe, British Illustrators and Caricaturists, *p. 377*
Judy, *29 March 1899, p. 146*
Thorpe, English Illustration

LYNCH, George 1868-1928
Lynch was born in Cork, Ireland, on 27 March 1868. He travelled widely in Australia and the Pacific islands. At the time of the Spanish-American War he represented the *Daily Chronicle*. At the start of the Boer War he was sent out from England to represent the *Morning Herald*, *Echo* and *The Illustrated London News*. He was present at the Battle of Elandslaagte and was wounded at Rietfontein. Like some of the other correspondents he was besieged at Ladysmith and early in December he asked General White's permission to go to the Boer lines to distribute copies of *The Ladysmith Lyre*.

This request was, of course, refused, but undaunted Lynch made an attempt anyway. He was soon captured by the Boers.

Lynch was sent to Pretoria and a flurry of telegrams concerning his capture was sent from both sides. After it was established that he was indeed a war correspondent, he was released and returned to England suffering from typhoid.

At least 13 of his sketches and photographs were inspiration for pictures which appeared in *The Illustrated London News* and 12 of these were reproduced in his book *Impressions of a War Correspondent* (1903).

Not long after his return to England Lynch was sent to China by *The Sphere*. He also represented the *Daily Express* there. He went to Macedonia for the *New York Journal* in 1903, Japan and Manchuria on behalf of the *London Daily Chronicle* in 1904, and Russia in 1905. During World War I he represented *The Illustrated London News* and *Westminster Gazette*.

Lynch was a keen inventor and patented several of his inventions, including gloves for handling barbed wire. Besides his *Impressions of a War Correspondent* he also published *The War of the Civilisations*, *Realities*, *The Path of Empire* and *Old and New Japan*.

Lynch died on 29 December 1928.

De Souza, No Charge for Delivery
Lynch, Impressions of a War Correspondent
Who was Who, *vol. 2, p. 654*

LYONS, Alfred fl. 1888-1919 1
South African cartoonist responsible for the illustrations on at least six anti-Boer envelopes produced in Johannesburg or Natal in 1901. They were: 1. *De Wet's Xmas pudding: with love from General French*; 2. *The Absent Minded Burgher*; 3. *Xmas on the veld: bringing in the Boer's head* (Kitchener); 4. *Xmas on the front* (Buller); 5. *Xmas greetings* (Cecil Rhodes and Kruger); and 6. *Seasonal greetings* (similar to number 5 but done in Natal not Johannesburg).

A postcard of the Bambata Revolution in 1906 bears Lyons's signature, and the Africana Museum catalogue lists Lyons's caricature of Victor Lewis done in 1919.

Lyons worked at various times for *The Lantern*, *The Port-folio*, *The Transvaal Truth*, *The Burlesque*, *The Standard* and *The Standard and Diggers News*. He also contributed to *The Daily Graphic* and *Pall Mall Budget*.

Lyons published *Rand People no. 1: Some Johannesburg Johnnies*. This publication, supposedly the forerunner of others, consisted of 15 caricatures of prominent Johannesburg personalities. It appeared before the War and no successors followed. In 1914 Lyons published *A South African alphabet of the War: cartoons and doggerel*.

MACAULEY, Charles R. 1871-?
Macauley was born in Canton, Ohio, in 1871. He worked as a cartoonist for *The Philadelphia Enquirer*, in which his Boer War cartoons were later published. He also lived and worked in New York for a while.

MACBETH, Robert Walker 1848-1910
Pastoral, landscape and rustic genre painter and etcher. The son of Norman Macbeth R.S.A., Macbeth was born in Glasgow on 30 September 1848. He studied art both in Edinburgh and in Friedrichsdorf, Germany. He later studied at the R.S.A. school. Macbeth went to London in 1870 where he was offered a job as an illustrator on *The Graphic*. He became an associate member of the Royal Academy in 1883 and a Royal Academician in 1903. Macbeth was made an R.E. in 1880 and an honorary member of the same society in 1909. He became a member of the R.O.I. in 1883 and an associate member of the R.W.S. in 1871, becoming a full member in 1901. He worked in Lincolnshire and Somerset and was much influenced by Frederick Walker and G.H. Mason. His *The Cast Shoe* was purchased by the Chantrey bequest in November 1890.

Macbeth's limited Boer War illustrations appeared in *With the Flag to Pretoria* and *The Graphic*. Only one appeared in

GEN. CRONJE   L° ROBERTS

2

the latter (28 April 1900); it was entitled *St. Patrick's Day with the wounded from the Front: In the hospital at Pietermaritzburg* and was done from a sketch by Agnes M. Johnstone.

Macbeth died on 1 November 1910 in Golders Green, London.

Hofmeyr, Matton and Roets, Graphic Picture Index
Waters, British Artists, *vol. 1, p. 212*
Who was Who, *vol. 1, p. 446*

MACPHERSON, Douglas 1871-? 1

Illustrator and 'special' for *The Graphic*. The son of John Macpherson, who was also an artist, Douglas Macpherson was born in Essex on 8 October 1871. He was educated privately, but later studied at the Westminster School of Art. He became a staff member of *The Daily Graphic* at its inception and worked continuously for both the daily and weekly until 1913.

Macpherson was a 'special' artist at home and abroad. He was present during the Spanish-American War in 1898, the St Petersburg Revolt in 1905, and the assassination of Don Carlos in 1908. In 1913 he joined *The Sphere*. He was a member of the Royal Naval Volunteer Reserve. In 1923 Macpherson was witness to the opening of Tutankhamen's tomb. He drew the coronation of King George VI for *The Daily Mail* in 1937 and did sketches during World War I for *The Sphere*, *The Daily Telegraph* and *The Daily Mail*. He was a member of the Langham Sketching Club.

During the Boer War Macpherson was very prolific for *The Daily Graphic*, but only one of his works was reproduced in *The Graphic* itself. *Reinforcements for the Cape station: Bluejackets going on board the S.S. Briton at Southampton* appeared on 11 November 1899 redrawn by Frederic de Haenen (see page 125).

The Royal Collection at Windsor has two works by Macpherson, done prior to the War, showing Queen Victoria's

Jubilee and another of the Queen in 1899. The National Army Museum has one pen-and-ink sketch by Macpherson depicting the surrender of Cronje. The author also has one of his pen-and-ink sketches. A postwar (1906) cartoon by a J.D. Macpherson can be found in the Africana Museum and it is likely that the two Macphersons are one and the same.

Dawnay and Miller, Military Drawings and Paintings
Houfe, British Illustrators and Caricaturists, *p. 382*
Waters, British Artists, *vol. 1, p. 221*

MADER, Percy Lionel 1873-? 1

Mader, a member of the Heilbron field cornetcy, was captured at Viljoensdrif on 15 October 1900. At the time he was 27 years old and must have been working on the railways as his address was c/o the railway station at Viljoensdrif. He was sent to Darrell's Island, Bermuda (P.O.W. no. 14592), where he drew a pen-and-ink sketch of a fellow prisoner, Jan van Tonder (11064), receiving a letter from his wife. This drawing is in the author's collection.

Personal communication with Mr J. Minnie, State Archives, Pretoria

MAGNE, Désiré-Alfred 1855-?

Genre, animal and flower painter. Magne was born in Vienna on 27 February 1855. He contributed to *Paris-Pretoria*.
Bénézit, Dictionnaire antique, *vol. 5, p. 693*

MAHUT, Maurice.

One of the illustrators of *La Guerre du Transvaal: Anglais et Boers*. He also contributed to *Le Petit Parisien*.

MAILICK, A. 1

A versatile German postcard artist who was well known for his 'Faith, Hope and Charity' series. During the Boer War Mai-

lick produced at least two illustrations which were published on postcards. There were at least six versions of *Fur Freiheit und Recht* published in Dutch and German either anonymously, by P. S.A.D. Erica or Paul Suss Dresden. *Hulde aan de Boeren* was also reproduced in several versions by different publishers in Dutch and German.

Holt, Tonie and Valmai, Picture Postcard Artists, *pp. 34-36 and* Stanley Gibbons Postcard Catalogue, *1984, p. 78*

MAIR, Maud

Miniature portrait painter. Mair, who was married to the painter Frank Eastman, exhibited more than 47 paintings at the Royal Academy. In 1904 her work, *Major General J.H. Bedford*, was shown there.

Graves, Royal Academy, *vol. 5, p. 167*
Johnson and Greutzner, British Artists, *p. 160*

MALTESTE, Louis Henri-Théodore ('Malatesta') 1870-1920

French lithographer, cartoonist, illustrator and poster artist. Malteste was born in Chartres on 20 October 1870. He contributed to several papers, including *Le Monde Illustré*, *La Vie en Rose*, *L'Assiette au Beurre* and *Le Rire*. He received recognition for his fine rapid illustrations during the Dreyfus trial and many of these drawings were reproduced in *The Daily Graphic*.

During the Boer War Malteste supplied cartoons to *L'Illustration*. One series of cartoons, entitled 'Opinion de quelques célébrités compétentes sur la Guerre du Transvaal', appeared on 6 January 1900. Other similar series of cartoons concerning the War were published in *Le Monde Illustré* (3 February 1900, 'Colonisation allemande'). One of his illustrations in *L'Assiette au Beurre* (22 August 1901) had Boer War relevance: *Vue prise au Transvaal ou en Chine, a moins que ce ne soit aux Philippines, au Maroc ou ailleurs, deux ans après la conférence de la Haye.*

Malteste died in Paris on 10 December 1920.

Selwyn Brinton (ed.), The Illustrators of Montmartre (A. Siegle, London, 1904)
Osterwalder, and Hubschmid and Bouret (eds.), Dictionnaire des Illustrateurs, *p. 657*

MANTE, Johannes Marte 1861-1920

Mante was born in Amsterdam in February 1861. He emigrated to South Africa where he became a building contractor. At the start of the Boer War he was attached to the field cornetcy of Melt Marais. Mante was captured at Elandslaagte on 21 October 1899 and sent to St Helena.

While on St Helena Mante manufactured and decorated at least two chessboards. One, which had 32 watercolour drawings on the lighter sections of the board, was presented to Mr K. Zwaardemaker, a pro-Boer Dutch philanthropist. Another, almost identical, board can be found in the Africana Museum. Two similar boards, possibly made under Mante's supervision, exist. One, signed 'D. Jansen', is in the author's collection, the other in the Totius Museum in Potchefstroom.

In a letter to Mr Zwaardemaker, Mante included a diagram showing how the various subjects appear on the board; the subjects, all St Helena views, are as follows:

3

Für Freiheit und Recht!

4

1 Alfred Lyons, the Johannesburg cartoonist, produced this pictorial envelope in 1901. Several others in this series have been noted.
2 Douglas MacPherson, 'special' artist for *The Graphic*, produced this pen-and-ink sketch of Cronje's surrender at Paardeberg. This important event in the War was depicted by several artists, of whom most were not present to witness it. Reproduced by courtesy of the National Army Museum, London.
3 Percy Mader did this pen-and-ink sketch of a fellow prisoner, Jan van Tonder, while in the Boer prisoner of war camp at Darrell's Island, Bermuda.
4 A. Mailick drew the illustration for this postcard *Fur Freiheit und Recht*, which was published in at least six versions in German and Dutch.

1. Jamestown from the sea.
2. Jamestown seen from the centre of the island.
3. The wharf: only landing place.
4. Jamestown with the ladder (800 steps leading up to the barracks cove).
5. Quoit-throwing in Deadwood Camp.
6. Flea-catching, a daily and absolutely necessary task in the camp.
7. Fetching water in the camp.
8. Deadwood Camp.
9. Emperor Napoleon's grave.
10. Longwood seen from the camp.
11. Napoleon's grave.
12. Near Napoleon's grave.
13. Street in Deadwood Camp.
14. Cooking in Deadwood Camp.
15. Blikkiesdorp (Tintown) in Deadwood Camp.
16. Part of the camp for English soldiers.
17. Highknol with citadel (fort).
18. Napoleon's grave.
19. At Knolcombe near the prisoner-of-war cemetery.
20. Highknol from the other direction.
21. Part of Jamestown.
22. Ruins and old slave cemetery in Rupperts Valley.
23. The Magistrate's house.
24. Religious Service in the camp, Pulpit and Sounding board (above the pulpit) made from branches and sacks. House in the background is the church made of the same material and used in rain and in the evenings.
25. Beach at Rupperts Valley with view of the condensation plant of sea water.
26. Near Knolcombe.
27. Entrance to Deadwood Camp.
28. St Matthew's Church.
29. English warship guarding us.
30, 31, and 32. Views from Deadwood Camp.

After his release Mante was repatriated to Holland where he married Jenneke Aalders. The couple had five children, and the family later returned to Pretoria, where Mante died on 5 October 1920.

Quarterly Bulletin, *vol. 36, nos. 3 and 4 (March and June 1982, Parts 1 and 2), 'Some artefacts and curios made by Boer prisoners-of-war' by F.R. Bradlow*

MANTON, G. Grenville 1855-1932

Manton was born in London in 1855. He was educated there and in Paris. He was a Royal Academy medallist and was elected a member of the R.B.N. in 1899.

In 1890 Manton visited America, where he painted portraits. On his return he worked as an illustrator for *Pall Mall Magazine* and, at its inception in 1900, for *The Sphere*. During the Anglo-Boer War Manton's illustrations appeared in

Black & White, Black & White Budget and *The Sphere*.
Houfe, British Illustrators and Caricaturists, *p. 383*
Thorpe, English Illustration
Waters, British Artists, *vol. 1, p. 223*

MARAIS, C. C.

A facsimile sketch by a Boer artilleryman appeared in *The Graphic* on 25 August 1900. It was entitled *Transvaal State Artillery in action before Ladysmith* and credit was given to 'C. C. Mavais'. This is probably a misprint and should have been Marais.

Hofmeyr, Matton and Roets, Graphic Picture Index

MARNIX

Cartoonist responsible for a postcard cartoon dated 6 January 1902 depicting Bismarck and Cecil Rhodes.

MARSHALL, J. Fitz 1859-1932

Animal, landscape and flower painter. Marshall was educated in Croydon and exhibited at the Royal Academy from 1883. He was elected R.B.A. in 1896. In 1900 he exhibited *Attack and Defence*, in 1901 *A frontal attack* and in 1902 *Victory*, at the R.B.A. The last-named picture fetched 18 guineas.

Waters, British Artists, *vol. 1, p. 225*

MARTIN, A. D.

A cartoonist by this name worked for the *St Louis Post and Despatch*. A reproduction of one of his cartoons appeared in *The King* on 20 January 1900.

MARTENS, Willem (Willy) 1856-1927   1

Dutch artist born in Semarang, Dutch East Indies, on 1 December 1856. He worked in both Paris and Amsterdam and was an exhibitor at the St Louis Exposition in 1904. At one time he was director of the Rijksmuseum in Amsterdam.

Martens was responsible for a photolithograph, *De Slag bij Krugersdorp* (Jacques Dusseau and Co., 20 Doelenstraat Amsterdam and 6 Kerk Street, Cape Town). The photolithograph, which is undated, probably refers to the Jameson Raid.

Scheen, Nederlandse Beeldende Kunstenaars
The Studio, *vol. 33, pp. 321-330, 'Dutch art at the St Louis Exposition' by M.I.G. Oliver*

MATANIA, Fortunino 1881-1963

Historical, battle and portrait painter. The son of Eduardo Matania, a professor of art, Fortunino Matania was born in Naples on 16 April 1881. He studied under his father and illustrated his first book at the age of 14, having contributed to a leading Italian paper from the age of 12. He worked in Milan as a 'special' artist for *Illustrazione Italiana*, before going to work for *L'Illustration Française* and then for *The Graphic* in London. He returned to Italy in 1903, at the age of 22, to

do military service after which he settled in London where he joined the staff of *The Sphere*. He was appointed 'special' artist for the paper in 1914 and saw action on several fronts. He produced several hundred pictures while working as a war artist and eventually he became *The Sphere*'s principal artist.

Matania was elected R.I. in 1917. He is reputed to have covered every coronation from Edward VII to Elizabeth II. Gibbons classifies him as a postcard artist, his most famous design being his World War I *Good Bye Old Man*.

During the Boer War one illustration by Matania appeared in *The Graphic* on 9 August 1902. At 21 he was probably one of the youngest professional Boer War illustrators. Entitled *The landing of ex-president Steyn at Southampton on his way to Holland*, the original drawing is owned by Argyll Elkin, the London firm of philatelic dealers.

Hofmeyr, Matton and Roets, Graphic Picture Index
Houfe, British Illustrators and Caricaturists, *p. 385*

MATHEWS, John Chester fl. 1880-1900

British artist known for his equestrian paintings. He was responsible for the heliochrome supplement showing Lord Roberts on his horse which appeared in *The Illustrated London News* on 9 June 1900.

Johnson and Greutzner, British Artists, *p. 345*

MAUD, William Theobald 1865-1903   4

'Special' for *The Graphic* and *The Daily Graphic*. Maud was born in England in September 1865. He studied at the Royal Academy schools and while he was still a student he contributed sporting sketches to *Punch*. He also illustrated *Rumford's Hounds*, *Hawbuck Grange* and other sporting books. In 1893 he was awarded the Landseer Scholarship, and soon afterwards travelled as a war artist through Armenia, Crete and Egypt, having joined the staff of *The Daily Graphic*.

In 1896, attached to the rebel side, Maud was sent to cover the conflict in Cuba, and in April the following year he accompanied the Greek army in Thessaly during the war against Turkey. His next assignment for *The Daily Graphic* was in the Sudan where he covered the march of the Sirdar to Abu Hamed in November 1897. At the end of the year Maud travelled to the north-western frontier of India and returned to the Sudan in May 1898 in time to cover Kitchener's march on Omdurman.

Maud left England for South Africa on 29 September 1899 aboard the *Tintagel Castle*. While on board he wrote:

We were 2 days from Cape Town when we met the *Dunvegan Castle* homeward bound. Word came down from the bridge that a vessel was in sight on the port side, and all crowded along the bulwarks to get a glimpse of her. The excitement of this moment was intense. Slowly but surely three masts and a big red funnel rose above the horizon. Presently the hull of the *Dunvegan Castle* came

into view. Captain altered course several points and closed in on her. We watched while the flags which made the query 'Is it peace or war?' fluttered up from the bridge on the mast head, and then we waited for the answer. Presently three flags fluttered above the bridge – a white pennant with a red ball in the centre then another pennant, half yellow and half blue; and below these two a square red flag with a yellow cross on it. A pause then again four others flew aloft to join their fellows. This was the message. The flags came tumbling down like a wounded bird upon a deck. Eyes turned instinctively towards the Captain and someone on the bridge said in a low voice 'War last Wednesday'.

This incident, which was reported in *The Graphic*, was redrawn by H.M.Paget and reproduced in *The Graphic* on 11 November 1899.

Shortly after his arrival in Cape Town Maud left for Natal where he was later trapped in Ladysmith, sharing a house there with George Steevens of *The Daily Mail*. When the latter became ill with typhoid Maud nursed him and remained with him to the end, acting as pallbearer at Steevens's night funeral.

During the siege Maud managed to send a few of his morale-boosting sketches out of Ladysmith by means of black runners. These included sketches entitled *Playing with the Boers* and *The Man of Straw*. The delivery of most of his sketches had to wait, however, until the town was relieved.

H.W. Nevison, a representative of *The Daily Chronicle*, related in his *Ladysmith: Diary of a Siege*: 'The narrowest escape was when a great fragment flew through an open door and cut the leg clean off a table where Mr Maud of *The Graphic* sat at work'. Maud was not injured. The battle of Caesar's camp on 6 January 1900, when the Manchester and Devonshires prevented the Boers from taking the town, inspired Maud to produce one of his best-known drawings.

Maud took the rather unusual step of volunteering his services as aide-de-camp to Ian Hamilton, but assured his head office that his new duties would not interfere with his responsibility to the paper.

When the siege was over Maud resigned his commission and then on his way home he contracted enteric fever at Durban. He was invalided there for some time before he returned to England, where he continued to illustrate as a home-based artist for *The Graphic*. On 8 December 1900 *The Graphic* reported on a lecture he had given on his war experiences. The proceeds of the lecture were in aid of the Ear, Nose and Throat Hospital in London.

Maud represented both *The Daily Graphic* and *The Graphic* at Queen Victoria's funeral and King Edward VII's coronation. He also covered the Somali Campaign, his sketches and drawings of which appeared regularly in *The Graphic*. He was a vigorous writer and one of his last despatches describing the fierce attack on Gough's column was the first full account to reach England and had the distinction, according to *The Graphic*, of being read in parliament.

Maud exhibited one painting at the Royal Academy in 1897. Two of his sketches were reproduced in Carter's *The Work of War Artists in South Africa*: *A candidate for the V.C.* and *The Charge of the Devons at Wagon Hill*. Both *The Graphic History of the South African War* and *The Graphic* special double number of 2 April 1900 were liberally illustrated with Maud's work.

The author has three paintings by Maud: *The Charge of the Devons at Wagon Hill* (*The Graphic* special double number, 2 April 1900); *A Tight fit on the Road to Lydenberg* (sic) (*The Graphic*, 29 September 1900); and *Sport and War: shooting partridges from an armoured train*, from a sketch by Lionel James (10 August 1901). The Africana Museum has *British Troops and Street musicians in Pretoria 1900* and the Royal Collection *King Edward VII presenting colours to Lord Strathcona's Horse, Buckingham Palace 15 February 1901*.

Maud was awarded the Queen's South Africa medal on 12 February 1903. He died in Aden on 12 May the same year, at the age of only 38. He had married in 1898 and he left his widow with two small children. He was on his way home from Somaliland when he died of, according to *The Times*, 'syncope'. Even though he died after the War, the memorial by Goscombe John in St Paul's Cathedral to the special correspondents who died in the War includes his name.

Carter, War Artists in S.A.
Dawnay and Miller, Military Drawings and Paintings
The Graphic (obituary), *16 May 1903*
Graves, Royal Academy, *vol. 5, p. 214*
Hodgson, The War Illustrators
Johnson, Front Line Artists
Personal communication with Kintracers
The Orders and Medals Research Society, *Summer 1986*, 'War Correspondents: South Africa 1899-1902', by Patrick Street Waters, British Artists, *vol. 1, p. 227*

MAURELL, F.
One of the illustrators of *La Guerre du Transvaal: Anglais et Boers*.

MAY
A cartoonist who worked for the *Detroit Mail*.

1 *Die Slag bij Krugersdorp*, by Willy Martens. This illustration was used on several postcards, including one published by Kotting of Amsterdam. One of them has a postmark of 16/10/99, making it one of the earliest of the War.
2 William Maud, 'special' artist for *The Graphic* and *The Daily Graphic*, smuggled this sketch out of Ladysmith during the siege of that town. Titled *How news is brought from Ladysmith: Correspondents despatching a runner*, it was redrawn by George Scott and published in *The Graphic* on 24 February 1900. Maud, Lynch and G.W. Steevens are the correspondents depicted.
3 This watercolour by William Maud, *A Tight fit on the Road to Lydenberg* (sic) was reproduced in his paper *The Graphic* on 29 September 1900.
4 Phil May's versatile talents were used to design the back of this pack of playing cards manufactured by Goodall and Son Ltd, London.
5 A caricature of the celebrated cartoonist Phil May.
6 Phil May's cartoon about John Bull and the Transvaal, based on the well-known Pears Soap advertisement.

MAY, Phillip William 1864-1903   3

Cartoonist. May was born on 22 April 1864 in Leeds. He was educated at St George's School, Leeds, and later became assistant scene painter at the Grand Theatre. He joined *The Society* and *St Stephen's Review* as an artist in 1883. He was offered a lucrative position in Australia where he worked for the *Sydney Bulletin* from 1885 to 1888. When he returned to Europe he studied art in Paris. He worked for *The Graphic* and *Punch* in 1895. He was elected a member of the R.I. in 1897. He published the *Phil May Annual* from 1892 and was a prominent member of both the Savage Club and the Langham Sketching Club.

May's Boer War work is not very prolific and relatively few War-related cartoons appeared, mostly in *Punch*.

A cartoon by May also appeared in *The Illustrated London News* on 16 December 1899 entitled *He won't be happy 'till he gets it*. This was a parody of a similar Pears Soap cartoon advertisement.

The author has several of May's cartoons including one undated pencil drawing of Kruger shedding crocodile tears on his departure from the Transvaal. The Africana Museum in Johannesburg has a similar pen-and-ink cartoon.

An unusual pack of playing cards with the backs designed and drawn by May, entitled *Nicely done*, shows Kruger, Chamberlain, Roberts and Baden-Powell. One Boer War scene by May, entitled *More for your money*, was depicted in the 'Cartoons from Punch' series of postcards (No. 10008).

May lived a Bohemian life and died of the combined effects of cirrhosis of the liver and tuberculosis on 5 August 1903.

Cuppleditch, *Phil May*

Illustrated London News, *(15 Aug. 1903), vol. 122, p. 230*

The Sketch, *(10 Oct. 1900), vol. 31, p. 485*
Thorpe, English Illustration
Thorpe, Phil May
Watson, The Savage Club
Who was Who, *vol. 1, p. 484*

MAYER, (Ernst Karl) Erich 1876-1960   1

Pro-Boer artist. Mayer was born in Karlsruhe, Germany, on 19 April 1876. He studied architecture at the Berlin Charlottenburg Technische Hochschule. These studies had a strong formative influence on his art and gave him the necessary facility for mastering the problems of perspective. A serious illness forced him to abandon his studies and he emigrated to South Africa in 1898 in order to regain his health. In South Africa he was appointed assistant surveyor at Vrede in the Orange Free State. In December 1899 he joined a Boer commando but during the assault on Mafeking in May 1900 he was captured and sent to St Helena.

Mayer spent nearly two and a half years in exile on the island, during which he produced several sketches of his fellow prisoners which can be found in the Africana Museum. One of the pictures he painted at this time was an oil of President Kruger in exile. Today it is housed in the War Museum of the Boer Republics in Bloemfontein.

After the War, despite his protests, Mayer was repatriated to Europe, via London and Tunis, in December 1902. He ar-

rived in Germany in May 1903 and his health again deteriorated. He had in the meanwhile continued his lessons in decorative art, for which he showed considerable talent. In December 1904 he found an opportunity to emigrate to South West Africa where he finally decided to devote himself exclusively to painting southern African scenes. Twice after his return to South West Africa, in the summer of 1907 and again from 1909 to 1911, he visited Germany to advance his art training. On the first occasion he studied in Karlsruhe and on the second in Stuttgart.

In October 1911 Mayer went to Port Elizabeth where he stayed for six months. He spent a further six months in Potchefstroom before he eventually settled in Pretoria. The Africana Museum has a number of studies dating from this Potchefstroom period, together with sketches and a picture book design created during his captivity on St Helena. At this time Mayer worked as an illustrator for the press and did book illustrations. He became acquainted with Pierneef and Wenning, among others, who had a strong influence on his work. His first notable success as an artist was at an exhibition held in Johannesburg in 1914.

When World War I broke out Mayer was once again arrested as an alien and he was interned in Pietermaritzburg for 21 months. In January 1928 he married Margaretha Gutter and in 1938 he and his wife founded the Pretoria spinning and weaving school.

The Africana Museum in Johannesburg has a collection of pencil drawings and sketches done by Mayer while on St Helena. They can be found in a loose leaf album of 117 pages. There is no title or general inscription and it was donated by Mrs J.M. van Drumelin, his sister-in-law. The Boer War titles are as follows:

M264 (1.) *Napoleon 1. His house. His tomb painted by E. Mayer – Vrede, prisoner of war, St. Helena, 1902.* Watercolour.

M265 (3.) *Mafeking 12/5/1900.* Pen and ink. Initialled in pencil 'E.M.'. On the back of this sketch are pencil and ink sketches of the heads of 12 men (M266).

M267 (4.) Four drawings, each signed Erich Mayer and entitled *Boer POW's, Mafeking.*

M268 (5.) *Map: the Island of St. Helena 1902.* Inscription: 'Made by a prisoner of war 1902'. Pen and ink and watercolour. Unsigned.

M269 (6 upper) *By rail as a prisoner from Mafeking to Cape Town 19.6.1900.* Inscription: 'Auf der Eisenbahnfahrt als Gefangener von Mafeking nach Kapstadt 19.6.1900'. Pencil. Unsigned.

M270 (6 lower) *Battle front, Mafeking.* Inscription 'Woche 1900 Heft 12'.' Pencil. Initialled 'E.M.'. A sketch of the dead on the field. On the back is another pencil sketch of the battlefield and other drawings.

M271 (7.) *St. Helena-Walking stick.* Inscription on carved walking stick: 'Mr. d'Albion P.O.W. – Lena'. Pencil. Signed 'EM 1901'. This consists of two sketches on one sheet: a building presumably on St Helena and, below, a walking stick carved by a prisoner of war. On the back are two small pencil sketches.

M272 (8.) *General Louis Botha – Portraits 1900*. Inscription on a) 'Louis Botha' and on b) 'Comdt.- Genrl. Louis Botha. 1900'.
a) Black paint touched with white and b) pen and ink, unsigned. There are four sketches on one sheet: two of General Botha and two landscapes. On the back is a landscape with trees initialled 'E.M.'.

M273 (9.) *St. Matthew's Church, St. Helena 1900*. Inscription on mount: 'St Mathaus Kirche 2000 fuss über . . .' Pen and ink. Signed 'Erich Mayer – Vrede, Prisoner of War Okt. 1900'.

M274 (11.) *Deadwood Camp-Plan*. Inscription on mount: 'Deadwood camp'. Pencil and crayon. Unsigned.

M275 (12.) *St James Church, St Helena*. Inscription on mount: 'Marktplatz mit Kirche en Jakobsleiter'. Pencil. Initialled 'E.M.'.

M276 (13a.) *View from Longwood Mill*. Inscription: 'View from Longwood mill'. Pen and ink. Unsigned; (b) *Longwood Camp*. Pen and ink. Unsigned. On the back of these pictures are (M277a) *Longwood Mill* Pencil, initialled 'E.M.', and (b) *Napoleon's House and Fish-pond*. Inscription: 'Napoleons haus u. Fischbassin'. Pencil. Unsigned.

M278 (16 upper) Pen-and-ink landscape, *Jamestown*. On the same sheet a pencil drawing, initialled 'E.M.', A Mansion, Jamestown'.

M280 (17.) *P.O.W.'s going out to work – St. Helena*. Pencil. Initialled 'E.M.'.

M281 (18 upper) *High Knoll Fort, St. Helena*. Inscription on mount: 'Fort High Knoll'. Watercolour. Signed 'Erich Mayer'.

M282 (18 lower) *Street in Jamestown, St. Helena*. Inscription: 'Strasse in Jamestown'. Pen and ink. Signed 'E. Mayer'.

M283 (19.) *Deadwood Camp, St. Helena*. Inscription on mount: 'Deadwood Laager'. Pencil and wash. Initialled 'E.M.'.

M284 (20.) *P.O.W.'s working in a hut*. Unsigned.

M285 (21.) *Ruperts Bay and Turk's Head, and details of St Paul's Church*. Inscription in ink: 'St. Helena – Uferlandschaft gez. von Erich Mayer – Vrede – Ruperts Bay and Turk's Head' and below 'Details von der St. Paul's Kirche'. Unsigned.

M286 (22.) *See front (sic) house St. Helena*. Pencil. Initialled 'E.M.'.

M287 (24.) *Boers in front of house*. Pencil and wash. Initialled 'E.M.'.

M288 (25.) *Deadwood*. Pencil. Initialled 'E.M.'.

M289 (26 upper) *A Cannon, St. Helena*. Sepia wash. Unsigned.

M290 (26 lower) *Jamestown, St. Helena*. Pen and ink. Initialled 'E.M.'. On the back is a sketch of a landscape.

M291 (27.) *Two POW's fishing in Rupert's Bay*? Initialled 'E.M.'.

M292 (28 upper) *Deadwood Camp, St. Helena 1902*. Inscription on back: 'Prisoners tents, Deadwood Camp, St. Helena, in the background and house where Napoleon died'. Pencil.

M293 (28 lower) *British Soldiers on parade*. Watercolour. Initialled 'E.M.'.

M294 (29.) *Camp fire, St. Helena*. Watercolour. Initialled 'E.M.'. On back is a pen-and-ink sketch of a prisoner of war camp.

M295 (31.) *A house in St. Helena 1900*. Inscription: 'Aan die pad na die Hawe St. Helena'. Pencil. Signed 'deur Erich Mayer 1902'.

M296 (32.) *Mr Deason's mill, St. Helena*. Inscription: 'Longwood & Mr. Deason's Mühle' and on mount 'Alte Windmühle hinter Napoleons Haus'. Watercolour. Initialled 'E.M.'.

M297 (33 upper) *Lot St. Helena 1902*. Inscription: 'Lot'. Pencil and wash. Initialled 'E.M.'.

M298 (33 lower) *Bay – with Jacob's Ladder 1902*. Pen and ink. Initialled 'E.M. 1902'.

The author has a pencil sketch, *Broadbottom Camp Vrijstaat Krijgsgevangene*, signed 'E.M. 1902'. The National Cultural History and Open-Air Museum in Pretoria also has several watercolours and pencil sketches done by Mayer during his captivity on St Helena.

Mayer died in Pretoria in August 1960.
Kennedy, Pictures in the Africana Museum, *vol. 7, pp. 58-62*
Lantern, 1984
Van der Westhuizen, Erich Mayer Album

MAYER, Henry ('Hy') 1868-?
Cartoonist and magazine editor. Mayer was born in Worms, Germany, in 1868. His parents emigrated to Britain when he was quite young, and in 1886 he went to the United States. He was considered a very versatile artist and his work was featured in satirical and humorous papers in the United States, England, Germany and France. Mayer returned to Worms to further his education and then went to London where he started work as a clerk. He travelled widely in North America, visiting Texas, Cincinnati, Chicago and Mexico. On his first return trip to Europe in 1890 Mayer became a part-time cartoonist with *Fliegende Blätter*. His series 'Worms' Eye Views' and 'Upside downery' caused quite a stir in the United States when they first appeared in *Life*. Mayer became editor-in-chief of *Puck* in 1914.

Mayer's Boer War work could be found in *Fliegende Blätter*, *Le Rire*, *Punch*, *The King*, *Illustrated Bits*, *Pick-Me-Up*, *Black & White* and *Black & White Budget*. One of his 'upside down' cartoons of Kruger appeared in *Black & White Budget* on 14 April 1900. This cartoon was possibly the inspiration for the Eysler postcard *John Bull before and after Ladysmith*.
Fielding, American Painters, etc.
The Strand, *vol. 23 (1902), pp. 311-313*

M'CRACKEN, Donald E.
An illustration by this artist, entitled *Crossing the Komati River*, was reproduced on the frontispiece of Louis Creswicke's *South Africa and the Transvaal War*, volume 7. Nothing is known about the artist.

MCCORMICK, Arthur David 1860-1943
McCormick was born in Coleraine, Ireland, on 14 October 1860. He was educated in Coleraine and Belfast before studying at the South Kensington Schools of Art from 1883 to 1886. He was official artist with Sir Martin Conway's expedition to the Himalayas from 1892 to 1893 and with Clifton Dent's expedition to the Caucasus in 1895. He was elected a member of the R.B.A. in 1897, the R.O.I. in 1905, and the R.I. in 1906. Several of his paintings were exhibited at the Royal Academy. He was a fellow of the Royal Geographical Society from 1895 and published *An Artist in the Himalayas* in the same year.

McCormick's relatively few Boer War illustrations can be found in *The Fight for the Flag in South Africa* by Edgar Sanderson. In 1903 his painting *War* was exhibited at the Royal Academy. It was presumably of Boer War interest.

McCormick often signed his sketches 'A.D.McC.'. He died in St John's Wood, London, in March 1943.
Graves, Royal Academy, *vol. 5, p. 132*
Waters, British Artists, *vol. 1, p. 214*
Who was Who, *vol. 4, p. 718*

MCCORMICK, Harry 1874-1917 [1]
'Special' artist for *The Graphic*. McCormick was born of Irish parents in Komga in the eastern Cape Colony. Before the Boer War he worked on the mines in Johannesburg. Very little is known about him, but he was almost certainly in Ladysmith during the siege. (Some sources say he was with the relieving forces, but this is unlikely.) Carter mentions McCormick briefly and reproduces one of his sketches on p. 24: '*Correspondents watching the Big Gun duel at Ladysmith* made by Mr. H. McCormick, the three figures in which are the late Mr. G.W. Steevens, Mr. G. Lynch and Mr. W.T. Maud'.

McCormick acted as correspondent for *The Graphic*, *The Daily Graphic* and *The Illustrated London News*, which reproduced one prewar illustration by him in Durban on 23 September 1899. *The Graphic* published 29 others up to 16 June 1900 and *The Graphic* special double number fea-

---

tured 11 of these, many depicting scenes of the siege. Some of them appeared in facsimile, including the one reproduced in Carter.

Verbeek lists two McCormick pictures. One, signed 'Harry McCormick' and entitled *Correspondents watching a big gun duel at Ladysmith*, is probably the original of the illustration referred to above. The other, signed 'H.Mc.C.', is in the Africana Museum. Entitled *Chat with 5th D.G. Carbineer Patrol* (1901), the illustration bears the following inscription in ink on the back: 'Wednesday. Riet. A. 10.4.01. A few days ago a Patrol of 12th Lancers, doing escort duty to conv[oy] to Kaalfontein passed our mine. So we had a few minutes ch[at] as the men stopped to enquire the way to their destination. We don't get much opportunity of having a chat with outside corps'. Below this comment is a cartoon entitled *Most disastrous Effect of today's washing. Put my shirts etc. with my blue socks and this is the effect of boiling them!!!*.

After the War McCormick became cartoonist for *The Rand Daily Mail* in Johannesburg and at the same time did illustrations for *The State*. He is assumed to have been the cartoonist ('H.Mc.C.') who contributed sketches to *The Transvaal Leader*. He left South Africa to study in Paris after favourable comments on 'his shrewd powers of observation'. He was friendly with and probably influenced by Charles Crosland Robinson and the latter's wife, Constance Penstone. A sketch book done by McCormick between 1899 and 1913 including Boer War and Cape Town suburban scenes is in the possession of his son, David, who lives in Fish Hoek near Cape Town.

McCormick joined the Artists' Rifles at the outbreak of World War I but died of wounds sustained as a P.O.W. during German raids in 1917.
Carter, War Artists in S.A., *p. 24*
De Wet, Illustrated London News Index
Hofmeyr, Matton and Roets, Graphic Picture Index
Kennedy, Pictures in the Africana Museum, *vol. 4, p. 1*
Schoonraad, Spot- en Strookprent Kunstenaars, *p. 158*
Verbeek, Early Natal Art

MCCUTCHEON, John Tinney 1870-?
McCutcheon was born in Indiana in 1870. He attended Purdue College and worked for the *Chicago Record* from 1889 to 1901, when the paper changed its name to *Record Herald*. In 1903 he joined the *Chicago Tribune* where he stayed for the rest of his working life.

In January 1898 McCutcheon embarked on a world tour aboard the despatch boat *McCulloch*. He was present at the battle of Manila Bay and sent home reports and drawings to his paper. He joined the Boer forces in April 1900, and, according to *Comic Art in America*, came out of the War 'with a whole skin, with hundreds of drawings behind him, and with hundreds of thousands of words of highly respectable prose to his credit'.
The Studio, *vol. 26 (1902), p. 286, 'American Press Illustrators' by W. Jenkins*

---

1 This wash drawing by Gordon Browne was based on a sketch by *The Graphic* 'special' artist Harry McCormick. It depicts the Rifle Brigade at Caesar's Hill. Reproduced by courtesy of the National Army Museum, London.
2 A pencil drawing by Erich Mayer, a German artist who fought on the side of the Boers. The sketch was produced while Mayer was a prisoner on St Helena and shows Broadbottom Camp, where Free State prisoners were interred.
3 Phil May's cartoon of Kruger, subtitled 'Mr Kruger shed tears on having to leave the Transvaal (Daily Paper). Mr Kruger has forwarded £2 000 000 to Europe (Daily Paper)'. The comment refers to the 'millions' that Kruger was said to have sent out of the Transvaal when he went into voluntary exile.
4 Lieutenant George McLean painted this watercolour in his diary. It shows the principal medical officer Lieutenant Colonel Watts carrying out his inspection of a camp hospital with the major and sister who McLean refers to as 'Major overworked and Sister Prettyone'. McLean was hospitalized in Pretoria on 29 September 1900.

MCDONALD, A. K. fl. 1898-1925

Cartoonist for *Moonshine*. His cartoons are also found in *Longbow*. McDonald often signed his work 'A.K.M.'.

MCFARLANE, John

This Scottish illustrator contributed occasional illustrations to *Black & White* and *Black & White Budget*. Some are reproduced in Brown's *War with the Boers*.

Wood, Victorian Painters, p. 298

MCKENZIE, Frank J.

Soldier-artist. McKenzie had sketches of the Boer War published in *The Graphic* and *The Illustrated London News*. He was probably with the Rhodesian forces stationed in that country prior to the War, since some of his sketches of the Matabele Rebellion were reproduced in *The Graphic*. During the War McKenzie published sketches in *The Graphic*, chiefly of Col. Plumer's relief column. *The Times History of the War* says that a Lt. McKenzie of the Gloucesters was taken prisoner at Nicholson's Nek. An illustration by McKenzie published in *The Graphic* on 30 November 1901 was called *How Boers treat their prisoners* and it is just possible that the two McKenzies are one and the same.

De Wet, Illustrated London News Index
Hofmeyr, Matton and Roets, Graphic Picture Index

MCLEAN, George Gilbert Creswick 1880-1928   2

Born on 28 August 1880, McLean was first commissioned on 16 February 1900 and served in the Boer War from July 1900 to May 1902 with the Royal Inniskilling Fusiliers. He went to India early in 1903. During World War I he served with the expeditionary force on the Western Front and later in Iraq, holding various appointments, including assistant military secretary and deputy military secretary to the commander in chief. He was mentioned in despatches and at the close of the war was made brevet major.

McLean took the command of the 36th Rajputana Rifles, formerly the 122nd Rajputana Infantry, in April 1925. His term would have been completed in March 1929, but he was drowned in a yachting accident at Secunderabad, Madras, on 19 June 1928.

The author has in his collection McLean's illustrated diary, which is entitled *2nd Lieutenant Squirt, being a 2nd Lieutenant's experiences in South Africa as told in his letters home*. The diary consists of 49 typewritten pages relating to the Boer War, and a further 23 manuscript pages describing McLean's experiences in India from 1903 to 1904. Of the watercolour illustrations and topographical drawings in the diary, 23 refer to South Africa. In addition, four hand-coloured lithographs of the City Imperial Volunteers are pasted into the diary. Included with the pages of the diary are copies of orders, telegrams, letters and photographs. The diary has several watercolours and pen-and-ink drawings done in Mesopotamia during World War I between 1914 and 1916.

McLean arrived in Durban on 14 July 1900. He moved up to Pretoria on 13 September 1900 where his regiment went to a Mounted Infantry training camp. He took ill at the end of September and was sent to the General Hospital in Pretoria. On 17 October McLean and his companions were transferred to the convalescent home in Johannesburg but by 10 November they had been discharged and were with the 4th Coy 120 Battalion Mounted Infantry with Col. Dandy's column, at Middelburg in the Eastern Transvaal. McLean was a keen photographer and in a letter to his sister he mentions that he would be sending some films home to be developed and asks her to look after them until his return. In his letter of 18 November he states that they have been ordered 'to do some farm burning as there are a whole lot of women out here giving the show away and harbouring Boers when they are not on the run'. He mentions in his letter of 19 November that

> We fetched in a cartload of women yesterday afternoon after burning the farm-house and demolishing the place. The women cried like anything and then changed their minds and began to sing hymns, and they've been singing ever since . . . they don't all sing on the same key which is rather a drawback but they occasionally strike a note together. There is one old lady — she is rather a fine specimen of a woman but her daughter is finer! I didn't think there were pretty girls like that out here. She would look better if she was cleaner. They'll be put in the concentration camp when we get in.

McLean includes a sketch of the old Boer woman and her daughter.

On 29 November he relates that again they 'went out with six waggons to fetch in some women and to burn the farms'.

> When we got to the place we found all the houses deserted and for the most part useless, and no families or any thing left. We took what there was and got a lot of potatoes and about a dozen horses we found around. On the way back the Boers came up like flies and we legged back into camp as fast as we could as we were an awfully small party. We got a waggon load of mealies which will come in useful for the horses.

The following day he mentions that they 'fetched in about 20 women — some of them are quite good looking. They are rather awful at night — they will insist upon singing hymns, and one can't go to sleep'. On 1 December he continues 'It's getting a bit monotonous here. We sent in the women by a convoy today. Hope when it comes back there'll be some letters and papers'.

On 13 December his letter relates

> We arrived here (in Carolina) late yesterday and I never saw such a hole or smelt such a smell in my life. The place is simply a mass of dead and dying oxen and sheep with vultures swarming all over the place. We picked out the cleanest spot we could to camp on and dragged as many dead horses and cows as far away as possible.

He mentions that most of the houses had been pulled to pieces for firewood and that night he admits they cooked their food on part of the organ which Micky, their cook, had brought in from a church with great pride. He had also brought some of the pews. He acknowledges that it was rather a pity 'but what can one do. One must get wood somewhere'.

At this stage McLean mentions that they were to take part in Bruce Hamilton's operations with Colonel Wools Sampson, the intelligence officer. In another letter home he says that the Boers had captured a few of their men but they had 'only stripped them, however, and sent them back. The women we took were asked which they would do, stay out or come in. They remained where they were! They seem to have a horror of the Concentration Camps — I can't make out why? They are far better off in the Camp than out on the veldt.'

In his letter of 19 January 1901 McLean writes that he had a chance to speak to one of the 'Boger' prisoners and he asked him about the foreign Legions and what they were worth.

> The Germans, he said, were useless except to give horses sore backs and look after the transport. The Irish-Americans were the best and made excellent scouts, remaining out for two or three days at a time and bringing in valuable information. The French, what there were of them, were not particularly keen about getting into the firing line — they preferred to give advice. The remainder, he went on, were as much use as a dummy would have been under the circumstances and showed great inclination after their first show to get back to their various countries, finding rough campaigning not such a picnic as they had imagined.

McLean asked the prisoner how long he thought the War would last. 'Till the English give in' he replied. McLean laughed and said the country 'was practically ours now . . .

> but he retorted by saying, we had the towns but the veldt we could never take, or venture on to without being armed. He is one of Botha's men and has great faith in his general. He said that Botha allowed anyone who chose to go in and surrender, reminding them at the same time that when he got the country back he would make it hot for them! Most of them are so simple that they really believe that Botha will be as good as his word and that in the end the Transvaal will be given up to them again.

> One prisoner we took a short while ago in a farm told me that he knew me well, by sight, and on several occasions I had passed him on the flank while he was hiding in the rocks! In future I shall keep my weather eye lifting for lurking Boers!

In the letter of 10 February McLean relates that 'there is a very pretty Boer girl living in the town whom I occasionally go and see. Her husband is an ex-commandant, and at present a prisoner at St Helena. She is quite nice and doesn't seem to miss him much.'

On 17 February he writes that they are to move over to the Western Kopjes to join Kekewich. On 11 April 1902 one of the columns was attacked by the Boers and charged through them. The Boers, he claimed, suffered heavy losses and two of their commandants were reported killed, together with 50 men. The British losses were 2 officers killed, 3 wounded, and 5 men killed, 14 wounded. But the British forces captured two 15-pounder guns and a pom-pom. McLean was one of those severely wounded, being hit in the left thigh and right

MODERN TACTICS

(STRAGGLING HIGHLANDER) — "WAIT TILL I GET THIS PEBBLE IN POSITION, THOSE BOERS WILL SEE STARS!"

3   4   5

arm. He was transferred to the military hospital in Wynberg, Cape Town, where he takes up the story and manages to write his first letter on 25 May 1902. He describes how they left camp early on the morning of 11 April with the Mounted Infantry as advance guard.

We hadn't gone more than two miles, when, on coming to a long rise, we were met by a regular hail of bullets. Fortunately most of them went high – I, unluckily, got one that went low in my arm, and my horse was shot dead under me. Naturally we were all extended, and the order was given to take any cover we could find – (there was absolutely none) and open fire. Of course all this happened in about one minute. We had barely thrown ourselves down on the ground when the Boers appeared over the ridge, mounted, and almost knee to knee. They charged down on us, firing their rifles off their hips, and some from their shoulders . . . others clubbed them and, as they passed through us, dealt savage blows. I was again hit, just before this, in the thigh and narrowly escaped being squashed by the horses' hoofs (sic) as they passed over me! The whole thing was over in about half an hour, but in the meanwhile I must have fainted for I can't remember any more until I came to and found myself jolting along in an ambulance waggon . . . The pain from my wounds was awful and I begged the doctor to give me morphia, but he wouldn't. I fainted again several times that day and was delirious the next. On the 14th we reached Klerksdorp and I went into hospital . . . I remember little of that time. Since I've been here of course the Sisters have written to you for me and you know I have been getting on . . . I hoped to be shipped off home next week. I'll write again shortly.

He left Cape Town for England on 15 June on the hospital ship *Tamar*. He arrived in Southampton on 24 June.

The remainder of McLean's diary is devoted to a manuscript description of his life in India and sketches and drawings done during World War I when he was appointed assistant military secretary to Maj. Gen. Sir G.F. Gorringe, commander of the Tigris Corps.

The National Army Museum has a microfilm of McLean's diary.

The Times, *28 June 1928*
The Times History of the War, *vol. 5, pp. 368-371*

MCNEILL, Angus John 1874-1950   3

Soldier-artist. McNeill, sometimes also known as M'Neil, was born on 31 May 1874. He was educated at Harrow and joined the Seaforth Highlanders in 1895, becoming a lieutenant in 1897 when he served in Crete. He saw action in the Sudan under Kitchener in 1898, being present at the battles of Atbara and Khartoum, and he was mentioned in despatches. McNeill was appointed aide-de-camp to General Gatacre, and on the death of its founder, Raymond de Montmorency V.C., he took command of Montmorency's Scouts.

Winston Churchill, writing in *My Early Life*, relates how, when riding with McNeill near Dewetsdorp, he had become dismounted in a skirmish and had been saved by the swift

action of one of McNeill's Montmorency's Scouts. Churchill's *River War* was illustrated by McNeill.

According to an article entitled 'A day's lion shooting', which appeared in *The Graphic* on 20 July 1901, McNeill was in Somaliland with the 93rd Highlanders in April that year. From 1904 until 1905 he was on the staff of the school of instruction for Mounted Infantry, Longmoor Camp. He retired in 1910 but joined Lovatt's Scouts at the outbreak of World War I. He was mentioned in despatches five times and was promoted to brigadier general in 1917. In 1915 he was present at Gallipoli. He received several decorations during the war, including the D.S.O. in 1918. Between 1920 and 1922 he commanded the Norfolk and Suffolk Infantry Brigade and from 1926 until 1931 he was chief stock breeding officer to the government of Palestine.

During the Boer War McNeill sent several sketches to *The Graphic* and *The Illustrated London News*. Some were redrawn but most were reproduced in facsimile, as were his sketches made in the Sudan. The author has 24 of McNeill's sketches, both from the Boer War and the earlier Sudan Campaign. On 25 January 1908 *The Graphic* used McNeill's sketches in an article written by him entitled 'Hunting Notes'. In 1983 pencil sketches by McNeill done during World War I were sold at Bonhams in London.

The Africana Museum, Johannesburg, has a wash drawing by George Soper, entitled *Friend or Foe – Scouts at work*, which was based on a sketch and report by McNeill. The report describes an action carried out by Montmorency's Scouts.

McNeill died on 22 June 1950.

Churchill, My Early Life, *pp. 354-355*
Creagh and Humphris, The D.S.O., *p. 299*
De Wet, Illustrated London News Index
Hofmeyr, Matton and Roets, Graphic Picture Index
The Times (obituary), *1 July 1950*
The Times History of the War, *vol. 3, p. 490*
Who was Who, *vol. 4, p. 744*

MCNEILL, John 1872-?   2

Soldier-artist. McNeill is listed in the records of the Lancashire Headquarters of the Royal Regiment of Fusiliers as follows:

3477 Cpl J McNeill enlisted at Bury on 28/10/1890 aged 18½. Fresh Complexion, Brown Eyes, Brown Hair, 5' 5½" tall, Chest 32", Weight 111 lbs. He was born in Manchester, a labourer by trade and a Roman Catholic

His records state that he deserted on 24 January 1891 and rejoined on 27 October of that year. He was finally discharged on 10 August 1903 and his character was described as 'Very Good'.

McNeill took part in the Battle of Omdurman (Sudan) and was probably with 2nd Battalion of the Lancashire Fusiliers at Spioenkop. He was awarded the Queen's South Africa medal with clasps for Cape Colony, Orange Free State, Transvaal and Laing's Nek; and the King's South Africa medal with clasps.

After the War he became a well-known postcard artist and contributed several illustrations which were used on the Gale & Polden regimental series of postcards published in 1909. Some of his illustrations also appeared on the Falkner series of military cards.

The Lancashire Headquarters of the Royal Regiment of Fusiliers has one watercolour by McNeill, *Corporal Skinner, Blockhouse Tvl 1901*. This painting was reproduced on a Falkner postcard. The author has two of his watercolours: *Modern Tactics* and *How we took Pieters Hill*.

Byatt, Picture Postcards
Personal communication with Maj. J. Hallam (Ret.), Regimental Secretary, the Royal Regiment of Fusiliers, Wellington Barracks, Bury, Lancashire

---

1 A pencil drawing of Montmorency's Scouts by soldier-artist Angus John McNeill, aide-de-camp to General Gatacre. On the reverse is a description of how the Scouts are picked, written by McNeill. Not long after this was written Montmorency was killed and McNeill was appointed commander of the Scouts in his place.
2 A pencil sketch by soldier-artist Angus John McNeill of the Mounted Infantry in action.
3 Angus John NcNeill's sketch *Tommy Log: – Sorry you were out when I called* shows a British trooper looting an unoccupied farmhouse. This was probably done for reproduction in *The Graphic*.
4 *Modern Tactics*, a watercolour done by John McNeill, the well-known postcard artist who was probably in South Africa during the War.
5 *How we took Pieter's Hill*, a watercolour by the postcard artist John McNeill.

1

2

3

MÉAULLE, Fortuné Louis 1844-? 1

Méaulle was born in Angers on 11 April 1844. He studied under Suiton and d'Isabey. He first exhibited at the Salon des Artistes Français in 1861. During the Boer War his engravings of other artists' work appeared on the covers of *Le Petit Parisien*.

Bénézit, Dictionnaire antique, *vol. 6, p. 32*

M., B.J. *see* **B.J.M.**

MEES, J.

Painter who was a member of the committee that produced the *Antwerpen-Transvaal Gedenknummer*.

MEIKLEJOHN, Ronald Forbes

Meiklejohn was a second lieutenant in 1st Warwickshire Regiment attached to the 2nd Devonshires. In Sawyer's catalogue for 1981 two illustrated diaries by Meiklejohn were offered. Nothing further is known about him.

MEINET, Marie François Lucien 1863-1930

Meinet's Boer War cartoons were published in *Le Rire Belge*.

MELVOMITCH, M.

Nothing is known about this artist except that one of his sketches was redrawn by Herbert Johnson in the special double number of *The Graphic* (2 April 1900). It is assumed that he was in Ladysmith during the siege.

MENARD, G.

Cartoonist for *La Caricature*, *Le Gavroche* and *L'Indiscret*. One of Menard's Boer War illustrations appeared in issue 1058

4

of *La Caricature*, dated 7 April 1900. His *Soulagement*, showing Edward VII and Chamberlain, appeared on page 13 of the *Le Gavroche* special number, 'La Paix à la mode John Bull', dated 16 June 1902.

MENPES, Mortimer 1860-1938 6

Menpes was born in Port Adelaide, South Australia, on 22 February 1860. He was educated at a private school and his art training began in 1878 after his arrival in London, where he studied at the South Kensington School of Art. He himself claimed that he was 'inartistically born' in Australia. He did, however, attend classes at the school of design in Adelaide and his entry in *Who was Who* mentions he had started drawing at the age of one. He exhibited in dry point at the Royal Academy exhibition in 1880. During the next 20 years he showed 35 etchings and paintings at the Academy. It was claimed that (at the time) he had held more one-man exhibitions in London than any other living artist. He was elected a member of the R.E. in 1881, the R.B.A. in 1885, the N.E.A. in 1886, and the R.I. in 1897.

He was an inveterate traveller and visited, among other places, Japan, India, Mexico, Burma, Kashmir, France, Spain, Morocco, Egypt, Italy and South Africa. For the last few years of his life, Menpes retired to the Menpes Fruit Farms, which he had founded and managed in Pangbourne, England.

Menpes was a follower and pupil of Whistler and it is often said that he tried to imitate him in his flamboyant method of dress and speech. His daughter collaborated with him on some of his publications, which included: *War Impressions* (1901); *Japan* (1901); *World Pictures* (1902); *World's Children* (1903); *The Durbar* (1903); *Venice* (1904); *Whistler as I knew him* (1904); *Brittany* (1905); *Rembrandt* (1905); *India* (1905); *Thames* (1906); *Sir Henry Irving* (1906), and *Portrait Biographies of Lord Roberts and Lord Kitchener*. During the preparation of *World Pictures*, in which he included South Africa, 'he travelled the world in record time being unsurpassed even by Jules Verne'.

Menpes married Rose Grosse, a fellow Australian, in London and the couple had two daughters. Maud helped found the Menpes Press while Dorothy, as previously mentioned, collaborated on some of his publications. Many of these publications were illustrated by Menpes's own special process of coloured etching. From 1900 he also published a large number of reproductions of paintings by old masters in this form. He donated 50 of these copies to form the nucleus of the Commonwealth Art Gallery in Australia.

During the War Menpes was engaged by *Black & White Budget* to accompany Lord Roberts.

Menpes travelled to South Africa on the SS *Briton* and learned of the relief of Ladysmith en route. Also aboard were Gen. Archibald Wavell and Col. Hugh Cholmondeley of the C.I.V. On arrival in Cape Town Menpes found that the military

were not very keen on helping artist-correspondents to accompany them.

His brief from *Black & White* included the production of paintings for an 'Exhibition of the War in South Africa', so he travelled around the Cape Peninsula sketching the tourist sights. He had a friend in Cape Town who gave him a letter to the Staff Officer and on presentation of this letter Menpes was immediately given a pass to travel by rail to Modder River. He had no previous experience of war corresponding, even though he managed to deck himself out in a uniform which resembled that of a field marshal. He was constantly mocked by his fellow travellers when they realized that, not only had he made no other transport arrangements, but he was also totally ignorant of the logistics of travel in wartime.

On arrival at Modder River he was promptly ordered to return by the officer to whom he showed his pass. Returning to Cape Town he met an old friend, Admiral Maxse, who was able to provide him with the proper licences and passes which allowed him to travel anywhere with Lord Roberts's column. Major Bagot sent a telegram to Lord Stanley, censor at the front, who gave Menpes the authority to travel anywhere he wanted.

While in Jacobsdal they were guided by another war artist/correspondent who is only identified as the 'Veteran' in Menpes' book, but was undoubtedly Frederic Villiers. On the suggestion of Villiers they left Jacobsdal in an effort to get to Kimberley before Lord Roberts reached the town. They thought that they had managed to get behind the Boer lines when they were approached by a group of men resembling Boers. Imagining they had been taken prisoner they were relieved to discover that their 'Boer capturers' were in fact the Kimberley Town Guard, who escorted them into the recently relieved town. On arrival in Kimberley they made straight for Rhodes's headquarters. Rhodes was delighted to see them and invited them to stay for lunch. Menpes spent two weeks in Kimberley, having managed to secure accommodation at the Kimberley Club next to the suite occupied by Col. Kekewich.

Menpes relates how Rhodes was extremely kind to him and he allowed him to sketch him on several occasions. After two weeks in Kimberley they went on to Klipdrift to rejoin Roberts. Here Menpes met and sketched Gen. Pole-Carew. Menpes and his colleagues travelled to Bloemfontein despite several delays along the way. Here he was introduced to Lord Roberts by Admiral Maxse and he was given permission to sketch him in his study. Several sketches of Roberts are reproduced in his book. Menpes claims he was very nervous when he approached Roberts with the request to draw him. Roberts went out of his way to put him at ease. Needless to say, Menpes hero-worshipped Lord Roberts and heaps lavish praise on him throughout *War Impressions*.

From Bloemfontein Menpes returned to Cape Town where he lost no time seeking out Alfred Milner, the high commissioner and governor of the Cape. Menpes spent some time at Government House sketching Milner in various poses and attitudes. While in Cape Town he renewed his acquaintance with Rhodes and visited him at Groote Schuur where he was able to do many other portraits of him. One of these is in the South African National Gallery and another is in Rust-en-Vreugd in Cape Town. Menpes was also invited to visit the Rhodes Fruit Farms, where he did sketches of the farmhouses.

Other personalities sketched by Menpes included the Duke of Norfolk, Prince Francis of Teck, Rudyard Kipling (whom he had met travelling from Bloemfontein to Cape Town) and Arthur Conan Doyle whom he sketched at the Langman's Hospital in Bloemfontein. He also sketched Winston Churchill, who he found 'a very sympathetic individuality; not arrogant, not an egoist, but a good listener and modest'.

Menpes was impressed by Hector McDonald's dislike of luxury: 'His sympathies are with the private, and he prefers to rough it on the ground rather than enjoy, as other officers did, the comparative luxury of Bloemfontein'. McDonald, he says, praised the Australian illustrated journals as being the most factual in contrast to 'the constant inaccuracy and folly of the illustrated London papers, so greatly inferior to the frank photographs that appear in the Australian journals'. Needless to say, he reports that the one English paper McDonald found some excuse for was *Black & White*.

Also in Bloemfontein, Menpes met and sketched Gen. French, who he describes as 'quite the shyest man in the British Army, and looks less like a cavalry officer than any one I ever saw . . . He would rather face a legion of Boers than my palette.' French promised to sit for Menpes although he could not understand why anybody would want to sketch him.

Menpes found Gen. Pole-Carew to be 'the handsomest man in the Army'. Others to impress Menpes were Col. Maxse and Maj. O'Meara, who later became Burgomaster in Johannesburg.

In his chapter entitled 'The War and Philately' Menpes mentions how he was given the privilege of watching misprinted copies of the Victoria overprints stamps being destroyed under the watchful eye of O'Meara while the latter was director of posts and telegraphs in Bloemfontein. The craze for collecting these stamps and the disappointments and triumphs of the collector are graphically described.

The relationships between the war correspondents intrigued him. One moment they were very friendly and the next they had quarrelled and were not on speaking terms. Menpes relates amusing incidents of his collaboration on *The Friend*.

Menpes says that a complete set of *The Friend* was very hard to come by and he was very pleased that Julian Ralph, one of the editors, gave Rudyard Kipling and Menpes himself a set, which in 1901 was worth £30. This set was recently sold in London for well over £1 000.

Menpes relates how impressed he was with Frederic Villiers – 'he has fought many battles on the platforms of our English lecture halls'. He was also very grateful to Villiers for giving him hints on nourishment while campaigning: 'You must only wet the mouth and not drink; second you must always carry with you a certain tinned meat which is invaluable.' Villiers in his book *Five Decades of Adventure* does not display the same high regard for Menpes.

Menpes was very critical of the junior British officer and deplored his lack of knowledge of the rifle and felt that his education (gathered from the Red Book) certainly did not endear him to his men as the conditions were completely different in South Africa to what he had been taught overseas. One thing Menpes does enthuse about in the British officer is his knowledge of watercolour, even though he is derogatory about the effeminate way in which some of the officers would like to discuss this medium.

He feels that the ordinary 'Tommy' should have had more artistic training. If this had been the case, he says, landmarks would have impressed themselves on the soldiers' minds and they would have remembered the placing of one kopje against the other. 'Whole scenes would have been carried away in Tommy's artistic eye while a slight sketch by his officer would have explained a situation to him in a moment.' In contrast Menpes suggests that the Boers had this artistic sense which comes about not through training but through habit. 'The retina of their eyes through habit is so much more delicate than ours that from a distance they can distinguish the colour of a mass of men, and would be able to tell you whether they were Kaffirs or Englishmen in a moment.'

Menpes concludes his book with the reproduction of a series of complimentary letters from Roberts, French, Pole-Carew, Hector McDonald and Archibald Graham Wavell, all praising his book. However another letter, written by Dr Steinmetz, a Boer doctor, is very scathing and accuses the British of being murderers, saying that from now on 'all civilised men (will) hate you'.

Among the highlights of Menpes's visit was the sight of Cronje and the other 4 000 Boer prisoners who were captured at Paardeberg. He sketched them on their arrival at Klipdrift and their spontaneous singing of a psalm impressed him enormously.

On 28 July 1900 *The King* comments that 'had he not been a painter, Mortimer Menpes would have done great things as a writer. He can describe all that he sees and hears with the same vivid touch and facility with which pictures grow beneath his brush.' Carter devotes more than two pages to praising Menpes: 'It was a happy thought of the proprietors of *Black & White* to despatch Mr. Mortimer Menpes to the seat of the war in order that he might portray the leaders of our side as they appeared amongst their men. The portraits which this distinguished artist was able to make, and the many sketches of the stirring scenes he saw, cause one to regret that more painters, as such, did not avail themselves of opportunities which the war provided . . .'

The pre-publicity for *War Impressions* proudly stated that 'There is good reason for believing that this work will attain a unique position in the literature of the South African campaign'. Two thousand five hundred copies of the ordinary edition of *War Impressions* were published in 1901, together with 350 special signed deluxe editions on large paper. It is believed that the first 25 copies of this edition contained a signed 'original watercolour frontispiece especially drawn for the purpose by Mr. Menpes'. Portraits of McDonald and Roberts have been noted in some of these editions. A second edition appeared in 1903.

The Africana Museum, Johannesburg, has the following paintings, all reproduced in *War Impressions*: *At Jacobsdal 1900* (reproduced opposite p. 28); *Orange Free State Farmhouse 1900* (reproduced opp. p. 62); *In the Garden of the Convent, Bloemfontein 1900* (reproduced opp. p. 64); *Departure of Cronje from Klipdrift 1900* (reproduced opp. p. 84); *Mule Waggon in difficulties 1900* (reproduced opp. p. 192); *Boer Prisoners 1900* (reproduced opp. p. 204); *Prince Francis of Teck – portrait 1900* (reproduced opp. p. 228).

The author has three paintings by Menpes: *Sir Alfred Milner addressing an audience* (reproduced opp. p. 98); *Boer Prisoner led into Klip Drift by C.I.V.* (reproduced opp. p. 198); and *General Hector McDonald*.

It is the general consensus that Menpes was probably more famous as a personality than as an artist. He was described as being alert and resourceful; an opportunist who was never at a loss for a retort in an argument. He was awarded the Queen's South Africa medal on 3 June 1904. Menpes died on 1 April 1938.

Carter, War Artists in S.A.
Kennedy, Pictures in the Africana Museum, *vol. 4, pp. 15-17*
Menpes, War Impressions
The Orders and Medals Research Society, *Summer 1986, 'War Correspondents: South Africa 1899-1902', by Patrick Street*
Waters, British Artists, *vol. 1, p. 230*
Who was Who, *vol. 3, pp. 930-931*

MENZIES, A.

At least two different illustrated postal covers done by Menzies in Bloemfontein in 1902 are in existence. One is entitled *Steyn escapes in his shirt* and is signed 'A. Menzies, Bloemfontein 1902'. The other carries the inscription 'A long start. Boer Staff officer: The British are 80 miles off. General De Wet: saddle up!'. It is also signed 'A. Menzies, Bloemfontein 1902'.

Postally used and unused specimens have been noted. The earliest date of use recorded on this type of envelope is 23 March 1902.

MENZIES, McGregor

Cartoonist whose work appeared in both *The South African Review* and *The Owl*. It is not known whether there is any connection between McGregor and 'Alpine' Menzies, the cartoonist who worked for *The Lantern* (1890). McGregor Menzies often signed his work with the initials 'M.M.'.
Schoonraad, S.A Cartoonists, *p. 244*

MERRY, Godfrey fl. 1883-1915

Merry, who was originally a figure and landscape painter, also worked as an illustrator for *The Illustrated London News* and *The Regiment*. One of his Boer War related illustrations appeared in *The Illustrated London News* on 16 December 1899 with the title *No enemy after all!*. The *Illustrated War Special* also featured cartoons by him.
De Wet, Illustrated London News Index
Johnson and Greutzner, British Artists, *p. 350*

MERRY, Tom 1852-1902

British cartoonist and caricaturist whose work appeared in *St Stephen's Review*, for which he became chief cartoonist. Later he worked for *Puck and Ariel*. At the time of the War he was a contributor to *Lloyd's News*.

Merry was responsible for two very large posters (approximately 1 000 x 600 mm): *Only Bubbles* (printed and published by Edward Weller and Graham Ltd, 42 Denmark Hill, London) and *Fads Before Empire* (printed by Knight and Forster, Leeds and London). Both were published in 1900 and while they had more relevance to the 'Khaki Election' of that year, they also refer to the Boer War.
Houfe, British Illustrators and Caricaturists, *p. 388*
Thorpe, English Illustration

MERSON, Luc-Olivier 1846-1920

Historical painter. The son of the artist and art critic Charles-Olivier Merson, Merson was born in Paris on 21 May 1846. He exhibited at the Salon des Artistes Français for many years, winning several awards.

Merson contributed a charcoal drawing of Jesus Christ to the special edition of *Le Monde Illustré* (17 November 1900). The drawing, which appeared on page 320, was dedicated to President Kruger.
Bénézit, Dictionnaire antique, *vol. 6, p. 74*

MERTE, O.

Illustrator of the *Ein Englischer Sieg* postcard published by Ludwig Franck and Co. of Munich.

---

1 *Punishment being inflicted on the Boer traitors.* De Wet looks on approvingly. This illustration by F. Méaulle appeared on the front cover of *Le Petit Parisien* on 17 February 1901.
2 Lieutenant General Hector McDonald was the subject of this watercolour by Mortimer Menpes. This was probably one of the watercolours given away with the first 25 special numbered copies of his book *War Impressions*.
3 Mortimer Menpes, one of the most famous 'special' artists of the War, depicted by the British artist Walker Hodgson in a wash drawing dated 26 January 1892.
4 Mortimer Menpes's watercolour entitled *Sir Alfred Milner Addressing an Audience* appeared in his book *War Impressions*.

MERTENS, Charles 1865-1919
Landscape and marine painter and illustrator. Mertens was born in Antwerp in 1865. He was a pupil of Verlat and later a member of the committee that produced the *Antwerpen-Transvaal Gedenknummer*. He died in London on 20 February 1919.

Bénézit, Dictionnaire antique, *vol. 6, p. 75*

MESPLÈS, Paul-Eugène 1849-1924
Painter, lithographer and engraver. Mesplès was born in Paris in 1849. He studied art under Gérôme. One of his engravings incorporating a medallion of President Kruger was published on p. 318 in the special number of *Le Monde Illustré* which appeared on 17 November 1900 and which was dedicated to Kruger. This engraving was also reproduced in Philippe Deschamps' *Le Livre D'or du Transvaal*. Mesplès also worked for *La Caricature* at the time of the War but none of his cartoons noted in this magazine thus far depict the conflict.

Bénézit, Dictionnaire antique, *vol. 6, p. 79*

METHFESSEL, Adolf 1836-1909
Painter, lithographer and illustrator. Methfessel was born in Berne, Switzerland, on 12 May 1836. In 1860 he travelled to Argentina with the German naturalist, Burmeister, and remained in South America. During the Paraguay-Argentinian War in 1865 he recorded the action from the front lines.

Methfessel had an important influence on Argentinian art. In 1890 he was appointed draughtsman to the Museum of La Plata in Buenos Aires. In the course of his duties he made numerous field trips, accompanying naturalists to the wilds of the country. Twenty of his South American paintings were sold at Sotheby's, London, in 1982.

Methfessel provided illustrations for Capt. A.T. Mahan's *The War in South Africa*.

He died on 6 November 1909.

Bénézit, Dictionnaire antique, *vol. 6, p. 82*
Sotheby's Catalogue, *10 Feb. 1982, p. 72*

MÉTIVET, Lucien-Marie-François 1863-1932
Artist, cartoonist and illustrator. Métivet was born in Paris on 19 January 1863. He studied at the Académie Julian under G. Boulanger and J. Lebfebvre. He exhibited at the Salon des Artistes Français. Métivet was closely associated with Grün, Cheret, Willette and Steinlen in the execution of the decorations for the 'Taverne de Paris' for the 'Exposition Universalle 1900' in Paris.

Métivet worked extensively for *Le Rire* and during the War several of his cartoons appeared in this publication.

Métivet died in Paris in 1932.

Bénézit, Dictionnaire antique, *vol. 6, p. 82*
Fanelli and Godoli, Art Nouveau Postcards
Osterwalder, and Hubschmid and Bouret (eds.), Dictionnaire des Illustrateurs, *p. 694*

MEUNIER, Georges 1869-1934
Painter, illustrator and poster artist. Meunier was born in St Claude, France, on 3 November 1869. He studied under Fleury at the École National des Beaux-Arts, and exhibited at the Salon des Humoristes from 1909 to 1913 and at the Salon des Artistes Français. He worked at various times for *L'Assiette au Beurre* and *Le Rire*.

During the War Meunier contributed the coloured front cover of the Christmas 1900 number of *La Vie Illustrée*. It was entitled *Le Dernier Noël du vieux siècle — De Bonaparte à Kruger*.

Meunier died in St Claude in 1934.

Bénézit, Dictionnaire antique, *vol. 6, p. 90*
Osterwalder, and Hubschmid and Bouret (eds.), Dictionnaire des Illustrateurs, *p. 695*

MEUNIER, Henri (Georges Jean Isidore) 1873-1922
Painter, etcher, lithographer, and poster and postcard artist. The nephew of the sculptor, Constantin Meunier, Henri Meunier was born in Ixelles, Belgium, on 25 July 1873. He studied at the Academy in Ixelles and exhibited at the Salon de Mons. At one time he worked for *Le Petit Bleu*.

Meunier's best-known Boer War work, dated 'Christmas 1901', appeared on a rare French postcard pre-addressed to Queen Victoria appealing for her intervention to end the suffering of the Boer women and children in the concentration camps.

Meunier died in Ixelles on 8 September 1922.

Bénézit, Dictionnaire antique, *vol. 6, p. 90*
Osterwalder, and Hubschmid and Bouret (eds.), Dictionnaire des Illustrateurs, *p. 696*

M.F.C.S. (or M.F.G.S.)
The *Evening News* illustrator who contributed portraits drawn from photographs of British and Boer generals to that paper.

MICHÄEL, A.
L'Assiette au Beurre cartoonist who provided at least two cartoons with Boer War relevance: *Au Transvaal* (9 May 1901) and *Le Char de la liberté* (1 August 1901). Both were signed with initials only.

MICHEL, G.V.
Le Journal Illustré and *Le Figaro* cartoonist.

MIGNOT, Victor 1872-1944   1
Belgian poster artist, cartoonist and sports illustrator who was born on 20 June 1872. He worked for *Le Cénacle, Le Sillon, Le Cycliste Belge, La Libre Critique* and *Le Petit Bleu*. He became well known for his sporting postcards published by Dietrich and Co., Brussels, and he did many postcards with a cycling theme.

During the War Mignot's anti-British cartoons appeared in *La Caricature*, often on the magazine's cover. Six of these cartoons were used to illustrate the 'Bon Vivant' series of French postcards (see nos. 1-6 below).

The coloured covers noted in *La Caricature* are as follows:

1. *Nos amis Les Anglais: La Reine n'a plus besoin de m'envoyer du chocolat: tous les jours je reçois des pruneaux!* (1048, 27 January 1900)
2. *Nos amis Les Anglais: Messieurs les Anglais, vous vous tirez les premiers* (1049, 3 February 1900)
3. *Nos amis Les Anglais: C'est vous qui m'avez forcé à jouer au foot-ball, messieurs les Anglais, vous voyez que je ne m'en tire pas trop mal . . .* (1051, 17 February 1900)
4. *Nos amis Les Anglais: Notre artillerie avait été placée à la portée de l'ennemi . . . Le Gènéral Joubert — Merci* (1052, 24 February 1900)
5. *Nos amis Les Anglais: John Bull — c'est pas le tout de les raccommoder . . . Faudrait que la colle soit solide!* (1055, 17 March 1900)
6. *Nos amis Les Anglais: Chamberlain — Majesté, vos locataires du Cap font du tapage . . . Pouvez-vous me prêter votre balai pour mettre ces gens-l la raison? . . .* (1056, 24 March 1900)
7. *Lendemain de Victoire* (1069, 23 June 1900)
8. *Le Petit Noël de Victoria* (1095, 22 December 1900)

Mignot died in Paris on 5 March 1944.

Bénézit, Dictionnaire antique, *vol. 6, p. 124*
Fanelli and Godoli, Art Nouveau Postcards
Osterwalder, and Hubschmid and Bouret (eds.), Dictionnaire des Illustrateurs, *p. 698*
Weill, Art Nouveau Postcards, *p. 11*

MILLS, A. Wallis 1878-1940
Illustrator. Mills trained at the South Kensington School of Art where he became associated with F.H. Townsend and George Stampa. From about 1898 his work appeared in various magazines. Among these were *The King, Punch, The Strand Magazine, The Humorist, The Royal Magazine* and *The Graphic*. During World War I he was in the Royal Artillery and was one of the official British war artists.

Mills's Boer War work is confined to the frontispiece of the novel by Bertram Mitford entitled *Aletta: A tale of the Boer Invasion* (F.V. White and Co., London, 1900).

Mills died in April 1940.

Houfe, British Illustrators and Caricaturists, *p. 392*
Thorpe, English Illustration

MINNS, Benjamin Edward fl. 1875-1923
Minns was born in the 'Australian bush' and went to Sydney at the age of 19 to work for the *Sydney Bulletin*. Several of his paintings are in the Sydney Art Gallery collection. He went to London in about 1895, but still continued to send home work to the *Sydney Bulletin*. In London Minns worked

1

2

To B.T. Price. In consideration of his patriotism in providing a unit to the C.I.V. from the artist. "The Star" Aug 9-1900

for *The Idler*, *St Paul's*, *Boy's Own Paper*, *The Minister*, *Pearson's Magazine* and *Punch*.

One of his cartoons was reproduced in *The King* on 30 June 1900. Entitled *Quite Safe*, it shows an army surgeon leaning over a soldier saying 'You've been very brave to stand all that probing. I'm so sorry I could find no bullet.' Wounded Tommy: 'Oh the bullet's all right, sir. I've got it in me 'aversack.'

Houfe, British Illustrators and Caricaturists, *p. 392*
Kornan, Australian Postcard Catalogue, *1984*
The Strand, *vol. 23 (1902), p. 662*
Thorpe, English Illustration

MITCHELL, Hutton fl.1892-1925 1

Mitchell is best known as the creator of Billy Bunter in *The Magnet*. He also worked as a cartoonist for *Fun*, *The Daily Graphic*, *Longbow* and *The Gem*.

Mitchell's Boer War work is not common; one drawing can be found on p. 80 of George Lynch's *Impressions of a War Correspondent*. This appeared in *The Illustrated London News* on 17 November 1900, as did one other by Mitchell. *The Sketch* reproduced one of Mitchell's cartoons on 14 February 1900; entitled *The rising generation*, it lampooned the war artist. *Judy* also occasionally featured Mitchell's cartoons.

De Wet, Illustrated London News Index
Houfe, British Illustrators and Caricaturists, *p. 392*

M.L.C.

An illustrator with these initials did a series of 'Ogdens Guinea Gold' cigarette advertisements with a Boer War theme.

MOGINIE, A.H.

Moginie contributed a drawing, later redone by Charles de Lacy, which appeared in *The Illustrated London News* on 9 December 1899 entitled *Our loyal colonies: Departure from Wellington of the New Zealand Contingent for South African service on board the Waiwera*.

MOLONY, F.

One illustration by this artist, who was presumably a soldier, appeared in *The Graphic* on 28 April 1900. It was entitled *How a river is crossed in South Africa: Interesting engineering operations at Norval's Point*.

Hofmeyr, Matton and Roets, Graphic Picture Index

MONCRIEFF, M.M.

Moncrieff was possibly the officer in the 6th Dragoon Guards who was an extra aide-de-camp to Baden-Powell. An illustration which appeared in *The Graphic* on 27 January 1900 entitled *With General French at Rensburg: Colonel Porter's successful engagement near Arundel* was by a Lt. Moncrieff.

A photograph of a Lt. Moncrieff, seated in front of the group, appeared on p. 297 of *Black & White Budget* on 9 June 1900. Some doubt exists as to whether this is the Lt. Moncrieff who was responsible for the illustration.

Black & White Budget, *9 June 1900*
Hofmeyr, Matton and Roets, Graphic Picture Index

MONNIER, G.

French artist who provided one cartoon, *Le prix du Sang*, to the *Le Gavroche* special number of 16 June 1902, 'La Paix à la mode John Bull'. Monnier also worked for *L'Indiscret* during the War. An engraver of the same name had worked for *The Illustrated London News* in 1875.

Engers, Victorian Wood Engravers, *p. 184*

MONTBARD, Georges (Charles Auguste Loye) 1841-1905 1

Landscape painter, illustrator and caricaturist. Born Charles Auguste Loye in Montbard, France, on 2 August 1841, Georges Montbard took his professional name from his birthplace. His first position as an illustrator was for *La Chronique Illustrée* and later he worked for *Le Journal Amusant* and *Petit Journal Pour Rire*. In 1868 *The Illustrated London News* began publishing his work. After the Franco-Prussian War Montbard

left France for political reasons and settled in England in 1871. There he contributed to *The Illustrated London News*, *The Graphic*, *Judy*, *Vanity Fair*, *Good Words*, *English Illustrated Magazine*, *St James Budget*, *Windsor Magazine* and *Pall Mall Magazine*. His work in *Vanity Fair* included a caricature of H.M. Stanley and six others which were signed 'M.D.'.

During the War at least 12 of Montbard's works appeared in *The Illustrated London News*. One of these, *Transport near Mafeking*, was reproduced anonymously as part of a Picture Postcard Co. Boer War cards series (5d). Montbard often signed with his characteristic monogram 'GM' intertwined and consequently *The Illustrated London News Index* did not give him full credit for all his illustrations.

His Boer War work also appeared in *Illustrated War Special* and *Defenders of the British Empire*.

Besides the Boer War works other Africana illustrations by Montbard appeared in *The Illustrated London News* between 1889 and 1904.

Montbard wrote at least three books: *The Land of the Sphinx*, *Among the Moors*, and *The Case of John Bull in Egypt*, *The Transvaal, Venezuela and Elsewhere* (Hutchinson and Company, c.1896). The last-named is illustrated with sketches done by the author-artist.

Montbard died in England on 5 August 1905.

De Wet, Illustrated London News Index
Houfe, British Illustrators and Caricaturists, *p. 393*
Matthews and Mellini, In Vanity Fair
Osterwalder, and Hubschmid and Bouret (eds.),
Dictionnaire des Illustrateurs, *p. 709*
Thorpe, English Illustration

MOORE, Richard Hewitt fl.1863-1900

The Illustrated Sporting & Dramatic News and *Lady's Pictorial* illustrator who specialized in drawing dogs. He worked for *The Illustrated London News* from 1875.

Some of the famous Monkey Brand soap 'won't wash clothes' advertisements with a Boer War theme were his creation. They appeared in most of the contemporary illustrated papers during the early part of the War.

Moore was also known as a sculptor.

Engers, Victorian Wood Engravers
Houfe, British Illustrators and Caricaturists, *p. 393*
Thorpe, English Illustration

MORA, Francis Luis 1874-1940

Mora was born in Montevideo, Uruguay, in 1874. He studied art in Boston and New York. From 1892 he worked as an illustrator for leading American periodicals. On 16 September 1899 *Harper's Weekly* had his picture of Paul Kruger entering the 'Central Bureau' on its front cover. Mora died in New York in 1940.

Fielding, American Painters, etc., *p. 246*
Samuels, Artists of the American West, *p. 331*

MOREHEN, Horace fl.1880-1902

Cartoonist and illustrator. Morehen was a pupil of Alfred Bryan. He worked for *The Illustrated Sporting & Dramatic News*, *Moonshine* (providing theatrical drawings), and *Cassell's Saturday Journal*. During the War Morehen supplied cartoons to *Moonshine* and *The Sketch*.

Thorpe, English Illustration

MORELAND, Arthur 1

Moreland was a cartoonist for *The Morning Leader*. His cartoons were published in a book entitled *Humours of History*. Moreland later became well known for his comic and political postcards, working for, among others, C.W. Faulkner.

The author has a pen-and-ink sketch depicting six members of the C.I.V. in comic uniform and is inscribed 'To B.T. Price in consideration of his patriotism in providing a unit to the C.I.V., from the artist'. In a different hand the following is written: ' "The Star" August 9 1900'. The reverse bears the note 'This drawing is held by Mr. B.T. Price on the under-

standing that while it is otherwise his sole property he cannot without the consent of the undersigned reproduce or publish it in any way. Arthur Moreland, Star offices, Stonecutter Street, EC'.

Houfe, British Illustrators and Caricaturists, *p. 394*

MORGAN, Cecil Buckley 1860-1918

Soldier-artist. The son of Thomas Morgan F.S.A., Cecil Morgan was born in Streatham, London, on 18 November 1860. He was educated at Dulwich College and Sandhurst. He entered the West Indian Regiment on 23 August 1884. He served in West Africa in 1892, 1893, and 1895, took part in the operations in the Niger Territories and was wounded twice. Morgan served in West Africa again from 1898 to 1899, taking part in operations in Sierra Leone and in the Mendiland Expedition where he was severely wounded, and commanded an expedition up the Jong River during which he was mentioned in despatches. While on his tour of duty in Sierra Leone he supplied *The Graphic* with sketches of the action. One of these, which was redrawn by Joseph Nash jnr., is in the author's possession. Morgan was promoted to major on 20 January 1898. He was awarded the D.S.O. in 1900 in recognition of his services in Sierra Leone.

Morgan served in the Boer War from 1901 to 1902, taking part in operations in the Cape Colony. He received the Queen's medal with three clasps. After the War he retired and joined the reserve officers. He remained on in South Africa to farm in the Orange Free State.

Two sketches by Morgan appeared in *The Graphic* during the War: *Englishmen stalking hartebeeste in South Africa: result – flight of the game* and *Natives stalking hartebeeste in South Africa: result – a good bag*. Both were redrawn by J. Nash jnr. and appeared on 23 November 1901.

Morgan served in World War I and died on 29 March 1918 as a result of wounds received in action.

Creagh and Humphris, The D.S.O.
Hofmeyr, Matton and Roets, Graphic Picture Index
The Times *(obituary), 8/9 April 1918*
Who was Who, *vol. 2, p. 747*

MORGAN, Frederick 1856-1927

Animal and child portrait painter. Morgan exhibited at the principal London galleries, particularly at the Royal Academy where he exhibited 50 works.

In 1900 *The hero of the hour* and in 1901 *Homewards*, both presumably of Boer War interest, were shown at the Royal Academy.

Morgan's wife, Alice Mary Havers, was also an artist.

Graves, Royal Academy, *vol. 5, p. 290*
Johnson and Greutzner, British Artists, *p. 362*
Waters, British Artists, *vol. 1, p. 238*

MORISS

La Caricature, *L'Indiscret*, *Le Rire* and *Polichinelle* cartoonist. His work appeared on at least one French postcard cartoon of Edward VII, entitled *Edouard VII ou L'Intrépide... vide Bouteilles*.

Moriss also provided a cartoon, *Entriacte*, for the *Le Gavroche* special of 16 June 1902, 'La paix à la mode John Bull'. Once again the cartoon shows Edward VII surrounded by bottles of liquor.

---

1 Georges Montbard provided illustrations for several French publications during the War.
2 Cartoonist Arthur Moreland's pen-and-ink sketch of six C.I.V. members in strange clothes was reproduced in *The Star* on 9 August 1900.

1

MORRIS, W.

Soldier-artist. Quartermaster sergeant Morris is responsible for at least 12 sketches for *The Illustrated London News* done in South Africa between 1899 and 1901. Judging from the titles of the illustrations, some done in facsimile, Morris was stationed in Cape Town before the outbreak of war and depicted the arrival of some of the troopships. One of his sketches shows the opening of the first church for British troops guarding the Boer prisoners on Diyatalawa. This appeared on 27 July 1901.

One of his best-known illustrations shows the presentation of the Queen's chocolate to members of the Duke of Edinburgh's Own Volunteer Rifles in Beaufort West on Sunday 25 January 1900. It was redrawn by Amedée Forestier and appeared on 31 March 1900. The Dukes was, and still is, a Cape Town regiment and it is possible that Morris was one of its members. He is not to be confused with Colour Sergeant E. Morris of the 3rd Middlesex Regiment who was wounded at Spioenkop and who provided photographs for the illustrated press.

De Wet, Illustrated London News Index

MORROW, Albert George 1863-1927

Illustrator. Morrow was born in County Down, Ireland, in 1863. He was from the well-known Morrow family of painters, the father George and the brothers Edwin, Jack, Norman and George. (The other three sons in the family were apparently not artistically inclined.) Morrow was educated in Belfast and at the Royal College of Art, London. At the age of 16 he won a prize offered by *The Graphic* for a 'black and white drawing'.

Morrow's career as an illustrator began in 1884 when he joined the *English Illustrated Magazine*. He was well known for his theatrical and commercial posters, which he did while working for *Answers*, *Lloyd's News* and the firms of Cassell and David Allen and Sons. He exhibited at the Royal Academy between 1890 and 1904. Examples of his work can be found in the British Museum and the Victoria and Albert Museum.

Morrow's relatively few Boer War illustrations appeared in *With the Flag to Pretoria* and *After Pretoria: the Guerilla War*.
Personal communication with the Curator, Ulster Museum, Belfast
The Poster, *vol. 3, no. 7, 11 Jan. 1899*
Waters, British Artists, *p. 239*
Who was Who, *vol. 2, p. 751*

MOSCHELES, Felix Stone 1833-1917   1

The son of the composer Ignaz Moscheles, Felix Stone Mo-scheles was born in London on 8 February 1833. He studied painting in Paris and in Antwerp under Van Lerius. He exhibited at the principal galleries in England from 1862.

Moscheles painted a picture entitled *Bethlehem stormed and captured in the year of our Lord 1900*. This painting was reproduced in vol. 22, p. 314 of William Stead's *Review of Reviews* (June-December 1900). The caption on p. 313 summed up Stead's well-known pro-Boer sympathies:

In England the wild boar, by a play on words, has been adopted as the National symbol of the South African Republics. In these last months an abominable picture entitled "The National Cartoon" has been extensively placarded throughout England. It represents the British lion triumphing over the prostrate bodies of boars who symbolise the Transvaal and the Orange Free State. Provoked by this insolent and vulgar exultation in the victory gained by an Empire of 400 000 000 over the tiny Republics of South Africa, Mr. Moscheles has painted a picture which is reproduced in miniature on the other side of the page. He adopted the central group of the "National Cartoon" but filled in details which bring into prominence the real truth of the situation. Upon the corpses of the murdered Republics he flung the broken cross. In the foreground lies the body of a British soldier united with the slaughtered boar in the sad brotherhood of death. Near them a bugler boy is writhing in agony. A cannon stands in the midst of the slain, half concealed in the smoke of battle. High aloft waves the Union Jack, the proud emblem of British glory and British pride. But from the centre of St. George's Cross, which is blazoned on every English flag, the crowned head of the Man of Sorrows looks down with infinite pity and reproach upon the scene of carnage and of victory. It is a great sermon in colour and a reproduction, also in colours, is being circulated by scores of thousands in England during the election.

Moscheles died in Tunbridge Wells on 22 December 1917.
Bénézit, Dictionnaire antique, *vol. 6, p. 237*
Stead [ed.], Review of Reviews, vol. 22, pp. 313-314
Waters, British Artists, *vol. 1, p. 240*

MOUCHOT, Charles

The author has a wash drawing signed by Mouchot and dated 1902. It is entitled *Transwaal* (sic) and has the inscription 'Tartuff je crois que je suis Victorieux!!!'

MOULTRAY, John Elder 1865-1922

Moultray was born in Edinburgh in 1865 and studied at the Edinburgh School of Art. He went to New Zealand with his parents in 1883. Both his mother and father were artists who painted historical scenes and incidents, chiefly reconstructions from eyewitness accounts. Watercolours of New Zealand scenes by John Moultray were sold by Christie's in October 1980.

During the Boer War Moultray went to South Africa with the 1st New Zealand Contingent as a newspaper correspondent. After six months he was invalided home. He later made sketching tours through several countries. The Alexander Turnbull Library in Wellington, New Zealand, has a collection of newspaper cuttings and cartoons taken from contemporary New Zealand newspapers which show life aboard the troopship *Waiwera* on the way to South Africa. The regiment depicted was the New Zealand Mounted Rifles which saw action in South Africa between 1899 and 1902.
Manuscript book of accredited correspondents from the personal papers of Capt. F. B. Maurice (in the author's collection)
Personal communication with the Curator, Alexander Turnbull Library, Wellington, New Zealand

MOWLEM, E. J.

One illustration by Mowlem appeared in *The Graphic* on 24 February 1900 entitled *Keeping watch over Boer Prisoners:*
H.M.S. Doris turning her searchlight onto the S.S. Catalonia.
Hofmeyr, Matton and Roets, Graphic Picture Index

M., S. *see* S.M.

MULOCK, Frederick Charles 1866-1933

Landscape and figure painter. Mulock studied in Brussels and at Bushey, England, under Herkomer. From 1888 he exhibited at leading galleries, including the Royal Academy.

A Boer War illustration by Mulock appeared in *The Graphic* on 27 January 1900. It was from a sketch by Capt. H. P. Leader and was entitled *With General French's Force: general view of the Boer position at Taaibosch Laagte before our advance on Colesberg*.

The 1904 Puttick & Simpson auction catalogue offered one untitled illustration by Mulock, which fetched two guineas.
Hofmeyr, Matton and Roets, Graphic Picture Index
Johnson and Greutzner, British Artists, *p. 367*
Puttick & Simpson catalogue (1904)
Waters, British Artists, *vol. 2, p. 38*
Wood, Victorian Painters, *p. 333*

MÜNZER, Adolf 1870-1952

Landscape and postcard artist and illustrator. Münzer was born in Pless, Silesia (now part of Poland) on 5 December 1870. He worked in Breslau, Munich and Paris.

Münzer's Boer War work, often signed 'M. Paris', appeared in *Jugend*. *Die Schlacht von Tweefontein 24 Dezbr. 1901* was published on 19 February 1902 (No. 9). It shows De Wet riding a horse with the 'Grim Reaper' cutting down the British soldiers and it accompanied a poem by Edgar Steiger.

Münzer died in Holzhausen am Ammersee in 1952.
Bénézit, Dictionnaire antique, *vol. 6, p. 278*
Fanelli and Godoli, Art Nouveau Postcards
Osterwalder, and Hubschmid and Bouret (eds.),
Dictionnaire des Illustrateurs, *p. 734*

MUSCHAMP, F. Sydney ?-1929

Historical and landscape artist. Muschamp was born in Hull. From 1870 he exhibited several works at the principal London galleries, including the Royal Academy. He was elected a member of the R.B.A. in 1893.

In 1900 Muschamp's *Ordered South* was shown at the Royal Academy.
Graves, Royal Academy, *vol. 5, p. 333*
Johnson and Greutzner, British Artists, *p. 370*
Waters, British Artists, *vol. 1, p. 243*

MUSGRAVE

An illustrator who worked for *Black & White Budget*.

MUSGRAVE, R. R.

The Owl cartoonist.

NANKIVELL, Frank Arthur 1869-?

Illustrator. Nankivell was born in Victoria, Australia, in 1869. He studied art for a while in Japan before settling in San Francisco. He produced and published *Chic*, a fortnightly magazine. After working for the San Francisco *Call*, *Examiner* and *Chronicle*. Nankivell moved to New York in May 1896 and joined the staff of *Puck*. During the Boer War he was still working for that periodical.
Fielding, American Painters, etc., *p. 254*

NAPER, L. A. D.

The National Army Museum, London, has a topographical drawing entitled *Cronje's laager at Paardeberg, looking E from Gun Hill*. The drawing is annotated as being from 'a sketch by Lieutenant Naper RFA'. A second lieutenant L.A.D. Naper appears in the *Army List* for 1900 as being a member of the Royal Garrison Artillery. He fought in World War I with the rank of major.
Army List *1900*

2

NASH, Joseph (jnr.) ?-1922

Marine and landscape painter and illustrator. Joseph Nash jnr. worked in London from 1859 and later in Bedford. (His father, who shared the same name, was also a well-known artist and illustrator.) He started working for *The Graphic* in about 1874 and remained with the magazine for most of his working life. He was elected a member of the R.I. in 1886, having exhibited in London from 1859. His work was shown at the Royal Academy from 1877 to 1885. Nash depicted South African scenes in his work from as early as the Zulu War in 1879, and at least 30 of his Africana pictures appeared in *The Graphic* up to 1899. *The Graphic* special double number which appeared on 2 April 1900 also contained several illustrations by Nash. The National Army Museum, London, has the original of one of these illustrations, entitled *The scene of desolation: Cronje's laager at Paardeberg, as it was when our men entered it*. Two further illustrations by Nash are in their collection: *On board the transport Bavarian on her way to the Cape: the troop deck* (25 November 1899) and *The pipe and coffee of peace: Boers and Britons fraternising round a blockhouse watch-fire* (30 August 1902).

Nash often signed his work with the initials 'J.N.', but more frequently his illustrations were unsigned, so much of his work is not credited to him. *After Pretoria: the Guerilla War* and *South Africa and the Transvaal War* frequently borrowed Nash's work, usually without acknowledgement.

The author has one non-Boer War watercolour by Nash: *With the Sherbro Expeditionary force in Sierra Leone: an attack on the 3rd West India Camp*.

Nash died in Somerleyton, Suffolk, on 24 May 1922.
Hofmeyr, Matton and Roets, Graphic Picture Index
Houfe, British Illustrators and Caricaturists, *p. 397*
Who was Who, vol. 2, p. 769

NAUDÉ, Pieter Hugo 1868-1941

South African civilian artist. Naudé was born in the Worcester district of the Cape on 23 July 1868. Olive Schreiner was one of the first to recognize his artistic talent, and in 1889 he accompanied her to Europe where he was introduced to Havelock Ellis. He studied at the Slade School, London, under Alphonse Legros and in Europe under Franz von Lenbach. In 1896 Naudé returned to South Africa and settled in his birthplace, Worcester, where today a major part of his collection is housed (the Hugo Naudé Collection).

Naudé visited Europe on several occasions and his work was favourably received by the critics and public alike.

Besides his portraits of presidents Kruger and Steyn, two of Naudé's watercolours dated 1900, showing the Duke of Wellington's West Riding regiment in camp at Worcester, were offered for sale by the firm of Frank Thorold in 1985.
Berman, Arts and Artists, *p. 302*
De Kock (ed.), DSAB, *vol. 1, p. 584*

N.C.

The initials of an illustrator who signed one of two illustrations which appeared on p. 1 of the supplement to *The Sphere* on 31 March 1900. The page is entitled 'Sketches and photographs – from our Special Artist in Pretoria'.

The uppermost illustration is entitled *Two British officers being conducted to the State Model School at Pretoria* and the other *Boers leaving Pretoria for Ladysmith*. The artist is not Johann Schönberg, *The Sphere's* artist on the spot, but he may have supplied the originals to be redrawn by a possibly home-based 'N.C.'.
The Sphere, vol. 1, 31 March, 1900

NEILLY, James Emerson

The son of a Dublin journalist, Neilly served for some time in an Irish militia regiment. He visited South Africa twice before the War and interviewed Paul Kruger. He was later sent to cover the War by *Pall Mall Gazette*. He was besieged in Mafeking and his experiences are described in his book *Besieged with B.P.* Although primarily a photographer he managed to send a few sketches to *The Graphic* which were redrawn before publication.
Leslie's Weekly, vol. 90, p. 50, 20 Jan. 1900

NESHAM, Thomas Peere William 1880-1902

Soldier-artist. The only son of Admiral Nesham, Thomas Nesham was born in May 1880. He was educated at Harleybury and received his first commission in December 1898. Philip Ziegler in the book *Omdurman* records a Lt. Nesham who had a narrow escape in one of the Sudan battles. Nesham joined the 38th Battery of the Royal Field Artillery and was promoted to lieutenant in February 1901. He was killed near Tweebosch on 7 March 1902. Both Methuen and Kitchener – on 13 March and 8 April respectively – mentioned Nesham in despatches. In *After Pretoria: the Guerilla War* (vol. 2, p. 953) there is a drawing by Ernest Prater entitled *The Death of Lieutenant Nesham*. The text describes the scene near Tweebosch as follows:

The flight of the mounted men did not cease till they regained the railway line many miles from the scene of action. It left the guns of the 38th Battery quite unprotected, but the gunners, under the heroic Lieutenant Nesham, rose to the occasion and sacrificed themselves with a devotion which is above all praise. The weapon continued to fire till every man in the section was down with the exception of Lieutenant Nesham. Then the Boers rushed the gun, and called upon the officers to surrender. He refused to obey the summons and, fighting desperately to the last, fell gloriously, thus setting a noble example to all those who had abandoned this fight in dismay.

Nesham had earlier contributed a sketch to *The Sphere* which was redrawn by A.S. Hartrick and published on 1 September 1900. It was entitled *What our soldiers have had to suffer: Sleeping Out in the Rain*.

The Kimberley Club has a series of 15 caricatures done by 'Lt. Nesham RFA'. Most are monogrammed 'TN', although one has the full initials 'T.N.'. All the caricatures are Boer War related.
After Pretoria: the Guerilla War, vol. 2, pp. 953-954
Dooner, The Last Post, *p. 284*
The Graphic, vol. 65, p. 404, 22 March 1902

NEUMANN, F.

Six chromolithographs by Neumann have been noted: *Colenso 15th Dec 1899, Battle of Elandslaagte, Surrender of Paardeberg, Roberts & Cronje, De Wet breaking through blockhouse lines* and *Battle of Tweebosch*. Verbeek records F. Neuman (one 'n') as having done a monochrome entitled *Elandslaagte 21/10/99*.
Personal communication with Fiona Barbour, Ethnologist, McGregor Museum, Kimberley, and E.W. Wessels, War Museum of the Boer Republics, Bloemfontein
Verbeek, Early Natal Art

NEWNHAM, J. S.

The author has two naive watercolours of Boer War scenes done by an artist of this name, probably a soldier. One is signed in full 'J.S. Newnham 1900' and depicts a soldier watering his horse next to a waterfall. The other, which is signed 'J.S.N. 1901', depicts a wagon crossing a river with soldiers wading across carrying their clothing and rifles on their heads.

NICHOLSON, Sir William (Newzam Prior) 1872-1949

Painter in oil of portraits, still life and landscapes. Nicholson was born in Newark-on-Trent on 5 February 1872. His art education was under Herkomer at Bushey in Hertfordshire between 1888 and 1889, and he also studied at the Académie Julian in Paris two years later.

Nicholson and his brother-in-law, James Pryde, collaborated on a series of posters and illustrated books. They copied the style of the Art Nouveau French posters and admired the work of Henri Toulouse-Lautrec. The artists became known as the 'Beggarstaff Brothers'.

After 1900 Nicholson's career was almost entirely devoted to portrait painting. He was knighted in 1936. Nicholson visited the United States, India and South Africa and travelled widely in Europe.

Nicholson's contribution to Boer War art takes the form of his *Twelve Portraits*. Included among these are lithographically reproduced wood blocks of portraits of Lord Roberts and Cecil Rhodes. A woodcut of Kitchener done in 1898 is of peripheral interest.

Nicholson died on 16 May 1949 in Blewbury, Berkshire.
Feaver, Masters of Caricature, *p. 118*
Hofstätter, Art Nouveau Prints, etc., *pp. 82-83*

---

1 The painting *Bethlehem stormed and captured in the year of our Lord 1900* by Felix Moscheles was painted as an answer to the jingoistic *National Cartoon*.
2 A pen-and-ink cartoon drawn by E. Nicolson for an unidentified publication.

1

3

National Army Museum Catalogue
Osterwalder, and Hubschmid and Bouret (eds.),
Dictionnaire des Illustrateurs, *p. 759*
Waters, British Artists, *vol. 1, p. 247*
Who was Who, *vol. 4, p. 850*

NICOLSON, E. 1
Le Charivari and *La République Illustrée* cartoonist. Nicolson's Boer War work also appeared in the *Le Charivari* Album: *Boers et Anglais*. Reproductions of his Boer War cartoons all appeared on the back-page feature, 'La Guerre et la Caricature', of the Belgian publication *L'Illustration Européenne.*

The author has one untitled pen-and-ink drawing by Nicolson.

NOBLE, Ernest
Illustrator of 'Dick Gosport's Last Ride', an adventure story which appeared in *Boys of the Empire* on 11 January 1901.

NORIE, Orlando 1832-1901
Military painter. Norie came from a family of artists in Edinburgh. Between 1876 and 1889 he exhibited battle scenes at the Royal Academy, including *The Battle at Ulundi* in 1882

and *Tel el Kebir* in 1884. He became well known for his watercolour studies of military uniforms, and his best work was done during the 1860s and 1870s. His later work on uniform and regimental life was done mainly on commission. Norie's work commands relatively high prices on auction nowadays.

The Royal Collection at Windsor has a watercolour of the Rifle Brigade done by Norie in 1900. The Africana Museum, Johannesburg, has a work by him in its collection, but it is not of the Boer War. Alfred Gordon-Brown, in *The Narrative of Private Buck Adams*, mentions that Norie went to India prior to the Indian Mutiny and that he probably called at the Cape en route.

In common with other military uniform artists such as Harry Payne, Norie's dates often refer to the period and not the date on which the painting was done.
Dawnay and Miller, Military Drawings and Paintings, *vol. 2, p. 221*
Houfe, British Illustrators and Caricaturists, *p. 402*
Kennedy, Pictures in the Africana Museum, *vol. 4, p. 39*
Mallalieu, British Watercolour Artists, *p. 191*

NORTON, Eardley B. 1
Vanity Fair cartoonist. Two cartoons by Norton were pub-

lished in that periodical, one of which, *De Wet* (31 July 1902) was of Boer War interest. Norton signed his work with the initials 'E.B.N.'.
Matthews and Mellini, In Vanity Fair

NORWIN'S, Les
Norwin's was responsible for a series of French hand-coloured postcards which lampooned the British involvement in the War. A similar series which made fun of French politicians of the time was also published. Variations in similar cards exist, indicating a possible hand-drawn or cyclostyled origin. The publisher's name does not appear on the cards and the earliest postmark is January 1900. All are signed 'Les Norwin's'. The numbers do not appear on the cards. The titles are:
1. *Chamberlain tire la Ficelle et Le Pantin Marche* (a variation exists with the word 'Marche' replaced by 'S'Agite').
2. *(Air Connu) C'est un Oiseau qui vient de Lon...dres.*
3. No title but card shows Boer tweaking Queen Victoria's ear.
4. *En Evant.*
5. *Kruger.*
6. *Le president Kruger.*
7. *Gal Joubert.*
8. *SM Victoria.*
9. *Cecil Rhodes.*
10. *Blindage de Trains.*
11. *Chamberlain et son Ombre.*
12. *Leur Cauchemar 9e Serie (Les Ministres Responsables) Chamberlain.*
13. *Leur Cauchemar 9e Serie (Les Ministres Responsables) Lord Salisbury.*
14. *Leur Cauchemar 9e Serie (Les Ministres Responsables) Duc du Devonshire.*
15. *Leur Cauchemar 9e Series (Les Ministres Responsables) Lord Lansdowne.*

A 'P.H.' Norwins', often signing himself 'P.N.H.', was responsible for a non-Boer War postcard entitled *La Danse du Macaroni.* The card was signed in full.

NOTT, W.H.
An illustration by this artist entitled *Dumping the President aboard the Ongaba* appeared, redrawn by Gordon Browne, in *The Graphic* on 16 December 1899.

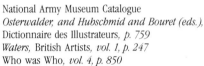

2

4

5

NUMA, B.
Illustrator of *Quelques mots sur le Transvaal* by Jean Varney. This pamphlet — which consisted of sheet music, verse and illustrations — was published by *Echo de Paris* as part of the series 'La Chanson à Montmartre'. Some of Numa's illustrations are signed 'B.N.'.

O'BEIRNE, F. 1
Postcard artist who worked for Blum & Degen Ltd. His work featured on both signed and unsigned cards depicting some British regiments that took part in the War. Occasionally he signed his work with the initials 'F.O.B.'. In 1984 the Parker Gallery offered three of O'Beirne's military watercolours, including one of an 11th (Prince Albert's Own) Hussars mounted officer in full dress. The painting was dated 1899.
> *Byatt*, Picture Postcards, *p. 46*
> *Parker Gallery*, Catalogue II

OERDER, Frans David 1867-1944 2
Pro-Boer artist; South Africa's first official war artist. Oerder was born in Rotterdam in the Netherlands on 7 April 1867. He was the youngest of seven children of a municipal employee, Johannes Carolus Oerder, who opposed his son's choice of art as a career, but who allowed him to study decorating, for which the initial training was similar. Oerder attended the Academy of Visual Arts in Rotterdam. He completed the six-year course in only five years, winning the King William III gold medal and a bursary which enabled him to tour Italy. On his father's death Oerder used his inheritance to study further in Brussels under Ernest Blanc-Garin.

In 1890 he went to Pretoria and became a house painter for the firm of De Wijn and Engelenburg. He was later employed to paint telegraph poles on the Lourenço Marques railway line between Komatipoort and Krokodilpoort. This experience enabled him to become familiar with the Transvaal landscape and local inhabitants. In 1894 Oerder was appointed art teacher at the Girls' Secondary School in Pretoria, where he rented a studio in order to earn a supplementary income drawing cartoons for 'newspapers'. At this stage he became friendly with Anton van Wouw and Pierneef, both of whom received art lessons from him. In 1896 he became a Zuid-Afrikaansche Republiek burgher (citizen).

In 1899 Oerder joined the Boer forces and sketched in the field. He is regarded as South Africa's first official war artist. He was accompanied by Nicolaas Hofmeyr, a history lecturer at the Staats Gymnasium in Pretoria. Hofmeyr was appointed as official chronicler of the War by Kruger. This led to his writing *Zes Maanden bij de Commandos*, which was published in The Hague in 1900. Oerder was interned as a P.O.W. at the camp on Meintjieskop. During his internment he continued with his drawings and paintings. His artistic ability came to the notice of the British authorities, who approached him to do sketches and portraits. Consequently he was allowed certain privileges not normally granted to prisoners. He was eventually allowed to return to his studio, where he continued to work. He was however still kept under house arrest.

The Africana Museum has the following Boer War sketches by Oerder:
02. *Vlucht over Vaalrivier by Warrenton 1900.*
03. *Opbrengen van Long Tom op Bulwana Hill.* Inscription on back in pencil: 'Opbrengen van Long Tom op Bulwana Hill'. Sepia wash touched with white. Signed 'F.D. Oerder'.
04. *Bridge Destroyed by the Boers 1900.* This is either the Bethulie or Norval's Pont bridge.
05. *Portrait of a Man.* The man might be a hospital patient or an orderly.
06. *Man on Crutches.*
07. *Mounted Boer c.1900.*
08. *Studies of Three Men.*
09. *Group of Boers Sitting Outside a Tent 1900.*
010. *The Haircut.*
011. *We weten dat er een God is.*

012. *Naby Magersfontein.* Inscription in pencil: 'Naby Magersfontein'. Pen and ink, charcoal and white. Depicts Boers round a camp fire. On the back is a charcoal sketch for 02.
018. *Six British Soldiers and their Mounts.*
019. *Meintjies Farm, Pretoria c.1900.*
021. *Johannesburg versus Boer.* Cartoon. Inscription: 'Illustratie Nr. 4 Boven Hoofstuk II Johannesburg versus Boer'.
029. *Colonial Mounted 1900.*
030. *Seaforth Highlander 1900.*
031. *Mounted Infantry 1900.*
032. *British Infantryman 1900.*
033. *Lancer 1900.*
034. *British Artillerymen 1900.*
035. *Irish Hospital, Pretoria 1900.* Oil on canvas. On the back of the canvas an inscription reads: 'The Irish Hospital provided by the 1st Earl of Iveagh and sent out to the South African War in charge of his eldest son The Hon. Rupert Guinness'. In Pretoria the hospital was in the Palace of Justice.

The War Museum of the Boer Republics, Bloemfontein, has 10 sketches by Oerder. They were done while on a visit to the Boer forces on the western border of the Orange Free State in late 1899 and early 1900.
1. *Schansen by Magersfontein.*
2. *Pretoriase ambulans by Modderrivier.*
3. *In die loopgraaf by Magersfontein.*
4. *Portrait studies of Burgers in the field at Magersfontein.*
5. *Brood-bakkery in die loopgrawe by Magersfontein.*
6. *Schansen by Magersfontein.*
7. *Midden Modderrivier Lager.*
8. *In die loopgraaf by Magersfontein.*
9. *Vrystaatse laer by Magersfontein.*
10. *General P.A. Cronje se laer by Magersfontein.*

The University of Pretoria has a further 37 sketches and drawings by Oerder, done in Ladysmith, Colenso, Modder River and Matjiesfontein.

On 31 October 1975 Sotheby's in Johannesburg sold nine Oerder sketches at an Africana sale. Two were inscribed 'Grikwa Vluchtelingen, Magersfontein' and 'Informatie bureau Magersfontein'. It was stated in the catalogue that similar sketches had been destroyed by fire in Holland. The lot, which had belonged to a Dutch vendor, fetched R2 000. In a letter dated 29 December 1979 Tom Oerder, the artist's son, wrote to the author to explain what had happened to these pictures:

> I can only give you a little more information about the works destroyed in the school fire. This happened in Utrecht, Netherlands, at the primary school which I attended at the time nearly 60 years ago and involved 8 or 10 Boer War sketches similar to the ones in the Bloemfontein Museum. The pictures had been brought to the school to show my classmates and had been left overnight when the school caught fire and burnt down, destroying the school and its contents.

The author has an oil painting entitled *British Mounted Infantry*. It is signed 'F.D. Oerder Pretoria 1901'. On 25 May 1983 *A Scouting Party*, signed 'F.D. Oerder 1901', was offered for sale by Christie's in London and in April 1992 Stephan Welz & Co. sold '*Bayonet' with his groom, Lance Corporal Childs, Pretoria 1901*.

Between 1908 and 1938 Oerder lived in Holland. In 1938 he returned to South Africa and exhibited in Cape Town. Oerder died in Pretoria on 15 July 1944.
> *Berman*, Art and Artists, *pp. 311-315*
> Bloemfontein War Museum Catalogue
> Christie's South Kensington Catalogue, 25 May 1983, lot 92
> *De Kock*, DSAB, *vol. 4, pp. 418-420*
> *Kennedy*, Pictures in the Africana Museum, *vol. 4, pp. 40-44 and vol. 7, pp. 86-87*
> Sotheby Parke Bernet S.A. Catalogue, *31 Oct. 1975, lot 53*
> Stephan Welz & Co. Johannesburg, Catalogue 13 April 1992
> *Personal communication with Prof. A.E. Duffey, Dept. of Art History, University of Pretoria.*

O'GALOP 1867-1946 1
Pseudonym of Marius Rossillon, the French painter and illustrator born in Lyon in 1867. He worked for *Le Rire, Revue Mâme, Le Charivari* and *L'Assiette au Beurre*. His Boer War work is found in *L'Illustré National* and *Le Franc Normand Illustré*. O'Galop died in Carnac on 2 January 1946.
> *Bénézit*, Dictionnaire antique, *vol. 6, p. 413*
> *Osterwalder, and Hubschmid and Bouret (eds.),* Dictionnaire des Illustrateurs, *p. 772*

OGÉ, Eugène
French lithographer, postcard artist and designer who was responsible for a cartoon lithograph of Kruger and Queen Victoria (Charles Verneau, 114 Rue Oberkampf, Paris).
> *Bénézit*, Dictionnaire antique, *vol. 6, p. 413*
> *Fanelli and Godoli*, Art Nouveau Postcards, *p. 358*

OPPER, Frederick Burr 1857-1937
Cartoonist. The son of an Austrian immigrant, Opper was born in Ohio, U.S.A., in 1857. After working for *Leslie's Weekly* for three years he joined *Puck*, forming an association which lasted for 18 years. In 1899 Opper left to work for Hearst's *New York Evening Journal*. Some Boer War work by Opper has been noted in this magazine. He retired in 1932 when his eyesight began to fail.
> *Feaver*, Masters of Caricature, *p. 121*
> The Strand, *vol. 23, pp. 304-305*

ORCHARDSON, Charles 1873-1917
Portrait and landscape painter. Orchardson exhibited at many of the principal British galleries, including the Royal Academy where 30 of his works were shown. In 1901 *Capt. Blunt, Lancashire Fusiliers* was exhibited at the Royal Academy.

Orchardson was killed in action in the Middle East during World War I.
> *Graves*, Royal Academy, *vol. 6, p. 21*
> *Johnson and Greutzner*, British Artists, *p. 384*

ORENS (Charles O. Denizard) 2
Postcard artist who was also known as 'Denizard' or 'Godillot'. He was reputed to be the French artist Charles O. Denizard. His postcards are very sought-after, especially as they were usually issued as limited editions. Orens contributed to the 'Collection des Cent', the well-known Art Nouveau postcards published by E. Gréningaire. His anti-British cards were quite venomous, particularly against Chamberlain. Even as late as Kruger's death in July 1904, he portrayed Chamberlain walking over the lifeless body of Paul Kruger.

Orens's known Boer War related cards are as follows (not numbered on the cards):

---

1 General Christiaan de Wet featured in this caricature by Eardley Norton ('E.B.N.') in *Vanity Fair* on 31 July 1902.
2 *In die loopgraaf by Magersfontein*, a pencil drawing by Frans Oerder. Reproduced by courtesy of the War Museum of the Boer Republics, Bloemfontein.
3 *La Dépêche*, 22 October 1899, by French artist 'O'Galop' (pseudonym of Marius Rossillon).
4 Denizard Orens drew this portrait of General De Wet to commemorate the Boer general's visit to Europe. He did similar studies of De La Rey and Botha.
5 Although most of Denizard Orens's work is done in black and white he produced this scatological card of King Edward in colour, published by M.Y. Paris. Titled *Une tempête sur un crâne* (A storm on a skull), it mocks the British defeats of Spioenkop, Tugela, Magersfontein and Tweebosch.

1. *General De La Rey*. Undated.

2. *General De Wet*. Dated 9/10/02.

3. *General Botha*. Dated 9/10/02.

4. *Colonel De Villebois-Mareuil Mort au Transvaal à Boshof*. Dated 5/11/02.

5. *Une Tempête sur un crâne* ('V.H. Les Miserables') (coloured).

6. *Mort de Kruger 14 Juillet 1904* 'Le Burin Satirique No. 26 2 anneé.

7. *Chez les English* (Lt. edit. 250) Dated '7/03'.

8. *Le Quadrille Franco-Anglais*. Dated '7/03'.

9. *L'Angleterre Artistique. Statue en peau de balles dumdum. Elevée à John Bull en Souvenir du Transvaal'*. Dated '7/03'.

10. *La Victoire. Statue offerte a l'Angleterre par le monde civilisé*. Dated '7/03'.

11. *Le Roi Fantome 27 Juin . . .*

12. *A Buckingham Bon Appetit Messieurs*. Dated '7/03'.

13. *Le Lion Brittannique Retour du Transvaal 2 Juin 1902*

14. *Dernier Rencontre*

15. *Gloria Victis*. Dated '2 Juin'.

16. *Kruger* (no title). Dated '11/10/02'.

17. *Les Anglais sont nos meilleurs clients*

18. *Ronde du Veau d'Or*.

19. *L'arrivée*

Bénézit, Dictionnaire antique, *vol. 3, p. 183*
Fanelli and Godoli, Art Nouveau Postcards
Holt, Tonie and Valmai, Stanley Gibbons Postcard Catalogue

ORR, J.

This illustrator was responsible for one sketch which appeared in *The Graphic* on 30 June 1900. It was entitled *A native siege wedding at Kimberley* and may have been copied from a photograph. The artist was possibly Jack Orr, whose brothers Monro and Stewart were also illustrators.

Hofmeyr, Matton and Roets, Graphic Picture Index

OST, Alfred 1884-1945

Belgian-born postcard artist. The 'Pour les Boers' postcards (A.D. & A.D., 35 Boulevard des Capucines, Paris) has a monogram similar to that of Ost. He was possibly too young, however, to have been responsible for the illustrations.

Holt, Tonie and Valmai, Stanley Gibbons Postcard Catalogue

OULESS, Walter William 1848-1933

Portrait painter. Ouless was born in St Helier, Jersey, on 21 September 1848. He was educated at Victoria College, Jersey, and

went to London in 1864, where he was a student at the Royal Academy schools from the following year. He exhibited several works at the Royal Academy from 1869. Ouless was elected A.R.A. in 1877 and R.A. in 1881.

His portraits of generals of both sides in the War were reproduced in *With the Flag to Pretoria*.

Graves, Royal Academy, *vol. 6, pp. 28-31*
Waters, British Artists, *vol. 1, p. 253*

OWLES, D. C.

Three sketches by Owles appeared in *The Graphic* between 9 December 1899 and 24 February 1900. They had been redrawn by the home-based artists F. Dickinson and F. Dadd.

Hofmeyr, Matton and Roets, Graphic Picture Index

PAGET, Henry Marriot 1856-1936 1

Home-based artist for *The Graphic* and *The Daily Graphic*. Henry Paget was born in Clerkenwell on 31 December 1856. He was educated at Atherstone Grammar School and the City Foundation schools. In 1874 he entered the Royal Academy schools. His first picture at the Royal Academy, *Enid and Geraint*, was exhibited in 1879. He travelled in Italy and Greece during 1879 and 1880. He worked in western Canada in 1909 and 1910 and was in Constantinople for *The Sphere* during the Balkan War of 1912-13. Paget was a member of the 20th Middlesex (Artists') Volunteers from 1875 to 1884. An expert in camouflage, he went to France as a captain in the Royal Engineers with the British Expeditionary Force in January 1916. He was mentioned in despatches. Two of Paget's brothers, Walter and Sidney (see below), were also well-known artists. At least 53 of Henry Paget's Boer War illustrations were reproduced in *The Graphic*; others appeared in the *The Daily Graphic* and *The Graphic* special double number of 2 April 1900. Paget's first Africana works were published in *The Graphic* in 1896, after the Jameson Raid.

The Africana Museum has three works by Paget:
P79. *Native of South Africa suspected of being a spy*. Inscription on the back: 'Native of South Africa suspected of being a spy'. Date stamp '23rd December 1899'. Wash drawing. Signed 'H.M.P.'. Reproduced in *The Graphic* on 23 December 1899 captioned 'In danger of being shot – the black population makes the trouble in South Africa more complicated. Neither side will use the natives as fighting material. Many of them turn spies and sell their information for what they can get for it. Some Kaffir spies were caught the other day and brought up for examination at General Wolfe Murray's headquarters at Estcourt'. Inscription: 'Drawn by H.M. Paget from a photograph by H.W. Nicholls'.
P80. *General Buller receiving an address at Aldershot 1900*.

Inscription on back: 'General Buller receiving an address at Aldershot'. Date stamp '17 Nov 00'. Wash drawing. Signed 'H.M.P.'. Reproduced in *The Graphic* on 17 November 1900 captioned 'The return of Sir Redvers Buller: Receiving an address of welcome at Aldershot'. Inscribed 'Drawn by H.M. Paget from a sketch by F.C. Dickinson'.
P630. *The War Game 1901*. Wash drawing. Inscription on back: 'Aug 10/01 "The War Game" *The Graphic*'. Initialled 'H.M.P.'.

The Mendelssohn Collection in the Library of Parliament, Cape Town, has one picture, also signed 'H.M.P.', which is entitled *Collection of Boer Arms*. It was published in the special double number of *The Graphic* on 2 April 1900.

The author has one wash drawing entitled *Lord Roberts inspecting rescued prisoners at Pretoria*. This illustration appeared in *The Graphic* on 25 August 1900 captioned 'Lord Roberts at Pretoria. Reviewing released British prisoners'. The drawing also appeared in *The Graphic History of the South African War* and *Cassell's Illustrated History of the Boer War*.

The Royal Collection at Windsor includes two originals by Paget, done in 1897 and 1901 respectively, but the subject matter has no connection with the Boer War.

Paget signed most of his illustrations with the initials 'H.M.P.'. He died on 27 March 1936 in London.

Dawnay and Miller, Military Drawings and Paintings, *vol. 2, pp. 244-245*
Kennedy, Pictures in the Africana Museum, *vol. 4, p. 61; vol. 7, p. 157*
The Times (obituary), *3 April 1936*
Waters, British Artists, *vol. 1, p. 253*
Who was Who, *vol. 3, p. 1037*

PAGET, Sidney Edward 1860-1908 1

Illustrator and portrait, landscape and figure painter. Sidney Paget was born in London on 4 October 1860. He was educated privately and at the Cowper Street School. He studied at the British Museum, the Heatherley School of Art and the Royal Academy schools, where he was awarded several prizes including the Armitage Bronze medal. He tied as a gold medallist for historical painting in 1884. From 1876 he exhibited at the Royal Academy. Paget's best known works, however, are the illustrations of Sherlock Holmes done for the original editions of Conan Doyle's detective stories. Even though *The Dictionary of National Biography* denies that he used his brother Walter as the model for Sherlock Holmes, it seems widely accepted that this was in fact so. Paget worked at various times for *Pictorial World*, *Pall Mall Magazine*, *The Illustrated London News*, *The Graphic*, and *The Sphere*. Like his brother Henry, he was a member of the 20th Middlesex

(Artists') Volunteers, as well as the Middlesex Yeomanry and the Duke of Cambridge's Hussars.

The author has one watercolour by Paget entitled *Saving the guns at Colenso*. This painting, which is probably a copy of a wash drawing, was reproduced in the first issue of *The Sphere*. A photogravure of the picture (a double-page spread) was offered for sale by *The Sphere* on 10 March 1900 at the price of one shilling.

Paget's work is also found in *With the Flag to Pretoria*. He often signed his illustrations with the initials 'S.P.'.

He died on 29 January 1908 in London.
Dictionary of National Biography, *vol. 2, p. 2823*
The Times (obituary), *1 Feb. 1908*
Waters, British Artists, *vol. 2, pp. 253-254*
Who was Who, *vol. 1, p. 544*

PAGET, Walter Stanley (Wal) 1863-1935 [1]
Artist and illustrator. After studying at the Royal Academy schools he was sent out with the Gordon Relief Expedition as war artist for *The Illustrated London News*. From 1884 he was a frequent exhibitor at the Royal Academy. He became a regular contributor to *The Illustrated London News, Black & White, The Sphere, The Illustrated Sporting & Dramatic News* and other periodicals. As a book illustrator Paget is best remembered for his drawings in Rider Haggard's novels, including *King Solomon's Mines* and *She*, and his illustrations for *Robinson Crusoe* and *Treasure Island*.

Wal Paget did not produce as much Boer War work as his brothers, Henry and Sidney, but nevertheless *The Sphere* published several examples of his work, many of which were unsigned. Some of these illustrations were borrowed by Cassell and Newnes for *Under The Union Jack*.

During the War two of Paget's illustrations were reproduced in *The Graphic: 2nd Battalion Royal Dublin Fusiliers leaving Pietermaritzburg* (from a sketch by A.M. Johnson, on 4 November 1899) and *Transvaal Crisis: the exodus of British subjects from Boer territory* (7 October 1899). Capt. F.S. Brereton's *With Rifle and Bayonet: A story of the Boer War* (Blackie and Son, London, Glasgow and Dublin, 1900) has eight Paget illustrations.

The author has one Boer War drawing (unsigned) by Wal Paget entitled *The Queen, God Bless her! Rimington's Scouts drinking the health of her Majesty*. The drawing was reproduced in *The Sphere* on 5 May 1900. The same illustration also appeared in *Under The Union Jack* on 2 June 1900.

Paget signed his illustrations 'W.P.' or 'Wal Paget'. He died on 29 January 1935.
Graves, Royal Academy, *vol. 6, p. 40*
Magazine of Art, *1892*
SABIB, *vol. 1, p. 278*
The Times (obituary), *1 Feb. 1935*

PAQUE, Oliver 1846-1908 [2]
Illustrator and watercolourist of landscapes. This is the pseudonym adopted by William Pike. He was born in Plymouth, Devon in 1846. In 1874 and 1888 he exhibited at the Royal Academy, as well as several other leading galleries including the R.B.A. While still living in Plymouth Pike, who had become a competent amateur actor, contributed sketches of local scenes and events to the *Western Figaro*.

Pike went to London in 1881 and he worked for *The Daily Graphic* almost from its inception, adopting the same pseudonym 'Oliver Paque' that he had used on the *Western Figaro*. In 1894, six months after its founding, Pike, still using his pseudonym, contributed to *The Sketch*.

At the time of the War Pike was a prolific contributor of pen-and-ink drawings to *The Daily Graphic*. Only one illustration by him has been noted in *The Graphic: Back from the war: Welcome home at Knightsbridge Barracks* appeared on 8 December 1900. It is not listed in *The Graphic* index. He was an active member of the Savage Club and was responsible for the design of the menu for the dinner which welcomed the war correspondents home from South Africa. The dinner

took place on Saturday 13 July 1901.

The Africana Museum has one Boer War work by Pike: *De Wet's remarkable escape 1900*. Done in black paint with some Chinese white on lined grey paper, it is signed 'Oliver Paque after W.M.G.'. The inscription on the back reads: 'The Great Drive in S Africa — 4 cols immediate'. The date stamp is '18 Mar 92' but should of course be '02'. The reproduction in *The Daily Graphic* had the following caption: 'De Wet's remarkable escape: the Commander with a few men rushing the cattle through the fence on the Kroonstad Lindley blockhouse line (From a sketch by a British officer)'. The Africana Museum catalogue entry states that the signature is 'Oliver Papof'. This mistake is understandable as Pike's pseudonymous signature is not clear. The museum also has three Matabele Campaign works by him.

The author has two pen-and-ink drawings by 'Paque':
1. *The Defence of Mafeking: Col Baden-Powell and his troops reconnoitring* (signed 'Oliver Paque').
2. *Spion Kop January 24th: Thorneycroft's Infantry attacking (from a sketch by one of Thorneycroft's men)*. The caption, taken from *The Daily Graphic* of 6 March 1900, continues:

Spion Kop was stormed in the early hours of January 24 by a force under the command of Brigadier General Woodgate. Thorneycroft's Mounted Infantry played a conspicuous part in the assault and subsequent defence of the position, their Colonel being in chief command after the General was wounded. They lost no fewer than ten of their officers in killed and wounded. They helped to hold the position for twenty four hours, then, as everybody knows, were forced to abandon it to the enemy.
Africana Notes and News, *March 1990*
Watson, The Savage Club
Graves, Royal Academy, *vol. 6, p. 152*
Kennedy, Pictures in the Africana Museum, *vol. 7, p. 158*
Mallalieu, British Watercolour Artists, *p. 206*
Thorpe, English Illustration

PARENT, A.
One of the illustrators of *La Guerre du Transvaal: Anglais et Boers*. Some of the illustrations are signed 'A.P.'. Parent's work is also noted in *L'Indiscret*.

PARIS, Alfred Jean Marie 1846-1908
Battle and equestrian painter and illustrator. Paris was born in Tours, France. He illustrated *Les Libre Burghers* by Georges Saint-Yves (Maison Alfred Mame and Sons, Tours, 1901).

Paris died in Fontaine Bonneloure dans L'oise in October 1908 .
Bénézit, Dictionnaire antique, *vol. 6, p. 519*

PARKER, Gray
Cartoons by this artist appeared second-hand in *The King*, having originally been reproduced in *Life*, New York. No other information about Parker is available.

PARKES, Harry
An English cartoonist who worked for both *Black & White Budget* and *Judy*. Parkes produced regular full-page cartoons for the latter.

The Africana Museum has one original pen-and-ink cartoon by him entitled *President Kruger and John Bull*. It appeared in *Judy* on 11 October 1899. The cartoon is signed 'Harry Parkes 99' and on the back '7 in wide-*Judy*' is written in ink. The inscription reads: 'Oom Paul: "This business cuts me to the heart." John Bull: "I would it cut you to the conscience".'
Kennedy, Pictures in the Africana Museum, *vol. 7, p. 158*
Thorpe, English Illustration

PARRINGTON, A.J.
Sergeant in the 2nd Kings Royal Rifles who was stationed in Ceylon. As part of the British garrison at Diyatalawa P.O.W.

camp, Parrington produced a plan of the camp with vignettes of Boer and British troops which appears on p. 52 of both language versions of J.N. Brink's *Recollections of a Boer Prisoner-of-War at Ceylon*.

PARTRIDGE, Bernard 1861-1945
Painter and cartoonist. Partridge was born in London on 11 October 1861. He was the youngest son of Professor Richard Partridge who was at one time president of the Royal College of Surgeons. Partridge's uncle, John, was Portrait Painter Extraordinary to Queen Victoria.

Partridge was educated at Stonyhurst College. In 1880 he started work as a stained glass designer and decorative painter but from 1884 he devoted himself to illustration. He joined *Punch* in 1891 and worked continuously for this magazine until his death. In 1901 he became second cartoonist to Linley Sambourne after the principal cartoonist, John Tenniel, retired. Partridge succeeded Sambourne in turn in 1909.

He was a competent actor and adopted the stage name Bernard Gould. He appeared in the first production of George Bernard Shaw's *Arms and the Man*. Partridge painted in oil, watercolour and pastel, and exhibited at the Royal Academy, the R.I. and the N.E.A.C. Besides *Punch* he contributed to *The Quiver, The Illustrated London News, Black & White, The Illustrated Sporting & Dramatic News, Vanity Fair, Pick-Me-Up, Lika Joko, Judy, Lady's Pictorial, Moonshine, The Idler, New Budget, The Sketch* and *Illustrated Bits*.

His Boer War cartoons are found in *Punch*, with occasional illustrations appearing in *The Sphere*.

Partridge often signed his illustrations with the initials 'BP'. He was knighted in 1925 and died in London on 9 August 1945.
Houfe, British Illustrators and Caricaturists, *p. 409*
The Sketch, *vol. 31, p. 442*
The Strand, *vol. 23, p. 81 and vol. 32, p. 411*
Waters, British Artists, *vol. 1, p. 256*
Who was Who, *vol. 4, p. 889*

PASQUIER, H.
One of the illustrators of *La Guerre du Transvaal: Anglais et Boers*.

PATERSON, Andrew Barton ('Banjo') 1864-1941
Australian journalist, author and balladist. His journalistic career started when he accompanied the Australian forces to South Africa in November 1899 in the service of the *Sydney Morning Herald*. During the War he became friendly with Rudyard Kipling, who he met in Bloemfontein. He also became acquainted with Milner, Roberts, Haig, French, McDonald and Kitchener.

In 1900 Paterson was sent to China to cover the Boxer Rebellion. He also spent time in London where he renewed his friendship with Phil May, whom he had known when the latter was in Australia.

Paterson became editor of *The Evening News* and wrote his first novel, *An Outback Marriage*. He later resigned from *The Evening News* to take over *The Town and Country Journal*.

1 This watercolour and wash painting by Wal Paget shows 'Rimington Scouts drinking the health of her Majesty in the home of a rebel farmer'. The reference to the rebel farmer is probably meant to excuse the vandalism to his furniture.
2 Oliver Paque (William Pike) produced this stirring pen-and-ink drawing of Thorneycroft's Infantry attacking at Spioenkop. He based it on a sketch made by one of Thorneycroft's men.

THE FIRST LIFE GUARDS
RECONNOITERING THE ENEMY'S POSITION
SOUTH AFRICA 1899-02

He served with the Australians in World War I. In 1919 he joined the *Sportsman* as editor, a position he held until 1930. He composed the words of 'Waltzing Matilda'. His *Rio Grande's Last Race and other verses* (1902) contained a chapter on 'Poems of the South African War'.

It is believed, but not confirmed, that he supplied the *Sydney Morning Herald* with sketches as well as news reports during the War.

Paterson, Happy Despatches
SABIB, *vol. 3, p. 634*

PATON, Frank 1856-1909
Genre and animal painter whose work was often engraved. Paton exhibited several paintings at the Royal Academy and other principal London galleries from 1872. In 1902 Leggat and Sons of 83 Cheapside, London, published a signed engraving by Paton entitled *A deep Dream of Peace.*

Waters, British Artists, *vol. 1, p. 257*

PATTERSON, F. 1
Patterson produced at least seven illustrations for *The Illustrated London News* during the War. They were done from sketches by frontline artists between December 1899 and March 1901. Patterson's work was borrowed for use in *With the Flag to Pretoria, Cassell's Illustrated History of the Boer War, Black & White Budget* and *The Fight for the Flag in South Africa.*

De Wet, Illustrated London News Index

PATTERSON, George Malcolm 1873-?
Patterson was born in Twickenham on 13 May 1873. He exhibited at the Royal Academy and the R.S.A., among other galleries. He was educated at Clifton and worked in St An-

drews, where he was art master at St Leonard's School specializing in rustic scenes. He contributed to *The Regiment, Fun, The Dome, The Quiver, Punch, Illustrated Bits, Sketchy Bits, Windsor Magazine,* and *The Royal Magazine.*

During the War Patterson was a regular contributor to *Shurey's Illustrated, Shurey's Budget, Pick-Me-Up* and *Illustrated War Special.* One Boer War-related illustration by Patterson appeared in *The Illustrated London News* on 10 March 1900 entitled *Martial Law in Durban. Shutting up the 'Review and Critic' offices for indiscreet criticism of certain military movements.* From a sketch by F. Villiers.

De Wet, Illustrated London News Index
Houfe, British Illustrators and Caricaturists, *p. 411*
Thorpe, English Illustration
Waters, British Artists, *vol. 1, p. 257*

PAUL, Bruno 1874-1968
Painter, artist, art critic, architect and designer of graphic art. Paul was born in Saxony on 19 January 1874. He studied art in Dresden but moved to Munich where he worked for *Jugend* and *Simplicissimus.* He became well known as a poster and postcard artist. Besides his illustrative work he also designed furniture and glass. He was associated with the Vereinigte Werkstätten Für Kunst und Handwerk in Munich between 1893 and 1907. In 1907 he was appointed director of the Berlin Museum Art School.

Paul's Boer War work appeared in *Jugend, Simplicissimus* and the 1900 German pro-Boer publication *Der Burenkrieg.* One of his cartoons, depicting a wounded lion with Queen Victoria looking on in dismay, appeared on the cover of the last-mentioned.

Paul often signed his work with a distinctive monogram. He died in Berlin on 17 August 1968.

Bénézit, Dictionnaire antique, *vol. 6, p. 552*
Fanelli and Godoli, Art Nouveau Postcards, *p. 359*
Feaver, Masters of Caricature, *p. 137*

PAULAT 1
French postcard artist responsible for card published by 'S.P.' showing a seated Edward VII with India, Transvaal and Ireland in chains. Japan is offering him its navy, but his thoughts are on nude ladies in Paris.

PAXTON, Robert B. M. fl. 1895-1925 2
Portrait painter and illustrator. Paxton served as a 'special artist' for *The Sphere*. Hartrick, in *A Painter's Pilgrimage,*

mentions that he lived with him at 8 Wentworth Studios early in his career. Paxton, he says, was an old colleague from *The Daily Graphic*, but eventually 'Paxton married and departed'.

At the start of the War *The Sphere* sent him out to South Africa almost as an afterthought. The announcement at the beginning of June 1900 mentions 'We are glad to inform our readers that in addition to our other artists at the seat of the war, Mr. B. M. Paxton well-known black and white artist has now reached Bloemfontein on behalf of *The Sphere*'.

In *The Work of War Artists in South Africa*, Carter discusses Paxton: '*Colonel Thorneycroft on Spion Kop* (page 4) is another forcible sketch, and by the courtesy of *The Sphere* we are allowed to give on the same page Mr. R. Paxton's development of it. The observer will see at a glance how faithfully the original suggestion has been followed.' The picture had been redrawn after a sketch by Ernest Prater, and was probably done after Paxton's return.

On 7 July 1900 *The Sphere* again featured Paxton's work, this time reproduced in facsimile after he had sent some 'capital sketches of Christiana, which General Hunter occupied on May 15. Mr Paxton and the correspondent of *The Daily Express* were the only newspaper representatives present, and he has drawn the picture of himself and comrade congratulating one another on the invasion of Mr. Kruger's Kingdom.' On 4 August 1900 *The Sphere*, showing a photograph of Paxton, mentioned that he was now with Gen. Hunter's column. On 16 March 1901 (p. 269) *The Sphere* reproduced another example of Paxton's work entitled *Punishment of rebels in South Africa* and subtitled 'Our soldiers looting a store'. The picture shows Paxton's full-page sketch with the photograph from which it was drawn inset in the top left-hand corner.

In January 1903 seven of Paxton's drawings were used to illustrate an article in *The Wide World Magazine.* The article, by Willie Steyn, was apparently ghosted by R.D. Barbor, a British officer in the Army Service Corps. Entitled *How we escaped from Ceylon*, it described Willie Steyn and his four companions' experiences during their dramatic escape from the prison ship *Catalonia* in Colombo harbour. It also describes how they were taken by the Russian troop carrier *Cherson* to the Russian capital and how they eventually rejoined the Boer commandos back in South Africa.

Paxton was awarded the Queen's South Africa medal on 12 June 1903. See p. 188.

Carter, War Artists in S.A., *pp. 4 and 12*
Hartrick, A Painter's Pilgrimage, *p. 160*
Houfe, British Illustrators and Caricaturists, *p. 412*

PAYNE, Arthur Charles 1856-1933

Elder brother of prominent military artist Harry Payne, Arthur Payne was responsible for occasional military pictures drawn in conjunction with his brother during the Anglo-Boer War. Arthur often painted the background and architectural detail, while Harry executed the figures in the foreground. Arthur did many military designs but his postcard work was mainly of cathedrals, views, river scenes etc.

Holt, Tonie and Valmai, Stanley Gibbons Postcard Catalogue, *p. 89*

PAYNE, Charlie Johnson 1884-?

Sporting painter and illustrator. Charlie Johnson Payne adopted the pseudonym 'Snaffles'. It appears that he was christened 'Charlie', not Charles. His father, Ambrose, was a bootmaker's son who had an interest in music and painting. Two of Charlie's sisters also became painters.

At the outbreak of the War the 15-year-old 'Snaffles' tried to enlist, but because of his age he was rejected. He eventually succeeded, however, in getting into the Royal Garrison Artillery in 1901 or 1902. (It is doubtful if he reached South Africa.) He remained with the regiment until a hernia forced his discharge in 1906. At this time he did several watercolours of army officers, some in caricature and signed 'C.J.P.'.

Besides producing over 250 prints Payne provided illustrations for *Punch, The Illustrated Sporting & Dramatic News, The Tatler, Field* and *Blackwood*. At one time *Field* referred to him as 'one of the finest horse artists of today'. His World War I work is very sought after.

Payne's Boer War related work is not common as he was obviously very young at the time. Nevertheless in 1983 the Bourne Gallery offered a watercolour, which, although done *c.*1906, has Boer War relevance. *I don't know whose dam column I'm in, nor where we're trekking, nor why* shows a mounted British trooper in tropical kit and 'South Africa' is inscribed on the mount.

Houfe, British Illustrators and Caricaturists, *p. 412*

PAYNE, G. M.

Postcard artist who worked for Gale & Polden. He produced bathing and sporting cards, and some with the theme 'Before our Time'. Payne illustrated *From private to General*, a one-page picture story showing the life of Hector McDonald. This appeared in *Boys of The Empire* on 11 May 1901.

Holt, Tonie and Valmai, Stanley Gibbons Postcard Catalogue, *p. 89*

PAYNE, Harry 1858-1927 [5]

Harry Payne was born at Newington on 8 March 1858. His older brother, Arthur also developed into a successful artist. The only art instruction Harry ever received was a few months of evening classes in an art school. On leaving school and after spending two years in a merchant's office, Harry secured the post of art designer to a firm of Army and Navy clothing contractors. Here he learnt the meticulous attention to detail so necessary in depicting military uniforms and badges. He continued to produce illustrations and paintings in his spare time and in 1879 these came to the attention of Lionel Marks, a well-known London dealer. The two formed an association as a result of which Harry gave up his job to concentrate full-time on painting.

In 1883 Harry joined the West Kent Queen's Own Yeomanry, determined to make military art his career. In 1884 his long association with the postcard publisher Raphael Tuck commenced and it lasted for some 36 years until 1920.

In 1906, after 23 years' service, Payne retired from the West Kent Queen's Own Yeomanry and he and his wife moved to Forest Hill.

Payne's brother Arthur had specialized in architectural paintings and had reproduced a series of designs of English cathedrals for Tuck. He was thus well equipped to collaborate with Harry on the production of the 'Military In London' series. During this period Harry provided the illustrations for a number of Tuck's 'Toy' books and many of his illustrations were subsequently produced as postcards, the most famous being no. 9877 depicting King George V. He also designed a series of 24 cards for Stewart and Woolf.

The end of World War I and of the postcard boom also brought to an end Harry Payne's arrangement with Tuck. During 1918 he was commissioned by Gale & Polden to do a series of 67 postcards and these were completed in 1919, although only 24 were issued. These were the last of his postcard designs. The next three years were very difficult ones and commissions were few, although in 1921 and 1923 Payne writes of designs on cigarette cards. His health was not good and in 1927 he died after contracting influenza at the age of 69.

A self-portrait of Harry is noted in Tuck's British Army series, card no. 108, *Royal Horse guards* which is repeated in large format, no. 6448, entitled *On service*. Between 556 and 560 of Payne's designs were issued as postcards.

Payne very often dated his work as the period depicted, not the date of execution. Sally Carver, in *The American Postcard Guide to Tuck*, describes him as the 'Michelangelo' of military artists.

He did several military cigarette cards including 'Types of British and Dominion Regiments' issued by Gallahers in 1901 and 1902; 'Types of Volunteers and Yeomanry' for H. & G. Wood in 1899; and 'V.C. Heroes' (40) for Taddy & Co. *c.*1899. Several of these cards have peripheral Boer War interest.

Payne's Boer War postcards are as follows:
1. Tuck Empire series 280. *Wiping something off the slate.* Signed 'HP'.
2. Empire series 281. *Baden-Powell.* Signed 'Harry Payne'.
3. and 4. Empire series 1280 and 1282. *Sons of the Empire.* Horizontal and vertical format respectively. The National Army Museum has a coloured platinum print after Harry Payne dedicated to Lord Wolesley, entitled *Sons of the Empire* (Raphael Tuck, 1900). This is probably from the same painting as the postcard illustration.
5. Oilette 3015 *Our fighting Regiments: The Royal Artillery* 'South African war 1899-1902'. Signed 'Harry Payne'.
6. Oilette 3163 (5) *Our fighting Regiments: The 1st Life Guards* 'The First Life Guards reconnoitering the Enemy's Position South Africa 1899-1902. Signed 'Harry Payne'. This painting is a mirror image of John Charlton's *Keep quiet, signs of the enemy* and was probably copied by Payne.
7. Oilette 3165 *Our fighting Regiments: 1st (King's) Dragoon Guards* 'The first King's Dragoon guards Scouting at Dawn, South Africa 1902'. Signed 'Harry Payne'. These oilettes, which all have divided backs, were reputedly done *c.*1917.

A print of *Lord Roberts Entering Pretoria* by Payne was published by E.S. & A. Robinson of Bristol *c.* 1900. The author has a watercolour by Payne entitled *The Artists' (20th Middlesex) Rifle Volunteers in Marching Order.* This painting is signed and dated 1889. It is probably the original for the chromolitho print of the same name published by Raphael Tuck in 1893 (series 559). This chromolithograph was printed by the 'Rafolith' plates at the Fine Art works in Saxony.

Cane, For Queen and Country
Carver, Guide to Tuck, *p. 48*
Picton's Postcard Catalogue, *1981, supplement 'Harry Payne'*

PAYNE, T.?

A Corporal Payne, possibly with the initial 'T', of the Army Pay Corps is credited with the design of nine well-known patriotic envelopes produced in 1900 and 1901. These envelopes were produced by means of a hectograph, a primitive copying machine. While the designs on each envelope are similar, hardly any are identical and distinct differences are apparent in most cases. The titles of the envelopes are as follows: *The Assembly, Wiping something off a Slate, Carving Something on a Rock, Jack and Jill, Steyn's pantechnicon, The Lord Helps those who help themselves, Humpty Dumpty, Trek, Hold the fort for I am coming.*

In 1902, probably after the War, the Cape Town postcard publisher George Budricks produced a series of postcards based on these envelopes, but were not quite as crudely executed. They were issued in both coloured and uncoloured states. Both the cards and envelopes were signed with a monogram which was similar to one used by John Tenniel. The monogram had either '00' or '01' on either side, indicating the year of production.

The Anglo-Boer War Philatelist, *vol. 35 no. 1, March 1992*
Cartoon Patriotic Envelopes and Postcards of the Anglo-Boer War, *Stuart Duggan*

PEARCE, Thirkell fl. 1900-1929

Pearce worked as an illustrator for *Black & White* and *Black & White Budget* during the War. He is mentioned in Johnson and Greutzner as having exhibited one painting at the R.C.A. from a London address in 1929. In 1980 the Parker Gallery offered three of his drawings done during World War I.

Johnson and Greutzner, British Artists, *p. 395*

PEARS, Charles 1873-1958

Cartoonist and illustrator. Pears was born in Pontefract, Yorkshire, on 9 September 1873. He was educated at East Hardwick and Pontefract College. He claimed to have started drawing at the age of two. His career as an illustrator started in 1895 when he went to work for *The Yorkshireman*. Two years

---

1 An anti-King Edward postcard by Paulat, published by S.P., Paris. Edward is thinking about naked women in Paris rather than the Japanese naval treaty or India, Ireland and Transvaal chained to his throne.

2 Robert Paxton drew this illustration from the photograph appearing inset upper left corner. Published in *The Sphere* on 16 March 1901, it shows British soldiers dismantling the store of a rebel Boer.

3 Harry Payne's *First Life Guards* cartoon.

4 This postcard, with painting by Harry Payne, commemorated the relief of Ladysmith and was entitled 'Wiping something off the Slate'.

5 Harry Payne's postcard of Baden-Powell, Tuck's Empire series no. 281, bore the inscription: 'Well done, Gallant little Mafeking. The Empire is proud of you'. There was some confusion about the exact date of the relief of Mafeking: Tuck played it safe and brought out cards with *three* different dates – 16, 17 and 18 May.

later he went to London and worked for *Pick-Me-Up*, contributing theatrical sketches. He had previously sent work from his home town to *The Idler* and *Yellow Book*.

While on the staff of *Punch* he contributed mainly theatrical sketches and caricatures. He also wrote and illustrated *Mr. Punch's Book for Children*, as well as illustrating several other children's books. Later he became known as a marine artist. During World War I and II he was official war artist to the Admiralty.

One Boer War cartoon by Pears, *Roberts' Marionettes*, appeared in *The Sketch* on 21 March 1900.

Hammerton, Humorists of the Pencil, *pp. 149-155*
Houfe, British Illustrators and Caricaturists, *412*
Peppin and Micklethwait, British Book Illustrators, *p. 230*
Thorpe, English Illustration

PEARSE, Alfred 1856-1933   2

Black and white artist and illustrator; home-based artist for *The Sphere*. The son of J.S. Pearse, the well-known decorative artist, Alfred Pearse was born in St Pancras, London, in 1856. There were four previous generations of artists in the family. Pearse's early education was private but he developed a taste for drawing. Between the ages of 15 and 19 he studied wood engraving but later turned his attention to drawing. He stud-

ied at the West London School of Art for two years, gaining 25 prizes for drawing. In 1879 he submitted a sketch of the Battle of Isandhlwana to the editor of *Pictorial World*, who accepted it. This led to a long career associated with illustrated journals and Pearse was given the nickname of 'Punctual Pearse' because of his ability to meet every deadline.

Pearse's illustrations for *The Sphere*, for which he worked as a home-based artist during the Boer War, were prolific. (His work has also been noted in *The Penny Illustrated Paper*.) He accompanied the Duke and Duchess of Cornwall on their world tour in 1901 aboard the *Ophir*, and he submitted sketches to *The Sphere* from all over the world, including South Africa.

The Africana Museum, Johannesburg, possesses one work by Pearse entitled *Ladysmith Relieved Feb 8 1900*. The inscription on the back in pencil reads 'The meeting of Sir George White and Lord Dundonald'. It is a monochrome signed 'A. Pearse'. Also on the back there are instructions for the engraver and 'with the flag to Pretoria', probably the source used for his portraits. It was reproduced as a sepia engraving (same size as the original) with the lettering,'Colonel Duff – Lt. Haag – Gen. White – Lord Dundonald – Maj. Mackenzie – One of the Gen. White's bodyguard – The Relief of Ladysmith' (Frost & Reed, 2 April 1901). Other Boer War engravings by Pearse published by Frost & Reed include:
1. *British Generals*
2. *Mafeking Relieved 15 May 1900*
3. *Kimberley Relieved 19 (sic) February 1900*   (sic)
All are signed 'Alfred Pearse' in pencil on the mount.

At the Royal Academy in 1900 Pearse exhibited '*Bobs' Eyes; a sketch on the Orange Free State border*.

During World War I Pearse was special artist for the New Zealand Expeditionary Force. His captaincy was earned in the New Zealand Rifle Brigade. He also painted several military pictures during the War, as well as 160 V.C. portraits for the British Government.

Pearse was specially commissioned to sketch the coronation of King George V and Queen Mary at Westminster Abbey and to paint 20 pictures for the *Royal Historical Record* by H. Farnham Burke. Another of his commissions was a picture of a tank in action for King George V. He also designed Royal costumes for investitures. His publications include *50,000 miles under the Union Jack*; *The Good Old Days*; *Merrie England*, and *Stories old and new*.

Pearse often signed his work with the initials 'A.P.'. He died on 29 April 1933.

Graves, Royal Academy, *vol. 6, p. 91*
Kennedy, Pictures in the Africana Museum, *vol. 7, p. 158*
The Strand, *vol. 10, p. 790*
Verbeek, Early Natal Art
Who was Who, *vol. 3, p. 1057*

PEGRAM, Frederick 1870-1937

Genre painter, black and white artist and illustrator. Pegram was born in London on 19 December 1870. He was a first cousin of the brothers C.E. and H.M. Brock (see p. 113). He studied under Fred Brown and spent some time in Paris. Pegram joined the staff of *The Queen* and then *Pall Mall Gazette* in 1886. He was probably one of the most prolific and consistent magazine illustrators. He exhibited at the principal London galleries from 1889 and was elected a member of the R.I. in 1935.

Pegram's Boer War work is not common and only one illustration has been noted. It appeared in *The Sphere* on 3 February 1900 entitled *Suspicious natives under examination by an intelligence officer at Frere* and was done from a sketch by Ernest Prater.

Pegram died in London on 23 August 1937.
Waters, British Artists, *vol. 1, p. 259*
Who was Who, *vol. 3, p. 1061*

PEGRAM, Henry Alfred 1863-1937

Figure and portrait sculptor. Pegram was born in London on 27 July 1863. He studied at the Royal Academy schools from 1881 to 1887 and worked as assistant to Sir Hamo Thornycroft from 1887 to 1891. Pegram exhibited over 180 sculptures at the Royal Academy including *The late Rt. Hon. Cecil Rhodes* in 1903. The bust of Rhodes, done in marble, was for the City of London. He was elected A.R.A. in 1904 and R.A. in 1922.
Graves, Royal Academy, *vol. 6, p. 97*
Johnson and Greutzner, British Artists, *p. 397*
Waters, British Artists, *vol. 1, p. 259*

PEN

Pseudonym of an unknown British cartoonist who illustrated a series of copyright postcards at the end of the War. The cards have an undivided back, and the titles and captions are printed in red. The publisher is unknown. The unnumbered cards are as follows:
1. *Packing up.* Caption: 'Old Boer: I say Tommy have you seen anything of an "Independence' throwing about? Tommy: Why I do believe I've packed it with my things! Awful sorry, Hope it won't inconvenience you!'
2. *In Eclipse.*
3. *Sheathed at last.*
4. *Sunset.* (Kruger as Napoleon.)
5. *Happy now he's got it.* (Chamberlain in a bath holding a cake of soap – a parody of the contemporary Pears Soap advertisement.)

PENSTONE, Constance 1865-1928

Cartoonist and landscape artist in watercolours. Constance Penstone (née Jones) was born in Chesterfield, England, but

lived for some years in Australia (where she married and divorced Felix Roth) and the United States. She studied at the Derbyshire School of Art. In 1896 she went to South Africa and married the cartoonist Charles Penstone, who had established the periodical *The Owl* in Johannesburg in 1895. In June 1896 the publication moved to Cape Town and changed its name to *The Owl: Penstone's Weekly*. Constance, the joint owner, used the pen name 'Scalpel'. During the War she also worked for *The Cape Times* weekly edition, contributing illustrations and cartoons. Later she submitted cartoons to *The Cape* and *Cape Argus*.

In 1902 Constance Penstone became a founder member of the South African Society of Artists. After the death of her husband in August 1896 she married the artist George Crosland Robinson. From about 1910 she concentrated more on her landscape watercolours than on cartoons. Her signature on her early cartoons ('C. Penstone') is difficult to distinguish from that of her second husband. Her later illustrations and cartoons are often signed 'C.P.'. Her work is found in public collections in the South African National Gallery, the Albany Museum (Grahamstown) and the Africana Museum. As yet no original Boer War cartoons by Penstone have been traced.

Berman, Art and Artists, *p. 324*

Kennedy, Pictures in the Africana Museum, *vol. 4, pp. 67-68*

Schoonraad, Spot- en Strookprent Kunstenaars, *pp. 185-186*

PERARD, Victor Semon 1870-1957

Perard was born in Paris on 16 January 1870. He studied art at the École des Beaux-Arts in Paris under Gérôme and also at the Art Students' League in New York. He was an illustrator for *Harper's Magazine, Scribner's* and *Century*. Later he became an instructor at the Cooper Institute. Perard wrote at least four books on art instruction and illustrated numerous others, including the 1933 edition of *Rip van Winkle*.

His Boer War work appeared in *Harper's Monthly*, illustrating an article entitled 'Behind Boer lines'.

Perard died in Plainfield, New Jersey, on 9 July 1957.

Fielding, American Painters, etc., *p. 278*

PESTILLAC, S. 1

Illustrated an adventure story entitled *Aventures de Deux Petits Boers contées par L'Oncle Paul aux petits Français*, interpreted by Jacques de la Voie. The book was published by Le Livre Moderne, 6 Rue de la Chaussée-d'Antin, Paris 1900. This 16-page pro-Boer booklet of coloured sketches was aimed at French children. The full-page portrait of Kruger is captioned 'Apostle of Liberty and Justice'.

Mendelssohn, Mendelssohn's Bibliography, *vol. 2, pp. 381-382*

PETERS, G.W.

An American artist who worked for *Harper's Weekly* and *Monthly*. His Boer War illustrations can be found in both publications. One, *An intercepted message*, appeared on the front cover of *Harper's Weekly* for 17 March 1900.

PETHYBRIDGE, H. M.

Nothing is known of this artist except that he was responsible for two illustrations which appeared in *The Illustrated London News* entitled *De Aar showing railway line to Kimberley, with Tafelberg in the distance, about 35 miles off* (23 December 1899) and *Transvaal War: De Aar, on the line to Kimberley, showing the railway station and hotel* (30 December 1899).

It is not known if H.M. Pethybridge is the same individual as T. Ley Pethybridge, who worked for *Ludgate Monthly* and *The Temple Magazine*.

De Wet, Illustrated London News Index

PHILIP, George

Four illustrations by this artist appeared in *The Graphic* on 28 October 1899. They were entitled:
1. *Position of forces before the battle of Dundee, October 19*
2. *Position of forces after the battle of Dundee, October 20*
3. *Position of forces before the battle of Elands Laagte, noon, October 21*
4. *Position of forces after the battle of Elands Laagte, evening, October 21*

Hofmeyr, Matton and Roets, Graphic Picture Index

PIC, Marcel 1

The regimental museum of the Royal Irish Fusiliers in Belfast, Northern Ireland, has a series of cartoons depicting the Royal Irish Fusiliers in Ladysmith. The cartoons are signed 'Marcel Pic'.

On 26 September 1900 *The Sketch* published four 'Military Caricatures by Marcel Pic'. The caricatures, showing Lt. Col. F.C. Porter (6th Dragoon Guards), Lt. Col. C.M. Bulock (2nd Devonshire Regiment), Col. H.R. Roberts (2nd Lincolnshire Regiment) and Col. G.P. Brabazon (4th Hussars) were, however, dated between 1895 and 1898.

The author has a pencil and crayon cartoon by Pic dated 1898. The illustration shows an impoverished Kaiser Wilhelm surveying a group of armed Boers. An annotation on the cartoon says 'all M. Marcel Pic's Drawings are copyright'.

Personal communication with the Curator, Royal Irish Regimental Museum, Belfast

PICASSO, Pablo (Ruiz Blasco) 1881-1973 1

Picasso was born in Malaga, Spain, on 25 October 1881. His father, Don Ruiz Picasso, was a minor art master. He instruct-

ed his son in pencil and charcoal drawing and gave him his first lessons in oil painting. When his father was appointed teacher at the School of Fine Arts in Barcelona in September 1895, the family moved there, and in the following year, aged 15, Picasso opened his own studio in the city. He studied in Madrid until June 1898 and then in Horta until mid-1899 when once again he returned to Barcelona. In 1900 he contributed illustrations to *Arte Joven*.

The Picasso Museum situated in the Calle Montcada was established in 1954, but, because of his opposition to the Franco regime, Picasso refused to have anything to do with it. In 1968, however, on the death of his lifelong friend Jaime Sabates, Picasso's attitude to the museum changed and he donated several of his early works to the museum's collection in memory of his friend, who had been born in Barcelona. Included in this vast collection are three sheets which depict drawings, or rather doodles, of the youthful Picasso's impressions of the Boer War. All the Boers depicted on the three sheets are bearded but have no moustaches, which might indicate that Picasso had intended to portray Paul Kruger.

One sheet shows three caricatures of armed pipe-smoking Boers. Interestingly enough Picasso shows the Boers armed with swords as well as bayonet-bearing rifles. There are also caricatures of Highlanders inscribed 'Ingles'. Several other male and female busts, including one with Negroid features, make up this collection.

---

1 *The Sphere* home-based artist Alfred Pearse produced this monochrome wash drawing entitled *The meeting of Sir George White and Lord Dundonald*. It was reproduced for sale as a sepia engraving in April 1901. Reproduced by courtesy of the Africana Museum.

2 S. Pestillac's cover design for Jacques de la Voie's *Aventures de Deux Petits Boers contées par L'Oncle Paul aux Petits Français*.

3 A pen-and-ink doodle by Pablo Picasso, one of at least three that he did in 1900 showing his pro-Boer feelings. It shows, among others, a bagpipe-playing Highlander, a Boer armed incongruously (and incorrectly) with a sword, and a monocled man who must represent Joe Chamberlain. Reproduced by courtesy of the Picasso Museum, Barcelona.

4 This engraving by Alfred Pearse is entitled *Mafeking Relieved* and depicts Baden-Powell on the right meeting relieving forces. It was published by Frost & Reed of Bristol.

5 Marcel Pic drew this original pencil, crayon and chalk cartoon in 1898. It depicts an impoverished Kaiser Wilhelm being fired on by a party of Boers. The significance of this cartoon is unclear as, at that time, following his congratulatory telegram to Kruger after the failure of the Jameson Raid, the Kaiser was considered to be a staunch, if opportunist, ally of the Transvaal.

LA SALE FACE

1   2   3

The second sheet, which is covered mainly with female figures, also has two clear and one indistinct bust caricatures of pipe-smoking Boers.

The third sheet, which is signed 'Pablo Ruiz Picasso', is dedicated to his father. The caricatures on this sheet include two monocled individuals, almost surely representing Joseph Chamberlain, a bagpipe-playing Highlander and another armed pipe-smoking Boer.

It has been said that Picasso's oeuvre has influenced 20th century art more than that of any other individual. He died on 8 April 1973.

Africana Notes and News, *June 1974, 'Picasso and the South African War' by I. Norwich*
Lantern, *May 1981, 'Picasso and the South African War' by F. Snitcher*
Osterwalder, *and Hubschmid and Bouret (eds.),* Dictionnaire des Illustrateurs, *p. 828*

PICK, M.   1

This artist was responsible for a French peace card and another card entitled *La Sale Face* (S.P., Paris), showing a dog urinating on a portrait of Joseph Chamberlain.

PIFFARD, Harold H. fl.1895-1903

Military painter and illustrator. Piffard's work appeared in *The Quiver, Pearson's Magazine, Cassell's Family Magazine* and *Windsor Magazine*. He provided eight illustrations for *Dick Dale, The Colonial Scout – a tale of the Transvaal War of 1899-1900* by Tom Bevan (S.W. Partridge, London, 1900). His Boer War illustrations also appeared in *Black & White*.

After the War Piffard worked for the firm of Gale & Polden and one divided-back card showing an illustration of Strathcona's Horse in the Boer War was illustrated by him.

Byatt, *Picture Postcards, p. 100*
Houfe, *British Illustrators and Caricaturists, p. 416*
SABIB, *vol. 1, p. 187*

PIKE, William Henry *see* PAQUE, Oliver

PINNOCK, Herbert Louis (Lulu) 1881-?   1

Soldier-artist. Pinnock was born in England in 1881, the same year that his family emigrated to South Africa. He was the great uncle of Cedryl Greenland, the author of *A Century in Shreds*, which was published in 1980. In her account, Mrs Greenland relates that the family settled in Woodstock where Lulu, as she called him, became interested in sketching from a very early age.

At the outbreak of War Pinnock joined the South African Light Horse, eventually becoming sergeant. He was sent up to the Orange River Colony where his regiment was in close collaboration with the Imperial Yeomanry.

Pinnock's sketchbook was dedicated to 'Mrs Hain, Sea Point Cape Town, South Africa'. It is now in the author's possession. Several of the sketches were used in *A Century in Shreds*. There are over 70 pencil, pen-and-ink, and water-colour sketches or cartoons in total, some of which are mere doodles. Most are untitled but those with titles include:

1. *A destroyed Boer farm house 1902*
2. *The Battle of Tabaksburg, 30 January 1900*
3. *Pom Pom Horses being brought out of action after engagement, Tabaksburg Jan. 30 1900*
4. *The Royal Army Medical Corps*
5. *The Seaforth Highlanders in the Orange River Colony*
6. *De Wet's remounts, I am yours*
7. *Capturing Stock, ORC*
8. *Heliographing in 1902*
9. *Block Houses*
10. *Doctors, Kroonstad Hospital*
11. *Too Late*
12. *Boer prisoners of War*
13. *The burial of Lieutenant Jansen at Aberdeen in 1901*
14. *The girls I left behind me*
15. *The 2nd Dragoon Royal Scots Grays*
16. *Yes, let me like a soldier fall*
17. *Picquet*
18. *SALH*
19. *General De Wet escaping through the block house line at Lindley*
20. *Homeward Bound*
21. *Aristocracy*
22. *Boers attacking Block House*
23. *Transvaal Scenery 1902*
24. *A Scotch Lassie*
25. *SALH Scouting*
26. *Forget me not*
27. *A novel way of dismounting much affected by 'I Ys' during the present war*
28. *Boers surrendering*
29. *An armoured train*
30. *A court martial*
31. *Feathers to the front South African Light Horse*
32. *Field Battery in action*
33. *Motor transport on the veld*
34. *A rebel's house in the ORC*
35. *KR, Maximus Wepener*
36. *Home sweet home.*

Some of the sketches also show women wearing military uniform. Those with titles are:

37. *Miss Hutton*
38. *Miss Rosa Barnes*
39. *Miss Mary Belfast*
40. *Daisy, Gladys Pinnock*

After the War Pinnock enrolled in the Cape Mounted Police and his application form in the archives has been traced. He describes himself as being 5ft 7½ in tall, weighing 140 lbs. His prior occupation on 9 October 1902 was that of clerk. He mentions that he was a British citizen able to speak Dutch and English and some Zulu. His service with the Cape Mounted Police lasted until he was discharged as medically unfit on 28 February 1913. It was at this time that he became cartoonist for *Nonquai*, the South African Police journal. He continued in this capacity for a few years. Details of his later life are not known.

Greenland, A Century in Shreds
Personal communication with the Cape Archives

PISCHON, Marie 1856-?

German-born painter whose maiden name was Hünfield. She was born in a town of the same name on 21 January 1856.

Marie Pischon is reputed to be the artist of *Naar harden Strÿd*. This well-known painting of a Boer consoling his wife among the ruins of his farm was copied by several artists including Paul Baggie and Sarah Wilcocks. These copies are in the Potchefstroom and Bloemfontein museums respectively.

The painting itself was reproduced on both posters and postcards in the Netherlands just after the War.

Bénézit, *Dictionnaire antique, vol. 6, p. 708*
Kriel and De Villiers, *Rondom die Anglo-Boereoorlog, p. 152*

P.L.   1

Illustrator of an Art Nouveau postcard entitled *Heil den tapfern Buren und ihren würdigen vertretern*. Published by either H. Däumler, J. Bauer or V.A. Baasch in Germany, these cards had a preprinted address for Paul Kruger in Brussels.

PLINZNER, M.

Illustrator of at least two books on the War, Paul Groningen's *Der Heldenkampf der Buren* (Gebrüder Rauh, Grafräth Solingen, 1902) and Wilhelm Vallentin's *Der Burenkrieg* (Rheinisches Verlagshaus, Wald-Solingen and Leipzig, 1903). One of his illustrations was used on the dustjacket of the Africana Reprint Series (vol. 8) of J.D. Kestell's *Through Shot and Flame*, published in 1976.

SABIB, *vol. 2, p. 450 and vol. 4, p. 595*

PLUMENT DE BAILHAC, Paul C. M. 1866-?

Portrait and landscape artist. Plument was born on the Isle of St Denis on 1 August 1866. He studied art under Bouguereau and T. Robert-Fleury, becoming a member of the Society of French Artists from 1896. Plument was founder and president of the Salon de l'École Française.

L'Illustration of 4 May 1901 published photographs of

4

5

several of the paintings which appeared at the Salon des Artistes Français exhibition, presumably in 1901. On page 292 Plument's painting *Au Transvaal – La Petite Guerre* was reproduced.

A postcard with the same title was published by the French firm of N.D. Phot.

Bénézit, Dictionnaire antique, *vol. 6, p. 729*
L'Illustration, 4 May 1901, p. 292

PLUMET, Jean Louis 1871-?

Painter and cartoonist. Plumet was born in Mâcon, France, on 13 June 1871. He exhibited at the Nationale des Beaux-Arts and worked for *Le Gavroche* and *La Caricature*.

On 2 February 1901 a coloured cartoon by Plumet appeared on the front page of issue 1101 of *La Caricature*. Entitled *Les Deux Augures*, it showed Roberts and Chamberlain. Plumet's *La Raison du plus fort* was published on page 4 of the special number of *Le Gavroche* (16 June 1902), 'La Paix à la mode John Bull'.

L'Indiscret also published some of Plumet's Boer War cartoons.

Bénézit, Dictionnaire antique, *vol. 6, p. 730*

POCOCK, R. Noel

Pocock worked as cartoonist for *The American Leader*.

POILPOT, Théophile (jnr.) 1848-1915

Military and marine painter. The son of the painter Théophile Poilpot snr., Théophile Poilpot jnr. was born in Paris on 20 March 1848. He studied under Gérôme and Boulanger. He exhibited at the Salon des Artistes Français from 1874, receiving an honourable mention in 1883. Poilpot's pencil sketch showing Kruger directing his troops in battle was published in the special edition of *Le Monde Illustré* of 17 November 1900. The inscription on the illustration translates as 'to President Kruger with homage and respect and great admiration'.

Poilpot died in Paris on 6 February 1915.

Bénézit, Dictionnaire antique, *vol. 6, p. 739*

POIRÉ, Emmanuel *see* CARAN D'ACHE

POPE, E.T.

Illustrator of *Contraband of War* by B. Aitken. This adventure story, subtitled 'A serial story of the Boer War', was serialized in *Boys of the Empire*.

POPINI

Judy cartoonist who later specialized in romantic situation postcards.

Popini's Boer War work, which was characterized by highly decorative drawings and cartoons, also appeared in

Illustrated War Special and *War Pictures*.
Thorpe, English Illustration

PORTER, Paul

Cartoonist for *Detroit Free Press* and *The Boston Herald*.

POTT, Charles L. 1865-? 1

Landscape painter and illustrator of military and sporting subjects. Possibly a soldier-artist during the Boer War. The son of the artist Laslett Pott, Charles Pott was born in South Hampstead, London, on 9 January 1865. He contributed to many magazines including *Punch*, *The Illustrated Sporting & Dramatic News*, *Cassell's Saturday Journal*, *The Regiment* and *The Sketch*.

Pott's Boer War cartoons appeared in *Under The Union Jack*, *After Pretoria: the Guerilla War*, *Punch* and *The Sketch*.

Even though Pott's name does not appear in the official list of the City Imperial Volunteers it is possible that he travelled to South Africa with them. His self-portrait caricature in *Humorists of the Pencil* by J.A. Hammerton shows him in what appears to be the C.I.V. uniform. On the other hand, *Punch* was still reproducing the occasional Pott cartoon while the C.I.V. were in South Africa.

On 24 June 1900 *The Sketch* reported as follows: "Good bye comrade", Brandon Thomas's seasonable song fitly figured in the menu of the notable little dinner given by some cheery spirits 'Al at Lloyds' to their friends of the Artists' Corps at the Restaurant d'Italie on the eve of their departure with the second contingent of the C.I.V. It will be observed from my reproduction of Mr. Pott's smart caricature on the front of the menu that the gallant band of artists now voyaging to the Cape boast an excellent humorist of the pencil. Cordially wishing the artists bon voyage and a safe return, I would also express the hope that *The Sketch* may be favoured with a few War drawings with the dexterous pencil of Mr. Potts.

Five of his sketches, entitled *Life on a Transport*, appeared in *Under The Union Jack* on 20 December 1900.

Pott collaborated with Richard Simkin in Dean's 'Diploma' series no. 36, *Tommy Atkins*. This little booklet, with coloured and black and white pictures, was a humorous look at army life.

Pott often signed his work with the initials 'C.L. P'.

Hammerton, Humorists of the Pencil, *pp. 143-148*
Houfe, British Illustrators and Caricaturists, *p. 418*
Thorpe, English Illustration, *p. 121*

POTT, Johannes Adriaan ?-1926

Pro-Boer artist. Pott was an official in the office of the Staatssecretaris of the Zuid-Afrikaansche Republiek (Transvaal Republic). He served with the Boer forces during the War.

After being wounded at Ladysmith, he accompanied President Kruger to Europe, only returning to South Africa after Kruger's death in Switzerland in 1904. The Africana Museum possesses 18 cartoon sketches by Pott. These are bound in a book of 12 numbered and six supplementary sheets. The title page is inscribed 'Die Groot Sukses van Tommy Atkins in Zuid-Afriká: Twaalf platen geteekend door Een Transvaler'.

Pott died at Pretoria in 1926.

Kennedy, Pictures in the Africana Museum, *vol. 4, p. 93*

POULBOT, Francisque 1879-1946 1

Cartoonist and poster and postcard artist. Poulbot was born in St Denis, France, in 1879. As a cartoonist he contributed to *Le Sourire*, *Le Rire*, *La Vie Pour Rire* and *Chronique Amusante*. His coloured front cover cartoon, *L'Angleterre Semeuse de discorde*, appeared in *La Caricature* on 24 November 1900. A full-page cartoon by Poulbot, *Happy Christmas*, appeared in *Le Rire* on 29 December 1900. He contributed two cartoons to the special number of *Le Gavroche*, 'La Paix à la mode John Bull', on 16 June 1902. One of these cartoons was the coloured front cover *Traite de Paix*'; the other, on p. 5, was entitled *Le remords*.

Poulbot became well known as a World War I postcard artist and was responsible for several posters during the period. He died in Paris on 16 September 1946.

Barnicoat, History of Posters, *p. 196*
Bénézit, Dictionnaire antique, *vol. 6, p. 783*
Holt, Tonie and Valmai, Stanley Gibbons Postcard Catalogue
Osterwalder, and Hubschmid and Bouret (eds.), Dictionnaire des Illustrateurs, *p. 846*

PRATER, Ernest fl.1885-1937 3

'Special' artist for *The Sphere*. Prater was a Londoner of Cornish descent who took up drawing after being in commerce for some years. He worked as an illustrator for *St James Budget*, *Boy's Own Paper*, *Chums*, *Ludgate Monthly*, *The Idler* and *Pearson's Magazine*. He served in the 3rd Middlesex Artillery at one time.

Between 1897 and 1904 Prater exhibited at the Royal Academy. In 1899 *Nelson wounded at the Nile* appeared at the R.A. The other exhibits are paintings inspired by his apparent interest in rugby football and the titles reflect this interest. The frontispiece of *World Sports*, vol. 1, was done by him. In 1912 he illustrated Basil Joseph Matthews' *Livingstone the Pathfinder*.

At the start of the War Prater was working for *The Graphic* and three illustrations credited to him appeared during October 1899. *The Sphere* obviously appropriated him and he was sent out to South Africa on their behalf. Describing their artists they mentioned that 'Mr Ernest Prater has long had a reputation in the work of black and white art'.

He joined Buller in Natal and was present at Spioenkop and Vaal Kranz. The pictures he sent to his paper included vivid accounts of the scenes he had drawn. He also described the Battle of Monte Cristo (*The Sphere*, 31 March 1900). (In *The War Illustrators*, Hodgson mentions that none of his work was reproduced in facsimile. While most was redrawn

---

1 This postcard by 'Pick', published by S.P., Paris, was one of many violently anti-Chamberlain illustrations. Its title *La Sale Face* means 'the obscene countenance'.
2 Charles L. Pott supplied cartoons of the War to several contemporary publications. He may have been a soldier-artist with the C.I.V.
3 The death of soldier-artist Lieutenant Nesham at Tweebosch was drawn by Ernest Prater and reproduced in *After Pretoria: the Guerilla War*.
4 Ernest Prater's illustration *How the Boer Prisoners kill time* appeared in *The Sphere* on 6 April 1901. It shows Boer P.O.W.s making toys while aboard the *Kildonan Castle* bound for Ceylon.
5 A wash drawing entitled *Jack's keen eyes watching the Boers at Colenso* by Alfred Pearse. In the top right-hand corner is the sketch that Ernest Prater provided for the illustration.

quite a few illustrations were in fact reproduced in facsimile, some even alongside the redrawn illustrations.)

The Sphere mentioned that 'Prater, who spent 6 months with General Buller, was down in hospital with enteric fever for a month'. When Prater recovered he returned to *The Sphere* offices and continued working for them as a home-based artist. He contributed several illustrations of the War. One, which appeared on 6 April 1901, was entitled *How the Boer Prisoners kill time* and showed prisoners making toys and other articles which were later resold in England. In *The Work of War Artists in South Africa*, A.C.R. Carter devotes considerable space to Prater's work, reproducing *Colonel Thorneycroft at Spion Kop*, *Capture of Pieter's Hill by the East Surrey Regiment*, *Bringing in the Wounded*, and *The Meeting of the Two Battalions of the Devonshire Regiment*. Prater was awarded the Queen's South Africa medal on 12 June 1903.

Prater was apparently still working for *The Sphere* at the outbreak of World War I and became well known as a military postcard artist. After the war some of his illustrations were used on the S. Hildesheimer and Co. Ltd. War series, for example *Types of the Japanese army*.

Byatt, Picture Postcards
Carter, War Artists in S.A., *pp. 10-16*
Hodgson, The War Illustrators, *pp. 183-184*
Houfe, British Illustrators and Caricaturists, *p. 419*
Peppin and Micklethwait, British Book Illustrators, *p. 39*
SABIB, *vol. 3, p. 725*
The Orders and Medals Research Society, *Summer 1986,*
'War Correspondents: South Africa 1899-1902', by Patrick Street
Thorpe, English Illustration

PRINSEP, Valentine Cameron 1838-1904

Portrait and genre painter. Prinsep was born in Calcutta on 14 February 1838. He studied under Gleyre in Paris in 1859. He accompanied Burne-Jones in Rome from 1859 to 1860. He exhibited at the Royal Academy from 1862 and became professor of painting at the Royal Academy schools. Prinsep was elected A.R.A. in 1879 and R.A. in 1894. He visited India in 1876 to paint the declaration of Queen Victoria as empress. In 1879 he published *Imperial India: an Artist's Journal*. He is given further credit for two novels and two plays. At one time he was a major in the Artists' Volunteers.

The museum in Mafikeng (formerly Mafeking) has an oil painting by Prinsep entitled *Mafeking 1900*. This picture shows a shell penetrating a room with a frightened servant and a mother and child inside. A picture of Baden-Powell hangs askew on the wall.

Prinsep died on 11 November 1904
The Graphic (obituary), *19 Nov. 1904*
Graves, Royal Academy, *vol. 6, pp. 205-208*
The Strand, *vol. 12, p. 603*
Who was Who, *vol. 1, p. 577*

PRIOR, Melton 1845-1910   7

'Special' for *The Illustrated London News*. Melton Prior was born in London on 12 September 1845. He was educated at St Clement Danes Grammar School, where he received his early art training, and later attended Bleriot College in Boulogne. Prior readily attributed his artistic ability to his father, William Harry Prior, who had exhibited at the Royal Academy.

The name of Melton Prior is virtually synonymous with *The Illustrated London News*. The newspaper published its first drawings by Prior, of Princess Mary of Teck opening a bazaar, in 1868. For the next five years Prior remained on the inside staff, until 1873 when Sir William Ingram, owner of the paper, sent him to accompany Lord Wolseley's expedition to Ashanti. Until his death in 1910, Prior covered over 24 campaigns and revolutions for the newspaper, spending an unbroken year at home only in 1883.

Prior produced a great deal of Africana work — over 300 illustrations related to South Africa appeared in *The Illustrated London News*. He went to South Africa on five separate occasions: the last Frontier War (1878), the Zulu War (1879), the first Anglo-Boer War (1881); the Jameson Raid (1895-6), when he also went to Rhodesia; and during the second Anglo-Boer War, when the newspaper recalled him from the Dreyfus trial in September 1899.

Prior's first picture of the campaign was published in *The Illustrated London News* on 7 October 1899, when Samuel Begg redrew a sketch made on board the SS *Norman*, showing General French discussing the possibility of war with Kruger's cousin.

Prior described his experiences in South Africa in his book *Campaigns of a War Correspondent*, published posthumously in 1912.

On arrival in Cape Town Prior was strongly advised to go to Natal as local newspapers had already published telegrams to the effect that the Boers had crossed the Natal frontier. He heard that Gen. French was also on his way to Durban and the newspaper correspondents Bennet Burleigh and H. Pearse had already arrived in Natal. Once in Durban he heard that

hard fighting had occurred at Dundee. He joined up with Ernest Smith of *The Morning Leader* and together they purchased horses and started off by rail for Ladysmith. Prior described how by an extraordinary piece of luck they were allowed to travel on an armoured train which was attempting to get through the blockade. They arrived at Elandslaagte station while the Battle of Elandslaagte was already in progress. He describes the battle in great detail, as well as the subsequent battle of Lombard's Kop which caused the retreat of Sir George White's forces back into Ladysmith. Prior followed White into Ladysmith.

Having been in many previous campaigns in the past Prior was excited at the idea of 'being invested [besieged] for the first time in his career'. Everyone was very optimistic, however, that the town would be relieved within two weeks, and that at the very worst the siege would last for six weeks. Prior describes his experiences in Ladysmith very vividly, including how his friend, Dr Stark, lost his life only a few seconds after Prior himself had moved away from the very position in which Stark was killed.

The tragedies and the lighter side of the experiences of inhabitants of Ladysmith are also described. Eventually Prior

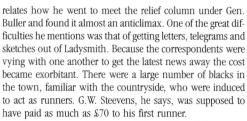

5 6

7

relates how he went to meet the relief column under Gen. Buller and found it almost an anticlimax. One of the great difficulties he mentions was that of getting letters, telegrams and sketches out of Ladysmith. Because the correspondents were vying with one another to get the latest news away the cost became exorbitant. There were a large number of blacks in the town, familiar with the countryside, who were induced to act as runners. G.W. Steevens, he says, was supposed to have paid as much as £70 to his first runner.

Prior made his sketches carefully and traced them onto the thinnest paper he had, folded them as small as possible and sent them out with a runner. (The first six sketches cost him £50.) The runners who undertook this journey left Ladysmith at night but hid during the day. Under cover of darkness they would either sneak through the lines or join the blacks employed by the Boers. In this way they hoped to escape detection. Once through the lines the runner had to take the envelope down to Colenso, get the receipt from the postmaster, and then return to Ladysmith where he was paid the amount promised on producing the receipt.

On 3 March 1900 *The Illustrated London News* reproduced in facsimile Prior's letter from Ladysmith dated 16 January 1900:

My Kaffir runner with the tracings of the Battle of Cesars Camp went out to get through the Boer lines but together with all the other correspondents' runners, had to return

— I sent him out again and now hear he was shot on the road. I have therefore made more tracings and sent them on again and trust this Kaffir will be more successful. At the end of the siege I shall send you over 40 originals (tracings of which I have sent you) in the event of your not having received them all.

Because of the high financial cost headquarters took the matter up and the press censor arranged for a regular post once a week. A regular stream of runners now became accustomed to running week after week in perfect safety, with the result that the price was fixed by the headquarters' staff at £15 for each letter. Prior was often asked how the correspondents could afford these enormous sums. Of course his head office was quite prepared to pay large amounts for the scoops.

After the relief of Ladysmith Prior travelled through Colenso to Durban, arriving on 2 March 1900. There he joined a steamer heading for the Cape, from where he intended to work his way up to Bloemfontein to join Lord Roberts en route to Pretoria. He had hoped to go to Kimberley and then to make the overland trip to Bloemfontein. Prior had heard, however, that small parties of Boers were patrolling the road and the only safe way to reach Bloemfontein was via Norval's Pont. Eventually he reached Bloemfontein. Here he met and spent time with Rudyard Kipling. He found him a 'charming man without an atom of "side"' and it was interesting to compare his natural manliness with the offensive style of some of the other men one met out there'.

Prior gives a good account of the retaking of the waterworks which had been captured by the Boers after Sanna's Post. His remarks on the Transvaal finish very abruptly, as he says 'I don't think the remainder of my visit to South Africa provided any more exciting incidents'. Prior describes one amusing incident, however, during the Battle of Elandslaagte. He could not understand why all the bullets and shells seemed to be coming in his direction. At last Bennet Burleigh spoke up: 'Confound your white helmet, Prior; you are drawing all the fire!' It had not occurred to him that his helmet, which was catching the sun, was a magnificent target, but he realized that if he were to take it off, his bald head would act like a heliograph. His solution was to place his waterproof cloak over his pate and to keep as low as possible. This had the right effect, for the shells chose another objective. His baldness and high-pitched voice earned him the nickname of 'screeching billiard ball'.

Back in England, Prior sketched the return of the C.I.V. to London in October 1900. He appears to have been sent out to Madeira in November 1900 to meet Roberts on his return to

England, as sketches of these scenes were reproduced in facsimile. After the War Prior attended the Delhi Durbar, then covered the Somali Campaign and, the following year, the Russo-Japanese War.

Prior made two round-the-world trips, and became so well acquainted with the United States on his four visits that he was classified as a Western artist.

Prior died in England on 2 November 1910. His funeral was attended by many mourners, including several of his colleagues: Richard Caton Woodville, Herman Koekkoek, Samuel Begg, Henry Nevison and René Bull. Under the chairmanship of Bennet Burleigh, Prior's friends decided to erect a bronze memorial to him in the crypt of St Paul's Cathedral. It was unveiled in October 1912.

During his career Prior also contributed to *The Sketch*. *The Dictionary of National Biography* says 'his art was not of the highest order (yet) was eminently graphic, and he had a keen eye for a dramatic situation'. His work was almost invariably done in black and white, but the author has a watercolour done in Brazil in 1878.

---

1 *C.I.V.s in a sharp engagement*, a pencil drawing by Melton Prior, was done after Prior had returned to London from South Africa. It refers to no particular incident and was used as a 'gap filler' in Prior's paper *The Illustrated London News*.
2 *The return of the C.I.V.: leaving Paddington Station* showed the welcome given by Londoners to the volunteers on their return to England at the end of October 1900. It was drawn by Melton Prior and appeared in *The Illustrated London News* a few days later.
3 Melton Prior produced the sketch from which Ernest Ibbotsen painted this scene of besieged Ladysmith. It was reproduced in *The Penny Illustrated Paper* on 10 February 1900.
4 To entertain the troops stuck in Bloemfontein during the typhoid epidemic, some artists did lightning sketches of War personalities. Robert Paxton depicted Melton Prior drawing Lord Roberts.
5 (Above) *Siege of Ladysmith: View of the Position we nearly lost*, sketched by Melton Prior, *The Illustrated London News* 'special' in South Africa. (Below) It was redrawn by Amedée Forestier and published under the title *View of Caesar's Camp and Wagon Hill, the Position we nearly lost*.
6 *Siege of Ladysmith: Shelling the enemy with 21 guns in honor (sic) of HRH the Prince of Wales's Birthday* was drawn by Melton Prior (right) and redrawn by Georges Montbard (far right) for the 31 March 1900 issue of *The Illustrated London News*.
7 The memorial to Colonel J.G. Scott Chisholme of the Imperial Light Horse, who was killed at the Battle of Elandslaagte on 21 October 1899. The memorial, in the town hall of Hawick in Scotland, used a reproduction of Melton Prior's pencil sketch of Chisholme which had originally appeared in *The Illustrated London News*.

In *The Work of the War Artists in South Africa*, A.C.R. Carter says:

> Mr Melton Prior and his adventurous colleague Mr. Frederic Villiers have long ago clinched their reputations as artists in the field. Each possesses an intimate acquaintance with military affairs and each has reduced his work to a perfect system. Mr Prior's sketches show a wonderful grasp of a general situation, and the abundant notes which cover his work are found invaluable to his London colleagues on *The Illustrated London News*. The portrait group of *Foreign Military Attachés* is very characteristic. There is much internal evidence of truthful detail, and the useful colour notes which can easily be read in our reproduction must have been found most serviceable to the artist to whom the task of making a finished drawing was allotted. Mr Prior may be described as the *doyen* of war specials . . .

Prior's original works are relatively rare. Many were supposedly destroyed when *The Illustrated London News* offices were hit during the Blitz in 1940. The largest collection is in the Brenthurst Library in Johannesburg. The medium is pencil unless otherwise stated and all are signed 'Melton Prior':

1. 6369(A) *Boer ambuscade Korn Spruit. Heroic Royal Horse Artillery saves the situation* (Bloemfontein).
2. 6369(B) *The surrender at Kroonstad. The march past Lord Roberts. The Guards leading* (Kroonstad).
3. 6369(C) *Lord Roberts' column crossing the Sand River drift* (Kroonstad).
4. 6369(D) *Battle of Lombard's Kop. General Sir George White's army being shelled during the retirement on Ladysmith – Oct. 30th, '99* (Ladysmith).
5. 6369(E) *The siege of Ladysmith. Battle of Cesar's Camp. The Devons charge on Wagon Hill. At Colonel Park's command the Devons dashed forward with a wild yell upon the rocky sangars occupied by the Boers* (Ladysmith, 1900).
6. 6369(F) *Siege of Ladysmith. Battle of Cesar's Camp. The Manchester Regiment repelling the Boer attack'* (Ladysmith, Jan. 1900). (This is a black and white watercolour painting with some Chinese white painted on it.)
7. 6369(G) *Battle of Elandslaagte. Dressing the wounds on the field* (Ladysmith).
8. 6369(H) *Battle of Elandslaagte. Devon, Manchester and Gordon Regiments. Charging the enemy's guns* (Ladysmith, Oct. 24th '99).
9. 6369(I) *Occupation of Pretoria. Release of 136 imprisoned officers from the "Bird Cage"* (Pretoria).
10. 6369(J) *Triumphal entry into Pretoria. Lord Roberts reviewing the troops* (Pretoria).
11. 6369(K) *Occupation of Pretoria. Hoisting the British flag. Lord Roberts leading three cheers for the Queen* (Pretoria).
12. 6374(A) *Siege of Ladysmith. Post Office closed and fortified.*
13. 6374(B) *Siege of Ladysmith. Killing cavalry horses for food* (Ladysmith).
14. 6374(C) *Siege of Ladysmith. Correspondents drawing half rations at the A.S.C. Issue store.*
15. 6374(D) *Siege of Ladysmith. General White congratulating the Natal Volunteer Forces on their gallant exploit in capturing the guns on Lombard's Kop.*
16. 6374(E) *Battle of Lombard's Kop. The Revd. Macpherson visited the wounded after the surrender of the Gloucester Reg. and Irish Fusiliers at Nicholson's Neck* (sic).
17. 6374(F) *Siege of Ladysmith. The Archdeacon of Ladysmith's cave – on the banks of the river, for protection against Boer shells* (Ladysmith).
18. 6374(G) *Siege of Ladysmith. The Day of Rest. Scene outside the Post Office on a Sunday afternoon.*
19. 6347(H) *Siege of Ladysmith. Issuing rations to the citizens of the town.*
20. 6374(I) *Bombardment of Ladysmith. Quarters of Mr Pearse (Daily News) after a shell had burst in them* (Ladysmith).
21. 6374(J) *Battle of Elandslaagte. Enemy's shell bursting by the side of General Sir George White* (Ladysmith).
22. 6374(K) *Battle of Elandslaagte. Tapping the telegraph wire and telephoning to Ladysmith for reinforcements required by Gen. French'* (Ladysmith, Oct. 27th '99).
23. 6374(L) *Battle of Elandslaagte. General advance on the Boer position* (Ladysmith).
24. 6374(M) *Britisher and Boer. Maj. Gen. French and Pres. Kruger's cousin having a friendly chat over the crisis on board the Union S.S. Norman.*
25. 6375 *Siege of Ladysmith. A mounted Boer who fired on Major Woods, R.A.M.C., while attending a wounded officer – shot by his corporal* (Ladysmith 1900).
26. 6375(A) *Siege of Ladysmith. A shell bursting in the Railway station, killing two and wounding four people.*
27. 6375(B) *Siege of Ladysmith. Helpmekaar Road advanced post. Officers discussing the situation.*
28. 6375(C) *Siege of Ladysmith – Capt. Hardy R.A.M.C. being fired on while dressing a wounded trooper of the 18th Hussars on the battlefield* (Ladysmith).
29. 6375(D) *Siege of Ladysmith. Advanced post, Helpmekaar Road – 'On the look out'.*
30. 6375(E) *Siege of Ladysmith. Captured Boer prisoners being brought into town* (Ladysmith).
31. 6375(F) *Relief of Ladysmith. General Sir George White calling for three cheers for the Queen in the main street of Ladysmith* (Ladysmith).
32. 6375(G) *Relief of Ladysmith. The advance guard of General Buller's column entering the town* (Ladysmith, Feb. 28th, 1900).
33. 6375(H) *Siege of Ladysmith. King's Post entrenched position of the 2nd Battn. Rifle Brigade* (Ladysmith, Jan. 1900).
34. 6375(I) *Siege of Ladysmith. Advanced post 2nd Battn. Rifle Brigade. Marksmen keeping down the fire of one of the enemy's guns.*
35. 6375(J) *Siege of Ladysmith. Shell bursting under a trooper of the 18th Hussars without injuring man or horse.*
36. 6375(K) *Relief of Ladysmith. Meeting of Generals White and Buller and their staffs in Ladysmith.*
37. 6375(L) *Boer ambuscade at Korn Spruit. Saving the guns – G. Battery, Royal Horse Artillery* (Bloemfontein).
38. 6375(M) Title partially obliterated (deliberately?): *The Boer Ambuscade at Korn Spruit . . . gallop* (Bloemfontein).
39. 6375(N) *Arrival of Sir Alfred Milner at Bloemfontein railway station, Orange Free State* (Bloemfontein).
40. 6376 *View looking towards Rhenoster drift. Showing Boer method of destroying the railway line.*
41. 6376(A) *Field Marshall Lord Roberts Headquarters at Brandfort* (Brandfort, 1900).
42. 6376(B) *The Foreign Attaché quartered in the railway station at Smaldeel* (Smaldeel).
43. 6376(C) *A Reconnaissance on the Water Works. Holding up two Kaffir boys from the Boer lines* (Bloemfontein).
44. 6376(D) *A Reconnaissance on the Water Works. The enemy's shells driving back our mounted infantry* (Bloemfontein).
45. 6376(E) *Headquarters Elandsfontein. Delegates from Johannesburg interviewed by Lord Roberts, Chief of the Staff.*
46. 6376(F) *Part of the Irish Rifles and Mounted Infantry delivering up their arms to the Boers at Reddersburg.*
47. 6376(G) *General Hamilton's Brigade capturing the Water Works and occupying the commanding hills* (Bloemfontein).
48. 6376(H) *Interior of 'Bird Cage' where 168 British Officers were imprisoned in Pretoria for over 4 months* (Pretoria).
49. 6376(I) *The March to Pretoria. Officers buying butter and forage on the road from a loyal Boer farmer.*
50. 6376(J) *Occupation of Brandfort. Capture of a Boer despatch rider by six of Rimington's Scouts (The first men into the town).*
51. 6376(K) *A Patrol examining Boer rifle pits at Rhenoster drift. (The pits were deserted on our approach).*
52. 6376(L) *Lord Roberts and staff watching the Boers retreat from Sand River with General French pursuing*

them on the extreme left. (Kroonstad)
53. 6376(M) *Head Quarters at Smaldeel. Lord Roberts and staff starting off on a reconnaissance (!).*
54. 6376(N) *Difficulties of crossing the Sand River. Way of getting convoy wagons up the steep drift.*

The Africana Museum, Johannesburg, has:

P273 *Correspondents' Carts and Wagons prevented from crossing the Sand River Drift 1900.* Pencil. Reproduced in *The Illustrated London News*, 23 June 1900.

P862 *Surrender of Johannesburg: Hoisting the British flag God save the Queen.* Pencil. Reproduced in *The Illustrated London News*, 21 July 1900.

P863 *Scene at the Drift, Kroonstad – President Steyn thrashing retreating Boers to compel them to return to the front 1900.* Pencil. Reproduced in *The Illustrated London News*, 23 June 1900.

P867 *Battle of Caesar's Camp 1900.* Pencil. Signed 'Melton Prior, Ladysmith'. Reproduced in *The Illustrated London News*, 3 March 1900.

The author has the following in his collection:

1. *The return of the C.I.V.: leaving Paddington Station Oct. 29th 1900.* Pencil. Reproduced in *The Illustrated London News*, 3 November 1900.
2. *C.I.V.s in a sharp engagement.* Pencil. Reproduced in *The Illustrated London News*, 27 October 1900.
3. *Siege of Ladysmith; view of the position we nearly lost.* Pencil. Reproduced in *The Illustrated London News*, 7 April 1900. Redrawn by A. Forestier.
4. *Siege of Ladysmith.; Shelling the enemy with 21 guns in honor (sic) of HRH The Prince of Wales's Birthday.* Pencil. Reproduced in *The Illustrated London News*, 31 March 1900. Redrawn by G. Montbard.

The National Army Museum has one pencil sketch by Prior: No. 20466 *'Hands up or we fire' (Boer treatment of our wounded at Korn Spruit).* Signed 'Melton Prior, Bloemfontein'. Reproduced in *The Illustrated London News*, 5 May 1900.

Both the Brenthurst Library and the Africana Museum also have several Africana pencil sketches relating to Prior's previous visits to South Africa. The Royal Collection at Windsor and the author have other non-Boer War works by Prior.

One interesting use for a Prior drawing is found in the memorial to Col. G.G. Scott Chisholme who was killed at Elandslaagte on 21 October 1899. This memorial, which is in the town hall in Hawick, Scotland, includes a framed facsimile of a drawing Prior did of Chisholme at Elandslaagte just before he was killed.

Prior was awarded the Queen's South Africa medal on 17 February 1903.

Carruthers, Melton Prior
Dawnay and Miller, Military Drawings and Paintings
De Wet, Illustrated London News Index
Dictionary of National Biography, *vol. 2, p. 2845*

Dixon, The Leaguer of Ladysmith
Kennedy, Pictures in the Africana Museum, *vol. 4, p. 98
and vol. 7, pp. 184-187*
Prior, Campaigns of a War Correspondent, *p. 192*
Samuels, Artists of the American West, *p. 383*
The Orders and Medals Research Society, *Summer 1986,*
'War Correspondents: South Africa 1899-1902', by
Patrick Street
The Times (obituary), *3 Nov 1910*

PROCTOR, John 1836-1902
Proctor was born in Edinburgh in 1836. He went to London
in 1859 to work for the *The Illustrated London News.* He
later worked for *The Sketch, Fun, Judy* and *Will o' the Wisp,*
before becoming principal cartoonist for *Moonshine* by succeeding Alfred Bryan. During the War Proctor contributed to
The Penny Illustrated Paper.
Hammerton, Humorists of the Pencil, *p. 54*
Thorpe, English Illustration

PRONIER, Alfred
French painter and illustrator who occasionally illustrated the
colour front covers of *La Semaine Illustrée, L'Impartial de
l'est* and *La Petit Méridional.*
Bénézit, Dictionnaire antique, *vol. 7, p. 35*

PROUT, Victor
Prout worked as an illustrator for *Windsor Magazine* and
Royal Magazine. His Boer War work appeared in *The Sphere.*

'PUNCH'
A French artist with this pseudonym illustrated the cover of
the pro-Boer French song 'Gloire aux Boers'.
Africana Notes and News, *June 1981, p. 211*

P.V.
Initials of postcard illustrator whose one card noted is entitled
A la fin du XIX siècle Les Enfants s'amusant.

PYM, Rowland
Pym was a theatrical designer who accompanied the Leonard
Rayne Theatrical Company to South Africa at the turn of the
century and was in Cape Town during the War. When Rayne's
company returned to Britain Pym stayed on in South Africa
where he concentrated on landscapes in oil and watercolour.
In about 1920 Pym produced an oil painting of Gen. de
Wet entitled *Uit Kÿkende.* Pym retained his copyright, but the
painting was reproduced as a limited framed edition in oils
and priced at 5 guineas. The manufacturers were the SA Kuns
Faksimile Ko. of 38 Church Street, Cape Town. An advertisement in *Die Huisgenoot,* August 1920, stated that 'no South
African household should be without a copy. This beautiful
and natural work of art shows an episode in the life of this
great fighter and statesman.'
Die Huisgenoot, *August 1920, p. 134*

R., A. *see* A.R.

RACEY, A. G.
Montreal Daily Witness and *Montreal Star* cartoonist and illustrator. *The Studio* refers to his work as 'always topical and
powerful'. It continues: 'In a comparatively short time he has
reached a high position in Canadian journalism. Besides his
work in Canada he is a well-known contributor to the American comic weeklies.'
The *Montreal Star* was one of the first dailies on the
American continent which featured illustrations regularly.
The Studio, *vol. 26, p. 288*

RACKHAM, Arthur 1867-1939
Illustrator. Rackham was born on 9 September 1867. He was
educated at the City of London schools and the Lambeth
School of Art. He married Edith Starkie in 1903 and they had
one daughter. Edith also studied art, at the Slade School in
London and later in Paris.
Rackham's illustrations of *Grimm's Fairy Tales, Aesop's
Fables, Rip Van Winkle, Peter Pan,* and *Hans Christian
Andersen's Fairy Tales,* among others, are well known and
much sought after by collectors. Prices for Rackham's original
illustrations reached a new height when an original paint-
ing for a children's story book fetched £6 500 at Christie's
in 1980.
His only known Boer War work is a pen-and-ink cartoon
which can be found in the Africana Museum. It is entitled
Toujours Soldat! and is signed and dated 'Arthur Rackham,
1901'. The cartoon depicts an ogre lifting a dish cover from
which soldiers escape. Prominent among them is a Boer.
Rackham died on 6 September 1939.
Kennedy, Pictures in the Africana Museum, *vol. 4, p. 100*
Who was Who, *vol. 3, p. 1115*

RADIGUET, Maurice 1866-1941   3
Cartoonist and illustrator. Radiguet was born on 12 July 1866.
He became known for his satirical drawings which appeared
in *Jugend* and several French magazines. He exhibited at the
Salon Des Humoristes et Des Independants in 1923.
His Boer War cartoons appeared in *Journal Pour Hu-
moristique, Le Bon Vivant, Le Rire, L'Indiscret* and *La Vie
Pour Rire.* The entire issue of the last-named magazine for
22 March 1902 (no. 100), subtitled 'La fin de la Guerre', was
devoted to his cartoons. The back page-coloured drawing, 'La
Fin' – La Joyeuse Farandole, showed King Edward and
Joseph Chamberlain on the gallows. This illustration was
crudely redrawn on an unsigned postcard by an unknown
French publisher.
Radiguet occasionally signed his work with the initials
'M.R.'. His son, Raymond, was a well-known author.
Bénézit, Dictionnaire antique, *vol. 7, p. 89*

Osterwalder, and Hubschmid and Bouret (eds.),
Dictionnaire des Illustrateurs, *p. 859*

RAINEY, H. William 1852-1936
Illustrator. Rainey was born in London on 21 July 1852. He
studied at the South Kensington School of Art and at the
Royal Academy schools before starting a career in book illustration. He exhibited at the Royal Academy from 1878, and
in 1893 he received a medal at the Chicago Exhibition. In 1900
he was awarded a medal at the Paris Exhibition. His work
appeared in *The Graphic, Black & White, The Strand Magazine, Ludgate Monthly, Cassell's Family Magazine* and
Chums.
Rainey illustrated several novels and short stories, many
of which related to the War: *The Boers Blunder* by Fox Rus-
sell (1900); *With Buller in Natal or A Born Leader* by G. A.
Henty (1901); *With Roberts to Pretoria: A Tale of the South
African War* by G. A. Henty (1902) and *Grit and Go* (1902).
The last-mentioned is a selection of short stories written by
Guy Boothby, G. A. Henty, D. Christie Murray, H. A. Bryden *et
al.* Eight illustrations by Rainey were used, several of which
depicted scenes of South Africa and the War.
Rainey died on 24 January 1936.
SABIB, *vol. 3, p. 771*
Thorpe, English Illustration
Waters, British Artists, *vol. 1, p. 273*
Who was Who, *vol. 3., p. 1117*

RALPH, Lester
'Special' for *Black & White* and *Black & White Budget.* Ralph
was sent by *Black & White* to South Africa to cover the War.
On 13 January 1900 *Black & White Budget* announced: 'With
Lord Methuen we have Mr. Lester Ralph, a brilliant young artist, son of Mr. Julian Ralph, the eminent American journalist'.
Ralph's work appeared in *Black & White, Black & White Budget, Harper's Weekly* and *War Pictures.*
Ralph was present at Graspan, Belmont, Modder River
and Magersfontein. During the occupation of Bloemfontein
he contracted typhoid fever. He did several illustrations for his
father's book *War's Brighter Side.* In the book Julian Ralph
describes how he got his son to design and illustrate the
menu for the dinner held by the staff of *The Friend* in honour of Lord Roberts. While working on this design Ralph became ill but didn't tell anyone. Gen. Pole-Carew noticed this
and warned his father that his son had a high fever and
should be admitted to hospital. He later recovered and left
South Africa soon after the occupation of Pretoria.
Ralph's illustrations were often reproduced in facsimile
and they were frequently signed 'L.R.'.
Ralph, War's Brighter Side

RALSTON, William 1848-1911   2
Cartoonist, postcard, genre and military artist. Ralston was
born in Milton near Dumbarton, Scotland, in 1848. He contributed to *The Graphic, Punch,* and *The Illustrated London
News.* He was described in *The Graphic* as follows:
Mr. William Ralston was born in 1841 (sic) and reared in
Glasgow. Leaving school at the age of 12 he was in turn
a warehouse boy, a gold digger in Australia, a photographer's assistant and a labourer in a vineyard, finally
returning home to settle down seriously as a photographer in which capacity he has been employed by Her
Majesty. When about thirty after doing some ill paid work
for publishers he was introduced to *The Graphic* for
which he has worked hard ever since.

1 *La Vie pour Rire* for 22 March 1902 published a special 'La Fin de
la Guerre' number. The whole issue was illustrated by Maurice
Radiguet. The back page showed Boer families celebrating the execution of the 'Last King of England'. Chamberlain's hanging is also
shown in the background.
2 Maurice Radiguet's cover of the *La Vie pour Rire* 'La fin de la
Guerre' edition, entitled *Le Mâle d'Amour.*
3 A self-portrait by Scottish cartoonist William Ralston.

TYPES OF
THE BRITISH
ARMY—XX CENT—
THE SEVENTEENTH LANCERS – REVIEW ORDER, S.A.

1

Caw, in *Scottish Painters Past and Present*, describes Ralston as 'primarily a comic man'. In 1902 he published some of his own pen-and-ink sketches as postcards. His company, William Ralston Ltd, continued to publish postcards until the 1930s.

Ralston's earliest Africana work in *The Graphic* appeared in 1896. His first Boer War work appeared on 3 February 1900 and a further 14 illustrations were published up to 31 May 1902. At least two comic British postcards in the 'Types of the British Army XX Century' series, *The seventeenth Lancers – Review order S.A.* and *The Gay Gordons during business hours*, were illustrated by him.

Ralston often signed his work with the initials 'W.R.'. He died in Glasgow on 2 October 1911.

> *Byatt*, Picture Postcards, *pp. 227-228*
> *Caw*, Scottish Painting
> *Hofmeyr, Matton and Roets*, Graphic Picture Index
> *Houfe*, British Illustrators and Caricaturists, *p. 426*
> *Hammerton*, Humorists of the Pencil, *pp. 93-98*

RANSOM, Sidney *see* YENDIS, Mosnar

RANSOME, Stafford
Illustrator. Ransome did the pictures for the satirical publication *Clara in Blunderland* by Caroline Lewis (William Heinemann, London, 1902). Caroline Lewis was the pseudonym for Harold Begbie and M.H. Temple, and the book is a skit on Lewis Carroll's *Alice in Wonderland*. The 40 illustrations are all signed 'S.R.', the initials of Stafford Ransome. He also illustrated two further books published by Heinemann: *The Coronation Nonsense-Book* (1902) and *Lost in Blunderland: the further adventures of Clara* (1903). The latter contains 50 illustrations.

> SABIB, *vol. 3, p. 108*

RAVEN-HILL, Leonard 1867-1942
Cartoonist. Raven-Hill was born in Bath on 10 March 1867. He was educated at Bristol Grammar School and Devon County School before entering the Lambeth School of Art where he met Charles Ricketts and Arthur Rackham (see page 191). Raven-Hill went to Paris and studied with Bouguereau and Aimé Morot. He exhibited at the Paris Salon from 1887, the New English Art Club from 1888, and the Royal Academy from 1889. He joined *Pick-Me-Up* as art editor in 1890 and founded his own publications, *The Butterfly* (1893) and *The Unicorn* (1895). In 1896 he started working for *Punch*, remaining on the staff until 1935. Failing eyesight caused his retirement after having been second cartoonist to Bernard Partridge for many years. He represented *Punch* at the Delhi Durbar in 1902-3, where the material he collected was exhibited with that of Inglis Sheldon-Williams (see pp. 204-206) at the Fine Art Society.

Raven-Hill was an enthusiastic volunteer in the 2nd V.B. Wiltshire Regiment and his cartoons often depicted the humour of 'citizen-soldiering'. His cartoons were frequently used on postcards. *The Strand Magazine* mentions that Raven-Hill combines the cultivation of art with the practise of agriculture on his estate in Wiltshire. His art lessons from Morot were especially applied to his horses. Raven-Hill generally invents his own jokes but sometimes takes them as a hint from Morot and they claim that he is one of the best living observers of rustic character in rural towns and his humour has a touch of subtlety and refinement all of his own.

His Boer War work was not prolific but can be found occasionally in *Punch* and *The King*. In 1902 he illustrated I. Zangwill's 'S. Cohen & Son or Anglicisation', a short story about a Jewish soldier's experience in the Boer War. The story appeared in *Pall Mall Magazine* (26, Jan-April 1902). In the same year *Our Battalion*, featuring some Boer War related illustrations by Raven-Hill, was published.

Among his publications is *Raven-Hill's Indian Sketchbook* (1903). Raven-Hill was a prominent member of the Savage Club. He died on the Isle of Wight on 31 March 1942.

> *Hammerton*, Humorists of the Pencil, *pp. 30-37*
> *Houfe*, British Illustrators and Caricaturists, *p. 427*
> *Peppin and Micklethwait*, British Book Illustrators, *p. 244*
> The Strand Magazine, *vol. 33, p. 86*
> *Thorpe*, English Illustration
> Who was Who, *vol. 4, p. 956*

RAWLINSON, Henry Seymour 1864-1925
The son of Maj. Gen. Sir Henry Creswicke Rawlinson, Henry Rawlinson jnr. was born in Dorset on 20 February 1864. Known as 'Rawly' to his friends, he became Lord Rawlinson in 1919.

After attending Eton, Sandhurst and Camberley, Rawlinson entered the 60th Kings Royal Rifles in 1884. He became aide-de-camp to Sir Frederick (later Lord) Roberts in India in 1887, a post he held until 1890. In 1898 he served with Kitchener in the Sudan and saw action at Atbara and Khartoum. During the Boer War Rawlinson served in Natal and was besieged in Ladysmith. He held the rank of lieutenant colonel at the time. He stayed on in South Africa after the relief, commanding a mobile column. During World War I he was mentioned in despatches on three occasions and was ultimately promoted to lieutenant general.

Among his several hobbies listed in *Who was Who* is 'drawing'. He used this talent to good effect while besieged in Ladysmith. On one occasion he went aloft in a balloon which was hit by a Boer shell. Despite the setback he managed to do three sketches of the surrounding panorama. These were published ('by permission of the Lady Rawlinson of Trent') in Victor Sampson and Ian Hamilton's *Anti-Commando*. Another of Rawlinson's panoramas, done before the investment of Ladysmith, including the scene of the Battle of Glencoe on 20 October 1899, appeared in *Black & White Budget* (Tvl Special No. 8 p. 12 and 13). These sketches were redrawn by Enoch Ward.

Rawlinson died in India on 28 March 1925.

> *De Kock (ed.)*, DSAB, *vol. 4, pp. 490-491*
> *Lines*, The Ladysmith Siege
> *Sampson and Hamilton*, Anti-Commando
> Who was Who, *vol. 2, p. 872*

RAWSON, M.A.
The Owl cartoonist.

R., B.C. *see* B.C.R.

READ, Edward Henry Handley 1870-?
Read studied at the South Kensington School of Art, the Westminster School of Art, and the Royal Academy schools where he won the Creswick prize. He was elected a member of the R.B.A. in 1895 and was an official war artist in 1918. Thorpe refers to him as a 'diluted Dudley Hardy'.

Read worked at various times for *The Graphic*, *The Royal Magazine*, *English Illustrated Magazine*, *The Illustrated Sporting & Dramatic News*, *The Sketch*, *Pick-Me-Up* and *Windsor Magazine*. He exhibited five works at the Royal Academy.

His Boer War work appeared in *With the Flag to Pretoria*, and a short story of Boer War relevance, 'Shot in the Back' by F. Talbot Townsend, had four illustrations by him. The story was published in *The Royal Magazine* (vol. 3, p. 353 ff).

Read occasionally signed his work with the initials 'E.R.'.

> *Houfe*, British Illustrators and Caricaturists, *p. 428*
> *Thorpe*, English Illustration

REAY, R. Martine
American illustrator who was a regular Boer War contributor to *Harper's Weekly*.

REDON, Georges 1869-1943
Flower painter, lithographer, postcard artist and cartoonist. Redon was born in Paris on 16 November 1869. He exhibited at the Salon des Humoristes and the Salon des Artistes Français, where he received an honourable mention in 1904.

During the War Redon worked for *La Vie Illustrée* and acted as its special artist in Marseilles when Kruger arrived in that city aboard the *Gelderland*.

> *Bénézit*, Dictionnaire antique, *vol. 7, p. 144*
> *Fanelli and Godoli*, Art Nouveau Postcards, *p. 360*

REED, Edward Tennyson 1860-19? 2
Cartoonist and caricaturist. The son of Sir Edward James Reed, a naval architect and M.P. for Cardiff, Edward Reed jnr. was born on 27 March 1860. He was educated at Harrow. Reed visited Egypt, China and Japan in 1880. He was appointed to the staff of *Punch* in 1890 and started his 'Prehistoric Peeps' series for that magazine in 1893. He was parliamentary caricaturist for *Punch* from 1894 to 1912 and was a well-known lecturer on caricature and humorous art. He drew

HIS MARK

2

weekly for *The Bystander*. His publications include *Mr. Punch's Prehistoric Peeps* (1896); *Unrecorded history etc. Mr. Punch's Animal Land* (1898); *Mr. Punch's Book of Arms* (1899), and *The Tablets of Azit-Tigleth-Miphansi; the scribe* (1900).

Reed's Boer War cartoons appeared in *Punch* and included cartoons from his 'Prehistoric Peeps' series. He signed his work with a distinctive 'ETR' monogram. The author has a small pencil cartoon sketch entitled *The Sower. What will he reap*. It was done by Reed for an unidentified publication after a painting by J.F. Millet.

Reed died on 12 July 1933.

Houfe, British Illustrators and Caricaturists, *p. 429*
The Strand, *vol. 32, p. 80*
Who was Who, *vol. 3, p. 1129*

REHNSE

St Paul Pioneer Press cartoonist. Several of his Boer War cartoons appeared in the American publication *Thrilling Experiences in the War in South Africa*, which was published by the Educational Company of Chicago, Illinois, in 1900.

REIJENGA, Jan Groningen 1867-?   1

A naïve drawing by Reijenga showing the Boer P.O.W. camp at Deadwood on St Helena was reproduced on a postcard. The card has the facsimile signature of several prisoners and is dated, also in facsimile, '13-3-01'. The message expresses thanks from the prisoners to the firm of Weinthal and Company, the Rotterdam cigarette manufacturing firm that had apparently provided comforts for the prisoners.

No trace of Reijenga has been found on the list of prisoners of war on St Helena. A Jan Groningen Rewenga is listed, however. It is likely that this is a transcription error and that the two individuals are one and the same. Rewenga, who hailed from Holland, was 33 when he was captured at Mafe-

king on 12 May 1900 prior to being sent off to St Helena.
Transvaal Archives, Pretoria, TKP 156, (p. 24)

REISACHER, Sylvester 1862-1916

Reisacher was born in Wolfertschenden, Allgäu, Germany, on 9 March 1862. His father, Gabriel Reisacher, was an artist but apparently abandoned his 'wife', Theresia Henkel, and newborn son. Reisacher jnr. never married and seems to have been a perpetual wanderer. He travelled to Turkey and twice to Russia and it is believed that he may have visited South Africa. Reisacher studied under well-known military art teacher Ludwig Braun (also known as Louis Braun), who was associated with the German Military Academy. Reisacher was responsible for five enormous canvases which are now housed in the National Cultural History and Open-Air Museum, Pretoria. The paintings are as follows:

1. *The Siege of Ladysmith. 2 November 1899-28 February 1900.*
2. *The Battle of Colenso 15 December 1899.*
3. *The Battle of Spion Kop 24 January 1900.*
4. *The Battle and Siege of Paardeberg. 17-20 February 1900.*
5. *Breakthrough of General De Wet through the British lines.*

In 1969 the paintings were found, rolled up in a trunk in Germany, by Mrs Kotie Roodt-Coetzee, director of the National Cultural History and Open-Air Museum in Pretoria. She had been told of their existence by Dr C.L. de Bruyn of Pretoria and Mr B. Heimann of Cape Town. Mr Heimann recalled that the paintings had been bought by a friend of his father who had a military clothing factory in Ludwigsberg near Stuttgart. He had bought these paintings to hang in the main entrance of the factory. The research into Sylvester Reisacher was done in Germany by Dr P. Anton Hendriks, formerly director of the Johannesburg Art Gallery. He searched the archives in Munich and Hamburg examining ships' passenger lists to see if Reisacher had ever visited South Africa. This seemed likely as the paintings are drawn with such accuracy as if done from life, but as yet no definite proof has been found.

In April 1972 the paintings were bought for the National Cultural History and Open-Air Museum. To mark the occasion of the opening of the exhibition by Dr Piet Koornhof (the then minister of education) on 2 September 1976, a brochure was published by Tom Hennings, senior educational officer of the museum.

Reisacher died on 19 March 1916.

Hennings, Vyf Skilderye oor die Tweede Vryheidsoorlog 1899-1902

REMINGTON, Frederic Sackrider 1861-1909   2

Illustrator, painter and sculptor. Remington was born in Canton, New York, on 4 October 1861. He was educated at the Episcopal Institute in Burlington, Vermont, and at the Yale School of Fine Arts between 1878 and 1880. He played football at university but did not graduate. When his father, who was editor of the *Ogdensburg Journal*, died, Remington (aged 19)

made a trip out to the West. He later returned when his business venture failed and studied at the Art Student's League in New York. During his travels in the West he worked as a cowboy and a scout, among other things. He also helped to run a sheep and mule ranch. His experiences there inspired him to become a Western artist. He later also became well known for his sculpture, which he described as 'illustration in bronze'.

Remington worked mainly for *Harper's Weekly* and *Century* but changed to *Collier's* in 1900. The Remington Art Memorial at Ogdensburg houses a collection of his work together with much of his equipment and other memorabilia. His library of Western history is in the Ogdensburg Public Library. Another large collection of his work is in the New York Public Library and his biographers, Peggy and Harold Samuels, have a large archive of his correspondence.

Even though Remington wrote to his lifelong friend, Julian Ralph, that he would love to have been in South Africa with him, he did not go and his Boer War work is rare. The British weekly, *War Pictures*, and *Harper's Weekly* featured his drawings done from sketches sent by Lester Ralph. One showing Rimington's Scouts was incorrectly titled Remington's Scouts in *Harper's Weekly* but correctly titled in Pearson's *War Pictures* (vol. 1, pp. 304-305, no. 10, 14 April 1900). Remington's best-known Boer War illustration is a full-page coloured reproduction which appeared in A.T. Mahan's New York publication *The War in South Africa* (1900). Entitled *General French's irregulars harassing the Boers after the Relief of Kimberley*, the illustration is signed and inscribed 'Frederic Remington, after photographs'. Unfortunately the irregulars are drawn to look more like Roughriders than colonial irregulars.

Poultney Bigelow's publication *White Man's Africa* (Harper Brothers Publishers, New York and London, 1898) has several illustrations by Richard Caton Woodville, three by De Thulstrup and three by the author's friend Remington from photographs taken during Bigelow's visit to South Africa.

Remington's talents also included writing and he was the author of several articles and books on the West and one play, *John Ermine of the Yellowstone*, which was an adaptation of his novel *John Ermine*.

---

1 William Ralston's drawing of *The seventeenth Lancers — Review order S.A.* appeared on a series of postcards published shortly after the end of the War.
2 A comic drawing of *Punch* cartoonist Edward Tennyson Reed.
3 Frederic Remington provided this coloured illustration entitled *General French's Irregulars harassing the Boers after the Relief of Kimberley* for Captain A.T. Mahan's *The War in South Africa*. Despite the fact that the illustration was drawn from a photograph Remington seems to have been influenced by his experiences in Cuba as the irregulars he portrays look like American Roughriders.
4 Frederic Remington, the famous Western artist, produced this cover illustration for *Harper's Weekly*. Titled *Boer Scouts on the Natal border*, it was the first Boer War related cover featured by the magazine.
5 Edward Tennyson Reed drew this pencil cartoon of Chamberlain in South Africa. Titled *The Sower. What will he reap*, it was for an unidentified publication.

In 1891 Remington was elected an associate of the National Academy of Design. He died of peritonitis following a ruptured appendix, in Ridgefield, Connecticut, on 26 December 1909.

Antiques in South Africa, no. 20, 1987
Baigell, The Western Art of Frederic Remington
Fielding, American Painters, etc., p. 299
Matthews and Mellini, In Vanity Fair, p. 429
Samuels, Frederic Remington

RENARD, Jules see DRANER

RENÉ, Albert 4
Artist and cartoonist who produced several front-page cartoons for La Republique Illustrée, Le Charivari and the Charivari Album: Boers et Anglais.

The author has a pen-and-ink cartoon, signed by René, entitled Au Transvaal: Lord Roberts et les généraux Anglais.

RENOUARD, Charles Paul 1845-1924
Painter, engraver and illustrator. Renouard was born in Cour-Cheverny, France, on 5 November 1845. He studied at the École des Beaux Arts after which he worked as a mural painter. His early black and white work was done for L'Illustration and Paris Illustré. In 1884 he joined The Graphic. Much of his work was done in pencil and chalk and was influenced by Degas. He exhibited at the Paris Salon from 1877 and was elected to the R.E. in 1881. Hartrick mentions that he became very friendly with Renouard when the latter was sent over by The Graphic's agent in Paris to make drawings of Ireland during the 'Land League troubles of a few years before'. Hartrick found him 'a very able and interesting man, to whose advice I owe much that has been of value to me'. In his article (see below), Gabriel Mourey describes Renouard 'as being the very highest type of the modern draughtsman. He draws as naturally as he breathes.'

Renouard did most of his Boer War work for The Sphere and one of his best-known portraits is that of Dr Leyds, which was published in facsimile. The original drawing was done 'from a sitting given to M Paul Renouard'.

Renouard often signed his work with the initials 'P.R.'. He died in Paris on 2 January 1924.

Hartrick, A Painter's Pilgrimage
Houfe, British Illustrators and Caricaturists, p. 431
Osterwalder, and Hubschmid and Bouret (eds.),
Dictionnaire des Illustrateurs, p. 881
The Studio, vol. 19, p. 165, 1900, 'A Master
Draughtsman: Paul Renouard' by G. Mourey

REUTERDAHL, Henry 1871-1925
Naval painter. Reuterdahl was born in Malmo, Sweden, in 1871. He served as a correspondent during the Spanish-American War in 1898 and during the early years of World War I. He was a contributor to several leading magazines. As a naval artist he was attached to the battleship Minnesota during the fleet's cruise around South America and during a cruise to the Mediterranean in 1913. He was present during the Veracruz Campaign in 1914. He is represented in the permanent collection of the United States Naval Academy by paintings of this cruise. His work is also in the National Museum, Washington, and the naval war collection at Newport, Rhode Island.

Reuterdahl won a silver medal for painting at the Panama/Pacific exposition of 1915. He was a member of the Society of Naval Architects and Marine Engravers.

Some of Reuterdahl's illustrations appeared in Black & White and The Graphic as late as 1907, but his Boer War work appeared mainly in The War in South Africa by A.T. Mahan. The illustrations include Landing troops at Cape Town, Sailors from the British Cruisers working the big naval guns at Ladysmith (colour), Arrival of a Transport, and The Deportation of Cronje (colour).

Reuterdahl died in Washington on 22 December 1925.
Fielding, American Painters, etc., p. 299
The Studio, vol. 64, p. 65, 1915

REYNOLDS, Frank 1876-1953
Reynolds was born in London on 13 February 1876. He studied at Heatherley School and exhibited at the R.I. and the Royal Academy. He became a member of the R.I. in 1903. He was a contributor to Judy, The Illustrated London News, Pick-Me-Up, The Sketch, Sketchy Bits, Longbow and Punch, which he joined in 1919, acting as art editor from 1920 to 1932. Among his book illustrations were those done for the 1911 Hodder edition of David Copperfield.

Reynolds' Boer War illustrations appeared in Shurey's Illustrated on 16 December 1899. James Thorpe dedicated his English Illustration: the Nineties, which was published in 1935, to Frank Reynolds.

He died on 18 April 1953.
Bradshaw, The Art of the Illustrator, p. 8.
Houfe, British Illustrators and Caricaturists, p. 431
Osterwalder, and Hubschmid and Bouret (eds.),
Dictionnaire des Illustrateurs, p. 885
Thorpe, English Illustration
Waters, British Artists, vol. 1, p. 277

REZNICEK, Ferdinand Freiherr 1868-1909
Painter, illustrator, cartoonist and postcard artist. Reznicek was born in Sievering, Vienna, on 16 June 1868. He worked for Simplicissimus (from the time of its founding in 1896) and Jugend.

Reznicek's Boer War cartoons appeared in Der Burenkrieg. He died in Munich on 11 May 1909.
Bénézit, Dictionnaire antique, vol. 7, p. 205
Fanelli and Godoli, Art Nouveau Postcards, p. 360
Osterwalder, and Hubschmid and Bouret (eds.),
Dictionnaire des Illustrateurs, p. 886

R.,H. see H.R.

RI,G.
Le Bon Vivant and La Caricature cartoonist. Several of his cartoons appeared in the latter publication on 27 January 1900.

RICHARDS, Mordaunt Cyril 1875-? 1
Cartoonist; soldier-artist. Richards was born on 7 January 1875. On 12 December 1894 he was commissioned as a second lieutenant in the Northumberland Fusiliers. A year later, on 1 January 1896, he was promoted to lieutenant. The following year Richards was transferred to the Wiltshire Regiment in which he saw service in South Africa, eventually becoming captain on 19 March 1902.

Richards was still in South Africa in 1913, but he saw action during World War I in France and Flanders. He was promoted to major on 25 January 1915. Richards distinguished himself during the retreat to the Marne on 27 August 1917. He retired with the rank of lieutenant colonel on 18 December 1919.

During his tour of duty in the Boer War Richards saw action in the Cape between 30 November 1900 and February 1901. Thereafter he was in the Transvaal. He also saw action in the Free State including Bethlehem and Wittebergen. Richards was awarded the Queen's South Africa medal with Bars of Wittebergen, Transvaal and Cape Colony. The King's South Africa medal was awarded with S.A. Bars (1901 and 1902). He was later awarded the British war medal and the Victory medal. All Richards' medals are in the possession of the regimental headquarters of the Duke of Edinburgh's Royal Regiment.

Richards had a series of cartoons published in The Owl. With one exception all of these caricatures were signed 'M.C.R.'. His first caricature appeared in The Owl on 24 January 1902, entitled Army Types (no number) and inscribed 'Egyptian pattern'. On 7 March and for 26 consecutive weeks a different 'Army type' appeared with an occasional extra cartoon or caricature:
7 March 1902: Army Types No. I – Thomas
14 March 1902: Army Types No. II – Ye Highlanders
21 March 1902: Army Types No. III – I.Y.
28 March 1902: Army Types No. IV – R.A.
4 April 1902: Army Types No. V – S.A.C.
11 April 1902: Army Types No. VI – K.F.S.
Extra caricature: Ministering Angels
18 April 1902: Army Types No. VII – M.I.
25 April 1902: Army Types No. VIII – A.S.C.
2 May 1902: Army Types No. IX – Bushman
9 May 1902: Army Types No. X – Infantry
16 May 1902: Army Types No. XI – Cavalry
23 May 1902: Army Types No. XII – R.A.M.C.
30 May 1902: Army Types No. XIII – The New Officer
6 June 1902: Army Types No. XIV – Newspaper Correspondent
13 June 1902: Army Types No. XV – A.P.D.
20 June 1902: Army Types No. XVI – Ye General
Extra cartoon: A wet holiday/Peace perfect peace
27 June 1902: Army Types No. XVII – A.C.D.
Extra full page of cartoons including Milner and Chamberlain, generally headed A Study in Expression; and they say 'God spare our King'.
4 July 1902: Army Types No. XVIII – R.E.
11 July 1902: Army Types No. XVIX – Civil Surgeon
18 July 1902: Army Types No. XX – R.S.O./The most abused staff billet in South Africa
25 July 1902: Army Types No. XXI – Padre
Extra full-page cartoon: Oom sweet oom
1 August 1902: Army Types No. XXII – Intelligence
Extra caricature: A study in silhouettes/Lt. Colonel Collenbrander C.B./The most successful Colonial commander.

Together with another full page of caricatures, signed 'M.C. Richards', with the general title Ye British Officer or Work v. Play.
8 August 1902: Army Types No. XXIII – Conductor/Weil's

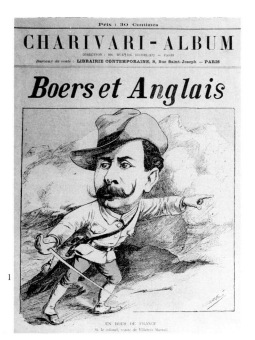

CHARIVARI-ALBUM
DIRECTION : 106, RUE DE RICHELIEU — PARIS
Bureaux de vente : LIBRAIRIE CONTEMPORAINE, 8, Rue Saint-Joseph — PARIS

Prix : 30 Centimes

Boers et Anglais

1

2

3

Man watching the wheeled transport.

15 August 1902: Army Types No. XXV — *Town Guard/The town guard dared de Wet to come and hold Cape Town in dread. The Mobile leader snapped his thumb and came and broke our bread.*

22 August 1902: Army Types No. XXVI — *Remounts/From week to week the war vote grew/But Britain met the piled accounts./The nation confidently knew/the strength of its far famed Remounts.*

29 August 1902: *After the War/Good bye, Girlies I must leave you.*

24 October 1902: *After the War/Repatriation.*

A series of divided-back cards, 'The South African Souvenir Series from copyright originals of MCR' was published after the War. The titles of these cards are as follows:

Repatriating
National Scout
Ye A.D.C.
Oh, its the Navy, the British Navy
S.A.C.
Mr. Atkins
Ye General
Civil Surgeon
Irregular (full facial view)
Irregular (profile)
Ubique

Types of English Beauty
Ye South African Butterfly
Ye Matron
Ye New Officer

In spite of the similar titles, the caricatures in *The Owl* and on the cards differ.

Wrench, the British postcard publisher, published a series of cards by M.C.R. entitled 'Caricatures of Army Types' (c.1904). It is not known if Wrench published the 'South African Souvenir Series' as well. Richards was responsible for a lithograph by an unknown publisher featuring a British soldier in South African kit. This is now in the collection of Mr Stephen Dance of England.

The Africana Museum, Johannesburg, has a sketchbook by Richards and the regimental headquarters of the Duke of Edinburgh's Royal Regiment has a collection of caricatures of military subjects and regimental officers. Some of these had been done in Pietermaritzburg during 1910 and 1911.

> *Personal communication with V. and A. Atkinson and Mrs B. Nagelgast, Director, Africana Museum*
> *Personal communication with Maj. John Price (Ret.), Regimental headquarters of the Duke of Edinburgh's Royal Regiment*
> *SPA auction catalogue, 4 July 1980*
> *SAPRG Newsletter, 10 Nov. 1983, 'The Cartoons of Captain Richards' by R. Greenwall*

RIDOUARD, Maxime
Ridouard was the chief compiler ('Sous la direction de M Ridouard Député de la Vienne') of *Paris-Pretoria*. His own illustrations appear on pages 20 and 26. Ridouard was a member of the French Chamber of Deputies.

RIGG, E.M.
This artist was responsible for illustrations in *With the Flag to Pretoria*.

RINS, P. H. *see* HELOURE RINS, P.

RINZNER, M.
Illustrator of pro-Boer postcard published in Germany in 1914 by C. A. Weller, Berlin, on behalf of Reichsverbandes zur Unterstützung Deutscher Veteranen. Its publication was probably meant to coincide with the 1914 rebellion in South Africa against Louis Botha's government and its decision to join World War I on the side of the allies by invading German South-West Africa. The title was *Der Ausstand der Buren*.

R.I.P., *see* HILL, Rowland

RIP
Pseudonym of French cartoonist whose Boer War work appeared on a postcard entitled *Marriages par Carte Postale*. Chamberlain was depicted on this card.

RIPP, P. H. 5
Illustrator responsible for many of the coloured supplements of *L'Impartial de l'est*, published in Nancy, *La Semaine Illustrée*, published in Paris, and *Le Petit Meridional*, published in Montpellier.

RIS, G.
A cartoon by Ris appeared in *Le Bon Vivant* on 30 December 1899.

RITCHIE, Alick P. F. fl. 1892-1913
Caricaturist who worked for several periodicals including *Pall Mall Budget*, *The Penny Illustrated Paper*, *Sketchy Bits*, *Eureka*, *Vanity Fair*, and *St Pauls*. Thorpe says Ritchie's work for *Pick-Me-Up* was 'forced humour from straight lines'.

During the War Ritchie contributed to *The King* (a caricature of Roberts on 15 December 1900) and *The Evening News*.
> *Houfe, British Illustrators and Caricaturists, p. 434*
> *Matthews and Mellini, In Vanity Fair*

RITTER, Eugen 1853-1922 1
Historic painter. Ritter was born in Gotha, Germany, on 19 June 1853. He was a student at the Weimar Art School and

---

1 The illustration of Colonel J. De Villebois-Mareuil was drawn by Albert René for the special *Le Charivari* publication entitled *Boers et Anglais*.

2 Albert René's drawing of Lord Roberts and the British generals depicts the generals as mules, a theme used on several occasions by European cartoonists. Reproduced by courtesy of the Africana Museum, Johannesburg.

3 Eugen Ritter's painting of the surrender of General Cronje to Lord Roberts at Paardeberg is now in the Africana Museum, Johannesburg.

4 P. H. Ripp's *Les Événements du Transvaal* was published in *La Semaine Illustrée* on 1 October 1899. It claims to show the death of Gen. Ben Viljoen. Since Viljoen died in 1917, it is more likely that the scene depicted is the death of Gen. Koch, who died on 31 October 1899, a few days after the battle of Elandslaagte.

5 P. H. Ripp's painting of President Kruger boarding the *Gelderland* was featured in *La Semaine Illustrée* on 4 November 1900.

4

ÉVÉNEMENTS DU TRANSVAAL
Mort du général boer Viljoen

5

Départ du Président Kruger

at the Academie de Linden Schmidt in Munich. One of his paintings, *Surrender at Paardeberg*, is in the Africana Museum. Although the painting is signed just 'E.R.' it is believed to be by Ritter. He died in Gotha on 15 July 1922.

Bénézit, Dictionnaire antique, *vol. 7, p. 262*
Kennedy, Pictures in the Africana Museum, *vol. 4, p. 101*

R.L.
Illustrator of at least three German postcards, one of which was published by Kunsanstalt Merkur of Dresden under the title *Vision Gieb Frieden – Konig von England*. The other two were titled *Hurrah Germania* (published by R. Langbein and R. Reinhart of Dresden) and *Vision*, which had no publisher's imprint. The illustrator could have been R. Langbein.

R.M.F.
A soldier-artist with these initials contributed a few sketches to *The Illustrated London News* between 21 June and 29 September 1900. They were redrawn by Samuel Begg and H.C. Seppings Wright. R.M.F. could have been a member of the Royal Irish Fusiliers.

De Wet, Illustrated London News Index

ROBERT, Earl 5
Illustrator, cartoonist and postcard artist. Contributor to siege publication *The Ladysmith Bombshell*. Robert was born in England. He went to South Africa in 1892 and he was initially employed by the *Cape Times*, at the same time acting as a correspondent for *The Illustrated London News*. In 1897 he illustrated the Johannesburg publication *A Souvenir of the Record Reign; illustrations of the Jubilee Festivities*. He also contributed to the Pretoria papers *De Pers* and *The Press*.

During the War Robert was besieged in Ladysmith, although he is not recorded on the official list of inhabitants. He illustrated one of the publications produced in Ladysmith during the siege, *The Ladysmith Bombshell*, and was undoubtedly responsible for the well-known Ladysmith Siege postcards and the Christmas, New Year and Valentine's Day cards which were published during the siege. An illustration by him appeared in *The Illustrated London News* on 31 March 1900; it was entitled *Bombardment of Ladysmith: room wrecked by shell-fire – Ruins of a furniture store*. *The Graphic* special double number published on 2 April 1900 also featured illustrations by Robert. The coloured illuminated addresses given to Sir George White and Redvers Buller by the inhabitants of Ladysmith were done by him.

In 1 February 1901, while in Pietermaritzburg, Robert established his own paper, *The Natal Caricature*. He was owner, publisher and cartoonist and even the advertisement illustrations were his work. The paper, which was published bi-monthly in Durban and Pietermaritzburg, was short-lived, although its date of closure is uncertain. Several of the cartoons were of Boer War relevance.

During the War Robert moved to Johannesburg where he became a commercial artist. He also taught art and contributed to local newspapers. He illustrated several books and published some of his own: *The Snow Age of the Transvaal* (CNA, 1909), *The Rand of Hope and Glory Under Martial Law* (Transvaal Leader, 1914) and *South Africa Under the Iron Heel* (Dawson, c.1914). *Ballads of Botha's Army* (1915) and *The Entente Nursery Rhymes: Oranges and Lemons* (CNA, c.1919) were also by him in collaboration with L.Y. Hastings and William Thomas respectively.

In the foreword to *The Rand of Hope and Glory*, Robert is described as '(someone) who occupies a deservedly high place among the humorous artists of South Africa, has portrayed (sic) the lighter side of Martial Law on the Rand'.

Robert was also responsible for some political postcards, among them the 'Colonial phrases' series published by the *Leader*. All the cartoons noted in this series are by Robert, but some are unsigned and others merely have the initials 'E.R.'.

The Africana Museum, Johannesburg, has three cartoons by him and the author has a caricature of a mounted soldier in tropical kit loaded with apparently looted goods.

It is believed that Robert died in about 1935.

De Wet, Illustrated London News Index
Kennedy, Pictures in the Africana Museum, *vol. 4, pp. 102-103*
SABIB, vol. 4, p. 49
Schoonraad, Spot- en Strookprent Kunstenaars, *pp. 198-200*

ROBERT, Paul
Contributor of two cartoons with English inscriptions to the Russian charity publication *St Petersburg-Transvaal*. A signed photograph of him is reproduced alongside them.

ROBERTS, J.
One of the illustrators of *La Guerre du Transvaal: Anglais et Boers*.

ROBERTS, J.H.
Formerly an architect, Roberts became a cartoonist and caricaturist. He worked for *Pall Mall Budget*, *Chums*, *Punch* (from 1896), *Fun* and *Judy*. Thorpe complains that his work for *Pall Mall Budget* was 'crudely drawn' and that his work for *Fun* was 'more humorous than artistic'.

During the War he contributed to *The Golden Penny*.

Houfe, British Illustrators and Caricaturists, *p. 435*
Thorpe, English Illustration

ROBERTSON, J.P.
One of the illustrators responsible for some of the illustrations in Israel Smith Clare's *British Boer War*. In his book the author claims that 'none of these illustrations can be found in any other publication as they have been drawn by our special artists from photographs and personal descriptions of the scenes portrayed at an expense of many thousands of dollars . . . the entire work is unique.' This is clearly untrue as the illustrations were almost without exception plagiarized from European and British newspapers.

ROBINSON, Charles 1870-1937
Robinson was born in Camden Town, London, on 22 October 1870. His father was the wood-engraver and illustrator, Thomas Robinson. His brothers, William Heath Robinson and Thomas Heath Robinson, were more famous as illustrators.

Charles Robinson was mainly self-taught but he did attend evening classes at the Heatherley School and the West London Art School. He was apprenticed to Waterlow and Sons. In 1895 he illustrated Robert Louis Stevenson's *A Child's Garden of Verses*. He worked for several illustrated periodicals including *Puck*, *Pan*, *The Queen*, *The Graphic* and *The Illustrated London News*.

Robinson was elected president of the London Sketch Club and became a member of the R.I. in 1932.

During the War an occasional Robinson illustration in the Art Nouveau style appeared in *Black & White*: on 31 March 1900 *Mafeking Waiting* was reproduced on p. 344.

Robinson died in Buckinghamshire on 13 June 1937.
Houfe, British Illustrators and Caricaturists, *p. 435*
Peppin and Micklethwait, British Book Illustrators
Thorpe, English Illustration

ROBINSON, S. A. H. fl.1890-1902
One of the few female illustrators of the War. She contributed work to *The Graphic* and *The Daily Graphic*. Two of her Boer War illustrations appeared in the former: *The convent at Mafeking: wrecked by Boer shells* (16 June 1900) and *Recreation for nurses in South Africa: a hockey match at Pretoria* (27 July 1901), from a sketch by Lionel James. Robinson's original painting of the former illustration is in the Mendelssohn Collection, Library of Parliament, Cape Town.
Hofmeyr, Matton and Roets, Graphic Picture Index
Thorpe, English Illustration, *p. 58*

ROBINSON, William Bennett fl.1892-1921 1
Starting out as an architectural draughtsman and illustrator, Robinson worked in Lincoln's Inn, London, in 1902, specializing in industrial subjects and views of international exhibitions and decorations. He contributed 15 illustrations to *The Illustrated London News* during the War, all of which appeared in 1900.
De Wet, Illustrated London News Index
Houfe, British Illustrators and Caricaturists, *p. 437*

ROEGGE, Wilhelm 2
Roegge provided the four coloured plates for *Die Buren und Der Südafrikanische Krieg* by Joseph Kürschner.

ROGERS, William Allen 1854-1931 2
Illustrator and cartoonist. Rogers was born in Springfield, Ohio, in 1854. His mother was also an artist. He was educated at Worcester Polytechnic. His career as a cartoonist began at the age of 14 when he drew for a Dayton, Ohio, paper. Rogers started work for *Harper's Weekly* in 1877 after having tried his hand at engraving. He made at least six trips to the West in 21 years, recording his experiences mainly for *Harper's Weekly*. He worked at various stages for the *New York Herald*, *St Nicholas*, *Century* and *Washington Post*. He was a member of the Society of Illustrators. His autobiography, *A World Worth While*, was published in 1921.

During the War Rogers did illustrations and cartoons for the *New York Herald* and *Harper's Weekly*. He often signed his work with the initials 'W.A.R.'.

Rogers died in Washington on 20 October 1931.
Fielding, American Painters, etc., *p. 307*
Osterwalder, and Hubschmid and Bouret (eds.), Dictionnaire des Illustrateurs, *p. 913*
Pitz, American Illustration, *p. 430*
Samuels, Artists of the American West, *pp. 406-407*

SLIM PIET:– SAY SURRENDER,
WACHT EEN BEETJE, SAYS TOMMY

3

4

ROGERS, W. G.

Reputedly a British cartoonist, whose oil painting *Lord Roberts on the March* (signed and dated 'W.G.R. 1902') fetched R700 at Sotheby's Johannesburg sale on Thursday 26 November 1981.

Sotheby's Johannesburg catalogue, *26 Nov. 1981*

ROMILLY, Frederick William 1854-1935

Romilly was born in Edinburgh on 22 July 1854. He was educated privately and at the Royal Military Academy at Woolwich. He entered the Scots Fusilier Guards in 1873 and passed the Staff College in 1880. In 1882 he served in the Egyptian Expedition and was present at the action of Mahuta and the battle of Tel el Kebir, winning a medal, clasp and bronze star. He was appointed aide-de-camp to the general commanding in Egypt from 1883 to 1888, and he served in the Suakim Campaign in 1884, once again as aide-de-camp to the general commanding. He was present at the battles of El Teb and Tamai, where he was mentioned in despatches and won two clasps. He served in the Guards Camel Regiment on the Nile Expedition from 1884 to 1885. He was present at the battles of Abu Klea and Goubat, as well as the action near Metemmeh where he won two clasps. He served in the Sudan Frontier Campaign from 1885 to 1886 as aide-de-camp to the general commanding. He was present at the action of Giniss where he was mentioned in despatches and awarded the fourth class of the Medjidie and D.S.O. He was created brevet major in 1888 and was D.A.A.G. Malta from 1890 to 1893. He was military secretary to the Governor of Madras from 1896 to 1898 and

Vol XLV
No 2299

10 Cents a Copy
$4.00 a Year

HARPER'S WEEKLY
A Journal of Civilization
NEW YORK JANUARY 12 : 1901

THE TAIL END OF THE CAMPAIGN

5

commanded the 2nd Battalion of the Scots Guards in South Africa from 1900 to 1902. During this time he was wounded and mentioned in despatches, and won the Queen's medal with three clasps, the King's medal with two clasps, and a C.B. He commanded the Scots Guards and Regimental district from 1906 to 1910 and retired in 1911 as he had reached the age limit. However, he served in the forces once again during World War I.

Ernest Prater redrew Romilly's illustration which was reproduced in Creswicke (vol. 6, p. 52), entitled *The surrender of Prinsloo's Force at the Caledon River.*

Romilly died on 23 September 1935.
Amery, Times History of the War
Who was Who, *vol. 3, p. 1168*

RONALD, J. McB.

Captain J. McB. Ronald submitted a sketch to *The Graphic* which was used by William Ralston as a basis for his illustration which appeared on 27 July 1901. It was entitled *The delight of campaigning in South Africa: The tale of a piece of soap.*

Hofmeyr, Matton and Roets, Graphic Picture Index

ROSE, Fred W.

Author and illustrator of *Two Bad Boer Boys* (George Vickers, c.1900) and *John Bull and his Friends* (G.W. Bacon, 1900).

SABIB, *vol. 4, p. 81*

ROSE, Hugh

Soldier-artist. Rose was an officer in the 42nd Regiment, the Black Watch. He was commissioned as lieutenant in 1884, and promoted to major in October 1901 and lieutenant colonel in 1914. He retired in 1914.

The Africana Museum, Johannesburg, has an album by Rose consisting of 24 leaves. There are a total of 152 items in this album, 91 of which are drawings of scenes, events and bird life done during and after the War in South Africa in 1902.

Kennedy, Pictures in the Africana Museum, *vol. 7, pp. 217-227*

ROSS, Charles 1864-1930

The third son of Gen. C.C. Ross K.C.B., Charles Ross was born on 10 March 1864. He was educated at Stubbington and gazetted to the Norfolk Regiment on 12 November 1884. He was promoted to captain and attached to the Egyptian Army from 1893 to 1894. He was at the Staff College between 1897 and 1899. Ross served in the Boer War from 1900 to 1902 and saw action in the Transvaal, Orange River Colony and Cape Colony. He was present at the relief of Kimberley and the battles at Paardeberg, Poplar Grove, Hout Nek and Zand River. He received the Queen's medal with five clasps, the King's medal with two clasps, and a D.S.O in 1901.

Ross was an instructor at Woolwich and a company commander at Sandhurst. He was promoted to colonel on 4 Octo-

ber 1911. He served in World War I, during which he was mentioned in despatches. He was created a C.B. and became brevet major general on 15 November 1915. He commanded the 6th Division of the British Expeditionary Force during the First World War from November 1915 to September 1917. He was transferred to the 69th Division, which he commanded until his retirement.

Ross wrote *Representative Government and War* (1903), *The Problem of National Defence* (1907), and *An Outline of the Russo-Japanese War 1904 and 1905* (1912). He also wrote fiction: *The Haunted 7th, Every Man's Hand, When the Devil was Sick,* and *The Castle Fenham Case.*

Ross was responsible for one drawing which appeared in *The Graphic* on 16 June 1900 entitled *'Gunfire'. An early cup of tea in camp at Bloemfontein.* It was redrawn by Reginald Cleaver.

Ross died on 21 December 1930.
Creagh and Humphris, The D.S.O., *pp. 122-123*
Who was Who, *vol. 3, pp. 1170-1171*

ROSS, F. B.

Ross's cartoons appeared in *The South African Review* from as early as 1896. During the War he contributed to *The Owl* and *The Telephone.* He published *A Dutch Courtship* in 1908. Ross signed his work with the initials 'F.B.R.'.

Schoonraad, Spot- en Strookprent Kunstenaars, *p. 206*

ROSS, L. C.

Major Ross was responsible for two topographical sketches done in South Africa during the War: *A panorama of Driefontein from a hill on which Lord Roberts stood at Schaaplatz* and *Panorama of the Modder River from a small kopje 2 miles north-east by north of Cronje's laager.* Both of these sketches are in the National Army Museum, London.

---

1 The front cover of the facsimile edition of *The Ladysmith Bombshell*, the 'newspaper' produced during the Ladysmith siege, was designed by Earl Robert. The Boer with the Long Tom is General Piet Joubert.
2 William Bennett Robinson, contributor of Boer War illustrations to *The Illustrated London News.*
3 *Buren attacke*, a coloured illustration by W. Roegge taken from the German publication *Der Buren und der Südafrikanische Krieg* by Joseph Kürschner.
4 *Boer artillery on the March* by W. Roegge, the frontispiece to Joseph Kürschner's *Der Buren und der Südafrikanische Krieg.*
5 William Allen Rogers did this cartoon for the 12 January 1901 *Harper's Weekly.* Depicting the British Lion with its new acquisitions Bloemfontein and Pretoria, it was titled *The tail end of the campaign.*

ROSS, Percy T.
Soldier-artist. Ross was a corporal in the 69th Sussex Company Imperial Yeomanry. He wrote and illustrated *A Yeoman's Letters* (Simpkin Marshall, 1901). He arrived in South Africa aboard the SS *Delphic* in April 1900. He finally left South Africa on 29 March 1901 aboard the *Aurania*. While waiting at the Maitland camp to return to England the soldiers published a 'magazine' entitled 'Latest Developments Gazette incorporating The Cookhouse News'. Ross drew the cartoons for the publication. The day before the men finally broke camp the proceeds of the 'Gazette' were donated to the No. 1 Hut Annual Ball. This grand affair was in fact a weekly dinner with 'no dancing allowed' and at the final dinner Ross was presented with a silver cigarette case in appreciation of his 'humble efforts'.
SABIB, *vol. 4, p. 85*

ROSSILLON, Marius *see* O'GALOP

ROSTKO
Cartoonist responsible for a satirical French postcard cartoon entitled *Death to the Beast; death to the poisoner Chamberlain.*

ROTIDA, A.
Cartoonist and illustrator who contributed an illustration (p. 319) to the special number of *Le Monde Illustré* which was published on 17 November 1900 and dedicated to President Kruger.

ROTTEMBOURG, Valerie
Illustrator of Marie Lera's *Les Petits Boers: Episode de la Guerre du Transvaal en 1900* (Libraire Gedalge, Paris). Some of Rottembourg's illustrations were signed 'V.R.'.

ROTTMAYER, H.
Artist of a postcard sold in aid of 'poor Boer women' at a pro-Boer women's meeting held in Berlin on 9 February 1902. The card was inscribed 'Frauen Europa helft Eueren armen Buren Schwestern!'

ROUAULT, Gustave
Cartoonist who was responsible for Boer War cartoons in *La Vie Illustrée.*

ROUBILLE, August Jean-Baptiste 1872-1955 1
Painter, engraver and cartoonist. Roubille was born in Paris on 15 December 1872. He started his career as a cartoonist in 1897 when he went to work for *Le Courrier Français*. He later contributed to several satirical journals, among them *Le Rire, Le Sourire, Cri de Paris, Fantastic* and *Cocorico.*
Roubille exhibited at several galleries including the Salon des Independants, Salon de la Comédie Humaine, and Salon des Humoristes.
His Boer War work appeared in *Le Sourire*. A caricature drawn by Roubille of 'Sir Paul Kruger' appeared in an 1899 publication by Antonin Reschal, *Feuille de Caricatures Politiques*. This illustration is reproduced in Sidney Mendelssohn's *South African Bibliography* (vol. 2, opposite p. 367) and was also used in a postcard series published by A. & Cie, 19 Rue de Paradis, Paris.
Roubille's signature is a characteristic monogram.
Bénézit, Dictionnaire antique, *vol. 7, pp. 382-383*
Osterwalder, and Hubschmid and Bouret (eds.), Dictionnaire des Illustrateurs, *p. 924*

ROUILLY, A. 1
French postcard artist who produced a series of numbered cards by an unknown publisher. These cards were based on anti-British cartoons which had appeared in the contemporary press including *Burenstreiche* and *Neue Burenstreiche*. Some of the originals had been done by F. Grätz, F. A. Jüttner and others, but no acknowledgement is given. Rouilly often signed in full and a 'AR' monogram is also invariably present.

ROUVEYRE, André 1879-1962
Artist and engraver. Rouveyre was born on 29 March 1879 in Paris. He contributed cartoons and illustrations to *Le Rire*. Rouveyre often signed his work with the initials 'A.R.'.
Bénézit, Dictionnaire antique, *vol. 7, p. 396*

ROWLANDSON, George Derville 1861-?
Equestrian and military illustrator and military postcard artist. Rowlandson was born in India in 1861. A sporting illustrator who studied art in Gloucester, Westminster and Paris, he worked extensively for *The Graphic, The Daily Graphic* and *Illustrated War Special*. In 1980 the Parker Gallery offered some of his World War I illustrations.
During the Boer War 11 of Rowlandson's illustrations appeared in *The Illustrated London News* between November 1899 and April 1900. Other illustrations appeared in *War Pictures*, including *Going into action – Royal Horse Artillery.* Rowlandson often signed his work with the initials 'G.D.R.'.
De Wet, Illustrated London News Index
Houfe, British Illustrators and Caricaturists, *p. 439*
Johnson and Greutzner, British Artists, *p. 439*

ROWLANDSON, Samuel M.
Rowlandson was a land agent who served with the Durham Light Infantry. The National Army Museum has 28 pencil and pen-and-ink cartoon sketches by him. The collection is entitled 'Sketches of the infant Samuel' and subtitled 'Incidents in the life of an officer in the Campaign in South Africa circa 1900'. Rowlandson's diary deals with the extremes of climate, the flies, the hostile civilian population, and the ability of the Boers to appear and disappear at will, usually unexpectedly.
Hugget, Cartoonists at War, *pp. 122-123*

ROWORTH, Edward 1880-1964
Painter. Roworth was born in Heaton Moore, Mersey, Lancashire in 1880. He studied under Tom Moston at Hearton near Manchester, under Hubert Herkomer at Bushey, and under Henry Tonks at the Slade School.
Roworth went to South Africa in 1902 with the British forces. He stayed on after the War, settling in Cape Town where he established a teaching studio in Burg Street. He soon became very active in art circles and in 1908 he was elected president of the South African Society of Artists. In 1909 he received an important commission, the painting of the National Convention. This was a 5 x 6 m panel portraying the group of delegates that led South Africa to Union. The painting, which took him until 1911, was hung at Buckingham Palace before being installed in the House of Assembly in Cape Town in 1912. Roworth later became a highly influential and controversial figure in South African art.
His Boer War related work included portraits, many of them generals, done after the War. Roworth did paintings of Gen. Botha, Cecil Rhodes, and Hertzog, as well as a picture of Gen. J.H. de la Rey (1910) which is in the War Museum of the Boer Republics, Bloemfontein. It is almost certain that he painted while he was a soldier, but regrettably none of this work has been traced.
Roworth died in Somerset West in 1964.
Berman, Art and Artists, *pp. 368-370*

ROZE, Leon
Cartoonist for *Le Bon Vivant* and *La Caricature*. Roze was

1 es anglais chics jouent au lawn-tennis... Moi aussi

LE MUSÉE DE SIRES N°2
2 SIR PAUL KRUGER

responsible for the uncoloured pictorial cover of the pro-Boer French song, *Prenz Garde a la Peinture*, the words of which were written by A. d'Halbert.

Africana Notes and News, June 1981, p. 211, 'French pro-Boer Songs' by A. Smith

RUCHERT

Engraver or illustrator of a series of French postcards, 'Guerre Anglo-Boer Croquis sur place', by L'Hoste and Cassegrain of Paris. The six unnumbered cards noted are as follows:
1. *Mort du Général Wautschope (sic) à l'Attaque de nuit de Maggersfontein (sic)*
2. *Capture d' une reconnaissance Anglaise par les Boers*
3. *Reprise de Spion-Kop*
4. *Le Général Buller repoussé sur la Tugela*
5. *Bas les armes! Prise d'un convoi Anglais par les Boers*
6. *Reddition du Général Cronje*

RUCTLER, M.

Illustrator of a postcard, *Buren Wichse — (Boer polish) Wichs-Fabrikation von Paul Kruger*, printed by Schneider & Lux of Vienna. Three other cards in the same series, *Buren wichse, Olnerkannt Vorzüglich* and *Curs London Glanz-Wichse*, are unsigned but are probably by the same hand.

RUDAUX, Henri Edmond ?-1927

Genre painter and illustrator. Rudaux was born in Paris where he died in 1927. His father, Edmond Adolphe Rudaux, was one of his teachers, as were Benjamin Constant and Jules Lefebvre. He was a member of the Society of French Artists from 1893 and he received an honourable mention at the Salon in 1897.

His Boer War work appeared in *Le Petit Journal* and *The Daily Graphic*.

Bénézit, Dictionnaire antique, vol. 7, p. 416

RÜNCKEL, F.

Illustrator of *Voor Vrijheid En Recht*.

RUSSELL, Walter Westley 1867-1949

Portrait, landscape and genre painter. Russell was born in Epping, Essex, on 31 May 1867. He was educated at the Westminster School of Art under Frederick Brown. He exhibited at the N.E.A.C. from 1893 and became a member in 1895. From 1895 to 1927 he was assistant professor at the Slade School and Keeper of the R.A. from 1927 to 1942. He exhibited at the Royal Academy from 1898. Russell was elected R.S. (1906), N.P.S. (1911), A.R.A. (1920), A.R.W.S. (1921), R.A. (1926) and R.W.S. (1930). He was made a C.V.O. in 1931 and knighted in 1935.

Russell's Boer War contribution consisted of three illustrations which appeared in *The Graphic*. *Breakfast for the 'Fighting Fifth': The field bakeries of the Northumberland Fusiliers with Lord Methuen's Force* and *In memory of fallen comrades: A self-imposed duty* (from a photograph by Lt. Girdwood) appeared on 5 May 1900. The third illustration, which appeared in the special double number of *The Graphic* on 2 April 1900, was entitled *The Heliograph station on Observation Hill, 16 miles from Thaba Inyama* (from a sketch by H. McCormick).

Russell died in London on 16 April 1949.
Hofmeyr, Matton and Roets, Graphic Picture Index
Waters, British Artists, vol. 1, p. 288

RUTHERFORD, F.

Corporal Rutherford was a member of the Army Post Office Corps stationed at one time at the field post office in Kroonstad. Two of his sketches, *The field post office at Kroonstad* and *A visit to Roodewal*, were reproduced in the post office staff magazine, *St Martins-Le Grand*, in 1901. These sketches also appeared in Archie Batten's *The Post Office Militant* (pp. 223 and 237).

S., A. *see* A.S.

SABATTIER, Louis Rémy fl.1894-1918

Portrait painter and illustrator. Born in Annonay, France, Sabattier studied in Paris with Gérôme and Boulanger. He exhibited at the Salon des Artistes Français from 1890, receiving an honourable mention in 1894. He worked as an illustrator for *The Graphic*, *The Illustrated London News* and *L'Illustration*.

Most of Sabattier's Boer War work appeared in *L'Illustration* and at least three signed illustrations, taken from this paper, appeared on the Adolphe Weick 'La Guerre au Transvaal' series of postcards. The dates in brackets indicate publication in *L'Illustration*:

822 *Batterie d'artillerie protégeant la retraite des Boers* (19 May 1900).

825 *Parlementaire Anglais dans le Camp Boer*fl20(28 April 1900).

1668 *Pillage d'un habitation Boer* (19 October 1901).

On 15 January 1901 a series of photogravures by Sabattier of King Edward VII appeared in *The Illustrated London News*. One of his postwar illustrations – showing generals Botha, De la Rey and De Wet on the balcony of the Hôtel De Hollande, Rue de la Paix in Paris on 13 October 1902 – appeared in *The Illustrated London News* on 25 October 1902. In 1904 Sabattier's illustration of Chinese labourers landing in Durban was reproduced in *The Illustrated London News*.
Bénézit, Dictionnaire antique, vol. 7, p. 455
De Wet, Illustrated London News Index
Houfe, British Illustrators and Caricaturists, p. 442
Osterwalder, and Hubschmid and Bouret (eds.), Dictionnaire des Illustrateurs, *p. 937*
SAPRG Newsletter, Aug. 1984, 'Journal L'Illustration and La Guerre au Transvaal' by R. Greenwall

SALMON, J. M. Balliol 1868-1953

Painter and illustrator. Salmon was born on 1 June 1868. He studied art under Frederick Brown at the Westminster School of Art and thereafter at the Académie Julian in Paris. As an illustrator he contributed to *The Graphic*, *The Quiver*, *The Illustrated Sporting & Dramatic News*, *Pall Mall*, *Pall Mall Budget*, *New Budget*, *Cassell's Monthly* and *Ludgate Monthly*. Salmon often used the media of pencil and Russian chalk. He worked as an illustrator during World War I.

At least six of Salmon's Boer War illustrations appeared in *The Graphic* (including *The Graphic* special double number of 2 April 1900) from March 1900 to November 1902. Inglis Sheldon-Williams, in an article on illustrators which appeared in *The Sphere* in 1937, mentions that Hatherell and Salmon often collaborated on an urgent illustration, each working on a separate half of the picture before piecing it together in the morning to meet the deadline.

One of Salmon's illustrations appeared in *The Sphere*'s 3 February 1900 supplement entitled *Latest from the front. Those who have been laid low. The effect of a shell fired by the Royal Horse Artillery on a Boer maxim and its crew*. The sketch was by W. B. Wollen.

Two of Salmon's works depicting British royalty are in the Royal Collection at Windsor. Both are dated 1903.

Salmon died on 3 January 1953.
Dawnay and Miller, Military Drawings and Paintings, vol. 2, p. 246
Hofmeyr, Matton and Roets, Graphic Picture Index
Houfe, British Illustrators and Caricaturists, pp. 442-444
Thorpe, English Illustration
Who was Who, vol. 5

SALVADORI, R.

L'Illustrazione Italiana illustrator. One of his paintings was reproduced in *After Pretoria: the Guerilla War* (vol. 1, p. 519).

SAMBOURNE, Edward Linley 1845-1910 [1]

Illustrator and cartoonist. Sambourne was born in London on 4 January 1845. He was educated at the City of London schools and Chester College. Although he was originally apprenticed to a marine engineer he gave up his chosen career when his work first appeared in *Punch* in 1867. He understudied Sir John Tenniel as a cartoonist for several years, eventually becoming first cartoonist for *Punch* when Tenniel retired in January 1901. Sambourne, who signed his work 'Linley Sambourne', was highly accurate and took great care over details of dress and construction. Several of Sambourne's original cartoons are housed in the Victorian Society's head office in London, which was at one time Sambourne's home. The author has five original non-Boer War *Punch* illustrations by him.

Sambourne's Boer War work is represented by cartoons in *Punch*.

His daughter, Maud, was also an illustrator. He died in Kensington on 3 August 1910.
Houfe, British Illustrators and Caricaturists, p. 444
Spielmann, The History of Punch
Who was Who, vol. 1, p. 624

SANCHA, José

Sancha was a Spanish artist who spent time in Paris at the turn of the century. One of his cartoons, *Les Loisirs de Kitchener*, appeared in the special number of *Le Gavroche* of 16 June 1902, 'La Paix à la mode John Bull'. The 3 January 1903 issue of *L'Assiette au Beurre*, 'Les Anglais chez Nous', was devoted entirely to Sancha's works. Although published after the War some of these cartons relate to it. Sancha also worked for *Le Rire*.
Bénézit, Dictionnaire antique, vol. 7, p. 497

SANDERSON-WELLS, John Sanderson 1872-1955

Portrait and sporting subjects. Sanderson-Wells studied art at the Slade School and the Académie Julian in Paris. He exhibited at the Royal Academy from 1895. He was elected a member of the R.I. in 1903. Sanderson-Wells became president of the Langham Sketching Club in 1904 and it is recorded that he was 'quite one of the most modern of the younger members and is noted for his cleverness in flat colour-work of sporting scenes'.

Sanderson-Wells's Boer War illustrations can be found in *With the Flag to Pretoria*.

He died in London on 16 March 1955.
The Studio, vol. 32, p. 298, 'The Artists' Society and the Langham Sketching Club' by L. van der Veer
Thorpe, English Illustration
Waters, British Artists, vol. 1, p. 291

SARGENT, John Singer 1856-1925

Portrait artist. The son of an American doctor who travelled widely in Europe and America, Sargent was born in Florence in 1856. In 1874 he met Whistler in Venice and later that year became a pupil of Carolus-Duran in Paris. He visited Spain to study the work of Velasquez in 1879 and exhibited at the Salon des Artistes Français, Paris. In 1886 he settled in London and, following his success at the Royal Academy, was soon in demand as a portrait painter. During World War I Sargent was an official war artist and did a large oil entitled *Gassed* for the Ministry of Information. He was elected A.R.A. (1894), R.A. (1897), A.R.W.S. (1904) and R.W.S. (1908). Rodin referred to him as the 'Van Dyck of our times'. His output, which was huge, amounts to over 800 paintings.

---

1 One of a large series of numbered cyclostyled cards by A. Rouilly, who based his cartoons on the work of other cartoonists. This one is copied from a cartoon by Fritz Grätz, first published in *Humoristische Blätter*.
2 August Roubille's postcard of Sir Paul Kruger, published as no. 2 in a postcard series by A. & Cie of Paris. It was originally used in Anton Reschal's *Feuille de Caricatures Politiques*.
3 Linley Sambourne was principal *Punch* cartoonist when this cartoon appeared on 27 August 1902. It shows the defeated Boer generals De la Rey, Botha and De Wet being welcomed to Britain by John Bull during their postwar visit to Europe.

Sargent's Boer War work includes a portrait of Gen. Ian Hamilton (which was reproduced as the frontispiece in Winston Churchill's book *Ian Hamilton's March*), and the frontispiece depicting the author in the Constable and Scribner editions of C.R. de Wet's *The Three Years' War*. Sargent was pro-Boer and even though his usual fee was over 5 000 guineas he offered to do this portrait free of charge. This charcoal drawing is in the New York Metropolitan Museum of Art.

The Africana Museum has an unsigned portrait of Roberts by Sargent.

Graves, Royal Academy, *vol. 7, p. 26*
Kennedy, Pictures in the Africana Museum, *vol. 4, p. 117*
Rosenthal, General de Wet, *pp. 126-127*
Waters, British Artists, *vol. 1, p. 291*

SAVAGE, Reginald fl. 1886-1905
Portrait and figure painter and illustrator. He worked for and was closely associated with the Essex House Press. His subjects were usually historical and poetic. He worked at various times for *Ludgate Monthly, Black & White, Butterfly, Pageant, Fun* and *St Paul's.*

Savage's Boer War illustrations appeared in *Under The Union Jack.* He often used a distinctive 'RS' monogram.

Houfe, British Illustrators and Caricaturists, *p. 446*
Thorpe, English Illustration

SAYERS
Lloyd's News illustrator.

SCHAUPP, Richard 1871-? 1
Illustrator and postcard artist. Schaupp was born in St Gallen, Switzerland, on 17 November 1871. He studied under K. Raupp, W. von Lindenschmidt and W. Diez at the Munich Academy. He worked as an illustrator for *Jugend* and on 29 May 1901 his portrait of De Wet, *De Zwarte Christian*, appeared on the cover of issue 24.

Bénézit, Dictionnaire antique, *vol. 7, p. 568*
Fanelli and Godoli, Art Nouveau Postcards, *p. 362*

SCHEFFLER, Herman 1879-?
Berlin-born artist whose painting *Death of de Villebois Mareuil* was featured on a French postcard.

SCHLETTE, Engelina Helena 1875-1954 1
Postcard artist. Schlette was born in The Hague on 20 August 1875. She lived and worked in The Hague, Munich, Paris, Nice, and England. She was a pupil of Von Lenbach and was known for her watercolours and figure drawings.

In 1900 the firm of N.J. Boon & Co. produced a series of 17 'Groet Uit' postcards. The cartoons on the cards lampooned the early British defeats and the sieges of Kimberley, Ladysmith and Mafeking, as well as alleged atrocities against the black population. Seven of the cards, which are all by the same hand, are signed 'E.H. Schlette fec.'. It is assumed that Engelina Schlette was responsible for the drawings.

'Boer-en Rooinek Speel', a type of Ludo published by Gebroeders Koster of Amsterdam, was drawn by an 'F.G. Schlette'. The soldiers depicted are identical to those on the postcards. The plate was lithographed by Gebroeders Braakensiek in Amsterdam.

The titles of the unnumbered cards are as follows:
Groet uit:Elandslaagte (2 different cards)
Basutoland (signed)
Kimberley
Kaapstad (signed)
Ladysmith (signed)
Magersfontein
Lady-Smith (sic)
Derdepoort (signed)
Mafeking
Engeland (signed)
Pretoria
Durban (signed)
Transvaal
Natal (signed)
Langs-Nek (sic)
Pietermaritzburg

Quarterly Bulletin, *no. 3, p. 74, 3 March 1980*
SAPRG Newsletter, *Nov. 1984, 'Groet uit Cards of N.J. Boon' by R. Greenwall*

SCHLITTGEN, Hermann 1859-1930
Painter, engraver, illustrator and caricaturist. Schlittgen was born in Roitzsch, Saxony, on 23 June 1859. He was a student at the Leipzig Academy and the École des Beaux-Arts at Weimar with Theodor Hagen. He worked at the Munich Academy and with Lefebvre at the Académie Julian in Paris.

Schlittgen's Boer War cartoon depicting Highlanders with flags portraying them as stockbrokers, appeared in the German publication *Burenkrieg.* The cartoon is dated 1900.

Schlittgen died in Wasserbourg on 9 June 1930 .

Bénézit, Dictionnaire antique, *vol. 7, p. 601*

SCHMIDHAMMER, Arpad 1857-1921 1
Painter, illustrator and cartoonist. Schmidhammer was born in Saint-Joachimsthal, Bohemia, on 12 February 1857. He studied in Gratz under Liposchutz and in Vienna and Munich with Löfftz, Hackl, Herterich and Diez. He contributed to several German periodicals including *Der Getreue Eckart, Berliner Illustrierte Zeitung, Jungbrunnenhefte Knecht Ruprecht,* and *Jugenland.* From 1896 he worked for *Jugend.*

Schmidhammer's Boer War cartoons in *Jugend* were prolific, but he also contributed Boer War material to *Der Floh, Der Scherer* and *Münchener Odinskarte.* He usually signed his work with one of three monograms. One had the appearance of a frog, another was like a mushroom or champagne cork, and the third had his initials intertwined. It is not known why he varied his signature especially as two or more of his cartoons appearing in the same issue of *Jugend,* even on the same page, would have different monograms.

One of his cartoons, *Hande weg,* appeared on an Odinskarte postcard published in October 1899, making it one of the earliest of the War.

Schmidhammer died in Munich on 13 May 1921.

Bénézit, Dictionnaire antique, *vol. 7, p. 607*
Osterwalder, and Hubschmid and Bouret (eds.), Dictionnaire des Illustrateurs, *p. 954*

SCHMIDT, Hugo Carl 1856-?
Swiss-born painter and caricaturist who contributed satirical sketches on French and Swiss postcards. One card, entitled *Lâche,* depicts a drunk Edward VII with foot on dead Boer woman and child. Another shows a pack of bulldogs attacking a fallen Kruger with 'Justice' rising with the sun in the background. A variation of this card has Kruger labelled 'Pour la justice et la liberté', while the dogs are 'Pour l'or et les diamants'.

Bénézit, Dictionnaire antique, *vol. 7, p. 610*

SCHOLL, Fritz
Jugend cartoonist.

SCHÖNBERG, Johann (John) Nepomuk 1844-1914 2
Schönberg was born in Vienna in 1844. He received his art training in both Vienna and Munich, where he studied under Piloti. Schönberg's career as a war artist began while he was working for *The Illustrated London News* in 1866. His first drawings depicted incidents in the Austro-Prussian War. He was later present during the Servo-Turkish War (1876-7) and the Russo-Turkish War (1877-8), and at Szegedin (1879). He represented *The Illustrated London News* again during the Egyptian Campaign (1882) and the Servo-Bulgarian War (1885). In addition he reported on the serious cholera epidemic in Hamburg and the wedding of the Crown Price of Rumania at Sigmaringen. On his return from South Africa Schönberg rejoined the staff of *The Illustrated London*

4

News and was sent to cover the Boxer Rebellion in China.

On 14 July 1900 *The Illustrated London News* described Schönberg's success: '(His) paintings are not the ordinary war-pictures — all struggling men and horses: he prefers to deal more fully with the strategical movements of a great battle, and the success with which he has met shows that his aim is a good one.'

Schönberg's involvement in the Boer War is remarkable in that it was done clandestinely from behind the Boer lines. *The Sphere* for 16 June 1900 carried the following report: 'In November last it occurred to the editor of this journal that it was desirable to illustrate the war from another aspect than that practicable from the point of view of the special correspondent with the British Army.'

It is interesting to note that this editorial policy was made even before the first copy of *The Sphere* appeared in January 1900. The editorial board discussed the possibilities of sending an artist behind the Boer lines but realized that it would be impossible for an Englishman to go. The report continues: 'It was remembered, however, that there resided in London an artist of considerable reputation and talent, who had worked for many illustrated newspapers at home and abroad.'

'John Schonberg', as he was called in England, or Johann Schönberg in his native Austria, had lived in England for over 20 years. The report continues:

'Will you,' Schönberg was asked, 'go to Pretoria for *The Sphere*? You are to set aside for the moment all interest in England; you are to forget the English language from the hour you arrive in South Africa; you are to carry an Austrian passport with you to Pretoria, and to speak nothing but German from the moment you arrive until the hour of leaving the enemy's country. You are to represent, nominally, a German newspaper if one will consent to accept occasional drawings from you.'

Schönberg readily accepted the offer. *The Sphere* continues; 'He sailed on the *Guelph* to Cape Town as special artist for the German publication *Gartenlaube* on 18 November 1899. On board the *Guelph*, which carried troops, was also a contingent of nurses. Schönberg spent much of his time aboard doing sketches of the nurses and the way in which 'Tommy Atkins amused the fair sisters of mercy *en route*'. Trouble was experienced when the ship left Durban for Delagoa Bay. Captain Percy Scott, the commander of H.M.S. *Terrible*, who was in charge of shipping intelligence and passenger regulations in the Mozambique Channel, suspected Schönberg of being a German officer. Even though Scott had been told of the reason for Schönberg's journey to the Transvaal he ordered him to leave the ship within 24 hours. While in Durban Schönberg sketched the arrest of the *Bundesrath* by the H.M.S. *Terrible* on suspicion of carrying contraband.

Schönberg boarded a French steamer, *Campania*, using the name Jean Beaumont (the French translation of John Schönberg) and sailed ostensibly for Beira. When the ship called at Delagoa Bay on 10 January 1900 he disembarked. From there he travelled on to Pretoria. Unfortunately the Boer officials did not understand precisely what a special war artist was. After an introduction to Transvaal State Secretary Grobler, however, he was referred to F.W. Reitz and was given a 'permit for sketching and drawing' by General Joubert's secretary, De Souza. He was granted an interview with General Joubert at Modderspruit. Schönberg was allowed to accompany Joubert through the Boer field of operations but after a few days returned to Pretoria where he sketched British prisoners of war and such incidents as came to hand. *The Sphere* reported, however, that an unfortunate telegram was sent to him through Germany: 'London requests you to remain'. The Boer officials immediately suspected that something was wrong and Schönberg, who had been wounded in an earlier incident, was sent back to England via Lourenço Marques.

Mrs L. de Wet, writing in *Africana Notes and News* in December 1961, discusses the remarkable story as her introduction to the article on the Africana Museum's acquisition of a number of Schönberg drawings which had been done during his stay in the Transvaal. These pen-and-ink wash drawings are as follows:

1. S20 *The Guelph 18 Nov. 1899 at 5 o'clock. Departure from Southampton*. Signed 'J Schönberg'. Wash drawing.
2. S21 *Regimental Conjuror on board the Guelph 1899*. Inscription: 'Regimental Gaff (sic) of the Army Ordnance Corps on board of the *Guelph*' and faintly 'Regimental Gauf'. Wash drawing.
3. S22 *Model School at Pretoria 1900*. Inscription: 'Die Staat Modelschule für die gefangenen englischen Officiere'. Wash drawing. Signed 'J. Schönberg Pretoria 21.1.1900'. This was reproduced in *The Sphere* on 17 March 1900, with a caption 'The Model School in Pretoria where the British Officers are imprisoned. It was here that Winston Churchill was gaoled. Three officers have just escaped, Captain Haldane, DSO, of the Gordons, Lieutenant Brockie, and Lieutenant Le Mesurier. The first two tried to escape with Mr Churchill, but could not elude the vigilance of the guard. All three are men of daring and determination' — 'the officer in charge of the prisoners is Commandant R.W.F. Opperman whose portrait appears in the corner'. The reproduction is in facsimile, but, obviously to avoid detection, his signature was removed. This was done in all the illustrations which were reproduced in *The Sphere* prior to Schönberg's return.
4. S23 *Two British Officers being conducted from Railway Station to the State Model School, Pretoria*. Wash drawing. Signed 'J. Schönberg, 30 1 1900, Pretoria ZAR'. Inscription on the back in German. This sketch was reproduced in *The Sphere* on 31 March 1900, with the inscription: 'Two British Officers being conducted to the State Model School at Pretoria. The taller officer is Lieutenant H.A. Chandos-Pole Gell of the 2nd Coldstreams who was captured by the Boers at Modder River while out under flag of truce. The other is Lieutenant

M.H. Tristram of the 12th Lancers who was also captured at Modder — on December 6. Both of them got their captors to send to the English camp for things that were absolutely necessary. This was done and Lieut. Tristram changed his khaki uniform in the railway carriage for a tennis suit.'
5. S24 *Boers leaving Pretoria for Ladysmith 1900*. Wash drawing. Signed 'J. Schönberg Pretoria 1,25 1900'. This was redrawn for *The Sphere* in the 31 March 1900 supplement with the caption 'Boers leaving Pretoria for Ladysmith — the boys, fourteen or fifteen, are very good shots and have already been in several battles. They were home for Christmas holidays and are going back again. The man in the middle is Mr. Wabeck, Chief of the Railway. The two girls are sisters who went to see their brothers off.'
6. S25 *Camp for British Prisoners Waterval, near Pretoria 1900*. Inscription below in German. Wash drawing. Signed 'Waterval 4.2.1900' and below the inscription 'John Schönberg'. It was reproduced without the German inscription and signature in *The Sphere* 31 March 1900 supplement with the inscription 'General view of the Camp where the Prisoners are kept'. The text says 'Waterval is a few miles north of Pretoria'.
7. S26 *General Botha's Headquarters on the Tugela*. Inscription in German. Wash drawing. Signed 'J. Schönberg, ZAR 18 Feb. 1900'. Re-drawn for *The Sphere* of 5 May 1900 with the caption 'General Botha's Quarters on the Tugela: — The larger tent in the centre of this view was used for business by the military headquarters staff. General Botha slept at night in the small tent behind. The tents shown to the left hand were occupied, one by his secretary, Mr. Otto, the other by our special artist and a Russian comrade. There were several holes in these tents caused by fragments of British shells.' 'Sketch by our special artist with the Boers — Drawn by A. Pearse.'
8. S27 *General and Mrs Joubert welcome Schönberg*. Inscription in German. Wash drawing. Reproduced in *The Sphere* on 5 May 1900 with the caption: 'Our special artist being received by the late General Joubert. — Our artist and a Russian officer were hospitably entertained by the late General Joubert and his wife at Modderspruit, Natal on February 18 (sic). They were given breakfast at 4.30 a.m. General Joubert also offered them a waggon for sleeping quarters so long as they stayed at his camp.'
9. S28 *President Kruger leaving Pretoria for Kroonstad 1900*. The inscription on the back is in German. Wash drawing. Signed on the back in pencil 'J. Schönberg Pretoria 21 Maart ZAR'. Reproduced in *The Sphere* on 19 May 1900 with the caption 'Mr. Kruger starting from Pretoria to meet Mr. Steyn at Kroonstadt. The president left Pretoria at 8 o'clock on the evening of March 21 [should be 14 March]. Mr. Reitz, the State Secretary; Mr. Smuts, the Attorney General; and Mr. A.D.W. Wolmarans, another member of the Executive Council, had a parting consultation with the President in the saloon carriage. He was accompanied on his journey to the Orange Free State by Mr. P. Grobler, Dr. Heymans, and Mr. Bruijn.'
10. S29 *Boer outpost escaping an attack 1900*. Inscription on top in ink: 'A Boer Outpost Hastily Escaping an Attack,

---

1 *Groet uit Derdepoort*, a postcard illustrated by Engelina Helena Schlette and published by N.J. Boon & Co. British troops under Colonel Holdsworth are alleged to have used members of the Linchwe tribe as 'shields' during their attack on the Boers at Derdepoort in the north-western Transvaal.

2 Arpad Schmidhammer's violently anti-British illustration *Der Kindermord in Süd Afrika*, based on Peter Paul Rubens' *Kindermord zu Bethlehem*, was published in *Jugend* on 10 July 1901.

3 Richard Schaupp's front cover portrait of De Wet entitled *De Zwarte Christian*, used on the front cover of *Jugend* on 29 May 1901.

4 Johann Schönberg's wash drawing of the Model School in Pretoria, where captured British officers were imprisoned. It was reproduced in *The Sphere* on 17 March 1900. Reproduced by courtesy of the Africana Museum, Johannesburg. Schönberg's signature was erased in the reproduction, because he was still in the Transvaal.

near Ladysmith, March 25'. A faint German inscription in pencil follows. Pen-and-ink wash drawing. Signed 'J. Schönberg Z.A.R. 25 Maart 1900'. Also on the back in pencil "4 in wide x 4 in high 12396 – Sphere slight border – take out Schönberg's name Saturday 10 o'clock'. Reproduced in *The Sphere* on 19 May 1900 with the caption 'Boer Outpost hastily escaping an Attack near Ladysmith March 25'.

11. S30 *How Captive English Officers were guarded at Night 1900*. Inscription in German. Wash drawing. Signed 'J. Schönberg'. Reproduced in *The Sphere* on 16 June 1900 with the inscription 'How the Eng. Officiers (sic) (Prisoners [sic] of War) were guardit (sic) in night time in Pretoria where the new Barracks are now erecaidet (sic)'. 'The whole place is lightend (sic) with electric light. Instead of Boers are now Dutch Volluntiers (sic) on Guard.' Reproduced in *The Sphere* on 16 June 1900 with the incription: 'How the English Officers were guarded at night-time in Pretoria – The officers were removed several weeks ago from the town to a spot on the Aapies, the river which makes Pretoria so verdant. The enclosure was surrounded by electric lights, and the guard was composed of Dutch Volunteers instead of Boers – Drawn by our special artist in Pretoria, Mr. John Schönberg.'

12. S31 *Concert on board the Guelph 1899*. Inscription in German. Drawn for *The Sphere* on 16 June p. 657 with the inscription 'Our Special Pretoria Artist going out on the *Guelph*: a concert on Board, sketch by J. Schönberg. Drawn by G. Grenville Manton'. S32 and S33 are also by Schönberg but are of his trip to China to cover the Boxer Rebellion for *The Illustrated London News*.

13. S275 *Boers spreading the news*. Inscription on back in blue pencil. Grey wash. Signed 'J. Schönberg 1899'. On the back is written 'Very urgent – 7 inches wide – please make this very urgent; block must be delivered to printer by Thursday midday'. There is also a printed label on the back 'St. Pauls. Granville House, Arundel Street, Strand'.

14. S276 *Boers Farewell to Home 1899*. Inscription on the back in pencil: 'Boers farwell (sic) from home-Boers Abschied by John Schönberg'. Also on the back is written 'Original to be returned – Block by Tuesday evening – 6½ wide'. The St Paul's label has been partially removed. It is assumed that both this and the previous picture were intended for publication in *St Paul's*, the periodical which ceased publication in January 1900.

Africana Notes and News, *Dec. 1961, vol. 14, no. 8, pp. 303 ff. 'Schönberg's Drawings of The Anglo Boer War' by L. de Wet*
De Wet, Illustrated London News Index
Hodgson, The War Illustrators
Illustrated London News, *14 July 1900, p. 61*
Johnson, Front Line Artists
Kennedy, Pictures in the Africana Museum, *vol. 4, pp. 117-121 and vol. 7, p. 232*
The Sphere *16 June 1900, p. 256*

SCHULZ, Wilhelm 1865-1952   1

Illustrator. Schulz was born in Lüneburg on 23 December 1865. He studied at the academies in Hamburg, Berlin, Karlsruhe, and Munich. In 1897 he began to work for *Simplicissimus*.

Three of Schulz's Boer War illustrations appeared in *Der Burenkrieg*. One illustration shows a young Boer saying farewell to his wife, another lions snatching British soldiers, and the third Boers marching to war.

Schulz died on 16 March 1952.

Bénézit, Dictionnaire antique, *vol. 7, p. 659*
Osterwalder, and Hubschmid and Bouret (eds.), Dictionnaire des Illustrateurs, *p. 963*

SCHULZE, Hermann

Cartoonist who drew a German postcard lampooning Chamberlain (Gustav Kohl, Leipzig).

SCHWARTZE, Thérèse (Van Duyl) 1852-1918   1

Genre and portrait painter. Schwartze was born in Amsterdam on 20 December 1852. Her father, the artist Johan Georg Schwartze, taught her initially and she later studied under G. Max, Piloty and Lenbach in Munich. Her married name was Van Duyl and she is frequently referred to as 'Van Duyl Schwartze'.

The War Museum of the Boer Republics in Bloemfontein has three portraits by Schwartze: two of General De Wet (one an oil [unfinished], the other a charcoal) and an oil of General De la Rey. The charcoal portrait of De Wet was used in the Dutch version of his *The Three Years War*, entitled *De Stryd Tusschen Boer en Brit* (Hoverkerk and Wormser). The portrait of De la Rey was donated by the Netherlands Zuid-Afrikaansche Vereniging in Amsterdam to the Bloemfontein museum in 1962.

A portrait of Joubert by Schwartze was reproduced on the front page of *The Sphere* on 3 February 1900. The portrait was also reproduced on a Jos Nuss postcard and in J.B. Atkins' *Relief of Ladysmith*. The caption to the illustration in *The Sphere* says that the painting was then on exhibition at the Society of Portrait Painters in the Grafton Galleries. *The Sphere* announced rather remarkably but incorrectly that 'Petrus Jacobus Joubert is a native of Louisiana and fought with the Confederates in the American Civil War'. The portrait is now in the National Cultural History and Open-Air Museum in Pretoria.

Recently her portrait of Kruger was rediscovered in Schwartze's home town. It is believed to have been offered to the South African Government for 400 000 Dutch guilders (approximately R300 000). If the offer is accepted it would make this painting the highest-priced Africana work of art to date. This portrait had been reproduced on the cover of the 19 February 1902 issue (no. 9) of *Jugend*. Prints of it were advertised by the magazine as being available at a price of DM1,50.

Schwartze died in Amsterdam on 23 December 1918.

Bénézit, Dictionnaire antique, *vol. 7, p. 670*
Bloemfontein War Museum Catalogue
The Studio, *vol. 52, p. 119 (1911)*

SCOTSON-CLARK, George Frederick

Anglo-American cartoonist and poster illustrator who worked for *Judy*, *New York Recorder*, *World* and *The Journal*. Scotson-Clark illustrated the lithograph music cover of 'Britons and Boers: Verses by Hubert Ives' (John Lau, London and New York).

Thorpe, writing about Scotson-Clark's work for *Judy*, refers to him as a 'weak cartoonist'.

Byatt, Picture Postcards, *p. 160*
Osterwalder, and Hubschmid and Bouret (eds.), Dictionnaire des Illustrateurs, *p. 969*
Thorpe, English Illustration, *p. 101*

SCOTT, Georges Bertin 1873-1948(?)   2

Painter and illustrator. He was also known as Scott de Plagnolles. He studied under Detaille, the French military painter. He was a special correspondent during the Balkan War and he acted as an official French military artist during World War I. His paintings of the Balkan War were exhibited at Petit's Gallery.

During the Boer War Scott contributed to *The Graphic* (at least 12 illustrations between 21 October 1899 and 9 June 1900) and *L'Illustration* (even more numerous). At least four illustrations from the latter were reproduced on the 'Guerre du Transvaal' series of postcards. They were:

751 *Highlanders Montant L'assaut d'un Kopje* (24 February 1900).
819 *Les Boers Hissant le Long Tom à Volksrust* (sic) (13 January 1900).
1662 *Retour à Londres de Lord Roberts* (untraced in *L'Illustration*).
1663 *Incendie d'une Ferme Boer* (16 November 1901).

In January 1901 Arthur Tooth and Sons Gallery of Haymarket, London, held an exhibition of three of Scott's oil paintings. The catalogue, which ran to 12 pages, was entitled *Incidents in the South African War*. The paintings were *Elandslaagte*, *Buller's Final crossing of the Tugela*, and *The surrender of Cronje*. The catalogue gave a vivid description of all three incidents. Admission fees for the exhibition were 'for the benefit of *The Daily Telegraph* war fund'. During the exhibition visitors were invited to subscribe for photoengravings of Scott's pictures. The 350 artist's proofs were priced at eight guineas each and the India prints at two guineas each.

After discussing the merits of the special artist's drawings vis-à-vis the 'grey, monotonous events afforded to us by the one-eyed camera', *The Graphic* for 19 January 1901 praised the exhibition thus:

> ... For this reason we draw special attention to the three pictures by M. Scott now on view at Tooth's gallery in the Haymarket – These are all 'actual', dramatic in a high

3 *Victory*

Royal Academy Pictures, *1901, p. 17*
Who was Who, *vol. 2, p. 953*

SHEARD, Thomas Frederick Mason 1866-1921
Sheard was educated at Magdalen College School and Keble College, Oxford. In 1899 he went to Paris where he studied painting under Courtois, Rixens, Lefebvre and Rigolot. In 1891 Sheard began exhibiting at the Royal Academy, the Paris Salon and the R.I. He was honorary secretary of the R.B.A. from 1899 to 1904. Many of his works featured oriental subjects. He was a professor of art at Queen's College, London. In 1900 Sheard exhibited two pictures at the R.B.A. entitled *A victim of the war* and *War victims* (a triptych). In the absence of contrary evidence it is assumed that these two paintings had Boer War relevance.

Sheard died on 1 October 1921.
R.B.A. Catalogue, vol. 2, p. 91
Who was Who, *vol. 2, pp. 953-954*

SHELDON, Charles Mills 1866-1928 1
Sheldon was born at Lawrenceburg, Indiana, U.S.A. on 24 June 1866. He studied in Paris under Constant and Lefebvre and at the Académie Julian from 1890 to 1891. In 1889 he travelled through the southern states illustrating articles for the Associated Press.

Sheldon went to England in about 1892, working as an illustrator on *Pall Mall Budget* (1892-5). He was in South Africa at the time of the Jameson Raid and sent back sketches to *Black & White*. Later that year he joined the Dongola Expedition in Sudan. In 1898 he became artist-correspondent for *Frank Leslie's* and *Black & White* in Cuba.

Sheldon was artist-correspondent at the opening of the Aswan barrage in Egypt and at the Delhi Durbar in (1902-3). In 1918 he was appointed special artist on the British front for the Northcliff Press. He was a fellow of the Royal Geographical Society.

Hodgson contends that Sheldon was in South Africa during the War, but this seems highly unlikely as *Black & White*, which was very proud of its correspondents and featured stories about their exploits, does not include his name in the lists it published. The illustrations which do appear in that paper under his signature are drawn from 'Sketches and photographs received from the front'.

The National Army Museum has a wash drawing done by Sheldon entitled *Sanna's Post: The Mounted Infantry Brigade under Colonel Alderson covering the retirement 1900*. This was drawn from a sketch by Capt. S.E. St Leger. Sheldon's Boer War work appeared in *The King*, *Black & White*, *Black & White Budget* and *With the Flag to Pretoria*. One of Sheldon's illustrations of Gen. Buller taken from *Black & White* was used on the Picture Postcard Company's card number 3d. Acknowledgement is given to the newspaper but not to Sheldon, whose signature is cropped.

A Reverend Charles Sheldon is mentioned in *The Golden Penny* as having been the author of a religious article 'In His

---

degree, bearing upon them the impress of truth. Not only have we the very spirit of the war, the essence of the great incidents themselves, but we see how the sky looked at the time, we know what the weather was, we observe the colour of veldt or tree, and how the Boers fought and the British charged, how Roberts stood as he received the tatterdemalion general, how the long, thin, khaki line of an army advanced across two great pontoon bridges on the Tugela to death and victory. We care nothing for the painting as we look at these canvases — only at the tragedies they depict, moved with a deeper passion than any aesthetic emotion could arouse; and what greater compliment could we pay to the clever artist than this?

The National Army Museum, London, now owns the oil *Final crossing of the Tugela*. It was reproduced on the cover of the paperback edition of Rayne Kruger's *Good Bye Dolly Gray*. Frank Thorold, the firm of antiquarian book dealers, owns *The surrender of Cronje*, which has been reproduced in the recent publication, *The Spectacle of Empire*, by Jan Morris.

The author has the wash drawing *Baden-Powell inspecting sick horses near Mafeking*. This appeared in *The Graphic* on 11 November 1899 and was exhibited at the Military Exhibition in London in 1901.

Arthur Tooth and Sons Galleries Catalogue, Incidents in the South African War
Bénézit, Dictionnaire antique, *vol. 7, p. 683*
Dawnay and Miller, Military Drawings and Paintings, *vol. 2, p. 246*
Hofmeyr, Matton and Roets, Graphic Picture Index
Osterwalder, and Hubschmid and Bouret (eds.), Dictionnaire des Illustrateurs, *p. 970*
SAPRG Newsletter, Aug. 1984, 'Journal L'Illustration and Guerre du Transvaal Postcards' by R. Greenwall

SEARELLE, Blanche
A Mrs Searelle provided a sketch for *The Illustrated London News* on 9 September 1899 entitled *The Transvaal crisis: Field cornet's messenger handing over commandos to Boer farmers to be ready for war*. This sketch was redrawn by P. Frenzeny. It was possible that Mrs Searelle was the wife of William Luscombe Searelle (Isaac Israel) whose book, *Tales of the Transvaal*, was illustrated by Frenzeny. Mrs Searelle was a dancer in her husband's theatrical company. Her maiden name was Blanche Fenton and she came to South Africa from Australia with her sister, Amy, and a tenor, Vernon Reid, in 1887.

De Wet, Illustrated London News Index

SEIBER
Designer and artist responsible for a postwar painting of Kruger and Steyn with the respective flags and coats of arms of the two Boer republics, dated 1899-1902. The painting was photographically reproduced, mounted and framed for distribution by an unknown publisher.

SEM 1863-1934
Sem was the pseudonym adopted by the caricaturist Georges (or Serge) Goursat. He based the pseudonym on the name of the early French caricaturist 'Cham' (Amédée de Noée), whom he greatly admired.

Goursat was born in Périgueux, France, on 23 November 1863. He moved to Paris in 1900 after having worked in Bordeaux and Marseilles and published an album on the racing world which he called *Le Turf*. In 1914 he published another book, *Un Pékin sur le Front* (a civilian at the Front). 'Sem' was well known for his characteristic style which captured the *belle époque* of the early 20th century. He was a frequent visitor to England and Edward VII was a favourite subject. He was a noted postcard artist and a contributor to the 'Collection des Cents'.

Goursat worked for *Le Journal* and *Le Cri de Paris*. Other albums by him include *Album Sem*, *La Ronde de Nuit*, *Le Vrai et le faux chic*, *Périgueux-Revue*, *Sem à la Mer*, *Monte-Carlo* and *Le nouveau Monde*.

The author has a sheet of nine pen and black ink and crayon caricatures by 'Sem'.

Bénézit, Dictionnaire antique, *vol. 7, p. 708*
Feaver, Masters of Caricature, *p. 128*
Houfe, British Illustrators and Caricaturists, *p. 449*
Osterwalder, and Hubschmid and Bouret (eds.), Dictionnaire des Illustrateurs, *p. 973*
Weill, Art Nouveau Postcards, *p. 9*

SEPPINGS WRIGHT, H.C. see WRIGHT, Henry Charles Seppings

SHAW, John Byam Liston 1872-1919
Oil and watercolour painter. Shaw was born in Madras, India, on 13 November 1872. He came to England in 1878 and was educated privately and at the St John's Wood School of Art. He entered the Royal Academy schools in 1889. His first picture, *Rose Mary*, was accepted by the Royal Academy in 1893.

Among Shaw's publications were the illustration of Browning's poems in 1898, *Tales from Boccaccio* (1899); *Chiswick Shakespeare* (1899); *Old King Cole's Book of Nursery Rhymes* (1901); *Pilgrim's Progress* (1904); *Coronation Book* (1902); *The Cloister and the Hearth* (1909); *Tales of Mystery and Imagination* by Edgar Allan Poe (1909), and *The Garden of Kama* by Laurence Hope (1914). Shaw, who was a follower of the pre-Raphaelite style, was mainly a painter in oils and watercolours. He became a partner with Rex Vicat Cole in a school of art at Campden Hill which is still in existence today.

Shaw exhibited a painting at the Royal Academy in 1901 entitled *Boer War, 1900*, which featured a pensive lady gazing into a pond. The painting is illustrated in *Royal Academy Pictures* (1901).

Shaw died on 26 January 1919.
Houfe, British Illustrators and Caricaturists, *p. 450*

---

1 Georges Scott's watercolour of General Baden-Powell inspecting sick horses at Mafeking was sold for three guineas at a sale of work from *The Graphic* in 1901.
2 The oil *Buller's Final crossing of the Tugela* by Georges Scott. Reproduced by courtesy of the National Army Museum, London.
3 Charles Mills Sheldon's wash drawing *Sanna's Post: The Mounted Infantry Brigade under Colonel Alderson covering the retirement 1900* was produced from a sketch by Captain S. E. St Leger. St Leger's original sketch, which seems far more competent than Sheldon's, was reproduced in his book *War Sketches in Colour*. Reproduced by courtesy of the National Army Museum, London.

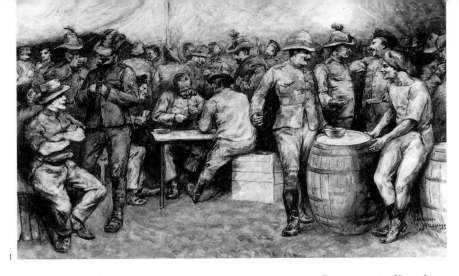

steps'. It is most unlikely that the two Sheldons are the same.
Sheldon died on 13 March 1928.

Fielding, American Painters etc., *p. 330*

Hodgson, The War Illustrators

Picture Postcard Monthly, *July 1983, 'The artists and sources of the illustrations in the Picture Postcard Company Ltd series on the Anglo Boer war' by R. Greenwall*

SHELDON-WILLIAMS, (Harry) Inglis (Jodrel) 1870-1940 4
Soldier-artist; illustrator and artist in civilian life. Inglis Sheldon-Williams was born in Elvetham, Hampshire, on Christmas Day, 1870. His father, Alfred, was a well-known artist who contributed sporting scenes to the illustrated journals of the day. He died in 1880 and his widow, Harriet, emigrated to Canada with her six young children in 1887. After first visiting Germany and Belgium, they settled at Cannington Manor in Saskatchewan. After his mother's death in 1891 Inglis went to Europe to study art at the École des Beaux-Arts in Paris. He returned to Canada in 1895 but a year later enrolled at the Slade School in London. His fellow students at the time included Augustus John, John's sister Gwen, and William Orpen. He left the Slade School in 1898 without (according to records) having won any prizes. He studied extensively in Europe and England; under Theophile Lybaert in Ghent, Belgium, under Sir Thomas Brock in London, at the Colarossi Academy in Paris, and at Karlsruhe in Germany.

When the Boer War broke out Sheldon-Williams was lecturing to students at Frank Calderon's School of Animal Painting. The events of 'Black Week' in South Africa encouraged him to enlist in Compton's Horse Volunteers. A postcard (dated 24 December 1899) which is in his daughter's possession and was addressed to her father, reads 'Please be at the parade riding school Knightsbridge barracks on Thursday at 9.45 — from Lord A. Compton'. Compton's Horse Volunteers were assembled at Liverpool Street Station before being sent to Landguard Fort and then on to Colchester for training.

The regiment spent about a month there before leaving London aboard the ship *Kent* on 7 February 1900. The Duke of Cambridge reviewed them prior to their departure. On arrival in Cape Town on 5 March 1900 they were greeted with the news that Kimberley had been relieved and that Cronje had surrendered at Paardeberg a few days before. The regiment disembarked with their horses and marched, dismounted and leading the horses, the five miles to the Yeomanry staging camp at Maitland where another 2 000 newly arrived troops had encamped. A few days later they rode via Durban Road to the remount camp at Stellenbosch where Sheldon-Williams produced a few drawings, one of which is in the Africana Museum. They spent ten days there before being sent to Piketberg Road Station, and on 11 April, following Roberts's orders, they proceeded by train to Springfontein, from where it was a further 10 days' march to Bloemfontein. They accompanied Roberts into Johannesburg, pursuing the

retreating Boers via Kroonstad to Vereeniging.

Sheldon-Williams, in his unpublished memoirs entitled *The Track of a Rolling Stone*, mentions that he spent '16 months on the veld'. He also mentions that he was introduced to Lord Roberts by Sir Rice Edwards who had known Sheldon-Williams' future wife's parents in India. Through the good offices of Sir Rice Edwards he was able to transmit letters via Lord Roberts's diplomatic pouch to his fiancée in England. At Roberts's headquarters Sheldon-Williams was invited to sketch portraits of General (then Captain) Wilson (who, he mentions, was reputed to be the ugliest man in the army), Sir Henry Rawlinson, Sir Ian Hamilton, and F.C. Stanley. General French, who was said to be very shy, refused to sit for him. Sheldon-Williams reports that he was laid low with dysentery and spent some time in a convalescent home before being sent back to England.

On 20 November 1937 *The Sphere* published an article by Sheldon-Williams entitled 'The war correspondent then and now. Some personal reminiscences by Inglis Sheldon-Williams. One time *Sphere* artist and veteran of many campaigns.' Sheldon-Williams discusses in some detail 'the rise and fall of the special artist' and how, with military censorship, the advancing power of the camera, and 'living news on screens attended by trained announcers', the *coup de grâce* of this breed of correspondent was finally administered. He describes the heyday of the war correspondent's adventurous life that closed with the Boer War:

> We know that Kitchener first sounded the warning in the Sudan, and with polite ruthlessness the Japanese rang down the curtain in 1904. But in South Africa all that was required of the duly accredited war correspondent was the submitting of his copy to the censor, who entered into the sport of the thing and played the game.
> 'I do not care' said Major Altham, chief censor in Ladysmith, 'if you get a hole through your body, as long as you don't go outside our lines'. More, in the person of Lord Stanley, now Earl of Derby, he actually started a newspaper himself, in Bloemfontein, it being gleefully contributed to for the edification of Lord Roberts, when prior claims permitted, by Percival Landon of *The Times*, H. A. Gwynne, Reuter's, F. W. Buxton, Johannesburg *Star* and Julian Ralph of *The Daily Mail*.
> The correspondent was at liberty to attach himself to any column, be ahead of the main force with the cavalry and infantry, or to visit any outpost. Admittedly this freedom of movement occasionally led to embarrassments, as when Bennet Burleigh complained fretfully that Melton Prior's bald head was drawing the enemy fire, or when the Gordons pelted with turf G.W. Steevens, 'Prince of special correspondents', for riding across their front on a white horse, like Napoleon to Austerlitz, and drove him to seek for a pot of brown paint, but generally speaking it made for pleasant amenities all round. It was still possible to carry on the torch lit by their great forerunners.
> All kinds of little incidents flock to the memory — once a corporal of ours in charge of half-a-dozen troopers

came unexpectedly upon a party of Boers for once as surprised as he was. The problem whether we came under the drill-book words of command as cavalry or infantry was never solved in the Boer War. With a masterstroke of genius our corporal gave the order 'Fix bayonets — charge!' The correct motions for fixing bayonet while on horse-back, whether 'by numbers' or 'judging the time' have not yet been drawn up. Executed on the spur of the moment without any precedent they can be complicated, and much depends on your horse. But it was done. For Queen and country, for Kimberley and the Rand, 'With spears in rest and hearts on flame that panted for the shock', the gallant band charged the Boers who incontinently turned and fled. The Boer loathes the bayonet. I don't blame him. It's the tickling association. As the Frenchman said of the flea — 'C'est moins le pique; c'est le promenade'.

Another article (unpublished) which is in his daughter's possession was entitled 'Infants in arms, or When horses mattered'. It is an interesting document and sets out modestly, and humorously at times, the experiences of Sheldon-Williams and his fellow troopers under fire, real or imagined, while campaigning against the Boers after the capture of Johannesburg.

He tells how on one occasion his preoccupation with sketching saved his life. When on patrol he noticed a girl talking to someone hidden in the vegetation. He did not report this to his sergeant, however, and two days later when it was his turn to ride again, the sergeant noticed that he was working on a drawing. He was told to carry on and that he need only go on patrol the following day. 'That day at the spot I have described — and where I should have been — devoid of any vestige of cover, chatting together, as likely as not joking amicably with those woman patriots, our patrol was ambushed. Two men were shot, one killed instantly, the sergeant stuck by the other until he too was dead, and escaped miraculously with the other three.'

During his service in South Africa Sheldon-Williams was awarded the Queen's medal. It had three state bars: the Cape Colony, Transvaal and the Orange Free State.

Soon after his return to England he arranged an exhibition which was held in October 1902 at the rooms of the Fine Arts Society, 148 New Bond Street. The catalogue is entitled 'An exhibition of watercolours illustrating Types of Brethren in Arms South Africa 1900-1902 by Inglis Sheldon-Williams (late of Compton's Horse Imperial Yeomanry)'. Thirty-eight paintings and one statuette were on sale:

1. *On Parade – Brabant's Horse*
2. *Scout Drawing Fire*
3. *The Gun Team*
4. *The Salted Yeoman*
5. *Mount!*
6. *Lord Roberts Crossing the Vaal at Viljoen's Drift*
7. *A Vicarious Remount*
8. *Dawn on an Outlying Patrol*
9. *Shrapnel*
10. *A Supplement to Bully Beef*
11. *Good Cover – Skirmishing Through a Mealie Field*
12. *A Long Drink*
13. *A Raw Article – Stellenbosch*
14. *Clear and Cool*
15. *After Many Days*
16. *Fall In!*
17. *The Farrier Sergeant*
18. *On the Veld – Kitchener's Fighting Scout*
19. *Lord Kitchener's Orderly*
20. *A Big Handful – Stellenbosch Remount Camp*
21. *Under Fire at Six Mile Spruit*
22. *Grim Earnest*
23. *Squadron Gallop! (Hussar Officer)*
24. *Brand New*
25. *A Few Words on a Frosty Morning*
26. *Staff Officer Reconnoitring*
27. *Rough Road to Water*
28. *Old Hands*
29. *Crossing a Drift*
30. *Wayside Refreshment*
31. *At Home on Coronation Day (9 August 1902)*
32. *At the Cape – On Active Service*
33. *Hands Up!*
34. *A Sore Back and a Dusty Road*
35. *Steady, Boy!*
36. *Special Service*
37. *Halt!*
38. *Off Duty at Pretoria*
39. Statuette: *The Scout*.

A note which preceded this list said:
Never probably in the history of the world's campaigns, certainly never in those of Great Britain, have Colonies so diverse and widely separated made common cause with the Mother Country as in the war in South Africa. A proper portrayal of this varied host by one qualified for the task therefore approaches an historical value, and consequently apart from any artistic merit the drawings comprised in this little show may claim a right to public exhibition. Their author, Mr Sheldon-Williams, was one of the earliest to enlist in the Imperial Yeomanry, and in Compton's Horse he saw a lengthened service, out of which an observant eye and a facile pencil were able to perpetuate a multitude of incidents, of which those now represented are but a small minority.

Most of these Boer War pictures eventually found their way to the Glenbow Museum in Alberta, Canada, where as recently as October 1981 they were used in a retrospective exhibition of Sheldon-Wiliams's works. For many years these remained in Sheldon Williams's possession as evidenced by a letter, dated 12 April 1938, that he wrote to James McMasters, the honorary secretary of the South African War Veterans Association in London:
Dear Sir,
I have a set of 24 Mounted Infantry coloured drawings of men and horses doing things, which I did during the Boer War from sketches and notes I made while serving as a trooper in the 20th Coy. Imperial Yeomanry. I call this 'When horses mattered'. They make a lively show but the interest for the general public today is doubtful. In 1903 (actually October 1902) I had an exhibition based on them at the Fine Arts Society when the Earl of Derby lent me a set of portrait sketches I did for him in Johannesburg of Lord Roberts and his Mess.

It had occurred to me that these 24 drawings might interest Veterans if shown at one of the dinners or smokers, and might yield a little revenue for the association from percentages on sales – if any. A few are framed the rest mounted. If you thought the idea interesting I would be pleased to call and show you some. I am out of town from Thursday until the 19th.
Yours truly,
I. Sheldon-Williams.
P.S. I think it is possible that the Earl of Derby might be willing to lend the portrait sketches for such an occasion. These include Lord Roberts, the Earl of Derby, Lord Stanley the late General Wilson – then Captain Wilson, the late Brigadier general Stanley – then the Hon. Ferdinand Stanley our adjutant, Sir Ian Hamilton, the late Field Marshal Lord Rawlinson – then Sir Henry Rawlinson.

At the end of 1902 Sheldon-Williams was commissioned by *The Sphere* to cover the Delhi Durbar. This lasted from Monday 29 December 1902 until Saturday 10 January 1903. Many of these sketches were used in facsimile on the cover of the magazine. In May 1903 he held a joint exhibition with L. Raven-Hill of his experiences there. Again this exhibition was held in the rooms of the Fine Arts Society. Of the 120 items on offer, 54 were by Williams. *The Times* (11 May 1903) mentioned the exhibition but did not comment on it.

Soon after his return from India Sheldon-Williams accompanied King Edward on his European tour, arriving with him at Lisbon on 2 April 1903. Problems with the post were not unusual and *The Sphere* lamented that 'the beautiful work by our special artist Mr. Sheldon-Williams picturing the King's visit to Lisbon, owing to delays at the Post Office arrived too late for publication in this number. The illustrations will appear next week'. And to whet the appetite of its readers *The Sphere* mentioned that King Carlos had accepted one of the drawings from the artist. Nevertheless the post office 'work to rule' must have been settled quickly because Sheldon-Williams's 'beautiful pictures' appeared regularly thereafter as he followed the King through Portugal, Italy and France.

Sheldon-Williams continued to work for *The Sphere*. (In 1904 he married his fiancée, Ina Maud Thompson, a flower painter who had also studied at the Slade School, where they had met.) During the Russo-Japanese War *The Sphere* engaged his services again and he was appointed special correspondent with the Japanese forces. His voyage to Japan, via San Francisco, enabled him to send back sketches of Chinatown which were published on 13 February 1904. With half-inch headlines *The Sphere* proclaimed that 'Mr Sheldon-Williams, a first class artist correspondent, was the first English artist at the seat of the war and would be sending back sketches of actual incidents from the scene of operations'. 'The Sphere', it continued, 'will publish no imaginary drawings.' The undeclared war started on 8/9 February 1904 with the Japanese attack on Port Arthur. Inglis arrived in Tokyo early in February and immediately sent back pictures of the Japanese cavalry leaving for Korea. He himself travelled to Korea with the Japanese and sketched a party of British Marines arriving at Seoul soon after. He described his experiences in Newchwang (Yinkou) in Manchuria and on one occasion, on 19 May 1904, he relates how he entered the town believing it in Japanese hands only to find that the Russians were still well in control. His sketches at that time were eagerly awaited back in London and reproduced directly without the assistance of the usual home-based artist.

During the Russo-Japanese War Sheldon-Williams was one of the few correspondents who was able to get to the front. He also recalls an incident with fellow correspondent Lionel James. Sheldon-Williams related one of his Boer War stories to him. James asked permission to use it as his own, but the artist refused.

Sheldon-Williams had a painting accepted by the Royal Academy in 1906. He subsequently ran a country art school with nude models despite objections from local obstructionists. He returned to Regina, Canada, in 1913 and was invited to establish a school of art, which is still in existence today. His appointment lasted until 1917. He returned to England to bring out his family but the war intervened and he was rejected for service. His friend, Norman McKenzie, was able to use his influence, however, to get Sheldon-Williams the position of official war artist with the Canadian forces in France in 1918. In a letter to Mr J. Calder, Minister of Colonization, McKenzie writes how Sheldon-Williams had tried unsuccessfully to join the Canadian forces, even as an orderly with no pay. He had been rejected, however, because of his age. (He was now over 45.) McKenzie mentioned Sheldon-Williams' war experiences in South Africa and the Russo-Japanese War and also his fine artistic ability. It appears that the appeal was successful and he was appointed.

Sir Max Aitken, later Lord Beaverbrook, had at this time formed a Canadian War Memorials Fund which among other things commissioned artists to paint scenes of the Canadian participation in the war. Sheldon-Williams was commissioned and two of his paintings, *The Return to Mons* and *Canadians Arriving on the Rhine*, were later exhibited at the Royal Academy in 1921 and 1922. They are now in the Canadian War Museum in Ottawa. Some of the watercolours he did in France were later reproduced in a book he published jointly with his brother Ralf, *The Canadian Front in France and Flanders* (A. & C. Black, London, 1920). In a foreword entitled 'Artist's Note' Sheldon-Williams thanks the committee of the Canadian War Memorials for granting him the 'privilege of being their guest with the Canadian Forces in Flanders, France and Germany during a momentous period'. Although he was not living in Canada at the time he was invited to submit work to the jury to select Canadian art for the British Empire Exhibition in 1923. He had stated at this time that he considered himself 'a Canadian artist by adoption'.

Sheldon-Williams suffered a severe nervous breakdown after completing his Canadian War Memorial paintings. He spent a few years in Porto Maurizio in Italy until he recovered his health. He wrote and illustrated two books: *A Dawdle in France*, which was published by A. & C. Black in 1926, and a companion volume, *A Dawdle in Lombardy and Venice*, which followed two years later. In 1922 he had been elected a member of the Royal Institute of Painters in London.

Sheldon-Williams died in Tunbridge Wells on 30 November 1940.

His Boer War works include his 22 illustrations in the two volumes of *After Pretoria: the Guerilla War*. His drawing *Ride for Life* was featured on the cover of Part 67. These illustrations are mainly equestrian scenes and often bear the caption 'drawn from life'. The Africana Museum possesses one of his works, *The Sinews of War* (W251). This, or an identical drawing but possibly larger, appeared as a facsimile on page 300 of *After Pretoria: the Guerilla War* (it was the first illus-

1 I. Sheldon-Williams' *Soldiers in a Mess Tent* was probably done for reproduction in an as yet unidentified publication.
2 Inglis Sheldon-Williams often portrayed himself in his work. This is one of two self-portraits in *Soldiers in a Mess Tent*. The other is the figure seated on the extreme left.
3 This wash drawing by I. Sheldon-Williams depicts Boers in British uniforms attacking the 17th Lancers at Elands River Poort.

tration of his to appear in the book). Strangely enough the facsimile is signed, but the original — which is damaged — is not. (Sheldon-Williams signed most of his works characteristically with his initial through the first letter of his name, almost like a dollar sign. Occasionally only the initials 'I.S.W.' were used.)

The Sinews of War has an inscription on the label below reading: "The Sinews of War" from a watercolour by Inglis Sheldon-Williams and drawn in black and white by himself. A draught of horses being brought by Indian coolies from Cape Town to the base remount camp at Stellenbosch, Boer War – 1901 Cape Colony.' When the catalogue of pictures was compiled, all that the note on the artist said was 'Nothing is known of the artist'.

Apart from the 39 works offered at his exhibition in London, a few of Sheldon-Williams's other Boer War works are extant. The National Army Museum in London has four works of that period:
1. *Passage of the Vaal*. Signed and dated 1 Johannesburg 1900.
2. *An aide-de-camp on horseback in tropical dress*. Pencil and watercolour.
3. and 4. Two sketches of mounted horses. Pencil and watercolour.

The Imperial War Museum has no Boer War works by Sheldon-Williams (its collection starts with World War I) but it has one watercolour done by him in France at that time. Others of that period were offered for sale to the museum by his daughter in 1957 but, because of a lack of funds, were not purchased.

The British Museum has five Sheldon-Williams pictures in its collection, one English and three Italian landscapes and a watercolour sketch of Field-Marshal Sir Henry Wilson inscribed 'Captain Wilson, Headquarters Staff 1900'. This drawing was presented by Mrs Sheldon-Williams and a note in the departmental inventory, presumably based on information supplied by her, states that her husband 'was a trooper in Compton's Horse and did a series of portrait drawings of officers at headquarters'.

His works come up at auctions from time to time. At Sotheby's, Johannesburg, sale on 16 February 1978 two pencil drawings were sold. They were signed and inscribed: *Boer War Sergeant Major, S.A. War* and *Ford, S.A. War*.

The author has four watercolours by Sheldon-Williams, one of which was used in facsimile on page 305 of *After Pretoria: The Guerilla War: Third Man, an Uncoveted Distinction* is signed and dated 1901. The caption under the facsimile mentions that it was sketched from life. A further note adds:

When a party of Mounted Infantry or Yeomanry goes into action one man of each four holds the horses of his companions, two with his right hand, one besides his own with his left hand, which explains why 'No. 3' is the unfortunate man – and remains mounted himself, an excellent target for the enemy while the rest of his subsection seek cover. Among the Boers the horses are trained to stand still as soon as the reins are dropped over their heads, consequently all their men can fight instead of three out of four as with us.

Another watercolour, signed and dated 1902, was also used in facsimile, this time on p. 745 and is captioned 'Don't Fire; we're the 17th Lancers'. This picture depicts Boers clad in British uniforms attacking Captain Sandeman's 17th Lancers at Elands River Poort on 17 September 1901. A third watercolour purchased from the artist's daughter is untitled but shows 'Yeomen relaxing in a mess tent'. Mrs Eve Sheldon-Williams pointed out two self-portraits in the painting. Further examination of his illustrations reveal that he often used his likeness in his pictures. The fourth is entitled *Mule train near Johannesburg*.

The Glenbow Museum in Calgary, Alberta, Canada, has the following works by Sheldon-Williams. As can be seen, many of these were on offer at the Fine Arts Exhibition in 1902.

65.58.9. *Skirmishing in a Mealie Field, 1902*. (Two soldiers crawling in a field.) Watercolour and pencil.
65.58.10. *The Farrier Sergeant, 1902*. Watercolour.
65.58.11. *At the Cape – on Active Service, 1902*. (Soldier mounted.) Watercolour.
65.58.12. *A supplement to Bully Beef, Maitland Camp, 1902*. (Soldier carrying grapes and melon.) Watercolour.
65.58.13. *A Staff Officer, 1902*. Watercolour.
65.58.14R *A Day Off*. (Soldier seated smoking pipe.) Pencil and gouache.
65.58.14V *Native Woman with Umbrella Conversing with Mounted Soldier*. Pencil.
65.58.15R *Full Marching Order – a Sore Back* (Soldier standing and horse.) Pencil, gouache and watercolour.
65.58.15V *An Old Man in a Railway Station*. Pencil.
65.58.16. *Soldier Carrying Grapes and Melon* (study for 65.58.12.) Pencil and gouache.
65.58.17. *Hands Up*. Pencil and gouache.
65.58.18R *The Gun Team*. Pencil and gouache.
65.58.18V *Mounted Men Galloping Past Village*. Pencil and watercolour.
65.58.19R *Headlong*.
65.58.19V *Crowd of Indians, Soldiers, Lady*. Pencil and gouache.
65.58.20R *Hey! Any Milk?* Pencil and gouache.
65.58.20V *Signalling*. Pencil and gouache.
65.58.21. *Squadron-Gallop*. Pencil and gouache.
65.58.22. *Mounted Officer*. Pencil and gouache.
65.58.23R *Scout Riding in Under Fire*. Pencil and gouache.
65.58.23V *Figure Mounted on Camel and Elephants Walking through Crowded Town*. Pencil.
65.58.33.6 *Studies, South Africa*. 6 sheets – soldiers. Pencil.
65.58.33.7 *Bengalese Entraining at Naaupoort Junction, South Africa, April 1900*. Pencil and watercolour.
65.58.33.8 *Old Folks at Home, Johannesburg, 1900*. Pencil.
65.58.33.9 *Convoy at Dawn, South Africa*. Pencil.
65.58.33.10 *Sleeping Soldier, South Africa*. Pencil.
65.58.33.11 *Trouser Study, South Africa*. Pencil.
65.58.33.12 *Soldier, South Africa*. Pencil.
65.58.33.13 *Laughing Soldier, South Africa*. Pencil.
65.58.33.14 *Studies of Saddle and Hands, South Africa, 1899-1900*. Pencil.
65.58.33.15 *Soldiers, South Africa, 1900*. Watercolour and pencil.
65.58.33.16 *Figure, South Africa*. Conté.
65.58.33.17 *Figures and Horses South Africa*. Charcoal and pastel.
65.58.33.18 *At Ogilvie's Farm Klipfontein South Africa 2 October 1900*. Pencil.
65.58.33.19 *Lord Compton on Horseback, – Johannesburg, 1900*. Pencil.
65.58.24 *A Rough Road to Water, Kroonstad*. Pencil, gouache and watercolour.
65.58.25 *When Horses Mattered, a String of Remounts at Stellenbosch*. Pencil and gouache.
65.58.26 *Skirmish in a Mealie Field*. Pencil and gouache.
65.58.27 *A Vicarious Remount*. Pencil, gouache and watercolour.
65.58.28 *Pulling Hope*. Pencil and gouache.
65.58.29R *March at Ease*. Pencil and gouache.
65.58.29V *Three studies of the anatomy of a horse*. Pencil.
65.58.32R *We discuss the possibilities of replenishing our Larder, 1906*. Charcoal, pen-and-ink, and ink wash.
65.58.32V *Gnomes in a forest*. Pencil.
65.58.33.1 *Sketchbook, South Africa*. Pencil and watercolour.
65.58.33.2 *Scenes in South Africa*. Eleven sheets, various titles e.g. Pencil.
– *Lord Roberts' Column Marching into Pretoria*
– *Shrapnel*
– *Boer Wagon*
– *Trooper Foraging*
– *Trekking South*

– *Scouts Coming Back into Camp*
– *Viljoen's Drift from the Mealie Field*
65.58.33.3 *Studies, South Africa*. Eight sheets – landscape, figure studies, soldiers. Pencil.
65.58.33.4 *Studies, South Africa*. Twenty-seven sheets – scenes on board ship, soldiers, camp, ox-wagon, horses, weapons. Pencil.
65.58.33.5 *Studies, South Africa*. Twenty-five sheets – camp scenes, horse and figure studies. Pencil.

Africana Notes and News, June 1980, part 24, no. 2, pp. 56 ff. 'Inglis Sheldon-Williams, Frederick Judd Waugh: Two special artists of the Anglo Boer War,' by R. Greenwall; and March 1981, part 24, no. 5, pp. 170 ff. 'Some further notes on Inglis Sheldon-Williams' by R. Greenwall
Personal communication with Miss P. Ainslie, Art Dept., Glenbow Museum, Calgary, Alberta, Canada
Personal communication with Mrs E. Sheldon-Williams

SHEPARD, Newton, T.

Little is known about this artist, who was responsible for a poster which appeared in *The Sphere* on 3 March 1900, entitled *What children are doing for our soldiers*. An 'F.H.' Newton Shepard contributed to *The St James Budget* in 1898, *The Long Bow* in 1898 and *The Graphic* in 1902.
Thorpe, English Illustration, p. 125

SHEPPERSON, Claude Allin 1867-1921

Painter and illustrator. Shepperson was born in Beckenham, Kent, on 25 October 1867. He studied law before attending the Heatherley School in 1891. He furthered his art education in Paris, taking up mainly illustration and lithography, but watercolour painting as well. He was elected R.I. in 1900, A.R.A. in 1919 and A.R.W.S. in 1920.

Shepperson worked for numerous illustrated British magazines, including *English Illustrated Magazine*, *St Pauls*, *The Idler*, *Punch*, *Pick-Me-Up*, *The Sketch*, *Illustrated Bits*, *Cassell's Family Magazine*, *The Queen*, *Pall Mall Magazine*, *The Wide World Magazine*, *The Strand Magazine*, *Windsor Magazine*, and *The Illustrated London News*. Bradshaw, commenting on a *Punch* reader's remark that he was a 'Sketcher of Aristocrats', says he should rather be called 'an aristocrat who sketches'.

Shepperson's Boer War work is represented by two illustrations which appeared in *The Graphic*. One, on 7 April 1900, was entitled *The first man to arrive from Ladysmith: a scene in Maritzburg*, and the other, on 21 July 1900, *Soldiers of the Queen: A scene at Pietermaritzburg (railway station) on Mafeking day*.

Shepperson died in Chelsea on 30 December 1921.
Hofmeyr, Matton and Roets, Graphic Picture Index
Houfe, British Illustrators and Caricaturists, p. 452
Thorpe, English Illustration
Who was Who, vol. 2, p. 955

SHÉRIE, Ernest F.

Military illustrator. Shérie's work appeared in *Royal Magazine*, *Sketchy Bits*, *Pearson's Magazine* and *The Illustrated London News*. He also worked as a postcard artist for A. Mansel Vivian & Co. Details of his career are very sketchy, but he eventually became art editor of *The Strand Magazine* and in 1925 he contributed to A.W. Brown's *How to Draw for the Papers* (C. Arthur Pearson Ltd., 1925). He had this to say in the chapter on 'What Editors Want':

The budding illustrator can easily ascertain for himself the style of work required for *The Strand Magazine* by studying one or two recent issues.

It will be more helpful, therefore, if I confine these notes to a brief indication of the branches of illustration in which the demand is greater than the supply. An illustrator who wishes to produce work that will lift him out of the rut of the 'just-good-enough' artists should remember the following points:

Good draughtsmanship is not the only quality required of an illustrator. He should develop, with equal application, a sense of the dramatic. He should be able to imbue his characters with feeling and vitality, to convey, by the pose of a hand, the turn of a head or the flash of an eye, something of the emotional feeling that the author has created in the story. It must be remembered that the aim of an illustrator should be to arrest the attention of the reader as he carelessly turns the pages of the magazine, and (b) to arouse his interest in the characters or situation depicted, so that he is induced to read the story. These, of course, are not the sole purposes of magazine illustrators, but they are of primary importance.

There are exceptional opportunities for the illustrator who can draw a good type of modern young man, a charming and lady-like girl, dress them well and imbue them with sufficient feeling to obviate any impression that they have been carefully posed models. More often than not, the illustrator who draws a pretty girl cannot draw a good type of man — or vice versa; whilst the illustrator who can draw both cannot draw a horse, a dog, a motor-car, or some other item essential to the picture as described by the author. I mention this to emphasize the value of versatility.

There is also an inadequate supply of first-class pen draughtsmen. We would often like to have a really good line drawing as a change from the monotony of chalk and wash drawings, but so many line draughtsmen have turned their attention to the slightly cheaper style of work, for printing on coarse paper, that they have lost some of their delicacy of treatment.

For the *Wide World Magazine*, there are plenty of opportunities for capable illustrators who have good reference libraries and, if possible, a knowledge of foreign countries and 'types'. For instance, the ability to draw an African negro without making him look like a European with his face blackened, is a distinct asset. This magazine circulates largely among those interested in adventure, travel and exploration, and, therefore, correctness of detail in costumes, types, weapons, etc. is most important.

Artists who have a special knowledge of animals, birds, shipping, etc. and combine such qualifications with good figure drawing, are always in demand.

Shérie was fairly active during the War and contributed at least seven illustrations to *The Illustrated London News* between January and May 1900. Several others appeared in *Shurey's Illustrated* (often front page), *Shurey's Pictorial Budget* and *The Sphere*. He also illustrated *Briton or Boer* by George Chetwynd Griffith (T. V. White, London, 1897) and, by the same author, *Knave of Diamonds* (Arthur Pearson, London, 1899). His co-illustrator for this book was T. Ayton Symington.

Browne, How to Draw for the Papers
Byatt, Picture Postcards, *p. 181*
De Wet, Illustrated London News Index

Houfe, British Illustrators and Caricaturists, *p. 452*
SABIB, *vol. 2, pp. 443-444*
Thorpe, English Illustration

SHINDLER, H.L.

A children's book illustrator who contributed cartoons to *Judy* and *Fun* during the War.
Houfe, British Illustrators and Caricaturists, *p. 452*
Thorpe, English Illustration

SHUTE, A. Burnham

Illustrator of Edward Stratemeyer's *Between Boer and Briton; or, Two Boys' Adventures in South Africa*. The book, which had eight illustrations signed either 'A.B. Shute' or 'A. Burnham Shute', was published by Lee and Shepard in Boston in 1900.
SABIB, *vol. 4, p. 425*

SIJTHOFF, Gijsbertus Jan 1867-1949

Sijthoff was born in Delft on 6 August 1867. He was adept at lithography and his cartoons were produced in this manner for *Vooruitgang*. He was the only cartoonist who contributed to this periodical. Sijthoff married the painter Johanna Bastiana Van Rijswijk.
Scheen, Nederlandse Beeldende Kunstenaars, *vol. 2, p. 420*

SIME, Sydney Herbert 1867-1941

Draughtsman, caricaturist and book illustrator. Sime was born in Manchester in 1867. After working as a miner he eventually entered the Liverpool School of Art. After his graduation he worked for *Pick-Me-Up*. He was influenced by both Beardsley and Raven-Hill (see p. 192). He became editor of *Eureka* and joint editor of *The Idler*.

During the War Sime was responsible for the illustration, *At 'the Patriotic'*, which was published on p. 64 of *The Muster Roll of Angus*.

Sime died in Worplesdon, Surrey, in March 1941.
Houfe, British Illustrators and Caricaturists, *p. 454*
Waters, British Artists, *p. 301*

SIMKIN, Richard 1840-1926 1

Military painter and illustrator. Simkin was one of Britain's best-known Victorian painters of this kind and he even ran a studio at the military camp at Aldershot. His speciality was uniforms. He was also known as a designer of posters for military recruitment. Simkin died in Herne Bay, Kent, in 1926.

Besides contributing to *Army and Navy Gazette* he produced a number of 'shilling' colour books. The *Index to British Military Prints* lists the following publications which included examples of his work:
1. *Simkin's Great Powers of the World* (c.1898)
2. *Simkin's Indian and Colonial Forces*
3. *Simkin's Life in the Army* (1889)
4. *Simkin's Military Scraps* (1890)
5. *Simkin's Our Armies* (1890)

6. *Simkin's Our Soldiers* (1890)
7. *Simkin's Our Soldiers in Egypt* (1882)
8. *Simkin's Royal Military Tournament* (1895)
9. *Simkin's Soldiers of the Century* (c.1901) This publication features 'South Africa 1899-1901' and a 'Cavalry Trooper, South Africa, 1900'.
10. *Simkin's The Army*
11. *Simkin's Types of the British Army*. These were published as supplements to the *Army and Navy Gazette* between 7 January 1888 and 6 September 1902:
No. 148, published on 7 April 1900, showed Types of Naval Forces: Natal Mounted Police. Trooper, Review Order. Natal Carbineers Officer, Review Order. Officers: Durban Light Infantry, Review Order. Natal Police, Service Kit. Imperial Light Horse, Service Kit. Trooper, Natal Carbiniers, Service Kit.
No. 149, published on 5 May 1900, showed Imperial Yeomanry. City Imperial Volunteers, Private, Officer Imperial Yeomanry, Service Marching Order.
No. 153, published 1 September 1900, showed Types of Cape Colony and Rhodesian Regiments. Rhodesian Horse; Duke of Edinburgh's Own Rifles and Cape Mounted Rifles (Police).
12. *Simkin's Uniforms of the British Army* (1886)
13. *Simkin's War in Egypt* (1883)
14. *Simkin's where Glory Calls* (1887)
15. *Simkin's World's Armies* (1901)

The National Army Museum has two Boer War works by Simkin:
Charge of the Gordon Highlanders at Obelisk Kloof South Africa 1899 and *Across the Veldt: the Royal Inniskilling Fusiliers, on the march in South Africa*. The author has three of Simkin's watercolours: *The Battle of Talvera, Royal Fusiliers Service dress 1900*, and *Imperial Yeomanry in action South Africa 1900*.

In 1986 Maggs Brothers in London offered five Boer War watercolours by Simkin:
1. *British infantry attacking a Kopje, South Africa 1900*
2. *Crossing the Vaal River, South Africa 1900*
3. *British Infantry in Action — South Africa 1900*
4. *General Officer and Staff, South Africa 1902*
5. *Imperial Yeomanry in action*

The Royal Collection at Windsor has seven watercolours by Simkin, none of which represents the Boer War. The compilers of their catalogue mention that he 'was a prolific but spiritless painter and draughtsman', that 'his work is most unreliable' and that 'all the drawings in their possession contain palpable errors'.

Despite his obvious deficiencies, Simkin's prints and original watercolours are much sought after in England today.

Simkin was also noted as a postcard artist and contributed to C.W. Faulkner's 'Empire series'. These Boer War related cards were published in 1900 and used Simkin's work to illustrate the six cards in their '20 series'.
British Military Costume Prints
Byatt, Picture Postcards
Dawnay and Miller, Military Drawings and Paintings
Houfe, British Illustrators and Caricaturists, *p. 454*

SIMON, G. F.

Simon was a trooper in the Natal Carbineers. He is recorded as being a special service member who was in Ladysmith during the siege. He was responsible for some frontline artist sketches which were redrawn for publication in *The Sphere*. Carter comments (page 18): 'Another illustration of the war's amenity to be found on page 12 depicting the friendly meeting of General Buller and Christian Botha. Mr Finnemore's

Imperial Yeomanry in action South Africa 1900, a watercolour by Richard Simkin. Despite the wooden appearance of his soldiers, Simkin's works (both prints and originals) are very sought after nowadays. When the British mounted infantry went into action at least one soldier was always assigned to look after his comrades' horses.

work is based on a workmanlike sketch by Trooper Simon, who was present. The hill behind is the fateful Majuba, and the incident illustrated is the consultation, which proved to be fruitless, on terms of surrender; Botha eventually refusing to give in unconditionally.' This illustration was published on the front page of *The Sphere* on 7 July 1900.

Carter, War Artists in S.A., *pp. 12 & 18*
Stalker (ed.), Natal Carbineers

SIMPSON, Charles

This artist was responsible for a few facsimile Boer War illustrations in *The Sphere*. Many art dictionaries list a Charles Walter Simpson, but with a birth date of 1885. It is unlikely that someone this young would have been employed by a paper. *The Sphere* does mention, however, that Charles Simpson is 'our artist in Natal' which makes him more likely to be an amateur resident or soldier.

SINGFRAU

Cartoonist responsible for the satirical German postcard *Edward's Dream*.

SINGLETON, John

Illustrator, compiler and publisher of *The Battle-fields of Natal Revisited* (Durban, 1900). In the book Singleton, who describes himself as a lithographer, thanks 'Mr W.A. Squire, the correspondent of the *Natal Mercury* during the Natal Campaign, for his assistance'.

SABIB, *vol. 4, p. 218*

SKIP

Melbourne Outpost cartoonist.
Review of Reviews, *vol. 22, July–Dec. 1900*

SLEVOGT, Max 1868-1932   1

Genre painter. Slevogt was born at Landshut, Germany, on

8 October 1868. As a follower of the Impressionist school he was a friend of Cézanne. He studied in Munich and at the Académie Julian. He returned to Berlin in 1901 and became closely associated with Max Liebermann and the *Sezession*. Along with the latter and Corinth, Slevogt is considered the strongest exponent of Naturalism in Germany.

During the War he contributed a sketch entitled *Der Staatswagen Chamberlain* to *Der Burenkrieg*. The illustration, which is signed 'M.S.', shows dead bodies being transported on a horse-drawn cart.

Slevogt died in Neukastel on 20 September 1923.
Bénézit, Dictionnaire antique, *vol. 7, p. 799*
Der Burenkrieg, *p. 32*
Piper, Dictionary of Painting, etc., *p. 166*

S.M.

Postcard illustrator, possibly a soldier, who illustrated at least three postcards produced in South Africa before Christmas 1900 by an unknown publisher. All three are initialled 'S.M.'. The unnumbered cards are as follows:
1. *A Merry Christmas and a happy new year from the Boer Campaign, Christmas Eve on the Battle Field* (printed on green card; see back cover).
2. *Greetings from the Boer Campaign: Review on Church Square* (printed on lilac card).
3. *Greetings from the Boer Campaign* (printed on buff card).

SMALL, William 1843-1929   2

Artist and illustrator. William Small was born in Edinburgh on 27 May 1843. He exhibited at the R.S.A. schools before going to London in 1865. He had worked in Edinburgh in the art department of Messrs Nelson, Publishers. He was a very quick worker and very prolific and at one time was reputed to have been one of the highest paid artists for *The Graphic*, earning 60 guineas for a double-page illustration. Small was elected a member of the R.I. in 1883. He contributed to several illustrated periodicals and illustrated a number of books.

An engraving and accompanying article about Small in *The Graphic* in 1890 mentioned that

> he began life as a wood engraver to his thorough knowledge of which craft may, perhaps, be partly attributed the excellence of his drawing. No artist puts more "colour" into his black and white work than Mr Small. In regard to his all-round strength as a draughtsman we need merely say that Mr Black the novelist, in a recent article on the illustration of books, remarked that Mr Small seemed equally at home with every sort of scene from a Highland Salmon Stream to a London Ballroom.

During the Boer War several of Small's illustrations appeared in *The Graphic* and *With the Flag to Pretoria*. Two of Small's paintings are in the Africana Museum:
1. *S76. Entry of Troops into Mafeking 1900*. Inscription on the back in pencil: 'Entry of Troops into Mafeking (Small)'

and in ink 'June 30/00'. Wash drawing. Unsigned. Reproduced in *The Graphic* on 30 June 1900, with the caption:
> Drawn by W. Small from material supplied by Major F.D. Baillie, Special Correspondent of the *Morning Post* title: 'The Relief of Mafeking: the march past of the relieving forces before Lieutenant General Baden-Powell' – 'The relieving column,' Major Baillie writes, 'had previously camped out on the Imperial reserve, and had thence passed rapidly to the north of Mafeking to indulge the townspeople in the rare treat of seeing their foes bombarded and fleeing hastily from McMullen's laager, whence for months they had vexed us. The Town Guard were formed up facing Dixon's Hotel, where General Baden-Powell took his stand supported by Colonels Mahon and Plumer and their staffs. Then men from all quarters of the globe marched passed in this little African border town, dirty and unkempt, but the outward and visible signs of a mighty Empire, and Mafeking cheered itself hoarse. It was actually relieved, though it couldn't quite realize it even yet. With the exception of the RHA every man on parade was a volunteer.'

2. S77. *News from the Outer World – Ladysmith*. Inscription in pencil on the back: 'News from the Outer World Ladysmith (Wm Small)' and the date-stamp 2 April 1900. Wash drawing. Unsigned. The compiler of the catalogue says that there was no *The Graphic* on that date. There was, however, a 'Special double Mafeking and Ladysmith number' which was published out of sequence on that date and Small's illustration was reproduced in it.

Small often signed his work with his initials only. He died on 23 December 1929.
Caw, Scottish Painters
Hofmeyr, Matton and Roets, Graphic Picture Index
Houfe, British Illustrators and Caricaturists, *p. 457*
Kennedy, Pictures in the Africana Museum, *vol. 4, p. 129*
Verbeek, Early Natal Art

All right !....

6

7

8

Waters, British Artists, *vol. 1, p. 304*
Who was Who, *vol. 3, p. 1247*

SMEDLEY, A. Constance
This cartoonist produced work during the War for *The King.*

S., M.F.C. or G. *see* M.F.C.S.

SMITH, A.T. fl. 1899-1914 1
Cartoonist. Smith contributed wooden doll scenes for *Punch* between 1902 and 1914. He is also known to have contributed to *Fun*.

During the War Smith produced a cartoon, published in *The King* on 28 April 1900, which lampooned the home-based artist. In two parts, it showed him *As we fancy him: The shells burst around me with horrible slaughter, but I stood cool and firm in the midst of the carnage* and *As he really is: Mr. Jones wants two more sketches of Buller crossing the Tugela at once.* The whole is subtitled 'With our special artist at the front'.

Houfe, British Illustrators and Caricaturists, *p. 458*

SMITH, W. Thomas 1862-?
Portrait, figure and historical painter. Smith worked in London in 1890. He was a contributor to *The Quiver, Good Cheer,* and *Boy's Own Paper.* Houfe says he may have emigrated to Canada before 1927.

9

During the War Smith contributed an illustration to *The Illustrated London News.* Entitled *War in South Africa: Music in Camp,* it was drawn from a sketch by P. Kennedy and appeared on 3 August 1901.

Houfe, British Illustrators and Caricaturists, *p. 459*

SMYTHE, Ernest fl. 1896-1900
Illustrator and watercolourist specializing in hunting subjects. The Victoria and Albert Museum has examples of his work. He contributed to *The Sketch* in 1896 and *The Illustrated London News* in 1899.

His Boer War work can be found in *The Regiment* and *Under the Union Jack.*

Houfe, British Illustrators and Caricaturists, *p. 459*

SOMERVILLE, Howard 1873-1940
Painter, illustrator and etcher. Somerville was born in Dundee in 1873. He initially trained as an engineer but later became an artist. In 1899 he went to London where he contributed to *Punch* and *Moonshine.* He also worked in New York and Glasgow.

During the War Somerville's cartoons were published in *Moonshine.*

Houfe, British Illustrators and Caricaturists, *p. 461*
Thorpe, English Illustration

SOMM, Henry or Henri 1844-1907 3
This was the pseudonym used by François Clement Sommier. Somm was a genre painter, illustrator, caricaturist, etcher and silhouettist.

He was born in Rouen in 1844. He exhibited at the fourth Impressionist exhibition at 28 Avenue de l'Opéra, Paris, between 10 April and 10 May 1879. Among his fellow exhibitors were Degas, Gauguin, Monet and Pissarro.

Somm's Boer War work appeared in *Le Rire* in which his 'Echos du Rire' was a regular feature. Often his cartoons were unsigned.

The author has three of Somm's pen-and-ink caricatures relating to the Boer War: *All right, Lord Kitchener,* and *Au Transvaal.* These were published in *Le Rire* in the 'Echos du Rire' series on 31 March 1900 (281), 27 October 1900 (312), and 30 March 1901 (334) respectively.

Somm died in Paris on 15 March 1907.
Bénézit, Dictionnaire antique, *vol. 8, p. 18*
Osterwalder, and Hubschmid and Bouret (eds.), Dictionnaire des Illustrateurs, *p. 994*

SOPER, George 1870-1942 3
Etcher, wood engraver, watercolourist and illustrator. Soper

was born in London in 1870 and educated at Ramsgate. From 1894 he exhibited at leading London galleries, including the Royal Academy, R.E. and R.B.A. He was elected a member of the R.O.E. in 1918 and the R.E. in 1920.

In an article entitled 'The etchings and ground points of George Soper RE' in *The Studio* (vol. 80) the well-known art critic, Malcolm Salaman, goes into great detail about Soper's ability as an etcher. He mentions, among other things, that 'it is no easy thing for a practised book illustrator who has been habitually adapting his art to picture making at the suggestion or dictation of authors and publishers to emancipate his artistic outlook and embark upon the adventure of a pictorial free-lance, choosing at will the motive that appeals for the spontaneous utterance of the instinctive etcher'. Soper studied etching with Sir Frank Short.

During the War Soper's work appeared in *The Illustrated London News, Cassell's Magazine, Boy's Own Paper,* and *Chums.* It was in *The Graphic,* however, that most of his Boer War work was published, with over 40 illustrations being reproduced between December 1899 and 14 June 1902. Soper also contributed several illustrations to *The Graphic's* sister weekly, *The Golden Penny.* Each week, 'Heroes of the

---

1 Max Slevogt's gruesome illustration *Der Staatswagen Chamberlain* was published in the German publication *Der Burenkrieg.*
2 William Small, contributor to *The Graphic.*
3 A.T. Smith's cartoon *With our special artist at the Front* poked fun at the home-based artist passing himself off as a 'front liner'. It was published in *The King* on 28 April 1900. See entry on A.T. Smith for full caption.
4 A pen-and-ink caricature of Lord Kitchener by Henry Somm, used in *Le Rire* on 30 March 1901.
5 This pen-and-ink drawing of Chamberlain and Queen Victoria was done by Henry Somm for *Le Rire's* 27 October 1900 edition.
6 Henry Somm probably produced this pen-and-ink cartoon strip for reproduction in a publication. Note his depiction of De Wet (upper right).
7 George Soper's watercolour depicting Lord Roberts's son Freddie trying to save the guns at Colenso. Roberts jnr. later died of his wounds sustained in this battle and was awarded a posthumous Victoria Cross. Several artists depicted this heroic event.
8 A watercolour by George Soper showing Major Milton helping a dismounted soldier onto his horse, reproduced in *The Golden Penny.*
9 *The Graphic's* sister weekly *The Golden Penny* reproduced this watercolour by George Soper showing Lieutenant Brierly of the Lancashire Fusiliers holding a kopje against the Boers. The event took place on 7 December 1899 near Enslin.

Wat wenschen hem | Was wünschen ihm die | Qu'est-ce que les nations
de Volken van Europa? | Völker Europas? | de l'Europe lui souhaitent?

War' – stories of personal bravery accompanied by illustrations often done by Soper – was featured. Three of these original drawings are in the author's collection:

1. *Major Milton helping a dismounted trooper to his horse. Having himself to walk through a rain of bullets* (20 January 1900).

2. *The son of Lord Roberts attempting to save the guns at Colenso* (24 February 1900).

3. *The King's Own Yorkshire Light Infantry. Lieutenant E.C. Brierly of the Lancashire Fusiliers holding a kopje against the Boers for seven hours by which the communications were saved* (10 March 1900).

The Mendelssohn Collection in the Library of Parliament, Cape Town, has a number of original Boer War works by Soper:

1. *Christmas on the veld.* (This appeared in *After Pretoria: the Guerilla War* and in *The Graphic* on 18 January 1902.)

2. *Troops finding Boer clothing.* (*The Graphic*, 7 December 1901.)

3. *Traction engines at Maritzburg.* (The special double number, 2 April 1902.)

4. *Bound for the front. Transport for the relief column. Armoured train ready to reconnoitre.* (2 June 1900)

5. *Colonel Haigh reconnoitering the Stormberg Mountains in a blizzard. After a sketch by Lionel James.* (*The Graphic*, 6 July 1901, and *After Pretoria: the Guerilla War, p. 491.*)

6. *A civilian passes from military authorities during the Ladysmith siege.* (Special double number p. 7, from a 'sketch by W.T. Maud'.)

7. *Auction of loot taken at Lubbe's Farm held at Belmont.* (*The Graphic*, 24 February 1900.)

8. *Bethune's Decoys, in the Orange River colony: Beating the Boers at their own game.* (After a sketch by Lionel James. Appeared in *The Graphic*, 20 April 1901. There is an appeal from Soper to the art editor on the back of this illustration: 'Please make a very nice block Monday 3 o'clock'. This illustration also appeared in *After Pretoria: The Guerilla War*, p. 348.)

9. *Making the best of things. Johannesburg refugees at Durban at the beginning of the war.* (*The Graphic*, 16 December 1899, and *After Pretoria: The Guerilla War*, p. 514.)

10. *The Band, refugee camp in the Transvaal.* (*The Graphic*, 19 October 1901.)

11. *Men drinking rum on the Queen's birthday.* (*The Graphic*, 11 August 1900.)

12. *Colonel Benson's trek.* (*The Graphic*, 14 December 1901.)

13. *Rimington's Tigers taking a hill* (*The Graphic*, 7 July 1900.)

The Africana Museum, Johannesburg, has eight original drawings by Soper. Six are of Boer War interest:

1. S138. *Rush of the Leicesters for Lunch 1899.* Signed George Soper. It was reproduced in *The Graphic* on 30 December 1899. Drawn by George Soper from a photograph by the Hon. Mrs Evelyn Cecil.

2. S139. *With General French in the Transvaal 1901.* Inscription on the back in ink: 'With General French in the Transvaal' and in pencil 'March 9/01. Monday morning'. Wash drawing. Signed George Soper. Reproduced in *The Graphic* on 9 March 1901, p. 351. Captioned: 'Drawn by George Soper from a photograph by A.R. Smith. The General addressing the 1st Suffolk Regiment on parade at Middelberg. With General French in the Transvaal.'

3. S140. *Veterinary Captain Farrell Saving the Horses.* Inscription on the back in ink 'Veterinary Surgeon Capt. Farrell saving horses from the Boers – March 16/01'. Wash drawing. Signed George Soper. Reproduced in *The Graphic* on 16 March 1901, p. 396, with the title *Veterinary Captain Farrell saving Artillery horses from capture by the Boers. Captain Farrell was taken prisoner but escaped.*

4. S141. *Friend or foe? Scouts at Work 1900.* Inscription on the back in pencil 'Intercepting a convoy – Scouts at work Friend or Foe'. Date stamp 31 March 1900. Wash drawing. Signed George Soper. Reproduced in *The Graphic*, 31 March 1900, p. 458, with the inscription: 'Drawn by George Soper from a sketch by Lieutenant Angus MacNeill. Title 'Friend or Foe? Scouts at Work'. On February 19 Montmorency's Scouts went out to east of Molteno to endeavour to intercept a Boer Commando, who were reported retiring that way from Penhoek. It was getting dark, raining hard, and a party of mounted men were seen approaching about 150 strong. They were within 600 yards of the scouts, who were hidden on a Kopje, covering them with their carbines. Captain Montmorency, however, thinking there was first a chance of their being a patrol of the Cape Police, ordered his men not to fire. By their subsequent movements it was evident, though, the men were Boers. Capt. Montmorency, it will be remembered, was subsequently killed in a skirmish near Dordrecht and the famous little body of scouts is now commanded by Lieutenant Angus MacNeill.'

5. S142. *Taking of Ladysmith Hill 1900.* Inscription on back in pencil 'Taking of Ladysmith Hill' and in ink 'April 7/1900'. Wash drawing. Signed George Soper. Reproduced in *The*

Graphic on 7 April 1900, p. 491, with the caption 'Drawn by George Soper from a sketch by Capt. W.S. Carey', and the title *The taking of Ladysmith Hill by Kitchener's Brigade and the West Yorkshire Regiment.*

6. S143. *Departure of Sir George White from Ladysmith 1900.* Inscription on back in pencil 'Departure of Sir George White from Ladysmith' and date stamp '14 Apr 00'. Wash drawing. Signed George Soper. Reproduced in *The Graphic* on 14 April 1900, p. 535, with the inscription 'Drawn by George Soper – from photographs by S.S. Watkinson' and the title *Sir George White bidding farewell to his old regiment on leaving Ladysmith.* The text says that Sir George left Ladysmith for Pietermaritzburg on 9 March. The guard of honour and the pipers were from the Gordon Highlanders.

The Africana Museum has two further wash drawings by Soper which do not have Boer War relevance: S144 *Boer contingent in Somaliland 1903* and S307 *Capt. Brand's patrol Charging the Matabele 1896.*

Soper illustrated Fred Whishaw's *The Three Scouts: A Story of the Boer War* (Griffith Farran Browne & Co, London, 1900).

Soper's daughter, Eileen Alice (born in 1905), became a very well-known artist and at the age of 14 she was the subject of an article in vol. 84 of *The Studio*. Soper died in Welwyn, Hertfordshire, on 13 August 1942.

Hofmeyr, Matton and Roets, Graphic Picture Index
Houfe, British Illustrators and Caricaturists, *p. 46*
Kennedy, Pictures in the Africana Museum, *vol. 4, pp. 138-139 and vol. 7, p. 236*
SABIB, *vol. 4, p. 769*
The Studio, *vol. 80, p. 98 and vol. 84, p. 155*
Who was Who, *vol. 4, p. 1081*

SORANUS
Uilenspiegel cartoonist.

SOREL, A.
French cartoonist and illustrator whose Boer War work is noted in *Echo des Marches* and *Le Franc Normand.*

SOWERBY, Millicent 1878-1967
Watercolour painter and postcard artist. Her father was the owner of a glass factory that produced 'Sowerby Pressed Glass'. She worked for several postcard publishers during her career.

Her Boer War contribution is found on a postwar postcard showing a young boy in military uniform. The caption reads: 'South Africa: South Africa beyond the Sea. Oh that's the sunny home for me! But I have heard the British Drum, Beating *to Arms* and here I come !' The publisher was Henry Frowde, and Hodder & Stoughton produced this card as part of their Sons of the Empire series.

Coysh, A.W. The Dictionary of Picture Postcards in Britain 1894-1939

SPADA
French cartoonist whose work appeared in *La Caricature.* One cover cartoon illustration by Spada appeared on 28 June 1902 (issue 1174) entitled *Hantise* (obsession).

SPAVEN, A. H.
Spaven was responsible for a picture of the *Ariosto* conveying the City Imperial Volunteers to the Cape, which appeared in *The Graphic* on 6 January 1900.

Hofmeyr, Matton and Roets, Graphic Picture Index

SPEED, Lancelot 1860-1931
Black and white artist and book illustrator. Speed was born on 13 June 1860 in London. His education was at Rugby and at Clare College, Cambridge. He contributed to *The Illustrated London News, The Illustrated Sporting & Dramatic News, The Sphere, Punch, English Illustrated Magazine* and *Good Words.* He published *The Limbersnigs,* which he wrote and

illustrated, in 1896. Among the well-known books illustrated by him was the 1904 Pearson edition of *Grimm's Fairy Tales.*

Speed's Boer War work appeared in *With the Flag to Pretoria.* He was also responsible for the illustrations, which were in colour in some editions, of William Andrew Johnston's *The Kopje Farm* (Collins' Clear-Type Press, London, 1900).

Houfe, British Illustrators and Caricaturists, *p. 461*
Osterwalder, and Hubschmid and Bouret (eds.),
Dictionnaire des Illustrateurs, *p. 1001*
Peppin and Micklethwait, British Book Illustrators, *pp. 282-283*
SABIB, *vol. 2, p. 697*
Thorpe, English Illustration
Waters, British Artists, *pp. 309-310*
Who was Who, *vol. 3, p. 1269*

SPEENHOFF, Jacobus Hendrikus (Koos) 1869-1945

Speenhoff was born in Kralingen, the Netherlands, on 23 October 1869. After studying drawing at the Rotterdam Academy Speenhoff became a regular contributor of cartoons and illustrations to *Der Wahre Jacob, Woord en Beeld,* Rotterdam *Dagblad,* and Rotterdam *Weekblad.* He also illustrated H.G. Wells's *War of the Worlds.*

In an interview on 'Dutch humorous artists' by Arthur Lord in *The Strand Magazine* (vol. 24, pp. 90-97), Speenhoff mentions that he was influenced by Degas and Caran d'Ache, but his greatest idol was Edward Tennyson Reed of *Punch.* Speenhoff died in The Hague on 3 March 1945.

Bénézit, Dictionnaire antique, *vol. 8, p. 47*
Scheen, Nederlandse Beeldende Kunstenaars, *vol. 2, p. 375*
The Strand Magazine *vol. 24, p. 96*

SPENCE, Percy Frederick Seaton 1868-1933

Spence was born in Sydney in 1868, but he spent most of his youth in Fiji. He was a contributor to the *Sydney Bulletin* in about 1890. In 1895 he went to Britain where he worked for *Black & White* and *The Graphic* and later for *The Sphere, Punch, Harper's Monthly, Ludgate Monthly, The Illustrated London News, Pall Mall Magazine* and *Windsor Magazine.* Two of his pictures were exhibited at the Royal Academy during the exhibition of 1899 and his work was accepted for three consecutive years. In 1901 he was responsible for the illustrations to *Britain's Austral Empire* which comprised mostly portraits of leading Australian politicians of the time. He returned to Sydney in 1905 and in 1910 he provided 75 illustrations for a work entitled *Australia,* which was published in London the following year. Spence returned to London where he died in August 1933.

Spence's work is represented in the Australian National Gallery and the Mitchell Library in Sydney, and his pencil sketches of R.L. Stevenson and Phil May are in the National Portrait Gallery in London. Other portraits are at the University of Sydney and the Sydney High Court. A painting done in 1913, *Australian Fleet entering Sydney Harbour,* hangs in Buckingham Palace.

Spence's Boer War work appeared in *With the Flag to Pretoria* and *The Graphic.* He contributed over 20 illustrations to the latter between January 1900 and 13 July 1901.

Australian Encyclopaedia
Graves, Royal Academy
Houfe, British Illustrators and Caricaturists, *p. 461*
Thorpe, English Illustration

SPEX

An artist with this pseudonym was responsible for five anti-Boer cartoons (Suckling & Co., London, 1899) entitled *Mr. Kruger in Peace and War.* The five cartoons were entitled:
1. *Majuba: Mr. Kruger teaches the young Boer how to shoot the British.*
2. *Put your trust in Providence, but stick to your Mausers.*
3. *That ought to make Mr Bull sit up.*
4. *Staggering Humanity.*

5. *Finis.*
SABIB, *vol. 4, p. 365*

SPOONER, Horace H. (Jack) ?-1900

Sydney Evening News and *Town and Country Journal* correspondent who arrived in South Africa in 1899. He accompanied Gen. French into Kimberley and was present at Paardeberg when Cronje surrendered. He died in the Deelfontein hospital of typhoid fever in 1900, soon after the British occupation of Bloemfontein.

In 1978 Wright and Lloyd's catalogue of Boer War books offered a pen-and-ink self portrait of Spooner in khaki officer's drill on board ship en route to South Africa. The monument to the special correspondents in St Paul's Cathedral includes Spooner's name.

Wright, W.T. & H.H. Lloyd, The Great Boer War: Catalogue of Fine Africana relating to the South African War 1899-1902, *December 1978*
Wallace, R.L., Australians at the Boer War
Gildea, For Remembrance

SPURRIER, Steven 1878-1961

Landscape and figure painter, illustrator and poster designer. Spurrier was born in London on 13 July 1878. At the age of 17 he was apprenticed to a silversmith and studied art during the evenings at the Heatherley School. He worked as an illustrator for *The Illustrated London News* and *The Strand Magazine.* He exhibited at the Royal Academy from 1913. He was elected R.B.A. in 1933, A.R.A. in 1945 and R.A. in 1952.

Spurrier's Boer War works, which were not numerous, appeared in *With the Flag to Pretoria.*

He died in London in March 1961.
Houfe, British Illustrators and Caricaturists, *p. 462*
Peppin and Micklethwait, British Book Illustrators, *p. 283*
The Studio, *vol. 83, pp. 158-162 and vol. 84, pp. 95-98*

SRICK

Le Bon Vivant and *La Caricature* cartoonist.

STACEY, Walter Sydney 1846-1929

Landscape and figure painter and illustrator. Stacey was born in London in 1846. He studied art at the Royal Academy schools. He worked at various times for *The Cornhill Magazine, The Quiver, The Strand Magazine, Good Words, Chums, The Temple, The Wide World Magazine, Cassell's Family Magazine* and *Black & White.*

Stacey is best known as an illustrator, particularly of boys' adventure stories. Thorpe describes him as a 'deft and graceful artist with the pen' and his pen drawings as 'interesting, well drawn and splendidly adapted for reproduction.' Stacey occasionally signed his work with the initials 'W.S.S.'.

Stacey's only Boer War contributions noted are the illustrations to Phoebe Allen's *Mafeking Day: A Snapshot from Real Life* (The Society for the Propagation of Christian Knowledge, London, 1901 and E. and J.B. Young & Co., New York).

Houfe, British Illustrators and Caricaturists, *p. 462*
Osterwalder, and Hubschmid and Bouret (eds.),
Dictionnaire des Illustrateurs, *p. 1005*
Peppin and Micklethwait, British Book Illustrators, *p. 284*
Thorpe, English Illustration

STALLER, G. F.   1

Staller was responsible for an illustration on a double postcard, published in Amsterdam by C. Cnobloch. The trilingual card (Dutch, French and German) was entitled *Who is the most hated person in Europe? – Chamberlain.*

STAMPA, George Loraine 1875-1951

Stampa was born in London on 29 November 1875. The son of an architect, he was educated at the Lambeth School. He studied art at the Heatherley School in about 1892 and at the Royal Academy schools from 1895 to 1900.

Stampa worked for *Punch* from 1895 until 1950 and con-

centrated mostly on Cockney urchin and street scenes. His Boer War cartoons can be found in that magazine.

Stampa was described as a Bohemian with a similar lifestyle to Phil May. He died on 25 May 1951.
Houfe, British Illustrators and Caricaturists, *p. 462*
Peppin and Micklethwait, British Book Illustrators, *p. 284*
Thorpe, English Illustration

STANIFORTH, Joseph Morewood 1863-1921   1

Staniforth was a cartoonist and humorist who worked for *The Western Mail* in Cardiff. He was educated at St John's School, Cardiff, and was apprenticed to the lithographic department of *The Western Mail* in 1878.

After about 10 years Staniforth joined the editorial staff of the paper and began illustrating current events. He contributed daily cartoons to *The Evening Express* and in 1893 started drawing a daily cartoon for *The Western Mail,* which he continued to do until his death.

Staniforth was a member of the South Wales Art Society from its inception in 1888 and he exhibited regularly at its annual exhibition. He produced a series of postcards under the initials 'J.M.S.'.

His Boer War work is found in the newspapers he represented and in a special publication entitled *Cartoons of the Boer War* which was published by *The Western Mail* in 1900. The 101 pro-British cartoons, signed 'J.M.S.', were originally printed in *The Western Mail* from August 1899 to August 1900. At least three editions were published. The first cartoon, *The Silent Sphinx,* was dated 30 August 1900 in the first edition. The date was corrected to August 1899 in subsequent editions. The prewar cartoons were initially pacifist, but once the War started they became decidedly jingoistic.

Staniforth died on 17 December 1921.
Houfe, British Illustrators and Caricaturists, *p. 463*
Who was Who, *vol. 2, p. 988*

STANILAND, Charles Joseph 1838-1916

Genre, historical and marine painter. Staniland was born in Kingston-upon-Hull on 19 June 1838. He studied at the Birmingham School of Art, Heatherley School, R.C.A., and the Royal Academy schools in 1861. From that year he exhibited at the principal London galleries, particularly at the R.I. Staniland was elected a member of the R.I. in 1879 and the R.O.I. in 1883. He produced an enormous amount of work for *The Illustrated London News* and *The Graphic* in the 1870s and 1880s. (His first recorded Africana illustration in *The Graphic* was in 1880.) He worked at various times for several other illustrated papers. Apparently Van Gogh was an admirer of his work during his English years.

Staniland's Boer War output was not prolific. It includes black and white illustrations in C.N. Robinson's *Britannia's Bulwarks: The Achievements of our Seamen, The Honour of our Ships* (1901). Staniland's co-illustrator was Charles Dixon. The Africana Museum has one Boer War work by Staniland entitled *Refugees in Cape Town.* Another, dated 1895, shows the Volksraad in Pretoria. Staniland often signed his work with the initials 'C.J.S.'.

Houfe, British Illustrators and Caricaturists, *p. 463*
Kennedy, Pictures in the Africana Museum, *vol. 7, p. 237*
Osterwalder, and Hubschmid and Bouret (eds.),
Dictionnaire des Illustrateurs, *p. 1008*
Waters, British Artists, *vol. 1, p. 312*

STEELINK, Willem (jnr.) 1856-1928

Etcher, lithographer and illustrator. Steelink was born in Amsterdam on 16 July 1856. His Boer War contribution was the three illustrations in Louwrens Penning's *De Leeuw van Modderspruit.*

G. F. Staller did the illustration for this double postcard with extreme anti-Chamberlain feelings, expressed in Dutch, German and French.

STEINLEN, Théophile-Alexandre 1859-1923 2

Poster and postcard artist, genre painter, etcher, lithographist, and sculptor. Steinlein was born in Lausanne, Switzerland, on 10 November 1859. He moved to Paris in 1879 where he worked with M. Schrenhauser, composing designs for textile prints. Much of his later work was apparently influenced by the events of World War I and he engraved a series of prints depicting Belgian and Serbian refugees.

Steinlen was a very prolific poster artist and designer of Art Nouveau postcards. He was a friend of Henri Toulouse-Lautrec who had a marked influence on him. In Paris, Adolphe Willette introduced him to Rodolphe Salis who had opened a writer's and artist's cabaret at No. 8 Boulevard Roche-court. In 1883 Steinlen's first reproduced drawing appeared in the eighth issue of *Chat Noir*. It was the first of a series of pictorial stories which continued to appear until 1895. Later they were collected and published under the titles of *Les chats* (1898) and *Contes à Sarah* (1899). Steinlen collaborated with Toulouse-Lautrec on the magazine *Le Mirliton*, working at first under the pseudonym of 'Treclau' and later under the name of Jean Caillou, which was the French translation of Steinlen (little stone). It was even later that he used his own name. Aristide Bruant was the publisher of *Le Mirliton*, and he had a nightclub of the same name. Bruant's songs were illustrated by Steinlen, and they were collected and published in four volumes. The first two appeared in 1888 and 1895.

After *Le Mirliton* Steinlen drew for several other magazines, including *Le Croquis*, *La Vie Illustrée*, *Revue*, *La Caricature*, *Jugend*, *Echo de Paris*, *L'Assiette au Beurre*, *Le Chambard* and *La Feuille*. (For his work in the last-named publication he used the pseudonym 'Petit Pierre'.) In 1901 Steinlen became a nationalized Frenchman. In 1911 he was one of the founders — along with Forain, Willette, Léandre and Veber — of the short-lived magazine *Journal des Humoristes*.

Steinlen's Boer War work appeared in *La Vie Illustrée*. His

double centre-page cartoon, entitled *Le Transvaal presentant le president Kruger aux peuples Européens*, appeared in the 16 November 1900 issue (no. 109). Another Boer War related cartoon by Steinlen, *Un clou chasse l'autre*, appeared in the postwar issue of *Le Canard Sauvage* (no. 7) on 8 March 1903.

Steinlen signed his work either with his surname or with a monogram. He died on 14 December 1923.

Bénézit, Dictionnaire antique, *vol. 8, p. 108*
Bilbo, Toulouse-Lautrec and Steinlen
Emanuel, Illustrators of Montmartre
Osterwalder, and Hubschmid and Bouret (eds.), Dictionnaire des Illustrateurs, *pp. 1014-1015*
Weill, Art Nouveau Postcards, *p. 7*

STEPHANY, M.

Le Rire cartoonist who provided occasional Boer War related cartoons. The artist's signature has a 'y' on the end, but the credit in *Le Rire* is given as 'Stephane'.

STEPPE, Romain 1859-?

Landscape and marine painter. Steppe was born in Antwerp, Belgium, on 13 January 1859. He worked in his native country, as well as the Netherlands, England and Germany.

Steppe contributed an illustration to *Antwerpen-Transvaal Gedenknummer*.

Bénézit, Dictionnaire antique, *vol. 8, p. 115*

STEUB, Fritz 1844-1903

Artist, caricaturist and etcher. Steub was born in Lindau, Germany, on 11 November 1844. He worked as a caricaturist for *Fliegende Blätter* from 1864. *The Strand Magazine* described Steub as follows: '. . . while in Steub the German publication (Fliegende Blätter) still has the service of one of its old brigade, a man of amazing industry as well as of remarkable ability; in parallel, perhaps, with our own Linley Sambourne, whose work now takes the place of honour lately held by that of Sir John Tenniel'.

Steub's Boer War work appeared in *Der Burenkrieg*. He died in Patenkirchen on 5 August 1903.

Bénézit, Dictionnaire antique, *vol. 8, p. 118*
Osterwalder, and Hubschmid and Bouret (eds.), Dictionnaire des Illustrateurs, *p. 1018*
The Strand, *vol. 27, p. 449 (1901)*

STEVENS, Edward

Designer who worked for the Picture Postcard Co. He designed the flags and scrollwork on their 30-card series on the Boer War.

Byatt, Picture Postcards

STEVENS, William D.

An American illustrator who worked in New York and was responsible for some of the illustrations in A.T. Mahan's *The War in South Africa*.

STEVENSON F. Arthur 1

Sergeant of the Cape Garrison Artillery Volunteers. Stevenson and W.G. Duncan designed the poster 'For Queen and Empire' which was printed and published by William Stableford and Company Ltd., Cape Town. The poster is dated 1 May 1901. The design incorporates the names of all the Cape Irregular Volunteers and their regiments.

Stevenson was also responsible for the Patriotic Souvenir envelope published by George Budricks and Co. on 16 May 1900. At least five different versions exist.

STEVENSON, J.

Captain Stevenson was responsible for seven illustrations which appeared in *The Illustrated London News* between August 1900 and September 1905. His illustration published on 23 September 1905 showed the new railway bridge over the Zambezi River.

His *Map of the Pretoria and Rustenburg districts illustrating recent movements*, which appeared in facsimile on 1 September 1900, was accompanied by an article 'Transvaal Topography', which was written by Stevenson. Also in this issue were his four topographical sketches, *War in South Africa: de Wet's field of operations*, which had been redrawn by Holland Tringham.

De Wet, Illustrated London News Index

STEWART, Allan 1865-1951 1

Portraits, landscape, military and historical painter. Stewart was born in Edinburgh on 11 February 1865. He was educated at the Royal Scottish Academy schools where he won several prizes, including the MacLaine-Walters Medal, the Start Prize and the Chambers Prize. He also studied in Paris and Spain. He exhibited at the Royal Academy from 1892, and at the

5

6

R.S.A. Stewart was on the staff of *The Illustrated London News* for many years. He accompanied King Edward VII on one of his Mediterranean cruises.

To the memory of brave men: The last stand of Major Allan Wilson at the Shangani, 4 December 1893 was exhibited at the Royal Academy in 1896. In 1899 *The Mazoe Relief* was exhibited, and *The charge of the 21st Lancers at Omdurman* appeared in 1900. Both of these were reproduced as photogravures which proved very popular. Stewart's work is prolific for *The Illustrated London News* and over 30 illustrations appeared between December 1899 and August 1902. Stewart often worked in oils, which was an unusual medium for reproduction. *The Spear* used his work extensively and a special gratis photogravure plate, entitled *Brothers in Arms*, was included on 14 February (issue no. 4). The advertisement reported that Stewart was 'The painter of the celebrated picture "Major Wilson's last stand"'. 'This photogravure [Brothers in Arms],' it continued, 'represented the splendid charge of the Yorkshires and the New Zealanders driving the Boers down the face of a kopje at Colesberg at the point of the bayonet. It will be a companion picture to their first presentation photogravure by Caton-Woodville "All that was left of them".' The plates were sold at sixpence each.

Stewart designed the Men of Huddersfield and District Boer War memorial in Huddersfield, which was unveiled by General French on 20 May 1905.

De Wet, Illustrated London News Index
Personal communication with Mr. K. Hartley, Assistant Keeper, National Gallery of Modern Art
The Studio, *vol. 80, pp. 96-99 (1920)*
Waters, *British Artists, vol. 1, pp. 315-316*
Gildea, *For Remembrance*

STEWART, Charles Edward fl. 1887-1930

Genre and historical painter. Stewart was born in Glasgow in 1887. He studied art at the Royal Academy schools and the Académie Julian in Paris. He exhibited at the principal London galleries from 1887, including 37 works at the Royal Academy.

In 1902 *The Victoria Cross* was shown at the Royal Academy.

Graves, Royal Academy, *vol. 7, p. 260*
Johnson and Greutzner, British Artists, *p. 481*
Waters, British Artists, *vol. 1, p. 316*

STEWART, Frank Algernon 1877-1945   6

Painter of sporting subjects. Stewart was educated in Hastings and studied art at Rochester under George Ward, at the Slade School under Fred Brown, and at Frank Calderon's School of Animal Painting. He was appointed war artist to *The Illustrated London News* in October 1899 and went to South Africa. He also worked for *The Illustrated Sporting & Dramatic News*, and in fact his name is recorded as their representative only in Capt. F. B. Maurice's list of accredited war correspondents. An indistinct photograph of Stewart which appeared in *Under The Union Jack* also gave the same designation.

The Boer War was Stewart's only experience as a war correspondent and it seems as if he must have been sent out by, or seconded to, *The Illustrated London News* after Melton Prior had become besieged at Ladysmith. Stewart accompanied Buller's Natal Field Force and was present at Colenso, Spioenkop, Monte Cristo and the relief of Ladysmith. He was invalided home some time in 1900 but continued to draw for *The Illustrated London News* as a home-based illustrator. Stewart was awarded the Queen's South Africa medal on 2 September 1905.

In 1901 Stewart went to Paris where he studied at the Académie Julian. His subsequent work was almost exclusively of equestrian and hunting subjects. The art magazine *Apollo*, reviewing an exhibition of his in 1935, says 'The artist knows his job to perfection'.

He provided over 32 illustrations for *The Illustrated London News*, most of which were reproduced in facsimile, and an undisclosed number of illustrations for *The Illustrated Sporting & Dramatic News*. He illustrated J.B. Atkins's *The Relief of Ladysmith* and George Manville Fenn's *The Dash from Diamond City*. One of his own publications was entitled *Cross Country with the Hounds*. He is quoted as saying '(he) became a specialist in painting and illustrating hunting scenes, pursuing the image of war without guilt and only five and twenty percent of its danger'. Some of Stewart's sketches from the front were accompanied by letters which were often quoted in *The Illustrated London News*. One of these letters described his view of events leading up to the Battle of Colenso.

Stewart's Book of Soldiers was published in 1900 by Ernest Nister of London and C. P. Dutton & Co. of New York. There were 15 lithographs (of which one was uncoloured), some of Boer War interest including *Blue Jackets with 4.7 Naval Gun*, *5th lancers charging*, and *New South Wales lancers preparing to storm a hill*.

On 28 October 1981 Christie's, South Kensington, offered 12 of Stewart's Boer War pen-and-ink and wash drawings. All were signed and dated '1900':

1. *On the march. Troops crossing a spruit at Springfield South Africa*. Appeared in *The Illustrated London News* (supplement) on 24 February 1900.
2. *A wounded comrade.The taking of Monte Cristo on February 18. The King's Royal Rifles advancing through the mealies*. Appeared in *The Illustrated London News* on 24 March 1900, vol. 116, p. 400.
3. *Troops dispossessing a homesteader. With Sir Redvers Buller's force: arresting a treacherous Boer farmer*. Appeared in *The Illustrated London News* on 15 September, vol. 117, p. 372.
4. *Bringing in the wounded.*
5. *Building a Bridge.*
6. *Convoy of wounded moving out.*
7. *Cavalry in Retreat*. Watercolour.
8. *General Kitchener Directing Highlanders.*
9. *A cavalry charge.*
10. *The night attack on Spion Kop*. Appeared on p. 236 of *The Relief of Ladysmith*, and probably also in *The Illustrated Sporting & Dramatic News*.

7

8

1 T. Steinlen produced this double-page cartoon depicting in Biblical terms President Kruger's presentation to the European people for *La Vie Illustrée*.
2 This pen-and-ink sketch, showing naval guns covering the advance from the top of Swartkop at the battle of Vaal Krantz, was done by Frank Stewart, probably for *The Illustrated Sporting & Dramatic News*.
3 T. Steinlen's cartoon *Un clou chasse l'autre* appeared in *Le Canard Sauvage* after the War. Note Edward's portrait on the wall and Kruger's at her side.
4 The memorial to the men of Huddersfield and district in Huddersfield, designed by Allan Stewart. The memorial was unveiled by Lt. Gen. French on 20 May 1905.
5 Frank Stewart's pen-and-ink drawing showing Sir Redvers Buller's force arresting a Boer farmer suspected of treachery.
6 This drawing entitled *Dragoons Surprising a Boer Laager* was done by *Illustrated London News* artist Frank Stewart and reproduced in the magazine on 1 September 1900.
7 Frank Stewart's drawing of troops crossing a Spruit near Springfield during the War. It was reproduced in *The Illustrated London News* on 24 February 1900.
8 Frank Stewart did this wash drawing of a trumpeter in the Royal Horse Artillery when he was a 12-year-old pupil at the International College in Rochester.

11. *Attack on Vaal Krantz*.

12. *A surprise attack on a Boer laager*. This picture had a comment on the reverse that it was the property of Esmé Stewart, presumably a relative.

The author purchased numbers 1, 2, 3, 10, 11 and 12 at the Christie's sale. A further two pen-and-ink drawings are in the author's collection: *R.E. Welden Trestle Bridge Tricards (sic) Drift, River Tugela* (appeared in *The Illustrated Sporting & Dramatic News* on 28 February 1900) and *Mount Alice Natal, Colonel Byng SALH* (*The Illustrated Sporting & Dramatic News*, 14 March 1900). The author also has a very competent equestrian watercolour by Stewart. It was done when he was a 12-year-old boy at the International College at Rochester.

The Africana Museum has a pen-and-ink drawing, dated 1901, which is entitled *Indian stretcher Bearers conveying the wounded to an ambulance wagon*.

Stewart is recorded as a postcard artist for the Ernest Nister series 'Coaching Life' and several other World War I military subjects.

Apollo, vol. 22, p. 51 (1935)
Byatt, Picture Postcards, p. 192
Christie's South Kensington Sale of Africana *catalogue 28 October 1981*
De Wet, Illustrated London News Index
Index to British Military Costume Prints
Johnson, Front Line Artists
Waters, British Artists, vol. 2, p. 316

STICK
Le Rire cartoonist who occasionally produced Boer War related cartoons.

ST LEGER, Stratford Edward 1868?-1935 4
St Leger was born on 18 March in either 1867 or 1868. There is some confusion as to the year of his birth. SABIB, taking the information from *Who was Who 1929-1940*, gives the date as 18 March 1878, which is obviously incorrect. Both *The Times* and *The Cape Times* obituaries for October 1935 merely mention that he was 67 in that year. *The St Leger family and its South African Branch*, compiled by Col. A.Y. St Leger, mentions his birth in 1868, as does Creagh and Humphris. However, the Diocesan College School (Bishops) register for 1885 gives his date of birth as 18 March 1867. They received this information from his father, but, having eight children, he may well have confused the year of Edward's

birth. His daughter, Mrs Moira Gibbs, is also not sure where or when he was born but seems to think that England in 1868 is probably the correct place and year.

St Leger's father was the Reverend Frederick York St Leger, Bishop of Queenstown. He later founded and edited *The Cape Times*. His mother was Christian Emma May, daughter of John Muddells of Shirley, Hampshire. Neither the Bishop of Grahamstown nor the Archdeacon of Queenstown could find any record of St Leger's baptism between 1867 and 1871, nor any baptism done by his father from April 1867 to December 1867, which seems to indicate that St Leger snr. was on long leave during that year.

St Leger was educated at Tonbridge School in England but returned to South Africa where he took his university course at the Diocesan College in Rondebosch. He registered on 18 February 1885. St Leger was an outstanding athlete (he held the record for the half mile) and captain of the rugby team (in 1887) as well as the first cricket eleven. St Leger also excelled at art. While at Tonbridge School he won several drawing prizes including the school's top prize in his last year there. His art master at Bishops was James Ford, the painter of the well-known large futuristic oil *Holiday in Cape Town in the 20th Century in honour of the expected arrival of the Governor General of the United South Africa.*

In 1888 an army class was formed at Bishops and St Leger soon enrolled. *The Diocesan College Magazine* for 1890 mentions that St Leger completed the whole of his military course at the college: 'Passed with single success in geometrical drawing and professional subjects; Topography, Fortification, Law, Administration, and Tactics'.

After he matriculated, St Leger went to Ireland and was commissioned into the 18th Foot of the Royal Irish Regiment in 1890. When the War broke out in 1899 Col. E.A.H. Alderson was instructed to raise a brigade of mounted infantry and St Leger was appointed to the command of the Cork Company of the 1st Mounted Infantry Regiment. The regiment sailed aboard the *Gascon*, arriving in Table Bay on 11 November 1899. Despite the news of 'Black Week' the spirit of the Royal Irish was high. The Mounted Infantry spent most of their time after their arrival in South Africa languishing in De Aar waiting for orders which they hoped would give them some action. With the exception of occasional patrols to Philipstown, an expedition to Prieska, and guarding the Hanover railway bridge, there was nothing much to interest them.

On 22 January 1900, however, they received orders to join Col. Alderson's flying column at Prieska. One hundred

and thirty-eight officers and men with 151 horses moved out. On their arrival in Prieska they were ordered to make for the Orange River Station about 100 miles away. This they accomplished in three marches via Klipdrift and Hopetown. Their first action was on 12 February at Waterval Drift. Despite rearguard action from the Boers at Olifant's Laager they managed to reach Kimberley with French's column at about 4 o'clock in the afternoon. St Leger did not see the actual entry of Gen. French into the town but he remarks that from all accounts the general had a very enthusiastic welcome. St Leger kept his sketchbooks in his saddlebag and was dismayed to discover when he reached the camp that in his absence one of his ponies, which had been saddled up that morning had broken loose, and when she was recovered by his servant his saddle bags had been ripped open and everything they contained looted, including his papers and sketchbook. Virtually all his Prieska sketches were missing.

After spending a few days in Kimberley his company set off for Bloemfontein, reaching the Orange River Colony capital on Tuesday 13 March. They bivouacked about three miles outside the town at Lawton's Farm and two days later three companies of his regiment were sent to protect the waterworks on the Modder River at Sanna's Post, about 22 miles east of Bloemfontein. St Leger gives a very graphic account in his *War Sketches in Colour* of the Battle of Sanna's Post but modestly makes no mention of his own achievements during the battle.

Lt. Col. G. le M. Gretton in *The Campaigns and History of the Royal Irish Regiment from 1684-1902* gives a vivid account of St Leger's bravery:

As Captain St Leger was superintending the retirement of the rear section of the Cork Company he saw a big man, dismounted, running after the horsemen. St Leger called him, and ascertained that he was Corporal Parker, 1st Life Guards, who after escaping from the trap in the Korn Spruit had attached himself to the mounted infantry. While the corporal was speaking he was shot through the right shoulder, and at that moment St Leger's orderly, Drummer Radford, noticed that his officer was staying behind and rode back to him. Thinking he could manage the Life Guardsman alone, St Leger ordered Radford to return to the company, but when he tried to get the trooper onto his (St Leger's) horse, failed to do so, for the man's wound had made him incapable of helping himself, and he was too heavy to be lifted into the saddle. There was no time to be lost, so with his right arm around the trooper's waist, he half supported, half dragged him in the direction in which the Cork company had retired. With his left hand St Leger led his horse, which grew very restive under the pitiless hail of bullets that literally tore up the ground under the animal's belly. As the Boers followed up the little group, now completely isolated and a long way behind the last of the rearguard, the outlook seemed almost hopeless. Suddenly St Leger realized that if he could succeed in getting his wounded man a few hundred yards farther on, they would not only find temporary cover in some low-lying and broken ground, but be protected by the fire of a party of Roberts' Horse who, some distance off, were holding back the enemy on this part of the battlefield. The burghers came on fast and three of them galloped up to within a hundred yards of the fugitives, and emptied their magazines at them as they disappeared into cover. As the Boers fired from the saddle none of their bullets took effect. Bad as the situation was, it grew worse when the section of Roberts' Horse turned about, and galloped to a position farther to the rear. Happily St Leger managed to attract the attention of one of them – a gallant man, who raced back to him with a led horse, on which they managed to hoist the Life Guardsman, who, though faint from his wound, was still able to ride once he was in the saddle. Then they galloped hard, scattering in order to offer a smaller target to the shower of Mauser bullets by which they were pursued. Corporal Parker recovered from his wound completely; and neither the trooper in Roberts' Horse nor Captain St Leger was hit; indeed, good luck followed the latter throughout the day, for thanks to the resolution of his groom, Private Ward, his favourite pony was saved from the general wreck of the column.

A footnote on page 363 reads: 'St Leger's exploit would have remained unknown had not Corporal Parker written to his own commanding officer to report the matter. Unfortunately the non-commissioned officer's letter did not reach the War Office until the list of rewards for South Africa was finally closed.' Undoubtedly St Leger would have received an award for valour.

In his book *War Sketches in Colour*, St Leger discusses the northward advance to the Vaal after an irksome delay of a week in Kroonstad which they left on Sunday 20 May, marching north to Boschkoppies. Having crossed the Vaal River at Viljoensdrif they crossed the Riet Spruit on 26 May but encountered opposition at Kliprivier sberg. After the fierce battle of Klipriviersberg Ridge they bivouacked at Doornkop, where Jameson and his men had surrendered in 1896. When they finally reached Pretoria St Leger mentions that he was in fact carried into the capital and was given one of the two vacant beds at the Bourke Hospital, which indicates that he was probably suffering from typhoid. Robert Langham Carter points out in his article in the *Military History Journal* of June 1981 that St Leger drew pictures of the Wynberg Military Camp. The assumption is that from Pretoria he was sent to Wynberg Hospital before he returned to England.

St Leger describes how, while his fellow officers were taking a siesta or lighting their pipes, he employed his time in attempting to transfer the nearest thing to paper. In common with many soldier-artists St Leger earned a few extra pounds by sending some of these sketches back to the illustrated newspapers in England and his work appeared, sometimes in facsimile, in *The Sphere*, *Black & White* and *Black & White Budget*.

Long after the War, on 12 March 1908, St Leger was promoted to major, and during World War I, on 29 February 1917, he was made lieutenant colonel. Just before the outbreak of World War I, however, he was hospitalized with a leg injury sustained in a cricket match. Nevertheless he rejoined the Royal Irish at the outset and went across to France with the British Expeditionary Force. He was later cut off from his unit but was able to make his way through the German lines and after many narrow escapes got through Belgian lines at Oudenrade and returned to Britain.

St Leger was awarded the D.S.O. in June 1916 and the C.M.G. in 1918. He was posted as assistant adjutant to the general at the War Office. In 1920 he was appointed as a member of the Overseas Settlement Council. He retired in 1922 but was gazetted as full colonel in 1924. St Leger died in Hough, Sussex, on 12 October 1935.

St Leger was a very competent sketcher and his daughter Mrs Moira Gibbs, who lives in Cape Town, possesses a few well-executed pastels, as well as a Christmas card designed and painted by him. This card was used by his regiment at the barracks in Buttervant, County Cork, prior to the War.

In 1903 St Leger's book *War Sketches in Colour* was published by A. & C. Black in London. A two-guinea deluxe edition consisting of 250 signed copies appeared on 15 December 1903 and an 'ordinary' edition which had a print run of 2 150 copies appeared on 4 December 1903 at a price of 20 shillings. The blurb says that '160 illustrations were used, 50 in colour – 15 full page in line and the rest appeared in the text'. Both editions had cover designs by A. A. Turbayne. Among the press notices which appeared in the A. & C. Black advertising brochure were favourable comments from the *Northern Whig*, *Spectator*, *Academy*,, *Manchester Courier*, *Military Mail*, *United Services Magazine*, *Aberdeen Free Press*, and *South Africa*.

The last-mentioned, in particular, enthused that these were 'the best pictures of scenes incident of the war yet published. We have seen few finer South African Watercolour drawings at all.' *The Northern Whig* referred to 'his brilliant sketches admirably reproduced'.

Six months later the Bruton Galleries held an exhibition of the sketches used in the book. The exhibition opened with a private viewing on Friday 27 May 1904. Despite the publicity the book was still not sold out at that stage and the exhibition catalogue stated that 'both deluxe and ordinary editions were still available'. The exhibition finally closed on Saturday 18 June 1904. The paintings and drawings were as follows:

Watercolour drawings

1. *A Prisoner.*
2. *A Veldt Fire. Shells bursting in the Veldt at once set it alight. These fires were, often erroneously I am certain, put down to Boer strategy.*
3. *Outpost – Breakfast.*
4. *The Ox-Waggon. Slow but sure.*
5. *Mounted Infantry Stretcher-Bearers.*
6. *A Successful Day. Mounted Infantry watering their horses before bivouacking, having obtained both fuel for themselves and oat-hay for their ponies.*
7. *The End of the Day.*
8. *The Road out of a Drift. Great difficulty was frequently experienced in getting the heavily laden transport waggons up the rough roads leading from a drift, and at times the help of drag ropes had to be resorted to.*
9. *The Rush for Kimberley. The cavalry charge through the Boer lines on February 15, 1900.*
10. *Watering Horses.*
11. *A Mounted Infantry vedette. The heavy weight carried by the horse will not bear comparison with the light equipment of the Boer pony.*
12. *A Mounted Infantry Patrol-Dinner. Frequently only 4-lb tins of beef were available for issue to the men, and if anything happened to a man who had one of these on his horse it was a poor look-out for those whose dinners he was carrying.*
13. *A Corner of Cronje's Laager at Paardeberg.*
14. *War Balloon on the March.*
15. *An Ox-Convoy.*
16. *Transport crossing a swollen drift. The rivers in South Africa – one day a trickling stream, the next a raging torrent.*
17. *Abandoned. This was one of the saddest scenes during the campaign. An order was issued after Paardeberg that all horses unable to keep up with the column were not to be destroyed, but left in the veldt. Whenever possible this was done near water. Columns following found many of these abandoned horses sufficiently recovered to bring on.*
18. *After a Storm at Kimberley. First Mounted Infantry Officers' Mess after a thunderstorm on February 18, 1900.*
19. *Tapping Telegraph Wires.*
20. *A Baralong Fruitseller. The picturesque dress of these people is fast disappearing.*
21. *Examining a Boer's Pass. The Burghers of the Orange Free State who surrendered under Lord Roberts' Proclamation of March 15, 1900, were given passes and allowed to remain on their farms.*
22. *Baralongs at Thabanchu.*
23. *Buying Ponies from Baralongs at Thabanchu. The Baralongs are great horse dealers.*
24. *A Patrol on the Ladybrand Road. Towering up on the right is the Thabanchu Mountain, with dense mist rising up from the valley below.*
25. *Burma Mounted Infantry. These hardy little ponies do not average more than twelve hands.*
26. *Transport Formed Up.*
27. *Our Brigadiers' Buck-Waggon. This waggon was captured in the Koorn Spruit Ambuscade.*
28. *Transport, Lumsden's Horse. Entering Kroonstad the day after our occupation of the town.*
29. *Mule Transport Crossing a Drift.*
30. *Free State Burghers Surrendering at Kroonstad. In compliance with Lord Roberts' Proclamation of March 15, 1900.*
31. *Our Water Supply at Kroonstad.*
32. *General French's First View of The Transvaal. On May 24, 1900, the rugged mountain range overlooking the Vaal, north of Vredefort, was the first sight obtained of the Transvaal.*
33. *Saddling-Up at Viljoen's Drift. General Hutton's Mounted Infantry saddling-up in the early morning of May 25, 1900, preparatory to crossing the Vaal and setting foot for the first time in Transvaal soil.*
34. *Tongas Crossing a Drift.*
35. *Led Ponies.*
36. *Mounted Infantry coming down the Witwatersrand.*
37. *Under Shelter of a Kopje.*
38. *Shell falling among Tongas. An incident during the fighting at Kliprivier sberg on May 28, 1900.*
39. *First Mounted Infantry at Kliprivier sberg, May 29, 1900. Retiring under heavy shell fire after having accomplished their object by holding a position as a pivot for General French's turning movement. The rings of smoke are shrapnel bursting overhead.*
40. *Captured Boer Waggons. It was extraordinary how fast the Boers got their oxen to move. These teams, however, were unable to keep up with a commando retreating in great haste from the Witwatersrand to Pretoria.*
41. *The contents of a Captured Boer Waggon.*
42. *A Transvaal Burgher. From the up-country districts.*
43. *Some Types of Free State Boers.*
44. *A Cape Cart from Cronje's Laager. This cart and ponies we obtained from the laager the day after Cronje's surrender.*
45. *A Mid-Day Rest. Orderly and Ponies.*
46. *Shoeing in the Veldt.*
47. *Wire Cutters to the Front. As the whole face of the Orange Free State and the Transvaal was covered with a network of wire fences, we carried nothing more useful than our wire cutters.*
48. *Guard Mounting, Bloemfontein. In front of the Residency – the Commander-in-Chief's headquarters shortly after our occupation of the capital of the Free State.*
49. *Evening at Welgelegen. Ambulances of Colonel Alderson's corps of Mounted Infantry, the 1st M.I., Canadian M.R., and Roberts' Horse.*
50. *Nearing Pretoria. The Magaliesberg range of mountains is on the left. Daspoort Fort is at the end of the ridge on right of sketch. These forts, built at enormous cost, were never made use of, having been denuded of their heavy guns for service in the field.*

Pen-and-ink sketches

51. *The Bed of the River at Paardeberg. This was the scene at the drift at Paardeberg where Cronje crossed the Modder in his attempted flight to Bloemfontein. It was in the high banks of the river shown here that the Boers dug out shelters for their women who were with them.*
52. *Tommy's use for the Waterproof Sheet. Very weird occasionally were Tommy's attempts to keep dry in a storm.*
53. *A Tonga. Dhanjibboy, a Pindi contractor who keeps a large posting establishment, well known in the Punjaub, supplied a number of tongas, fully equipped, to be used as ambulances in South Africa. They were attached to the mounted corps. The caption explained: 'A tonga has the advantage of bringing no weight to bear on the ponies' backs, and also when going down a steep incline the body of the tonga more or less keeps its level'.*
54. *A Transport Driver.*
55. *General French halting at Sanna's Post, March 19, 1900. General French's flying column, on their way from Bloemfontein to Thabanchu, halted on the identical spot where they were ambushed when returning under Colonel Broadwood on 31st March. The caption reads: 'The convoy*

The end of the Day, a watercolour by soldier-artist Captain Stratford St Leger, was reproduced in his book War Sketches in Colour.

and main body may be seen halted between the Koorn Spruit, which is just below the rising ground on which the mounted infantry rear-guard in foreground is halted, and the waterworks (the building with the tall chimney) on the banks of the Modder.

The high peak on right of sketch is Thabanchu mountain. The Boers first shelled our bivouac on the 31st March from the ridge immediately over the river on the left, and occupied the low kopjes on right of waterworks'.

56. *In the Face of a Storm. Sketched on our way to Thabanchu, March 19, 1900.*

57. *Sanna's Post. This sketch represents the scene of the disaster immediately after the Boers had disclosed their ambush by opening a murderous fire on Roberts' Horse and the two batteries Horse Artillery. The former may be seen galloping back from the spruit. Colonel Alderson (directly over shell bursting in foreground), with his Brigade – Major, Capt. M'Micking, is watching them.* The caption describes the sketch in greater detail: 'The waterworks chimney will be noticed on right of sketch just below the Boer guns at foot of kopje beyond the Modder, the tree-lined banks of which will be seen over and to the left of the waterworks.

'A dark spot immediately over the left of Mounted Infantry led horses retiring as far as possible from firing line, denotes Q Battery R.H.A., which has just unlimbered and come into action. A shell from the battery is bursting over the spruit on left; the tin station buildings and tops of waggons of the now captured convoy will also be noticed just to the right of this shell.

'The Cork District Company 1st M.I. is doubling up to the firing line.'

58. *An Early Drink.*

59. *Boer Transport crossing a drift. The Boer transport, in addition to their ox-waggons, included a large number of Cape carts.*

60. *A Boer Vrouw.*

61. *Siege Gun shells destroyed by De Wet, Roodeval, June 8, 1900. These enormous shells were lying about the veldt for a considerable time afterwards.*

62. *The Vet River Fight as seen by the Boers. This sketch, made the morning after the fight from the kopje in foreground, represents the extreme right of the strong position taken up by the Boers at the Vet River on May 5, 1900. On the right of sketch in the distance the Brandfort hills may be seen.* The caption continues as follows: 'The Boers hurriedly left their laager on these hills, with tents standing, on our advance on the 3rd May.

'The course of the Vet River may be traced by its tree and shrub-fringed banks.

'General Hutton's line of advance, the left column of our army, took him over the plain in sketch. Lord Roberts, with the 11th Division and the naval guns, the centre column, advanced on extreme left of sketch, with General Ian Hamilton's column on his right.

'Shells from G Battery R.H.A., which came into action from a small kopje in centre of plain, may be seen bursting over Boer position; also the Boers' shells in reply falling near the battery.

'The Canadian Mounted Rifles are extended in advance of the battery, and the 1st Mounted Infantry are making for a crossing near the right of sketch, which was made known to us by a Boer prisoner. By crossing the river we were enabled to turn their otherwise practically impregnable position.

'An unpleasant experience awaited us after crossing the river. While working up the right bank a heavy fire was poured into my company from the shrub lining the river bank. This immediately stopped on my firing a few volleys into the bush. It was afterwards ascertained that we had been fired on by another portion of General Hutton's column. Fortunately the only casualties were six horses hit.'

63. *A Swarm of Locusts. A swarm of these pests to South*

Africa migrating is not unlike the cloud of dust showing the track of an army on the march. Swarms of locusts were on several occasions at first mistaken by us for a large force of Boers trekking.

64. *Colonel Rimington and some of his Guides. Col. Rimington is seated on the camp stool.*

65. *Ambulances at Wynberg Railway Station. This long row of ambulances awaited each hospital train as it arrived from the front.*

There are also various smaller pen-and-ink sketches. Some of these paintings still exist.

In 1986 Galago re-published *War Sketches in Colour* as *Mounted Infantry at War.* It was a facsimile reproduction of the text. Some of the colour plates were reproduced in colour but most were only in black and white.

The Mendelssohn Collection in the Library of Parliament, Cape Town, has two watercolours from the book:
1. *The Free State Burghers Surrendering at Kroonstad.* Reproduced opposite p. 140. (No. 30)
2. *Our Water Supply at Kroonstad.* Reproduced opposite p. 144. (No. 31)

The author has four watercolours from the book:
1. *A Veldt Fire.* Reproduced opposite p. 2. (No. 2)
2. *The End of the Day.* Reproduced opposite p. 24. (No. 7)
3. *The Road out of a Drift.* Reproduced opposite p. 26. (No. 8)
4. *A Transvaal Burgher. From the up-country districts.* Reproduced opposite p. 180. (No. 42)

These four watercolours were originally in the possession of the St Leger family. Mrs Gibbs relates that when her father died her mother sold all his possessions to a dealer. When Mrs Gibbs heard about this she contacted the dealer who offered to sell the pictures back to her at five shillings each. This offer she readily accepted. It is not known whether St Leger kept the paintings because they were unsold at the end of the exhibition or because he liked them so much. The former explanation is the most likely.

In 1972 Sawyer's offered *Guard Mounting, Bloemfontein* (No. 48) at the price of £150. In 1974 two of the pen-and-ink sketches and one watercolour were offered for sale by Sotheby's. They were *Mule Transport Crossing a Drift* (reproduced opposite p. 139 – No. 29) and *An Early Drink* (reproduced opposite p. 142 – No. 58).

One of St Leger's paintings, *Boer and Pony,* appeared on A. & C. Black's 'Beautiful Books' postcard series.

Creagh and Humphris, The D.S.O., *p. 336*
Diocesan College Magazine, *March 1890*
Gretton, Campaigns and History of the Royal Irish Regiment

McIntyre, Diocesan College
Military History Journal, *June 1981*
Personal communication with Mrs M. Gibbs
St Leger, A.Y., The St Leger Family and Its South African Branch
St Leger, S. E., War Sketches in Colour
The Times (obituary), *15 Oct. 1935*
Who was Who, *vol. 3, p. 1188*

STONE, G.

The Africana Museum in Johannesburg has a grey wash painting entitled *The Vedette: CIV watching for Cronje Reinforcements 1900* which was signed by 'G. Stone'.

Kennedy, Pictures in the Africana Museum, *vol. 7, p. 238*

STONE, Marcus 1840-1921

Historical genre painter and wood engraver. Stone studied under his father, Frank Stone. Stone jnr. won several medals at international exhibitions in Paris, Berlin, Vienna, Melbourne, Chicago and Philadelphia. He was elected A.R.A. in 1877, R.O.I. in 1883 and R.A. in 1886. He illustrated several books.

Stone exhibited over 49 works at the Royal Academy, including *A Soldier's Return* in 1900.

He died in London on 24 March 1921.

Graves, Royal Academy, *vol. 7, p. 275*
Johnson and Greutzner, British Artists, *p. 484*
Waters, British Artists, *vol. 1, p. 317*

STONOR, W. G.

Lieutenant Stonor was responsible for at least eight frontline sketches which were reproduced in *The Graphic* between 31 August 1901 and 30 August 1902.

Hofmeyr, Matton and Roets, Graphic Picture Index

STORCH, Carl 1868-?

Painter, caricaturist and portrait artist. Storch was born in Budapest on 7 March 1868. He was a student at the Munich Academy under Diez and Herterich. He worked in Salzburg, Austria.

Storch's Boer War cartoons appeared in *Lustige Blätter.*
Bénézit, Dictionnaire antique, *vol. 8, p. 140*

STRAHAN, Geoffrey ?-1916

Strahan was a member of the London Sketch Club and exhibited at the Royal Academy, R.B.A., R.I., and R.O.I., as well as the New Gallery. He was killed in action during World War I while holding the rank of colonel.

Strahan's work during the Boer War appeared in Edgar

Samson's *The Fight for the Flag in South Africa* (Hutchinson & Co., London, 1900). Strahan's three signed illustrations were among the few original works in this publication. The others had been borrowed from *The Illustrated London News*, *The Sphere*, *The Graphic* and *Black & White*.
Johnson and Greutzner, British Artists, *p. 485*

STRANACK, Horis W.
Stranack's illustration, *Goods turned out in Alexandra Square, Durban, by the military authorities*, appeared in *The Graphic* on 17 February 1900.
Hofmeyr, Matton and Roets, Graphic Picture Index

STROMQUIST, H. S.
Designer of the memorial to the men of the Artists' Corps (20th Middlesex Rifle Volunteers) who were members of both the C.I.V. and the Imperial Yeomanry. The memorial, which consisted of eight panels, was unveiled in April 1903 by Maj. Gen. W.H. Mackinnon at the Corps headquarters.
The Graphic, *9 May 1903, p. 628*

STURGES, W. E.
Major Sturges was a member of the 5th Northumberland Fusiliers. He was captured at Stormberg on 10 December 1899 and sent to Pretoria, where he became editor of the third and final number of the P.O.W. 'newspaper' *The Gram*.

STUTZ, Ludwig 1865-1917
Cartoonist. Stutz was born in Hohenech on 8 November 1865. He studied art at the Académie Julian and the Munich Academy. Stutz worked for *Kladderadatsch*. His Boer War cartoons appeared in this periodical and one, which was entitled *Momento More* and appeared on 6 May 1899, was reproduced in the Dutch series of postcards which featured pro-Boer cartoons from the contemporary press.
Bénézit, Dictionnaire antique, *vol. 8, p. 172*
John Bull Sur la Sellette, *p. 18*
Review of Reviews, *Jan-June 1901*

STYCHE, Frank fl.1898-1925
Black and white artist. He worked in Hendon and Golders Green and contributed illustrations to *London Opinion*.
During the War Styche's cartoons appeared in *Judy*.
Houfe, British Illustrators and Caricaturists, *p. 470*

SUMNER, Percy
St George's Gazette illustrator who also provided the historical text for his drawings.

SUPPLE, Hazel
One sketch by this artist appeared in *The Graphic* on 20 January 1900 entitled *Graves of officers at Wynberg*. It is possible that she was a relative of Col. James Francis Supple.
Hofmeyr, Matton and Roets, Graphic Picture Index

SUPPLE, James Francis 1843-1922
Soldier-artist. Supple was born in Waterford, Ireland, on 14 November 1843. He entered the army in 1867 as assistant surgeon to the 1st Royal Scots. He served in the Ashanti War (1873-4), where he received a medal with clasps, and in Afghanistan (1878-9), where he was awarded another medal. During 1886 and 1887 he served in Burma as principal military officer under Sir Robert Low. During the Boer War Supple acted as principal medical officer in Cape Town. He was mentioned in despatches and awarded the Queen's medal with a clasp and a C.B. In 1903 he was principal medical officer of the Durbar troops in India and was eventually awarded a Distinguished Service pension.
One Boer War illustration by Supple appeared in *The Illustrated London News* on 4 March 1900. It was entitled *A sketch of the Isambulwana Hill and Lombard's Kop whence the Boer guns are shelling Ladysmith*.
Supple gave evidence for the Medical Commission and his name appears in the Blue Book of this commission. While in Cape Town he produced a few landscapes and one of them is in the possession of the author. It is a very pleasing watercolour depicting False Bay.
Supple died on 8 August 1922.
De Wet, Illustrated London News Index
The Times (obituary), 12 August 1922
Wellcome, *Medical Officers in the British Army, vol. 1, p. 465*
Who was Who, *vol. 2, p. 1015*

SUTHERLAND, A. 1
Sutherland was responsible for at least 12 G.W. Bacon & Company chromolithographs, 'Bacon's Battle Pictures', which were published in London in 1900. Representing incidents in the War, they were priced at a shilling each. While some were signed in full and others only initialled 'A.S.', most were unsigned. The advertisement described them as 'being beautifully printed in oil colours'. Among those noted are:
1. *Battle of Dundee (Glencoe) October 20 1899*. Signed 'A. Sutherland 99' (not numbered on print).
2. *The Battle of Elandslaagte October 21 1899*. Signed 'A. Sutherland 99'. Two versions of this print are found, one with the British troops in tropical kit and the other with home service uniforms.
3. *The Defence of Mafeking*.
4. *Battle of Belmont, November 23 1899*. Signed 'S 99' (not numbered on print).
5. *Battle of Modder River November 30 1899*. Signed 'A.S. 99'.
6. *Siege of Ladysmith – A Bird's Eye View*. 'London G.W. Bacon & Co.'. Signed 'A.S. 1900'.
7. *The Battle of Paardeberg*.
8. *The Last Barrier (Battle of Pieter's Hill and Relief of Ladysmith)*. Signed 'A.S. 1900'.
9. *Bacon's South African Pictures No. 9. Heroes of Ladysmith: Meeting of Generals Buller and White*.
10. *Dashing advance of the Canadians at Paardeberg*. Signed 'A.S.'.
11. *Relief of Mafeking May 17 1900*.
12. *British Entry into Pretoria June 5 1900*. 'London G.W. Bacon's South African Battle Picture No. 12'.
Numbers 1, 2 and 3 were provided with 'a special and graphic description for pasting on the back when framed'.

SUTTON
Possibly W.J. Sutton. Amateur postcard illustrator. This individual painted watercolours on a series of British court size postcards which he numbered. All are titled 'VADE BYK CUM'.

Only one of the 14 cards seen has been postmarked (No. 2860), with the date 27 December 1899. The cards are all signed 'SVTTON' and have initials (possibly WJS) in reverse. The cards are:

1899	2463	*En route for Cairo: Oom Paul in Pretoria*
1899	2495	*Eendraght maak magt: Oom Paul at home*
1899	2630	*When do you expect them, Earl's Court*
1899	2860	*Cleopatra of the Vaal Voorlog* (sic) *12/10/99 Vrouw Kruger on the Warpath*
1899	2890	*The Transvaal Go. See Times March 25 '99*
19C	3012	*Shots from the Vaal Voorlog Oct 12 1899 Ogre of the Vaal M'Paul HYP*
19C	3021	*Don't Rouse the British Lion. Noli me Tangere*
19C	3051	*The Boer's Head. Latest from the Vaal*
19C	3057	*Let 'em all Come: Earl's Court Feast*
19C	3067	*Shots from Swaziland* (sic) *Ohino Kuko*
19C	3068	*Don't Rouse the British Lion. Noli me Tangere* (different from 3021)
19C	3069	*Shots from the Vaal. Flight of M'Paul*
19C	3070	*Return to Earl's Court.*

SYMONDS, William Robert 1851-1934
Portrait, genre and landscape painter. Symonds was born in Suffolk on 25 February 1851. He studied in London and Antwerp. He exhibited at the principal London galleries from 1876.
In 1902 Symonds's *Surgeon-General Jameson, CB* was shown at the Royal Academy.
Graves, Royal Academy, *vol. 7, p. 315*
Johnson and Greutzner, British Artists, *p. 491*
Waters, British Artists, *vol. 1, p. 321*

TAFFS, Charles H. fl.1894-1911 1
Illustrator. Taffs worked in Clapham, London, and contributed to, among others, *St Paul's*, *Lady's Pictorial*, *The Quiver*, *New Budget*, *Pick-Me-Up*, *Sketchy Bits*, *Royal Magazine*, *English Illustrated Magazine*, *The Illustrated London News* and *The Graphic*. He exhibited at the Royal Academy from 1896 to 1898.
Taffs' Boer War work appeared in *Shurey's Illustrated* (from October 1900), *With the Flag to Pretoria* and *Black & White Budget*.
The author has a signed and dated (1900) wash drawing entitled *A Boer Horse-Trap. Barbed-wire entanglements under water*. This was reproduced in *With the Flag to Pretoria*.
Houfe, British Illustrators and Caricaturists, *p. 475*
Thorpe, English Illustration

TAILLEFER
The illustrator of a postcard showing Edward VII looking for the Kruger millions in the Transvaal. The card, a limited edition of 250, was published by Favor of Paris. Bénézit lists a Taillefer working between 1850 and 1879. She married to become Mrs Fanny Gambogi.

TALVART, Hector 1
French postcard artist who produced a series of 12 numbered cards published in 1902. They were engraved by the firm of

---

1 *Battle of Modder River* was published by G.W. Bacon & Co., London, after a picture by A. Sutherland.
2 This dramatic wash drawing showing a horse and rider falling into a submerged barbed wire horse trap set by the Boers was done by illustrator Charles H. Taffs and reproduced in *With the Flag to Pretoria*.

L. Geisler and Co. The verses were written by N. Allemand and the package of the set was entitled 'La Dernière Épopée'. The cards are as follows:

1. *Pax et Labor* (Shows Kruger)
2. *À sa jeune Majesté: La Reine Wilhelmine*
3. *Les Camps de Concentrations*
4. *Mane Thecel Phares: Au Roi Edouard VII*
5. *De La Rey*
6. *Au Général de Villebois-Mareuil (1847-1900)*
7. *Les Kopjes*
8. *De Wet, L'insaisissable*
9. *Cecil Rhodes: Aux envers*
10. *Invitation dix*
11. *Chamberlain au plus meritant*
12. *Les Mules nerveuses*

TATHAM, C. M.

On 28 October 1899 *The Illustrated London News* published a picture of Ladysmith done by this artist, entitled *Ladysmith town hall, now a hospital*. She was possibly related to Mrs F.S. Tatham, the founder of the Tatham Art Gallery in Pietermaritzburg, and to the early Natal artist Edmund Tatham.

Berman, *Art and Artists*
De Wet, *Illustrated London News Index*
Verbeek, *Early Natal Art*

TATTEGRAIN, Henri 1874-?

Painter and etcher. Tattegrain was born in Paris on 29 August 1874. He was a pupil of Duval, G. Debrie and Mayeux. He exhibited at the Salon des Artistes Français from 1899.

During the War Tattegrain contributed to *Paris-Pretoria*.
Bénézit, *Dictionnaire antique, vol. 8, p. 231*

TAYLOR, C. E.

Australian cartoonist whose work appeared in *The Arrow* and *The Australian Sunday Times*.

A series of four of his cartoons was reproduced in *Black & White Budget* on 5 May 1900. The series was entitled 'Some Australian cartoons on the war' and the four cartoons depicted are:

1. *Wily Kruger*
2. *Fancy Meeting You!*
3. *The Advent of a Nation*
4. *Finis*

A C.E. Taylor is listed in the Australian Postcard Catalogue as a very sought-after postcard artist of 'Comic Bulletin' cards.

TAYLOR, Sydney 1870-1952

Taylor was born in England in 1870. Both his father and grandfather were artists. After studying at the Royal College he went to South Africa with the British forces in 1899, reputedly as an artist-correspondent, although no confirmation of this has been found. After the War he stayed on in South Africa. He was a popular landscapist working in the traditional style and did many Cape Dutch homesteads. He was referred to in Roworth's essay 'Landscape Art in South Africa'. His

work was included in the British Empire Exhibition at Wembley in 1924. He was president of the South African Society of Artists from 1930 to 1932 and 1937 to 1939. He is represented in the South African National Gallery, Cape Town, and the Durban art gallery.

The War Museum of the Boer Republics in Bloemfontein has an oil painting on canvas entitled *At Dawn*. The painting, which is undated, depicts Deneys Reitz with a Boer commando in Natal.

Berman, *Art and Artists, p. 128*
Bloemfontein War Museum Catalogue

TEBBY, Arthur Kemp fl. 1883-1928

Landscape, figure and flower painter. Tebby exhibited at the Royal Academy, the R.B.A. and the R.I. His illustrations appeared in *The Daily Graphic*, *Windsor Magazine* and *Pearson's Magazine*. He is also described as being a naval artist for *The Graphic*.

Tebby's Boer War illustrations appeared mostly in *With the Flag to Pretoria*. One illustration, *With Sir Redvers Buller's Force: Volunteer ambulance men at work*, appeared in *The Graphic* on 16 June 1900. The Royal Collection at Windsor has one of Tebby's wash drawings, dated 10 August 1899, showing *Queen Victoria reviewing the Hampshire Volunteers at Osborne on the Isle of Wight*.

Tebby often signed his work with the initials 'A.K.T.'.
Dawnay and Miller, *Military Drawings and Paintings*
Hofmeyr, Matton and Roets, *Graphic Picture Index*
Houfe, *British Illustrators and Caricaturists, p. 475*
Thorpe, *English Illustration*

TENNANT, C. Dudley fl. 1898-1918

Marine artist and illustrator. He worked in Liverpool in 1898 and in Surrey in 1913. He contributed illustrations to *Punch*, *The Graphic*, *The Idler*, *The Royal Magazine*, *The Penny Pictorial Magazine*, *Ludgate* and *Black & White*.

During the War Tennant contributed to *Black & White Budget*, *With the Flag to Pretoria*, and *After Pretoria: the Guerilla War*.

His son, Dudley Trevor Tennant (born 1900), became a well-known sculptor.

Houfe, *British Illustrators and Caricaturists, p. 476*
Peppin and Micklethwait, *British Book Illustrators, p. 297*
Thorpe, *English Illustration*

TENNANT, Douglas

The Sphere for 3 November 1900 reproduced an illustration of Private Martin Hanlon, *The only CIV to win the Victoria Cross*, drawn by Maj. Douglas Tennant. Tennant married the well-known South African artist, Alice Tennant (née Aubry), but nothing else is known about him.

Berman, *Art and Artists, p. 452*

TENNIEL, John 1820-1914   1

Cartoonist and illustrator. Tenniel was born in London on 28 February 1820. His father, John Baptist Tenniel, was a

teacher of fencing at the Angelo School. He taught his son to fence and during a bout with his father in 1840 a freak accident caused Tenniel jnr. to lose his right eye.

Tenniel's early art training probably came from the painter John Martin, whose sons were friendly with Tenniel. After joining the Clipstone Street Art Society and drawing living models, he attended anatomy lectures and studied sculpture at the British Museum. His first oil was exhibited at the Royal Academy in 1837 and from then on his work appeared regularly at the Academy until 1842 and then again in 1851. In 1845 he was given his first important commission by the British Government to design adornments for the Houses of Parliament.

A few years later Tenniel decided that he could supplement his income by working as an illustrator. He never drew from life and relied heavily on his excellent memory. For *Alice's Adventures in Wonderland* and *Alice Through the Looking Glass* Tenniel produced 90 drawings, of which Lewis Carroll is reported to have liked only one: *Humpty Dumpty*. Tenniel and Lewis Carroll were continually at loggerheads and the letters that passed between them provide much amusement over 100 years later.

It is said that Mark Lemon, the editor of *Punch*, was so impressed with the *Aesop's Fables* illustrations that he asked Tenniel to join their staff in 1850. Tenniel's first *Punch* drawings appeared in vol. 19, including, among others, the title and half-title pages. This relationship lasted for 51 years until Tenniel retired. Tenniel's cartoons were printed directly from the wood block until 1892 when process engraving took over. Up to that time the engraver Swain interpreted his work.

The Times once described Tenniel's work as follows: 'Many of the cartoons are in fact simply metaphorical art. *Dropping the Pilot* is a famous instance. Often the metaphor is witty and well chosen — sometimes very funny indeed.'

Gladstone was an admirer of his work and commented on the 'total absence of vulgarity'. Tenniel was knighted by Gladstone's government in 1893. He was very surprised to receive this honour although he knew his work was extremely popular, particularly among members of parliament. When Tenniel retired from *Punch* in 1901 the then prime minister, Arthur Balfour, arranged a great banquet for him.

Tenniel's Boer War cartoons were obviously produced towards the end of his working life but they reveal the same ability and talent that he had shown as a young man. The author has a pencil cartoon drawing, *Shifting his capital*, which appeared in vol. 119 on 13 June 1900. The Africana Museum in Johannesburg has three original cartoons, two of which are of Boer War interest:

1. T143 *To absent friends*. Depicts Father Christmas with British soldiers in the background. It appeared in vol. 119 of 26 December 1900.
2. T5 *Full of Resource!*. Shows Kruger. It appeared in vol. 118 of 14 March 1900.
3. *A Black 'White Elephant'* concerns the Zulu War and was done in 1879.

Tenniel is known to have used at least six similar mono-

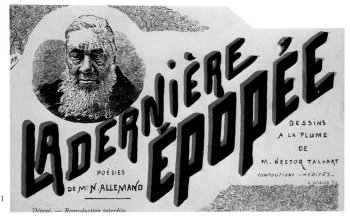

grams with the 'J' and 'T' interwoven. He died on 25 February 1914, three days before his 94th birthday. *Punch* issued a special supplement on 4 March 1914 to mark his death.

Dictionary of National Biography, supp., p. 2922
Houfe, British Illustrators and Caricaturists, *p. 476*
Kennedy, Pictures in the Africana Museum, *vol. 5, p. 2 and vol. 7, p. 239*
Osterwalder, and Hubschmid and Bouret (eds.), Dictionnaire des Illustrateurs
Sarzano, Sir John Tenniel
Spielmann, The History of Punch
Who was Who, vol. 1, p. 702

TÈSTELIN, N.
Illustrator of E. Harcourt Burrage's *Carbineer and Scout: A story of the Great Boer War* (Blackie & Son, London, 1901 and 1902).

SABIB, vol. 1, p. 341

TESTEVUIDE, Jehan 1873-1922
Cartoonist and caricaturist. Pseudonym of Jean Saurel who was born in Nîmes, France, in 1873. He worked for several French periodicals, and his Boer War work, along with that of Albert Guillaume, appeared in a regular feature, 'La Revue Comique', on the inside back page of *Le Monde Illustré*.

Bénézit, Dictionnaire antique, *vol. 8, p. 262*

TÉZIER
A cartoonist with this name or pseudonym was responsible for some of the cartoons in the *Le Charivari* Album: *Boers et Anglais*. Tézier was also responsible for the cartoon, *Encore La Perfide Albion*, on the front page of the 17 November 1899 issue of *Le Charivari*.

THACKERAY, Lance ?-1916   2
Painter, illustrator and author. Born in Yorkshire, Thackeray was a founder member of the London Sketch Club in 1898 after the group had broken away from the Langham Sketching Club. He was also a prominent member of the Savage Club and designed some of their menus. He held one-man exhibitions at the Leicester Gallery, the Fine Arts Society, and the Walker Gallery, and was elected a member of the R.B.A. in 1899. He became well known for his sporting prints.

Following his travels to the Middle East he published *The Light Side of Egypt* (1908) and *The People of Egypt* (1910). He was a regular contributor to *The Graphic, Punch, The Sketch, Tatler* and *Sketchy Bits*.

Thackeray became one of Tuck's leading comic artists and was the 'grand master' of 'write-away' postcards. He worked for Tuck from 1900 until his death in 1916, producing over 1 000 postcard designs. They were signed either 'Lance Thackeray', 'L. Thackeray' or 'L.T.'.

His first series of 'write-away' cards used the theme of the Boer War, and nine of the 13 cards (numbers 324 to 336) used illustrations relative to the War. The titles are as follows:
324 *To my great surprise . . .*
325 *I'm somewhat in a hurry . . .*
326 *There's always a little Scotch going . . .* (not Boer War)
327 *If I can possibly get round . . .* (not Boer War)
328 *A good deal of my time has been . . .* (not Boer War)
329 *It's a rather close shave . . .* (not Boer War)
330 *With the Flag to Pretoria* (unsigned)
331 *It is very good of you to . . .*
332 *This is the first opportunity I've had . . .*
333 *I wish I could see you . . .'*
334 *I trust this will reach . . .*
335 *I do hope I shan't miss . . .*
336 *In duty bound I . . .*

It is said that the four Hildesheimer & Co. Boer War cards — *CH-MB-RL--N, K-T-HE-ER, B-BS* and *HRH The PRI-CE OF W-LES* — with the unusual 'IHI' monogram were also by Thackeray. His other Boer War illustrations appeared in *With the Flag to Pretoria* and *The Sketch*, in which two full-page

illustrations representing *The return of the wounded* were published on 7 March 1900.

Thackeray died in Brighton on 11 August 1916 after having enlisted in the Artists' Corps during World War I.

Byatt, Picture Postcards
Holt, Tonie and Valmai, Stanley Gibbons Postcard Catalogue, *(1985)*
Houfe, British Illustrators and Caricaturists, *p. 477*
Johnson and Greutzner, British Artists, *p. 497*
Lawson and Warr, Postcards of Lance Thackeray
Peppin and Micklethwait, British Book Illustrators, *p. 297*
The Studio, *vol. 63, pp. 243 ff.*
Waters, British Artists, *vol. 2, p. 352*
Watson, The Savage Club, *p. 317*
Who was Who, vol. 2, p. 1032

THEWENETI, C.
The National Army Museum has group portraits of British Boer War generals by C. Theweneti.

THIELE, Julius Arthur 1841-1919   1
Postcard artist. Thiele was born in Dresden on 11 June 1841. He studied art under Ludwig Richter and Julius Hübner at the Dresden Academy from 1856 to 1864. He was initially a landscape artist but later became an extremely competent postcard artist whose cards are very popular with collectors. He died on 30 April 1919, but long after his death postcards bearing his signature were produced.

Some of the finest Boer War chromolithographic cards were designed by Thiele, almost invariably with 'Leipzig' under his signature. According to Howard Smith, writing in *Collector's World*, this indicates that the cards were printed by Adolf Klauss of that city; however, signed cards — identical except for language variations — produced by Emil Pinkau & Co. of Leipzig and Kunzli Frères of Zurich also exist. In some cases identical cards but with Thiele's signature deleted have been noted. His Boer War cards are as follows:
Une Surprise a`contretemps. Dutch, French and German versions, unsigned.
Les Pigeons courriers des Anglais. Dutch, French and German versions, signed. One Diehl & Cnobloch of Amsterdam card noted without signature. This card refers to Lionel James's captured carrier pigeons (see p. 28).
Chocolat anglais et des pâtés Boers. Dutch, French and German versions, unsigned.
Le Oncle Paul en peine. Dutch, French and German versions, unsigned.
Les Perspectives du Lord Roberts. French and German versions, signed. One Diehl & Cnobloch Dutch version, unsigned.
Une Retraite anglaise, bien organisée ou la marche-rétrograde. French and German versions. The latter by Ottmar Zieher of Munich, signed. Dutch version by Diehl & Cnobloch of Amsterdam, unsigned.
Les ânes effarouchés. German, Dutch and French versions, signed. Dutch version by Diehl & Cnobloch, Amsterdam, unsigned.
Mieux Laisser les cinq doigts que la pouce. French version, signed. Dutch version by Diehl & Cnobloch, Amsterdam, unsigned.
Lady-Smith le prude et l'aimable Joubert. German and French versions by Kunzli Frères, Zurich, unsigned.
Le Déblai Boer. French and German, Kunzli Frères and Dutch Diehl & Cnobloch versions, all unsigned.
La derniere Levée de troupes. French version by Kunzli Frères, signed.

Besides the above cards Thiele also illustrated some of the versions of the 'Homage to Kruger' cards which were published to mark Kruger's arrival in Europe. All the Kunzli cards bore his signature. Similar cards, but without the background of palm trees, were either signed by C. Lehr, or were unsigned. German, Dutch, French and Italian versions of the cards signed by Thiele are noted.

Thiele also designed postcards of the Boxer Rebellion.

On 24 February 1900 *Black & White Budget* featured an illustration showing aerial warfare of the future. This science fiction drawing was signed by Thiele and has a subtitle 'The airy navies grappling in central blue. The war of the future from a German point of view'.

The compilers of *Stanley Gibbons Postcard Catalogue* suggest that there were two artists of the same name and that the 'real Thiele' lived later. There is no evidence, however, to suggest that this theory is correct.

Bénézit, Dictionnaire antique, *vol. 8, p. 275*
Holt, Tonie and Valmai, Stanley Gibbons Postcard Catalogue, *(1985) p. 102*
SAPRG Newsletter, *March 1988, no. 27, 'The Boer War cards of Arthur Thiele' by R. Greenwall*

THIRIAT, Paul
As a London-based artist, Thiriat drew Boer War illustrations for *The Sphere, Le Monde Illustré* and *La Semaine Illustrée*. (During World War I, however, he was an artist-correspondent in France for *The Sphere*.) At the time of the Boer War Thiriat also worked for *Le Petit Journal*, but no illustrations relative to the War have been noted in this publication.

THÖNY, Eduard 1866-1950
Son of the sculptor Christian Thöny, Eduard Thöny was born in Brixen, Germany, on 9 February 1866. He studied with Gabriel Hackl in Munich. His cartoons were published in *Simplicissimus* and *Münchener Humoristische Blätter*.

Thöny's Boer War illustrations appeared in *Burenkrieg* and *Simplicissimus*.

Thöny died in Holtzhausen in 1950.

Bénézit, Dictionnaire antique, *vol. 8, p. 294*
Osterwalder, and Hubschmid and Bouret (eds.), Dictionnaire des Illustrateurs, *p. 1049*

THOMAS, William F. fl. 1894-1907
Landscape artist and cartoonist. After working for *Judy, Lika Joko* and *Punch*, he became chief cartoonist for *Ally Sloper's Half Holiday* in 1890. It was in this periodical that his Boer War cartoons appeared.

Houfe, British Illustrators and Caricaturists, *pp. 477-478*
Thorpe, English Illustration

THORNELY, J. H.   2
Thornely worked as an illustrator for *Pearson's Magazine, Royal Magazine*, and *Shurey's Illustrated* (some of his illustrations appeared on the cover (4 November 1899). Thornely's work also appeared in *With the Flag to Pretoria* and *After Pretoria: the Guerilla War*.

Thornely illustrated a short story, *Fiddle and I*, by F. Norreys Copnel which appeared in *Royal Magazine* (vol. 3, p. 156). The story had some Boer War relevance.

The author has two original wash drawings by this artist. One, *Thornhill, the Guide, apprising Colonel Stewart of Gough's Disaster*, was reproduced on p. 653 of *After Pretoria: the Guerilla War*. Interestingly the original is unsigned and differs slightly from the illustration reproduced in the text. The cover illustration had been altered by Thornely or another hand to enable the advertisement for *The London Magazine* to appear against a white background. The other wash drawing, dated 1899 and entitled *General Hunter relieving a wounded soldier*, was reproduced in *Shurey's Illustrated* on 11 November 1899.

---

1 The package of the *La Dernière Épopée* (The last epic) series of 12 postcards by Hector Talvart with verses by N. Allemand was published in 1902. As usual for this type of French postcard series, it was violently anti-British.

2 Lance Thackeray's 'Write-away' cards were part of the Tuck Empire series. This type of card with a preprinted message was meant to be completed by the sender.

An H. Thornely is noted in Thorpe's *English Illustration: the Nineties* as being a contributor to *The Penny Illustrated Paper*. Thornely, who occasionally signed with a 'JHT' monogram, had a distinctive signature. Very little else is known about him except that he was at the Slade School in 1881.

Personal communication with the Secretary of the Slade School, London

THORNTON, E.N.
An artist by this name was responsible for the original sketch of the Imperial Yeomanry Hospital at Deelfontein which was redrawn by W.B. Robinson for publication in *The Illustrated London News* on 7 April 1900.

De Wet, Illustrated London News Index

THORNYCROFT, (William) Hamo 1850-1925
Sculptor of portraits, figure subjects and monuments. Thornycroft was born in London on 9 March 1850. He studied sculpture at the Royal Academy schools, winning a gold medal in 1875. He exhibited at the Royal Academy from 1872. Thornycroft was elected A.R.A. in 1881 and R.A. in 1888. He became a member of the Royal Academy of Munich in 1889 and was knighted in 1917.

Thornycroft was responsible for the design of two Boer War memorials:
1. The memorial to the Manchester Regiment, Imperial Yeomanry, which was unveiled by Sir Ian Hamilton on 26 October 1908. The sculpture represents a wounded soldier of the Manchester Regiment passing up his last cartridge to a comrade standing over him in an attitude of defence. A report of the unveiling appeared on p. 527 of *The Graphic* for 31 October 1908.
2. The memorial to the men of Natal Regiment in front of the Town Hall in Durban. Included in the panels are scenes of Chieveley, Lombard's Kop, Elandslaagte and Pieter's Hill. It was unveiled by Sir H.E. McCallum on 9 April 1905.

Among Thornycroft's several other memorial statues of prominent people are the monument to Gen. Gordon in Trafalgar Square, the Lord Curzon Memorial in Calcutta, and the Queen Victoria Memorial in Karachi. He was also responsible for the First World War memorials in Durban.

Thornycroft died in Oxford on 18 December 1925.
Graves, Royal Academy,
Who was Who, vol. 2, p. 1040

THULSTRUP, Thure de *see* DE THULSTRUP, Thure

TILLY, E.
L'Illustration engraver.

TIPPEL, George W.
Lustige Blätter cartoonist whose unsigned work appeared on an Eysler postcard: 'Theatre de la Guerre' postcard No. 36 entitled *Chocolat de la Reine Victoria*. His work in *Lustige Blätter* was often signed 'G.T.'.

TINAYRE, (Jean Paul) Louis 1861-?
Illustrator, poster artist and painter. Tinayre was born in Neuilly-Sur-Seine, France, on 14 March 1861. He was a pupil of Cormon and exhibited at the Salon des Artistes Français from 1880, receiving an honourable mention in 1898. He worked for *Le Monde Illustré* and *Journal des Voyages.*

An illustration by Tinayre, *Hommage au President Kruger*, was published on p. 325 of the special issue of *Le Monde Illustré* on 17 November 1900.

He signed his work 'Louis Tinayre'.
Bénézit, Dictionnaire antique, vol. 8, p. 315
Osterwalder, and Hubschmid and Bouret (eds.),
Dictionnaire des Illustrateurs, *p. 1054*

TIRET-BOGNET, Georges 1855-? 2
Illustrator and cartoonist. Tiret-Bognet was born in Saint-Servan, France, on 13 January 1855. He worked for several illustrated and satirical journals including *Chronique Amusant, La Caricature, Le Rire* and *La Vie Pour Rire.* His Boer War cartoons were reproduced in all of these magazines.

On 31 March 1900 *La Caricature* published one of his coloured illustrations on the cover. It was entitled *Qui Sait? Haute situation que devrait occuper M. Chamberlain.*

On 3 August 1904 a cartoon dedicated to the recently deceased Kruger appeared in *L'Indiscret.* Tiret-Bognet's coloured cartoons often appeared on both the front and the back covers of *Chronique Amusant,* including the obscene Ultima Ratio on the back cover of issue 7 of 13 February 1902.

The author has a sheet of nine pen-and-ink cartoons entitled 'Cable grammes a la va-vite via Natal'. These undated cartoons, produced for an unidentified publication, are signed 'G.T.B.'. Tiret-Bognet often signed his work with his initials only.
Bénézit, Dictionnaire antique, vol. 8, p. 321

TITCOMB, William Holt Yates 1858-1930
The son of Jonathan Titcomb, Bishop of Rangoon, William Titcomb was born in Cambridge on 22 February 1858. He studied art at the Royal Academy schools, under Verlat in Antwerp, under Boulanger and Lefebvre in Paris, and under Herkomer at Bushey, Herts, England.

Titcomb exhibited at the principal London galleries, including the Royal Academy, from 1886. In 1900 *Good News from the War* was shown at the Royal Academy.

Both his brother, John Henry Titcomb, and his wife, Jessie Ada (née Morison), were artists in their own right.
Graves, Royal Academy, vol. 7, p. 398
Johnson and Greutzner, British Artists, p. 503
Waters, British Artists, vol. 1, p. 329

T.N.F.D.
The Illustrated London News artist whose work was published on 19 January 1901. He was almost certainly Lt. Talbot Neville Fawcett Davenport (see p. 124).

TODD, James Henry fl. 1898-1913
Landscape and flower painter. Todd worked in Glasgow. During the War an occasional illustration by Todd appeared in *Black & White Budget*, for example *The Boers' last assault on Mafeking* on 2 June 1900 .
Johnson and Greutzner, British Artists, p. 504

TOFANI, Oswaldo 1849-1915 2
Illustrator. Tofani was born in Florence on 18 September 1849. He worked for *L'Illustration Italienne* before going to Paris where he contributed to *L'Illustration.* His work also appeared in *Figaro Illustré, Revue Illustrée* and *Le Monde Illustré.*

During the War Tofani contributed an illustration to the *Le Monde Illustré* special issue, 'Hommage au President Kruger', which appeared on 17 November 1900. His front and back coloured illustrations appeared in *Le Petit Journal*; some of these are as follows:
472 21 November 1899 (back cover) *Événements du Transvaal: Les fugitifs de Ladysmith.*
476 31 December 1899 *En Irlande.*
477 7 January 1900 (back cover) *Meeting en faveur des Boers troublé par les antinationalistes.*
478 14 January 1900 *La Guerre au Transvaal: Le Général Joubert haranguant les Boers.*
491 15 April 1900 *Le Général Joubert Sur son lit de mort.*
524 2 December 1900 *Le Président Kruger.*
Bénézit, Dictionnaire antique, vol. 8, p. 331
Osterwalder, and Hubschmid and Bouret (eds.),
Dictionnaire des Illustrateurs, *p. 1057*

TOFT, Alfred 1862-1949
Portrait and figure sculptor. Toft was born in Birmingham on 3 June 1862. He studied at Hanley and Newcastle before winning a scholarship to the R.C.A. in 1880. There he became a pupil of Lanteri. Toft exhibited at the Royal Academy from 1885 and was elected F.R.B.S. in 1923. He was responsible for four Boer War memorials:
1. The memorial in Cannon Hill Park, Birmingham, to the

4

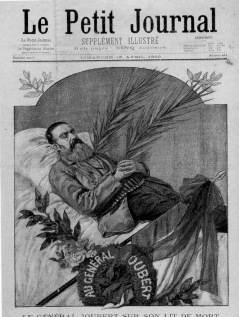

5

LE GÉNÉRAL JOUBERT SUR SON LIT DE MORT

Le Petit Journal

local men who fell in the War. It was unveiled by Lt. Gen. Ian Hamilton on 23 June 1906.

2. The Suffolk Soldiers' Memorial, Ipswich, unveiled by Gen. French on 29 September 1906.

3. A memorial to the Warwickshire Regiments in St Mary's Church, Warwick.

4. The Welsh National Memorial in Cathays Park, Cardiff. It was unveiled by Gen. French on 20 November 1909.

Toft died in Worthing on 18 December 1849.

Gildea, For Remembrance
Waters, British Artists, *vol. 1, pp. 329-330*

TONCER, George

Toncer was probably with Thorneycroft's Mounted Infantry. He was responsible for one illustration which appeared in *The Graphic* on 17 March 1900 entitled *With Thorneycroft's Mounted Infantry: A rest in camp after the Battle of Spion Kop*. The sketch was redrawn by George Soper.

Hofmeyr, Matton and Roets, Graphic Picture Index

TOPNALL, Frank J. 1870-1948

Topnall was born on the Isle of Wight on 27 April 1870. He produced a halftone print published by *The Spear* entitled *For Queen and old Ireland*. The National Army Museum possesses a copy of this print which is assumed to have Boer War relevance.

TOPPIN, H. S.

Lieutenant Toppin, a member of the Northumberland Fusi-

6

liers, was captured at Sanna's Post on 31 March 1900. He had come out to South Africa with his regiment, the 1st Battalion, aboard the SS *Gaul* and returned to England in 1901 to join the 3rd Battalion.

Stratford St Leger mentions him in his account of the Battle of Sanna's Post in his *War Sketches in Colour* (p. 128). While prisoners in Pretoria he and Capt. F. B. Morley formed an association, Morley, Toppin and Company, to print the prisoners' paper, *The Gram*. In his acknowledgement in the facsimile edition, Lord Rosslyn says 'Morley, Toppin and Company were our chief printers and were two officers in the Northumberland Fusiliers who worked indefatigably for hours every day'.

Toppin supplied at least six photographic illustrations to *The Graphic* from February to December 1900. One photograph of himself holding a pig, entitled *My Christmas Dinner at Modder River*, was published on 10 March 1900. Photographic contributions from Toppin also appeared in his regimental magazine, *St George's Gazette*.

The Gram
Hofmeyr, Matton and Roets, Graphic Picture Index

TORROMÉ, Francisco (Frank) J. fl. 1890-1908

Italian-born painter of landscape, military and figure subjects. He exhibited at the Royal Academy between 1898 and 1904. *Despatches* and *The Victor*, two of his paintings which were shown there in 1900, had Boer War interest. The Abe Bailey art sale in 1951 offered 'Two paintings depicting incidents of the Anglo Boer War 1900 by F.J. Turrome (sic)'.

Graves, Royal Academy, *vol. 8, p. 10*
Johnson and Greutzner, British Artists, *p. 505*

TOUBRAC, A.O.? 1

Artist with indistinct signature, as above, contributed an illustration to the special number of *Le Monde Illustré* of 17 November 1900. This issue was dedicated to President Kruger. The illustration, which appeared on p. 326, showed a seminude girl placing a portrait of Kruger just below the cross above her bed.

TOWNSEND, Frederick Henry Linton Jehne 1868-1920

Townsend was born in London on 25 February 1868. He studied at the Lambeth School of Art and among his fellow artists were Arthur Rackham, Leonard Raven-Hill, Reginald Savage, A.J. Finberg, Edgar Wilson, C. H. Aldin and Charles Ricketts. Townsend worked for *Punch* from 1903, becoming its first art editor in 1905. Besides *Punch* he contributed to many other illustrated magazines, including *Lady's Pictorial*, *The Illustrated London News*, *Windsor Magazine*, *Pall Mall*

Magazine, *Good News*, *Judy*, *Longbow*, *The Graphic*, *The Sphere*, *Tatler*, *The Queen*, *Gentlewoman*, *The Quiver*, *The Penny Illustrated Paper*, *Royal Magazine*, and *The Idler*. He illustrated several books including Kipling's *They* and *Brushwood Boy*.

Bradshaw describes the left-handed Townsend as 'a meticulous sketcher making several preliminary sketches for his drawings using models most thoroughly. He will not have a faked studio-made composition but a study of contemporary types, accessories, manner and customs which a future historian will find of value.'

Townsend's Boer War work was not prolific. He was responsible for some of the illustrations in *City of London Imperial Volunteers: Being the Story of the City Imperial Volunteers and Voluntary Regiments of the City of London 1300-1900*. It was published by George Newnes in 1900.

An illustration by Townsend entitled *Thirsty soldiers getting a drink at a native kraal in Natal* appeared in *The Sphere* on 26 May 1900.

Houfe, British Illustrators and Caricaturists, *p. 482*
Osterwalder, and Hubschmid and Bouret (eds.), Dictionnaire des Illustrateurs, *p. 1063*
SABIB, *vol. 2, p. 404*
Thorpe, English Illustration
Waters, British Artists, *vol. 1, p. 331*
Who was Who, *vol. 2, p. 1048*

TRENGLON, H.

Contributor to *The Illustrated London News*.

TREZONA, W.

W. Trezona, who was probably a member of the 3rd Battalion Middlesex Regiment, did a sketch which was published in *The Graphic* on 2 June 1900. It was redrawn by S.T. Dadd and entitled *The 3rd Battalion Middlesex Regiment manning the trenches before Jonono's Kop on April 10*.

Hofmeyr, Matton and Roets, Graphic Picture Index

TREIBER, W.

Illustrator of an embossed German card showing De Wet and a Boer family from the Transvaal. The card was published by A. Wohlmuth and inscribed: 'In aid of the poor women and children in the Transvaal' (translated).

TRINGHAM, Holland ?-1909   1

Painter and illustrator. Tringham studied art under Herbert Railton. He lived at Streatham and worked for several magazines until his death. Among others he contributed to *The Quiver*, *Black & White*, *The Illustrated Sporting & Dramatic News*, *The Illustrated London News*, *The Gentlewoman*, *The Sketch*, *Cassell's Family Magazine*, *Chums*, and *The English Illustrated Magazine*. *The Illustrated London News* referred to him as 'a pen draughtsman of singular felicity'.

Tringham exhibited two works at the Royal Academy in 1892 and 1894, and five works at the R.B.A. He was elected a member of the R.B.A. in 1894.

1 J. H. Thornely's wash drawing showing the guide Thornhill informing Colonel Stewart of Gough's disaster. It was reproduced in *After Pretoria: the Guerilla War*.
2 J. H. Thornely's work entitled *General Hunter relieving a wounded soldier* was reproduced in *Shurey's Illustrated*. It depicted General A. Hunter giving his horse to a wounded soldier after the battle of Farquhar's farm on 30 October 1899, just before the Siege of Ladysmith.
3 Georges Tiret-Bognet produced this pen-and-ink cartoon strip, entitled 'Cablegrammes', making fun of British troops landing in Durban, for an unidentified publication.
4 A. Toubrac produced this illustration, of a girl pinning up a portrait of Kruger above her bed, for *Le Monde Illustré*.
5 Oswaldo Tofani's *Le Petit Journal* front page tribute to General Piet Joubert, who died on 27 March 1900. The illustration appeared on 15 April the same year.
6 Holland Tringham, illustrator for *The Illustrated London News*.

Tringham's Boer War contributions were quite prolific and at least 25 works by him are identified in *The Illustrated London News*. (As some of his works were signed 'H.T.' only, they have not been included in the *ILN* Index.) Tringham seems to have been employed as retoucher of photographs and in one particular instance a signed photographic illustration which appeared in *The Illustrated London News* on 18 November 1899 shows an attempt to erase his signature. Thorpe describes his work for *The Illustrated London News* as 'excellent drawings of English scenes'.

De Wet, Illustrated London News Index
Houfe, British Illustrators and Caricaturists, *p. 482*
Johnson and Greutzner, British Artists, *p. 508*
Thorpe, English Illustration

TUCKER, Kidger ?-1913
Tucker was born in Canterbury. He went to South Africa in 1850 and served in the 8th Frontier War. He farmed in the King William's Town district, but later settled on the diamond fields in 1869. There he and his brother, Henry, took an active part in politics, and Kidger Tucker's political cartoons always drew admiring crowds when they 'were surreptitiously posted up in some popular canteen'. He settled in Johannesburg in August 1886 and lived there until his death on 23 August 1913. Soon after his arrival *Die Volkstem* of 15 October 1886 described him 'as that clever draughtsman'.

The Africana Museum has several watercolours by Tucker which are on loan by Mr and Mrs Hoernlé. (Mr Hoernlé is the great-grandson of Kidger Tucker.) All were done prior to the War or just after, but those dated 1897, 1898 and 1899 have political connotations and feature John Bull, Paul Kruger, Joseph Chamberlain, Rhodes and Hofmeyer.

Kidger Tucker's son, Senator W. Kidger Tucker, was mayor of Johannesburg from 1906 to 1907.

Kennedy, Pictures in the Africana Museum, *vol. 5, p. 726*
Schoonraad, S.A. Cartoonists, *pp. 361-362*

TURQUAND
The Owl cartoonist who satirized mostly local personalities.

TWEED, John 1869-1933
Sculptor. Tweed was born in Glasgow on 21 January 1869. He studied at Glasgow Art School. He became an associate of the Société Nationale des Beaux-Arts and was a friend of Rodin.

Tweed's works include the memorials to Earl Kitchener at the Horse Guards Parade, a monument to Sir George White, the Wilson memorial in Zimbabwe, Cecil Rhodes's statue in Bulawayo, and the statues of Alfred Beit in Harare and Jan van Riebeeck in Cape Town.

His Boer War memorials were to the members of St Mary's Hospital, Paddington, London, and to Lt. Col. George Elliott Benson (1861- 1901) of the Royal Regiment of Artillery who was killed at Braakenlaagte on 30 October 1901. The memorial, which was unveiled by Lord Methuen on 9 March 1904, is situated in Hexham, Northumberland.

Gildea, For Remembrance
Waters, British Artists, *vol. 1, p. 334*
Who was Who, *vol. 3, p. 1374*

ULLERSON, H. K.
One sketch by this artist appeared in *The Graphic* on 2 June 1900. It was redrawn by H.M. Paget and entitled *With General Buller's Force: An ancient uniform revived*.

Hofmeyr, Matton and Roets, Graphic Picture Index

VALLET, Louis 1856-?
Watercolourist and illustrator. Vallet was born in Paris on 26 February 1856. He worked for several periodicals, including *Le Charivari*, and became vice president of the French Society of Humorists.

One of his illustrations, dedicated to President Kruger, was published on p. 324 of the special issue of *Le Monde Illustré* on 17 November 1900 entitled *Hommage au Président Kruger*.

Bénézit, Dictionnaire antique, *vol. 8, p. 462*

VALLOTTON, Felix 1865-1925
Painter, engraver, and writer. Vallotton was born in Lausanne, Switzerland, on 28 December 1865. (He became a French citizen in 1900.) Vallotton studied under Boulanger and Lefebvre at the Académie Julian and the École des Beaux-Arts. From 1885 he exhibited at the Salon des Artistes Français. From 1891 to 1893 he wrote art reviews for the *Gazette de Lausanne* and from 1894 to 1903 he worked for the *Revue Blanche* in Paris. His work is also recorded in *L'Assiette au Beurre*.

Vallotton eventually concentrated on woodcuts and became associated with the Nabis group of artists. He became a founder member of the Committee of the 'Salon d'Automne' with Bonnard, Vuillard, Rousell and Collet. In 1908 his play *L'Homme Fort* was performed. His work was criticized in his native Switzerland and young girls were not admitted to his exhibitions. He was later to become a strong influence on German Expressionism.

Vallotton's only Boer War related work was a postwar woodcut on the back page of *Le Canard Sauvage* (2-8 May 1903). Entitled *Le Discours de Bienvenue*, it featured Kruger.

Vallotton often signed his work with the initials 'F.V.'.
Osterwalder, and Hubschmid and Bouret (eds.), Dictionnaire des Illustrateurs, *p. 1077*

VAN AKEN, Leo 1857-1904
Van Aken was born in Antwerp on 30 November 1857. He studied at the Antwerp Academy and his work was considered 'worth pausing to look at'. He contributed to *Antwerpen-Transvaal Gedenknummer*. Van Aken died on 11 January 1904.

Bénézit, Dictionnaire antique, *vol. 1, p. 64*
The Studio, *(1902) vol. 24, p. 292*

VAN AVERBEKE, E. M.
Van Averbeke was a member of the 'Skalden' Club, a group of energetic young Belgian artists who experimented with applied art forms. According to an article in *The Studio*, 'they were doing that which older and more influential societies dare not attempt'. Many of their members applied themselves successfully to the illustration of books and artistic postcards.

Van Averbeke used this type of illustration on postcards issued and sold by the Antwerp branch of the Algemeen Nederlandsche Verbond in aid of its pro-Boer appeal. One of the postcard cartoon illustrations, depicting a spider and a fly and entitled *Engeland-Transvaal*, appeared on the back cover of Louis van Neck's *Een Noodlottige Oorlog in het Boerenland*, and of the French version of the same book

(also published by De Vos and Van der Groen, Antwerp).

Van Averbeke often signed his work with the initials 'E.M.v.A.'.
SABIB, *vol. 3, pp. 478-479*
SAPRG Newsletter, *Sept. 1985 'Louis van Neck postcards' by R. Greenwall*
The Studio, *(1900), vol. 20, p. 60*

VAN BREDA, P.
Cartographer who drew the map used by Ben Viljoen in his *My Reminiscences of the Anglo Boer War* (London, 1902).

VAN DER MERWE, François (Rooi Faan) 1879-1958
Van der Merwe was born on the farm Metz in the Fauresmith district on 25 August 1877. His red hair earned him the nickname 'Rooi Faan' or 'Rooi duivel'.

During the War he was captured at Jagersfontein. For undisclosed reasons he was sentenced to death by a military tribunal under Maj. Kinghall. He was released when the Boers captured the town, but was later recaptured and sent to Bermuda.

While in Bermuda he did some fine artistic woodcarvings as well as work in iron, copper, leather and tin. He is best known for his sandstone monument on the island which he carved in memory of the 35 prisoners who died in captivity there.

Van der Merwe died at Krugerspos in May 1958.
Historica, *Sept. 1979 'Die Graveurder van Bermuda' by Dr C.A.R. Schulenberg*

VAN DER OUDERAA, Pierre Jan 1841-1915
Historical painter. Van der Ouderaa was born in Antwerp on 13 January 1841. He studied at the Antwerp Academy and visited Italy and the East. He was awarded medals in London and Antwerp.

Van der Ouderaa was a contributor to *Antwerpen-Transvaal Gedenknummer*. He died in Antwerp on 5 January 1915.

Bénézit, Dictionnaire antique, *vol. 6, p. 462*

VAN DOCK
Artist of an Italian Boer War postcard entitled *L'Anglais*. He was probably the Italian postcard artist Vincenzo Nasi, who used a similar pseudonym.

Fanelli and Godoli, Art Nouveau Postcards, *p. 77*

VAN DOOMAAL, Theo
Illustrator of a postcard dedicated to 'The women and children of the South African heroes'. The card, dated 1901, was published by P.J. van Melle Czn, Antwerp.

VAN DORT, E. F.
Two illustrations by Van Dort, who was possibly a Boer prisoner of war in Ceylon, appeared in *The Graphic*. One, redrawn by George Soper, was entitled *The Ceylon Contingent for South Africa: A Military Tattoo in its honour at Colombo* (3 March 1900). The other, redrawn by F.J. Waugh, was entitled *Boer prisoners cheering Kruger* (15 September 1900). The index to *The Graphic* refers to Van Dort as 'Evan Dort'.

Hofmeyr, Matton and Roets, Graphic Picture Index

VAN GELDORP, Petrus Johannes Antonius Christiaan 1872-c.1935
Cartoonist. Van Geldorp was born in Rotterdam on 11 September 1872. His father, Wilhelmus Petrus van Geldorp, was a well-known artist who was responsible for his son's art education. Van Geldorp jnr. used lithography and etching.

His Boer War cartoons appeared regularly in *Delftsche Courant, Amsterdamsche Courant* and *De Tijd*. Many of his *Amsterdamsche Courant* cartoons later appeared on postcards. Some of these unnumbered cards, which also advertised the paper's subscription rates, were as follows:
1. *Onderhandelingen tusschen Engeland en Transvaal.*

2. *John Bull's Reizen naar Transvaal en Vrijstaat.*
3. *John Bull in Zuid-Afrika.*
4. *Een spelletje skat.*
5. *Lady-Smith.*
6. *John Bull's Reis naar Pretoria.*
7. *Englesche overwinningen.*
8. *John Bull en de Mogendheden.*
9. *Op Glad Ijs.*

The earliest postmark date on these cards is September 1900. A separate card showing an illustration by Van Geldorp of De Wet was published by Mrs Amiot of s'Gravenhage.

Scheen, Nederlandse Beeldende Kunstenaars, vol. 2, p. 41

VAN HELSDINGEN, A.
A lithograph of *De Wet, Hero of Amajuba* by Helsdingen was sold at the Volks Auctions on 26 June 1981. Nothing else is known about this artist.

VAN KORSINKSKY, E.
A member of the Bethlehem commando during the War, Van Korsinksky was taken prisoner and sent to Diyatalawa, Ceylon. He produced an illustrated account, dated 1901, of some of his experiences in the camp, which included his views on the British presence in South Africa. Written in English, the manuscript was very anti-British, as were the caricatures, some of which attacked Boer prisoners who signed up for police duty on the Indian border. He labelled them 'rats' and showed no sympathy for one of their number who, filled with remorse, committed suicide.

The diary was dedicated to 'his honour President Steyn as a token of admiration'. The South African Library acquired the diary from Clarke's Bookshop in 1988.

VAN KUYCK, Frans Pieter Lodewyk 1852-1915
Illustrator, genre and landscape painter in watercolour. Van Kuyck was born in Antwerp on 9 June 1852. His father, Jean Louis, and brother, Pierre Lodewyk, were both artists.

He contributed to the pro-Boer souvenir publication *Antwerpen-Transvaal Gedenknummer* (in which his name is spelt 'Van Cuyck'). He died in Antwerp on 31 May 1915.

Bénézit, Dictionnaire antique, vol. 5, p. 333

VAN LEEMPUTTEN, Frans 1850-1914
Genre and landscape painter. Van Leemputten was born in Werchter on 29 December 1850. He won several medals and awards in Munich, Amsterdam, Brussels, Antwerp, Barcelona, Vienna and Athens.

Van Leemputten was a contributor to *Antwerpen-Transvaal Gedenknummer*. He died in Antwerp on 26 November 1914.

Bénézit, Dictionnaire antique, vol. 5, pp. 474-475

VAN LESNOUT
A cartoonist, apparently with this name, worked for the *Chicago Interocean*.

VAN MIEGHEM, Eugeen 1875-? [1]
Painter and engraver. Van Mieghem was born in Antwerp on 1 October 1875. He was a pupil at the Antwerp Academy.

Van Mieghem was a contributor to *Antwerpen-Transvaal Gedenknummer*. He is almost certainly the 'E.V.M.' who produced at least three cards for the Antwerp branch of the Algemeen Nederlandsche Verbond. They were: *Transvaal: Vrij of Dood, Transvaal: Gij Zult niet Dooden,* and *Transvaal: Overwinnen of Sterven.*

Bénézit, Dictionnaire antique, vol. 6, p. 115

VAN MOERKERKEN
Naby Ladysmith in January 1900, a watercolour by Van Moerkerken after W. du Toit jnr., is in the National Army Museum collection.

VAN NESTE, Alfred Joseph Auguste 1874-? [1]
Painter, illustrator and etcher. Van Neste was born in Bruges, Belgium, on 4 March 1874. He studied under his uncle, Flor M. van Acker. He was an active member of the 'Skalden' Club, a group of young artists who experimented with applied arts including postcard illustrations.

Van Neste contributed to *Antwerpen-Transvaal Gedenknummer.*

Bénézit, Dictionnaire antique, vol. 6, p. 335
The Studio, *(1900) vol. 20, p. 60*

VAN OFFEL, Edmond 1871-?
Illustrator and artist. Van Offel was born in Antwerp on 14 April 1971. He was a member of the 'Skalden' Club, a group of young Belgian artists who provided avant-garde illustrations for books and postcards.

Van Offel contributed to *Antwerpen-Transvaal Gedenknummer*, a souvenir publication issued by the Antwerp branch of the Algemeen Nederlandsche Verbond, in aid of the Boers.

Bénézit, Dictionnaire antique, vol. 6, p. 412
The Studio, *(1900) vol. 20, p. 60*

VAN PAPENDRECHT, Jan Hoynck *see* HOYNCK VAN PAPENDRECHT

VAN WELIE, Antoon 1866-1956
Portrait painter. Van Welie was born in Druten, the Netherlands, on 18 December 1866. Until 1885 he lived and worked in Vught. Later he moved to Den Bosch where he stayed until 1886 and then to Italy in 1893. Still later he worked in Paris, London and Greece. From 1886 to 1891 he studied at the Antwerp Academy under Grips and Stracke. At this time he became an international portrait painter, specializing in figure studies and religious subjects. When the Boer leaders visited Europe in 1902 he did several charcoal sketches and paintings of them. Often his subjects signed their names on his work.

When the Imperial Conference was held in London in 1909 an exhibition of Van Welie's paintings of former Boer leaders and their wives was opened in July by Sir Richard Solomon, Agent-General of the Transvaal, 'in the absence of General Botha'. Among the 45 works on view were five portraits of De Wet, and studies of Gen. de la Rey, Gen. G. D. Joubert, Gen. Kretzinger (sic), Gen. Ferreira, Mrs Ferreira, Gen. Louis Botha, and Mrs Louis Botha.

The War Museum of the Boer Republics in Bloemfontein has charcoal portraits by Van Welie of Gen. Kritzinger, Comdt. W. D. Fouche, A. D. Wolmarans and Gen. J. H. de la Rey.

Van Welie died in The Hague on 24 September 1956.

Bénézit, Dictionnaire antique, vol. 8, p. 704
The Graphic, *31 July 1909, pp. 138-139*
Bloemfontein War Museum Catalogue

VAN WOUW, Anthonie (Anton) 1862-1945 [1]
Van Wouw was born near Utrecht, the Netherlands, on 26 December 1862. He studied at the Academy for Art in Rotterdam and in the beginning was influenced by the French sculptor Auguste Rodin. He also studied under the Belgian sculptor Josef Grave. In 1890 he went to South Africa and, failing to find employment in his chosen field, worked for a gunsmith in Pretoria. In his free time, however, he gave lectures in painting and sketching. He eventually found employment with *The Press* and *De Pers*, for which he commenced work in 1892 on the death of Howard Schroeder, their original cartoonist. Van Wouw's cartoons were originally signed 'A. van Wouw', but later he used the initials 'A.v.W.' only. None of his original cartoons is extant and it is believed that they were done by lithography.

In collaboration with Frans Oerder, Van Wouw did the murals in the reception hall for the opening of the Pretoria-Lourenço Marques railway line in 1895. He also illustrated *Die Gedenkboek*, published to mark the occasion. In 1896 he was commissioned by Sammy Marks to do the statue of Paul Kruger which was eventually erected in Church Square, Pretoria, in October 1954. For this commission he travelled to Holland and Italy.

Van Wouw became a friend of Kruger and made several statues and busts of the president over a considerable period of time. One such bust was admired by the very religious Kruger who admonished the sculptor not to think he was God because he had modelled the figure so life-like, adding that only God could create life. Van Wouw worked without the use of sketches or drawings, preferring to model from the living object. Kruger, however, refused to sit for him and he was forced to use photographs.

Van Wouw returned to South Africa only two weeks before the outbreak of war in 1899, having supervised the casting of the Kruger statue in Italy. Throughout the War the statue remained in storage in Lourenço Marques, until after the peace declaration when the figures comprising the plinth were commandeered and sent back to England by Kitchener. They were eventually returned to South Africa many years later. When the British occupied Pretoria they requested Van Wouw to alter the Republic coat of arms which he had modelled for the Raadzaal and to construct a British coat of arms in its place. Van Wouw, who had signed an oath of allegiance to the Republic, refused to comply with the request.

Most of his Boer War work was done after the War, but in 1901 he did sketches of De Wet, De la Rey and Beyers, and probably also Louis Botha.

In 1907 he produced *Slegte Nuus* (bronze) and *Kruger in Ballingskap* (bronze). *Die Brandwag*, also in bronze, was done in 1910. His bronze bust of President Kruger was done in 1914, as were the bronze and plaster busts of De la Rey. De Wet's bust was completed in 1916 and that of President Steyn in 1917.

One of his most famous sculptures is the Vrouemonument which stands in the grounds of the War Museum of the Boer Republics in Bloemfontein. This monument, which was designed by the Pretoria architect Frans Soff, was unveiled by Rachel Steyn (the ex-President's wife) on 16 December 1913. The three panels by Van Wouw depict the suffering of the women and children in the concentration camps but nevertheless show hope for the future. Steyn, De Wet and Kestell are buried at the foot of the monument, as are the ashes of Emily Hobhouse.

Another sculpture by Van Wouw with Boer War relevance is his *Kruger na die vertrek van die eerste burghers na die front.*

During the visit of the Boer generals De la Rey, De Wet and Botha to Europe in 1902 the International Trading Company of Amsterdam published a card showing portraits of the three signed by Van Wouw and dated Pretoria 1901. Cards with the individual portraits by unidentified Dutch and French publishers were also produced.

Van Wouw died on 31 July 1945. In 1973 Anton Rupert bought the sculptor's house and presented it to the University of Pretoria as a museum to be known as the Van Wouwhuis.

Cohen, Anton van Wouw
SESA, *vol. 11, pp. 176 and 488*
Schoonraad, pp. 262 ff.
The Studio, *(1909) vol. 47, p. 158*
Bloemfontein War Museum Catalogue

Felix Valloton produced this woodcut, entitled *Le Discours de Bienvenue,* for the back page of *Le Canard Sauvage* of 2-8 May 1903.

1

2a 2b

VEBER, Jean 1868-1928 8

Cartoonist and lithographer. Veber was born in Paris on 13 February 1868. Initially he trained as a genre painter. Studying under Maillot and under Delauney and Cabanel at the École des Beaux-Arts, he later switched very successfully to satire. His brother, Pierre, was a journalist with *Gil Blas* and Jean Veber was persuaded to draw caricatures for that paper. Veber also revealed considerable talent as a lithographer and won several awards at the Salon des Artistes Français, including an honourable mention in 1894 and a silver medal in 1900. He contributed for many years to *Le Rire, Gil Blas, Le Journal* and *L'Illustration*. His work was not without controversy and in 1897 his composition *Butchery*, which depicted Bismarck as a butcher of people, caused an official outcry.

Veber's most famous cartoons, which also caused official censure, were those published in *L'Assiette au Beurre* (No. 26). Appearing on 28 September 1901, this issue of *L'Assiette au Beurre* was entitled 'Les camps de Reconcentration au Transvaal' and ran to at least 12 editions. According to Mendelssohn, the Paris police took action against the publication of the back cover cartoon *L'Impudique Albion*, which showed Edward VII's face superimposed on Albion's bare buttocks. Some issues in editions from the ninth onwards had the offending anatomy covered by a blue polka dot petticoat. A German version, *Das Blutbuch von Transvaal*, and a Dutch version, *De Boerenkampen*, were also pub-

lished. Dr Eysler, the *Lustige Blätter* publisher, produced the German version which had 24 caricatures and S.L. van Looy of Amsterdam published the Dutch version which had only 22 of the illustrations. Neither reproduced the offending cartoon.

In 1915 *La Satire: l'humor dans l'art* was published in Brussels. This was a reprint of the second edition of No. 26 '*L'Assiette au Beurre*'. It was published by the Germans as war propaganda, to remind the French of their attitude to the English 15 years earlier. The back page cartoon was omitted once more for the 'sake of decency' ('L'omission en a été dictée par des motifs de délicatesse'). A comment on the back page also draws attention to the fact that the cartoons were drawn 'by the hand of the master Jean Veber'.

The illustrations in the original were as follows:
cover *Le Silence* (coloured).
p. 394 *Le vieux Kruger*
p. 395 *Lord Kitchener* (coloured)
p. 396 *Les Progrès de la Science*
p. 397 *Le Verger du Roi Éduard*
p. 398 *La Revue de Bétheny: Le Nuage* (coloured)
p. 400 *Vers le Camp de Reconcentration*
p. 401 *Bravoure Brittanique*
p. 402 *L'insaisissable de Wet* (coloured)
p. 403 *Galanterie Brittanique*
p. 404-5 *L'Épave* (coloured)

p. 406 *Vers le Camp de Reconcentration*
p. 407 *S. M. Édouard VII, Roi d'Angleterre, Empereur des Indes* (coloured). *Le Foudre de Guerre.*
p. 408 *Les Camps de Reconcentration*
p. 409 *Le Deep-Level: L'honorable Chamberlain*
p. 410-11 *La Reine Victoria et Madame Kruger* (coloured)
p. 412 *La Visite du Tsar en France: Le Baiser sterile*
p. 413 *Les Acheteurs de Biens* (2 cartoons)
p. 414 *Les camps de Reconcentration* (coloured)
p. 415 *Le Royaume-Uni*
p. 416 *L'Impudique Albion* (back page) (coloured)

Sixteen of the illustrations were reproduced on postcards with both French and Dutch and Dutch-only inscriptions. J. Picot of 327 Rue St Honore in Paris had the publishing rights in France. His imprint, however, appears only some of the cards. The Dutch publisher is not identified.

As far as is known *Les Acheteurs de Biens, Les Progrès de La Science*, both *Vers le Camp de Reconcentrations* and *Les camps de concentration* on p. 408, and *L'Impudique Albion* were not reproduced on the postcards. However, coloured pirated crude copies of *L'Impudique Albion* and *L'Épave* by unidentified artists and publishers exist. Anti-British cigarette cards of Veber's drawings were produced in Germany in 1941.

It is said that Veber stopped drawing caricatures in about 1912 and devoted himself to his first artistic pursuit, lithography, and painting. Veber died in Paris on 28 November 1928.

Bénézit, Dictionnaire antique, *vol. 8, pp. 489-490*
Feaver, Masters of Caricature, *pp. 121-122*
Mendelssohn, Mendelssohn's Bibliography, *vol. 2, p. 562*
SABIB, *vol. 4, pp. 647-648*

VEDDER, Simon Harmon 1866-?

Painter, sculptor and illustrator. Vedder was born in Amsterdam, New York, on 9 October 1866. He was trained at the Metropolitan Museum School in New York before going to Paris

L'INSAISISSABLE DEWET

3

.... Seul un misérable fou refuse jusqu'ici de se rendre. C'est lui qui porte l'ESPÉRANCE des derniers rebelles.

4

2c   2d

and becoming a pupil at the Académie Julian under Bouguereau and Robert Fleury and at the École des Beaux-Arts under Crémone and Glaize. He received an honourable mention at the Paris Exhibition in 1899 and a second class medal at the Crystal Palace in London. After settling in London in 1896 he married the painter Eva Roos.

Vedder was a fairly prolific illustrator and worked for *Black & White*, *The Strand Magazine*, *Cassell's Family Magazine*, *The Idler* and *Pall Mall Magazine*. He also illustrated several books for A. & C. Black & Co.

Vedder's Boer War work appeared in *With the Flag to Pretoria*. His illustrations in G.A. Henty's *The Young Colonists* (Blackie and Son, 1885) related to the First Boer War and the Zulu war.

He often signed his work with the initials 'S.H.V.'.
Bénézit, Dictionnaire antique, *vol. 8, p. 493*
Houfe, British Illustrators and Caricaturists, *p. 485*
Thorpe, English Illustration

VENTER, Johannes H. 1871-?   1

Venter was born at Kaalfontein in the Ventersdorp district and fought on the side of the Boers. He was captured at Paardeberg on 27 February 1900 while a member of the Potchefstroom Commando. He is known to have done at least two naive watercolours. One, in the author's collection, is of the Battle of Modder River, and the other, dated 12 November 1900 is a diagrammatic representation in pen, ink, watercolour and blue chalk of the Green Point prisoner of war camp. This painting was sold at Christie's on 2 July 1980 and is now in the Africana Museum.

Personal communication with Roy Stockman,
Librarian of the Anglo-Boer War Philatelic Society

VERBER

Artist of the peace card entitled *Le jugement de l'Histoire Juin 1902*. The card, which was published by A.B., Paris, has both coloured and uncoloured states.

VERHAERT, Piet 1852-1908

Genre and landscape painter and etcher. Also known as Pieter

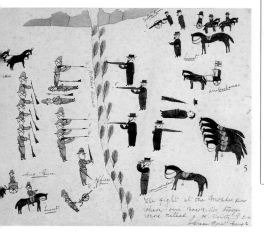

5

or Pierre Verhart, Verhaert was born in Antwerp on 26 February 1852. He contributed to *Antwerpen-Transvaal Gedenknummer*. He died in East Dunkirk on 4 August 1908.

VERNON, Frederick Charles Victor de 1858-1912

Sculptor and medal engraver. Vernon was born in Paris on 17 November 1858. He studied under Chaplain and Tusset. He was created Chevalier of the Legion of Honour in 1900.

In the same year, Vernon was commissioned to design and construct a plaque which was presented to President Kruger by Queen Wilhelmina of the Netherlands to mark his arrival in Europe. This plaque was illustrated in *Le Monde Illustré* on 15 December 1900 (p. 389).

Bénézit, Dictionnaire antique, *vol. 8, p. 535*

VICTA

Pseudonym of artist responsible for seven of the eight illustrations on the 'La Guerre du Transvaal' series of 'cartes postales satiriques'. These cards were also published in limited numbered editions. Others were hand-coloured.

Victa's cards were as follows:
La Guerre du Transvaal – Rôle de Salisbury
La Guerre du Transvaal – Rôle d'Edouard VII
La pieuvre Anglaise
Le Gouffre
La Guerre du Transvaal – Rôle des Tommys: Se rendre Evénement regrettable dû à l'affollement des mules et des ânes
La Guerre du Transvaal – Rôle de John Chamberlain: Encaisser.

The eighth card, *Eduard VII et Le Transvaal 7 Mars 1902*, was the work of 'Darsane' (see p. 124).

VIERGE, Daniel 1851-1904

Genre painter, watercolourist and illustrator. Vierge, whose full name was Daniel Urrabieta Ortiz Y Vierge, was born in Madrid on 5 March 1851. His father, Vincente, was a well-known Spanish illustrator.

Vierge worked for *Le Monde Illustré*, *The Idler* and *The Illustrated London News* and was responsible for the illustrations in several well-known classical works.

During the War he contributed illustrations to *Paris-Pretoria* (pp. 4 and 16). He also illustrated J.H. Rosny's *La Guerre Anglo-Boer* (*Revue Blanche*, Paris, 1902). Rosny was the pseudonym of Joseph Boëx-Borel and Sérphin Boëx.

Vierge died in Boulogne-sur-Seine on 16 May 1904.
Bénézit, Dictionnaire antique, *vol. 8, pp. 435-436*
Houfe, British Illustrators and Caricaturists, *pp. 485-486*
SABIB, vol. 4, p. 84
Thorpe, English Illustration

VIGORS, Philip Urban Walter 1863-1935

Soldier-artist. Vigors was born in County Carlow, Ireland, on 8 February 1863. He joined the Devonshire Regiment as a lieu-

tenant on 9 September 1882 and was promoted to captain on 4 February 1891. He served in Burma in 1891, taking part in operations in the Kachin Hills where he won a medal with clasp. He served in the Boer War, being present at the Relief of Ladysmith, Spioenkop, and Colenso, where he was slightly wounded. He saw action at Vaal Kranz in February 1900 and took part in the operations at Tugela Heights on 14 to 27 February, where he was wounded again. Vigors saw action once again, at Pieter's Hill, and his operations in Natal in March 1900 were followed by action at Laings Nek from 6 to 9 June 1900. At this stage he was appointed as railway staff officer. He was mentioned in despatches by Redvers Buller on 30 March and 9 November 1900 and in the *London Gazette* on 8 February and 10 September 1901. He received the Queen's medal with five clasps and the King's medal with two clasps and was created a Companion of the Distinguished Service Order on 27 September 1901. The entry in the *London Gazette* reads: 'Philip Urban Walter Vigors, Captain Devonshire Regiment. In recognition of services during the operations in South Africa.' The insignia were presented by King Edward on 24 October 1902. Vigors was promoted to major on 9 May 1902.

Although Vigors was primarily a photographer and several of his photographs were published in *The Illustrated London News* and *With the Flag to Pretoria*, some of his sketches were also used by the home-based artists. *The scene of the fighting at Monte Cristo Hill on February 19 1900* appeared in *The Illustrated London News* on 31 March 1900. It was redrawn by W.B. Robinson.

Vigors died on 30 October 1935. Another Philip Urban Vigors, who was with the Irish Regiment, is often confused with his namesake.

Creagh and Humphris, The D.S.O., *vol. 2, p. 188*
De Wet, Illustrated London News Index

VILLIERS, Frederic 1852-1922   1

Villiers was born in London on 23 April 1852. He was educat-

---

1 This illustration of King Edward VII wetting himself was done by Jean Veber for *L'Assiette au Beurre* in September 1901. Entitled *La Foudre de Guerre*, it was considered obscene and was omitted from the Dutch and German versions of this edition.
2a, b, c and d. Jean Veber's grim cartoons showing the suffering of Boer women and children in the concentration camps were featured in *L'Assiette au Beurre*.
3 Jean Veber's portrayal of Christiaan de Wet, 'the hero of the last rebels'. It was De Wet who carried on the guerrilla war for two years after the capitals of the two Boer republics had fallen. The cartoon was published in *L'Assiette au Beurre* on 29 September 1901.
4 One of the controversial cartoons drawn by Jean Veber for *L'Assiette au Beurre*'s special 'concentration camp' number. Kitchener's scorched earth and concentration camp policies are dramatically portrayed.
5 A naive watercolour of the Battle of Modder River by Boer P.O.W. J. H. Venter, done while he was being held at the Green Point Camp. A drawing of the camp by the same artist is in the Africana Museum, Johannesburg.
6 Veteran war correspondent Frederic Villiers.

6

ed at Guines, Pas de Calais (France). For a while he studied at the South Kensington schools of Art, and in 1871 he became a student at the Royal Academy. He joined *The Graphic* in 1876, serving as an artist-correspondent with the veteran correspondent Archibald Forbes in the Serbian Campaign. He also served in the Russo-Turkish War and was present at the battles of Plevna and Shipka. In the Afghan War he saw action at Gandamak. On 11 June 1882 he was on board the H.M.S. *Condor* with Lord Charles Beresford during the bombardment of Alexandria and the landing of the marines. Later he accompanied the Highland Brigade in the Battle of Tel el Kebir.

In 1883 Villiers attended the coronation of Tsar Alexander III in Moscow. In February the following year he was back in Egypt and the Sudan where he was present at the battles of El Teb and Tamai. As special correspondent for *The Daily News* he accompanied Admiral Hewett to Abyssinia in 1884 and the following year he was with the Khartoum relief expedition and saw action at the Battle of Abu Klea.

The Serbian and Bulgarian incidents in the same year provided Villiers with the opportunity to visit Eastern Europe. On his way home he was stopped in Venice by a telegram from *The Graphic* telling him to go to Burma. In 1894 he accompanied the Japanese army during its campaign against the Chinese and was present at the Battle of Pingyang and the taking of Port Arthur. He went on a lecture tour around the world in 1895 and a year later once again visited Moscow, for the coronation of Nicholas II.

During the Greco-Turkish War of 1897 Villiers represented *The Standard* and was the first correspondent to use the cinema camera in the field. In August 1898 he accompanied the Sirdar's army on its march to Omdurman. In that campaign he represented *The Illustrated London News* and *The Globe*. He rated the Battle of Omdurman and the memorial service to Gordon at Khartoum as his most memorable experiences. In his autobiography Villiers mentions that he introduced the bicycle to the Sudan.

Writing in the supplement to *The Illustrated London News* of 28 April 1900, *With a great army: an illustrated account of the campaign in South Africa*, Villiers mentioned that he was in the middle of a lecture tour in Australia when he was ordered to South Africa. He received the following telegram on 12 October 1899: 'War conditions with the Transvaal exist as from today'. He left immediately for South Africa and, weighing up the situation from information at his disposal, he felt that the relief of Kimberley and the rescue of Cecil Rhodes would probably be the most exciting events to be covered. In addition, he felt that the invasion of the Orange Free State, which he thought should be 'the principal strategic movement of the campaign', must take place in the comparatively open country between the Orange River and the Modder. He decided to land at Port Elizabeth and go by train to join Lord Methuen, who he believed was about to force his way through to relieve Kimberley.

In Port Elizabeth Colonel Fairholme, in charge of the lines of communication from Port Elizabeth to De Aar, gave him the necessary permits to proceed to the front. At the Orange River he reported to the commandant, who said he regretted very much that he could not allow Villiers to proceed further as the press censor at Modder River had wired that no more correspondents were to be sent on. Lord Methuen had become so fed up with war correspondents that 'he wanted no more'. Villiers, however, had been with Lord Methuen in Egypt in 1882 and decided to press his luck and petition the general himself for a pass to the front. Methuen did not seem to class Viliers with the others and he was delighted to receive a telegram from Methuen saying 'Glad to see you, come at once'. His companion, Frederick Wilkinson of the *Sydney Daily Telegraph*, was also granted permission to proceed to the front and they prepared to take the first available train, leaving at 9 o'clock that night. As Villiers was about to board the train an official handed him some despatches to deliver urgently to Lord Methuen, as no officers were available. The official warned him to destroy them 'if the enemy attacked the train *en route*, should (he) find the situation hopeless'.

At dawn they arrived at their destination, where 'puffs of our bursting shrapnel could be seen against the purple kopje of the enemy's position'. Villiers was so excited on his arrival at Modder River that he immediately hauled out his sketchbook, which he rapidly filled with sketches of the action. In the excitement he almost forgot about the special despatch he carried for Lord Methuen. When he remembered he tried to locate Methuen, but he was obstructed by the soldier on duty, who refused to let him see the general. He records in his memoirs that the production of his card, which he ordered the officer to take to the wounded Methuen, brought an immediate response and he was permitted to visit the commander who, having sustained leg wounds at the Belmont, was recuperating in his Cape cart. Methuen informed him that the setback at Magersfontein had delayed his advance and that they would not be able to resume the offensive for some weeks. Hearing that Buller was about to push on to Ladysmith Villiers decided to return to Noupoort and then to Port Elizabeth to rejoin his wife for Christmas.

He drove back in his Cape cart and was about half way to his destination when a patrol of Suffolks ordered him to halt. They examined his papers, his cart was searched and he could see that he was looked upon with considerable suspicion before eventually being allowed to proceed. Later, while dozing in his cart, he was awakened by the noise of gunfire. He jumped up to pull the reins from his driver, put his head out of the back of the cart and looked towards the adjacent koppie, when a rifle went off in the opposite direction. He saw British soldiers looking very businesslike with their rifles ready for any emergency. 'Why didn't you stop when we challenged?' asked the soldier. 'We never heard you,' replied Villiers, 'Why didn't you stop in the road instead of shooting 100 yards off?' 'Well,' sir, you nearly lost your horses,' said one of them. Villiers was probably more shocked than angry, especially when it was explained that the Boer officers always rode in Cape carts and that there had been a scare that day.

After reaching Noupoort without further adventure Villiers went down to Port Elizabeth by goods train. At Christmas further bad news came from the three fronts, but he was able to find an empty transport about to start for Natal en route for India, and, with the help of Captain Stewart of the B.I.S. *Lindula*, he was allowed to proceed with her to Durban. He attempted to make his way to the Natal front but the calamity at Spioenkop and the recrossing of the Tugela blocked his way. So once again he returned to Port Elizabeth, hoping to get back to the column heading for the relief of Kimberley.

In his report in the supplement of *The Illustrated London News* on 28 April 1900, Villiers mentions that one of the most imposing sights of the campaign was the march of the C.I.V.s with the captured Cronje to Modder River:

> In a quaint cart covered with khaki and pulled by four artillery horses, Cronje, his wife, secretary, and grandson, made their last march across their native veldt for many a month – perhaps years. On arriving at Modder River station, General Douglas met the distinguished prisoners, and Cronje introduced his wife, a meek little lady looking rather bedraggled in a black silk dress covered with dust.

He noticed, rather ungallantly, that her 'figure appeared rather unshapely'. This was accounted for on his return to Paardeberg when a greatly excited young officer rushed up to him and said, 'Villiers, Villiers! I have the most interesting loot in camp'. 'What is it?' he asked. Holding a mysterious scroll aloft the officer answered: 'Why, Mrs. Cronje's corsets!'. This incident was illustrated in *The Illustrated London News* by Ernest Shérie, drawn from one of Villiers' sketches.

Villiers reported the horror of the scene at Paardeberg, with the sight and stench of the rotting carcasses of the Boer horses and oxen. When the photogravure of the *Surrender of Cronje at Paardeberg* by Caton Woodville (after a sketch by Villiers) was published, *The Illustrated London News* announced proudly that Villiers was the only artist who had been permitted by Roberts to view the scene.

When he finally reached Kimberley he located Cecil Rhodes in his bath. Rhodes's secretary gave him a promise of a later interview. Not long afterwards Villiers met him and Rhodes offered to take him on a conducted tour of the recently beleaguered city. It was here that Villiers did his famous sketch, *The relief of Kimberley*, which was later redrawn by Samuel Begg, showing General French shaking hands with Cecil Rhodes. This illustration appeared in *The Illustrated London News* on 24 March 1900.

In April 1900 Villiers was back in England where he was in great demand as a lecturer. He was awarded the Queen's South Africa medal on 17 February 1903. In 1904, during the Russo-Japanese War, he was sent by his paper to Port Arthur with the Japanese forces. He was later with the Spanish army in Morocco in 1909 and the Italian army in Tripoli in 1911. In 1912 and 1913 he accompanied the Bulgarian army in the Balkan War and was also present at the siege of Adrianople. In 1914 Villiers, despite the fact that he was almost 62 years old, accompanied the French army and was present at the Allied retreat at Flanders and Ypres. He saw and reported the action at Neuve-Chapelle, La Boiselle, the Aisne and Verdun. After serving for two and half years with the British and French armies he left France on a lecture tour and to visit other fronts. He was unable to get into Mesopotamia but visited the North West Frontier and saw fighting in India before continuing his tour through the Straits Settlements, China, Japan, Canada, the United States and South Africa.

His publications, which he wrote and illustrated, included *Pictures of Many Wars* (1902); *Port Arthur* (1905); *Peaceful Personalities and Warriors bold* (1907); and *Villiers: His Five Decades of Adventure* (1921). His obituary in *The Times* records that 'the two volumes (of the last-mentioned publication) were full of entertaining anecdotes and hair-breadth escapes'. Villiers was not regarded as one of the better artists of the Boer War, but he was one of the more prolific and ubiquitous of the old school of war correspondents. He was a well-known lecturer and raconteur and was in great demand all over the world for his lectures.

Pat Hodgson in *The War Illustrators* mentions that none of his work was reproduced in facsimile. This is not quite correct. While most of his work for publication was redrawn by home-based artists, a few of his sketches, particularly of the march on Kimberley, were reproduced in facsimile in *The Illustrated London News*. As a contributor of sketches to that magazine and other publications, he certainly did not match Melton Prior; nevertheless nearly 50 of his works are recorded in *The Illustrated London News* Index.

Two of his battle paintings were exhibited at the Royal Academy: *The Road Home; the return of an Imperial brigade from Afghanistan* (1882) and *Fighting Arabi with his own weapons; an incident of the battle of TelelKebir* (1883).

Villiers died on 2 April 1922.

Hodgson, The War Illustrators
Houfe, British Illustrators and Caricaturists, *p. 486*
The Orders and Medals Research Society, *Summer 1986, 'War Correspondents in South Africa 1899-1902' by Patrick Street*
The Illustrated London News, *supplement 28 April 1900 and obituary 15 April 1922*
The Times (obituary), *6 April 1922*
Thorpe, English Illustration
Villiers, Villiers: His Five Decades of Adventure.
Who was Who, *vol. 2, p. 1074*

V.K.

Illustrator of a card in two forms by Behrendt & Wartenberger of Berlin. The card shows a Boer gazing up at an Angel of Peace. One of the cards is inscribed: 'In remembrance of the Peace agreement in the Boer War' (translated from German).

V.M. (or M.V.) 1

A cartoonist using this monogram was employed by Uitge-

wers van de Internationale Postkaartenhandel, 86 Rijn Street, Arnhem. A series of ten anti-British chromolithographic cards was published in about August 1900. J. A. Luii of Amsterdam was the lithographer. The unnumbered cards were as follows (the first five were vertical and the rest horizontal):

1. *Satan Chamberlain en zijn vriend Bachus*
2. *John Bull en die Mogendheden*
3. *Gouddelver Chamberlain*
4. *Twee Philantropen*
5. *John Bull: Na den Oorlog*
6. *Audiëntie bij Oom Paul*
7. *Diner bij Oom Paul*
8. *De Vlucht van Rhodes uit Kimberley naar . . . de Maan*
9. *Engelsche Beschavingsmiddelen*
10. *Chamberlain op het Gouden Koord*

VOGEL, Hermann 1856-1918

Painter and book illustrator. Hermann Vogel was born in Flensburg, Germany, in 1856. He became a naturalized Frenchman and exhibited at the Paris Salon from 1909. He worked for *La Caricature* from 1889, *Le Charivari* from 1890, *Le Courrier Français* in 1889, and *L'Assiette au Beurre* in 1901. His *Dans Macabre* was a regular feature in the last-named publication.

Vogel's Boer War work appeared in Leo Dex's (Édouard Deburaux's pseudonym) *Un Héros de Treize Ans*. This novel was published by Hachette & Co. in 1902 and had 17 illustrations by Vogel. He often used his initials only (in monogram form).

Vogel died in Paris on 14 October 1918.
Osterwalder, and Hubschmid and Bouret (eds.), Dictionnaire des Illustrateurs, p. 1098

VOLTZ, T.

Illustrator of a postcard published by J. Kocher's Kuntsverlag Reutingen. The card, entitled *Mitt Gott*, showed wounded Boers praying on the battlefield.

VON F, Laci

Cartoonist for *Humoristische Blätter*, Vienna.

VON LENBACH, Frans-Seraph *see* LENBACH, Frans-Seraph von

VON ZUMBUSCH, Ludwig *see* ZUMBUSCH, Ludwig von

V., P. *see* P.V.

WAIN, Louis William 1860-1939   1

Wain was born in London on 5 August 1860. He studied at the West London School of Art and between 1881 and 1882 he was an assistant master there. His first picture was accepted by the *The Illustrated Sporting & Dramatic News* in 1877.

Wain's obsession with cats is said to have begun when he bought a cat to amuse his wife during an illness. Throughout his life most of his illustrations for the leading papers and postcards for Raphael Tuck & Sons and other publishers depicted these animals. This obsession finally led to insanity and in 1923 he was committed to a paupers' asylum. A fund was started for him and he was moved to Bethlehem Hospital and later to Napsbury Hospital, where he died on 4 July 1939.

Although several of the illustrated weeklies carried Wain's illustrations during the War, none has any relevance to it. Nevertheless the Africana Museum has his large pen-and-ink drawing (56,2 x 76,3 cm) of a British encampment (probably Ladysmith) under Boer bombardment. Cats represent all the humans, and a wide variety of activities, from bathing to firing on the enemy, are taking place. Even three somewhat glum feline Boer prisoners are depicted in the scene.
Personal communication with Mrs Blanche Nagelgast, Director, Africana Museum, Johannesburg

WAIN, S.

Engraver who worked for *The Graphic* and who was responsible for some of the engraved illustrations of the War that appeared in this publication.

WAITE, James

Possibly the Australian artist James Clarke Waite, who provided the illustrations for two cards issued in Colmar, Alsace, in 1901 in aid of the Boers. One illustration shows a nurse comforting a Boer soldier, the other a nurse paying homage to Louis Botha. The second card is signed with a 'J.W.' monogram.

WAKE, G. R.

Wake was a second lieutenant in the Northumberland Fusiliers when he was captured at Stormberg on 10 December 1899 and sent to Pretoria. While in captivity he collaborated with others to produce *The Gram*. He was responsible for the illustrations on pages 25 and 43 and the bottom of the inside back cover of the first issue. In the second issue his illustrations appeared on pages 15, 25 and 27. Some of these illustrations he signed with the initials 'G.R.W.'.

Wake had been educated at Eton and his brother was on Lord Roberts's staff.
The Gram

WALENN, Gilbert Frederick Dudley fl. 1894-1930

Child and portrait painter. Walenn studied at the Royal Academy schools, the British Museum, and the Académie Julian in Paris. From 1870 he was principal of the St John's Wood School of Art.

One of Walenn's illustrations, *Boer Scouts*, appears in Pearson's *War Pictures* (p. 88). He was the donor of a picture (or pictures) sold in aid of the 'National Bazaar for Sufferers by the War' which was held in May 1900.
Johnson and Greutzner, British Artists, p. 522

WALKER, John Hanson 1844-1933   1

Portrait painter and illustrator. Walker exhibited at the principal London galleries, including the Royal Academy. He was responsible for some of the illustrations in Bessie Marchant's *Tommy's Trek: A Transvaal Story* (Blackie & Sons, London, 1901).

Walker died on 13 November 1933.
Johnson and Greutzner, British Artists, p. 524
SABIB, *vol. 3, p. 256*
Waters, British Artists, vol. 2, p. 341

WALLACE

The San Francisco Chronicle cartoonist.

WALLACE, Helen fl. 1900-1933   1

Wallace was reputedly an English artist who spent some time in South Africa, first going to King William's Town and then to East London. She taught at the Girls' High School there before opening her own teaching studio. She was a founder member of the East London Society of Arts and Crafts, and served as its chairman between 1926 and 1928. In 1927 she exhibited at the inaugural exhibition of the South African Institute. Wallace returned to England in 1928 and died in 1933.

The author has an oil painting by Wallace entitled *Table Mountain from Green Point Common* (1900). The painting depicts British troops on the common. The stretcher has an inscription to the effect that 'Mrs. Spilhaus of Arthur's Seat in Sea Point' bought the painting for two guineas.
Berman, Art and Artists, p. 131

WALLACE, R. J.

Wallace was one of the illustrators responsible for some of the illustrations in Israel Smith Clare's *British-Boer War* (1900). The author claims that 'none of these illustrations can be found in any other publication as they have either been drawn by our special artists from photographs and personal descriptions of the scenes portrayed at an expense of many thousands of dollars . . . the entire work is unique'. This is obviously untrue as the illustrations are, almost without exception, plagiarized from contemporary French, German and British newspapers.

---

1 *De Vlucht van Rhodes uit Kimberley naar . . . de Maan*, one of a series of ten postcards published by Internationale Postkaartenhandel, Arnhem. The besieging of Kimberley, with the arch-capitalist Rhodes in it, was gleefully depicted by European cartoonists. This card shows him wetting himself during his attempted escape. The artist is only identified by a 'M.V.' monogram.
2 Louis Wain, the British artist, was eventually driven mad by his obsession with cats. This delightful pen-and-ink depiction of Boers and British soldiers as cats, probably representing the Siege of Ladysmith, was done in about 1900. Reproduced by courtesy of the Africana Museum, Johannesburg.

WALTERS

This illustrator produced a series of 'alphabetical' cartoon drawings of Roberts and Kruger, among others, for *Boy's Own Paper*. The letters making up their names are incorporated into the caricatures.

Boy's Own Paper, *1 June 1901, vol. 23, p. 557*

WALTON, J. Ambrose

Illustrator of Harry Golding's *Between two fires: a Story of the Boer War* (Ward Lock, London, 1900).

SABIB, *vol. 2, p. 366*

WALRUS *see* CONOLLY, Walter Moorcroft

WARD, Enoch 1859-1922

Painter and illustrator. Ward was born in Parkgate, Yorkshire, in 1859. At the age of 11 he went with his parents to Chicago, returning to England only in 1880. He studied at the South Kensington School of Art and in Paris. He worked at various times for *The Illustrated London News* and *The Queen*. In 1907 Ward did a series of postcards for W.H. Smith and Son entitled 'Woodcuts of London'. He was elected a member of the R.B.A. in 1898. Ward's Boer War work appeared in *Black & White* and *With the Flag to Pretoria*.

Byatt, Picture Postcards, p. 251
Houfe, British Illustrators and Caricaturists, p. 490
Waters, British Artists, vol. 1, p. 343
Who was Who, vol. 2, p. 1091

WARD, Leslie Mathew 1851-1922   4

Portrait painter and caricaturist. Leslie Ward was born in London on 21 November 1851. Both his father, E. M. Ward, and his grandfather, James Ward, were Royal Academicians. He was educated at Eton and Barnes and later studied architecture with Sydney Smirke at the Royal Academy schools. While still at school he exhibited a bust at the Royal Academy. He contributed to *The Graphic* from 1874, but he is best known for his work in *Vanity Fair* from 1873 to 1909. During this time he contributed more than half of the caricatures published in the periodical. He became a member of the Royal Society of Portrait Painters. His publication *Forty Years of Spy* was published in 1915 and he was knighted in 1918. He died on 15 May 1922.

Ward found that at school he could no more resist caricaturing his schoolmates and masters than he could 'resist the temptation of cream tarts'. One such caricature of one of' his masters, Professor Owen, came to the attention of an old family friend, Sir John Everett Millais, which resulted in the start of his professional career with *Vanity Fair*. In an interview with *The Strand Magazine* in 1894, Ward describes how, when caricaturing a subject, he tries to 'catch hold of the leading feature and slightly, very slightly, exaggerate'. He admits that, with only one exception, he had never caricatured a woman. (The exception was Georgina Weldon.) In 1910, once again during an interview in *The Strand Magazine*, Ward describes how he prefers to take his victim unawares rather than have a formal sitting. This technique caused much annoyance on the part of politicians and other prominent figures caricatured by Ward. He describes how he came to adopt the *nom de crayon* 'Spy':

Mr Thomas Gibson Bowles, who was the proprietor of

Vanity Fair at the time I submitted my first cartoon, requested me to invent some characteristic signature consisting of three letters. I worked three initials into the form and semblance of a jester's bauble. But that did not please him. Thereupon he threw me over a dictionary and asked me to choose a three-lettered word which would constitute an appropriate signature. The book opened in the middle of the 'S' pages. Near the top of the first column was the word 'Spy', one of the meanings of which was given as 'to observe'. Whereupon I adopted the word as a pencil-name and I have caricatured under it ever since.

Ward's work relating to the Boer War consisted of at least 18 *Vanity Fair* caricatures showing various British generals, Boer leaders and British parliamentarians at the time. Cecil Rhodes, John X. Merriman and other Cape parliamentarians were also depicted in earlier editions. Ward occasionally signed his work using the palindrome of L. Ward – 'Drawl' and it is thought that he used this pseudonym when he hadn't drawn the sitter from life. Kruger and Baden-Powell, who Ward is not believed to have met, were both done by 'Drawl'. Several of Ward's caricatures were reproduced on postcards produced by Raphael Tuck and Stewart & Woolf.

Ward's Boer War related caricatures in *Vanity Fair* were as follows:

8:3:1900 *Stephanus Johannes Paulus Kruger*. Caption: 'Oom Paul'. Signed Drawl.
19:4:1900 *Lord Strathcona and Mount Royal*. Caption: 'Canada in London'. Signed Spy.
14:6:1900 *General Sir George Stuart White VC*. Caption: 'Ladysmith'. Signed Spy.

21:6:1900 *Field Marshal Lord Roberts VC KP.* Caption: 'Bobs'. Signed Spy.

28:6:1900 *Capt. the Honourable Hedworth Lambton RN.* Caption: 'HMS *Powerful*'. Signed Spy.

5:7:1900 *General Robert Stephenson Smyth Baden-Powell.* Caption: 'Mafeking'. Signed Drawl.

27:9:1900 *Winston Leonard Spencer Churchill.* Caption: 'Winston'. Signed Spy.

29:11:1900 *A General Group.* (Included Roberts, Buller, Kitchener, Hunter, Pole-Carew, French, White, Dundonald, Baden-Powell, Plumer, Carrington, and McDonald.)21: 2:1901 *General Reginald Pole-Carew CB.* Caption: 'Polly'. Signed Spy.

7:3:1901 *Joseph Chamberlain.* Caption: 'The Colonies'. Signed Spy.

2:5:1901 *General Sir Ian Standish Monteith Hamilton CB, DSO* Caption: 'Mixed forces'. Signed Spy.

18:7:1901 *The Secretary of State for War.* Caption: War. Signed Spy.

1:8:1901 *Surgeon-General Jameson.* Caption: 'Army Medical'. Signed Spy.

29:8:1901 *General Kelly-Kenny CB* Caption: '6th Division'. Signed Spy.

5:9:1901 *General the Hon Neville Gerald Lyttelton.* Caption: '4th Division'. Signed Spy.

5:12:1901 *General Smith-Dorrien DSO.* Caption: 'Doreen'. Signed Spy.

3:4:1902 *Lord Alwyne Frederick Compton DSO DL MP.* Caption: 'North Bedfordshire'. Signed Spy.

13:11:1902 *General Plumer.* Caption: 'Self Reliant'. Signed Spy.

25:12:1902 *General Sir Frederick William Edward Forestier Forestier-Walker GCMG CB.* Caption: 'Shookey'. Signed Spy.

Vanity Fair caricatures reproduced on postcards by Stewart and Woolf include:

Series 101 *General French*
Lord Chesham
Lord Kitchener
General Baden-Powell
Mr Kruger

Series 102 *Lord Roberts*
General Buller VC
General White
Rt. hon Jos Chamberlain MP

Series 117 *Dr L.S. Jameson CB*

All the cards were printed at the Fine Art works in Nuremberg and carried the *Vanity Fair* copyright.

The author has a watercolour by Spy of Capt. (later Lt. Col.) Francis Edward Lloyd Daniell (1874-1916), who saw action in the Boer War as special service officer in both the Transvaal and Cape Colony during 1900 and 1901.

Byatt, Picture Postcards, *p. 275*
S. Clarke, Vanity Fair in S.A., *Johannesburg, Brentburst Press, 1991*
Matthews and Mellini, In Vanity Fair
The Strand, *July-Dec. 1894, vol. 8, pp. 632-634; Jan.-June 1910, vol. 39, pp. 81-90*
Who was Who, *vol. 2, pp. 1092-1093*

WATSON

Colonel Watson of the Royal Field Artillery was responsible for an illustration which appeared on p. 245 of *After Pretoria: the Guerilla War*, entitled *The scene of the Nooitgedacht Disaster*. The illustration had been redrawn by G.K. Jones, which indicates that it probably first appeared in *The Daily Graphic*.

WATSON, George Mackie fl. 1901-1927

Scottish artist who exhibited at the R.S.A. He was responsible for the illustrations in Sir Francis Edward Fremantle's *Impressions of a Doctor in Khaki* (John Murray, 1901).

SABIB, vol. 2, p. 291

WATSON, James Hannan   1

Soldier-artist. Watson was a trooper in the 18th Company

(Glasgow) Imperial Yeomanry under the command of Capt. Coats. Together with the 17th Company (Ayr and Lanarkshire), the 19th Company (Lothians and Berwick), and 20th company (Fife and Forfar), Watson's company formed the Scottish Yeomanry Battalion under the overall command of Col. C. R. Burn.

Watson's company arrived in Table Bay on 19 March 1900. Like most of the other Imperial Yeomanry companies they were sent to the camp at Maitland on 1 April.

During his stay in South Africa Watson planned and illustrated *The Trooper's Sketch Book of the Boer War* (James Brown and Son, 1902). The book consists of 29 full-page illustrations with captions opposite. Watson also illustrated *Scottish Yeomanry in South Africa 1900-1901: A record of the work and experiences of the Glasgow and Ayrshire Companies* by Trooper A.S. Orr of the 18th Company of the Imperial Yeomanry. This book was published in 1901 by James Hedderwick and Sons, the Citizen Press, Glasgow. In his preface Orr mentions that, during their journey home on board the *Tintagel Castle*, the men of the Yeomanry expressed the desire to possess some record of their small share of 'the great South African struggle'. He says that thanks are due to 'Mr. J. Hannan Watson of our company, who has so enlivened the book with his sketches, and to Mr. R.E. Wilson for a chapter on the Bethlehem fighting'. Watson's sketches are found both within the text and as full-page plates, and the pictorial leather-bound cover is assumed to be by him.

On his return to Glasgow Watson exhibited paintings based on his experiences in South Africa, among which *The Empty Saddle* (1902) and *On Flank Guard, Bringing up the guns, 1902, The night patrol* and *Troop mates* (all 1903) were shown at the Royal Glasgow Institute of Fine Arts. (He had previously exhibited at the Royal Glasgow Institute in the early 1890s.) One of his oil paintings, *Returning to Camp*, based on one of his sketches in *A Trooper's Sketch Book*, was bought in England by Canon Wood. This painting is now in the University of the Witwatersrand library. Watson's other publications included *Military Glasgow* (Carter and Pratt, Glasgow, 1895).

Some of Watson's illustrations are signed with the initials 'J.H.W.'.

Dewar, With the Scottish Yeomanry
Orr, Scottish Yeomanry in S.A.
Personal communication with J.H. Thorburn, Keeper, Royal Scottish Regiment Museum, Edinburgh

WAUD, Leighton

Designer of a menu, depicted in both *Black & White Budget* and *The Sketch*, for a dinner given on 27 November 1900 at Hyde Park Barracks to welcome home the Cape Squadron returning from South Africa. He also designed Lady Glover's *Lest we Forget Them*, the proceeds of which were donated to the 'Fund for the widows and orphans of our sailors and soldiers'.

WAUGH, Frederick Judd 1861-1941   7

Marine painter. Waugh was born in New Jersey, U.S.A, on 13 September 1861. His father, Samuel Bell Waugh (1814-85), was a noted portrait and landscape painter who exhibited at the Royal Academy in the 1840s. His mother, Samuel Bell's second wife, was Mary Elizabeth Young, a miniaturist. Frederick's half sister Eliza was also a noted artist.

Waugh was referred to as 'a shy and sensitive youth and dreamer who disliked school preferring to roam the woods studying nature "at first hand" rather than from books'. This lack of interest in school got him into trouble with his elders. He showed no particular artistic talent as a child, but nevertheless studied art at the Philadelphia Academy of the Fine Arts from 1880 to 1883 under Thomas Eakens and Thomas Anshutz. He later continued his studies at the Académie Julian in France under Bouguereau and Lefebvre. For unknown reasons he was advised by friends to leave the academy and study on his own.

Waugh followed this advice but remained in Brittany for a while. After his father's death in 1885 he returned to Philadelphia where he was employed by the commercial art firm of Dakin and Petrie. In 1892 he married Clara Eugene Bunn (Gene), a fellow student at the Philadelphia Academy, and a year later settled on the island of Sark in the Channel Islands, where he began his long career as a marine painter. In 1894 his painting entitled *La Grande Grève, Sark* was accepted by the Royal Academy. A year later Waugh settled in St Ives, Cornwall, continuing to paint his marine-scapes. Economic pressure forced him to move, first to Leighton Buzzard near London, and then to Hendon in 1899 in the hope of selling more of his work.

George R. Havens, in his book *Frederick J. Waugh: American Marine Painter*, states that Waugh found employment, though at a small salary, on *Harmsworth Magazine*, which had just been started by Alfred Harmsworth, later Lord Northcliffe. This also led to a commission to provide illustrations for *With the Flag to Pretoria* and *After Pretoria: the Guerilla War*, both Harmsworth publications. According to Havens, Waugh approached *The Graphic* after the Boer War broke out, and was hired at a salary of one guinea an inch, more than he was receiving from Harmsworth, from which he had apparently then resigned.

At this point there is some confusion: the *Directory of American Biography* states that 'Waugh accepted a contract from his friend Alfred Harmsworth to illustrate this conflict for . . . *The Graphic*'. Clearly Waugh could not have resigned from Harmsworth's employ as he continued illustrating *With the Flag to Pretoria* and *After Pretoria: the Guerilla War* well into 1902 and there is no indication that Harmsworth ever owned or had anything to do with *The Graphic*. As was the custom of the day, however, many artists worked for various rival publications simultaneously so were sometimes not credited for their work. For example, on 23 June 1900 *The Graphic* published a facsimile of Waugh's illustration entitled *A Hailstorm on the Veldt* from a sketch by H. Lea. Waugh was not given credit, yet the same facsimile appears on p. 328 of *After Pretoria: the Guerilla War* with credits to both Lea and Waugh. The title in this case was *A South African Hail Storm*. In July 1900 *The Illustrated London News* used one of Waugh's works *Trekking home: The last of the Commando*.

Havens gives a vivid description of Waugh's work for *The Graphic*. Despatches and sketches came to him by courier from the front every Friday, and he worked under great pressure each weekend so that the finished pictures would reach the office of *The Graphic* at 190 the Strand by Monday morning. The rest of the week was his own to paint as he wished, or to freelance.

Havens remarks that none of *The Graphic*'s artists sketched on the spot in the midst of the horrors of war. This is not true. Charles Fripp, W. T. Maud and G. D. Giles were frontline artists employed by *The Graphic*. While they were not necessarily present at all the incidents they depicted they most certainly experienced some of the horror. Maud, who was besieged at Ladysmith, was nearly hit by a Boer shell.

1 Frederick Waugh's watercolour *A Friendly Burgher Seeking Information in the British Camp* was reproduced in *After Pretoria: the Guerilla War*.

2 The front cover of part 41 of *With the Flag to Pretoria*, entitled *The Disaster at Nooitgedacht*, from an original by F.J. Waugh.

3 American artist F. J. Waugh's wash drawing *Lord Roberts and the Innkeeper's Child* was reproduced in *With the Flag to Pretoria*. When Roberts occupied Johannesburg he established his headquarters at the Orange Grove Hotel. One evening while he was reading to the innkeeper's child he was approached by a soldier on urgent business. He looked up and jokingly said: 'Don't come now, can't you see I'm busy?'. This incident was used by several artists to show the 'humane' side of the commander-in-chief.

4 Cartoonist Leslie Ward, better known as 'Spy', produced this watercolour of Captain (later Lt. Col.) Frances Daniell, who saw action during the Boer War as special service officer.

5 *A Hurried Inspan*, a watercolour by Fred Waugh, was reproduced in *After Pretoria: the Guerilla War*.

When Queen Victoria died in 1901 Waugh contributed a full-page illustration entitled *The Procession on the Way to Paddington: passing Boundary Road* to *The Graphic* funeral supplement.

Simon Houfe says that Waugh was probably in South Africa during the Boer War. This seems highly unlikely as he was well established with his family in London at the time. All the while Waugh was working hard for *The Graphic*, *With the Flag to Pretoria* and *After Pretoria: the Guerilla War*, he continued to paint, and work was submitted to and accepted by the Royal Academy. In 1901 *Spring time and song* was exhibited. In 1903 three of Waugh's pictures were accepted by the Academy and in 1904 two were shown. One of these, *In the Heart of Great London*, was bought by the Durban art gallery in 1905 for £100 and is still in their collection today. Waugh is, however, listed in the gallery's catalogue as an English artist with an unknown date of death. Waugh's paintings were also exhibited in the Walker Art Gallery in Liverpool in 1901 and 1904.

In 1907 Waugh received his first rejection notice from the Royal Academy. It was a most upsetting experience for him and he decided to return to the United States, where he became an immediate success. He was elected an associate member of the American National Academy in 1909 and became an Academician in 1911. He experimented with various other subjects, including flower pieces and even abstracts. He wrote and illustrated a book entitled *Clan of Munes* in 1916. During World War I his knowledge of the sea was used by the U.S. Navy to design camouflage for their ships. For five consecutive years (1934-8) he won the popular award of the Carnegie Institute in Pittsburgh. *Time* magazine (17 December 1934), in an article entitled 'People's Choice' had the following to say about Waugh:

Before the public was admitted to Pittsburgh's Carnegie International, generally considered the most important annual art show in the U.S., the jury went through the galleries and awarded the $1 500 first prize to Peter Blume's colourful surrealist design entitled 'South of Scranton'. The award moved the U.S. Press to great bursts of sarcasm, but the Carnegie Institute directors bided their time. (*Time*, 29 October). Last week the show closed. All who visited it were given ballots and asked to vote for their favourite among the 356 paintings exhibited. With a total of 1 920 votes, more than twice as many as its nearest competitor, the people's choice was 'Tropic Seas' by Frederick J. Waugh. Depicted in a solid workmanlike way was a thoroughly banal study of green seas, white foam and brown rocks — a scene such as embellished the parlors of the country's leading hotels in the days when their

elevators had ropes to start them. It won $200. Artist Frederick Judd Waugh, Pittsburgh's favourite, is neither unknown, unrecognised nor impoverished. At 73 he is lean and fox-bearded and his dealers, Manhattan's Grand Central Galleries, are proud of him as one of their best sellers. He paints about 75 canvases a year — mostly marines and sells them for from $400 to $2 500 apiece.

A year later, on 16 December 1935, Time had another article about Waugh under the title 'Popular Prizeman'. It said:

If the ordinary U.S. citizen were given a blank check and told to go out and buy, according to his own taste, a new painting by a U.S. artist, he would probably pass up the works of Benton, Curry, Wood, Kroll and Speicher, and invest in a seascape by Frederick Judd Waugh. Later he would be considerably surprised to learn that the Bentons, the Currys, the Woods, the Krolls and the Speichers all looked disdainfully down their artistic noses at Oldster Waugh (pronounced Waw). Last week for the second successive year artist Waugh won the $200 prize for the most popular painting at the Carnegie International Exhibition in Pittsburgh. This award went to his 'Ante Meridian', not on the say so of any highbrow judges but by a majority vote of the 116 000 plain people who had visited the Carnegie show since October.

Frederick Waugh won the 1934 Popular Prize at Pittsburgh with another marine picture called 'Tropic Sea' (*Time* 17 December). Still another Waugh seascape entitled 'Post Meridian' took the $500 Palmer Prize for marine paintings at last Spring's National Academy. In Chicago last month bewildered Mrs Frank Logan, wife of the Art Institute's honorary President, picked a fourth Waugh seascape as the sort of picture she really liked, in contrast to the sarcastic canvas that had been awarded her $500 prize (*Time* 18 November).

Artist Waugh, spry at 74, produces about 75 canvases a year. The Grand Central Art Galleries, his Manhattan agents, never keep a Waugh canvas long in stock, wish they had more painters like him. Surf, sky and rocks are his only subjects. These he knows so well that he no longer bothers to leave his Provincetown, Mass. studio to look at them. However, all Waugh seascapes are not alike. *Ante Meridian* shows a wave breaking against a cliff in the right foreground. *Post Meridian* had waves breaking on rocks in the centre foreground. *Tropic Seas* had the rocks in the distance. In *Morning Tide*, Mrs Logan's favourite in Chicago, the rocks are on the left.

On 6 December 1937, *Time* featured Waugh again in a similar vein mentioning that "snotty" critics are accustomed to laugh out loud at the works of aged Waugh, 1) because they are

limited almost entirely to realistic paintings of surf, and 2) because his surf pictures are "all alike". The critics may have laughed out loud, but owners of his works were 'laughing all the way to the bank' when, at a Sotheby Parke Bernet (New York) sale of the John McDonough collection on 22 March 1978, a Waugh seascape entitled *Marine* fetched a record $10 000.

Waugh spent the last 15 years of his life in Provincetown, Mass., a popular and respected member of the community. Part of the main street was jokingly referred to as 'Waughville' because of his many business interests there. He died of cancer on 10 September 1940, just three days before his 79th birthday.

A few of Waugh's original Africana works are still extant. One entitled *Boers defending a Kopje* was sold on 18 January 1978 at Sotheby's in London for £160. In the catalogue only his initials were given, indicating that his first names were unknown to the auctioneer. Six of Waugh's paintings were purchased by the author at Sotheby's Johannesburg sale on 22 February 1979. They are:

1. *Disaster at Nooitgedacht: the End of a Brave Signaller*.
2. *A Hurried Inspan* signed and dated b.r. 1901. Reproduced on p. 220 of *After Pretoria: the Guerilla War*, incorrectly attributed to H. Dixon.
3. *Boer Treatment of Peace Envoys — the Flogging of Morgendaal*. Reproduced on p. 309 of *After Pretoria: the Guerilla War*, signed b.r.
4. *Fix bayonets Jack — Defence of a Trench by Two Survivors of the Fighting Fifth*. Reproduced on p. 385 of *After Pretoria: the Guerilla War*, signed and dated b. 1.1901.
5. *A Friendly Burgher Seeking Information in the British Camp*. Reproduced on p. 460 of *After Pretoria: the Guerilla War*, signed and dated 1901 b.l.6. *Lord Roberts and the Innkeeper's Child*. Reproduced on p. 647 of *With the Flag to Pretoria*, signed and dated b.r. 1900. Another painting, *The Faithful Picket at Zuurfontein*, dated 1901, is in the author's collection. It was reproduced on page 393 of *After Pretoria: the Guerilla War*.

The National Army Museum in London has two Boer War watercolours by Waugh: *British Troops entering a Farmyard* (signed and dated b.r. 1900) and *Cronje's Laager at Paardeberg*, not signed or dated but attributed to him by the Royal United Services Institution Museum, which owns the work.

Africana Notes and News, *vol. 24, no. 2, pp. 56-74, June 1980 'Inglis Sheldon-Williams, Frederick Judd Waugh: Two special artists of the Anglo-Boer War' by R. Greenwall*

Graves, Royal Academy, *vol. 8, p. 179*
Havens, Frederick J. Waugh
Houfe, British Illustrators and Caricaturists, *p. 493*

W.B.D.
Unidentified soldier who sent a sketch to *The Graphic*. It was redrawn by W. Ralston and published on 30 August 1902, entitled *An incident of camp Life in South Africa*.

WEIJMANN, Ottmar
Artist whose work appeared on 'Politische Postkarte' series of German Boer War postcards.

WEIL, Lucien-Henri 1873-1947
Cartoonist. Weil was born in Paris in 1873. He adopted the pseudonym 'Weiluc' when his first cartoons were published in *La Caricature* in 1896. From 1907 to 1909 he was one of the committee members of the French Society of Humorists and from 1911 he served as its president.

During the War Weil's cartoons were found in *La Caricature*, *La Vie Pour Rire*, *Le Petit Français Illustré*, *Le Bon Vivant*, and *Le Gavroche*.

Osterwalder, and Hubschmid and Bouret (eds.), Dictionnaire des Illustrateurs, *p. 1118*

WELLNER, W. A.

Lustige Blätter cartoonist and illustrator. *The Studio* describes his work as 'German' in style and says that he 'is strongly in love with Bocklin's fabulous types'.

Wellner provided one illustration, *In der Apotheke*, for the Eysler 'Gruss vom Kriegsschauplatz' postcard series. He often signed his work with the initials 'W.A.W.'.

The Studio, *vol. 51, pp. 164-165 (1911)*

WENZELL, Albert B. 1864-1917

Illustrator. Wenzell was born in Detroit in 1864. He was a pupil of Strahuber and Loeffitz in Munich. *The Studio*, commenting on his illustrations for *Vanity Fair*, remarks that 'Mr. Wenzell is notable for his monotint brush work. [He] possesses many brilliant qualities. He is vigorous, almost too unrestful and never dull. His figures are full of character, and his women are especially attractive'.

During the War Wenzell contributed coloured and black and white illustrations to A.T. Mahan's *The War in South Africa*.

He died in Englewood, New Jersey, in 1917.
Fielding, American Painters, etc., *p. 400*
The Studio, *vol. 9, p. 296 (1897)*

WESTMACOTT, Bernard

Moonshine cartoonist whose several cartoons parodying well-known advertising posters of the day often featured the Boer War. A few of his cartoons are signed with his initials only ('B.W.').

Johnson and Greutzner list him as a landscape artist who exhibited in 1902.
Johnson and Greutzner, British Artists, *p. 539*

W.F.

Initials of an illustrator of the famous Pioneer cigarette advertisements that appeared in *The Illustrated London News*. One example is noted on 27 October 1900.

W., H. *see* H.W.

WHISTON, Henry 1

An amateur artist of this name, possibly a non-commissioned officer or private, drew at least four pencil sketches of British generals: Roberts, Baden-Powell, French and Kitchener. The pictures were all 28 x 22 cm and were probably done from photographs.

WHITE, Geoffrey 1

Captain White of the Royal Horse Artillery was captured at Sanna's Post on 31 March 1900. He was sent to Pretoria where he provided illustrations for the P.O.W. magazine *The Gram*. Lord Rosslyn, in his introduction, thanks him 'for his co-operation and artistic assistance'.

White's illustrations, which were often signed 'G.H.A.W.', appeared in issue 1 on the front cover, the inside front cover and pages 13, 26, 27, 31, 32 and 33. In issue 2 he provided the front cover and inside front cover illustrations as well as those on pages 5, 17, and 23c. He also provided the front cover illustration on issue 3, as well as a cartoon of the camp bookmaker Lt. Neil Haig of the 6th Dragoons.
The Gram

WHITELAW, George fl.1900-1930

Artist and illustrator who worked in Glasgow in 1907. He contributed occasionally to *Judy* and *Punch*.

During the War Whitelaw provided cartoons for *Judy*. At least one cartoon taken from that magazine appeared in *War Pictures* (p. 69). He signed his cartoons 'Whitelaw'.
Houfe, British Illustrators and Caricaturists, *p. 496*
Johnson and Greutzner, British Artists, *p. 543*

WHITING, Frederic 1873-1962

Illustrator. Whiting was born in Hampstead in 1873. He was educated at Deal and St Mark's College. After four and a half years at the Royal Academy schools he went to Paris to study at the Académie Julian under Constant Laurens.

While still at the Royal Academy schools Whiting had work accepted by *The Graphic*. Even though he later did a considerable amount of military and sporting work for the paper he declined a permanent appointment. At the time of the Boer War he provided at least five illustrations to *The Graphic* and several others to *The Daily Graphic*, but when the Boxer Rebellion broke out in China in June 1900 he was sent out as special artist for *The Graphic*, remaining on in North China for a while after the uprising was suppressed.

In 1904 at the outbreak of the Russo-Japanese War Whiting was again sent out to the East where he accompanied the Japanese army in Manchuria. He returned to London via the U.S.A. He was elected a member of the R.B.A. in 1911, the R.O.I. in 1915, the R.I. in 1918, and the R.S.W. in 1921. In 1919 he became president of the Artist's Society.

His Royal Academy exhibit in 1900 was entitled *6th Dragoons leaving Albert Docks for South Africa*. He often signed his work with the initials 'F.W.'.

Whiting died on 1 August 1962.
Graves, Royal Academy, *vol. 8, p. 259*
Hofmeyr, Matton and Roets, Graphic Picture Index
Houfe, British Illustrators and Caricaturists, *p. 496*
The Studio, *vol. 61, pp. 109-121 (1914) 'Frederic Whiting RBA' by A. Reddie*

WHITING, Onslow fl.1900-1935

Sculptor and painter of portraits and animals. He studied at the Slade School and the Central School of Arts and Crafts. He exhibited at the Royal Academy.

Whiting is credited with two Boer War memorials:
1. The memorial in Plymouth to Prince Christian Victor of Schleswig-Holstein, in collaboration with Emile Fuchs;
2. The Gloucestershire Regiment memorial in Bristol, which was unveiled by Lord Roberts on 4 March 1905.
Gildea, For Remembrance, *pp. 37 and 59*
Waters, British Artists, *p. 354*

WHYTE, B.C.

On 6 October 1901 *The Illustrated London News* published Richard Caton Woodville's illustration *Guerilla Warfare in South Africa: an indaba held at the Kraal of the Chief Sipolilo by Captain Peake, 65th I.Y., in the north Lo Majunda District*. The illustration was based on a sketch by Capt. B. Whyte of the Imperial Yeomanry.
De Wet, Illustrated London News Index

WICHGRAF, Fritz 1853-c.1920

Historical painter. Wichgraf was born in Potsdam, Germany, on 9 May 1853. He was a pupil of A. Bauer in Weimar, H. von Angeli in Vienna, and Diez and Löfftz in Munich. Wichgraf concentrated mainly on historical paintings and portraits, and while in Germany he executed portraits of various German emperors.

Wichgraf arrived in Johannesburg in 1896. He received various commissions from the government and prominent personalities. In Johannesburg in 1898 an exhibition of his work was received favourably.

His best-known work, *De Deputatie* (*Die Deputasie*), was commissioned by the Transvaal Government for exhibition at the Transvaal pavilion at the Paris Exhibition of 1900. The painting was completed on 13 March 1900 but for various reasons could not be shown at the exhibition. Wichgraf had originally asked £2 000 for the work, but the exhibition committee settled on a figure of £500. Wichgraf was unhappy about this and both he and his son-in-law, Hugh Evans, attempted to collect the balance of £1 500.

Jan Ploeger, writing in *Africana Notes and News* (vol. 23, no. 6, 1979), reveals correspondence from Wichgraf to the Colonial Office in London requesting payment of the £1 500. Wichgraf states that as a German citizen he remained neutral during the War and, in any event, the painting (which he claims had no political motive) was done prior to the War. The colonial secretary replied that the British Government had no desire to purchase the painting.

The large painting (2,5 x 5 m) was eventually returned to Pretoria in 1910 and is now in the Provincial Administration building. It depicts an imaginary deputation of Boers requesting the Executive Council of the Transvaal Republic to act against the Johannesburg Reform Committee after the Jameson Raid of 1895-6. Portraits appearing in the picture include those of Kruger, Cronje, S. W. Burger and F. W. Reitz. A smaller preparatory study, about half the size of the finished painting, hangs in the old council chamber on Church Square, Pretoria. Several engravings of the painting, including one done in Germany in 1901 and a relatively recent one, are in existence. A copy of the painting was published in *The Graphic* on 14 December 1901 with the title *Never Again*.

W.J. Leyds had an individual portrait done by Wichgraf. The artist returned to Germany in 1900 and continued to exhibit there. He died in Germany c.1920.
Africana Notes and News, vol. 23, no. 6, pp. 248-254, June 1979, 'Wichgraf se bekende Deputasieskildery Aangebied aan die Britse Minister van Kolonies (1903)' by J. Ploeger
De Kock, (ed.), DSAB, vol. 4, p. 776
Hofmeyr, Matton and Roets, Graphic Picture Index
Rosenthal, National Biography, *p. 416*

WILD, Frank Percy 1861-1950

Genre, landscape and portrait painter. Wild was born in Leeds on 4 March 1861. Initially trained as an engineer, he took up art in 1884, studying at the Antwerp Academy, at the Académie Julian in Paris, and in Spain. Wild exhibited at the Royal Academy and the R.B.A., among others. He was elected a member of the R.B.A. in 1900. Wild's 54 exhibits at the R.B.A. included *A Gentleman in Khaki* in 1901 and *For the Flag* in 1902. Wild died on 14 April 1950.
Johnson and Greutzner, British Artists, *p. 545*
RBA Exhibitors 1893-1910, *vol. 2, p. 112*
Waters, British Artists, *vol. 1, p. 355*

WILDEY, A. Gascoigne

Wildey, who was in the Royal Navy, provided the sketch for *The Graphic* which was redrawn by J. Nash and published on 16 June 1900 under the title *Unfit for further service: an examination at the Naval Hospital, Haslar*.

Postwar illustrations by Wildey were published in *The Graphic* in 1903 (25 April).
Hofmeyr, Matton and Roets, Graphic Picture Index

WILKE, Rudolf 1873-1908*

Artist and illustrator. Wilke was born in Braunschweig, Bavaria, on 27 October 1873. He was a friend of Bruno Paul, with whom he shared a studio. Wilke's brother, Erich, was also a caricaturist.

Wilke studied in Munich and Paris before becoming a regular contributor to *Jugend* and *Simplicissimus*. Thomas Heine considered him the most gifted of all the artists working on his staff.

During the War Wilke contributed to *Simplicissimus* and *Der Burenkrieg*. His illustration *Morgenbesuch* showed a drunk Edward VII (as Prince of Wales) being told of Cronje's surrender by Chamberlain.

Wilke died on 4 November 1908.
Feaver, Masters of Caricature, *p. 134*
Osterwalder, and Hubschmid and Bouret (eds.), Dictionnaire des Illustrateurs, *p. 1129*

1 Amateur artist Henry Whiston drew a series of four pencil sketches of British generals. Lord Roberts is depicted here.
2 A drunk Prince of Wales is depicted receiving the news of Cronje's capitulation at Paardeberg. Rudolf Wilke did this illustration for *Der Burenkrieg*.

WILKINSON, Albert

Cartoonist and illustrator whose work appeared in *Black & White Budget* and *War Pictures*.

WILKINSON, Norman 1878-1971   1

Marine painter and etcher. Wilkinson was born in Cambridge on 24 November 1878. He was educated at Berkhampstead and St Paul's Cathedral Choir School. He worked for *The Illustrated London News*, *The Graphic* and *The Idler*, and was later employed by the R.N.V.R. during World War I to develop shipping camouflage. In 1918 he was awarded the O.B.E. for his contribution to the war effort.

Wilkinson was elected a member of the R.B.A. in 1902, the R.O.I. in 1908, and the R.I. in 1906, eventually becoming its president in 1937.

Despite the fact that he is not listed in *The Illustrated London News Index* Wilkinson contributed marine pictures to that paper, some of which had Boer War relevance.

He died in London in 1971.

Houfe, British Illustrators and Caricaturists, *p. 497*
Thorpe, English Illustration

WILKINSON, Tom fl. 1895-1923   3

Cartoonist who worked for *Judy*, *Fun* and *Illustrated Bits*. He occasionally contributed drawings to *Punch* during the War, such as that on p. 93 of the 8 August 1900 edition.

Houfe, British Illustrators and Caricaturists, *p. 497*
Thorpe, English Illustration

WILLETTE, Adolphe Léon 1857-1926   3

Painter, etcher, caricaturist and illustrator. Willette was born in Châlons-sur-Marne, France, on 31 July 1857. He studied under Cabanel at the École des Beaux-Arts. Henri Toulouse-Lautrec considered him one of the finest scene painters in Montmartre.

Besides illustrating several books Willette worked at various times for *Le Figaro*, *Père-Peinard*, *Trois Huit*, *Père-Duchesne*, *l'Echo de Paris*, *L'Assiette au Beurre* and *Pick-Me-Up*. He published his autobiography, *Pierrot*, in 1919.

Willette's Boer War work includes the illustration on the well-known postcard addressed to Tsar Nicholas II at the Château de Compiègne, Oise, when he visited Paris in 1900. The card carries an appeal to the Tsar, as sponsor of The Hague peace conference a year before, to mediate in the War. The illustration shows Kruger carrying a cross with his burning country in the background. Willette is known to have illustrated several other non-Boer War postcards.

Other Boer War cartoons by Willette appeared in *Le Rire*, *La Vie en Rose* ('Numero special', 29 December 1901), *Le Courrier Français*, *Le Pied de Nez* (several issues featured his work exclusively), and *La Semaine Illustré* (all cartoons in the issues of 6 December and 29 December 1901 were by

1

him). He sometimes signed with an 'AW' monogram.

Willette's work has also been found on a contemporary tapestry depicting Kruger barefoot and in tattered attire being supported by the young Queen Wilhelmina of the Netherlands. It is believed that these tapestries were woven from a design by Willette who had been commissioned by the French Government. They were sold on behalf of the Boer women and children in the concentration camps.

The author has two pen-and-ink and watercolour cartoons by Willette: *La joie fait peur*, showing Chamberlain with the peace treaty and King Edward with a chamberpot on his head, and *L'English et pendant ce temps*, which appeared on the cover of *Le Courrier Français* on 29 September 1901.

Willette's daughter, Anne, was also a prominent artist. He died in Paris on 4 February 1926.

Bénézit, Dictionnaire antique, *vol. 8, p. 752*
Osterwalder, and Hubschmid and Bouret (eds.), Dictionnaire des Illustrateurs, *p. 1132*
Thorpe, English Illustration

WILLIAMS, C. R. Fleming

Cartoonist who worked for *Sketchy Bits* and *Judy*. During the War some of his cartoons in this magazine were of Boer War relevance. Thorpe says that he was influenced by the American cartoonist Dana Gibson. His signature was an elaborate one incorporating an artist's palette.

During World War I Williams became a major in the Royal

Flying Corps. At this time he contributed to *The Graphic*, *The Illustrated London News* and *The War Illustrated*. He was later appointed official war artist with the Royal Air Force.

Thorpe, English Illustration, *pp. 101-102*

WILMER, John Riley

Judy cartoonist who was a regular exhibitor at the principal British galleries, including the Royal Academy, from 1905. He lived and worked in Falmouth, Cornwall. One of his cartoons in *Judy* (11 October 1899, p. 482) showed a 'suggested design for a stained glass window at Pretoria' (an armed Kruger is depicted). The Africana Museum has Wilmer's original black paint drawing of this picture.

Johnson and Greutzner, British Artists, *p. 551*
Kennedy, Pictures in the Africana Museum, *vol. 7, p. 280*

WILSON, David fl. 1895-1916

Draughtsman and caricaturist whose work appeared occasionally in *Punch* and later in *The Graphic*, where he became chief cartoonist. Boer War related cartoons by Wilson can be found only rarely in *Punch*.

Houfe, British Illustrators and Caricaturists, *p. 500*

WILSON, H. P.

The Africana Museum has a watercolour, *Saving the Guns at Colenso*, signed 'H. P. Wilson 1915'. An H. P. Wilson contributed to *The Illustrated Sporting & Dramatic News* (1890) and

2

La joie fait peur.

3

L'Englishmen Et pendant e'temps
Je tournai de la prunelle.

4

Black & White (1891). A Harry P. Wilson is listed in Johnson and Greutzner as a watercolour figure painter of 61 Tufnell Park Road, London. In 1895 his *An old salt* was exhibited at the Royal Academy. It is possible that these three Wilsons are the same artist.

Houfe, British Illustrators and Caricaturists, p. 500
Johnson and Greutzner, British Artists, p. 552
Kennedy, Pictures in the Africana Museum, vol. 7, p. 280

WILSON, H.W.

Wilson was responsible for a painting entitled *The Scout* which was published as a full-page illustration in *The Sketch* on 7 March 1900.

WILSON, Oscar 1867-1930

Portrait painter and illustrator. Wilson was born in London in 1867. He studied at the South Kensington School of Art and at the Antwerp Academy under Verlat and Beaufaux. He contributed to *St Pauls*, *Pick-Me-Up*, *Black & White*, *The Sketch*, *Madame*, *The Lady's Realm* and *The Illustrated London News*. He exhibited at the Royal Academy from 1888.

During the War Wilson provided *The Illustrated London News* (9 June 1900, p. 780) with an illustration entitled *Hoisting the Union Jack at Pretoria*.

Wilson died on 13 July 1930.

Houfe, British Illustrators and Caricaturists, p. 500
Peppin and Micklethwait, British Book Illustrators, p. 328
Thorpe, English Illustration
Waters, British Artists, vol. 1, p. 359
Who was Who, vol. 3, p. 1472

WILSON, Thomas Walter 1851-1912 1

Landscape painter and illustrator. Wilson was born in London on 7 November 1851. His father, Thomas Harrington Wilson, was also an illustrator. Wilson jnr. was educated at Chelsea and the South Kensington School of Art. He won a scholarship from the school in 1869 and was declared National Scholar in 1870. He was sent to study at Bayeux, after which he worked in Belgium and Holland. He was elected A.R.I. in 1877, R.I. in 1879 and R.O.I. in 1883. He exhibited at the Royal Academy from 1873. He worked for several magazines including *The Graphic*, *The Illustrated London News*, *English Illustrated Magazine*, *Good Words*, *The Sketch*, *The Minister*, and *The Idler*.

His Africana illustrations appeared in *The Illustrated London News* in 1888 and 1890 and Wilson depicted the Zulu War and the First Anglo-Boer War for *The Graphic* in 1879 and 1881 respectively.

During the Second Anglo-Boer War Wilson worked for *The Sphere* and several of his illustrations appeared in the magazine. On 21 July 1900 *The Sphere* published his sketch of *The Wily de Wet exhorting his Burghers*.

De Wet, Illustrated London News Index
Graves, Royal Academy, vol. 8, p. 315
Hofmeyr, Matton and Roets, Graphic Picture Index
Houfe, British Illustrators and Caricaturists, p. 501
Waters, British Artists, vol. 1, p. 360

WITHERBY, Arthur George fl. 1894-1919

Painter, illustrator and writer. Witherby became the owner of *Vanity Fair* and contributed caricatures initialled 'W.A.G.' or 'WAG'. On 9 August 1900 *Martinus Steyn: ex president Steyn* was published.

Houfe, British Illustrators and Caricaturists, p. 502
Matthews and Mellini, In Vanity Fair

WITHYCOMBE, John G.

An exhibitor at the R.B.A., Withycombe provided a sketch for *The Graphic* entitled *Buying horses in Somerset for mounted infantry in South Africa*. The sketch was redrawn by Fred Whiting and was published on 20 January 1900.

Hofmeyr, Matton and Roets, Graphic Picture Index
Johnson and Greutzner, British Artists, p. 555

W., J.R. *see* J.R.W.

WL-S *see* LEHMANN-SCHRAM, W.

WOLLEN, William Barnes 1857-1936 3

Special artist, military painter and illustrator. Wollen was born of English parents in Leipzig on 6 October 1857. He originally intended to join the army but decided on a career in art instead. He studied at the University College School in London where he took the first Goodall Scholarship. He went on to the Slade School where he studied under Poynter and Legros. He stayed there for five years, winning one of the school's scholarships. He was elected a member of the R.O.I. in 1888 and the R.I. in 1891.

Wollen illustrated for several magazines, starting his career with *Pictorial World* in 1882. Among those he contributed to were *The Illustrated London News*, *The Strand Magazine*, *Black & White*, *Chums*, *Boy's Own Paper*, *Daily Chronicle*, *The Penny Illustrated Paper*, *The Wide World Magazine*, *Cassell's Family Magazine* and *The Graphic*.

Wollen was engaged by *The Sphere* and sent out to South Africa even before its first issue appeared. On 27 January 1900 the first issue reported:

The Sphere has six well-accredited representatives at the seat of the war. One, Mr. W.B. Wollen, is with Lord Methuen at the Modder River, while Mr. Earnest Prater is with General Buller. Mr. Wollen and Mr. Prater are both well-known artists and some of Mr. Wollen's war pictures in the Royal Academy, particularly his Omdurman picture of last year, have attracted great attention.

Wollen reported on the events at Modder River and Magersfontein, and some of his sketches were reproduced in facsimile. He must have had very little else to report on, because *The Sphere* published his pictures from only these two battles repeatedly for over two months. On 31 March, however, he depicted the Battle of Paardeberg and thereafter the capture of Cronje and his men. On 21 April he reported on the entry of Roberts into Bloemfontein.

During their prolonged stay in Bloemfontein, Wollen and Melton Prior entertained the troops at the charity concert given in aid of the Widows and Orphans fund on 18 April 1900. Billed as the 'heavenly twins' they produced lightning cartoons which were put up for sale by auction and 'realised splendid prices among the crowd of distinguished officers who were present in the Town Hall on that memorable night'. R.M. Paxton, *The Sphere*'s 'new special artist', depict-

1 W.B. Wollen's oil painting *The Imperial Light Horse at Waggon Hill* was exhibited at the Royal Academy in 1901. Wollen was not present at the battle.
2 Norman Wilkinson, who provided mainly naval pictures to *The Illustrated London News*.
3 Adolphe Willette's pen, ink and watercolour cartoon gives a very derogatory depiction of King Edward VII with a chamberpot on his head and an overturned bottle of liquor on the floor. Chamberlain is at the door with the peace treaty between the British and the Boers.
4 This pen-and-ink cartoon by Adolphe Willette showing a greedy soldier (representing the British) getting his nose in a trap (representing the Transvaal), was reproduced in *Le Courrier Français* on 29 September 1901.
5 William Wollen's Christmas menu for correspondents at Modder River 25 December 1899.
6 Adolphe Willete's card addressed to Tsar Nicholas II during his visit to France in June 1901. It appealed to him to intervene to bring about peace in South Africa. The editor of *The Picture Postcard* deplored this use of postcards for propaganda purposes.
7 Thomas Walter Wilson, who produced illustrations for *The Sphere* during the War.
8 William Barnes Wollen.

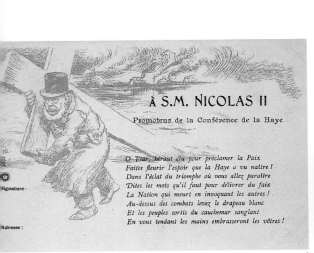

ed the scene showing Prior and Wollen at work. These sketches were published in facsimile on 2 June 1900 (p. 592).

Wollen also joined the team who produced *The Friend*, the newspaper compiled by war correspondents in Bloemfontein, and contributed a letter to its correspondence columns in support of the war artist. In a previous letter, correspondent H. Owen Scott had praised Wollen, Mortimer Menpes, Prior, and Lester Ralph because they represented actuality, but had criticized the 'old-fashioned war artist who draws on his imagination', saying that the camera would replace them. Wollen disagreed, replying 'to put the camera, which, after all, is only a fine piece of mechanism, on a par with a sketch is more than most people can put up with'.

When Roberts's army finally continued its march Wollen accompanied them through Kroonstad and on to Johannesburg and Pretoria. Facsimile sketches of the surrender of Johannesburg and Pretoria were featured in *The Sphere* on 4 August. By 11 August he was back in London painting scenes from memory. He had returned home on the same ship as his fellow artist-correspondents with *The Sphere*, Paxton and Prater. Also on board were Winston Churchill and several other newspaper correspondents. (A photograph of them on board ship was published in *After Pretoria: the Guerilla War*, vol. 1, p. 200.)

Wollen, who had contributed several military paintings to the Royal Academy since 1879, now produced three more based on his experiences in South Africa. *The Imperial Light Horse at Waggon Hill, January 6, 1900* was exhibited in 1901, *The Victoria Cross* in 1902, and *The 1st Battalion South Lancashire Regiment storming the Boer trenches at Pieter's Hill* in 1903. Strangely enough the 1901 and 1903 pictures were done of scenes in Natal to which he was not a witness.

Wollen's *The Victoria Cross* is now in the Durban art gallery. The National Army Museum possesses a similar watercolour of the same subject (7448) and the Africana Museum's *Sergeant James Rogers winning the V.C. 1901* (U562) by an unidentified artist is almost identical. When the Durban art gallery purchased *The Victoria Cross* Wollen explained his reasons for painting it.

The picture does not describe any actual instance of winning the Victoria Cross. I painted it as a tribute to 'Tommy' regular or irregular, Imperial or Colonial, and I also tried to show the public what it looks like to help another man into safety with a number of Boers — shooting at you at 400 yards. Had I painted any particular incident jealousies might have been caused.

Sir Abe Bailey is known to have commissioned *The Imperial Light Horse at Elandslaagte* which he presented to the headquarters of the Imperial Light Horse. Henrietta Dax of Clarke's Bookshop, Cape Town, owns a small oil by Wollen entitled *A Quiet Drink*. It was exhibited in London after the War. The National Army Museum has an oil, *An incident in the Boer War* (46717), and a watercolour, *The prospector and his pack horse* (51537). As mentioned earlier, Wollen often repeated his subjects and the author has a similar watercolour. Also in the author's collection is *The Scout*, dated 1901, and two pencil sketches of Boers. The author also has a menu designed and drawn in pencil by Wollen. Dated '25 December '99', the menu was for the war correspondents' Christmas dinner at Modder River. It is signed by several of the correspondents, including Lester and Julian Ralph. The Africana Museum possesses a pencil sketch, *Outside Johannesburg 1900* (W235), which was presented to the donor, Lawrence Whitehead, by the artist.

In *The Work of War Artists in South Africa*, Carter praises Wollen as follows:

Without suggesting any invidious comparisons it might be stated that Mr. W. B. Wollen, R.I., and Mr. Ernest Prater have displayed, besides this sense of usefulness, an unwonted power of draughtsmanship which has transformed a workable sketch into a work of art. Mr. Wollen's drawings, executed whilst accompanying the western force, are of singular ability. Naturally he had many opportunities at Magersfontein, and on page 6 is reproduced a spirited sketch of the attack of the 2nd Battalion of the Royal Highlanders. He has contrived in this to give the effect just before that period of dawn known to us in Caesar's language as 'prima luce'. As the Black Watch came abreast of the Boer position at 4.10 a.m. the whole of the trench was one sheet of flame from end to end, the kopje behind looming out black and indistinct in the faint flickerings of early morning light. The falling figure leading the attack is the gallant Major-General Wauchope.

To the solemn spectacle of the funeral of this hero, Mr. Wollen devoted a large sketch which is reproduced on page 27. The notes on this drawing can be easily deciphered, but without these, the masterly study is most effective and there is a convincing sense of motion in the advancing pipers who are playing the slow-step usual at the impressive function of the burial of a Highland chieftain.

Mr. Wollen is especially apt in portraying masses of men, and his power of realizing distances is given much scope in such an example as the departure of Cronje and the four thousand Boer prisoners under escort after Lord Roberts' brilliant capture of the Paardeberg stronghold (page 12). An admirable landscape effect is reproduced in the scene 'Cavalry patrol engaged with Boer Scouting Party' (page 29). Of a more exciting kind is his wash drawing of Boers stampeding under the merciless fire of a shell from the Naval Brigade (page 14), and a theme dear to admirers of the cool truculence of the Highland piper will be seen illustrated on page 6, showing how Corporal McKay of the Argyll and Sutherland Highlanders played that soul-stirring strain of Lucknow fame 'The Campbells are coming' at the Modder, to get the men together, as the officer's word of command could not be heard in the storm of bullets. Altogether Mr. Wollen's record in the war is of great achievement, and some of his huge panoramic scenes such as General French's action at Rooj Kop, the size of which prevents its reproduction on these pages, give a very lucid idea of the great range of country covered in most of the military operations.

Wollen was awarded the Queen's South Africa medal on 12 June 1903.

Wollen illustrated Rudyard Kipling's short story 'The Comprehension of Private Copper' which was published in *The Strand Magazine* (October 1902). He was also responsible for the illustrations in E. Small's *Told from the Ranks* (1897).

During World War I, besides doing a large number of postcard illustrations for Gale & Polden, Tuck and others, Wollen also produced some fine paintings of battles, such as *Defeat of the Prussian Guns*, *The Canadians at Ypres* and *Neuve Chapell March 10 1915*. He died on 28 March 1936.

Byatt, Picture Postcards, *p. 100*
Carter, Work of War Artists
Graves, Royal Academy, *vol. 8, p. 329*
Houfe, British Illustrators and Caricaturists, *p. 502*
Kennedy, Pictures in the Africana Museum, *vol. 5, p. 144 and vol. 7, p. 274*
Personal communication with J. Addleson, Curator, Durban art gallery
SABIB, *vol. 4, p. 815*
The Orders and Medals Research Society, *Summer 1986, 'War Correspondents: South Africa 1899-1902,' by Patrick Street*
The Strand Magazine, *vol. 10, p. 788, July-December 1895*
Thorpe, English Illustration
Ralph, War's Brighter Side
Who was Who, *vol. 3, p. 1480*

4

WOOD, Clarence Lawson 1878-1957 [1]
Cartoonist. Wood was born at Highgate, London, in 1878. His grandfather, Lewis John Wood R.I., was a landscape painter. Wood jnr. studied at the Slade School of Fine Art, the Heatherly School, and at the Frank Calderon School of Animal Painting. The publisher C.A. Pearson appointed Wood chief cartoonist for his publications, a position he held for six years. In about 1902 he dropped the use of his first name, which he disliked. He served in the Royal Flying Corps during World War I. He was a member of both the London Sketch Club and the Savage Club.

Wood was noted for his humorous sketches and cartoons. His postcard illustrations were published by, among others, Inter-Art Co., Valentine & Sons (for whom he did several annual studies, including the 'Gran'pop Series'), and the Pictorial Stationery Co. (whose Lawson cards date from 1902).

Wood worked for several magazines including *Pearson's Magazine, Royal Magazine, The Illustrated London News, The Graphic,* and *London Opinion*. Besides his Boer War illustrations in these publications, he was also responsible for the frontispiece to Harold Blore's novel *An Imperial Light Horseman* (1900), which was also published by C.A. Pearson.

Wood often signed his work with the initials 'L.W.'.
Byatt, Picture Postcards
Holt, Tonie and Valmai, Picture Postcard Artists *and* Picture Postcards of a Golden Age, *pp. 95 & 179*
Houfe, British Illustrators and Caricaturists, *p. 502*
Waters, British Artists, *vol. 2, p. 362*

5

WOOD, Stanley L. 1866-1928
Illustrator. Wood worked for the illustrated press and the publishing firm of Chatto as an illustrator of their boys' adventure stories. Wood exhibited at the principal galleries and had seven works shown at the Royal Academy, five of which had a military theme. His exhibit in 1897 was entitled *A surrender under protest; an incident in the Matabele war.*

In 1888 *The Illustrated London News* sent Wood to South Dakota, U.S.A., and his *Sketches from an Indian Reservation* were a result of this trip. Several of his illustrations were also published in *Harper's*. On his return to England he continued to draw cowboys and Indians. Jeff Dykes, in *Fifty Great Western Illustrators* (Flagstaff, Northland Press, 1975), praises him as follows: 'No better horse artist ever lived than Stanley L. Wood — there was more action in a Stanley Wood illustration than in the story itself'.

Among his Africana illustrations were those done for Bertram Mitford's books *The Gun-Runner* (1893); *The Luck of Gerard Ridgeley* (1894); *The Curse of Clement Waynflete* (1894); *Renshaw Fanning's Quest* (1894); *The King's Assegai* (1894); *A veldt official* (1895); and *The Expiation of Wynne Palliser* (1896). He also illustrated *With Shield and Assegai* (1899) and *One of the Fighting Scouts* (1903) by F.S. Brereton. He also illustrated *Men who have made the Empire* by George Chetwyn Griffith, published by C.A. Pearson in 1897.

During the Boer War Wood's work appeared in *Black & White* and *Black & White Budget, With the Flag to Pretoria* and *After Pretoria: the Guerilla War, The Fight for the Flag in South Africa, War Pictures, Cassell's History of the War in South Africa* and *L'Illustré Soleil du Dimanche*. During World War I he worked extensively for *War Illustrated*.

The author has an untitled wash drawing by Wood dated 1894. It shows a group of figures in Boer attire around a camp fire. The Africana Museum has a painting of the Matabele Rebellion by him.

Wood died on 21 March 1928.
Graves, Royal Academy, *vol. 8, p. 340*
Houfe, British Illustrators and Caricaturists, *503*
Johnson and Greutzner, British Artists, *p. 557*
SABIB, *vol. 4, p. 820*
Samuels, Artists of the American West, *p. 536*
Waters, British Artists, *vol. 2, p. 54*

WOOD, Starr 1870-1944
Caricaturist and illustrator who often used the pseudonym 'Snark'. Wood was born in London on 1 February 1870. (His father and grandfather also had the first name Starr.) Wood originally intended to be a chartered accountant, but he left the profession in 1890 to try his hand at illustrating, in spite of having no formal art training. He was founder and first art editor of *The Windmill* in 1898 and in 1910 he founded *Starr Wood's Magazine*. He was a member of the London Sketch Club and the Savage Club.

Among the periodicals to which Wood contributed were *Puck and Ariel, Fun, The Sketch, Judy, Pick-Me-Up, The Idler, Chums, The Parade, The English Illustrated Magazine, Punch,* and *Moonshine*. He drew postcards for Valentine & Sons and published various books including *The Snark's Annual, Rhymes of the Regiments* (1896), and *Cocktail Time* (1933).

Wood's Boer War work is not prolific and appeared in *Punch, Judy* and *The Regiment*. Hammerton reproduces a Boer War cartoon taken from p. 127 of *The Regiment*.

Wood often signed his work with the initials 'S.W.'. He was known for his snow white hair, which he acquired at the age of 26. He died on 2 September 1944.
Byatt, Picture Postcards, *p. 304*
Hammerton, Humorists of the Pencil, *pp. 124-129*
Houfe, British Illustrators and Caricaturists, *p. 503*
Who was Who, *vol. 4, p. 1259*

WOODHEAD, C. B. [1]
Presumably a member of the Duke of Edinburgh's Own Volunteer Rifles, whose watercolour heraldic drawing incorporates a picture of the Rifles' camp at Matjiesfontein in 1900.

WOODVILLE, Richard Caton 1856-1927 [7]
The son of an American father, Caton Woodville was born in London on 7 January 1856. He was educated in Düsseldorf, Germany, under Kamphaussen, and it is said that throughout his life he spoke with a German accent. Early in his career Caton Woodville joined *The Illustrated London News* and remained on the staff for almost 50 years. The magazine sent him to Turkey in 1878 and to cover the Egyptian campaign in 1882.

His first painting appeared in the Royal Academy in 1879 and the last just before his death. Most of these paintings depicted heroic British victories, such as *Maiwand: Saving the guns* (1882); *Badajos, 1812* (1894); *The Charge of the Light Brigade* (1895); and *Halloween 1914, Stand of the London Scottish on Messines Ridge* (1927). Only one with a Boer War theme, *Lindley: Whitsunday, 1900,* was shown at the Academy, in 1901.

Caton Woodville's Africana illustrations in *The Illustrated London News* were prolific and extend from 1878 to the end of the Boer War and beyond. His most famous Boer War work was *A gentleman in Khaki* (or 'Kharki' as it was often spelt), which was inspired by Rudyard Kipling's poem 'The Absent Minded Beggar'. This painting was reproduced on handkerchiefs, bottles, porcelain and bronze statues, mugs, copper plaques and many other articles. Most of these commemorative items were sold in aid of *The Daily Mail's* fund for the 'benefit of wives and children of the reservists fighting in South Africa'. A bronze statue, for example, was sold at £23 10s, of which 20 per cent was donated to the fund.

Caton Woodville's Boer War illustrations were borrowed by many other English and European journals and weeklies, often without acknowledgement. Many illustrations from *The Illustrated London News* and *The Spear* were repro-

---

1 C. B. Woodhead of the Duke of Edinburgh's Own Volunteer Rifles drew this heraldic design which includes a view of the regiment's camp at Magersfontein in 1900.
2 This wash drawing by Richard Caton Woodville of Queen Victoria inspecting a detachment of the Household Cavalry before their departure for South Africa is in the Royal Collection at Windsor. Reproduced by gracious permission of Her Majesty Queen Elizabeth II.
3 Richard Caton Woodville.
4 Richard Caton Woodville's dramatic paintings typified the British public's demand for patriotic and heroic pictures of the conflict. His photogravure *All that was left of them: The Highland Brigade at Magersfontein* was published by *The Spear* (an *Illustrated London News* publication given away free with the first issue of the magazine and subsequently sold separately at sixpence a copy). A second *All that was left of them* by Caton Woodville referred to a different incident — at the Battle of Modderfontein.
5 Richard Caton Woodville's proof print of *A gentlemen in Khaki*. The print is signed both by the artist and by Rudyard Kipling, the writer of 'The Absent Minded Beggar', the poem that inspired it.

duced as engravings. The engraving *Major General Baden Powell*, which appeared in *The Illustrated London News* on 26 May 1900 was sold for Lady Curzon's Mafeking Relief Fund. Other engravings which appeared in *The Spear* included *All that was left of them – the Highlanders at Magersfontein*. When *The Illustrated London News* published the *Transvaal War* in 1900, a limited deluxe edition was produced with the signature of Woodville, as well as those of Samuel Begg and Melton Prior.

Carter, in *The Work of War Artists in South Africa*, describes Caton Woodville as 'able to evolve a picture, if necessary, without the first aid of a sketch by a war "special". His experience in previous campaigns,' he continues, 'has endowed him with the requisite knowledge of the "image of war". As regards the hundreds of details that constitute military accessories, he has made the most patient study of these.'

The National Army Museum has one of Caton Woodville's original works entitled *The Surrender of Cronje at Paardeberg* (45495). The Africana Museum has a similar sepia wash drawing entitled *Surrender of Cronje to Lord Roberts at Paardeberg* (W236). It was done in 1901, a year after the event. The Royal Collection at Windsor has a wash drawing of *Queen Victoria Inspecting a Detachment of The Household Cavalry before their departure for South Africa, Combermere Barracks, Windsor, 11th November 1899*.

Verbeek records four of Caton Woodville's oils: *Battle of Biddulphsberg. Scots Guards, Biggarsberg, In the trenches at Ladysmith*, and *Majuba Hill Feb. 27 1881*. The Tatham Art Gallery in Pietermaritzburg ('Battle of Biddulphsberg'), the Local History Museum in Durban, the City Council of Pietermaritzburg, Mr Kenneth Griffith and the author also have works by Caton Woodville in their collections.

His work was used extensively on postcards and besides *A gentleman in Khaki*, at least seven illustrations were borrowed from *The Illustrated London News* for use in the Picture Postcard series on the War. His only recorded publication was *Random Recollections* in 1913.

Besides battle scenes Caton Woodville painted scenes of royalty (Queen Victoria, King Edward VII and King George V). He also accompanied the Duke of Clarence on his tour of India. He spent time in the U.S.A. in 1890 and 1891.

Caton Woodville often signed his work with the initials 'R.C.W.'. His attention to detail and speed of work were legendary. He was also a favourite of Queen Victoria who, however, reputedly disapproved of his reputation as a womanizer.

Like his father, who died from an overdose of cocaine before his son was born, Caton Woodville committed suicide, on 17 August 1927.

At the inquest it was stated by his sons, Anthony and William, that he had been depressed about the death of his wife a year earlier and 'because of his bad heart attack he would be unable to paint again'.

Carter, War Artists in S.A.
Dawnay and Miller, Military Drawings and Paintings
De Wet, Illustrated London News Index
Graves, Royal Academy, *vol. 8, pp. 349-350*
The Times (obituary), *24 August 1927*
Verbeek, Early Natal Art, *p. 9*
Who was Who, *vol. 2, p. 1146-1147*

WOOLLETT, Cresswell

Little-known artist whose painting *Cronje's first Night at St Helena* was reproduced in *The Sketch* (18 April 1900, p. 544). This painting is signed 'Cress Woollett'. He also worked as a postcard artist (after the War) for E. W. Savory Limited of Bristol and for C.W. Faulkner.

Byatt, Picture Postcards

WRIGHT, Alan fl. 1889-1925

Painter, illustrator and poet. Wright worked for *The Strand Magazine, Girls' Own Paper,* and *Pall Mall Magazine*. He wrote a book entitled *Climbing in the British Isles*. Wright's contribution during the Boer War was the cover illustration for six issues of George Newnes's *Khaki in South Africa*. His illustrations also appeared on the publisher's pictorial cloth cover of the bound volume.

Houfe, British Illustrators and Caricaturists, *p. 505*
Thorpe, English Illustration

WRIGHT, E. O. W.

He was responsible for three panoramas in C.S. Goldman's *With General French and the Cavalry in South Africa* (Macmillan and Company, London, 1902).

WRIGHT, Gilbert S. fl. 1900-1911

Painter and illustrator. Wright had one painting exhibited at the Royal Academy, *How he won the V.C.* (1900). Later that year it was published as a photogravure by Raphael Tuck and Sons.

The photogravure, which was 50 x 24 cm, was published in three states:
(a) Artist's proof (limited edition of 100) at 2 guineas.
(b) India prints at 1½ guineas.
(c) India print hand coloured at 1 guinea.

The incident depicted, that of Maj. Milton giving his horse to a wounded soldier, also inspired works by several other artists.

Wright contributed illustrations to *The Graphic* between 1910 and 1911.

Houfe, British Illustrators and Caricaturists, *p. 505*
Wood, Victorian Painters, *p. 531*

WRIGHT, Henry Charles Seppings 1849-1937

Artist and war correspondent. The eldest son of the Revd. F. H. A. Wright, vicar of St Stithians, Henry Charles Seppings Wright was born in 1849. After serving in the Royal Navy, he became special war correspondent for *The Illustrated London News* in about 1870 and saw action in Ashanti, Sudan, Benin, Greece, Cuba and the Balkans. He represented Armstrong, Whitworth and Company during the Russo-Japanese War in 1904 and the Central News Agency in Tripoli in 1911. During World War I he was in France when Antwerp was taken (1914) and in Russia at the fall of Przemysl (1915/16). Among his publications were *The Sudan* (1896), *With Togo* (1905), and *Two Years under the Crescent*.

Seppings Wright exhibited at the principal London gal-

leries, showing one seascape at the Royal Academy in 1901. He was an illustrator of general postcards and cards of a nautical nature for S. Hildesheimer and Co. It is believed that he contributed caricatures to *Vanity Fair* from 1891 to 1900 under the name of 'Stuff'. One such group caricature published in 1897 was entitled *Of Empire Makers and Breakers: A scene at the South Africa Committee, 1897*. His contributions to *The Illustrated London News* and *The Illustrated Sporting & Dramatic News* often had marine and naval themes, no doubt because of his Royal Navy association. Over 80 of these illustrations in *The Illustrated London News* were relevant to the Boer War.

Seppings Wright spent some time in Kimberley and Bloemfontein during the 1870s. He did at least two very large watercolours of the diamond fields, as well as other paintings of Bloemfontein and Kuruman. The William Fehr Collection (Cape Town) and the McGregor Museum (Kimberley) have examples of these works. Seppings Wright intended to have lithographs made of a large picture he had done of the Kimberley mine, as revealed in an advertisement in the *Diamond News* of 5 June 1887:

> Mr. H. C. S. Wright being about to proceed to England with his large Picture of the Kimberley Mine, to see it properly executed, begs the support of the Diamond Field Public for that proposal.
>
> The view will be reduced to about one-third so as to suit the size of Drawing Rooms.
>
> Subscribers will receive one copy for 22s, paying one instalment in advance, and one on delivery. Non-subscribers can obtain copies at 33s.
>
> Messrs. BIDEN & Co have kindly undertaken the Agency.
>
> Subscribers names received at the *News* Office.

Seppings Wright was sent out to accompany Buller to South Africa on 14 October 1899 aboard the *Dunnottar Castle*. Churchill and Pole-Carew were also on board. For some unaccountable reason Seppings Wright was ordered off the ship at Funchal in Madeira and returned to England. He describes how he regretfully watched 'the ship leave for the Cape without him'.

In about 1900 the Art Reproduction Company of London published his *The CIV's at Jacobsdal February 1900* as a platinum print.

The author has two watercolours by Seppings Wright:
1. *Watching and waiting*. Reproduced in *The Illustrated Sporting & Dramatic News* in February 1900.
2. *Parting shots. The West Yorkshires following the retreating Boers at 'Pieters Hill'*. Reproduced in *With the Flag to Pretoria* (vol. 2 p. 472). Probably first published in *The Illustrated Sporting & Dramatic News*.

Having visited the United States in the 1880s Seppings Wright is classed as a Western artist. He often signed his work with the initials 'H.C.S.W.'. He died in Sussex on 7 February 1937.

Africana News and Notes, *vol. 19, pp. 287-291, September 1971, 'The artist Seppings Wright on the diamond fields, and his friend George Hull' by O. McIntyre Byatt,* Picture Postcards, *p. 132*
De Wet, *Illustrated London News Index*
Matthews and Mellini, *In Vanity Fair*
Samuels, *Artists of the American West, p. 539*
Who was Who, *vol. 3, p. 1493*

WYLLIE, Charles William 1853-1923 [1]

Marine painter and illustrator. Charles William Wyllie was the second son of William Morison Wyllie (a genre painter) and younger brother of William Lionel Wyllie (see below). He was born in London on 18 February 1853. He studied at Leigh's and at the Royal Academy schools. He was elected a member of the R.B.A. in 1886 and the R.O.I. in 1888.

Wyllie worked for *The Graphic* for several years doing the same job as his brother William, a marine illustrator. Only one Boer War related illustration by Wyllie has been noted, but his Africana illustrations appeared from 1893.

Wyllie died in St John's Wood on 28 July 1923.
Hofmeyr, Matton and Roets, Graphic Picture Index
Houfe, British Illustrators and Caricaturists, *p. 505*
Who was Who, *vol. 2, p. 1153*

WYLLIE, William Lionel 1851-1931 [1]

Marine painter, etcher and illustrator. William Lionel was the eldest son of William Morison Wyllie (a genre painter), elder brother of Charles William Wyllie (see above), and half brother of Lionel Percy Smythe. He was born in London in July 1851. He was educated at the Heatherley School and the Royal Academy schools, where he won the Turner medal in 1869. His first painting at the Royal Academy was accepted in 1868. Most of those that followed had a nautical theme. He was marine painter to the Royal Yacht Squadron and was elected a member of the N.E.A. in 1887, A.R.A. in 1889, and R.A. in 1907.

The Graphic employed Wyllie for many years as a marine illustrator. It was in this capacity that he did the occasional Boer War related illustration.

In 1903 his *Peace driving away the horrors of war* and *June 1st 1902: peace proclaimed* were exhibited at the Royal Academy. Wyllie died on 6 April 1931.
Hofmeyr, Matton and Roets, Graphic Picture Index
Houfe, British Illustrators and Caricaturists, *p. 505*
Thorpe, English Illustration
Who was Who, *vol. 3, p. 149*

WYMER, Reginald Augustus 1849-1935

Wymer was commissioned into the 34th Foot in 1867 and transferred to the 91st Highlanders in 1870. He resigned in 1871. In 1892 he became a captain in the 2nd (Militia) Battalion, the Queen's Own Cameron Highlanders. In 1905 he retired as major. In 1915 he became a captain in the Territorial Force Reserve and was demobilized a year later.

Wymer drew several military uniform studies similar to the work of Richard Simkin (see page 207). Occasionally these paintings had Boer War relevance.

The Royal Collection at Windsor has three paintings by Wymer including *Review of Officers and Men of the Royal Navy and the Royal Marine from HMS Powerful, Windsor Castle, 2nd May 1900*, depicting the Naval Brigade which saw action in South Africa. The Brigade returned to England from Cape Town on 24 April 1900. A note in the catalogue states that the mayor of Kimberley was present at the review.
Dawnay and Miller, Military Drawings and Paintings, *vol. 2, p. 249-250*

WYSE, Henry Taylor 1870-?

Glasgow-born watercolour painter, pastel artist and potter. He studied at the Dundee School of Art, Académie Julian, and Colorassi's in Paris.

During the War, while Wyse was art master at the Ar-

broath High School, he and his pupils designed the cover and borders for *The Muster Roll of Angus* (edited by J.B. Salmond, Brodie and Salmond, Arbroath, 1900). He is thanked in the preface for his supervision given 'with characteristic care and good taste'. His pupils mentioned are J.K. Chapel, Helen Chapel, J.A. Bisset, Marguerite Bennet, Ida Leslie, P.K. Hanton, Charles Fowler, Albert Bisset, Roy Leslie, and Charles Paterson. Miss C.E. Dickson, who presumably was not one of his pupils, is also mentioned.
Johnson and Greutzner, British Artists, *p. 563*
The Muster Roll of Angus, *p. 8*

XAUDARO, Joaquin 1872-1933

Xaudaro was born in the Phillipines on 17 August 1872. He drew cartoons for *ABC* and *Blanco Y Negro*, the Madrid weekly in which his Boer War work appeared. Xaudaro died in Madrid on 1 April 1933.
Bénézit, Dictionnaire antique, *vol. 8, p. 819*
Osterwalder, and Hubschmid and Bouret (eds.), Dictionnaire des Illustrateurs, *p. 1146*

YENDIS, Mosnar [2]

Pseudonym (his name spelt backwards) of the *Fun* and *Moonshine* cartoonist and caricaturist Sidney Ransom. Some of his full-page coloured caricatures of politicians of the day were published in *Moonshine*. On 20 July 1901 Yendis published a cartoon which lampooned the penny-pinching attitude of the art editor to his artist-correspondents. He was also well known as a poster artist, having been responsible in 1899 for the cover illustration of the first volume of *The Poster*.
Barnicoat, History of Posters, *p. 4*

Y., F.H. *see* F.H.Y.

YOUNG, P. F.

The Daily Graphic illustrator. The author has two pen-and-ink sketches by him which were published in the *The Daily Graphic*.

1 H. C. Seppings Wright produced this drawing of the West Yorkshires following the retreat of the Boers at Pieter's Hill according to a sketch by F. A. Stewart. It was first published in *The Spear*.
2 *Watching and waiting*, a wash drawing by H. C. Seppings Wright, was reproduced in *The Sporting & Dramatic News* on 17 February 1900. Note the Bluejackets (British sailors) with their floppy hats manning the gun.
3 Henry Charles Seppings Wright.
4 Charles William Wyllie.
5 William Lionel Wyllie.
6 Mosnar Yendis shows the trials and tribulations of a home-based 'special' artist in this *Moonshine* cartoon. Note the caption.

5

6

Editor : " YOU MIGHT TAKE A RUN UP TO EDINBURGH AND INTERVIEW THE DUKE OF DUMDALE, GET A COUPLE OF HUNDRED WORDS, AND A FEW SKETCHES. THE USUAL RATE, YOU KNOW, 3/6 A COLUMN "
Contributor : " CERTAINLY, AND AS MONEY SEEMS SCARCE WITH YOU SHALL I SWIM OR WALK ? I AM ALWAYS READY TO OBLIGE."

ZIMMERMAN, Eugene ('Zim') 1862-1933

Zimmerman started his career as a caricaturist with *Puck* at its inception in 1876. He later worked for *Judge*, to which he contributed several Boer War cartoons.

> *Feaver*, Masters of Caricature, *p. 111*
> The Strand, *vol. 23, p. 440*

ZIMMERMANN, Alfred 1854-1910

Genre painter and etcher. Zimmermann was born in Munich on 16 May 1854. His double-page illustration *Die Schwestern*, published in issue 27 of *Jugend* in June 1901, showed nurses (sisters of mercy) attending to wounded Boers on the battlefield. Prints of this painting were sold by the publishers.

Zimmermann died in Munich on 21 May 1910.

> *Bénézit, Dictionnaire antique, vol. 8, p. 857*

ZODLER, M.

Illustrator of the postcard *Buren Siegfried's Kamp mit den Deutschen Drachen*, which was published by E. M. Porges, 17 Pilnitzer Street, Dresden.

ZUMBUSCH, Ludwig von 1861-1927   1

Historical, genre and portrait painter, illustrator and postcard artist. The son of the sculptor Kasper von Zumbusch, Ludwig von Zumbusch was born in Munich on 17 July 1861. He studied art at the Munich Academy under Lindenschmidt, Bouguereau, and Tony Robert Fleury. He exhibited in Vienna, Munich and Dresden. He was a member of the Munich Secession.

During the War Zumbusch worked for *Jugend*, and his portrait of De la Rey appeared on 18 March 1902 (issue 13).

Zumbusch died in Munich on 28 February 1927.

> *Bénézit, Dictionnaire antique, vol. 8, p. 872*
> *Fanelli and Godoli*, Art Nouveau Postcards
> *Hofstätter*, Art Nouveau Prints, etc., *p. 166*

ZWILLER, Marie Augustin 1850-?

Genre and portrait painter. Zwiller was born in Didenheim, Germany, on 10 July 1850. His contribution to *Paris-Pretoria*, showing a young girl at prayer, was published on p. 12.

> *Bénézit, Dictionnaire antique, vol. 8, pp. 876-877*

Ludwig von Zumbusch's portrait of De la Rey published in *Jugend* on 18 March 1902.

1 The obverse of a rare silver plaque with Richard Caton Woodville's illustration *The Absent Minded Beggar*.
2 Two examples of the Queen's South Africa medal, each with eight bars. The design was by G. W. de Saulles (see page 126).
3 The silver medal awarded to volunteers from the Borough of Portsmouth, including the crew of the H.M.S. *Terrible*.
4 The reverse of medal No. 3.
5 The obverse of the O'Okiep Cape Copper Company's bronze medal given to the men of the local garrison and company employees.
6 A tribute medal to volunteers of Willesden, Middlesex.
7 A tribute medal to volunteers of Doncaster, Yorkshire.
8 A tribute medal to volunteers of Londonderry, Ireland.
9 Avelino Belo's unique ceramic medallion showing Paul Kruger's image (see page 107).
10 The obverse of the Queen's South Africa medal, designed by G. W. de Saulles (see page 126).

Numbers 1 to 8 above were reproduced by kind permission of Mr M. G. Hibbard.

ADDENDUM: MEDALLISTS

BACHOVEN VON ECHT, K. A. Pro-Boer patron of the arts who initiated some of the medals designed by A. Scharff (see below).

BEETZ, ELISA. Dutch-born wife of A. Charpentier; known as a sculptor and medallist.

BEGEER, CAREL JOSEPH. Member of a Dutch family of medallists.

BOWCHER, FRANK 1864-?. Succeeded De Saulles at the Royal Mint in 1903.

CARABIN, FRANÇOIS RUPERT 1862-1932.

CARTAUX, F. Ran a factory in Paris that manufactured inexpensive medals.

DEVREESE, GODEFROI 1861-? Pupil of Simonis and Van der Stappen; produced medals of Boer generals.

DUBOIS, DANIEL 1849-1899. Painter who later became a medallist.

HAMILTON, MRS LILIAN 1865-? Wife of painter Vereker M. Hamilton and pupil of Legros. Sculptor and medallist. Produced medals of Roberts and Ian Hamilton.

HERBETTE, L.

JANVIER, VICTOR.

JORIS, FRANS JOZEF 1851-1914. Pupil of Jozef Geefs.

KEYZER, C. Boer P.O.W. in Ragama Camp, formerly employed by the N.Z.A. Spoorweg Maatschapij.

LAUER, LUDWIG CHRISTOPH. Die-sinking firm established in Nuremberg in 1729. Produced many popular medals.

LEFRANC, F. French P.O.W. on St Helena.

MAKKING, J. H. 1868-?. Sculptor and medallist. Produced a medal of Kruger.

MAYER, WILHELM and FRANZ WILHELM. Firm of die-sinkers, Stuttgart.

MENGER, JOHAN PHILIP MATHIAS 1845-? Chief engraver at Utrecht Mint until he retired in 1904.

NILSSON, SVANTE EDWIN 1869-1942. Medallist.

PASCAL, L. Engraver

PATEK, CARL.

PATEY, AUGUSTE 1855-1930. Chief medallist of the Paris Mint from 1896.

PAWLIK, FRANZ XAVER 1865-1906. Pupil of Scharff and later on staff of Vienna Mint.

PRUDHOMME, GEORGES HENRI 1873-? Sculptor and medallist.

RIVET, ADOLPHE 1855-? Sculptor and medallist.

SCHARFF, ANTON 1845-1903. Sculptor and medallist; Director of the School of Engraving at the Imperial Mint, Vienna. Designed many medals for the Bachoven von Echt family.

SCHULTZ, OTTO 1848-1911. A pupil of Wittig and Kullrich who worked in London and Berlin. Was second medallist at the Berlin State Mint. Responsible for the 1892 Transvaal coinage dies with the double shaft error. Kruger did not like the initials 'O.S.' on the truncation, because the word "os" means "ox" in Dutch.

WERNER, F. J. Dutch medallist working in Amsterdam c.1900. Produced commemorative plaquette.

WIENECKE, JOHANNES CORNELIS 1874-? Chief engraver at Utrecht Mint. Produced two medals of South African interest.

AFRICANA MUSEUM COMMEMORATIVE MEDALS OF THE Z.A.R., ANNA H. SMITH, CURATOR, 1958

APPENDIX 1: INITIALS OF SOME OF THE ARTISTS

A MA — Mary Ames
GDA — George Denholme Armour
B EB E. — Bahr
FOB — F. O'Beirne
GB — G. Bigot
DB — Daniel Boonzaier
DCB — Daniel Boonzaier
FB — Friedrich Boscovits
ASB — Alexander Stuart Boyd
FWB — F. W. Boyington
GB — Gustav Brandt
FB — Frank Brangwyn
GHB — G. H. Brennan
GB — Gordon Frederick Browne
TB — Tom Browne
Tom B — Tom Browne
AB — Alfred Bryan
C AEC — Algernon Essex Capell
C d'A — Caran d'Ache
JC — John Charlton
HC — H. Clark
KC — K. Collens
TSCC — T. S. C. Crowther
WC — (monogram) Walter Crane (incorporates a bird in the monogram)
D FD — Frank Dadd
STD — Stephen Dadd
TNFD — Talbot Neville Fawcett Davenport
DD — Douwes (Ernest) Dekker
BD — Bertrand Dete
FCD — F. C. Dickinson
CMD — Clive MacDonnell Dixon
TED — T. E. Donnison
Thomas D — Thomas Downey
du F — V. A. du Framont
E HE — Heinrich Egersdörfer
CEF — Charles Edwin Fripp
F FF — Frank Feller
AJF — Alexander Joseph Finberg
JF — Joseph Finnemore
AF — (monogram) Amedée Forestier
HF — (monogram) Harry Furniss
HyF — Harry Furniss
G OG — Otto Gerlach
GDG — Godfrey Douglas Giles
RGG — Robert Gwelo Goodman
FCG — Francis Carruthers Gould
FG — Fritz Georg Friedrich Grätz
FG — F. Griebner
H MH — Max Hagen
PH — Paul Halke
GRH — George Roland Halkett
SPH — Sydney Prior Hall
DH — Dudley Hardy
PH — Paul Hardy
ASH — Archibald Standish Hartrick
HH — Harold Harvey
JH — John Hassall
WH — William Hatherell
TTH — (monogram) Thomas Theodor Heine
H — Henriot
HP — (monogram) Hermann-Paul
JBH — J. B. Hess

MBH — Matthew Bede Hewerdine
RIP — Rowland Hill
EAH — Edgar A. Holloway
EH — Everard Hopkins
RAH — (monogram) Robert A. Hillingford
I IHI — (monogram) H. Innes
J AJ — Angelo Jank
MJ — M. Janzelow
HRJ — Harry R. Jay
JJ — John Jellicoe
BSJ — B. S. Johnson
HJ — Herbert Johnson
PJ — Paul Jouve
FAJ — Franz Albert Jüttner
FJ — Franz Albert Jüttner
K RK — (monogram) Rud Kauffmann
WRK — W. R. Kean
RK — Rudyard Kipling
EK — E. Klingebeil
RK — Richard Knötel
L HL — H. Law
EL — (monogram) E. Lauterburg
WLS — W. Lehmann-Schram
ML — Max Liebermann
TIL — T. Ivester Lloyd
FL — Frank Lynch
M WTM — William Theobald Maud
PM — Phillip William (Phil) May
EM — Erich Mayer
ADMcC — Arthur David McCormick
HMcC — Harry McCormick
M — Mortimer Menpes
MM — Mortimer Menpes
MM — McGregor Menzies
AM — A. Michäel
GM — (monogram) Georges Montbard
HM — Horace Morehen
AM — Arthur Moreland
M — Adolf Münzer
N JN — Joseph Nash (junior)
JSN — J. S. Newnham
EBN — Eardley B. Norton
PHN — P. H. Norwins (Les Norwin's?)
BN — B. Numa
O FOB — F. O'Beirne
AO — (monogram: unknown but possibly Alfred Ost)
P HMP — Henry Marriot Paget
SP — Sidney Paget
TP — (monogram) T. Payne
WP — Walter Paget
AP — A. Parent
BP — Bernard Partridge
BP — (monogram) Bruno Paul
HP — Harry Payne
AP — Alfred Pearse
CP — Constance Penstone
HLP — H. Pinnock
CLP — Charles L. Pott
R MR — Maurice Radiguet
SR — Stafford Ransome
LR — Lester Ralph
WR — William Ralston

LRH — Leonard Raven-Hill
ER — Edward Read
ETR — Edward Tennyson Reed
PR — Paul Renouard
MCR — Mordaunt Cyril Richards
ER — Earl Robert
WAR — William Allen Rogers
AR — A. Romilly
FBR — F. B. Ross
AJBR — August Jean-Baptiste Roubille
AR — A. Rouveyre
GDR — George Derville Rowlandson
S LS — Linley Sambourne
AS — (monogram) Arpad Schmidhammer
JS — Johann Schönberg
GS — Georges Bertin Scott
JAS — J. A. Shepherd
RS — Richard Simkin
MS — Max Slevogt
LS — Lancelot Speed
FS — Fred Spurgin
WSS — Walter Sydney Stacey
JMS — Joseph Morewood Staniforth
CJS — Charles Joseph Staniland
AS — A. Sutherland
T AKT — Arthur Kemp Tebby
JT — (monogram) John Tenniel
LT — Lance Thackeray
ET — Eduard Thöny
JHT — (monogram) J. H. Thornely
GT — George Tippel
GTB — Georges Tiret-Bognet
HT — Holland Tringham
V EMVA — E. M. van Averbeke
EVM — Eugene van Mieghem
SHV — Simon Harmon Vedder
FV — Frederic Villiers
HV — (monogram) Hermann Vögel
W JW — (monogram) James Waite
LMW — Leslie Ward
SPY — Leslie Ward
WAW — W. A. Wellner
GHAW — Geoffrey H. A. White
FW — Frederic Whiting
RW — Rudolf Wilke
W — Adolphe Willette
AW — (monogram) Adolphe Willette
ISW — Inglis Sheldon-Williams
WAG — Arthur George Witherby
LW — Clarence Lawson Wood
SW — Starr Wood
W — Starr Wood
HCSW — Henry Charles Seppings Wright
WLW — W. L. Wyllie
Z ZIM — Eugene Zimmermann

THE FOLLOWING INITIALS BELONG TO UNKNOWN ARTISTS

AF	DeV	FW	KG	NC	RB
AR	DWB	HE	KW	ND	RCB
A/S	EC	HTC	LC	OG	Rh
Jan C	EDB	HW	MFGS	Pen	Rip
CCLG	EH	IRF	MFR	PL	RK
CRB	EW	JAHC	MLC	PV	VK
CG	FHY	JM	MV or VM		
CL	FS	JRW	(monogram)		

THE ROYAL ACADEMY OF ARTS

Considering that the effects of the Boer War infiltrated almost every facet of British contemporary life it is understandable that the art of the time should reflect this influence. As early as February 1900, Marion Spielmann, author of *The History of Punch*, predicted in an article in *The Graphic* that the War would have a profound effect on art and he felt that one section of artists would suffer while others would benefit. Because of the national 'perturbation' less money would be available for art, particularly the anecdotal or 'art for art's sake' type of picture. On the other hand he forecast a marked increase in work for artists specializing in memorials, busts and medals. British military art was not as well developed as that on the Continent. The great French battle painter Edouard Detaille once remarked in an interview that he felt this was because the British had had no experience of war on their own soil as opposed to the artists in Europe where wars were a far more common occurrence during the 19th century.

He claimed to be a great admirer of the British black and white artist but was surprised to learn that the greatest British military artist was a woman. He was of course referring to Lady Elizabeth Butler, whose unfeminine exhibits at the R.A. caused quite a stir. Her husband Sir William Butler had had a great deal of military experience, including a spell in South Africa just prior to the War.

Exhibits at the Royal Academy had over the years depicted Africana military themes such as the Zulu War, the Matabele Rebellion and Major Allan Wilson's last stand in Rhodesia. South African and Africana painters such as Thomas Bowler (1860), Gwelo Goodman (1898-1904), James Morland (1877-1903), Sydney Carter (1894-1904), George Crosland Robinson (1884-1901) and Jean Rogier (1884-1903) all had works displayed. Even the architectural plans for the proposed new Port Elizabeth Library by C.E. Bateman and H.F. Buckland were exhibited in 1899. The Anglo-Boer War, however, inspired over 60 works by painters, sculptors, medallists and engravers which were exhibited at Burlington House.

Some of these paintings were illustrated in *Royal Academy Pictures* for the years 1899-1904. Others have not been seen so a certain amount of licence has been used in interpreting titles, which may in fact bear no relationship at all to the War. Others may not be listed, as some with such non-military titles as 'Morning' and 'The Return' proved, on viewing the illustration, to have Boer War relevance after all.

It was quite common for artists to sell the copyright of the paintings to publishing companies who would then publish and sell photoengravings, prints, and even postcards of them. A list of artists whose Boer War work was exhibited at the Royal Academy includes the following: (an asterisk after the title indicates that the picture is reproduced in this book)

ADAMS, DOUGLAS
Straight for the Guns (1900)
BACON, JOHN HENRY FREDERICK
Ordered South (1900)
For King and Fatherland, etc (1900)
The Return (1901)
Your sovereign, etc (1902)
BASTIN, A.D.
From the Front (1900)
BEADLE, JAMES PRINSEP
Reverie (1901)
*To the sound of the Guns (1901; Arrival of the 62nd Field Battery at the Modder River battle after a terrible forced march)
The victors of Paardeberg (1902)
BENNETT, WILLIAM B.
A Soldier's daughter (1900)
BERKELEY, STANLEY
Full Cry (1902)
BROWN, CECIL (sculptor)
The red badge of Courage (1901)
BRUCE-JOY, ALBERT
Field Marshal Lord Roberts of Kandahar V.C., etc (bust) bronze (1900)
BUTLER, ELIZABETH, Lady
Within sound of the guns (1903)
CARTER, SYDNEY
The list of casualties (1902)
CHARLTON JOHN
*Routed! Boers retreating (1900)
2 February, 1901 (1901)
CLACY, MISS ELLEN
War news in the streets, England, 1900 (1900)
CLARK, CHRISTOPHER
The attempt to save the guns at Colenso (1900)
Ubique (1901)
CLARKE, JOSEPH
War news at St Cross (1899)
COLE, P. TENNYSON
Lord Milner G.C.M.G., G.C.B., High Commissioner for South Africa (1902)
COPE, ARTHUR STOCKDALE
The Lord Kitchener of Khartoum (1900)
CUMMING, W. SKEOCH
The Black Watch on the Trek (1903)
Defence of a Kraal: 1st Life Guards at Diamond Hill, 11 June 1900 (1904)
DE LACY, CHARLES J.
With troops for Table Bay: Transport leaving the Royal Albert Docks (1900)
DICKSEE, HERBERT THOMAS
In the enemy's country (1901)
FARQUHARSON, DAVID
War News (1900)
FORMILLI, CESARE
My son's regiment (1903)
FOSTER, ARTHUR J.
Our young defenders: Children collecting for the Widows and Orphans Fund, May 1900 (1904)
FULLER, EDMUND G.
Peace! be still (1902)

FULLWOOD, A. HENRY
Table Bay, South Africa, during the Boer War, 1900 (1901)
GARRAT, ARTHUR
Wounded men at Wynberg, South Africa: A shady corner (1900)
Veterans reading the war news in Chelsea Hospital (1900)
The King's Yeoman (1901)
GOUGH, ARTHUR
Removing the limbers of the Guns at Tafel Kop (1903)
HARCOURT, GEORGE
*Goodbye! The 3rd Battalion Grenadier Guards leaving Waterloo station, October 21 1899 (1900)
HEARD, T.F.M.
A victim of the War (1900)
War's Victim (a tryptich)
HEDLEY, RALPH
The Reservist's wife (1900)
General H.R.H. The Duke of Connaught K.G. (1900)
Maj. General R.S.S. Baden-Powell, CB (1903)
HERKOMER, HUBERT VON
The Earl of Albemarle CB., M.V.O. Lieut. Colonel Commanding City Imperial Volunteers, South Africa (1902)
HESTER, EDWARD GILBERT
In time of War (1902)
HILLINGFORD, ROBERT ALEXANDER
*South Africa 1901: The dawn of Peace (1901)
HIRST, NORMAN
The Capture (1902)
JOHN, WILLIAM GOSCOMBE (sculptor)
The late Prince Christian Victor statue in bronze erected at Windsor Castle (1904)
Memorial to the officers, N-C officers and men of the Coldstream Guards who died in South Africa relief; St Paul's Cathedral (1904)
Model of a monument to commemorate the King's Liverpool Regiment (1904)
KEMP-WELCH, LUCY
*'In sight'; Lord Dundonald's dash on Ladysmith (1901)
*The Morning (1902)
Sons of the City (1903)
LESLIE, GEORGE DUNLOP
In time of war (1900)
LOMAX, JOHN ARTHUR
A Soldier ever! Assassin never! (1900)
LUCAS, JOHN SEYMOUR
News from the front (1899)
MAIR, MISS MAUD
Major General J.H. Bedford (1904)
McCORMICK, ARTHUR
War (1903)
MORGAN, FREDERICK
The hero of the hour (1900)
Homewards (1901)
MUSCHAMP, F. SYDNEY
Ordered South (1900)
ORCHARDSON, CHARLES
Capt. Blunt, Lancashire Fusiliers (1901)

PEARSE, ALFRED

'Bobs eyes'; A sketch on the Orange Free State border (1900)

PEGRAM, HENRY A.

The Late Rt. Hon. Cecil Rhodes (bust), marble for the City of London (1903)

SHAW, JOHN BYAM

Boer War, 1900 (1901)

STEWART, CHARLES E.

The Victoria Cross (1902)

STONE, MARCUS C.

A soldier's return (1900)

SYMONDS, WILLIAM ROBERT

Surgeon-General Jameson, C.B. (1902)

TITCOMB, WILLIAM HOLT YATES

Good news from the war (1900)

TORROMÉ, FRANK J. (FRANCISCO)

The victor (1900)

WATTS, GEORGE FREDERICK

Major General Baden-Powell (1902)

WELLS, HENRY TANWOTH

Colonel Sir Edward R.C Bradford G.C.B. (1900)

Major General Sir John F.D. Donnelly, K.C.B. (1901)

WHITING, FRED

6th Dragoons leaving Albert Docks for South Africa (1900)

WHITING, ONSLOW (sculptor)

Field Guns going into action – Colenso (relief; 1901)

WILSON, MISS BEATRICE J.

Major Best (1901)

WOLLEN, WILLIAM BARNES

*The Imperial Light Horse at Waggon Hill, January 6, 1900 (1901)

The Victoria Cross (1902)

The 1st Battalion South Lancashire Regiment storming the Boer trenches at Pieter's Hill (1903)

WOODVILLE, RICHARD CATON

Lindley: Whitsunday, 1900 (1901)

WRIGHT, GILBERT

How he won the V.C. (1900)

WRIGHT, H.C. SEPPINGS

The King's Ships (1901)

WYLLIE, WILLIAM LIONEL

Peace driving away the horrors of war (1903)

June 1st 1902: Peace proclaimed (1903)

ROYAL SOCIETY OF BRITISH ARTISTS

The exhibits at the Royal Society do not seem to have been as influenced by the War as their Royal Academy counterparts and only a few exhibits have Anglo-Boer War themes. Works shown included:

CRAFT, PERCY

The Pathos of War (1902)

FINNEMORE, JOSEPH

Peace: A Boer Vrouw of North Holland (1902)

LUKER, W. (JNR.)

Earl Roberts arriving at Buckingham Palace (1901)

MARSHALL J. FITZ

Attack and Defence (1900)

A frontal attack (1901)

WILD F. PERCY

A Gentleman in Khaki (1901)

For the Flag (1902)

OTHER EXHIBITIONS

Exhibitions of original works took place almost continuously at *The Illustrated London News*, *The Graphic* and other newspaper galleries. The exhibitions did not necessarily have Boer War themes but among those that did included Inglis Sheldon-Williams's 38 drawings and one statuette which were exhibited at the Fine Arts Society gallery, London, in October 1902. Stratford St Leger also held an exhibition of over 65 paintings and pen-and-ink sketches which had been used as illustrations for his book *War Sketches in Colour*. This exhibition, which opened on 27 May 1904, took place at the Bruton Galleries, London. Mortimer Menpes's pastel and watercolours used in his *War Impressions* were similarly exhibited and Georges Bertin Scott's three paintings *Elandslaagte, Buller's final crossing of the Tugela* and *The surrender of Cronje* were exhibited at the Tooth Gallery in the Haymarket in February 1901.

William Skeoch Cumming exhibited several Boer War watercolours at the Royal Scottish Academy between 1903 and 1906 and at the Walker Gallery in 1904. James Hannan Watson showed works influenced by his duty in South Africa at the Royal Glasgow Institute of Fine Arts every year from 1902 until 1906 and another of his works was sold at the Royal Scottish Academy. Robert Gwelo Goodman exhibited Boer War paintings done in South Africa in 1900, among other South African scenes done at the time, in Cape Town and later at Grafton Galleries, London, in 1901.

Another rich field of Boer War paintings were the numerous contemporary portraits of British generals and Boer personalities which were done at various times during and just after the war.

Some examples, many of which are housed in the National Portrait Gallery, London, include:

R. BADEN-POWELL

(1902) oil by J. F. Watts (Charterhouse School)

(1903) oil by Hubert von Herkomer (Cavalry and Guards Club)

SIR IAN HAMILTON

(1900) drawing by Inglis Sheldon-Williams (National Portrait Gallery)

KITCHENER

(1900) Arthur S. Cope (Royal Engineers) (1899) Heinrich von Angell (Royal Collection) (1899) Unknown (Royal Engineers)

DE WET

John Singer Sargent (New York Metropolitan Museum of Art)

ALFRED MILNER

(1901) oil by Hugh de Glazebrook (National Portrait Gallery)

LORD ROBERTS

(1904) oil by John Singer Sargent (National Portrait Gallery), (1899) Hubert von Herkomer (Herkomer Gravure; National Portrait Gallery), (1899) woodcut by William Nicholson (National Portrait Gallery), (1900) pencil and watercolour by Inglis Sheldon-Williams (National Portrait Gallery)

APPENDIX 3: POSTCARD ARTISTS

O ORIGINAL
C COPY
1 SINGLE
P PART
S SET

Most of the illustrations which appeared on postcards were borrowed from other sources. Some however were original and specially commissioned by the publishers.

Often cards were issued in sets, but on many occasions only individual cards or pairs of cards were issued.

The following list indicates in which category the artists and their illustrations appear, together with the publisher (if known) or the title or subject of the illustration, and the country or countries of origin. A plus sign after the set number indicates that there may be more cards in the set. Further information on the postcard sets appears under the name of the artist in the biographical section.

ARTIST		NUMBER AND SET	PUBLISHERS/ TITLE OF CARD	COUNTRY
A.F.	OPS	2/13	Bruno Bürger and Ottille	Germany
		2/6		Germany
A.O. (monogram)	OS	3/3	A.D. & A.D. Paris	France
AMATO, Gennaro	CPS	1/46	Imp Ad. Weick 1669 *Journal L'Illustration*	France
AR (monogram)	OS	8/8		Holland
BAETES, J.	OPS	1/11+	Algemene Nederlandsche Verbond	Germany, Belgium
BAGGIE, PAUL	C1		*Naar Harden Stryd*	Holland
BANNERMAN, ALEX	OS	8/8+	George Stewart & Co.	Scotland
BERKELEY, STANLEY	OPS		Raphael Tuck & Sons, Empire Series, 823: *CIV in action*	England
BERNHARD, F.	O1		Carl Otto Hayd	Germany
BIENERT, A.	O1		Kunsanstalt Minerva	Austria
BIGOT, G.	OPS	2/2+	J.P.	France
BIQUARD, ARMAND	OPS	2/30	Picture Postcard Co.	England
'BOBB'	OPS			France
BOUFFIER, MARGUERITE	OPS	3/3+	*Fur die Buren* Rud Bechtold & Co., Wiesbaden	
			L. Schellenberg'sche Hofbuchdruckerei Wiesbaden	Germany
BOYD, ALEXANDER	CPS		*Peace* 663	
			Peace with Honour 664	
			Peace with Honour 665	
			Raphael Tuck & Sons	England
BRAAKENSIEK, JOHAN	CPS		'Paul Kruger'	
			Jos Nuss	Holland
			Joh. J. Steinler	Holland
			J. C. Dalmeijer	Holland
BROWNE, TOM	OS	6/6	Davidson Bros.	England
BUCHANAN, FRED	O1		*Well over South Africa*	England
BUELINCX, HENRY	C1		*Pour l'Indépendence du Transvaal*	France
DA AMARAL, C.	O1		*De Slag op Modder River:* Ludwik Damrak	Holland
			J. G. Vlieger	Holland
DE CAMARA, LEAL	CS	8/8+	*L'Assiette au Beurre*	France
CAMPBELL, JOHN F.	OPS	6/6	*VC Heroes*	
			W. & A. K. Johnston Ltd.	Scotland, England
CHARBERT	O1			France
CHARLTON, JOHN	CPS		J. C. Dalmeijer	Holland
COLLENS, K.	OPS	3/11+	Algemene Nederlandsche Verbond	Belgium, Germany
'CULVER'	CPS			Holland
CUMMING, WILLIAM SKEOCH	CPS	1/6	Geo. Falkner & Sons	England
DARSANE	OPS	1/8		France
D'AURIAN, JEAN	CPS			Holland

ARTIST	NUMBER AND SET	PUBLISHERS/ TITLE OF CARD	COUNTRY
DE AMICIS, FRANCO	O1	*Figaro*	Holland, France
DEFREGGER, FRANZ VON	O1	Die Deutsche Centrale f Bestrebung z Beendigung der Burenkriege	Germany
DE HAENEN, FREDERIC	CPS 1/46	Imp Ad. Weick 757	
		Journal L'Illustration	France
DE LAMARRE, A. F.	OS 10/10 +	*Fantaisie Politique*	France
DE V, E	OS 5/5	J. C. auf der Heide	Holland
DORVILLE, NOËL	CPS		Holland
DU FRAMONT, V. A.	OS		St Helena
EDWARDS, LOUIS	OPS 2/30	Picture Postcard Co.	England
E.N.	C1	*Jugend*	Germany
ESPINASSE	OS 8/8		France
	O1		**France**
FAUSTIN, BETBEDER	CPS	Raphael Tuck & Sons, Empire Series 1286, 1288	England
FELLER, FRANK	CPS	Raphael Tuck & Sons, Empire Series 840	England
FHY	OPS	Max Marcus	Germany
FICKENSCHER	O1	L. Schlaf	Austria, Germany
FINNEMORE, JOSEPH	CPS	Raphael Tuck & Sons Empire Series 838	England
FORESTIER, AMEDEÉ	CPS 1/20	Picture Postcard Co.	England
FREDILLO	OPS 6/6		France
FRENZENY, PAUL	C1 1/30	Picture Postcard Co.	England
FRITZ	OS 2/2 +		France
FRITZCHEN	OS 6/6		Germany
FRKBCH, C. J.	O1	*Gruss aus Afrika*	Germany, Belgium
F.S. (possibly Fred Spurgin)	O1	*The girl he left behind him*	England
FURNISS, HARRY	OS 6/6	John Walker & Co Ltd	England
F. W.	O1	S.&G. Saulsohn, Berlin	Germany
GODFRIN	O1	'La Force Prime le Droit'	France
GOULD, FRANCIS CARRUTHERS	CS 6/6	Westminster Cartoon Series 1 & 2	England
GRÄTZ, FRITZ	CS 1/21	(Copy by A. Rouilly)	Holland, France
GRELLIER, HENRY HARLEY	OS 24 +	Sallo Epstein	South Africa
HASSALL, JOHN	O1	*Do you think you'll be in* (Write Away) Gale & Polden	England
HEINE, TH.	CS 2/2 +	Simplicissimus	Germany
HELOURE RINS, P.	OS 3/3 +	A. B. Paris	France
HEWERDINE, MATTHEW	OPS 6/6	C.W. Faulkner & Co. Patriotic Series 24	England
HOFFMANN, ANTON	OS 5/5	Hub Kohler, Munich	Germany
HOLLOWAY, EDGAR	OS	Gale & Polden	England
H.W.	OS 3/3 +	Regel & Krug	Holland, Germany
IBBETSON, ERNEST	OPS 56?/117	Gale & Polden	England
JAN, C.	O1		Belgium
J.C. or C.J.	OS 9/9 +	George Budricks & Co.	South Africa
JENEER, J.	O1	*Kruger et Wilhelmine* Salon Blanc 1901	Belgium
JENSEN, A.	O1	*Heil u. Sieg den Buren*	Germany
JILENO	CPS		Holland
JULIO, G.	CS 12/12	'Cartes Postales Artistique' par Julio	France
JÜTTNER, F. A.	CPS	J.C. Auf der Heide	Belgium
	OPS		Holland
	5/36	Dr Eysler & Co	Germany
K.G.	O1	'Illig & Moller, Goppingen: 'Chamberlain als Friedensengel'	Germany
KIENERCK, GIORGIO	O1	E.T. P.G. Obsner, Florence	Italy
KLEINHEMPEL, G.	OPS 7/13	Bruno Burger & Ottille	Germany
	OPS 1/6		
KNOTEL, RICHARD (R.K.)	CPS	J. C. auf der Heide	Holland
	CPS		France
KOSKI	OPS 1/24		France
KRÜGEN, A.	O1	*Deutschen Michel*	Germany
KUPKA, FRANÇOIS	CPS 1/46	Imp Ad. Weick *Journal l'Illustration* 1304	France
K.W.	O1	*Verlorne Gluck der Boeren*	Germany
L. (LENNY)	OS 6/6		France
LANGA, RATA	CPS		Holland
LAPLAGNE, GUILLAME	CS 4/4 +	A. N. Paris	France
LAUTERBERG, EMILE	O1	E. Lauterberg, Berne	Switzerland

ARTIST		NUMBER AND SET	PUBLISHERS/ TITLE OF CARD	COUNTRY
LÉANDRE, CHARLES	C1		Joss Nuss (*Paul Kruger*)	Holland
LECLERC	C1		'Journal des Voyages'	France
LEHR, C.	OS		'Homage to Kruger'	England, France
LEIGHTON, FREDERICK	OPS			England
LE ROY, HIPPOLYTE	CS		Albert Sugg a Gand	France
LEWIS, ROBERT	CPS	2/4	J.P., A.B. Paris	France
LION, G.	CPS	2/2 +	P.L. Paris *Edouard VII*	France
LOBEL, P.H.	OS	21/21 +	*Paix de Laches* par Lobel	France
M.V. or V.M.	OS	10/10	Internationalen Postkartenhandel	Holland
MAILICK, A.	OS	2/2	P.S.A.D. Erika 554	France, Holland
'MARNIX'	OPS	1/21		France
MARTENS, WILLY	C1		*Die slag bij Krugersdorp* Kotting	Holland
McNEIL, J.	OPS	3/6	George Falkner & Sons	England
MERTE, O.	O1		Ludwig Frank & Co	Germany
MEUNIER, HENRY	O1		'Appeal to Queen Victoria'	France
MIGNOT, VICTOR	CS	6/6	*Le Bon Vivant*	France
MONTBARD, G.	CPS	1/30	Picture Postcard Series	England
MORISS	O1		Edouard VII L'intrepide	France
NORWIN'S, LES	OS	15/15		France
O'BEIRNE, F.	OS	38/38 +	Blum & Degen	England
O.G.	O1		Richard Hauerstein, Attenburg	Germany
ORENS, DENIZARD	OS	2/2 +	M.Y., Paris	France
		6/6		France
		6/6		France
		6/6		France
PALMER, O.	OS		P.J. Fochtenberger Stuttgart	Germany
PAULAT	O1		S.P.	France
PAYNE, HARRY	OPS		Raphael Tuck & Sons *Wiping something off the slate* 280	England
	OPS		*Well done Gallant Mafeking* 281	
	OPS		Raphael Tuck oilette 1280, 1282, 3165, 3163	
			Sons of Empire 1280	England
			Sons of Empire 1282	
'PEN'	OS	5/5 +		England
PICK, A.	OS	2/2 +	S.P. Paris	France
PIFFARD, HAROLD	C1			England
P.L.	O1		*Heil den tapfern Buren* J. Bauer	Germany
PLUMET, PAUL	C1			France
PUEUBRAY	O1			France
P.V.	O1		*Les enfants s'amusant*	Belgium
RADIGUET, MAURICE	C1		*Fin de la Guerre*	France
RALSTON, WILLIAM	OS	2/2 +	*Types of the British Army XX Cent.*	England
REIJENGA, J.	O1		Weinthal & Co. Rotterdam	Holland
RINZNER, M.	O1		Reichsverband-Unterstutzung Dtsch. Veteranen	Germany
RICHARDS, MORDAUNT CYRIL 'MRC'	OS	14/14 +	Wrench?	England
RIP	O1		*Marriages par carte Postale* (Chamberlain)	France
RK (monogram)	O1		*Unser Mitgefuhl* Rud Kauffmann	Germany
R.L.	OS	3/3 +	*Vision* Kunsanstalt Merkur, Dresden	Germany
			Hurrah Germania R. Langbein & R. Reinhardt	
ROBERT, EARL	OS		Ladysmith siege cards	South Africa
ROSE, L.	CPS		P.L. Paris (*Edouard VII son cauchemar*)	France
ROSTKO	O1	1/21	'Wilhelmina welcoming Kruger'	France
ROTTMAYER, H.	O1		*Frauen Europas helft Euren Armen Buren-schwestern!*	Germany
ROUBILLE	CPS		*La Musée de Sires* A.C. Paris	France
ROUILLY, A.	OS	18/21 +		France
RUCHERT	OS	6/6	*Guerre Anglo Boer*	
			Croquis sur Place L.H. & C. Paris	France
RUCTLER, M	OS	3/3	Franz Schneider	Austria
RUPPE, M.	OS		J.A. Jetzelberger	Austria
SABATTIER, L.	CPS	3/46	Imp Ad. Weick 822, 833, 1668 *Journal L'Illustration*	France
SCHEFFLER, H.	C1		A. Hembo Nice	France
	O1		Villebois Mareuil, A. Hembo Nice	France

ARTIST	NUMBER AND SET		PUBLISHERS/ TITLE OF CARD	COUNTRY
SCHLETTE, ENGELINA HELENA	OS	17/17	N. J. Boon	Holland
SCHMIDHAMMER, ARPAD	C1		J. C. auf der Heide	Holland
	C1		Münchener Odinskarte	Germany
	C1		Schererverlag	Germany
SCHMIDT, HUGO CARL	OS	5/5 +	*Lache, Oncle Paul, 'Justice', Vaincre ou Mourir*	Switzerland
SCHULZE, HERMANN	O1		Gustav Kohl Leipzig	Germany
SCHWARTZE, THÉRÈSE	C1		*Piet Joubert* Joss Nuss	Holland
SCOTT, GEORGES BERTIN	CPS	4/46	Imp Ad. Weick *Journal L'Illustration* 751, 819, 1662, 1663	France
SIMKIN, RICHARD	OPS	6/6	C.W. Faulkner & Co. Patriotic Postcards Series 20	England
SINGFRAU	O1			France
S.M.	OS	3/3 +		South Africa
SOWERBY, M.	O1		*Sons of the Empire* Harry Frowde and Hodder & Stoughton	England
'SPY'	CS	6/6 x 4	Stewart and Woolf series 101, 102, 103, 117	England
G. F. STALLER	O1	(double card)	Cnobloch, Amsterdam	Holland
STEVENS, EDWARD	OPS	1/30	Picture Postcard Co.	England
ST LEGER, STRATFORD	C1		A. & C. Black	England
STUTZ, LUDWIG	CPS			Holland
TAILLEFER	O1		Favor, Paris	France
TALVART, HECTOR	OS	12/12	*La Dernière Epopée*	France
THACKERAY, LANCE	OPS	9/9 +	R. Tuck & Son	England
	OS	4/4	S Hildesheimer & Co.	England
THIELE, ARTHUR JULIUS	OS		Regel & Krug	Germany
		12/12	Kunzli Freres	Switzerland
			Diehl & Cnobloch	Holland
	O1	1/1	'Homage to Kruger'	Germany
			Kunzli	Switzerland
TREIBER, W.			A. Wolmuth	Germany
VAN AVERBEKE, E. M.	OPS	1/11	Algemeen Nederlandsche Verbond	Belgium
VAN DOCK	O1			Italy
VAN DOOMAL, THEO	O1		P. J. Van Melle	Belgium
VAN GELDORP, PETRUS	CS	9/9 +	*De Amsterdamsche Courant*	Holland
VAN MIEGHEM, EUGEEN	OS	3/11 +	Algemeen Nederlandsche Verbond	Belgium, Germany
VAN OFFEL, EDMUND	OPS	1/112	Algemene Nederlandsche Verbond	Belgium, Germany
VAN WOUW, ANTHONIE	CS	4/4	The International Trading Company	Holland, France
VEBER, JEAN	CS	16/16 +	M. Picot	France, Holland
VERBER	O1		A.B. Paris	France
VICTA	OPS	7/8		France
V.K.	OS		Behrendt & Wartenberger, Berlin	Germany
VOLZ, T.	OS		J. Kocher Kunsverlag, Reutlingen	Germany
WAG (ARTHUR WITHERBY)	CPS		Stewart and Woolf	England
WAITE, JAMES	OPS	2/2 +	*Fur der Buren* Colmar, Alsace	France
WARD, LESLIE (see 'Spy')				
WEIJMANN, OTTMAR	O		Peace	Germany
WELLNER, W.A.	OPS	1/36	Dr Eysler & Co	Germany, France, Holland
WILLEM, H.	O1		*Le Cauchemar de Joe Chamberlain*	Belgium
WILLETTE, ADOLPHE	O1		*à S. M. Nicholas II* La Litho Nouvelle, Asniers	France
W, JR	C1		Kruger and Steyn *Goodbye*	England
CATON WOODVILLE, R.	CPS		'A Gentleman in Kharki'	England
	CPS	7/30	Picture Postcard Co.	England
	OPS	4/4 +	Robert A. Thompson & Co. *Imperial Army Series*	England
WRIGHT, H. C. SEPPINGS	CPS	1/30	Picture Postcard Co.	England
	CPS	1/46	Imp Ad. Weick 1670 *Journal l'Illustration*	France
XAUDARO, JOAQUIN	CPS			Holland
ZODLER, M	O1		E. M. Porges, Dresden	Germany
			P. M. Friedemann, Dresden	Germany

APPENDIX 4: BOER WAR COVERS OF MAJOR FRENCH ILLUSTRATED NEWSPAPERS

LE PETIT PARISIEN

NO.	DATE	ARTIST	TITLE
363	19 JANUARY 1896	BERTRAND DETE	*'Anglais et Boërs': Le Filibustier Jameson et ses compagnons conduits à Pretoria après leur défaite.* (back cover) *Au Transvaal: une mine d'or. Types de cafres Employés aux travaux des Mines. Au Transvaal Campement de Boërs.*
556	1 OCTOBER 1899	B.D.	*Le Conflit Entre L'Angleterre et Le Transvaal. Une Troupe de Boërs en Marche vers la Frontière Transvaalienne.*
559	22 OCTOBER 1899	'B.D.'	*La Guerre au Transvaal. M. Paul Kruger Président de la République du Transvaal. Le Général Redvers Buller Commandant en chef des troupes anglaises. Le Général Joubert Commandant en chef de l'armée du Transvaal. Soldats et Volontaires du Transvaal – Une famille de Boërs en armes. Le Transport de Munitions par les Boërs – Les Boërs gardant la voie ferrée a la Frontière.*
560	29 OCTOBER 1899	BERTRAND DETE	*Les Événements du Transval. Les Boërs attaquant un Train blindé envoyé par les Anglais.* (p. 349) *La Guerre au Transvaal: carte des opérations Militaires.*
561	5 NOVEMBER 1899	BERTRAND DETE	*Au Combat de Glencoe. Le Général Anglais Symons Mortellement Blessé.*
562	12 NOVEMBER 1899	BERTRAND DETE	(back page) *La Guerre au Transvaal. Après le Combat de Ladysmith. Un Parlementaire Anglais conduit auprès du Général Joubert.*
564	26 NOVEMBER 1899	BERTRAND DETE	*La Guerre au Transvaal. Femme de Boërs faisant le coup de fusil.*
566	10 DECEMBER 1899	BERTRAND DETE	*Un Ambulance au Transvaal. Le Présidént Kruger visitant les Blessés Anglais.*
569	21 DECEMBER 1899	BERTRAND DETE	(back page) *Un détachment de Boërs traversant une Rivière.*
570	7 JANUARY 1900	F. MEÁULLE	*Anglais et Boërs: Le président Kruger et M. Chamberlain.* (coloured from here on)
571	14 JANUARY 1900	F. MEÁULLE & CARREY	(back page) *Prisonniers anglais conduits à Prétoria.*
574	4 FEBRUARY 1900	CH. CRESPIN & F. MEÁULLE	(back page) *L'Attente! Les Boers au guet dans Les Montagnes.*
575	11 FEBRUARY 1900	F. MEÁULLE	(back page) *Au War Office. Les Anglais lisant les Dépêches.*
577	25 FEBRUARY 1900	F. MEÁULLE & CARREY	(back page) *Le Patriotisme des Boërs. Les Femmes et les Enfants au Combat.*
580	18 MARCH 1900	F. MEÁULLE & CARREY	(inside, p. 8) *Le Général Kronje (sic) Lord Roberts*
		F. MEÁULLE & CARREY	(back page) *Un Capitulation Glorieux. Le Général Kronje (sic) Se rendant Au Général Roberts.*
583	8 APRIL 1900	CH. CRESPIN & F. MEÁULLE	*Vaincre ou Mourir. Le Président Steÿn Haranguant les Boërs.*
584	15 APRIL 1900	F. MEÁULLE & CARREY	(inside, p. 117) *Les Anglais surpris sur la Modder-River.*
		CH. CRESPIN & F. MEÁULLE	(back page) *Les Prisonniers Boërs à bord des Transports Anglais.*
585	22 APRIL 1900	F. MEÁULLE & CARREY	*La Mort d'un Brave: Le Colonel de Villebois-Mareuil au Transvaal.*
598	22 JULY 1900	F. MEÁULLE & CARREY	(back page) *L'Arrivée des délégués Boers à Paris.*
602	19 AUGUST 1900	F. MEÁULLE & CARREY	(back page) *Au Transvaal – Les tribunaux Anglais.*
605	9 SEPTEMBER 1900	F. MEÁULLE & CARREY	*Au Transvaal – Le Général de Wet.*
615	18 NOVEMBER 1900	F. MEÁULLE & CARREY	(back page) *Retour des volontaires Anglais.*
617	2 DECEMBER 1900	CH. CRESPIN & F. MEÁULLE	*Le Président Kruger en France.*
618	9 DECEMBER 1900	CH. CRESPIN & F. MEÁULLE	*Réception du Président Krüger par le Président de la République Français.*
		F. MEÁULLE	(inside, p. 389) *Arrivée du Président Krüger à L'Hôtel Scribe.* (back page) *Le President Krüger acclamé par la foule au balcon de l'hôtel Scribe.*
621	30 DECEMBER 1900	F. MEÁULLE & CARREY	*Dans L'Orange. Le Général De Wet Échappant Aux Anglais.*
628	17 FEBRUARY 1901	F. MEÁULLE & CARREY	*Châtiment infligé aux traîtres par les Boers.*
633	24 MARCH 1901	CARREY	*Au Transvaal: Entrevue des Généraux Kitchener et Botha.*
656	1 SEPTEMBER 1901	CH. CRESPIN	*La Proclamation de Lord Kitchener.*
667	17 NOVEMBER 1901	CH. CRESPIN	*Au Transvaal: Grave échec Anglais a Bergkelaagte (sic).*
675	12 JANUARY 1902	CARREY	*Pour les petits Boers. L'Obele de l'Écolier.*
686	30 MARCH 1902	CARREY & ANDRIEUX	(back page) *Au Transvaal: Defaite des Anglais à Tweebosch – Lord Methuen fait Prisonnier par Delarey.*
698	22 JUNE 1902	CARREY & ANDRIEUX	*Au Transvaal: Signature du Traître de Paix.*
706	17 AUGUST 1902	CH. CRESPIN	*Les Généraux Boers acclamés a Leur départ du Cap.*

LE PETIT JOURNAL

NO.	DATE	ARTIST	TITLE
270	19 JANUARY 1896	H. MEYER	*Au Transvaal: le docteur Jameson prisonnier des Boers.*
464	8 OCTOBER 1899	DAMBLANS	(back page) *A Londres: Meeting en faveur de la paix*
465	15 OCTOBER 1899	HENRI RUDAUX	*Les événements du Transvaal. Départ de troupes Anglaises.*
466	22 OCTOBER 1899		(inside page) *Évenéments du Transvaal: Carte de l'Afrique Australe*
467	29 OCTOBER 1899	DAMBLANS	*Les premiers prisonniers Anglais*
468	5 NOVEMBER 1899	DAMBLANS	*Événements du Transvaal Mort du général Boer Viljoen.*
469	12 NOVEMBER 1899	DAMBLANS	*Événements du Transvaal: Sommation aux Anglais.*
470	19 NOVEMBER 1899		*Le Lion Anglais et Le Taureau Boer.*
		TOFANI	(back page) *Événements du Transvaal: Les fugitifs de Ladysmith.*
471	26 NOVEMBER 1899		(inside, p. 381) *Carte du Theatre de la Guerre au Transvaal*
473	10 DECEMBER 1899	DAMBLANS	*La Guerre au Transvaal: Jonction des Boers et des Afrikanders (sic).*
474	17 DECEMBER 1899	J. BELON	*La Guerre au Transvaal: Ambulance indiennes.*
475	24 DECEMBER 1899	DAMBLANS	*A Pile ou Face! Le Boer – Si c'est 'Pile', ce sera pour toi?*
476	31 DECEMBER 1899	TOFANI	*En Irlande. Manifestation contre M. Chamberlain*
		J. BELON	(back page) *La Guerre au Transvaal: Courriers Boers annonçant la victoire.*

NO.	DATE	ARTIST	TITLE
477			(back page) *Meeting en faveur des Boers troublé les antinationalistes.*
478	14 JANUARY 1900	TOFANI	*La Guerre au Transvaal: Le général Joubert haranguant les Boers.*
480	28 JANUARY 1900	HENRI RUDAUX	(inside, p. 20) *Au Transvaal: Prise d'une batterie anglaise par les Boers.*
482	11 FEBRUARY 1900	DAMBLANS	(back page) *Reprise de Spion-Kop par les Boers.*
487	18 MARCH 1900		*Au Transvaal: Capitulation du général Cronje.*
488	25 MARCH 1900		(inside page) *Exposition de 1900: Pavillon du Transvaal.*
			(back page) *Entrevue des présidents Krüger et Steijn* (sic).
491	15 APRIL 1900	TOFANI	*Le Général Joubert sur son lit de Mort.*
492	22 APRIL 1900		(inside, p. 124) *Le Colonel de Villebois-Mareuil, Tué au Transvaal,* (not coloured).
493	29 APRIL 1900		(back page) *Honneurs rendus par les Anglais au Général de Villebois-Mareuil.*
496	20 MAY 1900		*Un Anglais irascible.*
523	25 NOVEMBER 1900		*M. Krüger sur le 'Gelderland'.*
524	2 DECEMBER 1900	TOFANI	*Le Président Krüger.*
525	9 DECEMBER 1900		*Les Hôtes de la France. Le President Krüger saluant les Parisiens.*
			(inside, p. 388; not coloured) *Débarquement du président Krüger a Marseilles.*
			(back page) *A Paris. Arrivée du President Krüger à la gare de Lyon.*
526	16 DECEMBER 1900		*Justice!!*
531	20 JANUARY 1901		(back page) *Au Transvaal: Les Prisonnièrs Boers.*
553	23 JUNE 1901	DOMANI	*La Guerre au Transvaal: Capitulation de la garrison anglais de Jamestown.*
569	18 OCTOBER 1901		*La Guerre au Transvaal: Les Camps de Reconcentration.*
572	8 NOVEMBER 1901		(back page) *Rixe entre régiments anglais.*
577	8 DECEMBER 1901		*Au Transvaal: Reddition de 180 Anglais.*
578	15 DECEMBER 1901		*Treize Français prisonniers a Sainte-Hélène*
583	19 JANUARY 1902		*La Guerre au Transvaal: Les exploits de de Wet.*
586	9 FEBRUARY 1902		(back page) *Mort d'un Héros. Le commandant boer Scheepters fusillé par les Anglais.*
593	30 MARCH 1902	DOMANI	*La Guerre au Transvaal. Lord Methuen pris et rendu aux Anglais par les Boers.*
605	22 JUNE 1902		*La Paix avec Les Boers. London en délire.*
623	26 OCTOBER 1902		*Arrivée des généraux Boers a Paris.* (back page) *Excès de Soldats Anglais dans une gare.*
624	2 NOVEMBER 1902	V. MICHEL	*Le Président Kruger A Menton.*
636	25 JANUARY 1903		(back page) *M. Joe Chamberlain visite L'Afrique du Sud.*
718	21 AUGUST 1904		(back page) *Dans l'Afrique du Sud. Travailleuis chinois s'engageant dans les mines.*
867	30 JUNE 1907		(back page) *Une chasse au Lion au Transvaal.*
870	21 JULY 1907		*Le Général Botha présente le nouveau drapeau du Transvaal au ministre des colonées d'Angleterre.*

BOER WAR RELATED COLOURED COVERS OF *LE RIRE*

NO.	DATE	ARTIST	TITLE
257	7 OCTOBER 1899	C. LÉANDRE	*L'Angleterre éternel Champion de la Justice, protégé les faibles.*
260	28 OCTOBER 1899	C. LÉANDRE	*Le Nouveau Macbeth. Lady Macbeth à Macbeth-Chamberlain – tu verras, toi aussi, que la tache ne s'en va pas et que tout l'or de la Charered 'ne pourra jamais laver ta jolie menotte'.*
264	23 NOVEMBER 1899	A. WILLETTE	*V'La Les English! Jeanne D'Arc.*
265	2 DECEMBER 1899	C. LÉANDRE	*– Ne te tourmente donc pas, mon vieux Kruger. Si je suis venu en Angleterre c'est seulement pour embrasser Grand-Mere.* (See front cover of this book.)
267	16 DECEMBER 1899	FERNAND FAU	(back page) *A Monsieur Chamberlain qui n'aime pas les images.*
271	13 JANUARY 1900	C. LÉANDRE	*Le Gotha du Rire XXVI Lord Salisbury.*
276	17 FEBRUARY 1900	C. LÉANDRE	*Le Gotha du Rire XXVIII Monsieur Cecil Rhodes.*
280	17 MARCH 1900	JEANNIOT	*La Dernière incarnation de Lohengrin. La Parole est d'argent, mais le silence est d'or (Proverbe Français).*
314	10 NOVEMBER 1900	C. LÉANDRE	*Krüger en Europe.*
315	17 NOVEMBER 1900	Entire issue CARAN D'ACHE	*Kruger Le Grand & John Bull Le Petit.*
322	5 JANUARY 1901	C. LÉANDRE	*Le Gotha du Rire XXXII Lord Roberts, voici mylord Roberts, vainqueuer de Cordua. On ne peut dénombrer les femmes qu'il tué!*
326	2 FEBRUARY 1901	C. LÉANDRE	*Le Gotha du Rire XXXIII Edouard VII roi d'Angleterre, empereur des Indes.*
333	23 MARCH 1901	C. LÉANDRE	*De Wet.*
339	4 MAY 1901	LÉAL DE CAMARA	*Il parait que Botha s'est rendu . . . Ah! Oui, dans la montagne pour voir sa femme.*
359	21 SEPTEMBER 1901	A. WILLETTE	*Les Mères à la Tsarine. Ton coeur de mère souflira-t-il qu'on égorge toujours nos enfants!*
390	26 APRIL 1902	DELAW	(back page) *Nos grands s'Amusent. (Jeux favoris de quelques notables personnages.)*
392	10 MAY 1902	GUILLAUME LAPLAGNE	(back page) *Monuments Anthumes II. SM Edouard VII Buste commemoratif du Couronnement souscription de L'Irlande ruinée, du Transvaal décimé et de L'Inde affamé.*
397	14 JUNE 1902	GUILLAUME LAPLAGNE	(back page) *Monuments Anthumes III Joe Chamberlain.*

BOER WAR RELATED COLOURED BACK AND FRONT COVERS OF
LA SEMAINE ILLUSTRÉE, L'IMPARTIAL DE L'EST and *LE PETIT MERIDIONAL*
(identical except for masthead and place of issue)

Volume 2

No 37   10 SEPTEMBER 1899   ALFRED PRONNIER   *Le conflit Anglo-Boer: Embarquement pour le Transvaal d'un régiment de hussards anglais.*

No. 40   1 OCTOBER 1899   P. H. RIPP   (front page) *Les Événements de Transvaal L'armée Boer.*

P. H. RIPP   (back page) *Les Événements du Transvaal: L'armée Anglaise de l'Afrique du Sud.*

No. 46   12 NOVEMBER 1899   LOUIS BOMBLED   *Bataille de Glencoe. Le général Symons mortellement blessé.*

No. 49   3 DECEMBER 1899   P. H. RIPP   (back page) *Scéne de désolation au 'war office'. La liste des soldats tués communiquée aux familles.*

No. 52   24 DECEMBER 1899   P. H. RIPP   *Le Combat de Modder River. Les Highlanders l'attaque du Pont.*

Volume 3

No. 1   7 JANUARY 1900   P. H. RIPP   (back page) *La Guerre dans l'Afrique australe. Une ambulance français de la Croix-Rouge.*

No. 6   11 FEBRUARY 1900   P. H. RIPP   (back page) *La Guerre dans l'Afrique australe. La General Joubert aux avant-postes.*

No. 7   18 FEBRUARY 1900   P. H. RIPP   *A quoi se résume la victoire des anglais a Spion-Kop.*

No. 9   4 MARCH 1900   P. H. RIPP   *Le conflit Anglo Boer. Le gardien du sémaphore de Durban éxécuté comme espion.*

No. 13   1 APRIL 1900   P. H. RIPP   *La liberté ou la Mort.*

No. 15   15 APRIL 1900   P. H. RIPP   (back page) *Les derniers moments d'un héros.*

No. 16   22 APRIL 1900   P. H. RIPP   *Mort au champ d'honneur. Le corps du Colonel de Villebois-Mareuil ramené au camp anglais.*

No. 17   29 APRIL 1900   P. H. RIPP   (back page) *Un fanatique de l'Hygiéne. Sir Charles Warren a la bataille de Spion Kop.*

No. 22   3 JUNE 1900   P. H. RIPP   *Guerre à outrance.*

No. 44   4 NOVEMBER 1900   *Départ du Président Krüger. L'arrivée à bord du 'Gelderland'.*

No. 47   25 NOVEMBER 1900   *Débarquement du président Krüger le 'Gelderland' salue la terre.*

No. 49   9 DECEMBER 1900   *Visite du président Krüger à M. Loubet: l'arrivée à l'Elysée.*

No. 50   16 DECEMBER 1900   PAUL THIRIAT   (back page) *Au Transvaal. Les Femmes boers Prisonnières de guerre chantant l'hymne national.*

Volume 4

No 3   20 JANUARY 1901   PAUL THIRIAT   (back page) *Un convoi Anglais capture par les Boers.*

BIBLIOGRAPHY

(SHORT TITLES USED IN TEXT ARE GIVEN IN
BRACKETS AFTER EACH PUBLICATION)

Africana Notes and News (Johannesburg, Africana Museum, quarterly 1942-)

Ainslie, Patricia *Inglis Sheldon-Williams* (Calgary, Glenbow Museum, Canada, 1982)

Amery, L. S., Editor *The Times History of The War in South Africa 1899-1902* (7 vols, London, Sampson Low, Marston & Co.
   Ltd., 1900-1909) (Amery, *Times History*)

Anglo, Michael *Penny Dreadfuls and other Victorian horrors* (London, Jupiter Books, 1977)

Antiques in South Africa (Cultural Press of South Africa, semi annually, 1976-1988)

Archer, Mildred *British Drawings in the India Office Library* (2 vols, London, H.M. Stationery Office, 1969)
   (Archer, *British Drawings*)

Armour, George Denholm *Bridle and Brush: Reminiscences of an Artist Sportsman* (London, Eyre & Spottiswoode, and
   New York, Charles Scribner's Sons, 1937) (Armour, *Bridle and Brush*)

Army List, (The War Office, London, monthly or quarterly)

Baigell, Matthew *The Western Art of Frederic Remington* (New York, Ballantine Books, 1976)
   (Baigell, *Frederic Remington*)

Baillie, F. D. *Mafeking: A Diary of a Siege* (Westminster, Archibald Constable & Co., 1900)

Baker, Charles (editor) *Bibliography of British Book Illustrators 1860-1900* (Birmingham, Birmingham Bookshop, 1978)
   (Baker (ed.), *British Book Illustrators*)

Barnard, C.J. *Die Vyf Swemmers* (Cape Town, Tafelberg, 1988)

Barnicoat, John *A Concise History of Posters* (London, Thames and Hudson, 1979) (Barnicoat, *History of Posters*)

Bateman, H. M. *Caran D'Ache the Supreme* (London, Methuen & Co. 1933)
   (Bateman, *Caran D'Ache*)

Baynes, Ken *War* (London, Arts Council of Great Britain, 1970.)

Benbow, Colin *Boer Prisoners of War in Bermuda* (Bermuda, Bermuda College, 2nd Edition, 1982)
   (Benbow, *Boer Prisoners*)

Bendiner, K. *An Introduction to Victorian Art* (New Haven, Yale University Press, 1985)

Bénézit, E. *Dictionnaire antique et documentaire des Peintres, Sculpteurs, Dessinateurs et Graveures* (8 vols, France,
   Libraire Gründ 1954) (Bénézit, *Dictionnaire antique*)

Berman, Esmé *Art & Artists of South Africa* (Cape Town, A. A. Balkema, 1983)
   (Berman, *Art & Artists*)

Bilbo, Jack *Toulouse-Lautrec and Steinlen* (London, Modern Art Gallery Ltd., 1946)

Bird, George L. *The Press and Society: A Book of Readings* (Englewood Cliffs, N.J., Prentice-Hall, 1987)

Boonzaier, D. C. *Owlographs* (Cape Town, Cape Times Ltd., 1901)

Bradshaw, Maurice *Royal Society of British Artists Members' Exhibition 1893-1910* (Leigh-on-Sea, T. Lewis Publications Ltd.,
   1975) (Bradshaw, *British Artists Exhibition*)

Bradshaw, Percy V. *The Art of the Illustrator* (20 vols, London, Press Art School, c.1917)

Breytenbach, J.H. *Die Geskiedenis van die Tweede Vryheidsoorlog in Suid-Afrika, 1899-1902* (5 vols to date, Pretoria, Government Printer, 1969-1983)

Index to British Military Costume Prints 1500-1914 (London, Compiled and published by the Army Museums Ogilby Trust,
   Northumberland House WC2 1972) (*British Military Costume Prints*)

Broder, Patricia Janis *Great Paintings of the old American West* (New York, Crown Publishers, 1979)
   (Broder, *Old American West*)

Brook-Hart, Denys *20th Century British Marine Paintings* (Woodbridge, Antique Collector Club, 1981)
   (Brook-Hart, *British Marine Paintings*)

Browne, A.W. *How to Draw for the Papers* (London, C. Arthur Pearson, 1925)

Burenstreiche: Der Transvaalkrieg in der Karikatur aller Völker (Berlin, Dr Eysler & Co., 1900) (*Burenstreiche*)

Butler, Elizabeth *An Autobiography* (London, Bombay, Sydney, Constable and Co., 1922)

From Sketch Book and Diary (London, Burns & Oates, 1909)
   (Butler, *Autobiography*; Butler, *From Sketch Book*)

Byatt, Anthony *Picture Postcards and their Publishers* (Malvern, Golden Age Postcard Books, 1978)
   (Byatt, *Picture Postcards*)

Cane, Michael *For Queen and Country. The Career of Harry Payne Military Artist 1858-1927* (Kingston, Surrey, Michael Cane,
   1977) (Cane, *For Queen and Country*)

The Cape (Cape Town, C.N.A., weekly 1907-)

Carpenter, Kevin *Penny Dreadfuls* (V. & A. Museum, 1983)

Carruthers, Jane *Melton Prior: War Artist in Southern Africa, 1895 to 1900* (Johannesburg, Brenthurst Press, 1987)
   (Carruthers (ed.), *Melton Prior*)

Carruthers, Jane *Thomas Baines: Eastern Cape Sketches: 1848 to 1852* (Johannesburg, Brenthurst Press, 1990)

Carter, A.C.R. *The Work of War Artists in South Africa* (London, Art Journal, 1900)
   (Carter, *War Artists in S.A.*)

Carter, Elizabeth *Sydney Carter* (Cape Town, C.N.A., 1948)

Carver, Sally *The American Postcard Guide to Tuck* (Massachussetts, Chestnut Hill, 1976)

Cassell's Magazine (London, Paris, New York and Melbourne Cassell & Company Ltd., monthly 1901-)

Catalogue of Pictures in the Bloemfontein War Museum of the Boer Republics

(Bloemfontein War Museum Catalogue)

Caw, J. L. *Scottish Painting Past and Present 1620-1908* (London 1908, reprint 1975)
   (Caw, *Scottish Painting*)

Churchill, W. S. *Ian Hamilton's March* (London, Longmans Green & Co., 1900)

Churchill, W. S. *From London to Ladysmith via Pretoria* (London, Longmans Green & Co., 1900)

Churchill, W. S. *My Early Life: A Roving Commission* (London, McMillan & Co. Ltd., 1941)
   (Churchill, *My Early Life*)

Churchill, W. S. *The River War* (Longmans, London, 1899)

Cohen, David A. *The Great War* (a catalogue of an exhibition of paintings & drawings at the Hahn Gallery, November 1985)

Childers, Erskine *In The Ranks of the C.I.V.* (London, Smith Elder & Co., 1900) (Childers, *The C.I.V.*)

Clare, Israel Smith *British Boer War* (London, Souvenir Publishing, 1900)

Clarke, Sonia *'Vanity Fair' in Southern Africa, 1869 to 1914* (Johannesburg, Brenthurst Press, 1990)

Cohen, Morris J. *Anton Van Wouw, Sculptor of South African Life* (Johannesburg, Radford Adlington Ltd., 1938)
   (Cohen, *Anton van Wouw*)

The Connoisseur: An Illustrated Magazine for Collectors (London, Edited by J. T. Herbert Bailey, monthly, 1901-)
   (*The Connoisseur*)

Coysh. A.W. *The Dictionary of Picture Postcards in Britain 1899-1902* (Woodbridge, Antique Collectors' Club, 1984)

Creagh, Sir O'Moore and Humphris E. M. *The Distinguished Service Order 1886-1923* (London, J. B. Hayward & Son, 1978)
   (Creagh and Humphris, *The D.S.O.*)

Creagh, Sir O'Moore and Humphris E. M. *The Victoria Cross 1856-1920* (London, J. B. Hayward & Son, 1985)
   (Creagh and Humphris, *The V.C.*)

Creswicke, Louis *South Africa and the Transvaal War* (8 vols Edinburgh, T.C. & E.C. Jack; London, Blackwood Le Bas & Co, 1903.)

Cuppleditch, David *The John Hassall Lifestyle* (Whitam, Essex, Dilke Press, 1979) (Cuppleditch, *The John Hassall Lifestyle*)

Cuppleditch, David *Phil May The Artist and his Wit* (London, Fortune Press, 1981) (Cupppleditch, *Phil May*)

Cuppleditch, David *The London Sketch Club* (Dilde Press, 1978)
   (Cuppleditch, *London Sketch Club*)

Darras, Daphne *Index to Pictures of South African interest in The Graphic 1915-1932* (Johannesburg, University of the Witwatersrand, 1968)

Davey, A. M. (editor) *Breaker Morant and the Bushveldt Carbineers* (Van Riebeeck Society, Cape Town, 1987)

Davies, Adriana *Dictionary of British Portraiture* (vol. 4, London, B. T. Batsford Ltd., 1981)
   (Davies, *British Portraiture*)

Dawnay, N. P. and Haswell Miller, A. E. *Military Drawings and paintings in the Collection of Her Majesty the Queen*
   (2 vols, London and New York, Phaidon Press, 1970) (Dawnay and Miller, *Military Drawings and Paintings*)

Debrett's Peerage and Baronetage (John Debrett, London, first published 1802)

De Graaf, Dr H. J. *De Boerenoorlog in oude Ansichten* (Zaltbommel, Nederland, Europese Biblioteek, 1972)
   (De Graaf, *De Boerenoorlog*)

De Kock, W. J. editor *Dictionary of South African Biography* (5 vols, Cape Town, Tafelberg Publishers, 1968-)
   (De Kock, (ed.), *DSAB*)

De Souza, L. *No Charge for Delivery* (Books of Africa, Cape Town, 1969)

De Wet, L. J. *Pictures of South African Interest in The Illustrated London News 1842-1949* (Johannesburg, Johannesburg Public Library, 1956) (De Wet, *Illustrated London News Index*)

Dickson, W. K-L. *The Biograph in Battle: Its story in the South African war: Related with Personal Experiences* (London, T. Fisher Unwin, 1901) (Dickson, *Biograph in Battle*)

Dictionary of National Biography (2 vols, compact edition, Oxford, Oxford University Press, 1975) (*DNB*)

Dixon, C. M. *The Leaguer of Ladysmith* (Eyre & Spottiswoode, London, 1900)

Dooner, Mildred *The Last Post* (London, Simpkin Marshall Hamilton Kent & Co., Ltd., 1903)

Drew, Sir Robert *Commissioned Officers in the Medical Services of the British Army 1660-1960* (2 vols, London, The Wellcome Historical Medical Library, 1968) (Drew, *Officers in Medical Services*)

Dum-Dum's der Publieke Opinie (Amsterdam, Uitgevers-Maatschappij 'Vivat', c.1899)

Edwards, Lionel *Reminiscences of a Sporting Artist* (London, Putnam and Co., 1947) (Edwards, *Reminiscences*)

Emanuel, Frank L. *The Illustrators of Montmartre* (London, A. Siegle, 1904)

Engers, Rodney K. *Dictionary of Victorian Wood Engravers* (Cambridge, Chadwyck, 1985)
   (Engers, *Victorian Wood Engravers*)

Esterhuysen, Matthy *Gedenkpennings ter ere van President S. P. Kruger* (Pretoria, National Cultural History and Open-Air Museum, 1973)

Evans, Margaret Jane *Index to Pictures of South African Interest in The Graphic 1875-1895* (Johannesburg, University of the Witwatersrand, 1966)

Fanelli, Giovanni and Godoli, Enzio *Art Nouveau Postcards* (London, Phaidon, Patrick Hawkey & Co., 1987)
   (Fanelli and Godoli, *Art Nouveau Postcards*)

Feaver, William *Masters of Caricature* Edited by Ann Gould (New York, Alfred A. Knopf, 1981)

Fehr, William *Treasures at the Castle of the Cape of Good Hope* (Cape Town, Trustees, William Fehr Collection, 1978)

Fido, Martin *Rudyard Kipling* (London, New York, Sydney, Toronto, Hamlyn, 1974)

Fielding, Mantle *Dictionary of American Painters, Sculptors and Engravers* (Greens Farms, Conn. Enlarged edition, Modern Books and Crafts, 1974) (Fielding, *American Painters, etc.*)

Fildier, André *Catalogue Cartes postales anciennes de Collecteur* (Paris, Fildier Cartophile, 1975) (Fildier, *Catalogue Cartes postales*)

Fleming, William *Art and Ideas* (6th edn., New York, Holt, Rhinehart & Winston, 1980)

Furneaux, Rupert *News of War* (London, Max Parrish, 1964)

Furniss, Harry *The Confessions of a Caricaturist* (2 vols, London, T. Fisher Unwin, 1901) (Furniss, *Confessions of a Caricaturist*)

Furniss, Harry *Harry Furniss at Home* (London, T. Fisher Unwin, 1904)

Gordon-Brown, Alfred *Pictorial Africana* (Cape Town, Rotterdam, A. A. Balkema, 1952)

Gildea, Sir James *For Remembrance and in Honour of those who lost their lives in the South African War 1899-1902* (London, Eyre & Spottiswoode, 1911) (Gildea, *For Remembrance*)

Grand-Carteret, John *John Bull Sur la Sellette* (Paris, Librairie J Straus, no date) (Grand-Carteret, *John Bull*)

Grand-Carteret, John *Eduard l'oncle de l' Europe* (Paris, Louis Michand, 1906) (Grand-Carteret, *Eduard*)

Graves, Algernon F.S.A. *The Royal Academy of Arts* (4 vols, London, reprinted SR Publishers Ltd., 1970) (Graves, *Royal Academy*)

Greenland, Cedryl *A Century in Shreds* (Fish Hoek, Cedryl Greenland, no date)

Gutsche, Thelma *The History and Social Significance of Motion Pictures in South Africa 1895-1940* (Cape Town, Howard Timmins, 1972) (Gutsche, *Motion Pictures in S.A.*)

Haldane, Aylmer *How we Escaped from Pretoria* (Edinburgh and London, Wm Blackwood & Sons, 1901) (Haldane, *How we Escaped from Pretoria*)

Hammerton, J.A. *Humorists of the Pencil* (London, Hurst and Blackett Ltd., 1905)

Hardie, William *Scottish Painting 1837-1939* (London, Christies, 1979)

Harmsworth Magazine (London, Harmsworth Bros. Monthly 1898 onwards)

Harper's Magazine (London, [European Edition] Osgood Mc Ilvaine, New York, Harper & Brothers, monthly 1880-)

Harries, Meirion and Susie, *The War Artists: British Official War Art of the Twentieth Century* (London, Michael Joseph, 1983)

Hart-Davis, Rupert *A Catalogue of the Caricatures of Max Beerbohm* (Cambridge, Mass., Harvard University Press, 1972) (Hart-Davis, *Caricatures of Max Beerbohm*)

Hartrick, R.W.S. *A Painter's Pilgrimage Through Fifty years* (Cambridge, University Press, 1939) (Hartrick, *A Painter's Pilgrimage*)

Heller, Steven *The Art of Satire* (U.S.A., Pratt Graphic Centre, 1984)

Hennings, Tom *Vyf Skilderye oor die Tweede Vryheidsoorlog 1899-1902* (Pretoria, Nasionale Kultuurhistoriese en Opelug Museum, 1976) (Hennings, *Vyf Skilderye*)

Heron, Roy *Cecil Aldin: The Story of a Sporting Artist* (Exeter, Webb & Bower, 1981) (Heron, *Cecil Aldin*)

Hibbard, M.G. *Boer War Tribute Medals* (Sandton, Constantia Classics, 1982) (Hibbard, *Boer War Medals*)

Historic Tableaux on Tiles (Johannesburg, SA Airways, 1970)

History of the War in South Africa, 1899-1902, compiled by F. Maurice *et al.*, (8 vols, London, Hurst & Blackett, 1906-1910)

Hobhouse, Emily *War Without Glamour* (Bloemfontein, Nasionale Pers, 1924)

Hodgson, Pat *The War Illustrators* (London, Osprey, 1977)

Hofmeyr, Adrian *The Story of My Captivity During the Transvaal War 1899-1900* (London, Edward Arnold, 1900)

*Hofmeyr, Janine *Index to Pictures of South African Interest in The Graphic July 1900 to December 1902* (Johannesburg, University of the Witwatersrand, 1974) (Hofmeyr, Matton and Roets, *Graphic Picture Index*)

*Hofmeyr's index often bound in one volume with those of Matton and Roets, so for the sake of convenience their works are referred to as one volume in the text, although each of them indexed a different period

Hofstätter, Hans A. *Art Nouveau Prints, Illustrations, and Postcards* (Hertfordshire, Omega Books, 1984) (Hofstätter, *Art Nouveau Prints, etc.*)

Hogarth, Paul *The Artist as Reporter* (London, Gordon Fraser Gallery Ltd., 1986)

Holt, Tonie and Valmai (compilers) *Stanley Gibbons Postcard Catalogue* (London, Stanley Gibbons Publishers 1987) (Holt, Tonie and Valmai, *Stanley Gibbons Postcard Catalogue*)

Holt, Tonie and Valmai *Picture Postcards of the Golden Age: a Collector's Guide* (London, Postcard Publishing Company, 1978) (Holt, Tonie and Valmai, *Golden Age Picture Postcards*)

Holt, Tonie and Valmai *Picture Postcard Artists: Landscape, Animals and Characters* (Harlow, Essex, Longman Group Ltd., 1984) (Holt, Tonie and Valmai, *Picture Postcard Artists*)
(Houfe, *British Illustrators and Caricaturists*)

Houfe, Simon *The Dictionary of British Book Illustrators and Caricaturists 1800-1914* (Woodbridge, Antique Collectors Club, 1978)

Houfe, *British Illustrators and Caricaturists*

Hugget, Frank E. *Cartoonists at War* (London, Book Club Associates, 1981)

Huyse, Wentworth *The Graphic History of the South African War* (London, *The Graphic*, 1900)

James, Lionel *High Pressure* (London, John Murray, 1929) (James, *High Pressure*)

James, Lionel *Side Tracks and Bridle Paths* (Edinburgh and London, Wm Blackwood & Sons, 1909) (James, *Side Tracks*)

(James, Lionel) (nom de plume 'The Intelligence Officer') *On the heels of de Wet* – (Edinburgh and London, Wm Blackwood & Sons, 1902)

Jeal, Tim *Baden-Powell* (London, Hutchinson, 1987)

Johnson, A.E. *Tom Browne* (London, A. & C. Black Ltd., 1909)

Johnson, A. E. *Lawson Wood* (London, A. & C. Black Ltd., 1910)

Johnson, A. E. *Dudley Hardy* (London, A. & C. Black Ltd., 1909)

Johnson, J. and Greutzner, A. *The Dictionary of British Artists 1880-1940* (Woodbridge, Antique Collectors' Club, 1976)
(Johnson and Greutzner, *British Artists*)

Johnson, Peter *Front Line Artists* (London, Cassell, 1978)

Jones, Adrian *Memoirs of a Soldier Artist* (London, Stanley Paul & Co. Ltd., 1933)

Jones, Mark *The Art of the Medal* (London, British Museum Publications, 1979)

Kandyba-Foxcroft, Elisaveta *Russia and the Anglo Boer War 1899-1902* (Roodepoort, Cum Books, 1981)
(Kandyba-Foxcroft, *Russia and the Anglo Boer War*)

Keegan, John and Darracott, Joseph *The Nature of War* (London, Jonathan Cape, 1981)

Kennedy, R. F. (compiler) *Catalogue of Pictures in the Africana Museum* (5 vols, Johannesburg, Africana Museum, 1966)
(2 vols [6 & 7], Johannesburg, Africana Museum, 1970) (Kennedy, *Pictures in the Africana Museum)*

Kery, Patricia Frantz *Great Magazine Covers of the World* (New York, Abbeville Press, 1984)
(Kery, *Great Magazine Covers*)

Knox, E. B. *Buller's Campaign with the Natal Field Force 1900*, (London, R. Brimley Johnson, 1902)

Koschatzky, Walter and Horst-Herbert Kossatz *Ornamental Posters of the Vienna Secession* (London, Academy Edition,
New York, St Martins Press, 1974) (Koschatzky and Kossatz, *Ornamental Posters*)

Kriel, C. and J. de Villiers (editors) *Rondom die Anglo-Boereoorlog 1899-1902* (Perskor, Johannesburg, 1979)
(Kriel and De Villiers, (ed.), *Rondom die Anglo-Boereoorlog*)

Kruger, C. (compiler) *Suid-Afrikaanse Oorlogskuns in Beeld/South African Images of War* (Johannesburg, South African
Museum of Military History, 1990)

Lalumia, Matthew P. *Realism and Politics in Victorian Art of the Crimean War* (Ann Arbor, Michigan, UMI Research Press, 1984)

Lantern Journal of Knowledge and Culture (Foundation for Education Sciences and Technology, Pretoria, quarterly 1950-)

Lawson, Ken and Warr, Tony *The Postcards of Lance Thackeray* (London, Postcards for Pleasure, 1979)
(Lawson and Warr, *Postcards of Lance Thackeray*)

Lawson, Ken and Warr, Tony *The Postcards of Tom Browne* (London, Postcards for Pleasure, 1978)

Lea, Henry *A Veld Farmer's Adventures* (London, Frederick Muller Ltd., 1936)

Leech, George W. *Magazine Illustration: The Art Editor's Point of View* (London, Sir Isaac Pitman & Sons Ltd., 1939)
(Leech, *Magazine Illustration*)

Le May, G. H. L. *British Supremacy in South Africa, 1899-1902* (Oxford, Clarendon Press, 1965)

Leyds, W. J. *Correspondentie 1900-1902* (9 vols, S'Gravenhage, N.V. Geuze, 1934)

Lines, G.W. *The Ladysmith Siege* (c.1900)

London Magazine (London, Amalgamated Press, monthly 1898-)

Lucie-Smith, Edward *The Art of Caricature* (London, Orbis Publishing, 1981)

Lye, William F. *Andrew Smith's Journal of his Expedition into the Interior of South Africa* (Cape Town, A.A. Balkema, 1975)

Lynch, George *The Impressions of a War Correspondent* (London, George Newnes Ltd., 1903)

Mabbet, B. G. *St Helena, The Philately of the camps for Boer Prisoners of War* (Anglo-Boer War Philatelic Society, 1985)

Maginnis, Charles D. *Pen Drawing: an Illustrated Treatise* (London, B.T. Batsford Ltd., 1899)
(Maginnis, *Pen Drawing*)

Mallalieu, H. L. *The Dictionary of British Watercolour Artists up to 1920* (Woodbridge, Antique Collectors' Club, 1976)
(Mallalieu, *British Watercolour Artists*)

Marais, J.S. *The Fall of Kruger's Republic* (Oxford, Clarendon Press, 1962)

*Matton, Carol Ann *Pictures of South African interest in The Graphic 1896-1899)* (Johannesburg, University of Witwatersrand,
1967) (Hofmeyr, Matton and Roets, *Graphic Picture Index*)

*Matton's index often bound in one volume with those of Hofmeyr and Roets, so for the sake of convenience their
works are referred to as one volume in the text, although each of them indexed a different period

Matcher, Janet Lynn *Index to Pictures of South African interest in The Graphic 1903-1914* (Johannesburg, University
of the Witwatersrand, 1968)

McDonald, Ian *The Boer War in Postcards* (London, Ian Suton, 1990)

McKenzie, J. M. *Imperialism and Popular Culture* (Manchester, University Press, 1986)

McMullin, Ross *Will Dyson: Cartoonist, Etcher, and Australia's Finest War Artist* (London, Sydney & Melbourne,
Angus & Robertson, 1984)
(McMullin, *Will Dyson*)

Mead, Ron, Venman, Joan, Whitney Dr J.T. *Picton's Priced Catalogue and Handbook of Pictorial Postcards and their
Postmarks* (London & New York, Longman, 1980) (Mead, Venman and Whitney, *Picton's Priced Catalogue*)

Matthews, Roy and Mellini, Peter *In Vanity Fair* (London, Berkeley and Los Angeles, University of California Press, 1982)
(Matthews and Mellini, *In Vanity Fair*)

Mendelssohn, S. *Mendelssohn's South African Bibliography* (2 vols, London, Kegan Paul, Trench Trubner & Co. Ltd., 1910)
(Mendelssohn, *Mendelssohn's Bibliography*)

Menpes, Mortimer *War Impressions: A Record in Colour* (London, A. & C. Black, 1901)   (Menpes, *War Impressions*)

Messum, David *Life and works of Lucy Kemp-Welch* (Woodbrige, Antique Collectors' Club, 1976)

Meyer, Susan E. *America's Great Illustrators* (New York, Galahad Books, 1978)

Military History Journal (Military History Society, Saxonwold, Transvaal, quarterly, 1969-)

Mockler, Ferryman A.F. *Military Sketching and Reconnoisance* (London, Edward Stanford, 1903)

Moore, William *The Story of Australian Art* (Sydney, A. & R., 1934)

Neudin, Joëlle et Gérard *L'officiel international des Cartes Postales De Collection*, France, Neudin, 1987)

Neue Burenstreiche: Der Transvaal krieg in der Karikatur alles Völker (Berlin, Dr Eysler & Co., 1900)

Newnes, George (editor) *The Strand Magazine* (monthly, 1890-)

Newspaper Press Directory (London, C. Mitchell & Co., published annually)

Newton, Eric *War Through Artists' Eyes: Paintings and Drawings by British War Artists* (London, John Murray, 1945)

Newton-Thompson, Joyce *Gwelo Goodman: South African Artist* (London, George Allen & Unwin Ltd., 1951)
    (Newton-Thompson, *Gwelo Goodman*)

Norgate, Matthew and Wykes, Alan *Not So Savage* (London, Jupiter Books, 1976)

Oorlogsmuseum van die Boererepublieke, Bloemfontein: Katalogus Kunsafdeling (Bloemfontein, no date) *see*
Catalogue of Pictures in the Bloemfontein War Museum of the Boer Republics

Oosthuizen, Pieter *Boer War Memorabilia* (Edmonton, Alderman Press, 1987)

Orr, A.S. *Scottish Yeomanry in South Africa 1900-1901* (Glasgow, James Hedderwick & Sons, the Citizen Press, 1901)

Osterwalder, Marcus *Dictionnaire des Illustrateurs 1800-1914* (Paris, Hubschmid & Bouret, 1983)
    (Osterwalder, and Hubschmid & Bouret (eds.), *Dictionnaire des Illustrateurs*)

Pakenham, Thomas *The Boer War* (Johannesburg, Jonathan Ball, 1979)

Pall Mall Magazine (Editor George R. Halkett, London, quarterly 1895-)

Paterson, A.B. *Happy Despatches* (Sydney, Angus and Robertson, 1984)

Paton, Robert *Memoir of W Skeoch Cumming* (Edinburgh, Constable, 1933)

Pearson's Magazine (London, C. Arthur Pearson)

Peppin, Brigid and Micklethwait, Lucy *Dictionary of British Book Illustrators: The Twentieth Century*
    (London, John Murray Ltd., 1983) (Peppin and Micklethwait, *British Book Illustrators*)

Piper, David *The Dictionary of Painting and Sculpture, Art and Artists* (vol 4, London, Mitchell Beazley Library
    of Art, 1981) (Piper, *Dictionary of Painting, etc.*)

Pitz, Henry C. *200 years of American Illustration* (New York, Random House, 1977)

Porter, A.N. *The Origins of the South African War; Joseph Chamberlain and the Diplomacy of Imperialism, 1895-1899*
    (Manchester, University Press, 1980)

Pound, Reginald *The Strand Magazine 1891-1950* (London, William Heinemann, 1966)
    (Pound, *Strand Magazine 1891-1950*)

Price, R.G.G. *A History of Punch* (London, Collins, 1957)

Prior, Melton *Campaigns of a War Correspondent* (London, Edward Arnold, 1912) (Prior, *Campaigns of a War Correspondent*)

Proud, Edward B. *History of British Army Postal Service: Vol. I 1882-1902* (Heathfield, Proud-Bailey & Co., no date)
    (Proud, *British Army Postal Service*)

Quarterly Bulletin (Cape Town, South African Library, quarterly, 1946-)

Ralph, Julian *War's Brighter Side* (New York, D. Appleton & Co., 1901)

Reed, Walt *Great American Illustrators* (New York, Abbeville Press, 1979)

Robinson, G. Chas *Illustrated Books: a guide to their Collection and Value* (Beaconsfield, Bookman Enterprises, 1979)

Roets, Rudolph *Pictures of South African Interest in The Graphic, January-June 1900* (Johannesburg, University of the
    Witwatersrand, 1971)

*Roets's index is often bound in one volume with those of Hofmeyr and Matton, so for the sake of convenience their
    works are referred to as one volume in the text, although each of them indexed a different period

Rosenthal, E. *General de Wet* (Cape Town, Unie-Volkspers Beperk, 1946)

Rosenthal, Eric *Heinrich Egersdörfer: An old time Sketch Book* (Cape Town, Nasionale Boekhandel, 1960)
    (Rosenthal, *Heinrich Egersdörfer*)

Rosenthal, Eric *Southern African Dictionary of National Biography* (London and New York, Frederick Warne & Co. 1966)
    (Rosenthal, *National Biography*)

Royal Academy Pictures (London, Paris, New York & Melbourne, Cassell and Co. Ltd., published annually 1897-)
    (*Royal Academy Pictures*)

Royal Magazine (London, C.A. Pearson, 1899-)

Samuels, Peggy and Harold *The Illustrated Biographical Encyclopedia of Artists of the American West* (New York,
    Doubleday & Co. Inc. 1976)
    (Samuels, *Artists of the American West*)

Samuels, Peggy and Harold *Frederic Remington* (New York, Doubleday & Co. Inc., 1982) (Samuels, *Frederic Remington*)

Sarzano, Frances *Sir John Tenniel* (New York, Pellegnni & Cudahy, no date)

Schardt, Herman *Paris 1900: The Art of the Poster* (London, Bracken Books, 1987)

Scheen, Pieter *Lexicon Nederlandse Beeldende Kunstenaars 1750-1950* (2 vols, The Hague, Pieter A. Scheen NV, 1969)
    (Scheen, *Nederlandse Beeldende Kunstenaars*)

Schoonraad, M. & E. *Companion to South African cartoonists* (Johannesburg, Ad. Donker, 1989)

Schoonraad, M. & E. *Suid-Afrikaanse Spot- en Strookprent Kunstenaars* (Roodepoort, Cum Boeke, 1983)

Schoonraad, Murray *Erich Mayer* (Pretoria, University of Pretoria, 1990)

Serullaz, Maurice *Phaidon Encyclopaedia of Impressionism* (New York, E.P. Dutton, 1978)

Shikes, Ralph E. and Heller, Steven *The Art of Satire* (U.S.A., Pratt Graphics Centre, no date)

Slythe, R. Margaret *The Art of Illustration 1750-1900* (London, the Library Association, 1970)

A South African Bibliography To the Year 1925: Being a Revision and Continuation of Sidney Mendelssohn's South African Bibliography (1910) Edited at the South African Library (5 vols, London, Mansell, 1979-1991)

Southern Africa Postcard Research Group Newsletter (quarterly 1981-) (*SAPRG Newsletter*)

Smith, Anna H. (compiler) *Commemorative Medals of the Z.A.R.* (Johannesburg, Africana Museum, 1970)

Spielmann, M.H. *The History of Punch* (London, Cassell, 1895) (Spielmann, *The History of Punch*)

Staff, Frank *The Picture Postcard and its Origins* (London, Lutterworth Press, 1966-1979)

Stalker, John (editor) *The Natal Carbineers 1855-1911* (Pietermaritzburg & Durban, P. Davis & Sons, 1912)

Standard Encyclopaedia of South Africa (SESA) (12 vols, Cape Town, Nasou, 1970)

Stead, W.T. Editor *Review of Reviews* (vol. 20 *et seq* London, Horace Marshall & Son)

St Georges Gazette Vol. 18, 19, 20 1900, 1901

St Leger, S.E. *War Sketches in Colour* (London, A.&C. Black, 1903) (St Leger, *War Sketches in Colour*)

Stroud, Richard *Ceylon, the camps for Boer Prisoners of War 1900-1902* (Anglo-Boer War Philatelic Society, 1989)

Stubbings, F.O. *Leyds Versameling van Nie-Boer Materiaal en die Unversiteits Biblioteek Stellenbosch* (Stellenbosch, no date)

The Studio: An Illustrated Magazine of Fine and Applied Art (London, monthly, 1892-)

Thieme, ü. and Becker, F. *Allgemeines Lexikon der Bildenden Künstler von der Antike bis Zur Gegenwart* (Leipzig, 1907)

Thorpe, James *English Illustration: The Nineties* (London, Faber & Faber, 1935) (Thorpe, *English Illustration*)

Thorpe, James *Phil May* (London, Art and Technics, 1945) (Thorpe, *Phil May*)

Thrilling Experiences in the War in South Africa (Illinois, Educational Company of Chicago, 1900)

Van Schoor, M.C.E. *Spotprente van die Anglo-Boere Oorlog* (Cape Town, Tafelberg, 1981) (Van Schoor, *Spotprente*)

Van der Westhuysen, H.M. *Erich Mayer Album* (Cape Town & Pretoria, HAUM J.H. & De Bussy, 1953)

Verbeek, J.A. *Early Natal Art* (privately printed, no date) (Verbeek, *Early Natal Art*)

Walton, Lt. Colonel P.S. *Simkin's Soldiers, The British Army in 1890* (2 vols, London, Victorian Military Society. 1981) (Walton, *Simkin's Soldiers*)

Waters, Grant M. *Dictionary of British Artists Working 1900-1936* (2 vols, Eastbourne, Eastbourne Fine Art, 1975) (Waters, *British Artist*)

Watson, Aaron *The Savage Club* (London, T. Fisher Unwin 1907)

Weill, Alain *Art Nouveau Postcards* (London, Thames & Hudson, 1977)

Wilkinson, Spenser, *The Transvaal War* (*Illustrated London News*, 1900)

Wilkinson-Latham, Robert J. *From our Special correspondent* (London, Hodder & Stoughton, 1979) (Wilkinson-Latham, *Special correspondent*)

Willcox, Walter Temple *The Fifth (Royal Irish) Lancers in South Africa 1899-1902* (York, Boer War Books, 1981)

Williams, Keith *The English Newspaper: an Illustrated History to 1900* (Springwood Books, 1977)

Who was Who
1897-1916 vol. 1
1916-1928 vol. 2
1929-1940 vol. 3
1941-1950 vol. 4
1951-1960 vol. 5
1961-1970 vol. 6
1971-1980 vol. 7 London, A.&C. Black, 1920 *et seq*

Windsor Magazine (London, Ward Lock & Co., monthly)

Wood, Christopher *The Dictionary of Victorian Painters* (Woodbridge, England. Antique Collector's Club, 2nd Edition 1978) (Wood, *Victorian Painters*)

INDEX

The index covers the artists, the publications their work appeared in, and the subjects of their work only in so far as the topic concerns the Anglo-Boer War. Their earlier and subsequent careers have not been covered. Italic page references refer to illustrations of a particular artist or his work. Bold page references refer to the Biographies. Bold italic page references indicate that there is an illustration in the Biographies.

A A.B., Paris 162
A.E.C. 102, 116
A.F. 102
A.N., Paris 160
A.R. 103
A.S. 103
Abbéma, Louise 69, *102*
Adams, Douglas 102
advertisements 93
    Bovril 39, *58-9*, 104, *115*, *144*
    cigarettes *104*, 175, 231
    golf 102, *103*
    Horlicks 149
    Michelin tyres 106, *107*
    soap *74*, *128*, *168*, 175, 184
    tobacco 124
After Pretoria: the Guerilla War 35, 62-3
Aitken, B. *Contraband of War* 187
Aldin, Cecil Charles Windsor 52, 58, 72, **102**
Alec, B. 102
Algemeen Nederlandsche Verbond 70, *94*, 105, 222
Allen, Phoebe *Mafeking Day. . .* 211
Allom, W.J. 102
Ally Sloper's Half Holiday 76, 77
Almond, William Douglas 58, **102**
Amaral, C. da (Tarsila) *84*, *85*, 92, *99*, **102**, 156
Amato, Gennaro 53, 65, **102**
American
    artists 56, 60, 117, 122, 129, 146, 156, 212;
        see also Western artists
    caricaturists 131, 137
    cartoonists 58, 106, 111, 115, 117, 122, 131, 132, 138, 150, 154, 157, 159, 162, 164, 166, 167, 179, 187, 196
    illustrated journals 68, 88; *see also* under names of journals
    postcard artists 137
    sculptors 111, 126
Ames, Ernest 99, 102
Ames, Mary Frances 99, **102**, *103*
Amsterdamsche Courant 86
Anderson, Martin *see* Cynicus
André 102
André, Richard *102-3*
Andreoli, Emile 123
Andrieux, Alfred-Louis 65, **103**
Antwerpen-Transvaal Gedenknummer 70-1, 127, 146, 222
Ardagh, John Charles **103**
Argyll and Sutherland Highlanders 122
Armée et Marine 64, 66
Armour, George Denholm 75, **103**
Aronson, Nachum **103**
The Arrow 80
Art Nouveau
    artists 109, 121, 126, 159, 196
    postcard artists 102, 152, 158
    postcards 116, 136, 140, 161, 179, 186, 212
Ashton, George Rossi 80, *103*
Ashwith, William *104*
Atkins, John Black 21, 29, 213
Au Transvaal 66-7
Aulent, A. 104
Austen, Edward G. 68, *104*
Australian
    artists 102, 129

cartoonists 162, 208
satirical press 80
troops 130, 135, 150, 162
The Australian Sunday Times 80
Austrian
    artists 25-6, 70, 194, 200-2
    caricaturists 155
    satirical press 88
    sculptors 117, 135, 155

B B., E.O. *see* E.O.B.
B.C.R. 106
B.J.M. 109
Bacon, John Henry Frederick *58*, *59*, 63, **104**, 145
Baden-Powell, Frank Smyth 104
Baden-Powell, Robert Stephenson Smyth **104-5**, 160, 236
    caricatures of 77-8, 229
    Mafeking, Siege of *39-41*, *53*, **104-5**, *202*, *203*
    portraits *52*, 146, 231
    post-and playing cards 105, 168, 183
Baer, Gil 105
Baetes, Jules 71, 94, **105**
Baggie, Paul 105, 186
Bahr, 87, **105**
Bailey, E.W.N. ('Omnibus') 19
Bailey, G.C. **105**
Baillie, Frederick David 29, 32, **105**, 208
Baines, Thomas *12*, 18
Ball, Alex C. 63, *105*
Banks, H.G. **105**
Bantjies, Jan Gerrit 45, **105**
Baragwanath, Fred *35*, **105**
Baragwanath, Tom 35, *105-6*
Barberton, Capture of 151
Barnard, J. Langton **106**
Barnes, W. **106**
Barnett, David 19, 23, 58
Barraud, Allan F. **106**
Barstow, Henry George Montague McLean 76, **106**
Bart **106**
Barton, Frank M. 60, **106**
Baseilhac, Jacques *106*, *107*
Bastin, A.D. **106**
Bates, Harry *106*
battlefields 32, 138
    Natal 37, 157; *see also* names of specific battles
Baunier **106**
Baxter, Giles 76
Baynes, T.S. 70
Baumer, Lewis 75
Beach, E.S. **106**
Beadle, James Prinsep Barnes *106*
Bechuanaland Protectorate Regiment *104*, 105
Bedford, Maj. Gen. J.H. 165
Beer **107**
Beer, John-Axel-Richard *42*, **107**
Beerbohm, Sir Henry Maximilian (Max) 78, **107**
Begbie, Harold *97*; *see also* Lewis, Caroline
Begg, Samuel, *19*, *21*, *22*, *49*, *52*, 60, 65, 80, *107*, 128, 196, 226, 236
'Beggarstaff Brothers' 177
Belgian
    artists 105, 111
    cartoonists 120, 155, 172, 174
    charity publications 70-1
    satirical press 88
    sculptors 115, 125, 127
Belgische Karikatur 88
Bell, Charles Davidson *12*
Bell, Charles Moberly 27
Bellemont, Léon 69, *107*
Bellevue Camp 46
Belmont, Battle of 217
Belo (or Bello), Avelino Soares *107-8*, *238*
Belon, José 64, **108**
Bendle, W. **108**
Bennett, William B. **108**

Benson, Lt Col George Elliott 222
Benyon, J.A. 108
Béraud, Jean 66, **108**
Beresford, Marcus de la Poer 36, **108**
Bergen, Fritz 108
Berkeley, Stanley 58, *108*
Bermuda Camp 46, 47, 146, 165, 222
Berne-Bellecour, Étienne-Prosper 66, **108-9**
Bernhard, F. 109
Bernhardt, Sarah 102
Berthon, Paul Emile 100, *108*, **109**
Bethlehem, capture of 176
Bevan, Tom *Dick Dale, The Colonial Scout . . .* 98, 186
Beyers, Gen C. 63, 223
Bienert, A. 94, *109*
Bigelow, P. *White Man's Africa* 193
Bigot, George 82, **109**
Bindley, Frank **109**
Binns 79, **109**
Biquard, Armand 75, *109*
Black
    artists 15
    population 180, 184, 200, 206, 215
    scouts (British) 18
Black & White 19, 37, 53, 88, 93
    artists with 23-4, 36, 57, 104, 111, 112, 119, 124
Black & White Budget 19, 44, 54, 80
    artists with 23-4, 758, 104, 108, 112, 119, 121, 124
The Black Watch (Royal Highland Regiment) 122, 131, 234
Blake, Phil 88, **109**
Bleach, C. Meredith 37, *109*
blockhouses 150
Bloemfontein, occupation of 23, 24, 62, 95, *112*, 131
Blomfield, Charles James 42, **109**
Blore, Harold *An Imperial Light Horseman* 98, 235
Blue, E.N. 68, **109**
Blum & Degen Ltd 179
Blumell, C. **109**
Blundell, W. **109**
board games 129, 200; *see also* chessboards
'Bobb' **109**
Boer
    artists 44-8
    generals *91*, *198*, *199*; *see also* under specific names
Bognet, Georges Tiret *see* Tiret-Bognet, Georges
Bois, J. 76
Boland Yostok 88
Bols, Louis-Jean 37, **109**
Bombled, Louis-Charles 67, *110*, **111**
Bonvoisin, Maurice ('Mars') 54, **111**
Boom, Karel 71, **111**
Boon, N.J. 68
Boon's Geillustreerd Magazijn 68
Boonzaaier, Daniel Cornelis 78, 79, *110*, **111**, 146
Booth, J.L.C. 37, 61, **111**
Border Mounted Rifles 114
Borglum, John Gutzon de la Mothe 111
Borione, Bernard Louis 69, **111**
Borszem-Janko 88, 107
Boscovits, Friedrich **111**
Botha, Gen Louis 122, 154, 180
    cartoons & caricatures 77, 78, 132
    portraits 32, 45, 100, 125, *198*, 223
Bouard, Ernest-Auguste 59, 66, 68, *110*, **111**
Boucher, William Henry 98, **111**
Bouffier, Marguerite **111**
Bowers, F. 88, **111**
Bowman, W.L. 88
Bowring, Walter Armiger **111**
Box, J. **111**
Boyd, Alexander Stuart 54, 57, 72, 75, *110*, **111-12**
Boyington, F.W. **112**
Braakensiek, Johan 70, 85-6, *87*, **112**, *113*, 163

Bradshaw **113**
Brabant, Maj Gen E. 78
Brabant's Horse 122
Brady, Matthew 18
Brandon, E.E. 43
Brandsma, A.C. **113**
Brandt, Gustav 88, **113**, 136
Brangwyn, Frank William 57, **113**
Brazilian artists 102
Brennan, G.H. **113**
Brereton, Frederick S. 97, *98*, 181, 235
Bridgman, George **113**
Brindley, Frank 62
British
    caricaturists 107, 114, 118, 119, 141, 143, 145, 164, 173, 177
    cartoonists 106, 109, 119, 121, 123, 128, 130, 135-6, 137, 138-9, 141, 144, 147, 150, 151, 152, 159, 162, 164, 168, 173, 175, 178, 181, 183, 184, 187, 192-3
    charity publications 71-2
    generals *194*, 219, 229 *see also* under individual names
    postcard artists 117, 123, 129, 133, 135-6, 138, 142, 145, 147, 150-1, 157-8, 163
    postcards 92-3
    satirical press 74-8
    sculptors 106, **113**, 114, 126, 128, 129, 134, 153-4, 160, 184, 220, 222
Brock, Charles Edmund **113**
Brock, Henry Mathew 65, 97, **113**
Broderick, John 77, 78, 107, 229
Brooks, Elbridge 98, 118
Brouillet, Pierre-André 69, **113**
Browell, Langton **113**
Brown, Cecil **113**
Brown, Dimmock F.N. 105, **113**
Brown, John Dimock **113**
Brown, Harold 53
Brown, T.R.J. 76
Browne, Gordon Frederick 55, 57, 72, 75, 97, *113-14*, 136, *168*, 178
Browne, Hablôt Knight (Phiz) 55, **113**
Brown(e), Henry Harris 72, **114**
Browne, John 75
Browne, Thomas Arthur (Tom) 53, 57, 75, *114*
Bruce-Joy, Albert **114**, 155
Bruestle, George M. **114**
Brun, A. 66, **114**
Brunet, Jean 69, *70*, **114**
Bryan, Alfred 75, **114**
Buchanan, Fred **114-15**
Buckland, William Harold **115**
Bucknall, Ernest Pile **115**
Buelinkx, Henry *114*, **115**
Bull, René 19, 22, 23, 58, *115*
Buller, Gen Sir Redvers 133-4, 180, 196, 202-3
    cartoons & caricatures 77-8, 134, 135, 140
    postcards 53, 95, 203
    Relief of Ladysmith 20, 150
    statues of 154, 160
Burger, Gen S.W. 45, 231
Bürger, Bruno 102, 158
Burgersdorp 106
Burleigh, Bennet 20, 52
Burma Mounted Infantry 215
Burn, Gerald Maurice **115**
Burrage, E. Harcourt 98, 219
Burret, Jean-Léonce 82, *83*, **115**
Burton, F.W. 63, *115*
Buscovitz, F. '88
Bush, C.L. 88, **115**
Butler, Lady Elizabeth Southerden **115-16**, 135
Butler, Mary Emily 16, **116**
Buval, E. **116**

C C., H.T. *see* H.T.C.
C., J.A.H. *see* J.A.H.C.
C., M.L. *see* M.L.C.
C.G. **118**
C.L. 41, **118**

C.L.G.-C. 119
Cadel, Eugène 84, **116**
Calkin, Lance 57, **116**
Camara, Tomás Júlio Leal de 83, 84, 85, *116*
Cameron, J.G. **116**
Cameron, John F. 63, *116*
Campbell, Colin 36, **116**
Campbell, John F. **116**
Canadian Light Horse 138
Canadian Mounted Rifles 216
Canadian troops 147
Cape Argus 78
Cape Mounted Police 50
Cape Mounted Rifles 130, 207
The Cape Register 78, 79
Capell, Algernon Essex 41, **102**, **116**
Carabineers 154
Caramba **116**
Caran d'Ache 16, 66, 82, 83, 85, 86, *116-17*, 155
Carey, John **117**
Carey, W.S. 210
Careye, Ward Sausmarez 36, **116**
Carl-Rosa, Mario Cornelleaiu 69, **117**
Carlegle, Charles-Emile 82, **117**
Carleton, Clifford **117**
Carnegie, Robert Francis **117**
Caronte **117**
Carrey, P. 65, 103, **117**, 121
Carruthers Gould, Francis *see* Gould, F. S.
Carter, F.A. 98, **117**
Carter, Sydney 16, 32, **117**
Carter, T.J. **117**
cartoonists *see* under specific countries or
 individual names
cartoons *see* under specific subjects or
 publications
Cassell's Illustrated History of the Boer War 53,
 61, 62, 63
Caton Woodville, Richard *see* Woodville, R.C.
Cauty, Horace Henry **117**
Celebrities of the Army 61
ceramic art 107-8
Ceylon Contingent 143, 222
Ceylon P.O.W. camps 45; *see also* Diyatalawa
 Camp; Ragama Camp
Chamberlain, Joseph 140, 168
 cartoons & caricatures
  and King Edward 191, 232
  and Lord Roberts 187
  and Queen Victoria 66, *208*
  British 75, 76, 77-8, 107, 145, 150, 164,
   184, *193*, 222, 229
  French 65, *73*, 102, 157, 163, 172, 179,
   195, 198
  German 87, 156
  South African 120, 128
 Picasso 100, 186
 postcards of *92*, 93, 159, *210*
  British 136, 184
  Dutch 127, 211
  French 134, 157, 162, 186, 195, 198, 218
Chambers, Mrs M.A. *118*
Chapellier, P. 100, *118*
Charbert *118*
Charlton, John 55, *57*, 72, **118**
Charron, Alfred-Joseph 69, **118**
Chase, Emerson C. 98, **118**
chessboards 46, 152, 165-6
'Chris Kras Kzn' *see* Feith, J.
Christian Victor, Prince 135, 153, 231
Christian Endeavour Society 45
Chronique Amusante 85
Church, Richard (Dicky) 43, **118**
Churchill, Winston Leonard Spencer 16, 26, *27*,
 29-31, 96, *118*, 173
 caricatures of 27, 78, 107, 119, 229
 escape 31, *56*, 118, 119, *125*
Churchill, Lord Randolph 119
Cinirin **118**
City Imperial Volunteers (C.I.V.) 24, 109, 152,
 154, 170, 187, 207, 210, 216, 218, 221, 237
 Baragwanath Brothers 35, 105-64
 cartoons of 174, 175
 postcards & postal covers of 93, 108, 119, 150

return of 20, 22, 69-70, 104, 124, 134, *188*,
 189, 190
Clacy, Ellen **118**
Clant van der Mijll-Piepers, Mrs J. 68
Clare, Israel Smith *98*, 146, 196, 227
Clark, Christopher 58, **118**
Clark, H.C. *119*
Clark, Joseph **119**
Cleaver, Dudley **119**
Cleaver, George 37
Cleaver, Hugh 37, **119**
Cleaver, Ralph 37, 58, 75, **119**
Cleaver, Reginald Thomas 37, 54, 57, *119*, 153,
 197
Clementél 69, **119**
Cock, Hylton **119**
Cock, Stanley 27, **119**
Cohen, Reuben 75, **119**
Cohl, Emil 85, **119**
Coke, Maj Gen John Talbot 37, **120**
Coldstream Guards 153
Cole, C.W. **120**
Cole, Philip Tennyson **120**
Colenso, Battle of 21, 32, 100, 101, 105, 107, 117,
 121, 125, 129, 135, 138, 177
 saving the guns *25*, 108, 119, 129, 181, *209*,
  210, 232
Colesberg 145, 176, 213
Coleskop 37
Collens, K. 94, **120**
Collier, John **120**
Collison-Morley, Harold Duke *35*, 36, 37, 68, 76,
 120
Colomb, Alphonse Hector 85, **120**
Comerford, E. **120**
Compton, Lord Douglas 206
Compton's Horse 57
Conan Doyle, Arthur 173
concentration camps *64*, 83-4, 150, 148, 150,
 223, 224-5
 postcards 95, 159, 218
concert programmes 114, 118
Conolly, Walter Moorcroft (Walrus) 79, 120
Cooke, W.H. **120**
Cooper, William Sidney 120-1
Cope, Arthur Stockdale **121**
Copnall, Frank T. **121**
Copp, B. 43
Corbould, Aster Chantrey 75, **121**
Core **121**
The Cossack Post 43
Coster, Dr H. 100, 125
Courtet, E. *see* Cohl, E.
Couturier, Léon-Antoine-Lucien 66, **121**
Cowham, Hilda 16, 53, 76, **121**, 159
Cowper, Max 72, *120*, **121**
Cox, A. *19*, **121**
Craig, Frank 55, 57, 72, *121-22*
Craig, Stuart E. **121**
Craig, William *12*
Crane, Walter 72, **121**
Crealock, John North 18
Crespin, Adolphe-Louis-Charles 65, 103, 117, **121**
Cresswell, Albert 69, **122**
Creswicke, Louis 53
Cri de Paris 85
Crispin, H.T. *see* H.T.C.
Crofts, Ernest **122**
Crompton, James Shaw 97, **122**
Cronje, Gen Piet 109
 portraits 45, 162, 231
 surrender of 23, 24, 64, *128*, 129, 131, 165,
  173, 176, 177, 202-3, *195*, 226, 233, 234,
  236; *see also* Paardeberg, Battle of
Crowther, T.S.C. 54, 55, 62, *122*
Cucuel, Edward **122**
'Culver' 88, **122**
Cumming, William Skeoch *33*, 122, *123*
Cundall, James A. **122**
Cuneo, Cyrus Cincinatto *19*, **122**
curios (P.O.W.) 45-6
Cusins, A.G.T. **123**
Cynicus (Martin Anderson) **123**
Czabran, Feodor 87, **123**

D D., J.A. *see* J.A.D.
D., N. **128**
D., W.B. *see* W.B.D.
D'Amato, Gennaro *see* Amato, G.
D'Aurian, Jean-Emmanuel 82, 84, *124*
Da Costa, Joseph Mendes 123
Dadd, Frank 50, *55*, 57, *69*, 72, 116, 118, *123*,
 134, 140, 149, 162
Dadd, Stephen 50, 54, 55, *123*, 221
The Daily Graphic 19, 22-3
 artists with 29, 32, 54-6, 105, 143
Dalmeijer, C.J. 118
Damblans, Eugène 64, *65*, **123**
Dancey, G.H. 80
Danes, Richard 61
Daniel, Vincent **123-4**
Daniell, Gordon 43
'Darsane' *94*, *124*, 225
Das, Pieter 86, **124**
Das Blutbuch von Transvaal 84
Das Goldene Büchlein 88
Däumler, H. *93*
Davenport, Talbot Neville Fawcett 36, **124**
Davidson, C. 72
Davie, K.M. 124, 130
Daviel, Léon 58, **124**
Davies, D. Dyer *see* Dyer-Davies, D.
Davis, G. 58
Davis, Joseph Barnard 58, **124**
Davis, Louis 72
Davis, Lucien **124**
Davison, Nora 72, **124-5**
De Aar 185
De Amicis, Franco 16, *124*, **125**
De Amsterdammer: weekblad voor Nederland
 67, 85
De Beauvais, Lubin 125
De Bruin, Cornelis *100-1*, **125**
De Bruin, W.K. 98, **125**
De Camara, Leal *see* Camara, T.J.L. de
De Capelli, Willem *12*
De Capol, H. 69, **125**
De Frick, Paul 69, **125**
De Haenen, Frederic 55, 65, 105, 120, *124*, **125**,
 147
De Jolar, Marie **125**
De Krijgsgevangene (Diyatalawa) 45, *46*, 105
De Krijgsgevangene (St Helena) 45
De la Rey, Gen J.H. 122, 180, 218
 bust 223
 portraits 32, *44*, 45, 67, 100, 198, 202, 223
De Lacy, Charles John *19*, 53, *126*, 175
De Lamarre, A.F. **126**
De Oorlog in Zuid Afrika 68
De Osarada, A. **126**
De Prikkeldraad 45
De Saulles, George William 126, *238*
De Sta, Henri **126**
De Strever 45
De Thulstrup, Thure (Bror Thure) 68, 127, *193*,
 220
De Tijd 67, 86
De V, E. 127
De Vernon, F.C.V. *see* Vernon, F.C.V. de
De Wabre Jacob 86
De Wet, Gen C.R. 64, 67, 101, 104, *107*, 122,
 148, 158, 176, 191, 193, 233
 bust 103, 123, 223
 cartoons & caricatures 77, 78, 85, *110*, *178*,
  224
 hunt for *30*, 162, 181
 portraits 45, 80, 100, 116, 117, 124, *178*, 200, 223
 postcards 95, 118, 218, 221
Deadwood Camp 47, 162, 193
Deckers, Jan Frans 71, **125**
Defregger, Franz von 70, *71*, 94, **125**
Dekker, Ernest François Eugène (Douwes Dekker)
 47, **48**, **125**
Delagoa Bay 150
Delannoy, Aristide 84, **126**
Delaw, Georges 82, **126**
Delftsche Courant 86
Deming, Edwin Willard 68, **126**
Den Hertog, G. 47, **126**

Denis, Maurice 67, **126**
Denizard, Charles O. *see* Orens
Der Burenfreund 70, 94
Der Burenkrieg 69-70
Der Floh 88, 102
Der Nebelspalter 88
Der Scherer 87, 88
Desauty, Henriette 69, **126**
Desbordes-Jonas, Louise-Alexandra 69, **126**
Detaille, Eduard 51
Dete, Bertrand 65, **127**
Deutscher Michel 159
Devonshire Regiment *14*, 135, 167, 188
Devriendt, Julien 71, **127**
Dewar, W. 63, **127**
Dewetsdorp 132
Dex, Leo 227
Diamond Hill, Battle of 127, 163
Dickinson, F.C. 105, *126*, **127**, 151, 180
Dicksee, Herbert Thomas 127
Dickson, Thorpe 75, **127**
Dickson, William Kennedy Laurie 127
Die Nederlandsche Spectator 86
Dierckx, Joseph 71, **127**
Dietrich & Co 174
Dietz, B.R. 36, **127**
Diez, Julius 87, **127**
Dixon, Charles Edward 56, 57, 123, 126, **127**,
 141, 211
Dixon, Clive MacDonnell 37, *38*, 39, *41*, **127-8**
Dixon, Harry 63, **128**
Dixon, Percy 72, **128**
Diyatalawa Camp 134, 175, 181, 223
Diyatalawa Camp Lyre 45
Diyatalawa Dum Dum 45
Domani 65, **128**
Donah, Ali 84, **128**
Donnison, T.E. 75, *128*
Dorville, Noel 83, 85, **128**
Dowling, W. 79, **128**
Downey, Thomas 75, **128**
Doyle, Richard 75
Doyle-Jones, F.W. **128**
Dragoons, 6th 231
Draner 82, 85, **128**
'Drawl' *see* Ward, L.M.
Dressel, A. 66, **128-9**
Driefontein 197
Drummond, Arthur 102, **129**
Drummond, N. **129**
Drury, Edward Alfred Briscoe 129
Du Bois 129
Du Framont, Victor Albert 48, *129*
Du Fresne, Paul 129
Du Maurier, George 78
Du Rand, Godefroy 54, **129**
Du Toit, W. 48, **129**, 223
Du Triac, George-Pierre 129
Dublin Fusiliers 105
Duch, Jan 85, 129
Dudeney, Henry Ernest 129
Duke of Edinburgh's Own Volunteer Rifles 176,
 207, **234**, 235
Duke of Wellington's West Riding Regiment 32,
 177
Duke of York's Own Bengal Lancers 157
Duncan, James Allen 54, **129**
Duncan, W.G. 212
Dundee, Battle of 185, 217
Dundonald, Lord 149, 156, *157*
Dunn, Joseph Smith 20
Dupray, Henri (Henri-Louis) *128*, **129**
Dutch
 artists 54, 103, 153, 166
 cartoonists 103, 112, 124, 159, 211
 charity publications 70
 illustrated journals 67-8
 novels 98
 postcard publishers 118, 156, 165
 satirical press 85-6
 sculptors 123
Dutriac, Georges Pierre 66
Dyer-Davies, D. 32, 80, *124*
Dyson, William Henry 80, **129**

E E.C. 129
E.H. 130
E.O.B. 130
East Surrey Regiment 188
Easton, Eugene E. 68
Ebbutt, Phil 129
Echo des Marches 85
Eckhardt, Oscar 76, 129
Edward VII, King 122, 199
  bust *160*
  cartoons 88, *178*
    and Chamberlain 191, 232
    French 83-4, *116*, 126, 130, 133, 162, 163,
      172, 175, 182, *224*
    German 208, *230*, 231
    Swiss 200
Edwards, George Wharton **129**
Edwards, (Henry) Dennis 79, **130**
Edy,wards, Lionel Dalhousie Robertson 130
Edwards, Louis 53, 72, **130**
Egersdörfer, Heinrich 32, 57, 70, 78, 79, *80*,
  130, 142, 145
Elandslaagte, Battle of 20, 51, 52, 53, 119, 177,
  185, 190, 202, 217, 234
Emmerson, H. Percy 36, **130**
Ener, R. 84, **130**
Engela, J.G. 48, **130**
envelopes (postal covers)
  illustrated 39, *140*, 164
  souvenir *90*, 96, 183, 212
Epstein, Sallo 140
equestrian
  scenes 55, 58, 103, 107
  statues 104
Erskine, W.C.C. 124, 130
Espinasse *130*
Ettling, L.E. 130
Evans, A. 130
Evans, Harry 130
Eysler & Co 87, *156*, 169

F F.,I.R. *see* I.R.F.
F.,R.M. *see* R.M.F.
F.H.Y. **132**
F.S. **135**
F.W. **136**
Fairhurst, Enoch 130
Faivre, Jules-Abel 82, 83, **130**
Falkner, G. 171
Farasyn, Edgard 71, **131**
Farquharson, David 131
Farquharson, John 36, *130*, **131**
Fau, Fernand 82, 83, **131**
Faulkner, C.W. & Co 147, 162
Faustin, Betbeder *89*, **131**
Fay, J. *99*
Fayard Frères 66
Fearon, Percy ('Poy') 75, *131*
Feininger, Lyonel 87, **131**
Feith, Johannes (Jan) jnr. 86, 87, *99*, **131**
Feldbauer, Max 85, 87, **131**
Feller, Frank 60, *131-2*
Fenn, George Manville 97, 111, 140, 213
Fenton, Roger 18
Fenwick **132**
Ferreira, Gen J.S. 223
Fertom 82, 84, 85, **132**
Festing, Arthur Hoskyns 36, **132**
Fickenscher **132**
Field, C.R.M. **132**
Field, D.H. **132**
Field Service Order 121
Figaro 88
Finberg, Alexander Joseph 53, 60, *132-3*
Finnemore, Joseph 58, 62, 63, 98, *132*, **133**
Fliegende Blätter 88
Flores, Ricardo 84, **133**
Flower, Clement 61, **133**
Forain, Jean-Louis 83
Forbes, Stanhope Alexander 133
Forestier, Amedée *19*, 53, 92, *133*, 176
Forestier-Walker, Gen F.W. 77
Formilli, Cesare T.G. 133
Forrest, Archibald Stevenson 58, 75, 99, **133**

Foster, Arthur J. 133
Foucar, George 133-4
Fouché, W.D. 223
Frampton, George James **134**
Francis of Teck, Prince 173
Franck, Ludwig & Co 173
François **134**
François, Leo Auguste 134
François, Louis 48, **134**
Frank Leslie's Illustrated Newspaper 19
Frankland, Thomas Hugh Colville 30, 37, 42
Fredillo *134*
Freeman's Journal 88
Fremantle, Sir F.E. 229
French, Gen J.D.P. 175, 210, 226, 234
  caricatures 77-8, 137
  portraits 52, 173, 231
French
  artists 53, 55, 64-7, 103, 108-9, 111, 122
  caricaturists 102, 130, 131, 136, 146, 153, 162,
    175
  cartoonists 105, 106, 108, 109, 115, 116-17, 120,
    124, 126, 128, 130, 133, 134, 136, 138, 139,
    140, 143, 146, 152, 153, 157, 159, 161-5,
    172, 174, 175, 178, 187, 192, 194, 211
  charity publications 69
  illustrated journals 64-7
  illustrated novels 99
  postcard artists 115, 125, 126, 130, 133, 134,
    136, 140, 162, 179-80, 187
  satirical press 82-5, 102
  sculptors 160, 162, 225
Frenzeny, Paul *52*, 53, 59, 92, **134**, 203
Frick, S. 84
The Friend 20, 25, 28, 158, 173, 234
Fripp, Charles Edwin 18, *22-3*, 24, 57, *134*, 229
Fritsch, Hans 134
Fritz, W.S. 135
Fritzchen 135
Frontier war artwork 12, 18, 19, 22
Frkbch, C.J. 134
Frument, Dudley 135
Fuchs, Emil(e) 72, *135*, 231
Fuller, Edmund G. 135
Fullwood, Albert Henry 80, **135**
Furniss, Harry 74, 75, *135-6*

G G., K. *see* K.G.
G.B. **136**
G.C. *see* C.G.
Gale & Polden 60, 149, 151, 163, 171, 183, 186
games *see* board games
Gandy, Herbert 136
Gann Keronec'h *see* Keronec'h, Gann
Garratt, Arthur Paine 58, 116, **136**
Garratt, R. 136
Gaul, William Gilbert 136
Geillustreerd Polietienieuws 67-8
Gemmell, Mrs 41, 136
George, Trooper **136**
George, Edward *136*
George Budricks & Co *90*, 96, 183, 212
George Stewart & Co Ltd 105
Georges, Léon 84, **136**
'Geoyo' 136
Gerardin, Auguste 66, **136**
Gerbault, Henri 67, 82, 83, 85, **136**
Gerlach, Otto 67, **136**
German
  artists 108, 123
  cartoonists 113, 130, 132, 134, 135, 139, 140,
    141, 146, 152, 153, 156, 158, 159
  charity publications 69-70
  illustrated journals 67
  illustrated novels 98
  satirical press 86-8
  sculptors 161
Gibb, Arthur **137**
Gibb, R.C. 36, **137**
Gibson, Charles Dana *136*, **137**
Giffey, P. *99*, **137**
Gilbert, John 19
Gilbert, René Joseph 100, **137**
Giles Maj G.D. 23, 77, *136*, **137**, 229

Gill, Arthur J.P. **137**
Gillam, F.Victor **138**
Gillett, Edward Frank **138**
Gillot, Rev. H. 71
Gilson, T. *138*
Glanville, Ernest 97, 122
Glencoe, Battle of *110*, 192
Glimpses of South Africa in Peace and War 68
Gloucestershire Regiment 231
Gocy, E. **138**
Godfin **138**
Godfrey, Herbert **138**
Godilot *see* Orens
Gog, H. 85, **138**
The Golden Penny 56, 132, 141
Golding, Harry 228
Goldman, C.S. 236
golf poster 102, *103*
Goodman, Robert Gwelo 16, 32, **138**
Gordon Highlanders 53, 107, 118, 129, 207, 210
Gottlob, Fernand-Louis 84, **138**
Gough, Arthur J. 60, 63, 72, **138**
Gould, Francis Carruthers 70, 75, *76*, 78, 88,
  97, 99, *138-9*
Gould, W. 80, **139**
Goursat, Georges *see* SEM
Gousse, Henri **139**
The Gram 42, *43*, 109, 140, 144-5, 149, 217,
  221, 227, 231
Grand-Carteret, John 88
'Grand Military and Patriotic Concert' 71-2
  programme for 114, 118
Grandjouan, Jules-Felix **139**
Grant, Gordon Hope 37, 61, 68, *139*
Grant, Hugh 75, **139**
Grätz, Fritz Georg Friedrich 88, **139**, *198*, 199
The Graphic 19, 31, 38, 41, 43
  artists with 22-3, 29, 32, 35-7, 50, 54-6
Gray, Tristram **139**
Greek
  artists 69, 150
Green Point
  military camp 31, 32, 227
  P.O.W. camp 48, 225
Greenfield, D.G. **139**
Greenland, Cedryl 37
greeting cards 38, 39, *40*, 196
Greiffenhagen, Maurice 76, **139**
Greig, James 58, 63, **139**
Grellet, Georges 84, **140**
Grellier, Henry Harley **140**
Grenadier Guards 113, 142
Grenfell, Charles M. 42, **140**
Gréningaire, E. 179
Griebner, F. 87, **140**
Griffith, George Chetwyn 235
Griffith, W.M. 36, **140**
Griset, Ernest-Henry **140**
Groningen, Paul 186
Groome, William Henry Charles 98, **140**
Grossi, A. **140**
Grun, Jules-Alexandre 100, *140*
Guerilla Oorlog in Zuid Afrika 68
Guignard, Alexandre-Gaston 69, **140**
Guillaume, Albert-André 66, *140-1*
Gülich, John 34
Gully, C. **141**
Gunn, D.D. **141**
Gwynn, Reginald P.J. 39, *140*, **141**
Gwynne, Howell Arthur 28

H H.E. 145
H.R. 150
H.T.C. 43, **150**
H.W. 150
Hagen, Max 87, **141**
Haldane, A. 42, 117
Hale, Maj George Ernest 43, *140*, **141**
Halke, Paul 87, **141**
Halkett, George Roland 75, **141**
Hall, Sydney Prior 55, 120, *140*, *141-2*
Halsted, A.E. 142
Hamilton, Angus 58
Hamilton, Gen Ian 52, 200, 229

Hampe, T. **142**
Hampshire Volunteers 218
Harcourt, George *142*
Hardy, Dudley 53, 60, 75, 76, *142*
Hardy, E.Stewart **142**
Hardy, Frank C. 60, **142**
Hardy, Norman H. 142-3
Hardy, Paul 61, *62*, **143**
Hare, Robert William *142*, **143**
Hare, St George 57, **143**
Haringus, Lui-Même **143**
Harmsworth, Alfred 62; *see also After Pretoria:*
  the Guerilla War; With the Flag to Pretoria
Harmsworth Magazine 63
Harper's Weekly 19, 37, 68, **88**
Harris, E.S. *143*
Harris, Owen 42, 43, **143**
Harrison, C. 75
Hartrick, Archibald Standish 22, 50-1, *52*, 53, 54,
  58, 72, *143-4*, 177
Harvey, Harold 37, **144**
Harvey, Sydney 75, **144**
Haserick, Alfred E. 42, *144-5*
Hassall, John 56, 62, *72*, 75-6, *144*, **145**
Hatherell, William 56, 57, 72, *144*, **145**
Hatos, Sandor **145**
Haug, Robert 98, **145**
Hayen, George 98
Hayward, Lucy Pearson **145**
Hebblethwaite, Sydney 76
Hedley, Ralph **145**
Heidbrinck, Oswald 84, 85, **146**
Heine, Thomas Theodor 16, *70*, 88, *146*
Heloure Rins, P. **146**
Helyar, C.W.H. **146**
Hencke, A.J. **146**
Hennessey, Richard 37, **146**
Hens, Frans 71, **146**
Henty, George A. 97, 98, 191
heraldic designs 162
Hering, E. **146**
Herkomer, Hubert **146**
Herle, D. **146**
Hermann-Paul **146**
Heron, Roderick 79, **146**
Herrmann, Dr Emmanuel 90
Hertzog, Gen J.B.M. 32, 198
Hess, J.B. 79, **146**
Hester, Edward Gilbert **146**
Het Huisgezin 68
Hewerdine, Matthew Bede 43, 72, *146-7*
Hey, E.G. & Co 138
Hickson, Robert Albert **147**
Higgins, Herbert **147**
Higham, B. **147**
Higham, Sidney 54, 55, 60, **147**
Highland Brigade 52, 127, 200, 202, 235; *see*
  also Magersfontein, Battle of
Hildesheimer & Co 92, 108, 117, 219
Hill, F.Jeffrey 32, **147**
Hill, Rowland (Rip) 78, **147**
Hillingford, Robert Alexander *147*
Hirst, Norman 148
Hobhouse, Emily 46, *148*
Hodgson, A. 75
Hodgson, Michael R.K. 148-9
Hoek, Henri Frits Marie 149
Hoffmann, Anton *148*, 149
Hofmeyer, Rev Adriaan Jacobus Louw 42, **149**
Hogg, H. Arthur 59, **149**
Holding, J.W. 149
Holloway, Edgar A. 60, **149**
Holloway, W.H. 149
Holmes, T.W. 53, 60, *149*
Holyoake, Rowland 149
Honourable Artillery Company *132*, 133
Hopkins, Arthur 57, 75, **149**
Hopkins, Everard 149
Hopkins, Livingston(e) (Hop) 80, *150*
Hoskier, Col F.H. 25
hospitals 139, 147, 165, *168*, 220, 222

Houghton, J.H. **150**
Howard, F. 61
Howard, S. 58, **150**
Hoynck van Papendrecht, Jan 54, 98, *150*
Hughes, Dr Alfred 154
Hughes, E.R. 72
Hughes, W.D. 54
Humoristike Listy 88
Humoristisch Album 86
Hungarian
    satirical press 88, 107
Hunter, Gen A. *220*
Hurst, Henry William Lowe (Hal) 58, **150**
Hutchison, Robert Genmell **150**
Hutton, R.W. **150**
Huyse, William 32
Hyde-Kelly, W. **150**

I I.R.F. 37, **151**
Iantitzmahias 69, **150**
Ibbetson, Ernest 60, *150-1*
The Idler 78
Il Fischetto 117, 118
Illig & Moller 157
Illustrated London News 18-22, 32, 36-7, 39,
    52-4, 92-3; *see also* under names of artists
The Illustrated Mail 59
The Illustrated Sporting & Dramatic News 21, 52
Illustrated War Special 60
Imperial Light Horse *232*, 234
Imperial Yeomanry 92, 147, 156, *207*, 220
Ingram, Herbert 19
Ingram, Joseph Forsyth **151**
Innes, H. 75, **151**
Inniskilling Dragoons 154
Irish-American Brigade 123
Isings, Johan Herman (jnr) 98, **151**
Islay 79, **151**
Italian
    artists 53, 56, 102, 133
    cartoonists 118, 140, 159
    sculptors 157

J J.A.D. **151**
J.A.H.C. *119*, **151**
J.R.W. **155**
Jackson, E.S. 36, **151**
Jackson, F.S. **151**
Jackson, Murray Cosby **151**
Jacomb-Hood, George Percy 56, **151**
Jalland, J.H. 75
James, George E. 75, **152**
James, Gilbert **152**
James, Lionel 20, 27-9, 38, **152**, 196, 210
Jameson, Dr L.S. 77-8, 119, 147
Jameson Raid 18, 65, 90, 141, 166
Jamet, Jean 84, **152**
Jank, Angelo 87, **152**
Jansen, Dirk 46, **152**
Jansen, Hendricus ('Henricus') 86, **152**
Janssens, Joseph-Marie-Louis ('Joz') 71, **153**
Janzelow, M. *87*, **153**
Jaquot, L. **153**
Jay, Harry R. **153**
Jeanniot, Pierre-Georges 82, 83, **153**
Jellicoe, John F. 62, **153**
Jeneer, J. **153**
Jennis, Charles Gurnell 37, **153**
Jensen, A. **153**
Jileno **153**
Job 66, **153**
Johannesburg, surrender of 190, 234
John, William Goscombe *153-4*
Johnson, B.S. 79, **154**
Johnson, Herbert 54, 68, *154*, 172
Johnson, W. & A.K. Ltd *92*
Johnston **154**
Johnston, Agnes M. **154**, 165, 181
Johnston, William 63
Johnston, William Andrew 97, *98*, 211
Jones, Adrian 58, *154-5*
Jones, George Kingston 54, *154*, **155**, 229
Jouas, Charles 69, *155*

Joubert, Gen Piet 26, 59, 65, 100, 109, 201, 202,
    221, 223
    death of 64, 94, 220
Journal des Voyages 67
Jouve, Paul 84, **155**
Joy, George William 114, **155**
Juch, Ernst 88, **155**
Judge 88
Judy 75
Jugend 66, 67, 87
Julio, G. 67, 88, **155**
Jüttner, Franz Albert 87, 88, *156*
Juven, F. 67

K K., V. *see* V.K.
K.G. **157**
Kakas Merton 88
Kampkruimels 45
Kaster, M. **156**
Kauffmann, Rud 66, **156**
Kean, W.R. **156**
'Kees' 99, **156**
Kelly-Kenny, Gen T. 77
Kemble, Edward Windsor 88, *156*
Kemp Tebby, Arthur *see* Tebby, Arthur Kemp
Kemp-Welch, Lucy Elizabeth 109, *156-7*
Kennedy, P. 37, **157**, 209
Keppler, Joseph (jnr) 88, **157**
Keronec'h, Gann 84, *157*
Kestell, John Daniel 108
Khaki in South Africa 62, 236
Kiekeriki 88
Kienerk, Giorgio **157**
Kimberley
    Siege of 41, 82, 107, 109, 118, 180, 200, *227*
    Relief of 20-1, 23, 131, 137, 158, 184, 226
King, Frank C. **157**
King, J. **157**
King, (William) Gunning 53, **157-8**
The King 50, 61, 74, 132
King's Dragoon Guards, 1st 183
King's Liverpool Regiment 154
King's Own Hussars, 3rd 130
King's Own Yorkshire Light Infantry 210
King's Royal Rifles 213
Kipling, Rudyard 16, 20, 142, **158**, 189, 234
    'Absent Minded Beggar' 69, *72*, 114, *119*, *144*,
        158, 235, *238*
    cartoons *30*, *32*, 78, 164
    portraits 120, 173
Kirton, Walter **158**
Kitchener, Gen Lord H.H. **160**, 177, 213
    cartoons 77-8, 79, 87, 107, 116, 132, 149,
        208, 209
    portraits 52, 120, 121, *144*, 146, 154, 159, 231
    postcards & postal covers 93, 130, 132
    return of 133, 139, 145
Kitchener's Brigade 117, 210
Kladderadatsch 88
Kleinhempel, Gertrud **158**
Klepper, Max Francis 68, **158**
Klingebeil, E. 98, **158**
Klinger, Julius 87, **158**
Kloods Hans 103
Knight, Charles 19
Knötel, Richard 67, **158-9**
Knox, Ernest Blake 37, **159**
Koch, E. **159**
Kock, Gen J.H.M. 100, 125, 195
Koekkoek, Hermanus Willem 19, 62, *158*, **159**
Köhler, Gustav **159**
Köhler, Hub 149
Kolstee, H.J. 68
Koppenol, Cornelis 86, 98, **159**
Koski **159**
Krejcik, K. 88, **159**
Kritzinger, Gen P.H. 223
Kroon, Patriq Heleen Joan 86, **159**
Krügen, A. **159**
Kruger, Paul 66, 86, 111, *195*, 201, 222
    arrival in Marseilles 64, 65, 67, 94, 102, 114,
        160, 192
    cartoons 155
    and Chamberlain *74*, 100, 128

and Queen Victoria 82, 100, 102, *124*
    American 66, 122, 157
    Australian 218
    British 75, 76, 77-8, 97, 107, 113, 114, 126,
        139, 141, *144*, 145, 147, 164, 181, 184,
        218, 222, 228, 232
    French 65, *81*, 85, 134, 138, 156, *160*, 161,
        162, 163, 179, 198, 220
    German 66, 131, 169
    Swiss 200, 212
    covers and posters 87, 140, 175
    lithographs *108*, 109
    medals, plaques & statues 108, 142, 223, 225
    portraits 45, 47, 67, 70, 100, 103, 137, 138,
        161, 168, 177, 185, 202, 231
    postcards & playing cards 92, 94, 95, 105,
        109, 116, 122, 125, 130, 153, 159, 161,
        168, *198*, 218, 232
    religious symbolism 16, 84, *124*, 125, 212
    75th birthday 68, 114
    tributes to 66, 108, 109, 121, 153, 163, 173,
        174, 187, 198, 219, 220, 221 222
Kunzli Frères 95, 161
Kupka, François 65, *66*, 68, 83, 84, 85, **159**

L 'L.' 159, *160*
L.,C. *see* C.L.
L.,P. *see* P.L.
L.,R. *see* R.L.
L'Agonie d'Albion 143
L'Assiette au Beurre 83-4
L'Illustratie Européene 68
L'Illustration 19, 55, 59, *65-6*, 68, 82
L'Illustré Nationale 66, 67, 85, 88
L'Illustré Soleil du Dimanche 67
L'Impartial de l'Est 65, 67
L'Indiscret 85
La Caricature 65, 84, 85, 99
La Garriage 84, *159*
La Guerre au Transvaal: Anglais et Boers 83
La Illustraçion 19
La Illustration 68
La Moderne Epopée les Boers 111
La Réforme 67, 68, 88
La République Illustrée 85
La Revue Mâme 85
La Semaine Illustrée 65, 66, 67
La Silhouette 85
La Vie en Rose 85
La Vie Illustrée 67
La Vie Pour Rire 85
Ladysmith 192
    Siege of 23, 27, 28, 37, 38-9, 44, 56, 100-1,
        107, *123*, 125, 128, 146, 169, *188-9*, 190,
        192, 193, 200
    Maud, W. *14*, 20, 22, 167
    greeting cards 38, 39, *40*, 196
    postcards & envelopes 39, *43*, 95, 141, 196
    Relief of 65, 93, 105, 127, 150, 156, 161, 182,
        184, 217
    Bacon, J.H. 58, 59, 104, *145*
    postcards 93, 115
The Ladysmith Bombshell 38-9, 196
The Ladysmith Lyre 27, 38, 127, 152
Lalauze, Alphonse 85, **159**
Lambdin, Vic 88, **159**
Lambton, the Hon H. 77, 229
Lancashire Fusiliers 134, 179, *209*, 210
Lancers, 17th 52, *192*, *204*, 206
Lander, Edgar 159
Langa, Rata 159
Lanos, Henri **160**
lantern slides 53-4, 59
Laplagne, Guillaume *73*, *160*
Laszlo de Lambos, P.A. de **160**
Lately, John 60
Laurence, Mervin **160**
Laurence, Sydney Mortimer 23, **160**
Lauterburg, Emil **160**
Law, H. 80, **160**
Lawrence, Jack **160**
Lawton, W.C. **160**
Le Bègue, René *66*, 67, *84*, 85, **161**
Le Bocain 84, **161**

Le Bon Vivant 84
Le Canard Sauvage 85
Le Charivari 81, 82
Le Courrier Français 85
Le Dépêche 85
Le Franc Normand Illustré 85
Le Gall, Maurice 47, 48, **161**
Le Gavroche 84
Le Grelot 85
Le Illustré National 68
Le Journal Amusant 85
Le Journal Illustré 64
Le Mesurier, Capt 42, *107*
Le Monde Illustré 19, 59, 66
Le Petit, Alfred 85, **162**
Le Petit Brayon Illustré 67, 85
Le Petit Journal 64-5
Le Petit Méridional 67
Le Petit Parisien 65, 102, 121
Le Rire 82-3, 88
Le Rire Belge 88
Le Sourire 85
Lea, Henry (Harry) 32, *160-1*, 229
Leader, H.P. **161**, 176
The Leaguer of Ladysmith 38, 39
Léandre, Charles-Lucien 67, 82-3, *160*, **161**
Leclerc 67, **161**
Lefèbvre-Lourdet, M. *see* Lourdey, M.
Legand, Jules **161**
Lehmann-Schram, W. 88, **161**
Lehr, Christian Wilhelm Jacob **161**
Leibl, W.M.H. 70, **161**
Leicester Regiment 210
Leigh, Chandos 36, **162**
Leighton, Frederick **162**
Leipziger Illustrierte Zeitung 19, 67
Leist, Frederik William 32, 80, **162**
Lempereur, François 82, 85, **162**
Lenbach, Frans-Seraph von **162**
Lenny *see* 'L'
Leroy, Hippolyte **162**
Leslie, George Dunlop **162**
Leslie's Weekly 68, 88
Lest We Forget Them 72
Levering, Albert **162**
Lewin, F.G. **162**
Lewis, Caroline 192
Lewis, Robert 84, **162**
Leyds, Dr W.J. 69, 194, 231
Liebermann, Max 70, **162**
Life 88
Life Guards, 1st 122, *182*, 183
Lindberg, Ernst Evert 47, **162**
Lindsay, Norman A.W. **162**
Lines, George Walter 39
Linse, Hendrik Jan Carel 86, 98, *162-3*
Lintott, Edward Barnard 59, 60, **163**
Lion, G. 65, 84, **163**
Lionel **163**
Lloyd, T. Ivester 63, 76, *163*
Lloyd's Weekly News 60
Lobel, P.H. 84, *163*
Lochard **163**
Lomax, John Arthur **163**
Lombard's Kop 37, 217
    Battle of 22, 23, 32, 50, *51*, 190
Longstaff, William Francis **163**
Looymans, Romain 71, **163**
Loraine, Nevison Arthur **163**
Lourdey, Maurice **163**
Lovett, Alfred Crowdy *163-4*
'Luc' 85, **164**
Lucas, Henry Frederick Lucas **164**
Lucas, John Seymour **164**
Lucas, Sydney Seymour 57, **164**
Lui-même, Haringus **164**
Luker, William (jnr) **164**
Lumley, Augustus Savile 60, **164**
Lustige Blätter 87
Lynch, Frank 75, 76, **164**
Lynch, George 20, 27, 37, 53, **164**
Lyon 85
Lyons, Alfred 96, *164*
Lyttleton, Gen the Hon G.N. 77

M M.,B.J. *see* B.J.M.
M.,S. *see* S.M.
M.F.C.S. 174
M.L.C. 175
Macauley, Charles R. 164
Macbeth, Robert Walker 38, 56, 57, **164-5**
MacKinnon, Gen W.H. 77
MacNeill, Angus *210*
Macpherson, Douglas 65, *165*
Mader, Percy Lionel *165*
Mafeking,
 Siege of 32, 39-41, 56, 93, 105, 107, 129, 136, 181, 188, 196, 200, 217, 220
 Relief of *29*, 57, 105, 122, 127, 129, 142, 184, *185*, 208, 217
 'Mafeking Mail Special Siege Slip' 40
Magersfontein, Battle of 44, 52, 100, 107, 125, 131, 151, 233, 236
Magne, Désiré-Alfred 69, *165*
Mahan, A.T. *War in South Africa* 127, 129, 136, 146, 174, *193*, 194, 212
Mahoney, Frank 80
Mahut, Maurice 65, *165*
Mailick, A. *165*
Mair, Maud 165
Majuba Hill 32, 114
Malteste, Louis Henri-Théodor ('Malatesta') 66, 84, *165*
Manchester Regiment 220
Mann, Harrington 72
Mante, Johannes Marte 46, 152, **165-6**
Manton, G. Grenville 58, 166
Marais, C.C. 166
Marc, Lucien 65
Marchant, Bessie 97, 227
Marcus, Max 132
Mareuil, Georges Villebois *see* Villebois-Mareuil, G. Comte de
marine artists 56, 60, 115, 126, 127, 141, 232, 237
Marnix 166
'Mars' *see* Bonvoisin, Maurice
Marshall, J. Fitz 166
Martens, Willem (Willy) *166*
Martin, A.D. 166
Matania, Fortunio 56, *166*
Mather, Percy 47
Mathews, John Chester 166
Maud, W.T. *14*, 22, 27, 38, 57, *166*-7, 210, 229
Maurell, F. 167
Maurice, Maj Gen Sir F. 124, 130
Maxwell, William 27, 38, 129
May 167
May, William Philip (Phil) 75, 76, 78, 80, 103, *143*, *167*, *168*, 210
Mayer, (Ernst Karl) Erich 16, 46-7, *168-9*
Mayer, Henry ('Hy') 58, 76, 88, *169*
M'Cracken, Donald E. 169
McCormick, Arthur David 169
McCormick, Harry 20, 23, 37, 38, 114, *168*, 169
McCutcheon, John Tinney 169
McDonald, A.K. 75, 170
McDonald, Maj Gen H. 52, *172*, 173, 183
McFarlane, John 170
McKenzie, Frank J. 170
McLean, George Gilbert Creswick *35*, 37, *168*, **170-1**
McNeill, Angus John 36, *170*, *171*
McNeill, John *171*
McPherson, Douglas 54
Méaulle, Fortuné-Louis 65, 117, 121, *172*
medals 107-8, 113, 122, *238*
 designers 126, 132, 134, 135, 162, 238
Mees, J. 71, *172*
Meikeljohn, Ronald Forbes 172
Meinet, Marie François Lucien 172
Meintjieskop camp 179
Meister, Frederich 98, 158
The Melbourne Outpost 80
The Melbourne Punch 80
Melvomitch, M. *172*
memorials 128, 129, 134, 135, 153-4, *189*, 190, 212, 213, 217, 220-1, 231; *see also* monuments
Menard, G. 84, *172*
Menpes, Mortimer *15*, 16, *18*, 21, 23-5, *172-3*, 234

menus *233*, 234
Menzies, A. **173**
Menzies, McGregor 79, *173*
Merry, Godfrey 53, *173*
Merry, Tom 60, *173*
Merson, Luc-Olivier 66, *173*
Mertens, Charles 71, **174**
Mesplès, Paul-Eugene 66, **174**
Methfessel, Adolf 174
Methuen, Lt Gen Lord 20, 64
Métivet, Lucien-Marie-François 82, *174*
Meunier, Georges 67, *174*
Meunier, Henri 174
SS Mexican 43, 118, 143
 sinking of 43, *140*, 141
The Mexican Mercury 42, 43, 118, 143
Meyer, H. 64, *65*
Michäel, A. 84, *174*
Michel, G.V. *174*
Middlesex Regiment 221
Middlesex Rifle Volunteers, Artists Corps 55, 183, 217
Mignot, Victor 84, *85*, 174
Mills, A.Wallis 75, 97, *174*
Milner, Alfred 24, 78, 120, 172-3
Minns, Benjamin Edward 80, **174-5**
Mitchell, Hutton *53*, *175*
Mitford, Bertram 97, 235
Modder River 197
 Battle of 48, 100, 106, 125, 127, 145, *216*, 217, 225, 226, 233, 234
Modderfontein 52
Moginie, A.H. *175*
Moloch, B. *see* Colomb, A.H.
Molony, F. *175*
Moncrieff, M.M. *175*
Monnier, G. 84, 85, *175*
Montbard, Georges 53, 66, 92, *174*, *175*, *189*
Monte Cristo, Battle of 187, 213, 225
Montmorency, Capt R. 108
Montmorency's Scouts *170*, 210
monuments 47, 222; *see also* memorials
Moonshine 58, 75-6
Moore, Richard Hewitt *175*
Mora, Francis Luis *175*
Morehen, Horace 75, *175*
Moreland, Arthur *174*, 175
Morgan, Cecil Buckley 37, *175*
Morgan, Frederick *175*
Moriss 84, *175*
The Morning Post 29-30, 32
Morris, W. 37, *176*
Morrow, Albert George 63, *176*
Moscheles, Felix Stone *176*
Mosquito 80
Mouchot, Charles *176*
Moultray, John Elder 32, *176*
Mounted Infantry Brigade *170*, 203
Mowlem, E.J. *176*
Mulock, Frederick Charles *176*
Münchener Odinskarte 87
Münzer, Adolf 87, *176*
Muschamp, F. Sydney *176*
Musgrave *176*
Musgrave, R.R. 79, *176*

N N.C. 177
Nankivell, Frank Arthur *176*
Naper, L.A.D. *176*
Nash, Joseph (jnr) *55-6*, 57, 113, 133, *175*, 177, 231
Nasi, Vincenzo *see* van Dock
The Natal Caricature 80, 196
Natal forces 127, 207, 220
Natal Volunteers 57
'National Bazaar in Aid of the Sufferers by the War' 72
National Convention 32, 198
National Scouts 108
Naudé, Pieter Hugo 16, 32, *177*
Naval Brigade 237
naval scenes 194; *see also* marine artists
Navy & Army Illustrated 61, 66

Nederland-Transvaal: Gedenkboek . . . 70
Neilly, James Emerson 177
Nesham, Thomas P.W. 37, *177*, 186
Neue Burenstreiche 87
Neue Glüblichter 88
Neumann, E. 177
Nevison, Arthur 58
Nevison, Henry Wood 20
The New Penny Magazine 61
New South Wales Lancers *109*, 151, 213
The New York Journal 68
New Zealand
 artists 111, 115
 troops 115, 126, 175, 213
New Zealand Mounted Rifles 176
Newnes, George 61-2, 66
Newnham, J.S. 177
Newnham-Davies, Lt Col N. 53
Nicholas II, Tsar 104, 232, 233
Nicholson, Sir William *177*-8
Nicholson's Nek 140
 Battle of *14*, *21*
Nicolson, E. 82, 85, *177*, *178*
Niemann, August 98, 117
Nieuwe Belgische Illustratie 68
Nijgh and Van Ditmar 68
Noble, Ernest 178
Noirfontaine, Baron v.d. 67
Nooitgedacht (Magaliesberg) *61*, *228*, 229, 230
Nooitgedacht camp 41, 116
Norie, Orlando 178
Northampton Regiment 131
Northumberland Fusiliers 43, 147, 150, 199
Norton, Eardley B. 77, *178*
Norval's Pont 175
Norwin's, Les 178
Norwood, Lt J. *116*
Nott, W.H. 178
Nuevo Mondo 68
Numa, B. 179

O 'O'Galop 67, 85, *178*, 179
O'Beirne, F. *92*, 179
O Seculo 68
Obsner, E.T.P.G. 157
Oerder, Frans David 16, 44, *45*, *178*, 179, 223
Og, G. 85
Ogé, Eugène 100, *179*
Opper, Frederick Burr 179
Oost, Harm 98, 125
Orchardson, Charles 179
Orens 95, 100, *178*, *179-80*
Orr, A.S. 34, *37*
Orr, J. 180
Ost, Alfred 180
Ouless, Walter William 180
The Owl 78-9, 185, 194
 cartoonists for 109, 111, 120, 222
Owles, D.C. 180

P P.L. *93*, 186
P.O.W. *see* prisoner of war
P.S.A.D. Erica 165
P.V. 191
Paardeberg, Battle of *24*, 93, 100, 101, 106, 125, *193*, 215, 217, 230; *see also* Cronje, Gen Piet
Paget, Henry Marriot 22, *54*, 55, 57, 167, **180**, 222
Paget, Sidney Edward *25*, 55, 58, 97, **180-1**
Paget, Walter Stanley (Wal) *34*, 55, 59, 97, *180*, **181**
Paget's Horse 43, 164
Pall Mall Magazine 78, 88
Palmer, Alfred 79
Paque, Oliver *53*, 54, 55, *180*, 181
Parent, A. **181**
Paris, Alfred Jean Marie 99, **181**
Paris-Pretoria 69, 70
Parker, Gray **181**
Parkes, Harry 58, 75, **181**
Parrington, A.J. **181**
Partridge, Bernard 58, 72, 75, 76, **181**
Pasquier, H. **181**
Patriotic Postcard Co. *93*

Paterson, Andrew Barton ('Banjo') **181-2**
Paton, Frank **182**
Patterson, F. 50, *51*, 53, **181**
Patterson, George Malcolm 60, 76, **181**
Paul, Bruno 69-70, 88, **182**
Paul, Hermann 67, 82, 83, 85, 88
Paulat **182**
Paxton, Robert B.M. *24*, 25, **182**, *188*, *233-4*
Payne, Arthur Charles **183**
Payne, Charlie Johnson **183**
Payne, G.M. **183**
Payne, Harry 92, 93, 119, *182*, **183**
Payne, T. 96, **183**
Peace, 1902 111, *112*, *155*
Pearce, Thirkell 58, 60, **183**
Pears, Charles 53, 75, 76, **183-4**
Pearse, Alfred 41, 58, 116, *184*, *185*, 187
Pearse, Henry 20
Pearson, Arthur C. 61
Pearson's Weekly 61
Pegram, Frederick 58, **184**
Pegram, Henry Alfred **184**
Pellegrini, Carlo ('Ape') 77, 107
Pen **184**
Penning, Louwrens 98, 211
The Penny Illustrated Paper 60, 133
Penstone, Charles 78-9, 80, **185**
Penstone, Constance 32, 70, 78-9, **184-5**
Perard, Victor Semon **185**
Pestillac, S. 99, *184*, **185**
Peters, G.W. 68, **185**
Pethybridge, H.M. **185**
Pfui Chamberlain 87
Philip, George **185**
Phillips, Laurence 72
photography, war 14, 18-19, 25, 50-1
 use of 58, 122, 177, 221, 225, 234
Pic, Marcel *185*
Picasso, Pablo 100, *184*, **185-6**
Pick, M. *186*
Pick-Me-Up 36, 37, 58, 76, 88
A Pictorial History of the Transvaal 61-2
Picture Postcard Co 53, 92-3, 109, 134, 175, 212
Piffard, Harold H. 98, **186**
Pike, William *see* Paque, Oliver
Pinnock, Herbert Louis (Lulu) *34*, 37, **186**
Pischon, Marie 105, **186**
playing cards 125, 168
Plinzner, M. **186**
Plument de Bailhac, Paul C.M. **186-7**
Plumer, H. 77, 170
Plumer's Scouts *105*
Plumet, Jean-Louis 84, **187**
Pocock, R. Noel **187**
Poilpot, Théophile (jnr) 66, **187**
Poiré, Emmanuel *see* Caran d'Ache
Pole-Carew, Maj Gen R. 172
Polichinelle 85
Pope, E.T. **187**
'Popini' 60, 75, 76, **187**
Porter, Paul **187**
Portuguese artists 83, 84, 85, 107, 116
postal covers 96, 108, 119, 130, 141, 173
postcard
 artists *see* under nationalities and Appendix 3
 publishers
  Belgian 70, *94*, 105, 222
  British 102, 162, 63, 183, 195
  Dutch 118, 156, 165
  French 160, 162, 163, 179
  German 102, 132, 156, 157, 158, 165, 173
  Italian 157
  Swiss 161: *see also* specific names of publishers
postcards *see* under specific subjects
poster
 art 100, 121, 173, 212
 artists
  Belgian 174
  British 142, 145, 237
  French 108, 118, 140, 165, 187
  German 182
Pott, Charles L. 53, 58, 75, *186*, **187**
Pott, Johannes Adriaan 44-5, **187**

Poulbot, Francisque 16, *84*, 85, **187**
Prater, Ernest *24, 25, 46, 177, 182, 184, 186, 187-8*, 197, 234
Pretoria, Fall of 20, 22, 95, 190, 217, 233, 234
Priem, C.H. 68, 100
Prince Albert's Own Hussars 179
Princess Royal's Dragoon Guards 127
Prinsep, Valentine Cameron **188**
Prior, Melton 15, 18, *19-20, 21*, 37, *41*, 50, 52, 60, 115, 151, ***188-91***, 233-4, 236
Prisoner-of-war camps
 Boer 16, 45-8, 125, 95, 108, 125, 128-9, 146
 British 41-3, 149, 201; *see also* names of camps
prisoners
 Boer *24*, 27, *109*, 149, 165, 168, 176, 182, 188, 215, 222
 British 26, 177, 180, 201-2
Probyn, Wilfred 72
Proctor, John 60, 75, **191**
Pronier, Alfred 67, **191**
Prout, Victor **191**
Puck 88, 157
'Punch' (artist) **191**
Punch 37, 74-5, 82, 88
Puttick and Simpson 57
Pym, Rowland **191**

Q Queen's Own Cameron Highlanders (79th Foot) 127
'Queensland Outlaws' 120

R R.,A. *see* A.R.
R.,B.C. *see* B.C.R.
R.,H. *see* H.R.
R.I.P. *see* Hill, Rowland
R.L. **196**
R.M.F. **196**
Racey, A.G. **191**
Rackham, Arthur **191**
Radiguet, Maurice 82, 84, 85, *86, 190*, **191**
Ragama camp 125, 130
Rainey, H. Wlliam 97, **191**
Ralph, Julian 20, 23, 61, **191**
Ralph, Lester 23, 37, 68, 102, **191**, 193, 234
Ralston, William 54, 56, 106, ***191-2***, 197, 230
The Rand Daily Mail 80
Ransom, Sidney *see* Yendis, Mosnar
Ransome, Stafford 99, **192**
Raphael Tuck & Sons *see* Tuck, R.
Ratby Tribute Medal 132
Raven-Hill, Leonard 54, 75, 76, **192**
Rawlinson, Lt Col Henry Seymour 39, **192**
Rawson, M.A. **192**
Read, Edward Henry Hadley 63, **192**
Reay, R. Martine 68, **192**
Reddersburg 100, 125
Redon, Georges 67, **192**
Reed, Edward Tennyson 75, 76, 86, ***192-3***
The Regiment 36
Rehse **193**
Reijenga, Jan G. *47*, 48, **193**
Reisacher, Sylvester *100-1*, **193**
Reitz, D. 218
Reitz, Gen F.W. 45, 78, *110*, 231
Remington, Frederic Sackrider 19, 68, 126, 129, *193-4*
Renard, Jules *see* Draner
René, Albert *81*, 82, 85, **194**
Renouard, Charles Paul 57, 58, **194**
Repina, Illia E. 71
Reuterdahl, Henry **194**
Review of Reviews 74
Rewenga, Jan G. *see* Reijenga, J.G.
Reynolds, Frank **194**
Reznicek, Ferdinand Freiherr 70, **194**
Rhodes, Cecil John 24, 102, 119, 172, 184
 cartoons 77, 78, *124*, 130, 139, *156*, 222
 Kimberley, Siege of 20-1, 82, 226, *227*
 portraits 32, 177, **198**
 postcards 127, 159, 166, 218
Rhodesian Regiment *104*, 105
Ri, G. 84, **194**
Richards, Mordaunt Cyril 79, 95, *96*, **194-5**

Ridouard, Maxime 69, **195**
Rifle Brigade *168*, 178
Rigg, E.M. 63, **195**
Rimington's Scouts *180*, 181,193, 216
Rimington's Tigers 210
Rins, P.H. *see* Heloure Rins, P.
Rinzner, M. **195**
Rip **195**
Ripp, P.H. *10*, *65*, *66*, 67, *195*
Ris, G. **195**
Ritchie, Alick P.F. **195**
Ritter, Eugen *195-6*
Robert, Earl 20, *38*, *40*, *43*, 60, 71, 80, 95, *196*
Robert, Paul **196**
Roberts, Field Marshall Lord 52, *54*, 111, 115, 129, 147, 166, 172, 180
 army of 20, 22, 37, 68, 139, 164, 183, 197
 cartoons 77-8, 94, 113, 132, 135, 147, 187, *194*, 195, 228, 229
 portraits 52, 102, 103, 127, 153, 154, 177, 200, *230*, 231
 postcards & playing cards 131, 132, 168
 sculptures 106, 114, 160
Roberts, Lt Frederick *209*, 210
Roberts, J. **196**
Roberts, J.H. **196**
Robertson, J.P. **196**
Robinson, Charles **196**
Robinson, C.N. 211
Robinson, George Crosland 32
Robinson, Miss S.A.H. 54, **196**
Robinson, William Bennett 53, 66, 147, *196*, 220, 225
Roegge, Wilhelm *196, 197*
Rogers, William Allen *66*, 68, 88, *196*, 197
Rogers, W.G. **197**
Rohida, A. 66
Roland, Paul 99, 137
Romilly, Frederick William **197**
Ronald, J. McB. **197**
Rose, Fred W. **197**
Rose, Hugh 37, **197**
Rosebery, Lord 77
Ross, Charles **197**
Ross, F.B. 79, **197**
Ross, L.C. 37, **197**
Ross, Percy T. 35, **198**
Rossillon, Marius *see* O'Galop
Rosslyn, Lord 25, 41-3, 78, 107, 109, 149
Rostko **198**
Rotida, A. **198**
Rottembourg, Valerie 99, **198**
Rottmayer, H. **198**
Rouault, Gustave **198**
Roubille, August Jean-Baptiste 82, 83, 85, *198*
Rouilly, A. **198**
Rouveyre, André 82, **198**
Rowan, M.A. 79
Rowlandson, George Derville 53, 66, **198**
Rowlandson, Samuel M. **198**
Roworth, Edward 32, 35, **198**
Royal Army Medical Corps 121, 153
Royal Artillery *132*, 183
Royal Dragoons, 1st 130, 163
Royal Dublin Fusiliers 181
Royal Engineers *92*, 123
Royal family 107, 236; *see also* under names of individual members
Royal Field Artillery 106
Royal Highland Regiment *see* The Black Watch
Royal Horse Artillery *119*, 151, 198, 199
Royal Horse Guards 183
Royal Irish Fusiliers 105, 185
Royal Irish Lancers 141
Royal Inniskilling Fusiliers 207
Royal Marines 154
Royal Naval and Military Bazaar
Royal Rifles 108
Royal Scots Fusiliers 122
Royal Welsh Regiment *55*
Royal West Kent Regiment 120
Roze, Leon 198-9
Ruchert **199**
Ructler, M. **199**

Rudaux, Henri Edmond 64, 66, **199**
ruins (farms) 140, 148
Rünckel, F. **199**
Rundle, Gen L. 52
Russell, Fox 191
Russell, Walter Westley **199**
Russian
 artists 71, 121
 charity publications 71
 postcards 94
 sculptors 103
Rutherford, F. **199**

S S.,M.F.C. *see* M.F.C.S.
S.M. **208**
Sabattier, Lionel 59, 65
Sabattier, Louis Rémy **199**
Saint-Saëns, Camille 66
Saint-Yves, Georges 181
Salisbury, Lord 77
Salmon, J. 138
Salmon, J.M. Balliol 56, 57, 58, **199**
Salvadori, R. **199**
Sambourne, Edward Linley 75, 76, *198*, **199**
Samson, Edgar 216-17
Sancha, José *84*, **199**
Sand River 131
Sanderson-Wells, John Sanderson **199**
Sanna's Post, Battle of 28, 45, 105, 203, 216
Sargent, John Singer **199-200**
Sass, Alek 80
Savage, Reginald 62, **200**
Savage Club 55
Sayers 60, **200**
Scandinavian Corps 47
Schaupp, Richard 67, *200*
Scheepers, Gideon 64
Scheepers Nek 134
Schleffler, Herman **200**
Schlaf, L. 132
Schlette, Engelina Helena *200*
Schlittgen, Hermann 70, **200**
Schmidhammer, Arpad 85, 87-8, *200*
Schmidt, Hugo Carl **200**
Scholl, Fritz 87, **200**
Schönberg, Johann *24*, *25-6*, 70, **200-2**
Schreiner, W.P. 78
Schröder, Howard 78
Schulz, Wilhelm *2*, 70, **202**
Schulze, Hermann **202**
Schwartze, Thérèse 59, *66*, 67, **202**
Schwarz, Samuel 83
Scotson-Clark, George Frederick **202**
Scott, Edward Daniel 21
Scott, Georges Bertin 59, 65, 92, *202-3*
Scott, H. Owen 25
Scottish Imperial Yeomanry 122, 229
Searelle, Mrs Blanche 32, **203**
Seiber **203**
Sem **203**
Seppings Wright, Henry Charles see Wright, H.C.S.
Sharpe, W.N. Ltd 163
Shaw, John Byam Liston **203**
Sheard, Thomas Frederick Mason **203**
Sheldon, Charles Mills 53, 63, 92, *203-4*
Sheldon-Williams, (Harry) Inglis *33-4*, 59, 62, 63, 192, **204-6**
Shelley, H.C. 19, 25, 50-1
Shepard, T. Newton 59, **206**
Sheppard, J.A. 75
Shepperson, C.A. **206**
Shérie, Ernest F. 53, 60, 76, **206-7**, 226
Shindler, H.L. 75, **207**
Shorter, Clement 24-5, 26
Shurey, Charles 59-60
Shurey's Illustrated 59
Shurey's Pictorial Budget 60
Shute, A.B.98, **207**
Sijthoff, G.J. **207**
silhouettists 111, 120, 140, 209
Sime, Sydney Herbert 76, B**207**
Simkin, Richard *207*, 237

Simplicissimus 88
Simon, G.F. **207**-8
Simpson, Charles 59, **208**
Simpson, William 18
Singfrau **208**
Singleton, John **208**
Sipy 88
Skip **208**
Sitjthoff, G.J. 86
The Sketch 21, 37, 52, 53
Sleppe, R. 71
Slevogt, Max 70, *208*
slides *see* lantern slides
Small, William 56, 57, *208-9*
 'The Relief of Mafeking' *29*, 32, 105, 208
Smedley, A. Constance **209**
Smith, A.T. *208*, **209**
Smith, Decost 126
Smith, Ernest W. 20
Smith, Walter 50
Smith, W. Thomas 157, **209**
Smith-Dorrien, Gen H.A. 77
Smuts, Gen J.C. 154
Smythe, Ernest 59, 62, **209**
Somerville, Howard **209**
Somm, Henri 82, *208*, **209**
Soper, George 56, 63, 97, 117, 134, 137, 140, 171, *209-10*, 221, 222
'Soranus' 86, **210**
Sorel, A. 85, **210**
South African
 cartoonists 111, 120, 124, 151, 153, 154, 156, 160, 164, 173, 176
 satirical press 78-80
South African Constabulary 105
South African Mounted Rifles 138
The South African Review 78, 79
South Australian National Memorial 154
The South Australian Critic 80
South Lancashire Regiment 129, 234
Sowerby, Millicent **210**
Spada 84, **210**
Spanish artists 153, 199
Spaven, A.H. **210**
The Spear 121, 235, 236
special correspondents 19-26
 memorial to *153*, 154
Speed, Lancelot 63, *98*, **210-11**
Speenhof, Jakobus Hendrikus 86, **211**
Spence, Percy F.S. 32, 108, 116, **211**
The Sphere 19, 24-5, 34-6, 50-1, 54, 58-9
Spioenkop 103, *149*, 213
 Battle of 32, 64, *65*, *86*, 100, 101, 107, 119, 125, *132*, *180*, 181, 182, 187, 193
Spooner, Horace H. (Jack) **211**
Springfontein, Battle of 137
Spurrier, Steven 63, **211**
'Spy' *see* Ward, Leslie
Srick **211**
St Clair-Erskine, J.F.H. *see* Rosslyn, Lord
St George's Gazette 43, 147, 150
St Helena P.O.W. camp 45, 46, 47, *48*, 126, 129, 152, 161, 162, 165-6, 168, 236
St Leger, S.E. *15*, 16, *34*, *36*, 79, 203, *214-16*
St Leger, F.Y. 79, 214
St Mary's Hospital, Paddington 222
St Petersburg Gazette 68
St Petersburg-Transvaal 71
Stable, W.G. 98
Stacey, Walter Sydney **211**
Staller, G.F. *210*, **211**
Stampa, George Loraine 75, **211**
Staniforth, Joseph Morewood 78, *79*, **211**
Staniland, Charles J. 57, **211**
Stead, W.T. 79
Steelink, Willem (jnr) 98, **211-12**
Steevens, George W. 20, 22, 23, 27, 38
Steinlen, Théophile-Alexandre 67, 82, 83, 85, *212*
Stephan, Heinrich von 90
Stephany, M. **212**
Steppe, Romain **212**
Steub, Fritz 88, **212**
Steub, Ludwig 70
Stevens, Edward **212**

Stevens, William D. **212**
Stevenson, F. Arthur *90*, 96, **212**
Stevenson, J. **212**
Stewart, Alan 22, 66, *212-13*
Stewart, Charles Edward **213**
Stewart, Frank Algernon 21, *22, 23, 24*, 37, 62, 66, 98, *212*, **213-14**
Stewart & Woolf 183
Steyn, Pres M.T. 56, 109, 166, 223
    cartoons 76, *77*, 78, 155, 233
    portraits *162*, 177
Stick **214**
Stone, G. **216**
Stone, Marcus **216**
Stonor, W.G. 36, **216**
Storch, Carl **216**
Stormberg, Battle of 100, 124, 125
Strahan, Geoffrey **216-17**
Stranack, Horis W. **217**
The Strand Magazine 60, 75
Stratemeyer, Edward 98, 207
Strathcona, Lord 77, 228
Strathcona's Horse 186
Stromquist, H.S. **217**
Sturges, Maj W.E. 42, **217**
Stutz, Ludwig 87, 88, **217**
Styche, Frank 75, **217**
Suffolk Regiment 210, 221
Sugg, Albert 162
Sullivan, J.T. 75
Sumner, Percy **217**
Sumner, Roy 43
Sundays River 109
Supple, Hazel 37, **217**
Supple, Col James Francis 37, **217**
Suss, Paul 165
Sutherland, A. *216*, **217**
Sutton **217**
Swiss
    artists 131, 222
    cartoonists 117, 161, 200
    postcard artists 131-2, 160, 200, 212
    satirical press 88
Sydney Bulletin 80
Symonds, William Robert **217**
Symons, Gen W. Penn 105, 110, 114, 129

T T.N.F.D. **220**
Taffs, Charles 58, 63, *217*
Taillefer **217**
Talvart, Hector *217-18*
Tatham, Miss C.M. 32, **218**
Tattegrain, Henri 69, **218**
Tavernier, Jules 134
Taylor, C.E. 80, **218**
Taylor, Sydney 32, **218**
Tebby, Arthur Kemp 54, **218**
The Telephone 78, 79, 111, 146
Tennant, C. Dudley 58, **218**
Tennant, Douglas
Tenniel, John 16, 74-5, *76*, 85-6, **218-19**
Tèstelin, N. 98, *219*
Testevuide, Jehan 66, 67, 140, **219**
Tézier 82, **219**
Thackeray, Lance 53, 58, 63, *92*, 93, *218*, **219**
Theweneti, C. **219**
Thiele, Julius Arthur *14*, *92*, *95*, 161, **219**
Thiriat, Paul 58, 65, 67, **219**
Thomas, William 19, 54
Thomas, William F. *76*, *77*, **219**
Thöny, Eduard 70, 88, **219**
Thorneycroft's Mounted Infantry 180, 221
Thornely, J.H. 60, 62, 63, *219-20*
Thornton, E.N. **220**
Thornycroft, (William) Hamo **220**
Thulstrup, Thure de *see* de Thulstrup, T.
tiles 125
Tilly, E. **220**
The Times 27-8
Tinayre, (Jean Paul) Louis 66, **220**
Tippel, George W. 87, **220**
Tiret-Bognet, Georges 82, 84, 85, *86*, **220**
Titcomb, W.H.Y. **220**
Todd, James Henry **220**

Tofani, Oswaldo 64, *65*, 66, **220**, *221*
Toft, Alfred **220-1**
Toncer, George **221**
topographical sketches 212, 222
Toppin, H.S. **221**
Torrome, Francisco (Frank) **221**
Toulouse-Lautrec 85
Toubrac, A.O. 66, *221*
Townsend, Frederick Henry L.J. 58, **221**
toys 46, 128-9, 188
Transvaal Album 68
The Transvaal War Album 61
Treibner, W. **221**
Trenglon, H. **221**
Trezona, W. **221**
Tringham, Holland 53, 212, *221-2*
Trotter, Maj Gen Sir H. 77
Truth 78
Tuck, Raphael & Sons 89, 93, 108, 117, 129, 131, 132, 133, 183
Tucker, Kidger **222**
Tugela River 108, 119, *202*
Turquand 79, **222**
Tweebosch, Battle of 177
Tweed, John **222**

U *Uilenspiegel* 86
Ulk 87, 141
Ullerson, H.K. **222**
Under the Union Jack 59, 61-2, 74
United States of America *see* American
Ustokos 88

V V.K. **226**
V.M. *226-7*
V.P. *see* P.V.
Valentine & Sons Ltd 102
Vallentin, Wilhelm 186
Vallet, Louis 66, **222**
Vallotton, Félix 85, *222*
van Aken, Leo 71, **222**
van Averbeke, E.M. *94*, **222**
van Breda, P. **222**
van der Aa *12*
van der Merwe, François 47, **222**
van der Ouderaa, Pierre Jan 71, **222**
van Dock **222**
van Dongen, Kees 83, 86, 156
van Doomaal, Theo **222**
van Dort, E.F. 143, **222**
van Geldorp, Petrus J.A.C. 86, 87, **222-3**
van Helsdingen, A. **222**
van Korsinsky, E. 48, **223**
van Kuyck, Frans P.L. 71, **223**
van Leemputten, Frans 71, **223**
van Lesnout **223**
van Mieghem, Eugeen *94*, **223**
van Moerkerken 48, 129, **223**
van Neck, Louis 94, 125, 222
van Neste, Alfred J.A. *71*, **223**
van Offel, Edmond *94*, **223**
van Papendrecht, Jan Hoynck *see* Hoynck van Papendrecht, J.
van Ponten, Kees 99
van Welie, Antoon 100, **223**
van Wouw, Anthonie (Anton) *44*, 45, 95, 137, **223**
Vanity Fair 16, 76-8, *228-9*
Veber, Jan 66, *83-4*, 87, 92, *116*, 117, *224-5*
Vedder, Simon Harmon 63, *224-5*
The Veldt 79-80
Venter, Johannes H. 48, *225*
Verber **225**
Verhaert, Piet 71, **225**
Vermont, M. 67
Verneau, Charles 179
Vernon, Frederick Charles Victor de **225**
Vet River 216
'Victa' *94*, **225**
Victoria, Queen *49*, 218, 230, *234*, 236
    cartoons *92*, *93*, **220**
        and Chamberlain 66, *208*
        and Kruger 100, 102, *124*, 160
        and Kaiser Wilhelm *134*

French 82, 84, 156, 161, 179
    German *70*, 146, 182
Victoria Cross 213, 234
    heroes 108, 116, 154, 218, 236
Vierge, Daniel 69, *225*
Vigors, Philip U. W. 36, *225*
Viljoen, Gen Ben 108, *195*, 222
Villebois-Mareuil, Georges Comte de 66, 81, 82, 100, 125, 180, *194*, 200, 218
Villiers, Frederic 20-1, *22*, 24, 37, *225-6*
Vizetelly, Frank 46
Vizetelly, Henry 19
Vogel, Hermann 83, 99, *227*
Voltz, T. *227*
von F, Laci *227*
von Lembach, F.S. *see* Lenbach, F.S. von
von Zumbusch, L. *see* Zumbusch, L. von
Vooruitgang 86
Vryheid, Relief of 134
Vsemirnaya Illyustratsiya 19

W W.,H. *see* H.W.
W. J.R. *see* J.R.W.
W.B.D. **230**
W.F. **231**
WL-S *see* Lehmann-Schram, W.
Wain, Louis William *227*
Wain, S. **227**
Waite, James **227**
Wake, G.R. 42, **227**
Walenn, Gilbert F.D. **227**
Walker, John Hanson 97, **227**
Wallace **227**
Wallace, Helen *31*, 32, **227**
Wallace, R.J. **227**
Walters **228**
Walrus *see* Conolly, W.M.
Walton, J. Ambrose **228**
Walton, J.G. 45, *46*
War Pictures 37, 61, *62*, 133
Ward, Enoch 58, 192, **228**
Ward, Leslie Mathew 16, *77*, *78*, *79*, *228-9*
Warwickshire Regiment 221
The Waterfall Wag 43
Watson **229**
Watson, George Mackie **229**
Watson, James Hannan 34-5, *37*, **229**
Wauchope, Maj Gen A. 133, 234
Waud, Leighton **229**
Waugh, Frederick Judd *28*, 56, 60, *61*, 62, 63, 102, 222, *228*, **229-30**
The Weekly Star 80
The Weekly Telegraph 60
Weick, Adolphe 65, 68
Weijmann, Ottmar 230
Weil, Julius 120
Weil, Lucien-Henri 84, 85, **230**
Wellner, W.A. 87, **231**
Wells, John Sanderson 59, 63
Welsh National Memorial 221
Wenzell, Albert B. **231**
Wepener, Defence of 132
Wêreldkroniek 68
West Yorkshire Regiment 117, 210, *236*, 237
Western artists 108, 111, 126, 127, 134, 136, 141, 147, 160, 189, 193, 237
The Western Mail 78
Westmacott, Bernard **231**
The Westminster Gazette 75, 76
Whishaw, Fred 97
Whiston, Henry *230*, **231**
White, Geoffrey H.A. 42, *43*, **231**
White, Lt Gen Sir George 20, 117, 133, 149, 150, 160, 196, 210
    cartoons 77-8, 228
Whitelaw, George 75, **231**
Whiting, Frederic 57, *231*, 233
Whiting, Onslow *135*, **231**
Whyte, B.C. **231**
Wichgraf, Fritz 45, **231**
Wiener Humoristische Blätter 88
Wigfull, Edward 60
Wilcocks, Sarah 186
Wild, Frank Percy **231**

Wildey, A. Gascoigne **231**
Wilhelm II, Kaiser *134*, 185
Wilhelmina, Queen 109, *124*, 218, 232
    and Kruger 66, 68, 225
Wilke, Rudolf 70, *230*, **231**
Wilkinson, Albert 58, **232**
Wilkinson, Norman *19*, 58, *232*
Wilkinson, Spenser *22*, 136
Wilkinson, Tom 75, **232**
Willette, Adolphe Leon 82, 83, 85, 92, *232*, *233*
Williams, C.R. Fleming 75, **232**
Willson, Leslie 76
Wilmer, John Riley 75, **232**
Wilson, David 75, **232**
Wilson, H.M. 53
Wilson, H.P. **232-3**
Wilson, Sir Henry 204, 205, 206
Wilson, Herbert Wrigley 62-3, **233**
Wilson, Oscar 76, *233*
Wilson, Thomas Walter 59, **233**
Winchester, Maj the Marquis of 154
With Roberts to the Transvaal 61
With the Flag to Pretoria 55, 58, 62-3
Witherby, Arthur George 77, **233**
Withycombe, John G. **233**
Wolf, W. 86
Wollen, William *17*, 25, 199, *232*, **233-4**
Wolmarans, A.D. 223
women artists 15, 16, *31*, 32, 37, 41
    Australian 203
    British 54, 109, 115, 118, 121, 124-5, 145, 156, 196, 209, 210, 217, 227
    Dutch 200, 202
    French 102, 111, 126
    German 158, 186
    South African 116, 154, 218
Wood, Sir Evelyn 119
Wood, Clarence Lawson 37, 61, *62*, 98, **235**
Wood, Lawson 37
Wood, Stanley L. 37, 58, 67, 72, 97, 235
Wood, Starr 75, **233**
woodcarvings 222
Woodhead, C.B. *234*, **235**
Woodville, Richard Caton *19*, *22*, *50-2*, 53, 60, 62, *63*, 72, 92, 99, 100, 149, 193, 234, *235-6*
    'Absent Minded Beggar' 158, 235, *238*
    redrawing 146, 153, 226, 231
Woollett, Cresswell *236*
Worcester 106
Worcester Regiment 137
The World 78
Wrench 195
Wright, Alan 62, **236**
Wright, E.O.W. **236**
Wright, Gilbert S. **236**
Wright, Henry Charles Seppings 21-2, 53, 66, 77, 92, *236-7*
    redrawing 109, 139, 146, 158, 196
Wyllie, Charles William 57, 59, **237**
Wyllie, William Lionel 56, *236*, **237**
Wymer, Reginald Augustus **237**
Wynberg Military Camp 215
Wyse, Henry Taylor **237**

X Xaudaro, Joaquin **237**

Y Y.,F.H. *see* F.H.Y.
Yendis, Mosnar 75, *76*, **237**
Yorkshire Regiment 213
Yorkshire Tribute Medal 113
Young, P.F. 54, **237**

Z Zangwill, I. 192
Zimmerman, Eugene (Zim) 88, **238**
Zimmermann, Alfred 67, **238**
Zivotoyskaye, S.V. 71
Zodler, M. **238**
Zumbusch, Ludwig von 67, 87, *238*
Zwaardemaker, K. 46
Zwiller, Marie Augustin 69, 238

Subscribers

Queen Wilhelmina of the
Netherlands and Paul Kruger
on a postcard by Rostke.

COLLECTORS' EDITION

G. K. H. Anderson

Steve Bales

Mr & Mrs F. J. Barrell & Shara

Arnold Benjamin

Eberhard Bertelsmann

The Brenthurst Library

Jim Gerard Paul Broekhuysen

Joy & Derek Butcher

Mrs S. W. Caroline

Jane Carruthers

Mr Andrew J. Cohen

Neville E. Constantine

Gilles Cristini

Danie, Daniel & Christiaan

Dr J. Dhansay

J. P. G. du Plessis

Kevin Dunkley

Dr H. B. Dyer

Fernwood Press (Pty) Ltd

First National Bank

John E. Franklin

Lydia Gorvy

Dr Ryno Greenwall

Glynn & Anne Herbert

J. Horowitz

M. F. Keeley

Helen Leibel

G. W. B. MacKenzie

O. J. Mackenzie

A. C. McCrindle

Peter Mitchell

Jan & Elizabeth Nel

David A. Nicholas O.B.E. MA

Carel A. Nolte

Rose & Oscar Norwich

L. S. Phelps

Bob & Alison Rightford

S A Library

I. G. Snelling

Pieter Struik

Mr W. van Rÿswÿck

C. & G. Villa

Michael John Walker

Inid Wengel

C. K. Williamson

J. A. Windell

H. D. Workman

R.J. Aberdein

Mr R.D. Ackerman

Africana Book Collectors

Keith Allen

Dr David R. Anderson

Dr Marion Arnold

Ashbey's Galleries

Mr & Mrs A.R. Aspoas

Mr & Mrs A. Atkinson

Paoletta Baker

Jonathan Ball

Thomas Barlow

Mrs Constance Barry

John G. Batsakis MD

Len & Fébé Becker

Reinher Behrens

Anne Marie Berry

Dr John Vivian Bickford-Smith

Paul & Jean Bingle

I.A.N. Bloy

Mr & Mrs H. Blumberg

Dr Paul M. Bower

Edna & Frank Bradlow

Dr David N. Brereton

G.G. Brereton-Stiles

Gillian & David Brock

Graham L. Brownrigg

S.F. Burger SC

Frank Stuart Butler

Andrew Cadman

Mr John Campbell

H. Cantor

C.J. Chorlton

B. Christopher

P.J. Cillié

T.M. Claassens

Mr George Clainos

Clarke's Bookshop

P. Coetsee SC

Dr & Mrs H. Cohen

Julian Collis

Neville E. Constantine

E.J. Cooper

Pietro Corgatelli

Graham & Jillian Cox

Mrs Margaret Coyles

Jock Craven

R.M. Crawford

R.B. Croft

Donald & Rosemary Currie

Major A.D. Damelin

Richard & Maureen de Beer

Dr Org de Bruin

Dr Jan de Kock

Johnnie & Ruth de Korte

H.R. de Lange

D. de Milander

J.C. (Kay) de Villiers

David de Villiers du Buisson Jnr

Dr Nic de Wet

Leicester Dicey

Chris Diedericks

Captain P.K.A. Digby JCD

Carol & Donald Dinnie

Don Africana Library

R.W.F. Droogleever

J.C.M.D. du Plessis

Enid du Plessis

Dr P.J. Dunn

Dr H.B. Dyer

Ellerman House

George, Brenda, Kathleen & Bronwyn Elliott

John Eloff

Anton O. Endres

Dr Alastair D. Ewart

John & Muff Featherstone

Ferdinand Postma-Biblioteek, PU vir CHO

J. Feyerick

E. Fick

Dorothy Foster

Beverley Anne Fourie

Eugene & Lalie Fourie

Raymond & Isabel Frankal

Dr S. Freedberg

R.M. Fritz

John H. Gaskell

J.S. Gericke Library

R. Gettliffe

David Gibbons

D.D.V. Gibson

Dr Rupert Gildenhuys

L. Glaser

Robert Goldblatt

Mrs Belinda Gordon

Mr & Mrs P.M. Goss

Lynne Greeff

Mrs Anne Greenwall

Joseph E. Grinnan

M.G.M. Guiney

Mr Ron Hackett

Mr Bertil Haggman

Leainne Hammergreen

Neville Harden

Derek Harraway

Mr & Mrs Ron Harrison

R.A. Harvey

Lisa & Giles Hefer

Dr David M. Heller

Commander E.F. Hendrikz, SA Navy (Retd)

Dudley Henn

Frank & Marjorie Heron

E.R. Hill

Josephine & Brett Hilton-Barber

Johannes P. Hoffman

Tony Hoffman

B.J.E. Human

Peter Hutterer

Toshihiro Inoue

Doug & Edna Jardine

John & Ann Jarvis

Ed Jernigan

Denis Keenan-Smith

Raymond Keeping

Brian L. Kieran

M.W. King

H.W. Kinsey

D. Klein

D.G. Knott

P.A.F. Knowlden Snr

C. Kotze

Reginald A. Lambert

P.J. & K.A.S. Latham

Johan Latsky

Robert E. Levitt

Pam & Irving Lissoos

Henk & André Loots

Clifford Lyons

Alan Macgregor

Ian Mackenzie

David Mann

Dr Paul Marchand

A. Mc A. Harvey

Ronnie Melville

William Grant Menzies

N. G. Meyer

Ruth & Walter Middelmann

Paul Mills

W. Moir

G. F. Moore

Alan & Jenny Mountain

Malcolm Murphy

Mr Neil Myers

Mrs Pat Myers

Nachman Family

Woody Nel

J. M. Neser

Mrs G. A. Nikschtat

Peter O'Connor

Dr H. F. Oberholzer

Karin Obojkovits

P. L. Olivier

Frikkie Oosthuizen

K. Palmer

David Paterson

Roydon C. Peden

Mr & Mrs D. J. Penwill

Jeffry Perlman

Colin, Charmaine, Kerry & Stephan Pinker

Brendan Pollard

Beryl & Lawrence Posniak

Allan Potash

Noel Potter

S. L. Pretorius

Henriëtte Prince

Paul Probert

Coenraad J. Raath

Dr A.W. R. Rademeyer

J. D. Rae

Gabriele Renz

Sally Reunert

Michael & Ruth Rice

M. J. Richter

Douglas Roberts

R. M. Robinson

Cedric Roché

A. D. Ross-Munro

J. P. Rourke

Fritz Ulrich Ruch

H. L. Schaary

Sylvia Schrire

Henry Arthur Schroeder

Albert Schultz

Norman Segal

Dr Johan A. Senekal

William Shirreffs

Sylvia & Bernard Shull

H. Sibul

Henry Sim

Mr & Mrs H. Simon

Thelma & Cecil Skotnes

Dennis & Ansie Slotow

Keith & Dorothy Smith

Tennyson Smith Bodill

Michiel & Morag Smuts

I. G. Snelling

P. W. St L. Searle

D. J. F. Stephen

Herman Stevenson

Michael Stevenson

Ian K. Stewart

Peter Steyn

Y. & M. T. Steyn

J. C. Strauss

John Stretton

B. W. Stroeve

Richard Stroud

B. M. Tanner

Carla Dayna Tanner

Dr Andrew Tarr

Colin & Ann Tedder

Mr Gilles Teulié

Neil Trollope

Dr Arnold van Dyk

Danie van Niekerk

J. F. van Reenen

P. L. J. van Rensburg

M. & M. A. van Rijswijck

Paul van Schalkwyk

Dr M. C. E. van Schoor

C. W. van Wyk

Elkie & Tommie van Zyl

Leo van den Heever

S. W. van der Merwe

Dr Gerdrie van der Merwe VDM

P. L. van der Spuy

Dr Johan van der Wat

Professor Albert Venter

Francois Viljoen

Dr A. A. Visser

Volks Art Auctions

Pieter C. Wagener

Anne Watt

Issa & Henry Werb

Dr David Westaby

Keith Cecil Whitfield

Cyril Wiggishoff

William Humphreys Art Gallery

Hilda & Jürgen Witt

E. J. Woodcock

Richard & Jason Woodward

J. W. Zahn

B. S. Zylstra